# Schools of the South 2006

**Concept Development**
Jim Balzer, Adam Burns, Chris Mason, and Kimberly Moore

**Cover Design**
McGinty

**Development**
Chris Mason, Kimberly Moore

**Editing**
Omid Gohari, Christina Koshzow, Kevin Nash, Joey Rahimi, Luke Skurman, and Rob Williams

ISBN # 1-59658-503-X
© Copyright 2005 College Prowler
All Rights Reserved
Printed in the U.S.A.
www.collegeprowler.com

**Special thanks to** Babs Carryer, Andy Hannah, LaunchCyte, Tim O'Brien, Bob Sehlinger, Thomas Emerson, Andrew Skurman, Barbara Skurman, Bert Mann, Dave Lehman, Daniel Fayock, Chris Babyak, the Donald H. Jones Center for Entrepreneurship, Terry Slease, Jerry McGinnis, Bill Ecenberger, McGinty, Kyle Russell, Jacque Zaremba, Larry Winderbaum, Paul Kelly, Roland Allen, Jon Reider, Team Evankovich, Julie Fenstermaker, Lauren Varacalli, Abu Noaman, Mark Exler, Daniel Steinmeyer, Jared Cohon, Gabriela Oates, David Koegler, Glen Meakem, and the College Prowler student authors.

College Prowler™
5001 Baum Blvd.
Suite 750
Pittsburgh, PA 15213

Phone:   (800) 290-2682
Fax:     (800) 772-4972
E-mail:  info@collegeprowler.com
Website: www.collegeprowler.com

College Prowler™ is not sponsored by, affiliated with, or approved by the colleges covered herein.

College Prowler™ strives faithfully to record its sources. As the reader understands, opinions, impressions, and experiences are necessarily personal and unique. Accordingly, there are, and can be, no guarantees of future satisfaction extended to the reader.

© Copyright 2005 College Prowler. All rights reserved. No part of this work may be reproduced or transmitted in any form or by any means, including but not limited to, photocopy, recording, or any information storage and retrieval systems, without the express written permission of College Prowler™.

# Welcome to College Prowler

During the writing of College Prowler's guidebooks, we felt it was critical that our content was unbiased and unaffiliated with any college or university. We think it's important that our readers get honest information and a realistic impression of the student opinions on any campus—that's why if any aspect of a particular school is terrible, we (unlike a campus brochure) intend to publish it. While we do keep an eye out for the occasional extremist—the cheerleader or the cynic—we take pride in letting the students tell it like it is. We strive to create a book that's as representative as possible of each particular campus. Our books cover both the good and the bad, and whether the survey responses point to recurring trends or a variation in opinion, these sentiments are directly and proportionally expressed through our guides.

College Prowler guidebooks are in the hands of students throughout the entire process of their creation. Because you can't make student-written guides without the students, we have students at each campus who help write, randomly survey their peers, edit, layout, and perform accuracy checks on every book that we publish. From the very beginning, student writers gather the most up-to-date stats, facts, and inside information on their colleges. They fill each section with student quotes and summarize the findings in editorial reviews. In addition, each school receives a collection of letter grades (A through F) that reflect student opinion and help to represent contentment, prominence, or satisfaction for each of our specific categories. Just as in grade school, the higher the mark, the more content, more prominent, or more satisfied the students are with the particular category.

Once a book is written, additional students serve as editors and check for accuracy even more extensively. Our bounce-back team—a group of randomly selected students who have no involvement with the project—are asked to read over the material in order to help ensure that the book accurately expresses every aspect of the university and its students.

This same process is applied to the 200-plus schools College Prowler currently covers. Each book is the result of endless student contributions, hundreds of pages of research and writing, and countless hours of hard work. All of this has led to the creation of a student information network that stretches across the nation to every school that we cover. It's no easy accomplishment, but it's the reason that our guides are such a great resource.

When reading our books and looking at our grades, keep in mind that every college is different and that the students who make up each school are not uniform—as a result, it is important to assess schools on a case-by-case basis. Because it's impossible to summarize an entire school with a single number or description, each book provides a dialogue, not a decision, that's made up of different topics and hundreds of student quotes. In the end, we hope that this guide will serve as a valuable tool in your college selection process. Enjoy!

OMID GOHARI 〇  CHRISTINA KOSHZOW 〇  CHRIS MASON 〇  JOEY RAHIMI 〇  LUKE SKURMAN 〇
*Founders of College Prowler™*

# What is a College Prowler *Off the Record Guidebook?*

### Explore the School of Your Dreams—Without Setting Foot on Campus!
Over 100,000 books are in circulation (and counting, fast!), with each guidebook providing a comprehensive, honest, in-depth portrayal that is dedicated to one school. Every college is a unique experience and therefore each college has an entire book dedicated to it.

### 55,000 Students Share Their Opinions
To maintain objectivity, we have refused investment from colleges. Instead, we let the students tell it like it is and fill each guide with over 300 student responses, both positive and negative.

### Students Rank 200 Colleges in 200 Guides
Our rankings represent student happiness, prominence, and satisfaction for each respective category. The higher the grade, the happier, the more prominent, or the more satisfied students are with the particular category. The ranking process is in the hands of current students and recent graduates the entire time.

### Students Speak Out About:
- Academics
- Athletics
- Campus Dining
- Campus Housing
- Campus Strictness
- Computers
- Diversity
- Drug Scene
- Facilities
- Girls
- Greek Life
- Guys
- Local Atmosphere
- Nightlife
- Off-Campus Dining
- Off-Campus Housing
- Parking
- Safety & Security
- Transportation
- Weather

### 200 Writers Dig for the Details You Care About
College Prowler has quotes from students about drugs on campus, Greek life, diversity, campus strictness and many other categories that don't usually pop up in traditional college guides. These quotes and categories are here to provide a helpful assessment of what's really happening on each campus. By including important, relevant facts and stats, like the average SAT score or the cost of a parking permit, you get a detailed look at the unique culture of each college.

It's like having an older friend show you around campus.

# Schools of the South 2006

### About This Book
College Prowler's line of over 200 guidebooks, each focusing on an individual school, have already become student favorites by providing unbiased, insider information on colleges and universities across the nation. You now hold in your hands the updated Schools of the South 2006 Compendium—all thirty-five of our Southern guidebooks collected in a single, easy-to-use reference, with plenty of advice on attending college in the Southern states. Whether as a starting point in the college search, or as a side-by-side comparison of a few favorite schools, this book is designed especially for the prospective student searching for that perfect school.

### Going to School in the South
Offering some of the largest, most well-known universities in the nation, located in charismatic and appealing college towns, the South offers a perfect learning environment for students looking to soak up a few rays of year-round sunshine while getting a great education. Many campuses in the South, whether large or small, are built around communities of trust and respect that deeply affect the relationships of students and non-students alike. Between community colleges, independent and private universities, historically black colleges and universities, and storied public degree-granting institutions, the South provides a network of resources to prospective students that cannot be found elsewhere in the United States.

# www.collegeprowler.com

**Did You Know?**
Visit our Website at **www.collegeprowler.com** and find out how you can enter our annual essay contest to win a $500 scholarship. While you're at it, check out rankings on top colleges across the nations, or order one of our in-depth, school-specific, student-written guides. Go ahead, get your prowl on!

## Save 10% Now!

**Order Online**
Save 10 percent on your entire order!
**www.collegeprowler.com**

→ Enter coupon code: **SOUTH**

→ The Truth About America's Top Colleges

# SCHOOLS OF THE SOUTH
# Table of Contents

How to Use This Book ...................................................................... 1

What's in This Book .......................................................................... 2

Southern Educational System ........................................................ 4

At a Glance ...................................................................................... 12

## Colleges In Depth

### Public Schools

Auburn University ................................................................ 40

Clemson University ............................................................. 60

College of Charleston ........................................................ 79

College of William & Mary ................................................. 98

Florida State University ..................................................... 119

Georgia Tech ........................................................................ 139

James Madison University ................................................ 159

University of Alabama ........................................................ 179

University of Central Florida ............................................. 199

University of Florida ........................................................... 218

University of Georgia .......................................................... 238

University of Kentucky..................................................................258

University of Mississippi............................................................278

University of North Carolina.....................................................297

University of South Carolina....................................................318

University of South Florida......................................................339

University of Tennessee ..........................................................358

University of Virginia ................................................................378

Virginia Tech...............................................................................398

## Private Schools

Davidson College ......................................................................419

Duke University .........................................................................439

Elon University ..........................................................................460

Emory University .......................................................................480

Furman University .....................................................................499

Guilford College ........................................................................518

Hampton University ..................................................................537

Loyola University New Orleans ..............................................557

Rhodes College .........................................................................577

Rollins College ...........................................................................597

Tulane University .......................................................................614

University of Miami ...................................................................632

University of Richmond ............................................................653

Vanderbilt University .................................................................670

Wake Forest University.............................................................688

Washington and Lee University..............................................708

# Southern USA Weather Map .................................................. 728

# Report Card Summary

    Academics ................................................................. 729

    Local Atmosphere ..................................................... 730

    Safety & Security ....................................................... 731

    Facilities ..................................................................... 732

    Campus Dining ......................................................... 733

    Campus Housing ...................................................... 734

    Diversity .................................................................... 735

    Guys ......................................................................... 736

    Girls ........................................................................... 737

    Athletics .................................................................... 738

    Greek Life ................................................................. 739

    Drug Scene .............................................................. 740

# Financial Aid .................................................................... 741

# Students with Special Needs ........................................ 742

# Southern Admissions Counseling ............................... 750

# Words to Know .............................................................. 753

# About the Authors ......................................................... 756

# How to Use This Book

### Self-Assess
First, decide what's important to you. Are you a party animal or straight-laced? Club kid? Homebody? Do you want to go Greek? Numbers and rankings can never provide the final answer, which is why College Prowler guidebooks are divided into sections covering everything from academics to dining. It might be helpful to make some notes detailing what each category means to you. It's your four years—make the most of it!

### Find the Schools
Dive into our in-depth sections, pages 40 to 727, where detailed, school-by-school information is provided in twelve distinct sections. Browse student quotes, statistics, and the authors' editorials. Find out why those schools you've got your eye on scored well in one category and poor in another. Just like the original College Prowler guidebooks, each school's section provides its own unique dialogue to help you discover if the college is right for you.

### Check the Grades
Check out our report card summaries, pages 729 to 740, for those aspects of college life that matter most. These summaries provide a side-by-side review of the schools, organized by section, with all 35 colleges right at your fingertips. Get a sense for which colleges suit you best—it couldn't be easier to find a school. We're confident we've provided an accurate comparison and a great starting point for your college search.

### Get the Guide
Now that you've narrowed your choices, check out the expanded College Prowler guidebooks—180 pages of inside information on each school with even more student quotes, key admissions statistics, and advice on everything from dorm life to the local club scene. A great companion for those campus visits, College Prowler guidebooks are your last stop in the college search process. For more info check out *www.collegeprowler.com*.

# What's In This Book?

> The following paragraphs explain what's included in each section of this book.

### School Systems
Southern schools offer strong, and often oppositional academic opportunities in both the public and private systems. The "Southern Educational System" section explains the different options available—public vs. private, religious schools, HBCUs, and so on. It's a great introduction to the academic scene of the South.

### Admissions Contacts
Not only does the South offer a rich and varied collection of universities to choose from, it also offers an astounding number of schools. The "At a Glance" section offers a few key pieces of information—not only on those colleges covered in-depth by College Prowler's individual guidebooks, but also several others we thought were worth a mention. It's information that can get you started on discovering those hidden gems.

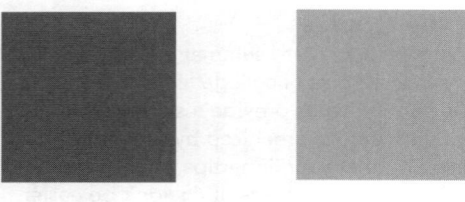

### Student Perspectives
"Colleges In Depth" is the most important section of this book, a highlight of our *Off the Record* guidebooks with honest, inside information, straight from the students' mouths. Even if the school is missing something you consider a must-have, it might compensate or really shine in another area. Get a sense of what your fellow students would be like, find out about a school's unique traditions or hidden drawbacks, and discover the opportunities available after graduation. You probably won't have the opportunity to visit every college that grabs your attention. Consider this a preview without ever having to leave your seat.

### The Weather Forecast
The "Southern USA Weather Map," located towards the back of the book, will tell you all you need to know when packing that suitcase.

### Rankings
The "Report Card Summaries" offer a side-by-side category comparison of the 35 schools. Flip to the summaries and check out two schools side by side, or compare the grades in one section to another. This section will help remind you where a school stands in the grand scheme. It's easy to move back and forth with each new question, so use this section as a worksheet and a quick index.

### Financial Advice
The "Financial Aid" section of this book offers advice and resources to get you started on finding the funds to pay for your education. The good news is that nearly 70 percent of students receive financial aid in some form. Not only is federal aid (FAFSA) available to those who qualify, there are also South-specific awards available to state residents. While the process of applying for aid can be confusing and sometimes discouraging, many students who believe they don't qualify in fact do.

### Students with Disabilities
Those with special needs should check out the "Students with Special Needs" section, which lists contact info and services available for individual schools.

### Admissions Counselors
Choosing the right college is a tough decision. Fortunately, there are professional admissions counselors to help you figure out which school is best for you. Flip to the "College Admissions Counseloring" section to find someone located near you.

### Glossary
Learn a few new words to stay in the know.

### Author Bios
Each college's section was written by its own student author. Good luck with your college search—maybe you'll be the next student to write a College Prowler guidebook!

# Southern Educational System

The following paragraphs explain the different sorts of schools available in the South.

### Public Schools
If you're a prospective college student looking for an academic environment that will enable you to receive a quality education, then one of the South's 122 public degree-granting institutions may be what you're looking for.

- **Accessible**
Public schools strive to provide a wide array of educational opportunities that are practical and affordable for students from all different economic, ethnic, and religious backgrounds.

- **Convenient**
Many public schools in southern states play the role of institutions for students seeking a bachelos degree in their respective states, as well as those who desire professional training in fields such as agriculture, business, engineering, nursing, and teaching.

- **Collective**
Some of the greatest, most infamous college towns in the United States are located around public universities in the South. Many college towns in the South provide an array of urban amenities, but most thrive on good ol' southern hospitality and small-town charm. Athens, GA, Chapel Hill NC, Charlottesville VA, Columbia SC, and Tallahassee FL are all top college towns. During football season, the population of these towns has been known to swell up to more than 50 times the normal numbers.

Check out *www.collegeprowler.com* for complete College Prowler guidebooks on these southern public schools:

- Auburn University
- Clemson University
- College of Charleston
- College of William & Mary
- Florida State University
- Georgia Tech
- James Madison University
- Louisiana State University
- University of Alabama
- University of Central Florida
- University of Florida
- University of Georgia
- University of Kentucky
- University of Mississippi
- University of North Carolina
- University of South Carolina
- University of South Florida
- University of Tennessee
- University of Virginia
- Virginia Tech

## Private Schools

Private schools in the southern states cover a wide array of institutions—one of which is sure to cater to your needs.

- **Accommodating**

  Private or independent institutions in the South really do run the gamut—from small liberal arts institutions tucked away in the foothills of the Appalachians, to large research institutions located smack dab in the middle of a bustling metropolis, to suburban based campuses located minutes from the Atlantic Ocean.

- **Respectable**

  Some southern private institutions, such as Washington and Lee University, Guilford College, and Davidson College, have long-standing "Honor Codes" that students devoutly adhere to. "The Code" is an unspoken agreement that students will not lie, cheat, or steal during their time on campus. While the system might sound a bit like something out of George Orwell's *1984*, it in fact bestows a feeling of mutual respect and admiration for fellow students.

- **Diverse**

  There are no "typical" private school students in the South, just as there is no "typical" private school experience. There are numerous liberal arts schools in the region as well as business, arts and design, technical, and all-girls schools. The one thing private school students do have in common, though, is the passion for lifelong learning and a desire to receive a solid, more personalized education.

Check out *www.collegeprowler.com* for complete College Prowler guidebooks on:

- Davidson College
- Duke University
- Elon University
- Emory University
- Furman University
- Guilford College
- Hampton University
- Loyola University New Orleans
- Rhodes College
- Rollins College
- Tulane University
- University of Miami
- University of Richmond
- Vanderbilt University
- Wake Forest University
- Washington and Lee University

## The Atlantic Coast Conference

Since 1953, the Atlantic Coast Conference (ACC) has been one of the premier athletic conferences in the United States. Ten of the twelve schools in the ACC are located in the South (Clemson, Duke, Florida State, Georgia Tech, Miami, North Carolina, North Carolina State, Virginia, Virginia Tech, and Wake Forest). ACC schools have captured 91 national championships, including 47 in women's competition and 44 in men's.

- **Established**

  The ACC has long enjoyed its reputation as one of the strongest and most competitive intercollegiate conferences in the nation. The conference expands to 12 members as of July, 2005, with the addition of Boston College.

- **Victorious**

  The ACC has captured five national college football championships, including the University of Maryland's title win in the conference's inaugural year (1953). Miami, a member since 2004, has laid claim to several national gridiron titles over the past 21 seasons.

- **Loyal**

  For the first time in league history, ACC schools surpassed the three-million mark in total attendance in 2004, and for the fifth-straight year the league set new single season records in attendance. In 58 home games season, ACC teams drew 3,006,841 fans, breaking the existing record of 2,944,936.

Check out *www.collegeprowler.com* for complete College Prowler guidebooks on:

- Clemson University
- Duke University
- Florida State University
- Georgia Tech
- University of Miami
- University of North Carolina
- University of Virginia
- Virginia Tech
- Wake Forest University

### The Southeastern Conference

The 2006 season marks the 73rd year of college football in the Southeastern Conference (SEC), and the fever hasn't lost a degree since it began. The 12 schools affiliated with the SEC are all located in southern states (Auburn, LSU, Mississippi State, U of Alabama, U of Arkansas, U of Florida, U of Georgia, U of Kentucky, U of Mississippi, U of South Carolina, U of Tennessee, and Vanderbilt).

- **Tenacious**

  Often, families divide and marriages dissolve when Alabama and Auburn square off on the gridiron on a Saturday afternoon—or, on a more recent note, when Florida and Kentucky go at it on the hardwood. In the last 16 years, the SEC has won 107 national team championships (an average of more than six per year).

- **Successful**

  In addition to winning six team championships in 2004, over 80 SEC student-athletes garnered individual national championships, while 498 individuals were awarded with first-team All-America honors.

- **Accomplished**

  Student-athletes around the league continued to excel in the classroom in 2004 as well with 1,954 earning recognition on the SEC Academic Honor Roll.

Check out *www.collegeprowler.com* for complete College Prowler guidebooks on:

- Auburn University
- Louisiana State University
- University of Alabama
- University of Florida
- University of Georgia
- University of Kentucky
- University of Mississippi
- University of South Carolina
- University of Tennessee
- Vanderbilt University

## Historically Black Colleges and Universities (HBCUs)

Thanks in large part to the tireless work of government organizations, black churches, missionary groups, and philanthropists, historically black colleges and universities are now a source of accomplishment and great pride for the African American community as well as the southern United States. The Higher Education Act of 1965, as amended, defines an HBCU as ". . . any historically black college or university that was established prior to 1964, whose principal mission was, and is, the education of black Americans." Seventy-three of the 105 HBCUs are located in the South.

- **Dynamic**
  HBCUs enroll over 14 percent of the nation's African American students in higher education, although they constitute only three percent of America's 4,084 universities. In 2000, these institutions matriculated 24 percent of all African American students enrolled in four-year colleges, awarded master's degrees and first-professional degrees to about one in six African Americans, and awarded 24 percent of all baccalaureate degrees earned by African Americans nationwide.

- **Significant**
  Historically Black Colleges and Universities have been responsible for training teachers and social workers, and their graduates include some of the most well-known public figures in America: Martin Luther King Jr. (Morehouse '48), Thurgood Marshall (Howard '33), and Oprah Winfrey (Tennessee State '75).

- **Progressive**
  Declining enrollments are leading some HBCUs to market themselves to a broader demographic, with low tuitions attracting an increasing number of students of different ethnicities.

Check out *www.collegeprowler.com* for the complete College Prowler guidebook on Hampton University, and look forward to upcoming titles on Morehouse College and Spelman College.

## Religiously-Affiliated Schools

Many religious affiliated schools in the South offer the best of liberal arts and professional studies in an academically-challenging and spiritually-refreshing environment. Many of these schools are coeducational, liberal arts institutions that provide opportunities for higher education in a traditional Christian or Southern Baptist atmosphere.

- **Committed**

  Many private schools in the South deliver a Christian-based, higher education in order to prepare well-grounded graduates for successful careers and significant lives. The missions behind many religious schools is primarily to impact the world for the sake of the common good.

- **Unified**

  Whatever their differences, most students that attend religious schools believe that, as one student put it, "we are really one people; we just have different ways of expressing truth." If you are fascinated by religious questions and traditions and enjoy exploring many points of view, perhaps you should consider one of the South's many religious institutions.

- **Receptive**

  When attending a religious-affiliated institution, it helps to be open-minded. Most religious colleges and universities in the South attract both students who practice various religious traditions, and those who aren't religious at all. If you can respect differences while seeking common ground, you'll enjoy your time at one of these institutions.

## Community Colleges

A community college can be an ideal choice for many students who might not be financially, academically, or personally ready to attend a four-year university. In fact, four out of 10 college-bound high-school graduates start their college education at a community college.

### • Extensive

With its vast community college network, the South offers an array of educational opportunities for prospective students. Composed of over 240 community colleges in the region, these institutions educate over five million students a year. The South's community colleges offer programs to meet the needs of almost every student.

### • Affordable

With four-year college tuitions often starting at $20,000 a year, many southern community colleges offer similar courses to those available at major universities at a fraction of the cost. Many occupational programs feature some of the best technology labs in the South and can prepare students for the workforce in only two years.

### • Transferable

Students who choose to attend community colleges can work towards an associate's degree in hundreds of academic and technical fields. After completion, students can transfer to a four-year college or university to complete a bachelor's degree or look for a job in their area of training. Many of the most popular degree programs revolve around health professions and modern technology.

# SCHOOLS OF THE SOUTH
# At a Glance

Over a hundred schools are listed below, with important information for the prospective student. Check out the in-depth sections to find out even more.

## Schools in Alabama

| College | Website | Phone | Tuition | Acceptance Rate | Application Deadline | Setting | GPA | SAT |
|---|---|---|---|---|---|---|---|---|
| Alabama A&M | www.aamu.edu | (256) 372-5245 | $3,872 in-state, $6,704 out-of-state | 45% | July 15 | Urban | N/A | N/A |
| Alabama State University | www.alasu.edu | (334) 229-4291 | $4,008 in-state, $8,016 out-of-state | 37% | July 30 | Urban | N/A | 690 – 904 |
| ✓ Auburn University | www.auburn.edu | (334) 844-4080 | $4,828 in-state, $14,048 out-of-state | 78% | August 1 | Suburban | 3.5 | 1030 – 1220 |
| Huntingdon College | www.huntingdon.edu | (334) 833-4497 | $14,560 | 59% | Rolling | Urban | 3.4 | 940 – 1200 |
| Jacksonville State University | www.jsu.edu | (256) 782-5268 | $4,060 in-state, $8,100 out-of-state | 89% | Rolling | Rural | N/A | 810 – 1060 |
| Judson College | www.home.judson.edu | (800) 447-9472 | $9,470 | 78% | Rolling | Rural | 3.1 | 980 – 1510 |
| Miles College | www.miles.edu | (800) 445-0708 | $5,717 | 39% | July 15 | Urban | N/A | N/A |
| Oakwood College | www.oakwood.edu | (256) 726-7356 | $11,298 | 47% | Rolling | Urban | 2.9 | 790 – 1050 |
| Samford University | www.samford.edu | (800) 888-7218 | $13,944 | 90% | Rolling | Suburban | 3.6 | 1030 – 1260 |
| Spring Hill College | www.shc.edu | (251) 380-3030 | $19,950 | 80% | July 1 | Suburban | 3.4 | 980 – 1235 |

**Get the guide at collegeprowler.com**

# Schools in Alabama

| College | Website | Phone | Tuition | Acceptance Rate | Application Deadline | Setting | GPA | SAT |
|---|---|---|---|---|---|---|---|---|
| Stillman College | www.stillman.edu | (205) 366-8814 | $8,718 | 47% | Rolling | Urban | N/A | 630 – 840 |
| Talladega College | www.talladega.edu | (256) 761-6235 | $11,842 | 42% | Rolling | Rural | 2.6 | 690 – 780 |
| Troy State University–Dothan | www.tsud.edu | (334) 983-6556 | $4,162 in-state, $8,012 out-of-state | 70% | Rolling | Urban | 3.1 | N/A |
| Troy State University–Montgomery | www.tsum.edu | (334) 241-9506 | $3,600 in-state, $7,130 out-of-state | 99% | Rolling | Urban | N/A | N/A |
| Troy State University–Troy | www.troyst.edu | (334) 670-3179 | $4,162 in-state, $8,012 out-of-state | 67% | Rolling | Rural | 3.2 | N/A |
| Tuskegee University | www.tuskegee.edu | (334) 727-8500 | $11,600 | 81% | March 15 | Rural | 3.2 | 710 – 1090 |
| ✓ University of Alabama | www.ua.edu | (205) 348-5666 | $4,630 in-state, $12,664 out-of-state | 87% | August 1 | Urban | 3.3 | 990 – 1220 |
| University of Alabama–Birmingham | www.uab.edu | (205) 934-8221 | $4,662 in-state, $10,422 out-of-state | 81% | July 1 | Urban | 3.2 | N/A |
| University of Alabama–Huntsville | www.uah.edu | (256) 824-6070 | $4,516 in-state, $9,518 out-of-state | 88% | August 15 | Suburban | 3.4 | 1030 – 1260 |
| University of Mobile | www.umobile.edu | (251) 442-2273 | $9,780 | 67% | Rolling | Suburban | N/A | N/A |
| University of Montevallo | www.montevallo.edu | (205) 665-6030 | $5,536 in-state, $10,726 out-of-state | 79% | August 1 | Rural | 3.2 | N/A |

## Schools in Alabama

| College | Website | Phone | Tuition | Acceptance Rate | Application Deadline | Setting | GPA | SAT |
|---|---|---|---|---|---|---|---|---|
| University of North Alabama | www.una.edu | (256) 765-4608 | $4,610 in-state, $8,620 out-of-state | 79% | Rolling | Urban | 3.0 | 820 – 1010 |
| University of South Alabama | www.southalabama.edu | (251) 460-6141 | $4,290 in-state, $8,100 out-of-state | 76% | August 2 | Suburban | N/A | N/A |
| University of West Alabama | www.uwa.edu | (205) 652-3578 | $4,196 in-state, $7,922 out-of-state | 78% | Rolling | Rural | N/A | N/A |

## Schools in Florida

| College | Website | Phone | Tuition | Acceptance Rate | Application Deadline | Setting | GPA | SAT |
|---|---|---|---|---|---|---|---|---|
| Baptist College of Florida | www.baptist-college.edu | (800) 328-2660 | N/A | 27% | August 1 | Rural | 3.0 | 850 – 1210 |
| Barry University | www.barry.edu | (305) 899-3100 | $21,350 | 70% | Rolling | Suburban | 3.0 | 850 – 1050 |
| Bethune-Cookman College | www.bethune.cookman.edu | (800) 448-0228 | $10,611 | 67% | Rolling | Urban | 2.8 | N/A |
| Clearwater Christian College | www.clearwater.edu | (800) 348-4463 | $10,850 | 89% | July 1 | Suburban | 3.5 | 940 – 1180 |
| Eckerd College | www.eckerd.edu | (727) 864-8331 | $24,362 | 77% | Rolling | Suburban | 3.3 | 1020 – 1260 |
| Edward Waters College | www.ewc.edu | (904) 366-2715 | $9,176 | 54% | Rolling | Urban | 2.9 | N/A |
| Embry Riddle Aeronautical University | www.embryriddle.edu | (800) 862-2416 | $22,190 | 82% | Rolling | Suburban | 3.3 | 1010 – 1230 |
| Flagler College | www.flagler.edu | (800) 304-4208 | $8,000 | 33% | March 1 | Suburban | 3.3 | 1040 – 1210 |

# Schools in Florida

| College | Website | Phone | Tuition | Acceptance Rate | Application Deadline | Setting | GPA | SAT |
|---|---|---|---|---|---|---|---|---|
| Florida A&M University | www.famu.edu | (850) 599-3796 | $2,852 in-state, $14,949 out-of-state | 71% | May 10 | Urban | N/A | 880 – 1100 |
| Florida Atlantic University | www.fau.edu | (561) 297-3040 | $3,092 in-state, $15,599 out-of-state | 72% | June 1 | Urban | 3.4 | 930 – 1130 |
| Florida Gulf Coast University | www.fgcu.edu | (239) 590-7878 | $3,150 in-state, $15,248 out-of-state | 72% | August 15 | Suburban | 3.5 | 940 – 1120 |
| Florida Institute of Technology | www.fit.edu | (800) 888-4348 | $23,730 | 85% | Rolling | Urban | 3.5 | 1040 – 1270 |
| Florida International University | www.fiu.edu | (305) 348-2363 | $3,157 in-state, $15,664 out-of-state | 43% | Rolling | Urban | 3.6 | 1070 – 1220 |
| Florida Memorial College | www.fmc.edu | (305) 626-3750 | $11,110 | 45% | Rolling | Suburban | 2.6 | N/A |
| Florida Southern College | www.flsouthern.edu | (863) 680-4131 | $17,740 | 75% | Rolling | Suburban | 3.3 | 900 – 1130 |
| Florida State University | www.fsu.edu | (850) 644-6200 | $3,038 in-state, $15,544 out-of-state | 64% | March 1 | Urban | 3.8 | 1050 – 1250 |
| International College | www.internationalcollege.edu | (239) 513-1122 | $8,540 | 98% | Rolling | Suburban | N/A | N/A |
| Jacksonville University | www.jacksonville.edu | (800) 225-2027 | $18,830 | 70% | Rolling | Suburban | 3.2 | 930 – 1170 |
| Lynn University | www.lynn.edu | (800) 888-5966 | $24,750 | 77% | Rolling | Suburban | 2.6 | 800 – 1030 |

**Get the guide at collegeprowler.com**

# Schools in Florida

| College | Website | Phone | Tuition | Acceptance Rate | Application Deadline | Setting | GPA | SAT |
|---|---|---|---|---|---|---|---|---|
| Northwood University–Florida Campus | www.northwood.edu | (561) 478-5500 | $14,529 | 61% | Rolling | Suburban | 2.9 | 840 – 1070 |
| Nova Southeastern University | www.nova.edu | (954) 262-8000 | $15,820 | 64% | Rolling | Suburban | 3.5 | 880 – 1100 |
| Palm Beach Atlantic University | www.pba.edu | (888) 468-6722 | $16,360 | 87% | Rolling | Urban | 3.4 | 980 – 1170 |
| Ringling School of Art and Design | www.ringling.edu | (800) 255-7695 | $21,620 | 67% | Rolling | Urban | 3.5 | N/A |
| ✓ Rollins College | www.rollins.edu | (407) 646-2161 | $27,700 | 66% | February 15 | Suburban | 3.4 | 1080 – 1260 |
| Southeastern College of the Assemblies of God | www.secollege.edu | (863) 667-5018 | $10,140 | 85% | N/A | Suburban | 3.3 | N/A |
| St. Leo University | www.saintleo.edu | (800) 334-5532 | $13,880 | 59% | August 15 | Rural | 3.1 | 888 – 1073 |
| St. Thomas University | www.stu.edu | (305) 628-6546 | $17,000 | 43% | Rolling | Urban | 2.9 | 770 – 988 |
| Stetson University | www.stetson.edu | (800) 688-0101 | $23,345 | 76% | Rolling | Suburban | 3.5 | 1030 – 1230 |
| ✓ University of Central Florida | www.ucf.edu | (407) 823-3000 | $3,180 in-state, $15,686 out-of-state | 60% | May 1 | Urban | 3.8 | 1050 – 1230 |
| ✓ University of Florida | www.ufl.edu | (352) 392-1365 | $2,780 in-state, $13,283 out-of-state | 52% | January 12 | Suburban | 3.9 | 1140 – 1340 |

# Schools in Florida

| College | Website | Phone | Tuition | Acceptance Rate | Application Deadline | Setting | GPA | SAT |
|---|---|---|---|---|---|---|---|---|
| ✓ University of Miami | www.miami.edu | (305) 284-4323 | $27,840 | 44% | February 1 | Suburban | 4.0 | 1120 – 1340 |
| University of North Florida | www.unf.edu | (904) 620-2624 | $3,100 in-state, $14,850 out-of-state | 66% | July 2 | Urban | 3.5 | 1000 – 1200 |
| ✓ University of South Florida | www.usf.edu | (813) 974-3350 | $3,166 in-state, $16,040 out-of-state | 62% | April 15 | Urban | 3.6 | 980 – 1190 |
| University of Tampa | www.ut.edu | (888) 646-2738 | $18,172 | 61% | Rolling | Urban | 3.2 | 980 – 1160 |
| University of West Florida | http://uwf.edu | (850) 474-2230 | $3,039 in-state, $15,546 out-of-state | 66% | June 30 | Urban | 3.5 | 1010 – 1210 |
| Warner Southern College | www.warner.edu | (800) 309-9563 | $11,830 | 71% | Rolling | Rural | 3.3 | 718 – 1137 |
| Webber International University | www.webber.edu | (800) 741-1844 | $12,900 | 50% | August 1 | Rural | 2.9 | 756 – 966 |

# Schools in Georgia

| College | Website | Phone | Tuition | Acceptance Rate | Application Deadline | Setting | GPA | SAT |
|---|---|---|---|---|---|---|---|---|
| Agnes Scott College | www.agnesscott.edu | (800) 868-8602 | $22,210 | 66% | Rolling | Urban | 3.6 | 1080 – 1320 |
| Albany State University | http://asuweb.asurams.edu | (229) 430-4646 | $2,774 in-state, $9,410 out-of-state | 24% | July 1 | Urban | 2.8 | N/A |
| Armstrong Atlantic State University | www.armstrong.edu | (912) 927-5277 | $2,734 in-state, $9,702 out-of-state | 65% | July 1 | Urban | 3.0 | 920 – 1120 |
| Atlanta College of Art | www.aca.edu | (800) 832-2104 | $17,500 | 64% | Rolling | Urban | 2.9 | 830 – 1140 |

# Schools in Georgia

| College | Website | Phone | Tuition | Acceptance Rate | Application Deadline | Setting | GPA | SAT |
|---|---|---|---|---|---|---|---|---|
| Augusta State University | www.aug.edu | (706) 737-1632 | $1,351 in-state, $4,654 out-of-state | 65% | July 18 | Urban | 2.8 | 860 – 1070 |
| Berry College | www.berry.edu | (706) 236-2215 | $16,240 | 83% | July 23 | Suburban | 3.6 | 1070 – 1280 |
| Brenau University | www.brenau.edu | (770) 534-6100 | $14,710 | 74% | Rolling | Suburban | N/A | N/A |
| Brewton-Parker College | www.bpc.edu | (912) 583-3265 | $11,820 | 96% | August 20 | Rural | 3.0 | 820 – 1070 |
| Clark Atlanta University | www.cau.edu | (800) 688-3228 | $14,036 | 53% | June 1 | Urban | 3.1 | 690 – 1190 |
| Clayton College and State University | www.clayton.edu | (770) 961-3500 | $2,802 in-state, $9,770 out-of-state | 71% | July 1 | Suburban | 2.9 | 890 – 1100 |
| Columbus State University | www.colstate.edu | (706) 568-2035 | $2,808 in-state, $9,776 out-of-state | 71% | July 28 | Urban | 3.0 | 850 – 1070 |
| Covenant College | www.covenant.edu | (706) 820-2398 | $19,320 | 61% | Rolling | Suburban | 3.6 | 1060 – 1320 |
| Emmanuel College | www.emmanuelcollege.edu | (800) 860-8800 | $9,600 | 49% | August 1 | Rural | N/A | N/A |
| ✓ Emory University | www.emory.edu | (404) 727-6036 | $29,322 | 42% | January 15 | Urban | 3.8 | 1300 – 1460 |
| Fort Valley State University | www.fvsu.edu | (478) 825-6307 | $2,916 in-state, $9,884 out-of-state | 48% | July 23 | Rural | 2.7 | 891 – 1333 |
| Georgia College and State University | www.gcsu.edu | (478) 445-5779 | $3,862 in-state, $13,318 out-of-state | 62% | July 15 | Urban | 3.2 | 1010 – 1160 |
| ✓ Georgia Tech | www.admission.gatech.edu | (404) 894-4154 | $4,278 in-state, $17,558 out-of-state | 63% | January 15 | Urban | 3.7 | 1250 – 1430 |

18 | AT A GLANCE

www.collegeprowler.com

# Schools in Georgia

| College | Website | Phone | Tuition | Acceptance Rate | Application Deadline | Setting | GPA | SAT |
|---|---|---|---|---|---|---|---|---|
| Medical College of Georgia | www.mcg.edu | (706) 721-2725 | $3,794 in-state, $13,418 out-of-state | N/A | Rolling | Urban | N/A | N/A |
| Mercer University | www.mercer.edu | (478) 301-2650 | $22,050 | 79% | June 1 | Urban | 3.6 | 1080 – 1280 |
| Morris Brown College | www.morris-brown.edu | (404) 739-1560 | N/A | 43% | May 1 | Urban | N/A | N/A |
| North Georgia College and State University | www.ngcsu.edu | (800) 498-9581 | $1,393 in-state, $5,573 out-of-state | 59% | July 1 | Rural | 3.3 | 983 – 1160 |
| Oglethorpe University | www.oglethorpe.edu | (404) 364-8307 | $20,900 | 66% | Rolling | Suburban | 3.7 | 1070 – 1300 |
| Paine College | www.paine.edu | (706) 821-8320 | $9,626 | N/A | August 1 | Urban | 2.8 | 680 – 870 |
| Piedmont College | www.piedmont.edu | (800) 277-7020 | $13,500 | 54% | July 15 | Rural | 3.0 | 880 – 1140 |
| Reinhardt College | www.reinhardt.edu | (770) 720-5526 | $12,150 | 68% | Rolling | Rural | N/A | 880 – 1080 |
| Savannah College of Art and Design | www.scad.edu | (912) 525-5100 | $20,750 | 75% | Rolling | Urban | N/A | 960 – 1200 |
| Savannah State University | www.savstate.edu | (912) 356-2181 | $2,940 in-state, $9,908 out-of-state | 42% | September 1 | Urban | 2.7 | 810 – 950 |
| Shorter College | www.shorter.edu | (800) 868-6980 | $12,770 | 83% | Rolling | Urban | 3.3 | 950 – 1160 |
| Southern Polytechnic State University | www.spsu.edu | (770) 528-4188 | $3,134 in-state, $11,144 out-of-state | 85% | August 1 | Suburban | 3.2 | 1010 – 1190 |

**Get the guide at collegeprowler.com**

# Schools in Georgia

| College | Website | Phone | Tuition | Acceptance Rate | Application Deadline | Setting | GPA | SAT |
|---|---|---|---|---|---|---|---|---|
| Spelman College | www.spelman.edu | (800) 982-2411 | $14,940 | 39% | February 1 | Urban | 3.4 | 990 – 1160 |
| State University of West Georgia | www.westga.edu | (770) 836-6416 | $2,906 in-state, $9,874 out-of-state | 62% | July 1 | Rural | 3.0 | 910 – 1100 |
| Thomas University | www.thomasu.edu | (229) 227-6934 | $9,800 | 100% | Rolling | Urban | N/A | N/A |
| Toccoa Falls College | www.tfc.edu | (706) 886-6831 | $11,900 | 75% | Rolling | Rural | 3.4 | 930 – 1160 |
|  University of Georgia | www.uga.edu | (706) 542-8776 | $4,272 in-state, $15,588 out-of-state | 75% | February 1 | Urban | 3.6 | 1120 – 1300 |
| Valdosta State University | www.valdosta.edu | (229) 333-5791 | $2,860 in-state, $9,496 out-of-state | 68% | July 15 | Urban | 3.1 | 930 – 1110 |
| Wesleyan College | www.wesleyan-college.edu | (800) 447-6610 | $10,900 | 77% | N/A | Suburban | 3.6 | 960 – 1210 |

# Schools in Kentucky

| College | Website | Phone | Tuition | Acceptance Rate | Application Deadline | Setting | GPA | SAT |
|---|---|---|---|---|---|---|---|---|
| Alice Lloyd College | www.alc.edu | (888) 280-4252 | $990 | 58% | July 1 | Rural | 3.3 | 800 – 1120 |
| Asbury College | www.asbury.edu | (800) 888-1818 | $17,808 | 73% | Rolling | Suburban | 3.6 | 1020 – 1270 |
| Bellarmine University | www.bellarmine.edu | (502) 452-8131 | $19,980 | 82% | August 15 | Urban | 3.5 | 960 – 1230 |
| Berea College | www.berea.edu | (800) 326-5948 | $516 | 25% | April 30 | Rural | 3.4 | 978 – 1196 |
| Brescia University | www.brescia.edu | (270) 686-4241 | $11,600 | N/A | Rolling | Urban | N/A | N/A |
| Campbellsville University | www.campbellsville.edu | (270) 789-5220 | $13,952 | 80% | August 1 | Rural | 3.2 | 860 – 1130 |
| Centre College | www.centre.edu | (859) 238-5350 | $21,800 | 75% | February 1 | Urban | N/A | 1090 – 1340 |
| Cumberland College | www.cumberlandcollege.edu | (800) 343-1609 | $11,858 | 72% | August 15 | Rural | 3.4 | 860 – 1110 |
| Eastern Kentucky University | www.eku.edu | (800) 465-9191 | $3,792 in-state, $10,464 out-of-state | 76% | August 1 | Suburban | 3.1 | 880 – 1103 |
| Georgetown College | www.georgetowncollege.edu | (502) 863-8009 | $17,290 | 80% | August 1 | Suburban | 3.5 | 920 – 1140 |
| Kentucky Christian College | www.kcc.edu | (800) 522-3181 | $10,640 | 76% | Rolling | Rural | 3.2 | 870 – 1090 |
| Kentucky State University | www.kysu.edu | (800) 325-1716 | $2,828 in-state, $8,472 out-of-state | 47% | July 15 | Urban | N/A | N/A |
| Kentucky Wesleyan College | www.kwc.edu | (800) 999-0592 | $12,510 | 75% | August 21 | Urban | 3.3 | 865 – 1075 |
| Lindsey Wilson College | www.lindsey.edu | (270) 384-8100 | $13,140 | N/A | Rolling | Rural | 3.0 | N/A |

# Schools in Kentucky

| College | Website | Phone | Tuition | Acceptance Rate | Application Deadline | Setting | GPA | SAT |
|---|---|---|---|---|---|---|---|---|
| Mid-Continent College | www.midcontinent.edu | (270) 247-8521 | $9,350 | 88% | Rolling | Rural | 2.9 | 810 – 1010 |
| Midway College | www.Midway.edu | (800) 755-0031 | $12,825 | 74% | Rolling | Rural | 3.0 | 890 – 1110 |
| Morehead State University | www.morehead-state.edu | (606) 783-2000 | $3,840 in-state, $10,200 out-of-state | 71% | Rolling | Rural | 3.1 | N/A |
| Murray State University | www.murray-state.edu | (270) 762-3741 | $3,984 in-state, $6,592 out-of-state | 63% | Rolling | Rural | 3.5 | N/A |
| Northern Kentucky University | www.nku.edu | (800) 637-9948 | $4,368 in-state, $9,096 out-of-state | 89% | August 1 | Suburban | N/A | 840 – 1070 |
| Pikeville College | www.pc.edu | (606) 218-5251 | $10,500 | 100% | August 19 | Urban | 3.2 | N/A |
| Spalding University | www.spalding.edu | (502) 585-7111 | $13,950 | 76% | Rolling | Urban | 2.9 | N/A |
| Thomas More College | www.thomasmore.edu | (800) 825-4557 | $17,320 | 61% | August 15 | Suburban | 3.2 | 920 – 1180 |
| Transylvania University | www.transy.edu | (859) 233-8242 | $18,590 | 86% | February 1 | Urban | 3.6 | 1055 – 1230 |
| Union College | www.unionky.edu | (800) 489-8646 | N/A | N/A | August 1 | Rural | N/A | N/A |
|  University of Kentucky | www.uky.edu | (859) 257-2000 | $5,315 in-state, $12,095 out-of-state | 81% | February 15 | Urban | 3.6 | 1020 – 1250 |
| University of Louisville | www.louisville.edu | (502) 852-6531 | $5,040 in-state, $13,752 out-of-state | 79% | Rolling | Urban | 3.4 | 970 – 1210 |
| Western Kentucky University | www.wku.edu | (270) 745-2551 | $4,468 in-state, $9,316 out-of-state | 93% | August 1 | Urban | 3.2 | 910 – 1110 |

# Schools in Louisiana

| College | Website | Phone | Tuition | Acceptance Rate | Application Deadline | Setting | GPA | SAT |
|---|---|---|---|---|---|---|---|---|
| Centenary College of Louisiana | www.centenary.edu | (318) 869-5131 | $17,360 | 74% | February 15 | Suburban | 3.2 | 1030 – 1270 |
| Dillard University | www.dillard.edu | (800) 216-6637 | $11,550 | 64% | July 1 | Urban | 3.2 | 820 – 1030 |
| Grambling State University | www.gram.edu | (318) 274-6183 | $1,639 in-state, $4,314 out-of-state | 62% | July 15 | Rural | 2.7 | N/A |
| Louisiana College | www.lacollege.edu | (318) 487-7259 | $9,700 | 85% | Rolling | Suburban | 3.5 | 880 – 1170 |
| Louisiana State University–Baton Rouge | www.lsu.edu | (225) 578-1175 | $4,226 in-state, $11,026 out-of-state | 81% | April 15 | Urban | 3.5 | N/A |
| Louisiana State University–Shreveport | www.lsus.edu | (318) 797-5061 | $3,270 in-state, $7,600 out-of-state | 100% | August 1 | Urban | 3.1 | N/A |
| Louisiana Tech University | www.latech.edu | (318) 257-3036 | $3,069 | 92% | July 31 | Rural | 3.2 | N/A |
| Loyola University New Orleans | www.loyno.edu | (800) 456-9652 | $21,078 | 69% | Rolling | Urban | 3.7 | 1130 – 1310 |
| McNeese State University | www.mcneese.edu | (337) 475-5356 | $3,098 in-state, $6,066 out-of-state | 88% | Rolling | Urban | N/A | N/A |
| Nicholls State University | www.nicholls.edu | (985) 448-4507 | $3,239 in-state, $8,687 out-of-state | 99% | Rolling | Rural | 3.0 | 840 – 1090 |
| Northwestern State University of Louisiana | www.nsula.edu | (318) 357-4503 | $3,241 in-state, $9,319 out-of-state | 98% | Rolling | Rural | 3.0 | 858 – 1150 |
| Our Lady of Holy Cross College | www.olhcc.edu | (504) 398-2175 | $6,240 | 97% | July 20 | Suburban | N/A | N/A |

# Schools in Louisiana

| College | Website | Phone | Tuition | Acceptance Rate | Application Deadline | Setting | GPA | SAT |
|---|---|---|---|---|---|---|---|---|
| Southeastern Louisiana University | www.selu.edu | (985) 549-2066 | $3,191 in-state, $8,519 out-of-state | 96% | July 15 | Rural | N/A | N/A |
| Southern University and A&M College | www.subr.edu | (225) 771-2430 | $3,168 in-state, $8,960 out-of-state | 57% | July 1 | Urban | 2.8 | 750 – 950 |
| Southern University–New Orleans | www.suno.edu | (504) 286-5314 | $2,872 in-state, $6,610 out-of-state | 69% | July 1 | Urban | N/A | N/A |
| ✓ Tulane University | www.tulane.edu | (504) 865-5731 | $31,210 | 55% | January 15 | Urban | 3.5 | 1240 – 1420 |
| University of Louisiana–Lafayette | www.louisiana.edu | (337) 482-6467 | $3,124 in-state, $9,304 out-of-state | 87% | Rolling | Urban | 3.1 | N/A |
| University of Louisiana–Monroe | www.ulm.edu | (318) 342-5252 | $3,075 in-state, $9,028 out-of-state | 99% | April 1 | Urban | 3.0 | N/A |
| University of New Orleans | www.uno.edu | (504) 280-6595 | $3,464 in-state, $10,508 out-of-state | 70% | August 31 | Urban | 3.0 | 910 – 1210 |
| Xavier University of Louisiana | www.xula.edu | (504) 520-7388 | $11,400 | 84% | July 1 | Urban | 3.1 | 870 – 1100 |

# Schools in Mississippi

| College | Website | Phone | Tuition | Acceptance Rate | Application Deadline | Setting | GPA | SAT |
|---|---|---|---|---|---|---|---|---|
| Alcorn State University | www.alcorn.edu | (601) 877-6147 | $3,872 in-state, $6,237 out-of-state | 22% | Rolling | Rural | 2.9 | N/A |
| Belhaven College | www.belhaven.edu | (601) 968-5940 | $13,440 | 56% | Rolling | Urban | 3.3 | 960 – 1250 |
| Blue Mountain College | www.bmc.edu | (662) 685-4161 | $6,820 | 64% | Rolling | Rural | 3.3 | N/A |
| Delta State University | www.deltastate.edu | (662) 846-4018 | $3,582 in-state, $8,522 out-of-state | N/A | August 1 | Rural | 2.4 | N/A |
| Jackson State University | www.jsums.edu | (601) 979-2100 | $3,841 in-state, $8,570 out-of-state | 42% | August 1 | Urban | 2.7 | N/A |
| Millsaps College | www.gomillsaps.edu | (601) 974-1050 | $19,518 | 84% | June 1 | Urban | 3.5 | 1050 – 1270 |
| Mississippi College | www.mc.edu | (601) 925-3800 | $11,836 | 58% | August 15 | Suburban | 3.4 | 1020 – 1280 |
| Mississippi State University | www.msstate.edu | (662) 325-2224 | $4,106 in-state, $9,306 out-of-state | 75% | August 1 | Rural | 3.2 | N/A |
| Mississippi University for Women | www.muw.edu | (662) 329-7106 | $3,298 in-state, $7,965 out-of-state | 60% | Rolling | Urban | 3.3 | N/A |
| Mississippi Valley State University | www.mvsu.edu | (662) 254-3344 | $3,411 in-state, $7,965 out-of-state | 99% | August 1 | Rural | 2.7 | N/A |
| Rust College | www.rustcollege.edu | (662) 252-8000 | $6,000 | 47% | Rolling | Rural | N/A | N/A |
| Tougaloo College | www.tougaloo.edu | (601) 977-7764 | $8,860 | 24% | Rolling | Suburban | N/A | N/A |
|  University of Mississippi | www.olemiss.edu | (662) 915-7226 | $4,110 in-state, $9,264 out-of-state | 80% | July 20 | Urban | 3.4 | N/A |

# Schools in Mississippi

| College | Website | Phone | Tuition | Acceptance Rate | Application Deadline | Setting | GPA | SAT |
|---|---|---|---|---|---|---|---|---|
| University of Southern Mississippi | www.usm.edu | (601) 266-5000 | $2,035 in-state, $2,585 out-of-state | 49% | Rolling | Urban | 3.0 | 930 – 1230 |
| William Carey College | www.wmcarey.edu | (601) 318-6103 | $8,115 | 59% | Rolling | Urban | N/A | 870 – 1060 |

# Schools in North Carolina

| College | Website | Phone | Tuition | Acceptance Rate | Application Deadline | Setting | GPA | SAT |
|---|---|---|---|---|---|---|---|---|
| Appalachian State University | www.appstate.edu | (828) 262-2120 | $3,199 in-state, $12,641 out-of-state | 66% | Rolling | Rural | 3.7 | 1020 – 1210 |
| Barber Scotia College | www.b-sc.edu | (704) 789-2900 | $9,200 | 51% | July 1 | Urban | N/A | N/A |
| Barton College | www.barton.edu | (800) 345-4973 | $15,363 | 74% | Rolling | Urban | 3.3 | 820 – 1130 |
| Belmont Abbey College | www.belmontabbeycollege.edu | (704) 825-6665 | $15,778 | 69% | August 15 | Suburban | 3.0 | 860 – 1110 |
| Bennett College | www.bennett.edu | (336) 370-8624 | $11,801 | 74% | Rolling | Urban | N/A | N/A |
| Brevard College | www.brevard.edu | (828) 884-8300 | $14,740 | 82% | Rolling | Rural | 2.9 | 770 – 1193 |
| Campbell University | www.campbell.edu | (910) 893-1320 | $14,420 | 58% | September 3 | Rural | 3.5 | 1005 – 1250 |
| Catawba College | www.catawba.edu | (800) 228-2922 | $17,600 | 64% | Rolling | Suburban | 3.1 | 950 – 1130 |
| Chowan College | www.chowan.edu | (252) 398-1236 | $14,100 | 67% | Rolling | Rural | 2.9 | 760 – 970 |

 **Get the guide at collegeprowler.com**

# Schools in North Carolina

| College | Website | Phone | Tuition | Acceptance Rate | Application Deadline | Setting | GPA | SAT |
|---|---|---|---|---|---|---|---|---|
| ✓ Davidson College | www.davidson.edu | (800) 768-0380 | $27,171 | 32% | January 2 | Suburban | N/A | 1270 – 1440 |
| ✓ Duke University | www.duke.edu | (919) 684-3214 | $30,720 | 25% | January 2 | Suburban | 3.9 | 1330 – 1520 |
| East Carolina University | www.ecu.edu | (252) 328-6640 | $3,454 in-state, $13,668 out-of-state | 77% | March 15 | Urban | 3.4 | 950 – 1130 |
| Elizabeth City State University | www.ecsu.edu | (252) 335-3305 | $2,950 in-state, $11,214 out-of-state | 76% | August 1 | Rural | 2.7 | 720 – 900 |
| ✓ Elon University | www.elon.edu | (800) 334-8448 | $17,555 | 45% | January 10 | Suburban | 3.6 | 1070 – 1250 |
| Fayetteville State University | www.uncfsu.edu | (910) 672-1371 | $2,279 in-state, $11,715 out-of-state | 85% | July 15 | Urban | 2.8 | 770 – 950 |
| Gardner-Webb University | www.gardner-webb.edu | (800) 253-6472 | $15,130 | 74% | Rolling | Rural | 3.4 | 900 – 1140 |
| Greensboro College | www.gborocollege.edu | (336) 272-7102 | $16,820 | 74% | Rolling | Urban | 3.0 | 860 – 1090 |
| ✓ Guilford College | www.guilford.edu | (800) 992-7759 | $20,290 | 69% | February 15 | Suburban | 3.0 | 1020 – 1270 |
| High Point University | www.highpoint.edu | (800) 345-6993 | $15,700 | 87% | Rolling | Urban | 2.8 | 920 – 1130 |
| John Wesley College | johnwesley.edu | N/A | $8,210 | 69% | August 1 | Suburban | 2.8 | N/A |
| Johnson C. Smith University | www.jcsu.edu | (704) 378-1010 | $13,712 | 48% | Rolling | Urban | 2.9 | 825 – 1009 |
| Lees-McRae College | www.lmc.edu | (828) 898-8723 | $15,228 | 80% | Rolling | Rural | 3.0 | 860 – 1080 |
| Lenoir-Rhyne College | www.lrc.edu | (828) 328-7300 | $17,550 | 81% | Rolling | Urban | 3.4 | 900 – 1150 |

# Schools in North Carolina

| College | Website | Phone | Tuition | Acceptance Rate | Application Deadline | Setting | GPA | SAT |
|---|---|---|---|---|---|---|---|---|
| Livingstone College | www.livingstone.edu | (704) 216-6001 | $13,527 | 15% | August 2 | Urban | 2.6 | 680 – 890 |
| Mars Hill College | www.mhc.edu | (800) 543-1514 | $15,922 | 81% | Rolling | Rural | N/A | 850 – 1080 |
| Meredith College | www.meredith.edu | (919) 760-8581 | $19,000 | 87% | Rolling | Urban | 3.0 | 940 – 1130 |
| Methodist College | www.methodist.edu | (910) 630-7027 | $16,710 | 76% | Rolling | Urban | 3.2 | 870 – 1110 |
| Montreat College | www.montreat.edu | (800) 622-6968 | $15,108 | 78% | Rolling | Suburban | 3.1 | 928 – 1143 |
| Mount Olive College | www.moc.edu | (919) 658-7164 | $11,220 | 74% | Rolling | Rural | 3.0 | 850 – 1040 |
| North Carolina A&T State University | www.ncat.edu | (336) 334-7946 | $2,722 in-state, $12,089 out-of-state | 81% | Rolling | Urban | N/A | N/A |
| North Carolina Central University | www.nccu.edu | (919) 530-6298 | $3,524 in-state, $12,968 out-of-state | 81% | July 3 | Urban | 2.7 | 740 – 920 |
| North Carolina School of the Arts | www.ncarts.edu | (336) 770-3291 | $4,307 in-state, $15,587 out-of-state | 40% | March 1 | Urban | N/A | 1040 – 1260 |
| North Carolina State University–Raleigh | www.ncsu.edu | (919) 515-2434 | $4,294 in-state, $16,192 out-of-state | 62% | February 1 | Urban | 4.0 | 1100 – 1300 |
| North Carolina Wesleyan College | www.ncwc.edu | (800) 488-6292 | $12,443 | 83% | July 30 | Suburban | N/A | N/A |
| Peace College | www.peace.edu | (800) 732-2347 | $16,880 | 78% | August 1 | Urban | 3.0 | 688 – 1258 |

# Schools in North Carolina

| College | Website | Phone | Tuition | Acceptance Rate | Application Deadline | Setting | GPA | SAT |
|---|---|---|---|---|---|---|---|---|
| Pfeiffer University | www.pfeiffer.edu | (800) 338-2060 | $14,570 | 72% | Rolling | Rural | 3.1 | 880 – 1110 |
| Queens University of Charlotte | www.queens.edu | (800) 849-0202 | $17,008 | 74% | Rolling | Urban | 3.3 | 1000 – 1170 |
| Salem College | www.salem.edu | (336) 721-2621 | $16,490 | 70% | Rolling | Urban | 3.5 | 1020 – 1250 |
| Shaw University | www.shawuniversity.edu | (800) 214-6683 | $9,438 | 44% | July 30 | Urban | 2.4 | 645 – 885 |
| St. Andrews Presbyterian College | www.sapc.edu | (800) 763-0198 | $15,725 | 84% | Rolling | Rural | N/A | 870 – 1105 |
| St. Augustine's College | www.st-aug.edu | (919) 516-4016 | $10,388 | 60% | July 1 | Urban | 2.4 | 660 – 840 |
| University of North Carolina–Asheville | www.unca.edu | (828) 251-6481 | $3,392 in-state, $12,592 out-of-state | 73% | March 15 | Urban | 3.7 | 1060 – 1270 |
| ✓ University of North Carolina–Chapel Hill | www.unc.edu | (919) 966-3621 | $3,205 in-state, $16,303 out-of-state | 37% | January 15 | Suburban | 4.0 | 1190 – 1390 |
| University of North Carolina–Charlotte | www.uncc.edu | (704) 687-2213 | $3,419 in-state, $13,531 out-of-state | 72% | July 1 | Suburban | 3.5 | 970 – 1160 |
| University of North Carolina–Greensboro | www.uncg.edu | (336) 334-5243 | $3,830 in-state, $15,262 out-of-state | 77% | August 1 | Urban | 3.5 | 940 – 1140 |

✓ Get the guide at collegeprowler.com

# Schools in North Carolina

| College | Website | Phone | Tuition | Acceptance Rate | Application Deadline | Setting | GPA | SAT |
|---|---|---|---|---|---|---|---|---|
| University of North Carolina–Pembroke | www.uncp.edu | (910) 521-6262 | $1,689 in-state, $11,129 out-of-state | 86% | Rolling | Rural | 3.0 | 850 – 1030 |
| University of North Carolina–Wilmington | www.uncwil.edu | (910) 962-3243 | $3,626 in-state, $13,336 out-of-state | 54% | February 1 | Suburban | 3.7 | 1020 – 1200 |
| ✓ Wake Forest University | www.wfu.edu | (336) 758-5201 | $28,310 | 45% | January 15 | Suburban | N/A | 1240 – 1390 |
| Warren Wilson College | www.warren-wilson.edu | (800) 934-3536 | $17,738 | 79% | March 15 | Rural | 3.3 | 1050 – 1290 |
| Western Carolina University | www.wcu.edu | (828) 227-7317 | $3,448 in-state, $12,884 out-of-state | 74% | August 1 | Rural | 3.3 | 920 – 1110 |
| Wingate University | www.wingate.edu | (800) 755-5550 | $16,000 | 82% | Rolling | Suburban | 3.4 | 920 – 1150 |
| Winston-Salem State University | www.wssu.edu | (336) 750-2070 | $2,675 in-state, $11,015 out-of-state | 77% | August 30 | Urban | 2.8 | 780 – 940 |

✓ **Get the guide at collegeprowler.com**

# Schools in South Carolina

| College | Website | Phone | Tuition | Acceptance Rate | Application Deadline | Setting | GPA | SAT |
|---|---|---|---|---|---|---|---|---|
| Allen University | www.allenuniversity.edu | (803) 376-5735 | $7,518 | 61% | Rolling | Urban | 2.3 | N/A |
| Anderson College | www.ac.edu | (864) 231-5607 | $14,225 | 79% | July 1 | Urban | 3.6 | 930 – 1140 |
| Benedict College | www.benedict.edu | (803) 253-5143 | $12,256 | 72% | Rolling | Urban | 2.4 | 680 – 900 |
| Charleston Southern University | www.csuniv.edu | (843) 863-7050 | $15,292 | 80% | Rolling | Suburban | 3.3 | 930 – 1130 |
| Claflin University | www.claflin.edu | (803) 535-5747 | $10,452 | 40% | Rolling | Urban | 3.0 | 845 – 1110 |
| ✓ Clemson University | www.clemson.edu | (864) 656-2287 | $8,012 in-state, $15,610 out-of-state | 61% | May 1 | Rural | 3.9 | 1120 – 1290 |
| Coastal Carolina University | www.coastal.edu | (843) 349-2026 | $6,100 in-state, $14,200 out-of-state | 71% | August 15 | Suburban | 3.3 | 940 – 1130 |
| Coker College | www.coker.edu | (843) 383-8050 | $16,800 | 61% | Rolling | Rural | 3.2 | 880 – 1090 |
| ✓ College of Charleston | www.cofc.edu | (843) 953-5670 | $6,202 in-state, $14,140 out-of-state | 60% | April 1 | Urban | 3.7 | 1120 – 1280 |
| Columbia College | www.columbiacollegesc.edu | (800) 277-1301 | $17,990 | 86% | August 1 | Urban | 3.2 | 850 – 1060 |
| Columbia International University | www.ciu.edu | (800) 777-2227 | $13,206 | N/A | Rolling | Urban | N/A | N/A |
| Converse College | www.converse.edu | (864) 596-9040 | $19,960 | 69% | August 1 | Urban | 3.5 | 980 – 1210 |
| Erskine College | www.erskine.edu | (864) 379-8838 | $18,128 | 70% | Rolling | Rural | 3.6 | 1005 – 1243 |

# Schools in South Carolina

| College | Website | Phone | Tuition | Acceptance Rate | Application Deadline | Setting | GPA | SAT |
|---|---|---|---|---|---|---|---|---|
| Francis Marion University | www.fmarion.edu | (843) 661-1231 | $5,540 in-state, $10,945 out-of-state | 76% | Rolling | Rural | 3.3 | 860 – 1050 |
| ✓ Furman University | www.engage-furman.com | (864) 294-2034 | $24,408 | 60% | January 15 | Urban | 3.8 | 1190 – 1370 |
| Johnson & Wales University-Charleston | www.jwu.edu/charles | 843-727-3018 | Varies | N/A | Rolling | Urban | N/A | N/A |
| Lander University | www.lander.edu | (864) 388-8307 | $5,628 in-state, $11,537 out-of-state | 81% | August 1 | Suburban | 3.5 | 900 – 1090 |
| Limestone College | www.limestone.edu | (864) 488-4554 | $13,200 | 60% | August 26 | Suburban | 2.9 | 830 – 1050 |
| Medical University of South Carolina | www.musc.edu | (843) 792-2300 | Varies from $7,242 - $18,600 | N/A | Rolling | Urban | N/A | N/A |
| Morris College | www.morris.edu | (803) 934-3225 | $7,785 | 94% | Rolling | Urban | 2.6 | N/A |
| Newberry College | www.newberry.edu/ | (800) 845-4955 | $17,470 | 58% | Rolling | Urban | N/A | 820 – 1090 |
| North Greenville College | www.ngc.edu | (864) 977-7001 | $9,760 | 95% | Rolling | Rural | 3.8 | 930 – 1150 |
| Presbyterian College | www.presby.edu/ | (864) 833-8230 | $21,622 | 78% | Rolling | Rural | 3.4 | 1040 – 1240 |
| South Carolina State University | www.scsu.edu | (803) 536-7185 | $3,085 in-state, $6,489 out-of-state | 55% | July 1 | Urban | 2.9 | 730 – 910 |
| Southern Wesleyan University | www.swu.edu | (864) 644-5550 | $14,750 | 68% | Rolling | Rural | 3.6 | 880 – 1160 |

# Schools in South Carolina

| College | Website | Phone | Tuition | Acceptance Rate | Application Deadline | Setting | GPA | SAT |
|---|---|---|---|---|---|---|---|---|
| The Citadel | www.citadel.edu | (843) 953-5230 | $6,828 in-state, $15,446 out-of-state | 67% | Rolling | Urban | 3.3 | 1003 – 1210 |
| University of South Carolina–Aiken | www.usca.edu | (803) 641-3366 | $5,116 in-state, $10,256 out-of-state | 65% | August 20 | Suburban | 3.4 | 890 – 1110 |
| University of South Carolina–Columbia | www.sc.edu | (803) 777-7700 | $6,356 in-state, $16,724 out-of-state | 64% | February 15 | Urban | 3.8 | 1030 – 1250 |
| University of South Carolina–Upstate | www.uscs.edu | (864) 503-5246 | $6,261 in-state, $12,505 out-of-state | 49% | Rolling | Urban | 3.4 | 890 – 1070 |
| Voorhees College | www.voorhees.edu | (803) 703-7111 | $7,276 | 35% | Rolling | Rural | N/A | 700 – 800 |
| Winthrop University | www.winthrop.edu | (803) 323-2191 | $7,816 in-state, $14,410 out-of-state | 66% | Rolling | Suburban | 3.6 | 960 – 1160 |
| Wofford College | www.wofford.edu | (864) 597-4130 | $20,610 | 80% | February 1 | Urban | 4.0 | 1140 – 1340 |

Get the guide at collegeprowler.com

# Schools in Tennessee

| College | Website | Phone | Tuition | Acceptance Rate | Application Deadline | Setting | GPA | SAT |
|---|---|---|---|---|---|---|---|---|
| American Baptist College | www.abcnash.edu | (616) 256-1463 | N/A | N/A | N/A | N/A | N/A | N/A |
| Aquinas College | www.aquinas-tn.edu | (615) 297-7545 | $12,240 | N/A | Rolling | Suburban | N/A | N/A |
| Austin Peay State University | www.apsu.edu | (931) 221-7661 | $4,224 in-state, $12,712 out-of-state | 93% | September 3 | Urban | 2.9 | 850 – 1120 |
| Belmont University | www.belmont.edu | (615) 460-6785 | $16,220 | 75% | May 1 | Urban | 3.4 | 1030 – 1240 |
| Bethel College | www.bethel-college.edu | (731) 352-4030 | $9,630 | 49% | Rolling | Rural | N/A | 470 – 1411 |
| Bryan College | www.bryan.edu | (800) 277-9522 | $14,100 | 81% | July 31 | Rural | 3.6 | 1000 – 1290 |
| Carson-Newman College | www.cn.edu | (800) 678-9061 | $14,420 | 88% | August 1 | Rural | 3.3 | N/A |
| Christian Brothers University | www.cbu.edu | (901) 321-3205 | $18,230 | 85% | March 1 | Urban | 3.4 | 960 – 1200 |
| Crichton College | www.crichton.edu | (901) 320-9797 | $12,095 | 55% | Rolling | Urban | N/A | N/A |
| Cumberland University | www.cumberland.edu | (615) 444-2562 | $12,280 | 66% | Rolling | Suburban | 3.1 | 790 – 1040 |
| David Lipscomb University | www.lipscomb.edu | (615) 269-1776 | $13,486 | 73% | Rolling | Urban | 3.4 | 990 – 1306 |
| East Tennessee State University | www.etsu.edu | (423) 439-4213 | $4,172 in-state, $9,452 out-of-state | 82% | Rolling | Urban | 3.2 | 890 – 1160 |
| Fisk University | www.fisk.edu | (888) 702-0022 | $12,450 | 66% | June 1 | Urban | 3.0 | 800 – 1030 |

# Schools in Tenessee

| College | Website | Phone | Tuition | Acceptance Rate | Application Deadline | Setting | GPA | SAT |
|---|---|---|---|---|---|---|---|---|
| Free Will Baptist Bible College | www.fwbbc.edu | (800) 76-FWBBC | $8,880 | N/A | April 15 | Urban | N/A | N/A |
| Freed-Hardeman University | www.fhu.edu | (800) 630-3480 | $11,960 | 99% | Rolling | Rural | 3.4 | N/A |
| Johnson Bible College | www.jbc.edu/college | (865) 573-4517 | $5,800 | N/A | Rolling | Rural | N/A | N/A |
| King College | www.king.edu | (423) 652-4861 | $17,040 | 92% | Rolling | Urban | 3.5 | 993 – 1258 |
| Lambuth University | www.lambuth.edu | (731) 425-3223 | $12,490 | 65% | Rolling | Urban | 3.2 | 920 – 1230 |
| Lane College | www.lanecollege.edu | (731) 426-7533 | $7,176 | 17% | August 1 | Urban | 3.1 | N/A |
| Lee University | www.leeuniversity.edu | (423) 614-8500 | $9,075 | 56% | September 1 | Urban | 3.4 | 930 – 1180 |
| LeMoyne-Owen College | www.lemoyne-owen.edu | (901) 942-7302 | $9,360 | 45% | April 1 | Urban | N/A | N/A |
| Lincoln Memorial University | www.lmunet.edu | (423) 869-6280 | $12,600 | 85% | Rolling | Rural | N/A | 890 – 1110 |
| Martin Methodist College | www.martinmethodist.edu | (931) 363-9804 | $13,000 | 95% | August 2 | Rural | N/A | N/A |
| Maryville College | www.maryvillecollege.edu | (865) 981-8092 | $21,065 | 81% | March 1 | Urban | 3.6 | 960 – 1260 |
| Memphis College of Art | www.mca.edu | (800) 727-1088 | $15,860 | 76% | August 3 | Urban | 2.8 | N/A |

# Schools in Tennessee

| College | Website | Phone | Tuition | Acceptance Rate | Application Deadline | Setting | GPA | SAT |
|---|---|---|---|---|---|---|---|---|
| Middle Tennessee State University | www.mtsu.edu | (615) 898-2111 | $4,130 in-state, $12,618 out-of-state | 75% | July 1 | Urban | N/A | N/A |
| Milligan College | www.milligan.edu | (423) 461-8730 | $16,360 | 76% | August 1 | Urban | 3.5 | 990–1250 |
| O'More College of Design | www.omorecollege.edu | (615) 794-4254 | N/A | N/A | N/A | Urban | N/A | N/A |
| ✓ Rhodes College | www.rhodes.edu | (800) 844-5969 | $24,274 | 72% | February 1 | Urban | 3.7 | 1190–1360 |
| Sewanee–University of the South | www.sewanee.edu | (800) 522-2234 | $25,580 | 72% | February 1 | Rural | 3.4 | 1160–1320 |
| Southern Adventist University | www.southern.edu | (423) 238-2844 | $13,410 | 76% | September 7 | Rural | 3.3 | N/A |
| Tennessee State University | www.tnstate.edu | (615) 963-5101 | $4,038 in-state, $12,526 out-of-state | 59% | August 1 | Urban | N/A | 820–1020 |
| Tennessee Technological University | www.tntech.edu | (800) 255-8881 | $3,900 in-state, $8,542 out-of-state | 80% | August 1 | Rural | 3.2 | 1000–1250 |
| Tennessee Temple University | www.tntemple.edu | (800) 553-4050 | $13,430 | N/A | N/A | Urban | N/A | N/A |
| Tennessee Wesleyan College | www.twcnet.edu | (423) 746-5286 | $12,340 | 83% | Rolling | Urban | 3.2 | N/A |
| Trevecca Nazarene University | www.trevecca.edu | (615) 248-1320 | $12,792 | 67% | Rolling | Urban | 3.2 | N/A |
| Tusculum College | www.tusculum.edu | (800) 729-0256 | $15,110 | 78% | Rolling | Rural | 2.9 | 820–1082 |

# Schools in Tennessee

| College | Website | Phone | Tuition | Acceptance Rate | Application Deadline | Setting | GPA | SAT |
|---|---|---|---|---|---|---|---|---|
| Union University | www.uu.edu | (800) 338-6466 | $15,370 | 84% | March 1 | Urban | 3.5 | 1020 – 1250 |
| University of Memphis | www.memphis.edu | (901) 678-2111 | $4,392 in-state, $13,116 out-of-state | 73% | August 1 | Urban | N/A | 925 – 1200 |
| ✓ University of Tennessee | www.tennessee.edu | (865) 974-2184 | $4,748 in-state, $14,528 out-of-state | 71% | February 1 | Urban | 3.4 | 3.4 |
| University of Tennessee Health Sciences Center | www.utmem.edu | (901) 448-5500 | Varies with field | Varies | Varies | Urban | N/A | N/A |
| University of Tennessee–Chattanooga | www.utc.edu | (423) 425-4662 | $4,094 in-state, $12,350 out-of-state | 52% | Rolling | Urban | 3.2 | N/A |
| University of Tennessee–Martin | www.utm.edu | (800) 829-8861 | $4,044 in-state, $12,140 out-of-state | 56% | Rolling | Rural | 3.3 | N/A |
| ✓ Vanderbilt University | www.vanderbilt.edu | (800) 288-0432 | $29,990 | 40% | January 2 | Urban | N/A | 1250 – 1430 |

# Schools in Virginia

| College | Website | Phone | Tuition | Acceptance Rate | Application Deadline | Setting | GPA | SAT |
|---|---|---|---|---|---|---|---|---|
| Averett University | www.averett.com | (800) 283-7388 | $18,430 | 89% | September 1 | Suburban | 3.0 | 860 – 1045 |
| Bluefield College | www.bluefield.edu | (276) 326-4214 | $10,615 | 67% | Rolling | Rural | 3.0 | 820 – 1030 |
| Bridgewater College | www.bridgewater.edu | (800) 759-8328 | $17,990 | 88% | Rolling | Rural | 3.3 | 910 – 1120 |
| Christendom College | www.christendom.edu | (800) 877-5456 | $14,420 | 80% | Rolling | Rural | 3.6 | 1130 – 1330 |
| Christopher Newport University | www.cnu.edu | (757) 594-7015 | $5,314 in-state, $12,626 out-of-state | 58% | March 1 | Suburban | 3.3 | 1040 – 1220 |
| ✓ College of William and Mary | www.wm.edu | (757) 221-4223 | $7,096 in-state, $21,796 out-of-state | 34% | January 5 | Urban | 4.0 | 1260 – 1440 |
| Eastern Mennonite University | www.emu.edu | (800) 368-2665 | $18,220 | 82% | August 15 | Urban | 3.4 | 930 – 1235 |
| Emory and Henry College | www.ehc.edu | (800) 848-5493 | $16,690 | 81% | Rolling | Rural | 3.4 | 922 – 1135 |
| Ferrum College | www.ferrum.edu | (800) 868-9797 | $16,870 | 74% | Rolling | Rural | 2.7 | 780 – 970 |
| George Mason University | www.gmu.edu | (703) 993-2400 | $5,580 in-state, $16,680 out-of-state | 66% | January 15 | Suburban | 3.3 | 1000 – 1210 |
| Hampden-Sydney College | www.hsc.edu | (800) 755-0733 | $22,946 | 71% | March 1 | Rural | 3.1 | 1030 – 1240 |
| Hollins University | www.hollins.edu | (800) 456-9595 | $21,675 | 86% | Rolling | Suburban | 3.4 | 1040 – 1260 |
| ✓ James Madison University | www.jmu.edu | (540) 568-5681 | $5,476 in-state, $14,420 out-of-state | 62% | January 15 | Urban | 3.7 | 1080 – 1250 |

# Schools in Virginia

| College | Website | Phone | Tuition | Acceptance Rate | Application Deadline | Setting | GPA | SAT |
|---|---|---|---|---|---|---|---|---|
| Radford University | www.radford.edu | (540) 831-5371 | $4,762 in-state, $11,762 out-of-state | 74% | May 1 | Urban | 3.1 | 3.1 |
| Randolph-Macon College | www.rmc.edu | (800) 888-1762 | $22,625 | 77% | March 1 | Suburban | 3.3 | 1000 – 1200 |
| Roanoke College | www.roanoke.edu | (540) 375-2270 | $22,109 | 77% | March 1 | Suburban | 3.2 | 1020 – 1210 |
| Shenandoah University | www.su.edu | (540) 665-4581 | $19,240 | 73% | Rolling | Suburban | 3.1 | 880 – 1130 |
| St. Paul's College | www.saint-pauls.edu | (434) 848-1856 | $9,816 | 81% | Rolling | Rural | 2.1 | 620 – 820 |
| Sweet Briar College | www.sbc.edu | (800) 381-6142 | $21,080 | 88% | February 1 | Rural | 3.4 | 990 – 1190 |
| University of Mary Washington | www.mwc.edu/admissions | (540) 654-2000 | $4,670 in-state, $12,800 out-of-state | 60% | February 1 | Suburban | 3.6 | 1130 – 1300 |
| ✓ University of Richmond | www.richmond.edu | (804) 289-8640 | $26,520 | 42% | January 15 | Suburban | 3.5 | 1240 – 1390 |
| ✓ University of Virginia | www.virginia.edu | (434) 982-3200 | $6,600 in-state, $22,700 out-of-state | 39% | January 2 | Suburban | 4.0 | 1230 – 1430 |
| Virginia State University | www.vsu.edu | (804) 524-5902 | $4,412 in-state, $11,272 out-of-state | 66% | May 1 | Suburban | 2.7 | 710 – 890 |
| ✓ Virginia Tech | www.vt.edu | (540) 231-6267 | $5,838 in-state, $16,531 out-of-state | 69% | January 15 | Rural | 3.6 | 1120 – 1280 |
| ✓ Washington and Lee University | www.wlu.edu | (540) 463-8710 | $25,760 | 31% | January 15 | Rural | N/A | 1300 – 1440 |

# Auburn University

**DISTANCE TO...**
Atlanta: 108 mi.
Panama City: 203 mi.
Savannah: 283 mi.
Nashville: 335 mi.

202 Martin Hall, Auburn University, AL 36849-5145
www.auburn.edu          (334) 844-4080

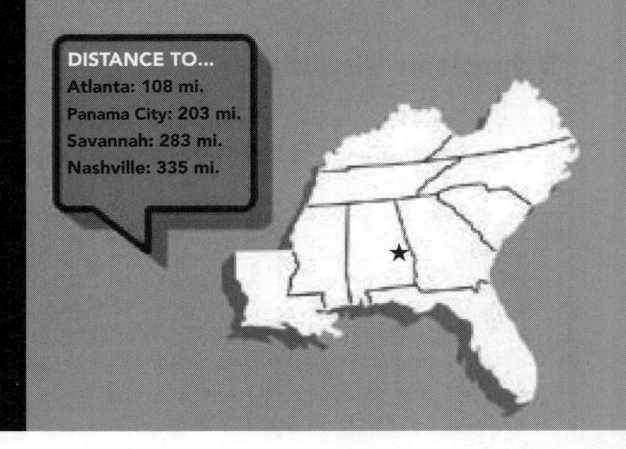

*"It's hard not to get swept up in all the excitement. Students here are full of school spirit and proud to attend AU."*

**Total Enrollment:**
17,584

**Top 10% of High School Class:**
31%

**Average GPA:**
3.5

**Acceptance Rate:**
78%

**Tuition:**
$4,828 in-state, $14,048 out-of-state

**SAT Range (25th-75th Percentile)**
| Verbal | Math | Total |
|---|---|---|
| 510 – 620 | 520 – 620 | 1030 – 1220 |

**ACT Range (25th-75th Percentile)**
| Verbal | Math | Total |
|---|---|---|
| 21-28 | 20-26 | 22-27 |

**Most Popular Majors:**
28% Business
11% Engineering
9% Education
6% Health Professions
4% Psychology

**Students also applied to:***
Clemson University
Florida State University
Georgia Tech
University of Georgia
University of Tennessee

*For more school info check out www.collegeprowler.com

## Table of Contents

| | |
|---|---|
| Academics | 41 |
| Local Atmosphere | 42 |
| Safety & Security | 44 |
| Facilities | 45 |
| Campus Dining | 47 |
| Campus Housing | 49 |
| Diversity | 51 |
| Guys & Girls | 52 |
| Athletics | 54 |
| Greek Life | 56 |
| Drug Scene | 57 |
| Overall Experience | 58 |

## College Prowler Report Card

| | |
|---|---|
| Academics | B- |
| Local Atmosphere | C+ |
| Safety & Security | A- |
| Facilities | B+ |
| Campus Dining | B+ |
| Campus Housing | C |
| Diversity | D- |
| Guys | B+ |
| Girls | B |
| Athletics | A |
| Greek Life | B+ |
| Drug Scene | A- |

# Academics

## Did You Know?

The building known as the Haley Center is where the majority of freshman classes are held. This building is also one of the hardest to navigate. Room numbers are split into three sections: floor number, quadrant number, and room number. So, for example, room 3122 would be on the third floor, first quadrant, in room 22. Good luck!

## The Lowdown
### ON ACADEMICS

**Degrees Awarded:**
Bachelor, Master, Doctorate

**Undergraduate Schools:**
Agriculture, Architecture, Design & Construction, Business, Education, Engineering, Forestry and Wildlife Sciences, Honors College, Human Sciences, Liberal Arts, Nursing, Pharmacy Sciences and Mathematics, and Veterinary Medicine

**Full-time Faculty:**
1,064

**Faculty with Terminal Degree:**
93%

**Student-to-Faculty Ratio:**
16:1

**Average Course Load:**
15 credit hours per semester

**AP Test Score Requirements:**
Possible credit for scores of 3, 4, or 5

**IB Test Score Requirements:**
Possible credit for scores of 5, 6, or 7

**Best Places to Study:**
Ralph Brown Draughon Library

## Students Speak Out
### ON ACADEMICS

"**The teachers are good overall. Math teachers are usually foreign, English teachers are usually anal, history teachers enjoy history, and communication teachers like to talk.**"

Q "In my experience, **the teachers have varied from department to department**. All the math and science professors are going to speak a different language. I am in the business department and I like most of my professors. It also depends on the class. It doesn't matter who I have for accounting; I'm going to hate the class."

Q "As with any place, it all depends on who you get. I have yet to have a teacher I have loathed and I have had only a few that I just didn't care for. **I have had excellent teachers.**"

Q "Most of my teachers have been very **good, helpful, and approachable**. There's also a good program if you need help in a particular class; it's free and not embarrassing because there are a ton of people there. I went there for physics. Overall, the teachers are good."

Q "When you're a freshman, you have pretty large lecture classes and really don't get to know your teachers at all. Once you get into your major, you will find that the teachers are more personal and **willing to help out if you ask**."

> "During my undergrad, my professors were awesome. Just keep in mind that **you can and should ask them anything**. They are there to help you. About the only problem I saw was with my chemistry lab professors. Usually these guys are foreign grad students so they have real problems with English anyway. That's pretty much how it goes at other schools, too."

## The College Prowler Take
### ON ACADEMICS

Most students seem satisfied with their teachers at Auburn. However, as with any university, there are some teachers that don't meet the standard. The biggest problems that students encounter with their teachers are difficulty understanding foreign teachers and getting stuck in lecture classes. As a freshman or sophomore, large classes are usually hard to avoid. However, students feel that personally approaching any teacher with a problem you might have will definitely be a benefit to you. Also, while it may be difficult to understand a teacher with a foreign accent, that doesn't mean they are any less willing to help you in the class. Students claim that most teachers are approachable and helpful, so don't be afraid to take advantage of this. Their job is to help you do the best that you can do during your time at Auburn.

**B-**

**The College Prowler™ Grade on**
## Academics: B-

A high Academics grade generally indicates that professors are knowledgeable, accessible, and genuinely interested in their students' welfare. Other determining factors include class size, how well professors communicate, and whether or not classes are engaging.

# Local Atmosphere

## The Lowdown
### ON LOCAL ATMOSPHERE

**Region:**
Southeast

**City, State:**
Auburn, Alabama

**Setting:**
Rural

**Distance from Montgomery:**
1 hour, 15 minutes

**Distance from Atlanta:**
2 hours

**Points of Interest:**
Chewacla State Park, The Arboretum, football games

**City Websites:**
http://www.auburnalabama.org
http://www.auburnnow.com

**Major Sports Teams:**
None in Alabama; however, many Auburn citizens pay tribute to the Atlanta Braves.

**COLLEGE PROWLER™**

Need help finding things to do? For a detailed listing of all local attractions, check out the College Prowler book on Auburn at *www.collegeprowler.com*.

## Students Speak Out
### ON LOCAL ATMOSPHERE

"**The atmosphere around Auburn is very laid-back and friendly. It's a small college town with no other major schools nearby and one community college in a neighboring town.**"

Q "Auburn is a small town, so it has that small town atmosphere. **Sometimes the smallness will get on your nerves**, but Atlanta is only an hour and a half away, so you get your city fix and come back."

Q "**Auburn is a great little town**. There's plenty to do to keep you occupied. The nightlife is pretty good and overall it's just a classic 'college town.' We are about an hour and a half drive from Atlanta, which has so much to do there. One of the best bar scenes in the country is in Atlanta at Buckhead. I always end up going to Atlanta for concerts and Braves games. We are also only like three hours from the beach—Destin, Panama City, Ft. Walton, etc.—so we go down there for the weekend every once in a while. I love that. New Orleans is only six hours away. Holla!"

Q "The city of Auburn is awesome. They are so supportive of the University and everything that we do. Auburn is a very small town, so when the University was built in it, **the University became the major focal point of the city**. It is really cool to see how the people of the town act toward students. It's awesome to be in a place where the people around you love it as much as you do."

Q "Auburn is a great location. **You can be in four different states within a three-hour drive**. If you are into outdoors stuff, then you will be in heaven. There is great backpacking, kayaking, rock climbing, and mountain biking close by."

Q "My friends that have gone to other universities have told me that they have been **impressed with how nice people are at Auburn.** I can't think of anything to absolutely stay away from, but if you do come down here, definitely visit all of the local Auburn traditions, such as Toomer's Corner, the Arboretum, and football games."

## The College Prowler Take
### ON LOCAL ATMOSPHERE

Most students claim to feel right at home with Auburn's warm and friendly atmosphere. They enjoy the slow pace of the southern university town and at the same time are able to engage in a variety of activities. While there are a few drawbacks, such as lack of entertainment during the breaks, larger cities are just a short drive away. Some students may feel bored at times with what Auburn has to offer, but that doesn't mean that there isn't anything to do here.

**C+**

The College Prowler™ Grade on

### Local Atmosphere: C+

A high Local Atmosphere grade indicates that the area surrounding campus is safe and scenic. Other factors include nearby attractions, proximity to other schools, and the town's attitude toward students.

# Safety & Security

## The Lowdown
### ON SAFETY & SECURITY

**Number of AU Police:**
55

**Phone:**
(334) 844-4158

**Health Center Office Hours:**
Monday 8 a.m.-6 p.m.
Tuesday, Wednesday, Friday 8 a.m.-5 p.m.
Thursday 9 a.m.-6 p.m.
Saturday 8 a.m.-12 p.m.

**Safety Services:**
Emergency call boxes, Tiger Transit, Police escort

## Students Speak Out
### ON SAFETY & SECURITY

"I've never once felt threatened here. People leave their dorm room doors open in the day and at night. It's more social that way I guess, and people don't feel threatened."

Q "For the most part, security and safety are really good. **Crime is not a major attribute of Auburn**. All day and all night you can find people jogging and hanging around outside without worrying."

Q "Auburn is a safe campus, but like any town it has had its fair share of rapes. The basic thing to remember in any college atmosphere, and in general, is to have a good head on your shoulders and be wise to the situation you are in. **Auburn has a personal escort service** and police that patrol the campus."

Q "The security and safety are good on campus. **They have the Tiger Transit**, which runs at night to and from the parking lot to the dorms. And, if you are walking by yourself, there are several safety stations, which have a phone and will make noises and flash lights if you press the emergency button. You can also have a campus police escort."

Q "Auburn is a really safe town for the most part. Of course, crime happens here just like it does anywhere else in the world. There were a few rape attempts back in 2001, and **there were a couple of break-ins this summer**. But, I know what I have to do to stay safe, so if you just use common sense, you should be fine. Don't walk alone at night, especially in unlit areas. Anyone around campus will be happy to give you a ride out to your car or to escort you somewhere. Just ask."

Q "In the fall of 2001, there were three sexual attacks on campus, but after that, security and safety became a huge priority. There have been none since. There are **security shuttles and escorts available anytime** you need them."

## The College Prowler Take
### ON SAFETY & SECURITY

Students agree that they feel very safe at Auburn, especially on the campus itself. Like any other town, Auburn has its bouts with crime, but students advise that if you take the necessary precautions, your time at Auburn will be a safe and enjoyable one. Because of Auburn's friendly atmosphere, it may be easy to take safety for granted. While Auburn is an overall friendly and safe town, you still shouldn't let your guard down, especially when out late at night.

**A-**

The College Prowler™ Grade on
### Safety & Security: A-

A high grade in Safety & Security means that students generally feel safe, campus police are visible, blue-light phones and escort services are readily available, and safety precautions are not overly necessary.

# Facilities

## The Lowdown
### ON FACILITIES

**Student Center:**
Foy Student Union

**Athletic Center:**
Student Activities Center

**Libraries:**
3

**Movie Theatre on Campus?**
Yes, Langdon Hall, College Street

**Bar on Campus?**
No

**Coffeehouse on Campus?**
No

**Popular Places to Chill:**
Foy Student Union
Haley Center/Concourse

### Computers
**High-Speed Network?** Yes
**Wireless Network?** Yes
**Number of Labs:** 11
**24-Hour Labs:** None
**Charge to Print?** Yes

### Favorite Things to Do

Students who want to enjoy a night of relaxation can catch a movie at Langdon Hall, which constantly plays new releases. Many students enjoy staying in shape, so it's not uncommon for students to spend a lot of time working out at the Student Activities Center. And, of course, what would Auburn be without its varsity sports? The most popular activity for Auburn students is to attend a football game during football season. Baseball and basketball are also fairly popular during the rest of the year.

## Students Speak Out
### ON FACILITIES

"The facilities are beautiful here. The athletic facilities are awesome, especially the baseball stadium, Plainsman Park, which was voted consistently one of the top collegiate baseball stadiums in the nation."

"Facilities are great. The whole Student Union area is scheduled to be redone and expanded in the next two or three years. It's adequate now, but does need to be bigger. **Our library is huge** ... something like the biggest on-campus library in the nation [other than Harvard.] It's pretty impressive. The student activities center is great: weight room, basketball courts, volleyball, racquetball, swimming, and tennis. It is an extremely clean campus. Obviously, the sports facilities like Jordan-Hare Stadium and Plainsman Park [baseball] are top-notch."

"The facilities are what you would expect from a school from the SEC; **they are state-of-the-art**, enormous, cost a ton to build, and keep the student body busy the whole year round."

"As far as buildings on campus, they are all in great shape. **All the classrooms have the newest technologies**, as far as projectors and computers, and they are comfortable to stay in for the whole class. Foy Student Union is also a really cool place. On the middle floor, there is a large lobby with several TVs where you can sit and relax. Downstairs is the War Eagle Food Court as well as a game room, a computer lab, the Tiger Club office, a Copy Cat, a small store, and the Freshman Year Experience office."

"**The dorms on campus have been redone in the last two years,** so they are really nice and not that bad to stay in. Also, our library is ranked number two in the nation, after Harvard. It is five stories tall and is full of every book, magazine, and newspaper that you could imagine. There are also computer labs on each floor and several private group study rooms. There is a small snack area in the basement where you can take a break after long hours of studying."

"The campus is really nice. It is clean and safe. **It is an old southern campus**. It has big trees and lots of landscaping. A lot of the facilities are getting makeovers. There is a new women's sports center that has just been built. They are getting ready to build a new student center, and they just finished redoing a lot of the dorms. They put a little shopping center up at the dorms on the hill, which I love. Computer labs are fine. We have a huge library, and they just finished making it more user friendly."

"One of the main reasons I came here was because of the **top-notch facilities**. They are like nothing I have ever seen!"

## The College Prowler Take
### ON FACILITIES

Auburn University knows what it has to do to make the campus a pleasant place for students and faculty. The campus is under constant revision. While that often means that a lot of construction is going on, students feel that it's worth it. Most students rave about the facilities on campus, especially the athletic facilities. Some may feel that too much attention is being focused on the athletic facilities in Auburn. However, work is also being done to update a lot of the older, run-down academic buildings on campus, so that the students can have a better place to learn as well.

## Campus Dining

### The Lowdown
### ON CAMPUS DINING

**B+**

**The College Prowler™ Grade on Facilities: B+**

A high Facilities grade indicates that the campus is aesthetically pleasing and well-maintained; facilities are state-of-the-art, and libraries are exceptional. Other determining factors include the quality of both athletic and student centers and an abundance of things to do on campus.

**Freshman Meal Plan Requirement?**
No

**24-Hour On-Campus Eating?**
No

**Student Favorites:**
Chick-fil-A, Terrell Hall Cafeteria, War Eagle Food Court

**Meal Plan Average Cost:**
$2,200

**Did You Know?**
During finals, Terrell Hall has a midnight breakfast during the week so you can stay awake and keep studying on a full stomach.

## COLLEGE PROWLER™

Need help finding the best on-campus grub? For a detailed listing of all the campus eateries, check out the College Prowler book on Auburn available at www.collegeprowler.com.

## Students Speak Out
### ON CAMPUS DINING

"**People complain about on-campus food, but I like it. I ate at Terrell a lot.** It has a nice, friendly atmosphere. The food was pretty good, too. They served a nice variety and always had a salad bar available. I liked it."

Q "Food on campus is okay. Since campus and town are pretty much right there with each other, **I found myself eating many meals in downtown Auburn.**"

Q "On campus, there are several places to eat. Foy Student Union has a food court with a Chick-fil-A, a wrap place, sub place, Starbucks, grill, and a cafeteria line. **Terrell Hall also has basically the same type stuff.** There's a deli right there in the middle of the dorms, as well as some places at the bottom of Haley Center—the huge class building that you'll be in the majority of freshman year."

Q "**I only eat Chick-fil-A on campus.** Everything else pretty much sucks and it's too expensive."

Q "The food is excellent on campus and I love the way they do it. You have your Tiger Card and either have a descending or an ascending account and **you eat whenever and wherever you want**. A lot of places around town also take Tiger Card. Everywhere is good."

Q "There are actually some decent options on campus. Compared to other schools I've been to, [like] U. of Alabama, U. of Central Florida, **the food here is quite satisfying**."

## The College Prowler Take
### ON CAMPUS DINING

Opinions vary when it comes to eating on campus. Many students enjoy the food that AU has to offer. Terrell Hall and the War Eagle Food Court are the two most popular places for students to eat on campus. There are also several little snack and coffee stands throughout campus, if you need a meal on the run. While both Terrell Hall and War Eagle Food Court offer a variety of foods, some students prefer to eat off campus. This is made easy by being able to use their Tiger Card at almost all restaurants in the downtown area. Unfortunately, meal plans can only be used on campus.

## B+

**The College Prowler™ Grade on**
## Campus Dining: B+

Our grade on Campus Dining addresses the quality of both school-owned dining halls and independent on-campus restaurants as well as the price, availability, and variety of food.

# Campus Housing

### Did You Know?
Many of the dorms on campus are named after alumni, most of who have donated a large amount of money or made significant impacts on the University. One dorm is named after a famous Alabamian—Helen Keller.

## The Lowdown
ON CAMPUS HOUSING

## Students Speak Out
ON CAMPUS HOUSING

**Number of Dormitories:**
22

**Room Types:**
Quad: Suite-style
Extension: Apartment-style, rooms are separate and come with kitchen area
Village: On-campus family living area; 1- or 2-bedroom
Noble: Single bedroom

**You Get:**
Beds, dressers, desks, separate closets, and a suite-style bathroom

**Bed Type:**
Twin extra-long (can be bunked)

**Also Available:**
You can have carpeting installed in your room, but, of course, you have to pay extra for it.

**Cleaning Service?**
Nothing available on campus, but AU does have several laundromats that students have to pay for themselves to do their laundry. There are also several cleaners within close range of the University if you don't want to use the ones on campus.

"Dorms are all right. Try to get into the Quad because it's right in the middle of everything. The CDV Extension is pretty nice. They are more like two-bedroom apartments. The Tiger Transit runs by there, so it's no trouble getting to and from class."

"**Dorms are nice, but the rules suck.** You can live in the Hill, Quad, Extension, or Village. The Quad dorms are right in the middle of campus, a minute walk away from Haley Center. They are pretty nice and in the prettiest area of campus; they are also mainly coed by floor. I stayed there, [in] Harper Hall, my freshman year and it was great being able to sleep until 9:55 for a 10 o'clock class. The rules sucked though: no alcohol and a strict visitor policy, so I don't live there anymore."

> "The Hill Dorms are about **a five-minute walk from the center of campus [Haley Center]**. They are all girls' dorms and are where the sororities have their 'houses.' Each sorority gets one floor out of each dorm. There are fourteen dorms on the Hill. The Extension is the 'on-campus apartments' on the edge of campus, about a ten-minute walk from Haley Center. Rules here are not strict and it's pretty decent. The Village is an 'on-campus apartment complex' and it isn't that great ... kind of like the ghetto if Auburn has one. About a 15-minute walk from Haley Center, but Tiger Transit goes out there."

> "Dorms are okay, but **a dorm is a dorm**. All the dorms in the Quad have been redone and the ones on the Hill are good. Overall they're nice; they're just dorms. Stay away from Noble Hall and the Extension—bad living."

> "**Do not live in CDV Extension**. I had several friends who were stuck there. If they put you there, find off-campus housing ASAP. It is horrible and it is quaintly referred to as the ghetto."

> "Everyone complains about the dorms, but I personally don't see what's so bad about them. Sure, **you have to share a room with another person and a bathroom with three people**, but living in the dorms is a good experience for everyone. Everyone should live there at least for their freshman year. Off-campus housing is sometimes hard to come by and usually pretty expensive."

## The College Prowler Take
### ON CAMPUS HOUSING

**While students mostly agree that living in the dorms isn't a luxury, they do say that spending at least your freshman year there is a good experience. Students with experience in the dorms claim that the Quad and the Hill are the best choices, while the CDV Extension and the Village are not as pleasant. If you choose to live in the dorms, then make sure to apply early for them because they fill up fast and off-campus housing is not always a guarantee. The fight for housing at Auburn can be fierce.**

**The College Prowler™ Grade on**
### Campus Housing: C

A high Campus Housing grade indicates that dorms are clean, well-maintained, and spacious. Other determining factors include variety of dorms, proximity to classes, and social atmosphere.

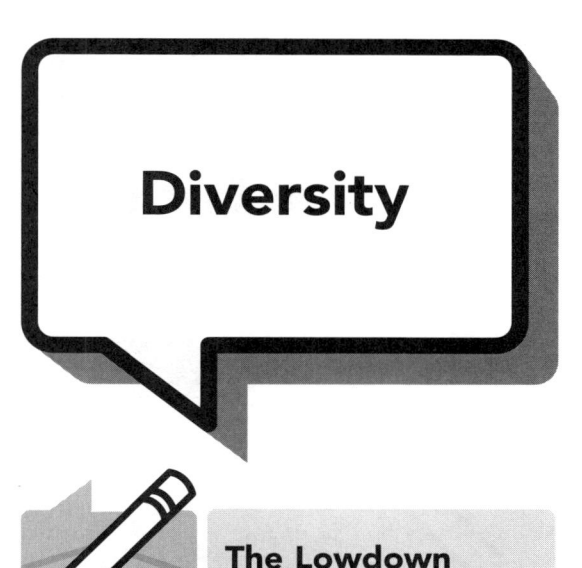

# Diversity

## Political Activity
The most prominent political groups on campus are the College Democrats and the College Republicans. Both groups are active and visible on campus. Check one or both out on the Concourse during special events.

## Gay Tolerance
Auburn has a few gay/lesbian clubs that will hold certain events, but Auburn's conservative atmosphere prevents them from having as large a presence as you might find at other schools.

## The Lowdown
ON DIVERSITY

**Native American:** 0%

**Asian American:** 1%

**African American:** 7%

**Hispanic:** 1%

**White:** 89%

**International:** 2%

**Out-of-State:** 37%

### Minority Clubs
Black Student Union, Indian Student Association, Bangladesh Student Organization, Chinese Student Association, Jewish Student Organization, Korean Student Association, International Student Organization, Auburn Gay/Lesbian/Bisexual Caucus

### Most Popular Religion
Southern Baptist, Methodist

### Economic Status
Lower- to upper-middle-class

## Students Speak Out
ON DIVERSITY

"Anyone who honestly believes that Auburn is that diverse is kidding themselves. I suppose for an Alabama university, it's not bad. But Auburn is largely white and conservative."

"Whether or not you think Auburn is diverse **depends on your definition**. Racially, not much at all. Auburn is well over 90 percent white. Other than that, though, there are a ton of people from out-of-state. I think like 40 percent of students are from outside Alabama. That's really high for a state school. I'm from Texas and there are lots of people from the Atlanta area, which is only an hour and a half away, and you generally meet people from all over the United States."

"**Diversity is something Auburn has been working on**. It's not San Francisco, but we are a diverse university and have something for everybody."

"Auburn's campus thrives on diversity. On our campus **there are members of every race, sex, and religion**. The great thing is that no one treats you any differently because of who you are and that's what made me fall in love with Auburn. The people here are second to none. You won't find a better atmosphere anywhere and I'll stand by that. It's also great that we have organizations for each group to be a part of. These groups cater to the special needs that each member has and does their best to help them out."

💬 "**Not at all diverse**. They're working on it, but you've probably heard of the racial incident that happened with a certain frat at Auburn. If not, then just check out *auburn.edu*, and it'll pretty much tell you what happened."

## The College Prowler Take
ON DIVERSITY

Unfortunately, Auburn University is not the multicultural hub that some think it is. The majority of students are overwhelmingly white, with just a fraction of minorities. Don't let that intimidate you, though. Auburn students all claim to be right at home in Auburn and praise the efforts of the administration to help diversify the University. Auburn has a welcoming and friendly atmosphere, but, as with any school, it's best to visit the school before making a decision to see if you think you'll be happy here.

## Guys & Girls

## The Lowdown
ON GUYS & GIRLS

**Women Undergrads:** 48%
**Men Undergrads:** 52%

### Birth Control Available?
Yes, Auburn University Medical Clinic

### Social Scene
Auburn students are very friendly and interactive with each other. Guys and girls love going out and having fun, so it's not hard to meet people here.

### Hookups or Relationships?
Random hookups and relationships are both prevalent at Auburn. Because of the largely conservative atmosphere, relationships are probably a little more common than hookups. You can make anything happen that you want to, though.

### Dress Code
Fashion is important to Auburn students, but not overwhelmingly so. Since a large part of college consists of rolling out of bed and going to class, casual is always in. The humidity that sticks around for most of the year leaves students usually donning T-shirts and shorts.

**The College Prowler™ Grade on**
## Diversity: D-

A high grade in Diversity indicates that ethnic minorities and international students have a notable presence on campus and that students of different economic backgrounds, religious beliefs, and sexual preferences are well-represented.

## Students Speak Out
ON GUYS & GIRLS

"You'll find all sorts of guys here: city boys, ravers, rednecks and lots of good ol' country boys, too. The girls are pretty much just southern belles."

Q "Guys are guys and girls are girls. There is someone for everyone, but what is most important is how nice and kind they are to each other. **Everyone is awesome**."

Q "Just like anywhere, you have different styles of people. That's what I liked so much about AU's campus. **There is a little bit of anything and everything**. You have preppies, fratties, hippies, punks, the poor, and the rich. People, in general, are great and friendly. Yes, the guys are hot. I was once told that AU has the most beautiful college women. The girls are really into staying in shape."

Q "Well the guys that I know, especially my fraternity bros, are awesome. **Most of the guys are real gentlemen** and respectful of everybody. There is the occasional nut, but overall they are great. The girls are incredible. I have never seen so many wonderful, attractive, genuinely nice girls anywhere. It truly is amazing. Everybody that comes and visits notices that I have made some great girl friends down there and they are all awesome. As far as looks, the ladies got it goin' on."

Q "Well, I am a male, and the girls here are a lot better-looking than from where I come from. Then again, there are 11,000 females my age in the space of less than a square mile. **Everyone I have met has been extremely friendly**. Even the Yankees and the foreigners have picked up on some southern hospitality."

Q "They are all incredibly hot, for the most part. If you aren't from around here, then I think it'll **take a little while for you to get used to the accent**."

## The College Prowler Take
ON GUYS & GIRLS

Well, there's no question about it: students at Auburn are looking pretty good and, if socializing is just as important to you as studying, then Auburn may be right for you. Guys and girls both generally tend to take good care of themselves by working out. On top of good looks, students at Auburn are also friendly and outgoing. If you're looking for a relationship or just a one-night stand, you can make it happen if you try. Most students lean toward relationships, but there are plenty of hookups that go on as well. Ahh … sweet home Alabama!

**The College Prowler™ Grade on**
### Guys: B+
A high grade for Guys indicates that the male population on campus is attractive, smart, friendly, and engaging, and that the school has a decent ratio of guys to girls.

**The College Prowler™ Grade on**
### Girls: B
A high grade for Girls not only implies that the women on campus are attractive, smart, friendly, and engaging, but also that there is a fair ratio of girls to guys.

# Athletics

## The Lowdown
### ON ATHLETICS

**Athletic Division:**
NCAA Division I

**Conference:**
SEC

**Most Popular Sport:**
Football

**Overlooked Teams:**
Rowing team, Rugby team

**School Mascot:**
Tiger

**Men's Varsity Teams:**
Baseball
Basketball
Tennis
Football
Golf
Equestrian
Gymnastics
Soccer
Softball
Swimming & Diving
Track & Field
Volleyball
Rugby
Lacrosse

**Women's Varsity Teams:**
Basketball
Golf
Tennis
Equestrian
Softball
Swimming & Diving
Track & Field
Volleyball
Gymnastics
Soccer
Lacrosse
Rugby

### Getting Tickets
If you want a place to sit at a football game, get your tickets early! Tickets go on sale for undergrad students usually during the summer. Sports like baseball and basketball are not as widely popular as football, so you can probably get your ticket right before the game starts.

### Fields
Plainsman Park, Beard-Eaves Coliseum, Jordan-Hare Stadium, Yarborough Farms, McWhorter Center for Women's Athletics, AU Soccer Complex, James E. Martin Aquatics Center, Luther Young Tennis Complex, Wilbur Hutsell Track Complex, and the Student Activities Center

## Students Speak Out
### ON ATHLETICS

"Football is Auburn's biggest thing in the world. During the fall, it's great. People come from everywhere to go to the games here. The atmosphere is so awesome."

Q "I could go on for days on this one. I couldn't imagine going to a school with more spirit than Auburn. It's unbelievable. Varsity sports, especially football, are huge. Football is essentially life at Auburn. When we played Alabama last year, there was something like 160,000 people in town. **Tailgating every weekend is unbelievable**; the stuff you'll see and the crazy fans that are everywhere will amaze you."

Q "**Basketball is pretty big when we're winning**. Baseball is pretty big. Lots of people go to the games and lots sit up on the Hill and tailgate, getting drunk during the game. I know we kick ass in swimming. IM sports are also huge at Auburn. I know this year AU got rated the number two intramural program in the country. Everyone plays. There are Greek leagues and normal leagues in flag football, basketball, soccer, and softball."

- "I'm not involved in any IM [intramural] sports, so I don't know. Sororities and fraternities do IM sports and those are a lot of fun, but I don't know about campus wide."

- "Varsity sports are big, especially football. Everyone goes to football games and the six or seven weekends when Auburn is at home are **the biggest party weekends of the year**. I played two intramural sports this year. A lot of people play because it's a nice break from all of the studying."

- "**Varsity sports are a major part of Auburn**. The football games are indescribable. It is so much fun. The student body is so supportive of all the sports. We have parades and pep rallies for games and the spirit is unbelievable. Tailgating before games is also an experience. It's just a lot of fun and something that makes Auburn what it is. And it's not just football; it's every sport: basketball, baseball, swimming, etc. They are all great. Intramurals are awesome, too. They have all different divisions, like male, female, coed, Greek, etc. They are very competitive, but they are so much fun. I really enjoyed them this year. I played football and softball and had a blast. Sports are definitely a major part of campus life."

- "Since varsity sports are so big at Auburn, **a good way to meet people is to get involved with a sport**. You don't necessarily have to play a sport to support it, however. Whether you decide to play in the band, or be a cheerleader or dance team member, or just sit in the student section at every game, I guarantee it will be a great experience."

## The College Prowler Take
### ON ATHLETICS

"Auburn is football," as some people say down here. Students rave about the high energy and school spirit that is displayed on game days. You don't have to worry about getting bored around here, especially if you're a sports fanatic! Attend a varsity game or get involved in an intramural sport, if that's your thing. Students promise that you'll have fun no matter what you choose. Just be advised that if you dislike football, you'll be part of a very small minority.

**The College Prowler™ Grade on**
## Athletics: A

A high grade in Athletics indicates that students have school spirit, that sports programs are respected, that games are well-attended, and that intramurals are a prominent part of student life.

Want to know what teams at Auburn are looking for a player like you? Check out www.collegeprowler.com for the guidebook full of Auburn info.

# Greek Life

## The Lowdown
ON GREEK LIFE

**Number of Fraternities:**
29

**Number of Sororities:**
18

**Undergrad Men in Fraternities:**
21%

**Undergrad Women in Sororities:**
35%

### Did You Know?

Alpha Tau Omega and Phi Delta Theta are the two oldest continuing fraternities on campus.

## Students Speak Out
ON GREEK LIFE

"**Greek life doesn't dominate the social scene.** It's obvious that it's there, but there is no definitive line that separates Greeks from independents."

"**Greek life is definitely present here.** I'm not in a sorority, myself, and I don't regret that decision. There is life outside of the Greek system, but if you're not in a sorority or fraternity, then don't plan on making that many friends with people who are. They tend to stay with their own kind."

"I'm Greek and I pretty much love it. Greeks are only 20 percent of the students at AU, but it seems like more than that to me since I associate mainly with Greeks. **Every girl I know is in a sorority.** Sororities have many more people in them than fraternities do. I'd recommend that you do rush because it is a great way to meet people. Pretty much every football weekend there are massive parties at fraternity houses on Old and New Row. Sororities do not have houses; they live in the Hill Dorms. There are always a lot of socials and date parties held downtown in the bars and everything. I wouldn't say that the Greeks 'dominate' the social scene, but we are prevalent."

"**You'll be aware of Greeks**, but won't be looked down upon if you're not one. I did not want to join a sorority at first, but I decided to give it a try. I enjoyed it while it lasted, but I could have done with or without it. I am glad I did it, but I'm not sure that it made a huge difference in my college life one way or the other. It kind of depends on your personality, I suppose. Some people love it; some hate it. I was in the middle."

"**Greek life can dominate the social scene**, if you let it. I think only 20 percent of the student body is Greek, which does not seem like a lot, but they are around and especially in certain academic schools, like business."

"I went through rush because **I wanted to see if it was for me**. I suggest that you do go through it because you might like it; if not, then don't waste the money. I withdrew from rush the second day. I am glad I did and it did not change the fun I had at school."

## The College Prowler Take
### ON GREEK LIFE

The general consensus is that going Greek is mostly your own personal choice. Greek life is prevalent but doesn't dominate the social scene. Some people never go through rush and are happy with their choice. Others stay with a particular fraternity or sorority throughout their entire college career and are equally happy. No matter what you choose, you should feel comfortable with what you do.

# Drug Scene

## The Lowdown
### ON DRUG SCENE

**Most Prevalent Drugs on Campus:**
Alcohol, Caffeine, Marijuana, Adderall, Ritalin

## Students Speak Out
### ON DRUG SCENE

"I don't do drugs or involve myself with it. I do know it's not wide open, but stuff goes on just like anywhere else. You do have 22,000 college-age kids in the same area."

"**Pretty much everyone smokes weed**. It's not like a drug-dealing ghetto, though; it doesn't take over the town. But, at least one person you meet knows someone who can get stuff for you, if that's your pleasure."

"The drug scene is there, of course, but it does not rule the school. The whole time I was there, I think **I saw cocaine only once**. Of course it is always around, and if that's what you want, you can find it. The pot isn't great, but if you find good stuff, they charge an arm and leg for it."

## B+

**The College Prowler™ Grade on**
### Greek Life: B+

A high grade in Greek Life indicates that sororities and fraternities are not only present, but also active on campus. Other determining factors include the variety of houses available and the respect the Greek community receives from the rest of the campus.

Q: "Off campus, it's become harder and harder to find any illegal substances in the past couple of years, but **if you look hard enough**, you can find whatever you're into."

Q: "I have seen drugs in small amounts at fraternity parties, but I wouldn't say that the majority of people here do drugs. Of course there are those people who do it, but I think that **the majority of people stick to drinking**. That's just what I've seen and what I've been told. Drugs are here, but they are not that prevalent. Not too many people use them."

## The College Prowler Take
### ON DRUG SCENE

Like any other college, Auburn does have to deal with the presence of drugs. Fortunately, if you're not looking for that kind of recreation, then you probably won't come across it. Most students cite alcohol and marijuana among the most commonly used drugs at Auburn. Caffeine and amphetamine drugs associated with concentration, like Ritalin and Adderall, are also common. If you find yourself in an uncomfortable situation, then don't hesitate to leave or contact someone for help, if necessary.

**A-**

### The College Prowler™ Grade on
### Drug Scene: A-

A high grade on Drug Scene indicates that drugs are not a noticeable part of campus life; drug use is not visible, and no pressure to use them seems to exist.

# Overall Experience

## Students Speak Out
### ON OVERALL EXPERIENCE

"I have met so many great people and made lifelong friends. I have learned so much about life in general in just one year that it blows my mind."

Q: "I think it is the best school to go to! My overall experience has been amazing. When I graduate, I am going to miss all my friends, **all the fun we had**, and everything else. I would never have wanted to go anywhere else!"

Q: "I'll admit that, for a while, I wished that I had gone to a different school, but everyone feels that way on whatever decision they make. Now, I love Auburn. The people are extremely nice and **it's really close to Atlanta**."

Q: "My experience at Auburn has just been indescribable. And I think that if you talk to anyone else that goes here, they'll sing you the same song. When I got to Auburn last fall, I fell in love with it. When I was home in the summer, I couldn't wait to go back. It's incredible. I wouldn't go anywhere else if you paid me to. **I bleed orange and blue now**."

Q: "I'm very happy here. **The people are nice and they treat you well**. All around, Auburn is a good school, but it has its flaws just like any other school. When it comes down to it, four years isn't as long as you think, so even if things get tough, just remember you don't have that long here. The only time I wish I was somewhere else is on some weekends."

Q "My overall experience here has been great. No problems at all. The one thing you'll notice if you come here is how friendly everyone on campus is. That **friendliness goes with you everywhere**. You can be walking down the street, in some place far away from Auburn, see a fan or alumni, and exchange a hearty War Eagle—the typical Auburn greeting. The campus is big enough for a large university experience, but small enough that you don't get overwhelmed."

## The College Prowler Take
### ON OVERALL EXPERIENCE

Overall, students are very happy to be at Auburn. They love the people around them and the experiences that they get to have. College is what you make of it. If you sit at home and don't do anything, then you won't enjoy yourself no matter where you go. But, with all the options offered to you at Auburn, you'd have to try pretty hard not to have a good time—with a student body that is so happy to be here, it's impossible not to get swept up in the excitement. Just live by the motto "work hard, play hard" and you'll be just fine at Auburn.

# Clemson University

**DISTANCE TO...**
Atlanta: 130 mi.
Savannah: 292 mi.
Charlotte: 138 mi.
Knoxville: 195 mi.

105 Sikes Hall, Clemson, SC 29634
www.clemson.edu          (864) 656-2287

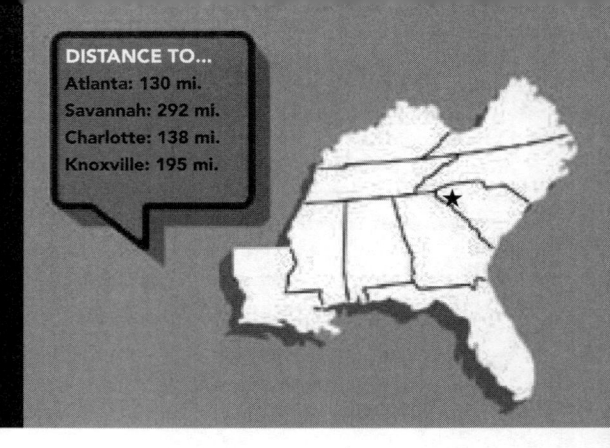

*"The town of Clemson owes its existence to the University—about 13,000 undergraduates keep the area alive with excitement."*

**Total Enrollment:**
12,857

**Top 10% of High School Class:**
41%

**Average GPA:**
3.9

**Acceptance Rate:**
61%

**Tuition:**
$8,012 in-state, $15,610 out-of-state

**SAT Range (25th-75th Percentile):**
| Verbal | Math | Total |
|---|---|---|
| 550 – 630 | 570 – 660 | 1120 – 1290 |

**ACT Range (25th-75th Percentile):**
| Verbal | Math | Total |
|---|---|---|
| N/A | N/A | 24-29 |

**Most Popular Majors:**
22% Business
14% Engineering
10% Education
7%   Social Sciences
6%   English

**Students also applied to:***
University of South Carolina
College of Charleston
University of North Carolina
University of Georgia
North Carolina State

*For more school info check out www.collegeprowler.com

### Table of Contents

| | |
|---|---|
| Academics | 61 |
| Local Atmosphere | 63 |
| Safety & Security | 64 |
| Facilities | 66 |
| Campus Dining | 67 |
| Campus Housing | 69 |
| Diversity | 70 |
| Guys & Girls | 72 |
| Athletics | 73 |
| Greek Life | 75 |
| Drug Scene | 77 |
| Overall Experience | 78 |

### College Prowler Report Card

| | |
|---|---|
| Academics | B |
| Local Atmosphere | B |
| Safety & Security | B+ |
| Facilities | A- |
| Campus Dining | C+ |
| Campus Housing | C+ |
| Diversity | D |
| Guys | A |
| Girls | A |
| Athletics | A+ |
| Greek Life | B+ |
| Drug Scene | B+ |

# Academics

## The Lowdown
### ON ACADEMICS

**Degrees Awarded:**
Bachelor, Master, Doctorate

**Undergraduate Schools:**
Agriculture, Forestry, and Life Sciences; Architecture, Arts, and Humanities; Business and Behavioral Science; Engineering and Science; Health, Education, and Human Development

**Full-time Faculty:**
970

**Faculty with Terminal Degree:**
84%

**Student-to-Faculty Ratio:**
16:1

**Average Course Load:**
5 courses

**AP Test Score Requirements:**
3 or higher

**IB Test Score Requirements:**
4 or higher

**Best Places to Study:**
Cooper Library—fourth floor, or the Hendrix Student Center lounge

## Special Degree Options
Pre-professional programs: Pre-law, pre-medicine, pre-veterinary science, pre-pharmacy, pre-dentistry. Combined-degree programs: Two-Three pharmacy and physical therapy programs. Host university for Three-Two engineering program with Coastal Carolina University.

Cooperative education programs: Agriculture, business, computer science, education, engineering, humanities, natural science, social/behavioral science.

## Sample Academic Clubs
Model United Nations, Speech and Communications Club, College Democrats, College Republicans, Clemson Bioengineering Society, Community & Rural Development Club, Psychology Club

### Did You Know?
*Kiplinger's Personal Finance* ranks Clemson as one of the nation's 20 best values among public universities.

Clemson's Department of Environmental Engineering and Science is ranked 14th in the country.

Clemson's Army ROTC program is in the top 15 percent in the nation, according to the U.S. Army Cadet Command.

## Students Speak Out
### ON ACADEMICS

"My professors are wonderful, and very willing to help. Some give out their home numbers, but e-mail is the best way to go. Don't be afraid to go visit during their office hours, either. It helps if they know your name and face."

> "Professors are on average really good at Clemson. You can go to a website that my honor fraternity, Phi Sigma Pi, runs: *http://people.clemson.edu/~psp/ryp.htm* and within it, there is a tool called 'rate your professor' where **you can look up how other students rate the teachers**."

> "**I've had really good experiences with my teachers**. There are a couple professors that I go out with for lunch, or for coffee. There are a lot of professors who I consider to be friends of mine first, and professors second. Shoot, one of my intramural teams is basically half professors and faculty members. Obviously all of them can't be good, and I've had my share of bad ones, but my good experiences with professors far outweigh the bad. Academically speaking, all of my classes here were taught by professors with the exception of one calculus class, which was taught by a grad student."

> "**Word of mouth is the way to find out if teachers are good or bad**. Thankfully, most of my teachers have been wonderful. Of course, I have had some not-too-cool professors. Be prepared for whatever kind of teacher you may get, but once you begin to register for spring classes, listen to what a lot of other students say about other professors."

> "Honestly, **I haven't been terribly impressed with my teachers**. I went to a parochial high school where it was very easy and common to casually get to know your teachers. They were all approachable, and it was great having a personal relationship with many of my teachers in high school. That is where Clemson differs. Granted, I'm learning a great deal, the professors are definitely 'teaching' me the book work; however, in many classes I feel like just another face. I'm sure, or at least I'm hoping, that once I get through the general ed classes my teachers will become more approachable and eager to get to know my name and more. Aside from the teachers, I do like the classes as a whole and really am learning; I find that most classes are pretty interesting, and I like to go to the majority of them."

## The College Prowler Take
### ON ACADEMICS

Students at Clemson seem to be satisfied with their professors and classes. To ensure the quality of the teaching staff, students are given the opportunity to evaluate their professors at the end of each semester. Although most students say they have had a "bad apple" or two, it is not uncommon for students to find a professor whom they get to know personally.

Although Clemson is no Ivy League school, it is still an outstanding public university devoted to educating and preparing its students for life after college. To accomplish this goal, Clemson requires all students to complete a series of general education classes that focus on communication, speaking, and computer skills, as well classes in mathematical science, physical or biological science, humanities, and social science. Under this system, freshmen have time to explore different academic areas before making a final decision. Clemson University is committed to maintaining its competitive public university status, but with state budgets running in the red, the road ahead may be a little rocky.

**The College Prowler™ Grade on**
## Academics: B

A high Academics grade generally indicates that professors are knowledgeable, accessible, and genuinely interested in their students' welfare. Other determining factors include class size, how well professors communicate, and whether or not classes are engaging.

# Local Atmosphere

## The Lowdown
ON LOCAL ATMOSPHERE

**Region:**
Southeast

**City, State:**
Clemson, South Carolina

**Setting:**
Rural

**Distance from Greenville:**
45 minutes

**Distance from Atlanta:**
2 hours

**Distance from Charlotte:**
2 hours

Q "If you are looking for nightlife and clubs, this isn't the school for you. **Don't get me wrong, it's a total party school**, if you want it to be. It's just that it's more of a college bar and frat party scene, and not a nightclub thing."

Q "There are a lot of places nearby where **you can go hiking and see waterfalls and camp**. It's also good to make friends with someone who has a boat or wave runner, because it's fun to go out on Lake Hartwell. Also, Lake Keowee is about 15 minutes away, and it's beautiful! Supposedly, Oprah has a lake house on it."

Q "It's a college town atmosphere; everyone here is related to Clemson in some respect, and understands the needs of college kids. Clemson itself is a small town, **the school doubles the town in population**, and on a football weekend, we have a city of 100,000 people. The opportunity to go to cities is always there, though. Atlanta and Charlotte are both two hours away. My favorite little city is Greenville, South Carolina, which is about 100,000 people, and it's about a half hour from Clemson. It's got a bunch of good restaurants, some minor league sports teams, and some pretty good-sized malls."

Q "Clemson is a fairly small town that has made itself into a great place to come to. People come from neighboring cities to party and go to sporting events. Anderson College, kind of a conservative Christian school, is about 15 miles away. Furman University is about an hour away, and **University of Georgia—awesome school as well—is about an hour away**. I'm not really sure that I can suggest places to stay away from. That is something you'll find on your own, I'm sure."

## Students Speak Out
ON LOCAL ATMOSPHERE

"Basically, Clemson University is the town. It's a typical college town. Seneca's pretty close but there's not much to do there. If we want to get off campus and go do something, we usually go to Anderson."

## The College Prowler Take
### ON LOCAL ATMOSPHERE

It's obvious to anyone who visits Clemson: life here revolves around the school. The towns of Anderson and Seneca are only short drives away, but few find them to be more interesting than the university atmosphere at Clemson. Some students say there isn't much to do in or around Clemson, but other more adventurous ones say they can't get enough of the outdoor activities the region has to offer. If nothing else, Clemson has a golf course and an enormous man-made lake on the outskirts of campus. Greenville and Atlanta are great for the club and bar scene, and the Appalachian Mountains offer everything from camping to water skiing.

# Safety & Security

## The Lowdown
### ON SAFETY & SECURITY

**Number of CU Police:**
28

**Phone:**
(864) 656-2222

**Health Center Office Hours:**
Monday-Friday: 8 a.m.-5 p.m.

**Safety Services:**
CU Fire Department, CU Police Department, Police escort service, blue emergency call phones on campus

## B

The College Prowler™ Grade on
### Local Atmosphere: B

A high Local Atmosphere grade indicates that the area surrounding campus is safe and scenic. Other factors include nearby attractions, proximity to other schools, and the town's attitude toward students.

## Students Speak Out
### ON SAFETY & SECURITY

"Clemson has its own police and fire department. The escort service is available 24 hours. They will pick you up and take you to your dorm. The CAT [Clemson Area Transit] also saves you a walk alone in the dark."

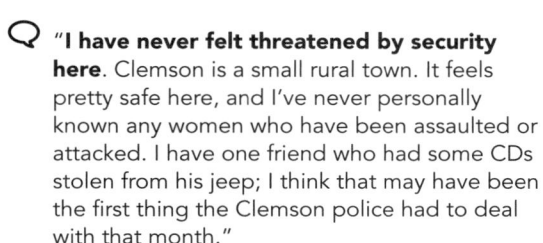

Q "**There are security phones all over campus, along sidewalks**, and on the sides of every building. Every path is also lit at night. Each dorm has a security guard or a hired student who sits at the dorm's front desk and makes sure that no one enters who isn't allowed."

Q "**I have never felt threatened by security here**. Clemson is a small rural town. It feels pretty safe here, and I've never personally known any women who have been assaulted or attacked. I have one friend who had some CDs stolen from his jeep; I think that may have been the first thing the Clemson police had to deal with that month."

Q "**I think safety is excellent here**. My best friend here served on student senate as the safety chairperson, and during his watch, I believe there were no major safety problems for the entire school year. The place is very well-lit at night, and I've had no problems with theft in my dorm or apartments."

Q "I feel very secure on my campus. Common sense tells anyone not to walk around at four [in the morning] by yourself anywhere, but if you and a couple of friends have a late night at the library, there's no problem walking down the sidewalk—they are all lit of course—to your dorm. Clemson wants to be safe. **The annual campus safety walk**, which involves students and police, checks for burnt-out lights, working phones, and areas that don't feel safe, and the problems are addressed."

## The College Prowler Take
### ON SAFETY & SECURITY

Security phones, police escorts, and lights all over campus help make Clemson a very safe environment for students. The annual Clemson "Safe Walk" involves students and members of the Clemson community who walk the campus and discuss ways to improve safety. Most students agree that Clemson is an extremely safe campus, as long as you take the basic precautionary measures, like walking in a group after dark and locking your doors. Clemson is a fairly large university located in a rural setting, which makes it an obvious target for theft by outsiders. However, most students will tell you they haven't had any trouble, and there really isn't too much to worry about.

**B+**

The College Prowler™ Grade on
### Safety & Security: B+

A high grade in Safety & Security means that students generally feel safe, campus police are visible, blue-light phones and escort services are readily available, and safety precautions are not overly necessary.

# Facilities

**Computers**
**High-Speed Network?** Yes
**Wireless Network?** Yes
**Number of Labs:** 15
**Numbers of Computers:** 1,000
**24-Hour Labs:** Brackett, Martin
**Charge to Print?** No

## The Lowdown
ON FACILITIES

**Student Center:**
Hendrix Student Center

**Athletic Center:**
Fike Recreational Center

**Libraries:**
Cooper Library

**Popular Places to Chill:**
Bowman Field, the Amphitheater

**Movie Theatre on Campus?**
McKissick Theatre is in Hendrix Center.

**Bowling on Campus?**
Yes, we have the Union Underground.

**Bar on Campus?**
Yes, there is Edgar's Bar.

**Coffeehouse on Campus?**
Yes, there's a Java City in the Hendrix Center and in the old student union.

## Students Speak Out
ON FACILITIES

"The student union is new. It has a bowling alley, hair salon, and lots of other things. The athletic building is called 'Fike.' There are weights, aerobic classes, exercise equipment, and an Olympic-sized pool."

Q "Our facilities are constantly upgraded to ensure that they are top-notch. **They just built a new student center**—The Hendrix Center—and it's a very nice building containing the bookstore, ballrooms, the campus radio station, and a food court, among other things."

Q "The facilities here are pretty good, and improving. **The recreation center is being renovated and expanded**, our student center has a huge bookstore, lots of places to eat, a coffee shop, a computer lab, meeting rooms, and a theater. There are lots of computer labs on campus, though they will be crowded. The varsity athletic facilities are all undergoing face-lifts right now, but in two years, wow, this place is going to look absolutely fantastic. They're tearing down the old dorms that are an eyesore this summer."

Q "**Well the University is old so a lot of the buildings are old,** but there are a lot of renovations taking place, and [renovations] have already taken place [on] a couple of the buildings on campus—the football stadium [and] the basketball arena. And the roads around campus are being widened so that traffic can flow in and out of campus better on game Saturdays."

💬 "Computers in the labs are fairly nice, although those currently in the library are hardly tolerable. The student center is absolutely wonderful, as is some of the campus housing—[like] Stadium Suites [and] New Lightsey. A lot of classes are in really old buildings that have been retrofitted with necessary technology such as wireless Internet and digital projectors. Many of these buildings don't look especially good on the interior, but **they serve their purpose**."

# Campus Dining

## The College Prowler Take
### ON FACILITIES

Students are satisfied with the facilities at Clemson, and they are eagerly awaiting the renovations that are underway. Already remodeled athletic facilities such as the Littlejohn Coliseum (basketball), Tiger Field (baseball), and Clemson Memorial Stadium, also known as "Death Valley," make any competition worth attending. Although a lot of the other facilities are aging, one must only walk across campus to see that Clemson is perpetually engaged in improving its services to students. Indeed, the construction is never-ending—it seems like there is always yellow tape somewhere on campus. So, after renovations, the facilities provided to incoming students should be incredible.

## The Lowdown
### ON CAMPUS DINING

**Freshman Meal Plan Requirement?**
Yes

**24-Hour On-Campus Eating?**
No. The Hendrix Center is open the latest, until 11 p.m. Monday through Friday.

**Student Favorites:**
Clemson House, Schilletter, Hendrix Center's east side food court

**Meal Plan Average Cost:**
$879-$1,046

## A-

### The College Prowler™ Grade on
### Facilities: A-

A high Facilities grade indicates that the campus is aesthetically pleasing and well-maintained; facilities are state-of-the-art, and libraries are exceptional. Other determining factors include the quality of both athletic and student centers and an abundance of things to do on campus.

## Students Speak Out
### ON CAMPUS DINING

"The first semester, you won't mind the food at all. However, that second semester you probably will be tired of it. There are also other choices aside from the meal plan."

> "**Food is actually not bad**. There are two cafeterias that are covered in the basic meal plan. There is cafeteria food; nothing more, nothing less. It's not bad, and they usually offer a good variety, and have theme days to try and spice it up. There are several other places on campus that are good—for instance, the student union has a food court with things like Burger King and Chick-fil-A."

> "Food in the dining halls is **absolutely average**, it's dining hall food. I ate at the dining halls my first two years, then when I went to apartments. I started cooking everything for myself. Definitely the better way to go if you've got any talent in the kitchen. But the dining halls have a good variety, and nobody can screw up cereal, so you've always got a safety net. In short, it's not bad, but it's not as good as cooking for yourself. There are a couple other places on campus, [like] Hendrix Student Center, the Canteen, and Fernow Street Cafe, that are a ton better than dining halls, but they're not on a meal plan. You either pay by cash or by your Tiger Stripe account."

> "The food on campus is all right, the cafeterias are, well, **typical college cafeteria food**. Then there are two places on campus, in the new and old unions, that serve subs, Chick-fil-A, Burger King, and other types of actual good food."

> "I personally do not like the food on campus. **Most of the good food is at the Hendrix Center**, but it is very expensive. I would recommend having food in your room that you can eat for meals if you need to."

> "The food court in the Hendrix Center, Fernow Street Cafe, and the Canteen in the student union are **great alternatives to the meal plan**."

## The College Prowler Take
### ON CAMPUS DINING

When at college, what you're given is what you eat. Clemson is no exception. Students say the food is tolerable, but there are certainly places that are better than others. It is generally agreed upon that Clemson House and Schilleter are better dining halls than Harcombe. Other alternatives to dining hall food are the Hendrix Center's east side food court and the Fernow St. Café. There are many options to choose from, and there is something for everyone.

**C+**

The College Prowler™ Grade on
### Campus Dining: C+

Our grade on Campus Dining addresses the quality of both school-owned dining halls and independent on-campus restaurants as well as the price, availability, and variety of food.

# Campus Housing

**Did You Know?**
The new Clemson House rooms and apartments used to be a University-owned hotel.

## The Lowdown
ON CAMPUS HOUSING

**Undergrads on Campus:**
48%

**Number of Dormitories:**
21

**Number of University-Owned Apartments:**
5

**Room Types:**
Doubles, suites, apartments

**Available for Rent:**
Micro-fridges

**Cleaning Service?**
No

**You get:**
Bed, desk, chair, closet, dresser, mirror, tack-board

**NOTE**
The "High-rise Dorms" include Lever, Byrnes, and Manning. The "Low-rise Dorms" are Barnett, Smith, and Mauldin. Holmes, McCabe, and Stadium Halls are the "Suites." The "Shoeboxes" refer to Geer, Cope, Benet, Young, and Sanders Halls.

## Students Speak Out
ON CAMPUS HOUSING

"If I had the chance to do again, I would pick the new West Campus [Clemson House rooms] housing. It's the newest, most amazing dorm—it's like a hotel inside!"

Q "I stayed in Sanders, one of the Shoeboxes, and it was fun. **Lots of girls to meet and hang out with**. Never a dull moment when you're in a single-sex dorm! Also, they are tearing down probably the worst dorm in Clemson. Johnstone has been here since my grandfather was here. My dad stayed there ... and they usually put all freshman boys there. Party central, but crappy! There is still one Johnstone unit left that isn't bad [at] all, so if you get it, don't get upset. There are also co-ed honors dorms and on campus apartments, too."

Q "The dorms are okay, I think. I stayed in Holmes Hall my first two years before moving into apartments, and **Holmes was excellent**. McCabe is just like Holmes, and the new West Campus dorm is outstanding. The other dorms like Barnett, Smith, Lever, Mauldin, Cope, Manning, Young—they're very much your typical college dorms: good, but not great."

Q "I lived in Johnstone, the worst dorm on campus. Everybody knows it, and **everybody makes fun of it**. The walls are all metal, for starters. However ... the experience is awesome. Right away, you bond over the terrible building and start friendships. You're in college, you don't need a room worthy of the Four Seasons; you need a place to socialize, meet tons of people, and have a great time. Any dorm will do that for you, as long as you leave your door open to visitors."

> "Dorms in descending order from good to bad: Stadium Suites, Holmes, McCabe, Shoeboxes, Johnstone, High Rises, Frat Quad. Apartments: Lightsey II is wonderful, Lightsey I is pretty nice, and Calhoun Courts, although **not in as pristine of condition**, is still a neat place to live."

## The College Prowler Take
### ON CAMPUS HOUSING

The best dorms for freshmen are the High-rises or the honors dorm, Holmes. If you must settle for less, the Shoeboxes are not a bad way to go. Students recommend avoiding Johnstone, but those who have lived there say it was a "bonding experience" due to the living conditions they all had to face. The dorms at Clemson range from outdated to top-of-the-line. A lot of construction has taken place in recent years to improve student living conditions, and if you can't find a dorm that feels like home after your first year, there are many off-campus housing options for you to choose from. If nothing else, the "dorm experience" will allow you to meet people with whom you will always share a common bond—be it good or bad.

**The College Prowler™ Grade on**
## Campus Housing: C+

A high Campus Housing grade indicates that dorms are clean, well-maintained, and spacious. Other determining factors include variety of dorms, proximity to classes, and social atmosphere.

# Diversity

## The Lowdown
### ON DIVERSITY

Native American: 0%

Asian American: 2%

African American: 7%

Hispanic: 1%

White: 89%

International: 1%

Out-of-State: 30%

**Minority Clubs**
Black Student Alliance, Hillel Jewish Center, Indian Students Association, Korean Student Association, Muslim Student Association, Turkish Student Association, Vietnamese Student Association

**Political Activity**
Organizations like the College Democrats and the College Republicans do exist, but they are seldom the center of attention on campus.

**Gay Tolerance**
There is a Gay-Straight Alliance club on campus, but the student body attitude tends to be less accepting of gays than it probably should be.

**Most Popular Religion**
Christianity

## Students Speak Out
### ON DIVERSITY

> "CU is diverse in some ways, but not in others. They are very encouraging about diversifying campus and we have a million cultural activities, but honestly, the majority of campus is white."

Q "**Diversity is a drawback here**. I have to admit, it took me awhile to adjust to the Deep South."

Q "**You'll meet some people who aren't aware the Civil War is over**, and you'll see a lot of Confederate flags flying in this part of the country. But not everyone is like that, and it doesn't dominate the school at all. It is just a completely different culture down here. That's just warning, though. It took me a couple of months to realize that, in the South, racism and things like that are issues you'll occasionally have to deal with."

Q "It is very diverse on campus. **There are people from all over the world**. In some computer labs I will hear people speaking in German, French, Spanish, Arabic, Chinese, and of course, English."

Q "Not very [diverse]. Campus is primarily white with **a sprinkling of blacks and Indians**. There are enough international [exchange] students that you'll inevitably meet, and even speak to one."

## The College Prowler Take
### ON DIVERSITY

Students find that, when looking around campus, they all look pretty much the same. They also note that foreign students and students of similar ethnicities tend to form their own groups. Although Clemson has students from many different countries, they make up a small proportion of the predominantly white student body population. Don't expect to see much diversity when you come to Clemson. Keep in mind that the school is located in rural northwestern South Carolina—not exactly a melting pot for diversity. If diversity is an important factor in selecting your school, you might want to look elsewhere.

Visit www.collegeprowler.com to find the Clemson University guidebook and read more about the student body.

The College Prowler™ Grade on
### Diversity: D

A high grade in Diversity indicates that ethnic minorities and international students have a notable presence on campus and that students of different economic backgrounds, religious beliefs, and sexual preferences are well-represented.

# Guys & Girls

## Dress Code

There is no set dress code, but this is what the majority of guys and girls wear. For guys, it's usually Rainbow sandals, polo shirts, sunglasses with "the strap," and John Deere hats. Girls can be often be seen in dresses, skirts, sorority T-shirts, and flip-flops.

## Students Speak Out
### ON GUYS & GIRLS

## The Lowdown
### ON GUYS & GIRLS

"Girls, you'll be running into some stiff competition. There are some hot girls here on campus—more than I've seen anywhere else."

**Women Undergrads:** 45%

**Men Undergrads:** 55%

Q "It all **breaks down to the North and South**: You've got the southern gentlemen, who wear khakis and a golf shirt, and the northern guys, who wear jeans and a T-shirt. Then, you've got the southern belles, who wear cute dresses and skirts, and the northern chicks ,who wear jeans and cute shirts."

## Birth Control Available?

Yes, at the Redfern Health Center. Free condoms are also available.

Redfern Health Center
McMillian Road, Clemson
(864) 656-2233
http://stuaff.clemson.edu/redfern/

Q "Since it's in the Southeast, **it's a whole 'southern hospitality' thing we've got going here**. The majority of people from the South talk to the people they pass whether they know them or not—or, if we don't talk, we will definitely smile."

## Social Scene

There's something for everyone, but binge drinking is definitely the most popular. Students flock to College Avenue, which runs through downtown Clemson, on Friday and Saturday nights to go to the bars. Sports team parties and Greek parties also occur weekly, at the very least. In general, students at Clemson are very outgoing and love to party.

Q "Giving an unbiased opinion, **the guys are handsome, gentlemanly, athletic** ... okay, just a touch biased. The girls I've found to be, for the most part, very sweet and easy to get along with. I think all the people here are fantastic, there are a lot of good-looking people on this campus."

## Hookups or Relationships?

Clemson is home to many attractive men and women. If you don't have a partner, you're sure to find someone you click with among Clemson's 14,000 undergrads.

Q "**Clemson has the hottest girls of any campus I've ever seen**, and I have probably been to over 20 large school campuses. They are even better than UF [University of Florida] and UGA [University of Georgia]."

## The College Prowler Take
### ON GUYS & GIRLS

Students at Clemson enjoy going to school with one another. As well as boasting a lot of "eye candy," the student body here is very hospitable and friendly. Southern "gents" and "belles" are the norm, and the students here take pride in their appearance. Although some say there is a certain degree of superficiality, it certainly isn't enough to detract from a generally enthusiastic opinion of the guys and girls at Clemson. Clemson students are very happy with the appearance of the student body, and rightfully so. Clemson has a good mix of southerners and northerners, and it's encouraging how well everyone gets along.

**The College Prowler™ Grade on**
## Guys: A

A high grade for Guys indicates that the male population on campus is attractive, smart, friendly, and engaging, and that the school has a decent ratio of guys to girls.

**The College Prowler™ Grade on**
## Girls: A

A high grade for Girls not only implies that the women on campus are attractive, smart, friendly, and engaging, but also that there is a fair ratio of girls to guys.

# Athletics

## The Lowdown
### ON ATHLETICS

**Men's Varsity Teams:**
Baseball
Basketball
Cross Country
Diving
Football
Golf
Soccer
Swimming
Tennis
Track (indoor)
Track (outdoor)
Track and Field

**Women's Varsity Teams:**
Basketball
Crew
Cross Country
Diving
Soccer
Swimming
Tennis
Track (indoor)
Track (outdoor)
Track and Field
Volleyball

## Club Sports

Aficionados of Alternative Recreational Games, Air Rifle Club, Bowling Club, Chidokwan Karate, Baseball, Golf, Ice Hockey, Cuong Nhu Oriental Martial Arts Association, Cycling Club, Dixie Skydivers, Equestrian Team, Fast-Pitch Softball Team, Fencers, Field Hockey Club, Flying Club, Gaming Guild, Hapkido Club, Roller Hockey Club, Lacrosse Club, Outdoors Club, Paintball Club, Rodeo Club, Rowing Association, Rugby Football Club, Sailing Club, Scuba Club, Dance Club, Soccer Club, Sport Bike Club, Sports Car Club, Tae Kwon Do Club, Tennis Club, Triathlon Club, Volleyball Club, Water Ski Club, Weight Club

**Athletic Division:**
NCAA Division I, NCAA Division I-A for football

**Conference:**
Atlantic Coast Conference

**School Mascot:**
Tiger

**Getting Tickets:**
All students receive free tickets to athletic events. However, for some big football games, you must stand in line a few weeks prior to the event.

**Most Popular Sports:**
Football and baseball generally draw the largest crowds.

**Overlooked Teams:**
Soccer attendance is low, considering their outstanding accomplishments.

**Fields:**
6 numbered intramural fields

## Students Speak Out
### ON ATHLETICS

"I hated football when I came, but being here had made me love it. At the games, it is like an orange wave in the stands and everyone goes nuts!"

Q "Varsity sports are huge here, which is one of the reasons I came to Clemson. I went to a small school in Indiana and wanted a big sports atmosphere. **Football is amazing here**; you've never lived till you've experienced a game at Death Valley with 100,000 people, all wearing orange with tiger paws painted on [their] faces. It's amazing."

Q "Football is huge. Partying the night before, tailgating the day of, and definitely wearing orange are all part of the deal. Aside from football, **there are tons of other sports to be a part of or support**, from club level ice hockey and crew, to ultimate Frisbee, soccer, baseball, and golf. We've got it all."

Q "Varsity sports are enormous. IM [intramural] sports are enormous. **If you like sports, there's no better place**. In the fall, there are two things you can bet on: people hardly ever miss church on Sunday morning, and they never miss football on a Saturday afternoon. College football is an absolute institution here. One of the most impressive experiences of my life was my first Clemson football game. I still get chills before every game."

Q "All the sports are pretty much awesome here. The baseball team—my love—was number one in the country for seven weeks this year; **the soccer team is always top 10**, both men's and women's. The basketball team is fun to watch, although we play a really tough schedule. The really nice thing is that as an undergraduate, you'll get free football and basketball tickets, and all the other sports you just have to show your ID to get in. You can play just about any sport you want through intramurals. The recreation center is state-of-the-art."

Q "**You will love football season**! People start tailgating and camping out on Thursdays. The stadium holds about 85,000 people, and it is usually packed!"

## The College Prowler Take
**ON ATHLETICS**

Clemson draws a lot of students who actively participate in or love to watch sports. Those freshmen that arrive without an understanding of the Clemson athletic tradition find themselves in awe at the first home football game as 80,000 fans cheer on the Tigers as they rush down "the Hill," a grassy area behind the home goalposts. Weekends at Clemson in the fall revolve around football, and students here wouldn't have it any other way. Sports are a way of life at Clemson. It is perhaps one of the best schools for you to watch or play any sport imaginable, from Division I to intramural.

# Greek Life

## The Lowdown
**ON GREEK LIFE**

**Number of Fraternities:**
24

**Number of Sororities:**
12

**Undergrad Men in Fraternities:**
15%

**Undergrad Women in Sororities:**
22%

**Multicultural Colonies:**
N/A

**Other Greek Organizations:**
Greek Council, Greek Peer Advisors, Interfraternity Council, Order of Omega, Pan-Hellenic Council

## A+

**The College Prowler™ Grade on**
### Athletics: A+

A high grade in Athletics indicates that students have school spirit, that sports programs are respected, that games are well-attended, and that intramurals are a prominent part of student life.

### Did You Know?
The Clemson Fraternity Quad is being renovated to offer new housing for Greeks on campus.

## Students Speak Out
### ON GREEK LIFE

"Greek people seem to be 100 percent total Greek freaks. For everyone else, it doesn't seem to be that important. You can still go to frat parties even if you don't join a sorority."

"Some people may say that Greek life dominates the social scene, others, like me, disagree. As a freshman, I chose not to rush and I was invited to many fraternity parties—girls rushing cannot do those things during rush, I guess, so they won't be pressured into a certain sorority—and had tons of time to do things. I honestly think I met more people. Last year, I was asked into a sorority on campus that is great. **It was just too time consuming**, and I didn't have the time to commit. You can always find a fraternity party, as a girl, but there are always, always other non-Greek things going on."

"**Greek life is very big**, but there is also more than enough for the non-Greeks. I am not Greek, I haven't regretted it, and I don't think I have missed out on anything. I have many friends that are Greek, and they love it."

"Greek life accounts for about 20 percent of the undergraduate population. **The Greeks throw the best parties**. Expect to have a lot of fun, because a lot of people with the same interests can combine their efforts."

"**Greek life does not dominate the social scene**. Greek life in Clemson is very much like a small subculture, rather than a dominating force. Greek organizations obviously still have the resources to throw some of the largest parties, but other groups, such as the largest clubs and club sports, also have the resources to do some of the same things."

## The College Prowler Take
### ON GREEK LIFE

Less than a quarter of the students at Clemson are Greek, but fraternities and sororities are still highly visible social scenes. In addition to becoming involved on campus, going Greek is a great way to meet a lot of people, fast. Although it can be time consuming and expensive, Greek life thrives at Clemson because enough students want it to. Becoming a member of the Greek community is entirely up to you. There are plenty of fraternities and sororities on campus, all different in their own way. If you are considering becoming a Greek, you should attend the rush functions in the fall to get to know some of the different fraternities and sororities on campus.

**B+**

The College Prowler™ Grade on
### Greek Life: B+

A high grade in Greek Life indicates that sororities and fraternities are not only present, but also active on campus. Other determining factors include the variety of houses available and the respect the Greek community receives from the rest of the campus.

# Drug Scene

💬 **"The drug scene is pretty underground**, in the sense that if you want to be part of it you can find your connections pretty easily, but if you don't want to be a part of it, you won't see it or be bothered by it."

💬 "I personally think that **the drug scene is what you make of it**. If you want to associate with the pot heads, then you can find them. However, you won't run into a lot of druggies on the campus."

💬 **"There is heavy alcohol usage and some other drug use**. One can definitely hang around Clemson and never see illegal drug use, and if one really wanted to; even alcohol could be avoided."

## The Lowdown
### ON DRUG SCENE

**Most Prevalent Drugs on Campus:**
Alcohol, Marijuana

**Liquor-Related Arrests:**
483

**Drug-Related Arrests:**
96

**Drug Counseling Programs:**
Counseling and Psychological Services at Redfern Health Center, Crisis Response, Rape Counseling, Victim Assistance

## The College Prowler Take
### ON DRUG SCENE

Apart from the heavy alcohol consumption, drugs are only available if you're looking for them. Those people who do drugs don't tend to pressure those who don't. Whether you see college as a time of experimentation, or as four years with your head in your books, drugs will influence your life only as much as you let them. Hard drug usage such as cocaine and heroin is rather scarce, which is a good sign for a school dedicated to becoming a top public university. At Clemson you will find that the students committed to academic success avoid drugs entirely.

## Students Speak Out
### ON DRUG SCENE

"If anything, people smoke marijuana, but that's about it. Lots of people either don't do drugs or hide it very well—drinking is a different story!"

💬 "**Nothing heavy such as heroin or cocaine**, but I've seen marijuana and some different pills. It's not that bad at all, especially for a major university."

**B+**

The College Prowler™ Grade on
### Drug Scene: B+

A high grade on Drug Scene indicates that drugs are not a noticeable part of campus life; drug use is not visible, and no pressure to use them seems to exist.

# Overall Experience

## Students Speak Out
### ON OVERALL EXPERIENCE

> "Clemson got inside me. You'll see bumper stickers around here that say 'my blood runneth orange,' but nobody really understands that's the way it works until you get here."

Q "I really didn't like the school when I first came here because it's such a small town, and a lot of the time **you feel like you're in the middle of nowhere**. But, after a semester here, I really started to like it more, and now I love it! It's a great school, and President Barker is really set on making constant improvements."

Q "I am definitely glad I picked Clemson, and it's not just me—**people love the school**. Clemson and South Carolina pride are definitely in the air. People are friendly and happy to be here. It's a little secluded, so it's kind of our own little world. I wouldn't have it any other way!"

Q "Quite simply, **coming to Clemson was one of the best choices I've ever made**. I fell in love with it from my first visit junior year of [high school], and it's given me nothing but great experiences and memories since. My mom didn't want me to go here, since it was 'too far from home,' but my parents have grown to love it, too, and plan to retire somewhere in this area in a few years."

Q "The easiest way to tell you about my experience here is that I've already done four years here, and I'm set to do five more, just because **I don't want to leave**. When I would go home for the summer, I would never want to leave, and would count the days until I could start back in the fall.

Q "I first knew I was going to school here during a visit in my junior year ... but before I even set foot on campus. We were about 10 minutes away, just having gotten off the interstate, and on the road were a series of 10 tiger paws painted. Every mile or two after that, you'd see another set of 10 tiger paws painted on the road, **letting you know you were going in the right direction**. Right at that first set of paws, I got the feel for what it meant to be a Clemson student. The passion has grown ever since."

Q "I didn't want to come to Clemson at first. My mind was set on UNC [University of North Carolina] my entire life, but UNC doesn't accept many out-of-state students. So, when I was deferred until May, I had to make a choice, and I went with Clemson—best **decision I've made regarding my education**."

## The College Prowler Take
### ON OVERALL EXPERIENCE

Clemson offers an amazing college experience. Even after graduating, students return for the rest of their lives to see how the campus has changed, and to support the Tigers. Although it is located in a small town, the school is big enough that there is never a dull moment. As anyone who has been to Clemson knows, the students' blood here is orange.

# College of Charleston

66 George Street, Charleston, SC 29424
www.cofc.edu          (843) 953-5670

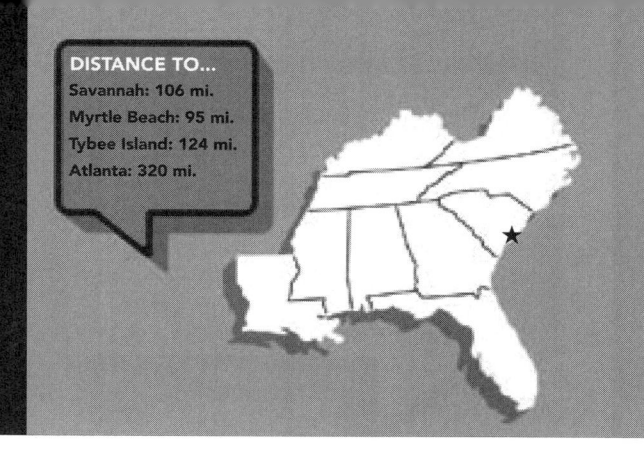

**DISTANCE TO...**
Savannah: 106 mi.
Myrtle Beach: 95 mi.
Tybee Island: 124 mi.
Atlanta: 320 mi.

*"I love the feeling of this school. It's just like Charleston—laid-back, relaxed, peaceful."*

**Total Enrollment:**
8,921

**Top 10% of High School Class:**
28%

**Average GPA:**
3.7

**Acceptance Rate:**
60%

**Tuition:**
$6,202 in-state, $14,140 out-of-state

**SAT Range (25th-75th Percentile):**
| Verbal | Math | Total |
|---|---|---|
| 560 – 640 | 560 – 640 | 1120 – 1280 |

**ACT Range (25th-75th Percentile):**
| Verbal | Math | Total |
|---|---|---|
| N/A | N/A | 22-25 |

**Most Popular Majors:**
18%  Communications
14%  Business
8%   Psychology
7%   Biology
7%   Elementary Education

**Students also applied to:***
Clemson University
James Madison University
University of Georgia
University of North Carolina
University of South Carolina

*For more school info check out www.collegeprowler.com

## Table of Contents

| | |
|---|---|
| Academics | 80 |
| Local Atmosphere | 82 |
| Safety & Security | 83 |
| Facilities | 85 |
| Campus Dining | 87 |
| Campus Housing | 88 |
| Diversity | 90 |
| Guys & Girls | 91 |
| Athletics | 93 |
| Greek Life | 95 |
| Drug Scene | 96 |
| Overall Experience | 97 |

## College Prowler Report Card

| | |
|---|---|
| Academics | B- |
| Local Atmosphere | B |
| Safety & Security | B |
| Facilities | B |
| Campus Dining | C+ |
| Campus Housing | B |
| Diversity | D |
| Guys | B- |
| Girls | A |
| Athletics | B- |
| Greek Life | C+ |
| Drug Scene | B |

# Academics

## Special Degree Options
The College of Charleston offers various interdisciplinary majors, in addition to a couple of pre-professional programs (pre-medicine and pre-dentistry) and teacher certification.

## Sample Academic Clubs
Biology Club, Arabic Club, Marketing Club, Visual Arts Club, Golden Key Honor Society, PETE (Physical Education Teacher Education), Historic Preservation Alliance, American Student Dental Association, Honors Program Student Association, MESSA (Master of Environmental Studies Student Association)

## The Lowdown
### ON ACADEMICS

**Degrees Awarded:**
Bachelor, Master, Post-Bachelor Certificate

**Undergraduate Schools:**
School of the Arts, School of Economics, School of Education, School of Humanities and Social Sciences, School of Science and Mathematics

**Full-time Faculty:**
487

**Part-time Faculty:**
366

**Faculty with Terminal Degree:**
85.6%

**Student-to-Faculty Ratio:**
14:1

**Average Course Load:**
15 credits (5 courses)

**AP Test Score Requirements:**
Possible credit for scores of 3 or higher

**IB Test Score Requirements:**
Possible credit for scores of 5, 6, or 7

## Did You Know?
Charleston's graduation occurs on Mother's Day every year, and, instead of caps and gowns, the girls wear white dresses and the guys wear tuxes.

Charleston's campus, as well as being scenic and beautiful, is full of places for outdoor studying, like the lawn in front of Randolph Hall or the center of campus near the Physician's Auditorium.

During final and midterm exams, Craig Cafeteria plays host to a midnight breakfast, so students can take a break, grab a bite to eat, and relax away some stress during exam cram-time.

The College of Charleston's On Course program is a flexible, easy-to-use audit processing program that makes it faster and easier for students to keep up with their degree, credits, scheduling, and GPA.

**Best Places to Study:**

Students looking for peace and quiet should head to the library, or the third or fourth floor of the Stern Center.

## Students Speak Out
### ON ACADEMICS

> "It's impossible to make a general statement about the faculty here. Some are awesome and you want to take their classes over and over again, but others are, plain and simple, not good professors."

Q "I don't think that the College of Charleston is negligent in their responsibility to hire professors who are **capable in their field, but sometimes professors are just unfair**—not giving enough warning before assignments, changing due dates, testing on things that weren't discussed in class, stuff like that. Some professors here just suck, but I guess that happens at every college."

Q "The college is really **devoted to the success of its students**. The professors know you by name, and they are always available. There are programs here to help you if you're struggling. There's never a time when you can't find help."

Q "I have to say I was a little **disappointed by the variety of classes provided** here. There should be more classes for film and writing, and they shouldn't be electives. I mean, this is a liberal arts college, right?"

Q "I really feel like the professors here, for the most part, treat their students like equals. I've had a couple **professors who insisted on being called by their first names**. That really takes the pressure off."

Want to find more info on majors offered by the College of Charleston? Visit www.collegeprowler.com for the full-length book.

## The College Prowler Take
### ON ACADEMICS

One thing can be said about the College of Charleston: students experience a range of emotions when it comes to their professors. Some professors may seem unqualified and unfair, while others become more of a mentor than just a professor. This is true no matter where you go, but what makes the College of Charleston unique is the relationship between professors and students. With a student-to-teacher ratio of 14:1, you can always be certain that personal attention will be provided in abundance. The vast majority of students at Charleston feel that their professors view them as equals and sincerely care about how they are doing in class.

With Charleston's reputation as a quality liberal arts college, the faculty here have earned the right to be trusted to help guide and develop your education. While Communications and Business are the most common degrees pursued at the College of Charleston, professors and staff in every other department are just as capable and ready to teach and encourage their students. Whether you hate or love your professor, he or she will always be there to help you in any way possible. Every department is the same in this respect, whether it is Theater or Biology, Communications or Jazz Piano.

**B-**

**The College Prowler™ Grade on**
## Academics: B-

A high Academics grade generally indicates that professors are knowledgeable, accessible, and genuinely interested in their students' welfare. Other determining factors include class size, how well professors communicate, and whether or not classes are engaging.

# Local Atmosphere

**City Websites:**
http://www.charleston.cvb.com
http://www.ci.charleston.sc.us
http://www.charleston.com

## Did you know?

Charleston, South Carolina's oldest city, ranks 16th out of 20 cites for the best quality of life in the nation, according to www.easidemographics.com.

## The Lowdown
ON LOCAL ATMOSPHERE

**Region:**
Southeast

**City, State:**
Charleston, South Carolina

**Setting:**
Medium-sized city

**Distance from Columbia:**
1 hour, 45 minutes

**Distance from Myrtle Beach:**
1 hour, 15 minutes

**Points of Interest:**
Market Street, Spoleto Arts Festival, Charleston Ghost and Dungeon Tour, Civil War Walk, South Carolina Aquarium, Patriots' Point Naval and Maritime Museum, Historical Old Exchange and Provost Dungeon, Waterfront Park, Dock Street Theater, the Hunley Submarine, the Charleston Symphony Orchestra

**Sports Teams:**
Charleston Battery (soccer)
Charleston Stingrays (hockey)
Charleston Riverdogs (minor league baseball)

## Students Speak Out
ON LOCAL ATMOSPHERE

"I love Charleston's location! It's not like a normal campus. It's right in the middle of the city, so you can walk anywhere you need to go."

Q "I love Charleston because we're in an urban setting, but it's not a big city that overwhelms you. The **beach is 20 minutes in practically every direction**, and so are the suburbs. There are so many places to go, but why would you want to go anywhere else? It's Charleston!"

Q "It's **hard with all the tourists sometimes.** Charleston isn't that big to begin with, and when huge buses clog the streets, it's pretty annoying. But it's cool that our home is interesting and beautiful enough to draw that much attention."

Q "Sometimes it's a little overwhelming to live in the city when you're from a small town. I know some people who have transferred because they didn't feel right here. There are **so many people from small towns here!** Imagine what they would do in New York City!"

Q "I'm from Atlanta, and **this city seems kind of small and quaint** in comparison. But it's peaceful and quiet. You can still get crazy though, don't get me wrong. It's fun. It's just not big."

## The College Prowler Take
ON LOCAL ATMOSPHERE

Charleston is a city preserved by care and untainted by change and novelty. This is not to say that Charleston is outdated or boring. Aside from being a beautiful and historic city, Charleston offers a variety of activities and events to choose from. Two other colleges, CSU and the Citadel are nearby, so even though Charleston is not a huge college town, there are enough college students to go around. Whether you're into sports or art, outdoor activities or indoor, shopping or surfing, there is always something to do. Shops on King and Meeting Streets are only blocks away from campus. Beaches (yes, more than one) are only a 20-minute drive away. And there are more restaurants downtown than anyone could ever eat at in a lifetime. If you are looking for skyscrapers, rush-hour traffic and the hustle and bustle of a metropolis, search elsewhere. But, if you are looking for laid-back, easygoing Southern culture, Charleston is just right for you.

# Safety & Security

## The Lowdown
ON SAFETY & SECURITY

**Number of C of C Police Officers:**
36 trained police officers
15 security guards assigned to residence halls

**Phone:**
(843) 953-5611

**Website:**
http://www.cofc.edu/publicsafety

**Health Center Office Hours:**
Monday-Thursday 8:30 a.m.-7 p.m.; Friday: 8:30 a.m.-5 p.m.

**Website:**
http://www.wellness.cofc.edu/health.htm

**Safety Services:**
Bicycle Registration, Campus Emergency Call Boxes, C.A.R.E (Crisis Assistance Response and Education), First Responder Unit, Parking Enforcement, RAD (Rape Aggression Defense)

**B**

The College Prowler™ Grade on
## Local Atmosphere: B

A high Local Atmosphere grade indicates that the area surrounding campus is safe and scenic. Other factors include nearby attractions, proximity to other schools, and the town's attitude toward students.

## Students Speak Out
### ON SAFETY & SECURITY

> "Campus police always seem to be watching you, but that means they're watching the shady people, too, which makes me feel more comfortable."

Q "Obviously, since the college is located downtown, there are going to be crimes and incidents that public safety can't always stop. But, when I am on campus, I know that **public safety officers are the ones around the street corner** at night, not a mugger."

Q "They piss me off sometimes, like when they **check everything in your bag if you're going into the dorm at night**. But I've heard some really horrible stories of what happens at other schools when security was lax. And if someone has a gun or a bomb in their bag, I'd rather have public safety enforcing all the rules instead of letting any psycho stroll by."

Q "**My bike has been stolen twice**. You're telling me public safety is doing a good job, and they can't even keep people's bikes from being stolen?"

Q "I like the fact that we have **emergency call boxes on campus.** You can call a public safety officer any time—day or night—and they'll take you wherever you want to go, even if you just have a bad feeling about the street or something. That makes me feel safe on campus."

## The College Prowler Take
### ON SAFETY & SECURITY

Statistics show that the College of Charleston, even with its urban setting, is no more dangerous than a college or university with a closed campus. Thirty-six professionally trained police officers (a large number in comparison to other colleges much larger than the College of Charleston) patrol the campus and surrounding areas 24 hours a day, and 15 security officers are stationed in the residence halls. This strong security presence makes most students feel safe on campus at all times of the day and night. Sometimes students feel that campus security is more like campus surveillance: police officers are on just about every corner, and security guards dig in to every corner of your bag when you enter the residence halls. Every dorm has a different color sticker that residents must have on their student ID. Without this sticker, you can't get in, except as a guest, and every guest's information is taken down by the guard at the front desk. Overall, students feel that security officers are doing a good job (in spite of occasional bike thefts here and there).

**B**

The College Prowler™ Grade on
### Safety & Security: B

A high grade in Safety & Security means that students generally feel safe, campus police are visible, blue-light phones and escort services are readily available, and safety precautions are not overly necessary.

# Facilities

## Computers

**High-Speed Network?** Yes
**Wireless Network?** Yes
**Number of Labs:** 16
**24-Hour Labs:** No
**Operating Systems:** Mac, PC
**Charge to Print:**
Printing is free in the library computer lab, but it costs 10 cents a page everywhere else on campus.

## The Lowdown
ON FACILITIES

### Favorite Things to Do

The center of campus, in between Maybank Hall and the Robert S. Small Library, is a popular place for students to hang out in between classes, and tables are usually set up by campus organizations, such as Greek life and the athletic teams. Napping on the lawn in front of Randolph Hall is always a popular way to pass time. The Stern Center Gardens plays host to live music functions. Several buildings on campus hold poetry readings, lectures, debates, and films.

**Student Center:**
Stern Center on George Street

**Libraries:**
The Robert Scott Small Library, the Marine Resources Library, the John Rivers Communications Museum, the Avery Research Center, and the Office of Media and Technology make up the college's library system. The Marlene and Nathan Addlestone Library was new for the fall 2004 semester.

**Athletic Center:**
Stern Center and F. Mitchell Johnson Center

**Movie Theater on Campus?**
Movies are shown twice a month in the Sotille Theater on George Street and in the Education Center.

**Bar on Campus?**
No

**Coffee on Campus?**
Yes, at the Port City Java in the Stern Center. Also there is a Starbucks and another Port City Java less than a block away from campus.

### COLLEGE PROWLER™

Want to hear more about campus facilities? For more student quotes, check out the guidebook on the College of Charleston at *www.collegeprowler.com*.

## Students Speak Out
### ON FACILITIES

"Sometimes the bathrooms make me feel like I'm in high school again. But that's just because they're kind of old. They're clean, and I'm not afraid to go into them or anything."

Q "I'm glad **they built a new fitness center**. The first one was always so crowded. You could never find a machine when you needed one. But now that there are two, you don't have to worry about finding equipment."

Q "**I love the arena**. The energy during a game is so high; you can't help but enjoy yourself, even if you're there only for social reasons."

Q "Since I've been here, they've built a new dorm, a new garage, remodeled the Stern Center, remodeled Berry Hall, and put in a new diner. And now they're building a brand new library. I love how they are **always trying to make things newer and better** for us."

Q "If you're not on an athletic team, the facilities here can be frustrating. **The pool hours for general use are ridiculous**, and unless you're on the team, you can hardly ever use it."

Q "I don't really have much to do with the athletic places. But, I like that they offer **yoga and dance classes for free**."

## The College Prowler Take
### ON FACILITIES

Most students feel, for the most part, that the facilities provided by the College of Charleston are suitable. And the school is making even further attempts to accommodate its students. Newly built residence halls will allow more housing for the ever-growing influx of students. The newly remodeled Joe E. Berry Hall shows that the college doesn't neglect its older buildings. With the exception of relatively new buildings (new meaning built within the last 100 years), the facilities that have stood in the city of Charleston for over 200 years are the ones used by the college. Even on campus, where the city has seen the most architectural change, the sights are pleasing to the eye.

**B**

**The College Prowler™ Grade on**
### Facilities: B

A high Facilities grade indicates that the campus is aesthetically pleasing and well-maintained; facilities are state-of-the-art, and libraries are exceptional. Other determining factors include the quality of both athletic and student centers and an abundance of things to do on campus.

# Campus Dining

## Students Speak Out
### ON CAMPUS DINING

"There's no reason to get a meal plan after your freshman year. If you get Dining Dollars, you have a lot more options, and you can still always eat at the cafeteria if you want to."

"I love the Champ Card! I can eat out any time I want. But you do have to be careful not to use it too many times too fast. If the Champ Card is all you have, you could find yourself **starving and broke at the end of the year**."

"I hate the HomeZone. If there wasn't a dorm above it I would want someone to burn it down. There is no excuse for our parents paying the money they **pay for the crap they call food** in the HomeZone. It makes me sick just looking at it sometimes."

"There could definitely be more places to eat on campus, and the food in the Hungry Cougar is **just plain pathetic, for the most part**. The food there reminds me of what I ate in my high school cafeteria, only then I wasn't paying for it."

"I don't know why, but I kind of like the cafeteria. Considering the fact that I can't really afford to eat out whenever I want, it's **pretty good for the bare minimum**."

"The Bistro is a good place to hang out and **chill between classes and grab a bite to eat**. It's a lot more convenient than going to the cafeteria and standing in line for a whole meal."

## The Lowdown
### ON CAMPUS DINING

**Freshman Meal Plan Requirement?**
No

**24-Hour On-Campus Eating?**
No

**Student Favorites:**
Kickin' Chicken, Moe's

**Meal Plan Average Cost:**
Between $360 and $1,030

### Did you know?

Meal plans at Charleston include Dining Dollars, money stored in a student's account that can be used like a credit card at dining halls.

The College of Charleston meal plan offers another option, called the Champ Card, which allows students to dine at various Charleston restaurants on a pre-paid plan.

## The College Prowler Take
### ON CAMPUS DINING

There will always be mixed emotions when it comes to campus dining, but every student can pretty much agree that the dining hall leaves much to be desired. Though the food at the HomeZone may be nearly inedible by students' standards, the quality of the food in Craig Café is quite good by cafeteria standards, and very good considering how much a meal plan costs. Once you're inside the Café and your student ID has been swiped, you can eat to your heart's desire. However, as very cheap and very common among freshmen and on-campus students as the Café is, it is not the popular choice for upperclassmen. As an alternative to campus eating, the Champ Card gives students access to a great variety of restaurants around Charleston, which are easy to get to regardless of where you are living.

**The College Prowler™ Grade on**
## Campus Dining: C+

Our grade on Campus Dining addresses the quality of both school-owned dining halls and independent on-campus restaurants as well as the price, availability, and variety of food.

# Campus Housing

## The Lowdown
### ON CAMPUS HOUSING

**Undergrads on Campus:**
26%

**Number of Residence Halls/Houses:**
25

**Number of College-Owned Apartments:**
2

**Available for Rent:**
Mini-fridge and microwave

**Cleaning Service?**
Cleaning services are only available in public areas. Community bathrooms are cleaned by staff members.

**Bed-Type:**
Single extra-long (39"x80"); some lofts, some bunk-beds; regular beds in Warren Place

**Also Available:**
Handicap-accessible housing, special interest housing

## Room Types

Residential housing on campus includes standard, suite-style, and apartment-style units. In standard units, students share a common bathroom facility and living area. In suite-style units, students share a bathroom and living area with no more than five people. In apartment-style units, students share a semi-private bathroom with no more than one person, and share a living area and kitchen with no more than six people.

The College of Charleston owns Warren Place, an apartment building off campus that offers approximately 287 single rooms in two- to five-bedroom apartments.

## You Get

Single bed (loftable/ bunkable), individual desks, desk chairs, wardrobes, blinds, air-conditioning, telephone hookup (one per bedroom), cable television, Internet service (one per student)

### Students Speak Out
ON CAMPUS HOUSING

"I don't recommend College Lodge. It's just disgusting. It's fun if you want to party every night, but it's not the kind of place you actually want to live. There's this feeling when you're inside that you're going to catch something."

Q "I'm so glad that most of the **dorms on campus don't have community showers**. I wouldn't mind one so much in a girls' dorm, but if I lived in McConnell and I had to use the same shower as 200 college guys, I would probably never shower."

Q "I never lived in a dorm with community showers, and I'm glad. I didn't do that normal college routine of carrying your little bath bucket down the hall and **showering with your flip-flops on**. I shared my shower with one other person and it was nice and clean all the time, right there in our room. Most of our dorms have private bathrooms anyway, which is a plus."

Q "The dorms are a great way to meet people your first year. But if you're an upperclassman and you're living in the dorms, you're practically never there because you're always over at your friends' apartments. **McAlister had a lot of upperclassman this past year**, and the only reasons I can think of is that they had nowhere else to go, and McAlister is the nicest one."

Q "**Yes, live in a dorm your first year**. There's really no reason not to. But if you can, move into your own apartment or into a historic house your sophomore year. The dorms are nice and all, but when you're 21 and you can't have a beer in your own living room, that's just lame."

### The College Prowler Take
ON CAMPUS HOUSING

On-campus housing is a good way to meet new people, form friendships, and find roommates for next year's housing plans. It's pretty much considered the norm among transfer students and freshmen, who make up the majority undergraduate students living on campus. Many students choose to live on campus their first year, even though freshmen aren't required to do so. But if you do choose to live on campus, here is what you're in for: relatively tight security at the entrances to the dorms, and RAs that either breathe down your neck about the rules, or don't care at all.

Charleston's residence halls vary from brand-new apartment-style suites, to ancient, fairly maintained standard rooms with common bathrooms and lounges. For the most part, students look back on their experiences in on-campus housing favorably.

**B**

The College Prowler™ Grade on
## Campus Housing: B

A high Campus Housing grade indicates that dorms are clean, well-maintained, and spacious. Other determining factors include variety of dorms, proximity to classes, and social atmosphere.

# Diversity

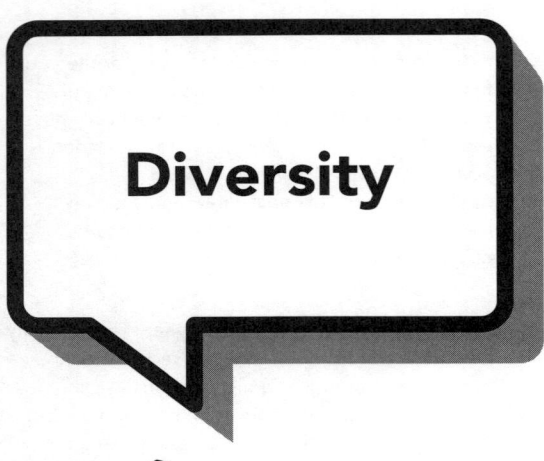

## The Lowdown
ON DIVERSITY

**Native American:** 0%

**Asian American:** 2%

**African American:** 8%

**Hispanic:** 1%

**White:** 86%

**International:** 2%

**Unknown:** 1%

**Out-of-State:** 29.6%

### Political Activity
There is a balanced mix of students who are liberal and who are conservative, but many students seem to be politically apathetic. The College of Charleston plays host to debates and events that are politically centered, but politics don't seem to play a large role in the student body.

### Minority Clubs
The college offers a variety of clubs for minorities, including the Student Union for Minority Affairs, Indian Cultural Exchange, and Black Student Union.

### Most Popular Religions
Being a southern college, the most popular religion is Christianity. There are many Christian groups on campus, such as Baptist Collegiate Ministries, Campus Outreach, Campus Crusade for Christ, and Fellowship of Christian Athletes, but all religions are encouraged to be involved in student organizations such as the Atheist-Humanist Alliance, COMPASS (Catholic Student Association), the Jewish Student Union, and the Muslim Students Association.

### Gay Tolerance
The Gay-Straight Alliance is the only student organization concerning gay students, and the gay community at the College of Charleston remains relatively low-key.

### Economic Status
Charleston welcomes students from all economic backgrounds and offers millions of dollars in scholarships every year. The majority of students on campus seem to come from upper-middle- or upper-class families though.

## Students Speak Out
ON DIVERSITY

"I think the fact that we're in the South has a lot to do with the [lack of] diversity here. Not even two percent of our students are Hispanic."

"Other schools are demonstrating the changing times, and the fact that **more non-white kids are going to college. Not here.**"

"I don't think that the diversity on our campus is that bad. I see **all kinds of people hanging out together**. I think there's a pretty good mix of people here."

"I was surprised to find that only nine percent of our students were black. That means there are **even more white kids at this school than I thought!**"

💬 "**I run into more international students** than I do Americans of different ethnicities. To me, that's kind of strange."

💬 "I know that a lot of kids are from the South, and even though **they're not exactly racist, they stick to their own kind**. I hate that. But, that's not true for everyone."

## The College Prowler Take
### ON DIVERSITY

The College of Charleston is not known for being a racially diverse school. But it's not completely behind in the times. More and more international students come here every year. It sometimes seems as if it will take forever for the college's percentage of minority students to come close to its percentage of white students, if indeed that will ever happen. This is unsettling to those students who feel they are surrounded by sameness and for those who feel that the college's student population does not reflect the changes in our society. Culturally, some students feel that they are immersed in a world of southern mind-sets, mannerisms, and ways of life, and wish to see some other influences on campus. In spite of the lack of diversity here, some students do make the personal effort of diversifying their own social circles.

**The College Prowler™ Grade on**
## Diversity: D

A high grade in Diversity indicates that ethnic minorities and international students have a notable presence on campus and that students of different economic backgrounds, religious beliefs, and sexual preferences are well-represented.

# Guys & Girls

## The Lowdown
### ON GUYS & GIRLS

**Women Undergrads:** 63.1%

**Men Undergrads:** 36.9%

### Birth Control Available?
No. Though the Health Center does not provide birth control to female students, it provides information and guidance for students who are seeking birth control.

### Social Scene
The College of Charleston doesn't necessarily have a well-known reputation for being a party school, but most students would agree that parties aren't hard to find. Even without the bars downtown, which are limited in number, students will celebrate, no matter what the occasion. Meeting people can be tough, and many freshmen have claimed that they have run into a lot of snobby girls and guys. Joining a sorority or fraternity is not the only way to meet people, and the key to forming friendships is universal: bite the bullet and be friendly. Everyone else wants to meet people just as badly as you do.

## Hookups or Relationships?

Many girls at the College of Charleston meet and stay with cadets from the Citadel, who are most likely looking for a hookup more than anything else. Sometimes, it seems like College of Charleston boys are never going to be boyfriend material, and commitment-free hookups are as common here as the typical keg party.

## Dress Code

With a vast majority of southern belles and debutantes at a school that is already overpopulated by females, it is the norm to see pearl necklaces, cardigans, and tennis skirts. But Charleston has a wide variety of students, and with that comes a wide variety of styles. When it comes to nightlife, expect to see lots of girls overdressing in stilettos and tiny skirts, while the guys seem to make absolutely no effort whatsoever. You want to see a well-dressed guy? Look for a man in uniform. There are plenty of Citadel cadets on the streets on Friday and Saturday nights.

Wanna know more about C of C hotties? For more opinions and info on C of C's luscious "student body," check out the College Prowler book on C of C available at www.collegeprowler.com.

# Students Speak Out
## ON GUYS & GIRLS

"For the most part, I'd say that the student body here is an attractive one. The girls all take care of themselves, and they're so cute in their little skirts."

Q "**Just because you put on a short skirt doesn't mean you're sexy**. Especially when every other girl is wearing one at a party. Showing off a lot of skin won't get you noticed when everyone else is showing off a lot of skin too. The girls at this school don't seem to realize this."

Q "**Pearl necklaces, cardigans, khaki shorts** ... I thought that only happened in movies. I didn't realize that people actually dress like that. It definitely took a while before I could look at some of these southern girls without laughing."

Q "I know that **guys here party and smoke weed a lot**, but that doesn't mean you have to look like it. A lot of the guys here are just disgusting. I don't understand how they get girls to even give them a second look."

Q "I always **enjoy meeting guys from the North**. There's something different about them. They stand out from the southern ones, not always in a good way. Like when they're from New Jersey. I haven't met a nice boy from New Jersey yet; still trying though."

Q "There's a good variety of people here. There are preppy guys in their collared shirts and then hippies with dreadlocks down to their shoulders. There are a lot of surfers and skaters, too. **Whatever your type is, you can find it here**."

## The College Prowler Take
### ON GUYS & GIRLS

For the most part, the College of Charleston campus is an attractive one, and with the nearly-constant warm weather, students are not afraid to display what they have to offer to the opposite sex. Usually what you will find is that girls are sweet and conservative during the day and provocative at night, while guys will most likely roll out of bed after an afternoon nap and wear the same thing to a party they wore all day. There seems to be an abundance of preppy girls, and preppy guys who have gotten a little bit lazy, but no student ever complains about a dearth of attractive people—they're everywhere.

**B-**

**A**

**The College Prowler™ Grade on**
## Guys: B-

A high grade for Guys indicates that the male population on campus is attractive, smart, friendly, and engaging, and that the school has a decent ratio of guys to girls.

**The College Prowler™ Grade on**
## Girls: A

A high grade for Girls not only implies that the women on campus are attractive, smart, friendly, and engaging, but also that there is a fair ratio of girls to guys.

# Athletics

## The Lowdown
### ON ATHLETICS

**Men's Varsity Teams:**
Baseball
Basketball
Cross Country
Golf
Sailing
Soccer
Swimming & Diving
Tennis

**Women's Varsity Teams:**
Basketball
Cross Country
Equestrian
Golf
Sailing
Soccer
Softball
Swimming & Diving
Tennis
Track & Field
Volleyball

## Club Sports
Crew, Fencing, Field Hockey, Rugby (men's/women's)

## Intramurals
Chess, Volleyball, Golf, Softball

## Getting Tickets
Students can get into some basketball games without buying tickets ahead of time. But basketball games at the College of Charleston are a big deal and certain games, like between C of C and the Citadel, are talked about for a week before they happen. Without tickets ahead of time, you'll be watching from your couch. Most other sporting events are not as popular, and students and spectators can buy tickets at the door.

**School Mascot:**
Cougar

**Athletic Division:**
NCAA Division III

**Conference:**
Southern Conference

**Most Popular Sports:**
Basketball, Soccer, Swimming

**Overlooked Teams:**
Sailing, Rugby

**Stadiums:**
Kresse Arena, Stadiums at Patriots Point (Baseball, Softball, Soccer, Tennis), Stern Student Center, Walker Sailing Complex

## Students Speak Out
### ON ATHLETICS

"Sporting events aren't like a school obsession or anything, but they're very popular. A lot of people go simply for the social factor. But, since it's free, there are always a lot of people at sporting events."

Q "Our gym, as well as our entire school, was used to film the basketball scenes in 'O.' Our gym is awesome. The **energy in there during a game is through the roof**, and even if basketball isn't really your thing, you can't help but get into it."

Q "There is **no hierarchy here amongst the athletes**. Yeah, a girl is going to like a guy who tells her he's a baseball player, but it's not like they strut around school like they own the place. That was for high school, thank you."

Q "The **girls' teams don't get enough recognition** here. The volleyball team is really good, and softball is always a good way to spend an hour or two of your life."

Q "It's **crazy here when there's a big game**. Tickets were sold out four days before one game. People were trying to pay each other for tickets. It is nuts. It's the closest we'll ever get to fanaticism here."

## The College Prowler Take
### ON ATHLETICS

While most of the teams on campus have their fair share of achievements, only with basketball do you get any real athletic excitement at Charleston. Being very arts-driven, the overwhelming majority of the student population didn't come here because of a certain team or because of the college's athletic reputation. The same can be said about the student athletes; they are laid-back, just like "regular" Charleston students, and do not strut about campus boasting about their achievements and talents. But, Cougar fans love to support their teams. Football fans, however, must satisfy their love of tackles and touchdowns by supporting the USC and Clemson teams, since Charleston doesn't have a team. If you're not a sports fan, then the College of Charleston is the place for you. If you are, then this is also the place for you.

**B-**

The College Prowler™ Grade on
### Athletics: B-

A high grade in Athletics indicates that students have school spirit, that sports programs are respected, that games are well-attended, and that intramurals are a prominent part of student life.

# Greek Life

> "Some **frats are like really close-knit groups of high school boys**. If you get involved with one brother, then the whole frat knows within a day."

> "There are a lot of cliques, and when I say cliques, I mean sororities. But **you don't have to be part of a clique to fit in**. There are lots of friendly and interesting people here. it's easy to meet people."

> "We are in the South, and we do have little girly girls who enjoy having to dress up for things and enjoy their girliness. **The rest of us don't rely so much on tradition**."

## The Lowdown
### ON GREEK LIFE

**Number of Fraternities:**
13

**Number of Sororities:**
11

**Undergrad Men in Fraternities:**
11.5%

**Undergrad Women in Sororities:**
16.5%

## The College Prowler Take
### ON GREEK LIFE

The scene and influence of sororities and fraternities on campus is pretty much contained within the group. Greeks don't run the campus. There is no pressure to join a sorority or fraternity, and there is no pressure if you join one and then quit. There is a trend that Charleston students who don't go Greek in their first year have a cynical, somewhat bitter, attitude towards Greeks. Some students think that pledging is selling away your soul, buying friends, and submitting to conformity. There are, of course, students who think oppositely, and see the good in joining an organization, or don't think anything of it at all. Even from a non-Greek perspective, one can admit that Greek life is a good way to make lasting friendships.

## Students Speak Out
### ON GREEK LIFE

> "There really is no separation between Greeks and non-Greeks. We can all be friends and mix in with each other. There isn't a dividing line or anything."

> "Sometimes I feel like fraternities and sororities rule this school. But, there are enough individuals to make up for the sheep. I've met so many interesting people here. The Greek thing is **just something you get used to after a while**."

### The College Prowler™ Grade on
## Greek Life: C+

A high grade in Greek Life indicates that sororities and fraternities are not only present, but also active on campus. Other determining factors include the variety of houses available and the respect the Greek community receives from the rest of the campus.

# Drug Scene

## The Lowdown
ON DRUG SCENE

**Most Prevalent Drugs on Campus:**
Alcohol, Marijuana, Caffeine, Ritalin, Adderall

**Drug Counseling Programs**
Counseling and Substance Abuse Services (CASAS) provides counseling for individual, couple, domestic, and relationship concerns as well as substance and alcohol abuse. Other psychiatric services are also available.

## Students Speak Out
ON DRUG SCENE

"I haven't run into that many kids doing anything dangerous. Just pot. Pot is everywhere here. We have a lot of hippies who smoke, and a lot of other kids too. It's easy to get here."

Q "I was surprised that kids can smoke in the dorms as much as they do. If you can manage it right so that it doesn't set off the smoke detector, you can smoke inside whenever you want. **College Lodge reeks of smoke all the time**."

Q "Kids do basically what they want here. I know **there are a lot of kids that probably try coke** or something more dangerous, and some that are just plain users. But, the people I've seen offering cocaine and ecstasy are not college students."

Q "I've heard people say that **cocaine is becoming really popular in South Carolina** and at Charleston. But I haven't seen any evidence of that with my own eyes."

Q "I don't really think that drug use here is a problem. Yeah, **kids smoke pot and drink,** but that's what college students do. Most kids shape up when their grades start to slip, and if they don't, they fail out."

## The College Prowler Take
ON DRUG SCENE

Alcohol and weed are the most common drugs used by students at Charleston, but students who really care about their education will do their best to stay away from anything more serious (i.e., cocaine or acid). It's not hard for students to find marijuana, or any other substance they might want to get into. Many students find that drugs are not a dominant force on this campus, despite growing talk that cocaine is becoming a popular accessory to College of Charleston life. Drugs are passed around at parties, and are used in the residence halls, but there is no pressure to use them. Alcohol, on the other hand, is a different story. Many students think that getting a little wild with drinking is a normal part of the college experience.

The College Prowler™ Grade on
## Drug Scene: B

A high grade on Drug Scene indicates that drugs are not a noticeable part of campus life; drug use is not visible, and no pressure to use them seems to exist.

# Overall Experience

## The Lowdown
ON OVERALL EXPERIENCE

"I can't imagine going anywhere else. I feel at home here, and I felt at home almost right away. There are things about the city that I don't really like, but the people and the atmosphere more than make up for that."

Q "C of C doesn't have a reputation for much of anything. **You're not getting the most exceptional education here**, you're not participating in the craziest parties, or supporting the most successful teams. But, I wouldn't want to go anywhere else. I feel like this is my home now."

Q "I met a lot of really unfriendly people when I first got here. I was thinking 'oh, southern hospitality will be nice,' and there wasn't any. **This is not a typical southern school**. It's about as metropolitan as you're going to get, except for Atlanta."

Q "**Don't expect Charleston to be like Atlanta or New York**. It's not like any other city I've ever been in. It has its own charm, its own appeal, its own taste. If you're here for a while and you can't adjust to Charleston for what it is, then there's a good chance you won't enjoy your time at this school."

Q "**The faculty is great, the school is great, the city is great**. I know there are people here who aren't gaga over the atmosphere, or don't love their professors, or whatever. But for me, I pretty much love everything about this place."

## The College Prowler Take
ON OVERALL EXPERIENCE

Most students acknowledge the fact that, at the College of Charleston, they are experiencing something unique and rare. Not only is the city an interesting and fascinating place, but the years students will spend at C of C will be radically different than they would be at most other schools. Many schools are not located in the heart of a city, as Charleston is, and many schools do not preserve the old while combining it with the new, the way the College of Charleston strives to. Although C of C may not have a well-known reputation for superior academics or sports, both the latter and the former are among the greatest in the nation, and many students come to care less and less about the acclaim that Charleston receives.

One cannot truly understand the appeal and rarity of attending the College of Charleston until they have been here a while, and though students do transfer out for various reasons (including simply not being happy as a C of C student), those who do remain here for all of their college years look back on their memories with nothing but contentment and pride. Charleston does its best to encourage its students and residents to enjoy the time they spend here, and students here will never be lacking in opportunities for their career or further education goals. Though it may be small and laid-back, the College of Charleston has many different qualities to be proud of, and the students themselves have said that Charleston has become their home.

Read more student opinions on their overall experience in the College Prowler book on C of C, available at *www.collegeprowler.com*.

# College of William & Mary

PO Box 8795, Williamsburg, VA 23187
www.wm.edu            (757) 221-4223

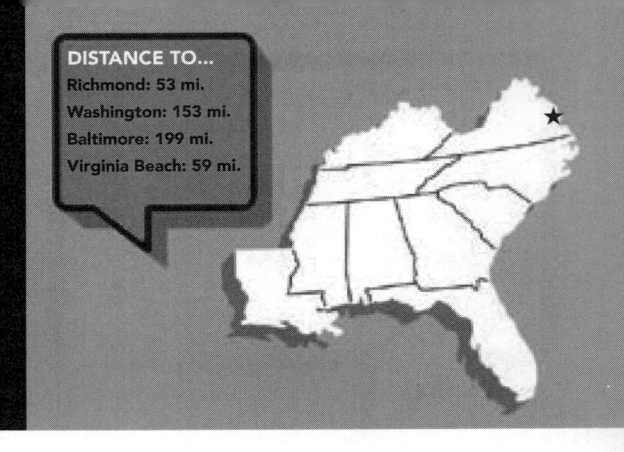

**DISTANCE TO...**
Richmond: 53 mi.
Washington: 153 mi.
Baltimore: 199 mi.
Virginia Beach: 59 mi.

"W&M is the perfect size for a close community of students, and everyone seems to be very involved in clubs and organizations."

**Total Enrollment:**
5,666

**Top 10% of High School Class:**
85%

**Average GPA:**
4.0

**Acceptance Rate:**
34%

**Tuition:**
$7,096 in-state, $21,796 out-of-state

**SAT Range (25th-75th Percentile):**
| Verbal | Math | Total |
|---|---|---|
| 630 – 730 | 630 – 710 | 1260 – 1440 |

**ACT Range (25th-75th Percentile):**
| Verbal | Math | Total |
|---|---|---|
| 28-33 | 28-31 | 30-32 |

**Most Popular Majors:**
- 14% Business
- 9% Political Science
- 9% Psychology
- 8% Biology
- 7% English

**Students also applied to:***
University of Virginia
Georgetown University
University of Richmond
Duke University
Washington and Lee University

*For more school info check out www.collegeprowler.com*

## Table of Contents

| | |
|---|---|
| Academics | 99 |
| Local Atmosphere | 101 |
| Safety & Security | 102 |
| Facilities | 104 |
| Campus Dining | 106 |
| Campus Housing | 107 |
| Diversity | 109 |
| Guys & Girls | 110 |
| Athletics | 112 |
| Greek Life | 114 |
| Drug Scene | 115 |
| Overall Experience | 117 |

## College Prowler Report Card

| | |
|---|---|
| Academics | A- |
| Local Atmosphere | C+ |
| Safety & Security | A- |
| Facilities | B |
| Campus Dining | B- |
| Campus Housing | C+ |
| Diversity | D+ |
| Guys | B- |
| Girls | B |
| Athletics | C |
| Greek Life | A |
| Drug Scene | A |

# Academics

## The Lowdown
### ON ACADEMICS

**Degrees Awarded:**
Bachelor, Master, Doctorate

**Full-time Faculty:**
577

**Faculty with Terminal Degree:**
93%

**Student-to-Faculty Ratio:**
12:1

**Average Course Load:**
14 Credits

**Special Programs:**
Interdisciplinary Majors, Double-Majors

**AP Test Score Requirements:**
Possible credit for scores of 3, 4, or 5

**IB Test Score Requirements:**
Possible credit for scores of 4, 5, 6, or 7

**Sample Academic Clubs:**
Anthropology Club, Classical Studies Club, Linguistics Club, the Society of Physics Students

### Did You Know?

William & Mary contributed to the education of three U.S. Presidents, Thomas Jefferson, James Monroe, and John Tyler, as well as four signers of the Declaration of Independence.

At the time of its foundation, in 1693, the college was contained in just one building—the Wren Building. Today, the Wren Building is the oldest building in continual use on a college campus in America.

**Best Places to Study:**
Swem Library, University Center lounges, the Daily Grind, the Sunken Gardens or Barksdale field in nice weather

### COLLEGE PROWLER

Need help choosing a major? For more info on W&M's classes and professors check out www.collegeprowler.com

## Students Speak Out
ON ACADEMICS

"**The professors rock! Okay, so you'll get the occasional boring loser, but mostly they're excited about what they are teaching and are good at it.**"

"Professors are awesome. They are there to teach, not to do research, and **they're incredible, intelligent, interesting people**. I've had a few duds, that I'll admit, but the rest of them totally made up for it."

"The teaching staff is probably one of the best qualities about W&M. I built great student-professor relationships. Since W&M is a smaller school, professors tend to give a lot **more personal attention to each student**."

"W&M tends to attract great minds and people who actually like to teach. There are no TAs here, so **you'll always be taught by a professor**, which is a huge advantage over most other schools where you get stuck being taught by a graduate student. W&M has a tremendous faculty, at least as far as I've seen."

"Excellent teachers. I was deciding between two schools, and I went to visit classes at each, and made my decision based solely on the teachers I encountered at W&M. The classes are small, all are taught by full professors, and the small number of grad students means the profs are interested solely in what you are doing. **You can't do better than the professors at W&M**."

## The College Prowler Take
ON ACADEMICS

Students adore the exceptionally committed faculty at William & Mary. In general, they are completely committed to teaching, and very accessible to their students. The professors' passion for their disciplines, as well as their love of teaching, leaves students feeling a connection to the faculty and the classes they teach. Class sizes are small at W&M, which makes it easy for teachers and students to bond. The faculty is accessible, but it goes beyond that—they make an effort to befriend and help any student who is willing to accept.

On the whole, students are very happy with their classroom experience at William & Mary. The faculty is focused on instruction, not research, and no classes are taught by teaching assistants. The professors really know their stuff, and students report only a few "duds." Mostly though, it's the relationships that students form with faculty that really stick with them and enhance their studies. Great teaching and a well-rounded liberal arts curriculum prepare students for any number of future endeavors.

**A-**

The College Prowler™ Grade on
### Academics: A-

A high Academics grade generally indicates that professors are knowledgeable, accessible, and genuinely interested in their students' welfare. Other determining factors include class size, how well professors communicate, and whether or not classes are engaging.

# Local Atmosphere

## The Lowdown
### ON LOCAL ATMOSPHERE

**Region:**
East

**City, State:**
Williamsburg, Virginia

**Setting:**
Small city

**Distance from Washington, DC:**
2 hours, 30 minutes

**Distance from Richmond:**
1 hour

**Points of Interest:**
Busch Gardens, Water Country USA, Colonial Williamsburg

**City Websites:**
http://www.ci.williamsburg.va.us/

## Students Speak Out
### ON LOCAL ATMOSPHERE

"It's Colonial Williamsburg, and it's amazing. You live right in the middle of history."

Q "The atmosphere in **Williamsburg is quiet and touristy**. Williamsburg is something like the number five most popular tourist attraction in the United States. So, especially in the warmer months, there are lots of people around. In some ways that's good, in others it's bad—[for instance] lots of random traffic."

Q "It's an hour in either direction from major cities, so you'll miss some conveniences if you're used to being in a big city. At the same time, it's not rural either. **There's everything you need close by**, and you won't feel stuck out in the sticks."

Q "There are some other universities close by, but not right there. Hampton University is in Hampton, about a half-hour away, and there's also **a nice movie theater and the Hampton Coliseum** and the Coliseum Mall there. Christopher Newport University is in Newport News, about 20 minutes away, Old Dominion University and the University of Richmond are in Richmond, and there's another school in Norfolk."

Q "The atmosphere is **pretty academic, with lots of interesting things to do**, especially for history buffs. However, Williamsburg has a tendency to completely die out around nine o'clock. With no other universities closer than 45 minutes, you're really on your own to find a fun time. 2 a.m. Wawa hoagie runs are a must—one of the few things to do after hours."

## The College Prowler Take
**ON LOCAL ATMOSPHERE**

Students label Williamsburg as quiet, touristy, and historic, but wouldn't call it a town with a thriving college atmosphere. While it's a beautiful city, it can become overrun with tourists at times, and can lack fun activities at other times. With enough creativity, however, students can make the best of the somewhat tepid atmosphere. Student organizations are always trying their best to bring interesting speakers, popular movie showings, and musical groups to campus to make up for the lack of off-campus attractions for the college crowd. Most students find that this arrangement suits them fine. There are no other universities in the immediate vicinity, but there are some within driving distance. Amenities such as shopping malls and clubs also require a bit of a drive. Despite that, Williamsburg remains a charming small town with a rich history.

## C+

The College Prowler™ Grade on
### Local Atmosphere: C+

A high Local Atmosphere grade indicates that the area surrounding campus is safe and scenic. Other factors include nearby attractions, proximity to other schools, and the town's attitude toward students.

# Safety & Security

## The Lowdown
**ON SAFETY & SECURITY**

**Number of W&M Police:**
22

**Phone:**
911 (emergency)
(757) 221-4596 (non-emergency)

**Health Center Office Hours:**
Monday, Tuesday, Thursday, Friday 8 a.m.-5 p.m.; Wednesday 10 a.m.-5 p.m.; Saturday 12 p.m.-4 p.m.

**Safety Services:**
Escort Service, Steer Clear shuttle, Emergency phones

### Did You Know?

All campus residences are protected by electronic key card locks that allow only students in during the day, while only admitting residents of the building in at night.

## Students Speak Out
### ON SAFETY & SECURITY

{ **"Safety on campus is pretty good. You've got all the standard stuff, like a student-run escort service, blue emergency lights, and 24-hour card-key access to the dorms."**

Q "Williamsburg is **not a very dangerous place,** so there's not much to worry about. Until recently, they worst crimes reported on campus were bicycles being stolen, and maybe one date rape per year. My roommate and I didn't lock our dorm room door for two years straight, and nothing was ever taken."

Q "We have an escort service available if you ever need someone to walk you somewhere at night. **The campus police are always available,** and drive around campus all the time, in case there are any problems. The dorms are secure, and you need an ID to get in. There are blue emergency lights scattered all around campus, and you just push a button if you have a problem, and it connects you to the campus police right away."

Q "Although there are incidents with robberies or worse on campus a few times a semester, I have not felt unsafe on the campus at anytime. Those who do, have a variety of options open to them, from campus escorts, to getting shuttled in vans, to simply calling Campus Police for rides at night. **The police are dedicated and extremely helpful** when needed. I usually leave my room unlocked and have even left book bags unattended with little fear of theft; the mood on campus encourages this trust."

Q "Safety is pretty darn good. We are in Colonial Williamsburg after all, which is fairly quiet and safe. There were some assaults on female students this year, but whenever that happens the administration makes it public really quickly to alert everyone and ask for help. I personally **never felt threatened on campus**, and even though I know it's a bad idea, I walked alone late at night without feeling unsafe."

Q "Campus Police is one of the most incompetent departments on campus. **They are unorganized and ill-informed.** However, they have a faster response time during a crisis than the city and state police. Campus is pretty safe. There are alarm boxes on all paths and campus is pretty well-lit. The place is safe, if you use your head."

## The College Prowler Take
### ON SAFETY & SECURITY

Students mostly say they're pleased with the Campus Police Department and other safety services. The small town atmosphere and tight-knit college community combine to create a sense of safety not present at larger universities. Lots of students leave their rooms unlocked and few have had anything stolen from them. Serious crime, such as assault or rape, is rare; most students don't fear this kind of incident, even late at night.

Williamsburg is a small town, and is therefore safer than many places. The police force seems to do an adequate job, though students sometimes complain that they spend more time writing parking tickets than doing anything else—though annoying, it's a good indication that there aren't any major threats to campus safety on a regular basis.

**A-**

### The College Prowler™ Grade on
## Safety & Security: A-

A high grade in Safety & Security means that students generally feel safe, campus police are visible, blue-light phones and escort services are readily available, and safety precautions are not overly necessary.

# Facilities

**Computers**

**High-Speed Network?** Yes

**Wireless Network?**
Yes, in Swem Library and various other academic buildings, but not in dorms.

**Number of Labs:** 11

**Numbers of Computers:** 300

**24-Hour Labs:** Yes (some, but not all)

**Charge to Print?** 5 cents per page

## The Lowdown
ON FACILITIES

**Student Centers:**
The University Center (UC) and Campus Center

**Athletic Centers:**
The Recreation Center, Adair Gym, Zable Stadium, Busch Field

**Libraries:**
Swem Library, which includes biology, chemistry, education, geology, law, marine science, music, and physics libraries, and a rare book and manuscript collection.

**Popular Places to Chill:**
The UC, Daily Grind, Campus Center, anywhere outside in nice weather

**Movie Theatre on Campus?**
No, but there are occasional movie showings.

**Bar on Campus?**
Yes, Lodge One is in the UC basement.

**Coffeehouse on Campus?**
Yes, the Daily Grind is in UC.

**Favorite Things to Do:**
Hang out on the Daily Grind patio, play pool or video games in Lodge One, have a jam session in Ewell Hall.

## Students Speak Out
ON FACILITIES

"Facilities are good, everything is clean. You always have access to computers. The Rec Center has lots of machines available for exercising. The football stadiums are nice, and we have new tennis courts."

"The facilities are pretty good, adequate for my needs. The University Center is awesome, they just remodeled it with **pool tables, air hockey, e-mail ports, video games, etc.** The Rec Center is also fairly well-equipped, although there are certain times when the gym is over-crowded. If you go at less crowded times, you'll be fine."

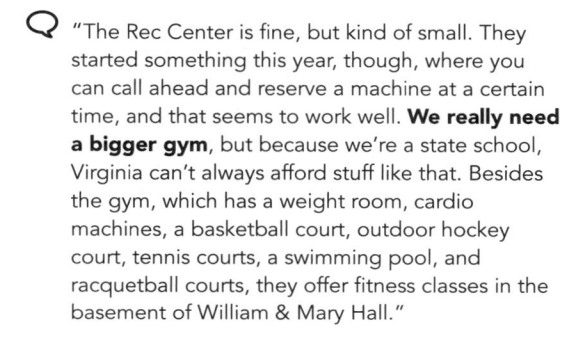

Q "The facilities are very nice. The University Center is a great central point on campus. It has a dining hall, mailroom, game room, store, and restaurant and sports bar, making it very convenient. The library will be nice once it is finished being remodeled. It will have a Starbucks and sandwich place. The library also has some computers for student use. **The Rec Center is also good, complete with weight rooms**, racquetball courts, a pool, and exercise rooms. The Rec will be also be renovated soon, so it will be even bigger."

Q "The Rec Center is fine, but kind of small. They started something this year, though, where you can call ahead and reserve a machine at a certain time, and that seems to work well. **We really need a bigger gym**, but because we're a state school, Virginia can't always afford stuff like that. Besides the gym, which has a weight room, cardio machines, a basketball court, outdoor hockey court, tennis courts, a swimming pool, and racquetball courts, they offer fitness classes in the basement of William & Mary Hall."

Q "The computers were just upgraded, and they are really nice—**a bit light on the entertaining software**, but for academics they have anything you could want. The Rec Center is really nice and we have tons of fields and tennis courts. You can always find a place to play something and if you need the equipment you can just go rent it really cheap from the Rec Center. The student center is nice, it has pool tables and game systems and places to get food. It's a fun place to spend some of your free time."

## The College Prowler Take
### ON FACILITIES

For hours of entertainment, students flock to the University Center basement, where there are foosball tables, air hockey, video games, and pool, as well as a food store, bar, and late night eatery. Students sweat away their stress at the Rec Center, which features a room with weight machines, two weight rooms downstairs, an indoor pool, racquetball courts, and indoor and outdoor basketball courts. It also has an outdoor equipment center where students can rent tents, sleeping bags, etc. for a minimal fee. Most students say the Rec Center is adequate, though crowded at times. Overall, students are pleased with the facilities. The most common complaint is that a few of the older academic buildings could use some improvement.

**B**

Check out www.collegeprowler.com for the College of William & Mary guidebook. Inside, you'll find more details on what the campus has to offer.

### The College Prowler™ Grade on
### Facilities: B

A high Facilities grade indicates that the campus is aesthetically pleasing and well-maintained; facilities are state-of-the-art, and libraries are exceptional. Other determining factors include the quality of both athletic and student centers and an abundance of things to do on campus.

# Campus Dining

## The Lowdown
ON CAMPUS DINING

**Freshman Meal Plan Requirement?**
Yes

**24-Hour On-Campus Eating?**
No

**Student Favorites:**
The Commons Dining Hall, The Marketplace

**Meal Plan Average Cost:**
$1,100

### Did You Know?

If students don't feel well enough to leave their room for food, they can fill out an "under the weather" form (available on the Dining Services Website) and a friend can use their ID card to pick up food for them.

## Students Speak Out
ON CAMPUS DINING

"The Caf has decent food and a great social atmosphere; however, like all the places on campus, the food lacks variety. I could only take one year of eating it."

"Food on campus is fine. **There are three dining halls: two all-you-can-eat, one à la carte.** All freshmen are required to get the biggest meal plan, so you won't starve, and there's always something you can eat, wherever you go. They've been making an effort in recent years to include more vegetarian and vegan options as well. There are some fast food places on campus, too. We have Pizza Hut, Burger King, and Chick-fil-A."

"Well, the food is pretty good as far as campus dining can go. The Caf recently changed hands so the food has gotten much, much better there. I find that it's worth it to walk the extra distance to eat there rather than the UC Center Court. Also, the Marketplace is very good. It is different from the other dining venues because it is à la carte. The **grilled deli sandwiches, wraps, pizzas, and smoothies are good** there."

"The food on campus isn't very good, but that's to be expected of cafeterias. **You can find something to eat, the variety is the only concern**. The Caf has gotten much better since my freshman year, and the Marketplace has some good meals, especially Chick-fil-A. Just make sure you don't overdose on the Marketplace, it gets really boring by the end of the year."

"The food is decent. The Marketplace has a lot of variety in its concepts and has great quality. The Caf has a lot of general variety in a different way, and its food and staff are both great. **The UC is my least favorite place to eat on campus**, but it still isn't bad."

## The College Prowler Take
ON CAMPUS DINING

Some students think the campus food is above average, some find it below par. There are two all-you-can-eat cafeterias, offering rotating menus, and several à la carte eateries. The fare ranges from a plentiful salad bar at the Caf to fried chicken at the Marketplace. Despite the apparent cornucopia of options, students still want more variety. Overall, the food is nothing special, but it's not horrible either. Freshmen are required to get a large meal plan, which can end up being a waste of money, and the greasy food won't help ward off the infamous freshman 15. On the positive side, the hours of operation are pretty accommodating, and most students admit that the food really isn't all that bad.

## B-

### The College Prowler™ Grade on
### Campus Dining: B-

Our grade on Campus Dining addresses the quality of both school-owned dining halls and independent on-campus restaurants as well as the price, availability, and variety of food.

# Campus Housing

## The Lowdown
ON CAMPUS HOUSING

**Undergrads on Campus:**
77%

**Dormitories:**
47

**University-Owned Apartments:**
131

**Room Types:**
Rooms are mostly doubles, triples, and quads in traditional hall-style dorms, with some small apartments and single rooms.

**Available for Rent:**
Microwaves, mini-fridges, lofts

**Cleaning Service?**
Hall bathrooms and common areas only, cleaned every weekday

**You Get:**
Bed, desk, chair, closet or wardrobe, dresser, some rooms have sinks and medicine cabinets

**Also Available:**
Smoke-free living houses, substance-free halls, and special interest housing (language houses, fraternity and sorority houses, etc.)

### Did You Know?

All freshmen are required to live on campus, and many form a strong bond with their freshman hallmates. The dorms are divided into upperclassmen and freshman housing.

## Students Speak Out
### ON CAMPUS HOUSING

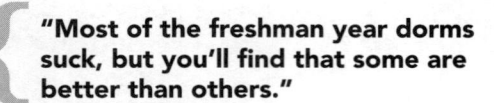

*"Most of the freshman year dorms suck, but you'll find that some are better than others."*

Q "The dorms are fine. Not the best, as W&M is a state school, but also certainly not bad. Freshmen live in freshman dorms. **You don't get much of a choice**, except for whether or not you want single sex or co-ed dorms. Co-ed means each hallway will be single sex, and the rooms aren't interspersed. Some freshman dorms don't have air conditioning. That's either tolerable or not depending on the weather that particular August—it was hot my freshman year—but if you get a note signed by a doctor from home that says you have allergies and need A/C, they'll let you bring a window unit."

Q "The dorms are generally all right, and **many are currently getting renovated or have recently been renovated**. As a freshman, the worst housing to get is in Botetourt. So try to request Dupont, Yates, or, if you are a girl, Barrett. As an upperclassman, you have much more of a choice about living arrangements. Your sophomore year is the worst year, because you don't generally get the best options."

Q "Dorms are really decent. Ask to **live in Yates freshman year; it's the 'party dorm' and very fun**. As an upperclassman, Old Dominion Hall and the Randolph Complex are the nicest, in my opinion. Make sure to try to get dorms with A/C; not all of them have it."

Q "All freshmen are required to live in a freshman dorm. This means everyone you live with freshman year will be in the same situation, which almost always results in the **creation of tight, long-lasting friendships between freshman hall mates**. As for the dorms themselves, they vary but they're all pretty nice. After freshman year you enter a lottery for housing and are given a number based on academic year. Thus, seniors get the best numbers and so on."

## The College Prowler Take
### ON CAMPUS HOUSING

Students say the quality of housing at William & Mary depends heavily on which dorm you end up in. All freshmen are required to live on campus, and some of the housing is less than luxurious. However, students often form strong bonds with their freshman hallmates, which helps everyone overcome the dingy conditions. Housing options range from Spartan and tiny, to spacious and comfortable. One of the biggest complaints students have is that many dorms are not air conditioned, which means they have to turn their room into a virtual wind tunnel to keep cool.

**C+**

### The College Prowler™ Grade on
## Campus Housing: C+

A high Campus Housing grade indicates that dorms are clean, well-maintained, and spacious. Other determining factors include variety of dorms, proximity to classes, and social atmosphere.

# Diversity

## The Lowdown
ON DIVERSITY

**Native American**: 0%

**Asian American:** 6%

**African American:** 6%

**Hispanic:** 3%

**White:** 81%

**International:** 4%

**Out-of-State:** 36%

### Minority Clubs
Cultural organizations have a significant presence on campus. They hold performances and events in addition to club meetings, and everyone is encouraged to join and participate in the organizations.

### Most Popular Religions
There are many active Christian organizations on campus, such as Agape Christian Fellowship and the Catholic Campus Ministry. There is also a Jewish organization and a Muslim organization.

### Political Activity
The Young Democrats and College Republicans are the two main political groups on campus. In addition, there are political activist groups, such as a chapter of Amnesty International and the Feminist Majority Leadership Alliance. Just before U.S. troops were sent to Iraq there were some of anti-war demonstrations that drew several hundred protesters.

### Economic Status
Though there is some diversity in this area, most students seem to be middle- or upper-middle-class.

## Students Speak Out
ON DIVERSITY

"On my freshman hall, we had one girl from Cyprus, one from Bulgaria, and one from Australia. I learned a lot about the rest of the world and gained a different perspective about a lot of things."

"Very diverse—we have people from **Richmond and northern Virginia**."

"The campus is not overly diverse. They're trying to fix that little by little, but the grand **majority of the students are white middle-class**. We have a lot of minority groups represented, however, and there are a lot of cultural student organizations. They can be a solid presence on campus, because they hold major events like the Chinese Student Organization's annual Lunar New Year Banquet, or 'A Taste of India,' which is a big dinner. There's also a Middle Eastern belly dancing club … I always wanted to check that out and never got a chance to."

"It's not diverse at all. **That is the one thing this college lacks**. It's almost a shock when I go home to see people of other nationalities. However, I have met more international students here than I have ever known before."

💬 "Diversity is a problem at W&M. The vast majority at W&M is white, though as a public school, it tends to be **more socioeconomically diverse—and cheaper!—than a private school**. Racially, W&M has a sizable Asian minority, a small but active Hispanic community, and an embarrassingly small black community, considering the population of Virginia. Still, I believe they are taking steps to improve this discrepancy, and your friends will probably be pretty diverse."

💬 "Not very. It's overall an upper-middle-class, white, southern school. I went to a very diverse high school in the north, so it was a bit of a culture shock. I have heard that there is a **decent gay and lesbian population on campus**, but that's as diverse as W&M gets."

## The College Prowler Take
### ON DIVERSITY

Students cite the lack of visible diversity as one of the major downsides to William & Mary. With 81 percent of the student body being white, and the majority of those from Virginia, there isn't much racial or social diversity. This is disturbing to some students, especially those who come from urban areas with diverse high schools, but others don't seem to mind the homogeny. Students do, however, say that there is a diversity of opinion and outlook at W&M that has given them new perspectives and enriched their experience at the college. Though the lack of diversity is pretty apparent at W&M, the number of minority students is on the rise—up two percent from last year. The school seems to make an honest attempt to draw in students from different backgrounds.

**D+**

The College Prowler™ Grade on
### Diversity: D+

A high grade in Diversity indicates that ethnic minorities and international students have a notable presence on campus and that students of different economic backgrounds, religious beliefs, and sexual preferences are well-represented.

# Guys & Girls

## The Lowdown
### ON GUYS & GIRLS

**Women Undergrads:** 56%

**Men Undergrads:** 44%

### Birth Control Available?
Yes, the Health Center offers gynecological exams and birth control prescriptions can be filled in the campus pharmacy. They also offer emergency contraception. There are containers of free condoms in the Health Center and at the FISH Bowl in the Campus Center.

### Social Scene
It all starts on the freshman hall. Students often bond strongly with their hallmates and form friendships that last throughout college. Beyond that, most social interaction takes place between people in organizations or classes. Of course, fraternities and sororities, which are big at W&M, are also hubs of social interaction, but joining one isn't a free ticket to a thriving social life.

## Hookups or Relationships?

There are usually several girls making the "walk of shame" from fraternity row back to their dorm rooms on Saturday and Sunday mornings after a night of hooking up, and they're not the only ones engaged in these pseudo-relationships. A lot of students continue hanging out and hooking up with the same person, but wouldn't call it dating, and wouldn't admit that they're "together." On the other end of the spectrum are the practically married couples. They start dating freshman year, and from that point on they can't be separated.

## Dress Code

In a word—casual. You won't find many William & Mary students dressed to the nines, especially for early morning classes. It is not frowned upon to show up for an eight, nine, or even 10 o'clock class un-showered and wearing pajama pants and an old T-shirt. A long-standing joke on campus is that you can tell when someone needs to do laundry because he or she is dressed up, but there is a small portion of constantly well-coiffed, made-up, Abercrombie-wearing kids. For the most part, however, it's basic jeans and T-shirts.

## Students Speak Out
### ON GUYS & GIRLS

> "Both sexes complain of the lack of hot members of the opposite sex, but loads of people date so it can't be that bad."

"I'll be shallow, but honest: there are some beautiful girls on this campus, but the majority is simply pretty and cute. The same probably goes for guys. **We're not winning any beauty contests here**, but we're not all hideous freaks either. Of course, beauty is only skin deep. W&M students of both genders tend to be highly intelligent, motivated, kind, and friendly people. There are the ubiquitous bad apples, but we're all pretty cool overall, I'd say."

"Guys, girls ... they're people like anybody else. Lots of people joke about 'William & Mary goggles,' since we're not supermodels, but you'd be surprised how many **good-looking people come out of nowhere** when the sun comes out."

"**The guys generally leave something to be desired**, in my opinion. That doesn't mean there aren't several who are smart and nice and funny and hot ... it just means they're usually taken. Something else I've observed is that there are a lot of people who find, like, the 'person of their dreams' freshman year and date them the whole time, and then there are people who hook up a lot and never really date anyone seriously. The girls are generally a little more attractive than the guys—more competition for dates. And there are very nice people either way you go. That's the one thing I love most about W&M—the awesome people I've met."

"We were voted **one of the ugliest campuses in some magazine**, I don't remember which. But go out in the Sunken Gardens or Barksdale field on a hot day, and you can get some eye candy."

## The College Prowler Take
### ON GUYS & GIRLS

Okay, so William & Mary isn't known for its exceptionally great-looking people. It is, however, full of interesting, nice, decently good-looking guys and girls. There are complaints from both sexes about the lack of eye candy, but enough people hook up or date that it really can't be all that horrible. At least students at W&M can be assured that their entire selection gets an A+ in the brains department. Superficiality aside, guys and girls at William & Mary are great people, and are definitely worth dating. They aren't the hottest students around, but there are more than a few very attractive people, and a whole lot of cuties.

**The College Prowler™ Grade on**
## Guys: B-

A high grade for Guys indicates that the male population on campus is attractive, smart, friendly, and engaging, and that the school has a decent ratio of guys to girls.

**The College Prowler™ Grade on**
## Girls: B

A high grade for Girls not only implies that the women on campus are attractive, smart, friendly, and engaging, but also that there is a fair ratio of girls to guys.

# Athletics

## The Lowdown
ON ATHLETICS

**Athletic Division:**
NCAA Division I

**Conference:**
Atlantic 10 and CAA

**School Mascot:**
The Tribe (frog-like Colonel Ebirt)

**Fields:**
Barksdale Field, Busch Field, Cary Field, Dillard Fields, Fraternity Field, IM Fields on Campus Drive, Yates Field

**Men's Varsity Teams:**
Baseball
Basketball
Cheerleading
Cross Country
Diving
Football
Golf
Gymnastics
Soccer
Swimming
Tennis
Track and Field (indoor)
Track and Field (outdoor)

**Women's Varsity Teams:**
Basketball
Cheerleading
Cross Country
Diving
Field Hockey
Golf
Gymnastics
Lacrosse
Soccer
Swimming
Tennis
Track and Field (indoor)
Track and Field (outdoor)
Volleyball

**Club Sports**
Badminton, Baseball, Field Hockey, Ice Hockey, Lacrosse, Martial Arts, Racquetball, Rowing, Rugby, Sailing, Soccer, Softball, Swimming, Synchronized Swimming, Ultimate Frisbee, Volleyball

**Intramurals (IMs)**
Aerobics, Badminton, Basketball, Billiards, Bowling, Flag Football, Frisbee Golf, Golf, Racquetball, Soccer, Softball, Swimming, Table tennis, Tennis, Volleyball, Walleyball, Wrestling

### Most Popular Sports
Football and varsity men's soccer are pretty much the only teams people support. As far as club sports, rugby is big for both sexes, and so is Ultimate Frisbee.

### Overlooked Teams
Both the men's and women's gymnastics teams are amazing and have won several titles over the last couple of years. William & Mary has also had swimmers who have placed nationally in recent years.

### Getting Tickets
Tickets to all athletic events are free to students. Everyone else can get tickets from the main ticket office, (757) 221-3340.

## Students Speak Out
ON ATHLETICS

"**Sports aren't huge.** Though many people like to go to football games, there are plenty that don't, as well. There are a lot of IMs and club sports, which are great!"

"**Football gets the most fan support.** Sometimes the games are crowded, other times not. People seem more interested in their studies than in sports. IM sports are pretty big. A lot of fraternities and freshman halls get teams together to compete."

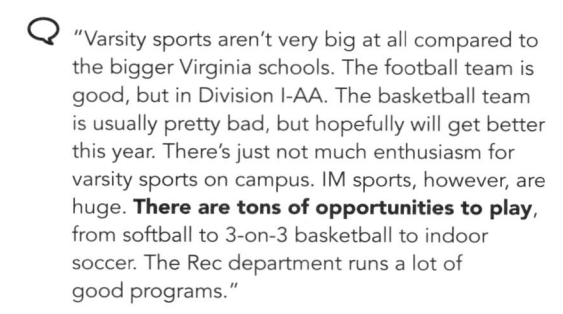

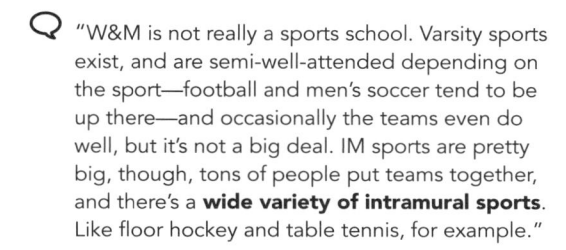

Q "Varsity sports aren't very big at all compared to the bigger Virginia schools. The football team is good, but in Division I-AA. The basketball team is usually pretty bad, but hopefully will get better this year. There's just not much enthusiasm for varsity sports on campus. IM sports, however, are huge. **There are tons of opportunities to play**, from softball to 3-on-3 basketball to indoor soccer. The Rec department runs a lot of good programs."

Q "W&M is not really a sports school. Varsity sports exist, and are semi-well-attended depending on the sport—football and men's soccer tend to be up there—and occasionally the teams even do well, but it's not a big deal. IM sports are pretty big, though, tons of people put teams together, and there's a **wide variety of intramural sports**. Like floor hockey and table tennis, for example."

Q "W&M has a lot of NCAA Division I teams, many of whom are nationally competitive. The glaring exceptions being our good I-AA football team and our embarrassing basketball team. **Hell will freeze over long before we see either a bowl game** or a trip to the Big Dance."

Q "Football games are popular and fun, as are the sports that don't draw big crowds, but actually win games. **All in all, W&M is not at all a jock school**, and we tend to focus our school pride in academic achievement, not athletics. IM sports are very popular and a lot of fun. Somewhere around 80 percent of the student body participates, and there are a variety of sports from football to floor hockey."

## The College Prowler Take
ON ATHLETICS

William & Mary students don't make much of an effort to attend varsity sports games. They do, however, participate in numerous club and intramural sports. The bottom line is that W&M is a school full of nerds: some are athletic, but a lot aren't. There is ample opportunity for those who want athletic action to get involved in something, though. The athletic facilities, such as the Rec Center and various fields, provide great places to stay in shape and let off steam. IM and club sports are big on campus, and students take advantage of them frequently. Unfortunately, due to budget cuts, the kinesiology department has been stripped down to bare bones, and they have severely reduced the number and variety of classes offered.

Want more info on the sports W&M has to offer? Check out the full-length College Prowler guidebook on W&M available at www.collegeprowler.com.

The College Prowler™ Grade on
## Athletics: C

A high grade in Athletics indicates that students have school spirit, that sports programs are respected, that games are well-attended, and that intramurals are a prominent part of student life.

# Greek Life

## The Lowdown
### ON GREEK LIFE

**Number of Fraternities:**
15

**Number of Sororities:**
11

**Undergrad Men in Fraternities:**
24.8%

**Undergrad Women in Sororities:**
26.7%

**Other Greek Organizations:**
Council for Fraternity Affairs, Inter Sorority Council, Order of Omega

### Did You Know?

Greek organizations gather every spring for the campus golf charity event, which consists of tipsy Greeks hitting tennis balls all over campus with golf clubs on a Saturday morning.

## Students Speak Out
### ON GREEK LIFE

"There's no pressure to be Greek. A lot of people are, but it's not exclusive (I can go to all the parties), so you don't need to be Greek to participate in Greek life on campus."

Q "**Greek organizations provide a lot of social outlets** on campus between frat parties and various philanthropies. For example, my sorority hosts a glow-in-the-dark volleyball tournament in the Sunken Gardens every fall to raise money for a camp for children with cancer, things like that."

Q "It doesn't dominate the social scene, I'd say it takes up a large-ish slice. **There isn't that much pressure to join frats**, but if you want to there are many to choose from, and if you don't, that's cool too. I'm not in a frat, and you don't really lose out on that much."

Q "Greek life does not at all dominate the social scene at the school. There are so many clubs that you are sure to find something of interest, or you can start your own! The campus is roughly 30 percent Greek, so it's there if you want it, but **you're not considered antisocial if you don't**."

Q "Greek life is most of the social scene at W&M. However, if you are female, you don't necessarily have to be Greek to take part. Most of the on-campus weekend 'party' activity occurs at fraternity row. It is a big pile of frat houses that are lined up in three rows on one end of campus. Unless the fraternity is having a private party with a sorority, they will pretty much let any female into their party. It can be a little harder for guys, if they aren't members or close friends with the members, to get in. For guys, I think about 40 percent are Greek, and for girls, I think it's about a third. It is a lot of fun to do, but if Greek life isn't your scene, then **there are plenty of other social circles to hang out in**. I had a lot of friends that didn't go Greek and I still hung out with them all the time."

## The College Prowler Take
**ON GREEK LIFE**

William & Mary has a thriving Greek community that includes a significant number of students. The fraternities are responsible for most of the on-campus nightlife. The Greek community, as much as it parties, also organizes a lot of charity events, which enhance the campus. While the Greeks are a large presence on campus, they don't dominate the social scene to the point that students must join them in order to have a social life. With around a third of students involved in Greek organizations, it's almost impossible for them to avoid being the center of social activities. All the same, students say they can find plenty of non-Greek social activities, and they don't feel pressured to join.

## Drug Scene

### The Lowdown
**ON DRUG SCENE**

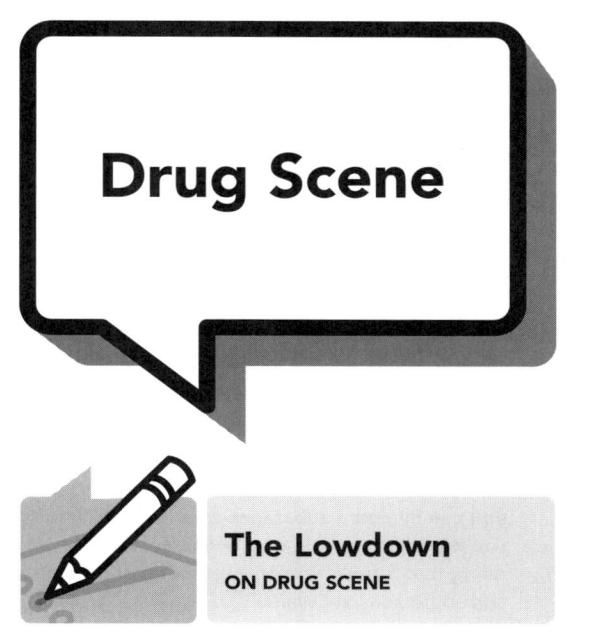

**Most Prevalent Drugs on Campus:**
Alcohol, Marijuana, Caffeine

**Liquor-Related Referrals:**
175

**Liquor-Related Arrests:**
6

**Drug-Related Referrals:**
1

**Drug-Related Arrests:**
18

## A

The College Prowler™ Grade on
### Greek Life: A

A high grade in Greek Life indicates that sororities and fraternities are not only present, but also active on campus. Other determining factors include the variety of houses available and the respect the Greek community receives from the rest of the campus.

## Drug Counseling Programs

**Drug Abuse Educator Mary Crozier at the FISH Bowl:**

Phone: (757) 221-3631

Services: There is a lot of information in the FISH Bowl office on drug and alcohol related problems. The OCTAA course that students must take if they have an alcohol offense is also run through this office.

**Counseling Center:**

Phone: (757) 221-3620

Services: Individual, couple, group, and family counseling is available for students free of charge.

## Students Speak Out
### ON DRUG SCENE

> "Pot is easy enough to find if you're interested, but if you're not the type, then you'd probably think that there wasn't any at all on campus. Other drugs are extremely rare."

Q "The drug scene is not too bad. You see weed here and there, but not much else. If you choose, **you can live on a substance-free hall**, which puts you with other people who definitely won't be doing that. Usually you only see weed at the frats and sometimes at Dillard."

Q "There is little or no drug scene on campus. The **most popular drug, naturally, is pot**, but you can seriously go all four years without even knowing anyone smokes up if it's not what your friends are into. But it's also not overly difficult to find people who do if that's what you are into—it's just a very low-key, non-blatant thing. And drugs don't get much harder than that."

Q "You don't see drugs, although I know they are there. **Only certain crowds get into that**, it depends on who you hang out with. For the most part, you don't see it at all."

Q "There really isn't much of a drug scene. Aside from alcohol, pot's the biggest drug, but not that many people smoke. Out of all my friends, I think three use it, and only one does frequently. **There are harder drugs being used**, but you really have to search for the people who use them."

## The College Prowler Take
### ON DRUG SCENE

William & Mary's drug scene is only really evident to those who participate in it. Students say marijuana is available if they look for it, but if they don't, they probably wouldn't even notice people using it. Like on many college campuses, alcohol use is pretty widespread, but use of harder drugs is almost nonexistent. Students can also ask to be placed in substance-free housing, which further reduces their exposure to drugs. In a small community like Williamsburg, there aren't too many drugs creeping onto campus, and the police keep things well under control.

**The College Prowler™ Grade on**
### Drug Scene: A

A high grade on Drug Scene indicates that drugs are not a noticeable part of campus life; drug use is not visible, and no pressure to use them seems to exist.

# Overall Experience

### The Lowdown
ON OVERALL EXPERIENCE

"People came here to learn, but they're also here to live and have a good time. It's impossible not to make friends, and as long as you don't mind working your butt off to get a good education, you'll like it."

Q "My overall experience of school has been wonderful. **There were good parts and bad parts, but such is life**, you know? I've never once wished I was somewhere else. Life is what you make of it; you have to make a choice and go with it. The only time I even came close to wishing I were somewhere else was right in the beginning of freshman year when I was homesick, and that had nothing to do with the school, I just missed my family and friends. The South takes a little bit of getting used to, but I had a great time at W&M. It's a good place to spend four years and I'm going to miss it. I already miss my friends a lot and I've only been gone two weeks!"

Q "I, personally, love the school. Sometimes I wonder if I should have gone to a bigger school, like UVA [University of Virginia], but I feel like **at W&M I make more of a difference in the community**. I stand out more as an individual. I have great relationships with most of my professors and find that that helps a lot academically. I've made a lot of great friends that I wouldn't give up for anything. This school is really what you make of it. It doesn't mold you like other schools do—it helps you mold yourself and allows you to grow as an individual."

Q "I can't imagine myself anywhere else—I'm so glad to be at William & Mary. I couldn't ask for a better group of people to make up my college community; **the students are great, the professors are great**. Plus, the background of everything that happens here is over 300 years of history. I love feeling like I'm part of that somehow. I hadn't even finished my first semester when I started dreading the day I'll graduate and they'll make me leave."

Q "I have loved my three years at William & Mary and I'm glad I'm there. It is the right school for me. W&M is an **academically demanding school, but with a great reputation and tons of assets** for whatever your interests are. The campus is one of the most beautiful in the nation. The student body is friendly and about the perfect size, as far as I'm concerned—just under 6,000. That means you'll never know everyone, but you'll always know someone wherever you go. In terms of history, W&M is hard to beat. W&M has educated three U.S. Presidents and has been around since the seventeenth century, which means it's filled with rich tradition, but is also very modern. There's something very cool about sitting in the same classrooms Thomas Jefferson sat in when he was a student here. I highly recommend W&M. I love it here and I'm sure you would, too."

## The College Prowler Take
### ON OVERALL EXPERIENCE

To say the least, William & Mary students have a strong affection for their school. They love the sense of history, the size, the faculty, and their fellow students. You hardly ever hear anyone expressing regret for choosing William & Mary. Alumni come back year after year and wish they could attend college here all over again. Williamsburg may not be a bustling hub of activity, but the students form their own community that cannot be beat.

W&M is academically challenging for sure, but students know all of that hard work is going to add up to a quality education. Most students agree that William & Mary is as close to perfect as they could hope for.

# Florida State University

Tallahassee, FL 32306
www.fsu.edu   (850) 644-6200

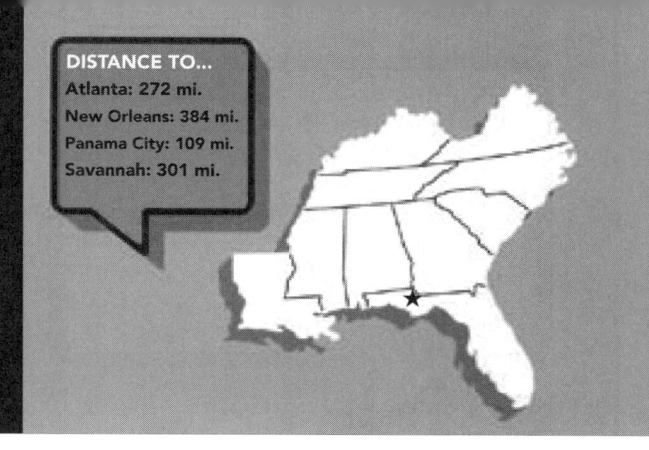

**DISTANCE TO...**
Atlanta: 272 mi.
New Orleans: 384 mi.
Panama City: 109 mi.
Savannah: 301 mi.

"Florida State is a unique school that has been able to find that elusive balance between fun and serious academia."

**Total Enrollment:**
25,959

**Top 10% of High School Class:**
55%

**Average GPA:**
3.8

**Acceptance Rate:**
64%

**Tuition:**
$3,038 in-state, $15,544 out-of-state

**SAT Range (25th-75th Percentile)**
| Verbal | Math | Total |
|---|---|---|
| 520 – 620 | 530 – 630 | 1050 – 1250 |

**ACT Range (25th-75th Percentile)**
| Verbal | Math | Total |
|---|---|---|
| 21-27 | 21-26 | 22-27 |

**Most Popular Majors:**
6% Finance
6% Psychology
5% Criminal Justice/Safety Studies
4% English Language and Literature
4% Communication Studies

**Students also applied to:***
Florida International University
University of Central Florida
University of Florida
University of Miami
University of South Florida

*For more school info check out www.collegeprowler.com

### Table of Contents

| | |
|---|---|
| Academics | 120 |
| Local Atmosphere | 122 |
| Safety & Security | 123 |
| Facilities | 125 |
| Campus Dining | 127 |
| Campus Housing | 128 |
| Diversity | 130 |
| Guys & Girls | 131 |
| Athletics | 133 |
| Greek Life | 134 |
| Drug Scene | 136 |
| Overall Experience | 137 |

### College Prowler Report Card

| | |
|---|---|
| Academics | B- |
| Local Atmosphere | B |
| Safety & Security | B |
| Facilities | A |
| Campus Dining | C+ |
| Campus Housing | B- |
| Diversity | B- |
| Guys | A- |
| Girls | A |
| Athletics | A |
| Greek Life | A- |
| Drug Scene | C+ |

# Academics

**Special Programs**
Online Learning offers undergraduate degrees in computer science, information studies, interdisciplinary social studies, and nursing.

**Sample Academic Clubs**
FSU Geological Society, Art History Association, Accounting Society, Tallahassee Bar Association

## The Lowdown
ON ACADEMICS

### Did You Know?
Current faculty members include Pulitzer Prize winner Robert Olen Butler, as well as former astronauts Dr. Norm Thagard and Cpt. Winston Scott, both of whom teach in the College of Engineering.

The Carnegie Foundation has designated FSU as a Research I University for the Advancement of Teaching. FSU's Center for Advanced Power Systems was recently awarded a $52-million grant by the U.S. Navy for use in testing propulsion systems.

**Best Places to Study:**
Student Union, Strozier Library, one of the many local coffeehouses.

**Degrees Awarded:**
Associate, Bachelor, Master, Doctorate

**Undergraduate Schools:**
Arts & Sciences; Business; Communications; Criminal Justice; Education; Engineering; Human Services; Information Studies; Law; Medicine; Motion Picture, TV, & Recording Arts; Music; Nursing; Social Sciences; Social Work; Theatre; Visual Arts & Dance

**Full-time Faculty:**
1,103

**Faculty with Terminal Degree:**
92%

**Student-to-Faculty Ratio:**
23:1

**Average Course Load:**
4 courses (12 credit hours)

**AP Test Score Requirements:**
Credit given for scores 3, 4, or 5

**IB Test Score Requirements:**
Credit given for a score of 5 or better

## COLLEGE PROWLER

Visit www.collegeprowler.com for the FSU guidebook packed with info about courses, professors, and academic life on campus.

## Students Speak Out
### ON ACADEMICS

> "In my four years, I would say that 90 percent of my teachers were great! I made a lot of great friendships and relied on many for recommendations."

Q "Teachers, I feel, are the same everywhere; some are great and some are not, it just depends who you get. Overall, I have had very good teachers. My number one piece of advice to you would be to **make sure the teachers know who you are**—that is always good to have on your side."

Q "The professors here are very good. Most seem to **really care about their students**, and, opposed to popular belief, you aren't just a number in all the classes. Some classes, depending upon your major and chosen classes, may be really large, but most times you will have TAs [teaching assistants] who will be familiar with you. Something important to note, also, is that they are pretty fair. Don't be afraid to confront a professor about a grade you have received, because if you have reasons to back-up why you deserve something better, they will often listen."

Q "The teachers fall into two categories, tenured and non-tenured/doctorate candidates. **The tenured professor has a well organized plan for teaching** the course materials. The non-tenured/doctorate candidate instructor, generally, has a poorer lesson outline, and several have complained that FSU does not teach them how to 'teach.' Also, many are extremely lenient regarding deadlines and test dates."

Q "While most undergraduate students around me seem addicted to bars and clubs and wet T-shirt contests, the instructors at FSU actually seem dedicated to their profession. Most are **friendly and available to students who need extra help** or attention. And if you don't like your teacher, just drop the class and enroll in another section."

Q "You would think that for a big school, it is hard to get special attention, but all of the teachers are very good about making themselves available. If you make and effort to know them, then they would be more than happy to get to know you. Make the effort, it helps a lot to get to know them personally. Overall, they were great!"

## The College Prowler Take
### ON ACADEMICS

The consensus among the Florida State University student body is that the faculty is both easy to get along with and dedicated to its profession. Most are readily available to meet with students outside of class and offer assistance when necessary. No professor wants to see a student fail, but don't expect them to come to you. Take the initiative and they'll respect you for it. Most students admit that the prolific number of teaching assistants can be problematic in lower level classes. However, word of mouth is an excellent way to find out in advance which professors to take and which to avoid.

Academics are important at Florida State University, especially among the tenured professors. Don't expect to coast through the higher level undergraduate classes. The teaching assistants and associate professors are more likely to cut you some slack, but even that isn't a guarantee. The school has recently received recognition for a broad range of scientific research projects, and they have just created a new College of Medicine.

**B-**

**The College Prowler™ Grade on**
### Academics: B-

A high Academics grade generally indicates that professors are knowledgeable, accessible, and genuinely interested in their students' welfare. Other determining factors include class size, how well professors communicate, and whether or not classes are engaging.

# Local Atmosphere

**City Websites**
http://www.co.leon.fl.us/visitors/
http://www.tallahassee.com/mld/tallahasse/
http://www.state.fl.us/citytlh/

## Students Speak Out
ON LOCAL ATMOSPHERE

## The Lowdown
ON LOCAL ATMOSPHERE

**Region:**
Southeast

**City, State:**
Tallahassee, Florida

**Setting:**
Medium-sized City

**Distance from Panama City:**
2 hours

**Distance from Jacksonville:**
3 hours, 30 minutes

**Points of Interest:**
Mary Brogan Museum of Arts and Sciences, FSU Reservation, Wakulla Springs State Park, Old City Cemetery, Challenger Learning Center, Maclay State Gardens

**Major Sports Teams (statewide):**
Marlins (baseball), Dolphins (football), Jaguars (football), Devil Rays (baseball), Panthers (hockey), Buccaneers (football), Lightning (hockey), Magic (basketball), Heat (basketball)

---

"There are two other colleges here, FAMU and TCC. Tallahassee is a big college town. There is a lot of stuff to do if you are creative, and sometimes this means driving an hour away to get to a beach."

"It depends on where you originated from. Tallahassee operates on the 'good ol' boy' system. As a native, I know the system and can accept some of its boundaries ... others I fight against. Tallahassee is the state capital, and **we are surrounded by government**. It is also quite picturesque. However, for those interested in shopping or worldly goods, this is definitely not the place to be."

"Tallahassee is a very low-key environment. It's a nice place to live while in school because it is relatively small, and navigating your way around is a snap. At the same time, you can always find something to do. There are museums, great parks, malls—if you're into that kind of thing—bars, and **the beach is only one or two hours away**. Everyone is really friendly and though it is still considered the South, there is a diversity of people including students and citizens."

"A lot of the new students complain that there isn't enough to do in Tallahassee, but I always find things to do. There are a couple of decent **museums, a science center, and there's usually something going on** at one of the many campus facilities."

"This is **one of those sleepy, southern towns**. It's country, no doubt about that, but it's also really laid-back. It's a cool place to be in the summer."

## The College Prowler Take
### ON LOCAL ATMOSPHERE

Like one of the quotes states, this is a southern town, so you can expect things to move at a slower pace. But don't be fooled into thinking that nothing happens here. During the spring and summer the state legislature is in session and the town is filled with movers and shakers. For political science, business, and communications majors, this gives you the opportunity to see the deal-making and schmoozing first-hand. Tallahassee is also home to two universities and a community college, so there is also a large student population. This means there are twice as many bars, parties, and other activities to keep the average student entertained. Keep in mind that appearances can be deceiving, and there is more to do in Tallahassee than meets the eye.

**B**

The College Prowler™ Grade on
## Local Atmosphere: B

A high Local Atmosphere grade indicates that the area surrounding campus is safe and scenic. Other factors include nearby attractions, proximity to other schools, and the town's attitude toward students.

# Safety & Security

## The Lowdown
### ON SAFETY & SECURITY

**Number of FSU Police:**
46

**Phone:**
(850) 644-1234

**Health Center Office Hours:**
8:00 a.m. – 5:00 p.m., Monday – Thursday
9:00 a.m. – 5:00 p.m., Friday

**Safety Services:**
S.A.F.E. Escort Service, emergency phones, Victim Advocacy Program, Rape Aggression Defense System

### Did You Know?

Thagard now serves over 32,000 students with its own pharmacy, x-ray, urgent care, women's care, and general medical services. Contract providers on-site include optometry, lab, and physical therapy.

## Students Speak Out
### ON SAFETY & SECURITY

"FSUPD seems to have a good presence around campus, and there are emergency lampposts scattered around campus, but I have yet to know anyone who has used one."

Q "Security and **safety on campus is good during the day,** but at night I would advise you to always walk with someone else. Never walk alone at night on the FSU campus. It's just like any other big city."

Q "In addition to the campus police, the University has made improvements to its campus safety by adding what is termed 'the blue-light trail,' which is a series of phones along the walkways of campus which link to the campus police department. **There are seminars related to personal safety** and date rape available to students as well."

Q "Although there have been incidents in the past, **FSU is well-lit and littered with emergency phones** everywhere you turn. During the summer, part of the fall, and the tail-end of spring, before daylight savings time kicks in, it doesn't get dark till nearly 9 p.m., so you can comfortably traverse the campus without fearing your life. But it's always nice to bring a buddy along anyway, just in case."

Q "Security on campus is very convenient, as **you need your ID to slide on a keypad to get into your dorm**, and there are always people around so you never feel unsafe, even at night when you're downstairs by yourself. There's also a night staff at the dorm from 11 p.m. to 7 a.m. making sure everything is cool."

## The College Prowler Take
### ON SAFETY & SECURITY

The FSUPD are highly visible on campus, and the school goes to great lengths to make sure that the student body is safe and secure. A nighttime escort service is available and emergency phones are located throughout campus, so there is never any reason for someone to have to walk alone at night. Crime does happen, usually muggings, but that usually occurs when someone decides to venture out after dark alone. FSU also offers a Victim Advocacy Program, Rape Aggression Defense System courses, and publishes an annual *Seminole Safety Guide* that is available to all students. Most crimes are easily prevented, and at FSU the police do their part to keep the campus safe.

The College Prowler™ Grade on
### Safety & Security: B

A high grade in Safety & Security means that students generally feel safe, campus police are visible, blue-light phones and escort services are readily available, and safety precautions are not overly necessary.

# Facilities

## The Lowdown
ON FACILITIES

**Student Center:**
The newly opened Student Life Building houses a movie theatre, the Cyber Café and Gaming Center (with the latest PC and Playstation games), the FSU Central Posting Office, and the Student Counseling Center.

**Athletic Center:**
The Leach Recreation Center/Stults Aquatic Center offers natatorium, gymnasium, spas, racquetball and squash courts, weight training and fitness rooms, and an indoor track.

**Libraries:**
13; Strozier Library, Dirac Science Library, Allen Music Library, Claude Pepper Library, Media Center, Engineering Reading Room, Special Collections, Career Center Library, Goldstein Library of Science, Law Library, Medical Library, Ringling Library

**Computers**
**High-Speed Network?** Yes
**Wireless Network?** No
**Number of Labs:** 3
**Numbers of Computers:**
197 Pentium PCs, 34 PowerMacs
**24-Hour Labs:**
One, located in the FSU Student Union.
**Charge to Print?**
No. Students are allotted 35 pages per day.

**Popular Places to Chill:**
Student Life Building, Oglesby Union, Landis Green

**Movie Theatre on Campus?**
Yes, in the Student Life Building, and it's free for students. In addition to the latest new releases and a mix of older films, the SLB Theatre also holds special screenings of FSU Film School projects.

**Bowling on Campus?**
Yes. Crenshaw Lanes is located in the Oglesby Union, and has twelve lanes with automatic scoring, a billiards room, and a complete pro shop.

**Bar on Campus?**
Yes, Club Downunder is located in the Oglesby Union.

**Coffeehouse on Campus?**
Yes, Java Blues is located in the Student Life Building.

**Favorite Things to Do**
With so many things to do on campus, it would be difficult to pin down specific favorites, but the majority of students enjoy breaking a sweat at the Leach Center, swimming, catching a movie at the SLB, or hanging out at Oglesby Union.

## Students Speak Out
### ON FACILITIES

{ "FSU is continually striving to improve and update the facilities on campus. The older buildings on campus are being updated with new technologies, as well as being restored to their original beauty."

Q "Some of the buildings are really old-looking. They look kind of grimy. The gym is nice, and **we have a really nice stadium!** Most of the facilities are decent."

Q "We have an awesome gym. It's three stories, has a **huge pool with diving boards, sauna, Jacuzzi, massages, athletic trainers** (free of charge), aerobics classes, indoor track, racquetball rooms, and basketball and volleyball courts. There are many computer labs throughout campus and they all have Ethernet, so you get a really fast connection. The student union is really nice, and it has events often throughout the year. There is a building that has a movie theatre in it, and, if you get tickets, you can go see movies before they go into theaters."

Q "Despite being an old campus, FSU has done a **good job of modernizing equipment and remodeling the buildings**. The downside to this is that there's a lot of construction going on, but once you know where it is, you can avoid it for the rest of the semester. Most people hang out at the gym or the Union. I like hanging out on Landis Green. There's usually some kind of protest or something going on, and people bring blankets and sit out and study. It's great on a sunny day."

Q "FSU has done a great job improving its facilities over the past 10 years and moving into the next 10 years. They have **plenty of new dorms that are great**, the workout place is second to none, in the nation, many new classrooms are state of the art, and the campus in general is very beautiful."

## The College Prowler Take
### ON FACILITIES

Florida State University offers a wide variety of entertainment for students, everything from cyber-gaming to bowling. Club Downunder brings in live music on a regular basis, and the newly completed Student Life Building is usually a good place to go and run into friends. FSU has been actively remodeling and renovating older buildings on campus, as well as providing students with modern entertainment venues. You don't have to worry if you don't have transportation because you can always find something to do around campus.

### The College Prowler™ Grade on
### Facilities: A

A high Facilities grade indicates that the campus is aesthetically pleasing and well-maintained; facilities are state-of-the-art, and libraries are exceptional. Other determining factors include the quality of both athletic and student centers and an abundance of things to do on campus.

# Campus Dining

## Students Speak Out
ON CAMPUS DINING

"I don't know about breakfast or dinner, but lunches are great on campus. If your classes are close to the court, there is a Pizza Hut, Burger King and Chick-fil-A. There's also a few sandwich shops around the campus."

Q "**Lots of high-fat and fried foods**. It's tough to eat healthy. If nothing else, there's always something to eat, and you do get a pretty good variety of food. I gained 10 pounds my first semester here. I'm just glad they have a gym on campus!"

Q "Food court in the union is okay ... pricey though. I don't really eat on campus if I can help it. I prefer some of the restaurants on the edge of campus. I get burned out on the **same fast food menu every day**."

Q "There are a **couple of cafeterias on campus and a food court.** It's enough, but the selection is not that great. Mostly fast food. I also tried the meal plan my first semester here, but I didn't care for it. I'd rather make food myself, or scrounge off my roommates."

Q "The union **food court pretty much stinks**. I've never eaten in the cafeteria or whatever it has recently been dubbed. There is a small coffee shop that I'm sure serves decent coffee and bagels, but the food court just has fast food like Burger King, Pizza Hut, and Chick-fil-A. The seating is pretty crappy and always crowded. It sometimes it makes you feel like you're back in high school, which is something no one wants."

## The Lowdown
ON CAMPUS DINING

**Freshman Meal Plan Requirement?**
No

**24-Hour On-Campus Dining?**
No

**Meal Plan Average Cost:**
$2,400 per year

### Did You Know?

The best times to hit the dining halls are first thing in the morning or late evenings. That is when they are less crowded and you can usually get in some quality study time while grabbing a bite to eat.

FSU now has a student dining website at http://www.seminoledining.com. This is where you will find everything you need to know about the cafeterias, dining halls, restaurants, and other food vendors on campus.

## The College Prowler Take
### ON CAMPUS DINING

Most students will complain about on-campus dining, but ironically, the restaurants and dining halls are usually busy. The loudest complaints are often from underclassmen who are still adjusting to not having a home cooked meal every night. Upperclassmen will grumble about the food, but they'll eat it, mostly out of convenience. Many of these establishments are open late, which is a boon to night owls and late-night revelers. The meal plans get mixed reviews. Students who are just looking for fuel to get through the day would probably do well with a meal plan, due to the buffet-style dining halls and all-you-can-eat options. Those who just grab a quick bite between classes, or who are interested in healthy dining, would be better off venturing off campus or waiting for the next care package from home.

**C+**

**The College Prowler™ Grade on**
### Campus Dining: C+

Our grade on Campus Dining addresses the quality of both school-owned dining halls and independent on-campus restaurants as well as the price, availability, and variety of food.

## Campus Housing

### The Lowdown
### ON CAMPUS HOUSING

**Undergrads on Campus:**
2,988

**Number of Dormitories:**
15

**Number of University-Owned Apartments:**
2

**Cleaning Service?**
The private and semi-private bathrooms are deep-cleaned by University Housing staff during breaks.

**You Get:**
Bed, desk and chair, closets or closet space, dresser, local telephone, direct computer connections, security card access

**Bed Type:**
Twin

**Also Available:**
In-room sinks, refrigerators, mirrors

## Room Types

Residence rooms include singles, doubles, suites, triples, quads, and apartments. The suites offer semi-private baths. There are two kinds of apartments offered. Efficiency apartments are one-bedroom apartments, and townhouse apartments have four bedrooms. Computer connections are offered in every dormitory. Television rooms, kitchens, recreational rooms, and laundry rooms can be found in every residence hall as well.

### Did You Know?

Florida State University just opened a new apartment-style residence hall. Landis Hall is being remodeled, and is temporarily closed. It will reopen in August of 2006 and be the new home of the Honors Community.

## Students Speak Out
### ON CAMPUS HOUSING

"Dorms are pretty good, but it depends on where you end up. Some are renovated and some aren't. You just have to see for yourself to decide what you want."

"I live in a nice dorm, but I have seen some bad ones on campus. My best friend lived in a dorm called Kellum, and I thought it was horrible. I have heard to **stay away from Smith and DeGraff.** The good ones are Murphree, Salley, and Cawthon, only because they are all newly renovated."

"As far as I know, Salley has been renovated, but I don't know if that really means it's all that great or not. When I lived in Salley as a freshman we couldn't decide if it was more **like living in a Mexican prison cell** or with the Teenage Mutant Ninja Turtles."

"The more money you spend, the better the dorms. I stayed in Kellum my first year. That wasn't going to happen my sophomore year. The dorms here suck. **Moldy, grimy, nasty** ...."

"Fifty percent of FSU's dorms are okay, and the other 50 percent are nasty. If you like living in a **shoebox complete with roaches and moldy ceiling tiles**, try Kellum Hall and Smith Hall. If you like living in a shoebox with nicer furniture try Deviney and Dorman. And if you can afford it, are in the honors program, or are just plain lucky, then you'll probably end up living in the rest of the dorms, which I've heard are quite lovely."

## The College Prowler Take
### ON CAMPUS HOUSING

As you can tell from the above quotes, on-campus housing can be hit-or-miss. A small percentage of students love living on campus, where they have all the amenities of home (minus Mom and Dad), and are close to their classes. Florida State is working hard to renovate the older dormitories, and within a year or two they should all be up to par with the newer facilities. As far as suggestions go, your best bet is to visit campus and see the dorms for yourself. It doesn't hurt to ask around. Some of the dorms are fairly quiet and are better suited for the serious student, while others tend to house the late-night revelers. If nothing else, dorm living is a great way to meet people and make friends. Just remember, don't expect it to be as nice as living at home.

**The College Prowler™ Grade on**
## Campus Housing: B-

A high Campus Housing grade indicates that dorms are clean, well-maintained, and spacious. Other determining factors include variety of dorms, proximity to classes, and social atmosphere.

# Diversity

## The Lowdown
### ON DIVERSITY

**Native American:** 0.4%

**Asian American:** 2.8%

**African American:** 11.8%

**Hispanic:** 8.5%

**White:** 71.1%

**International:** 4.1%

**Unknown:** 1.3%

**Out-of-State:** 23.8%

## Political Activity
The most visible political activity on campus, other than student government, is usually activists protesting either real or perceived injustices. Last fall, Florida State had a mass camp-out on Landis Green that lasted over a month.

## Minority Clubs
There are quite a few organizations on campus that represent minorities and offer them a voice in student affairs. The list of organizations includes: the African Student Association, the Chinese Student & Scholar Association, the Cuban American Student Association, and the South Asian Students Association.

## Most Popular Religions
Mostly Christian, but many other religions are also represented. Many consider Tallahassee to be part of the Bible Belt, and the city plays host to a number of churches.

## Gay Tolerance
While Florida State is in the South, both the FSU and the local community show a high degree of tolerance for alternative lifestyles. There have been no violent crimes against homosexuals in recent history. The university also hosts the Lesbian/Gay/Bisexual/Transgender Student Union and SafeZone.

## Economic Status
You'll hear the usually complaints about "rich kids," and more than a handful of students drive cars you know they didn't pay for themselves. However, the economic status of the student body varies, and FSU does a good job of bringing in students from all walks of life.

## Students Speak Out
### ON DIVERSITY

"The population is mainly white, but there are plenty of other races and cultures represented. Many clubs and organizations involve people from varying groups. There is definitely some diversity, but not a lot."

Q "Campus is pretty diverse, with **lots of organizations linking all types of people**. There are organizations for Jews, blacks, Hispanics, Muslims, Presbyterians, Catholics, and I'm sure many more."

Q "FSU is not that diverse, but FAMU is across the street, so **you get a mix of cultures**."

Q "I guess it depends on your viewpoint. Most of my white friends think the campus is diverse, but my **African American friends feel that they don't get much representation**. As far as other cultures go, they are around, but there aren't many."

"In the four years I've been here, **I've met people from all over the world**, so I would argue that the campus is very diverse. Sure, it is predominately white, but I feel that other ethnic groups are well-represented here."

### The College Prowler Take
ON DIVERSITY

Florida State appears to strive towards diversity among the student body. Recent statistics show that FSU has seen minority enrollment increase by 33 percent over the last five years. FSU also boasts a large number of international students, as well as over 250 student organizations. This broad range of representation will give students the opportunity to meet and hang out with people of various backgrounds. Also, keep in mind that Florida A&M University, a predominately minority school, is only a few blocks away, which serves to deepen the ethnic and cultural diversity of the area. Most students agree that attending FSU is a great way to broaden your horizons and gain exposure to a variety of people and cultures.

**B-**

**The College Prowler™ Grade on**
### Diversity: B-

A high grade in Diversity indicates that ethnic minorities and international students have a notable presence on campus and that students of different economic backgrounds, religious beliefs, and sexual preferences are well-represented.

# Guys & Girls

### The Lowdown
ON GUYS & GIRLS

**Women Undergrads:** 56%

**Men Undergrads:** 44%

### Birth Control Available?
Yes, its available at at Thagard Student Health Center

Due to the number of off-campus facilities available to students, Thagard Student Health Center does not keep track of sexually transmitted diseases (STDs) among the student body. However, they do provide testing, treatment, and counseling services for students. Thagard is also one of the few university health clinics in the nation that provides anonymous HIV testing.

Anonymous HIV Clinic: (850) 644-0579

### Social Scene
The majority of students will agree that Florida State is one of the friendliest places in the country. Sure, it can be awkward at first, but it won't take long to meet new people and find a crowd to hang out with.

## Hookups or Relationships?

While there are a number of couples on campus, there is also a thriving singles scene. There are several bars on the edge of campus—along the Tennessee Street Strip—that cater to the singles crowd with ladies-night drink specials and other events that offer the opportunity to mix and mingle.

## Dress Code

The students at FSU tend to dress casually. There are a few who are brave enough to dress up, but you have to remember, this is Florida, and the summer here can be warm and humid. From May to October most people will be wearing shorts, T-shirts, and flip-flops. This isn't to say that they dress like slobs—only that most students dress for comfort.

## Students Speak Out
### ON GUYS & GIRLS

"There are beautiful men and women here. The guys are incredible. There are so many different types to choose from. If you can't find your soul mate here, you probably never will."

Q "The guys are all gentlemen. The girls vary more. They can be **really sweet southern belles** or they can be snobby, but they're the types of people you will find anywhere you go."

Q "Actually, it seems to me that **a lot of the guys on campus are short**—somebody pointed that out to me, and now I can't help but notice that it's true. But FSU has been labeled one of the most attractive campuses in the country. If there was a nationwide rating for hotness at universities, we would kick Harvard's butt."

Q "It's the Sunshine State, so you know **there are some fine women here**. There's just something about a nice tan that can drive a guy crazy! Girls I hang out with say the guys here are pretty hot too, so I guess there's something for everyone."

Q "I don't know. I think that it would be the same at just about any campus. I mean, there are some good-looking people here, don't get me wrong. **I'm just not into just looks**."

Q "The **girl to guy ratio makes any woman sad**. There are many more women here, but the quality of guys makes up for it, if you can snatch one up!"

## The College Prowler Take
### ON GUYS & GIRLS

Most students at FSU will admit that one of the more popular pastimes on campus is admiring the student body. The warm weather offers ample opportunity to bask in the sun. It also gives people a chance to show a little more skin. It can sometimes be distracting during the summer months, but you'd be hard-pressed to find someone that complains about it. And as if that weren't enough, FSU students are also some of the friendliest in the South. Of course, in Tallahassee women outnumber men at a little over two-to-one, but that doesn't interfere with anyone making new friends.

**A-**

**A**

The College Prowler™ Grade on
### Guys: A-

A high grade for Guys indicates that the male population on campus is attractive, smart, friendly, and engaging, and that the school has a decent ratio of guys to girls.

The College Prowler™ Grade on
### Girls: A

A high grade for Girls not only implies that the women on campus are attractive, smart, friendly, and engaging, but also that there is a fair ratio of girls to guys.

# Athletics

## The Lowdown
### ON ATHLETICS

**Athletic Division:**
NCAA Division I

**Conference:**
ACC

**School Mascot:**
Seminole Indian

**Fields:**
Dick Howser Stadium, Doak Campbell Stadium, Intramural Sports Complex, Seminole Soccer Complex, Seminole Softball Complex

**Men's Varsity Teams:**

Baseball
Basketball
Cross Country
Football
Golf
Swimming
Tennis
Track-Indoor
Track-Outdoor

**Women's Varsity Teams:**

Basketball
Cross Country
Golf
Soccer
Softball
Swimming
Tennis
Track-Indoor
Track-Outdoor
Volleyball

## Getting Tickets

Getting tickets for most athletic events at FSU really isn't a problem. Football tickets, however, can be difficult to come by. Because the football games are such a big event on campus, the school has initiated a system by which students receive vouchers for tickets, but then must stand in line to redeem the vouchers. And possession of a voucher does not guarantee a ticket to the game.

## Students Speak Out
### ON ATHLETICS

"Everything at FSU and Tallahassee revolves around the FSU football team. I never cared for the sport until it sucked me in after the first year, and now I try to attend every game."

Q "Sports on campus are huge and nothing compares to FSU football games in the fall—nothing. Baseball games are always packed, and the **women's teams have started to become a lot more popular**. They are attracting a lot of fans. Basketball games are fun, and we are getting a new complex. They have [intramural] teams and leagues for every sport that you can think of, with great facilities for them all. There are some very competitive games in the higher leagues, but they also offer B and C leagues with easier play, and plenty of co-ed opportunities."

Q "Even if you aren't a sports fan, **you can't help but get caught up in the excitement** on campus when there's a big game. Tailgating in the fall is a serious tradition here. I would suggest attending at least one football game. You won't be disappointed."

💬 "Football and baseball are big. Volleyball is pretty good as well. **Basketball is pretty sorry, but big games are fun** to go to because you never know when there will be an upset."

💬 "Sports are crazy at FSU. We have **the number one baseball team in the country** and our football team is one of the best in the nation. IM sports are easy to get into—there are tournaments between teams made up of people from dorms, frats, sororities, and just groups of friends getting together."

# Greek Life

## The College Prowler Take
ON GREEK LIFE

**Varsity football at FSU is arguably the biggest thing on campus. When fall rolls around you can feel the excitement in the air. Tickets can be difficult to come by, especially for the big games, but everyone is usually able to attend the games they want.** For those who want to participate in sports, but aren't ready to try out at the varsity level, it's easy to get involved with intramural teams (IMs). There are a wide variety of IMs to choose from, and the warm weather allows for year-round competition. Florida State University prides itself on having one of the most competitive athletic programs in the country. Football does dominate the scene, but that doesn't mean the other sports are ignored. Even if you aren't interested in sports, you can't help but cheer when an FSU team takes the field.

## The Lowdown
ON GREEK LIFE

**Number of Fraternities:**
20

**Number of Sororities:**
14

**Undergrad Men in Fraternities:**
14%

**Undergrad Women in Sororities:**
13%

**Multicultural Colonies:**
Alpha Kappa Delta Phi Sorority, Inc., Lambda Theta Alpha Latin Sorority, Inc., Lambda Theta Phi Latin Fraternity, Inc., Sigma Lambda Beta International Fraternity, Inc., Sigma Lambda Gamma National Sorority, Inc., Theta Nu Xi Multicultural Sorority, Inc.

### COLLEGE PROWLER™

For listings of all Greek organizations on campus, check out the College Prowler book on Florida State University available at *www.collegeprowler.com*.

**The College Prowler™ Grade on**
## Athletics: A

A high grade in Athletics indicates that students have school spirit, that sports programs are respected, that games are well-attended, and that intramurals are a prominent part of student life.

## Students Speak Out
ON GREEK LIFE

> "Greek life does not dominate the social scene—it's not one of those things where if you're not in it you're nobody, but the frats do throw really good parties."

Q "In my eyes, Greek life plays a major role in the social scene, but this is coming from a Greek. You do not have to join a sorority to have fun in college, but it helps—you meet a lot of awesome people. I definitely recommend going through recruitment, and if you don't find a house that you are 100 percent sure about, you don't have to join. Greek life is everywhere at FSU. **We are the people in the paper for doing awesome philanthropic work**, and also for bad stuff like drinking. The community has mixed feelings about Greek life, but the sororities and fraternities are working hard to get a better image. All student organizations can participate in events like homecoming, but Greeks dominate all the competitions. We always do a lot of service work and have a lot of socials."

Q "Greek life is something unique to be experienced at FSU. **There's a house for everyone**. Greeks have the best parties, the loudest music, and of course you can always find companionship. It dominates the scene for people already in it. As for the rest of campus, they're missing out."

Q "I did not join a sorority and I found that most of the **guys I talked to prefer girls that aren't in a sorority**. Believe me—you'll spot a sorority girl right away. Greeks don't dominate the social scene. I went to some great parties and none of them involved sorority members or frats guys."

Q "There are lots of fraternities and sororities to join on campus, but **they definitely don't control things**. You can choose to join, but you don't have to; if you don't, you will still have a life."

## The College Prowler Take
ON GREEK LIFE

Greek organizations are both very active and visible on the FSU campus. They tend to have a partying reputation, but many students don't notice all the volunteer work the Greeks perform. Despite many of the preconceptions, Greek organizations at FSU set the standard for leadership and community service. As far as the social scene is concerned, Greek life is not the dominant force on campus. Some students enjoy the camaraderie and lifelong friendships they develop through membership in a fraternity or sorority. The Greeks do dominate student government and homecoming elections, but that is to be expected. The majority of students at FSU do not belong to a fraternity or sorority, and many would agree that their social lives are just as active as any Greek's.

**A-**

The College Prowler™ Grade on
### Greek Life: A-

A high grade in Greek Life indicates that sororities and fraternities are not only present, but also active on campus. Other determining factors include the variety of houses available and the respect the Greek community receives from the rest of the campus.

# Drug Scene

## The Lowdown
### ON DRUG SCENE

**Most Prevalent Drugs on Campus:**
Alcohol, Marijuana, Caffeine, Ritalin

**Liquor-Related Referrals:**
151

**Liquor-Related Arrests:**
223

**Drug-Related Referrals:**
12

**Drug-Related Arrests:**
98

## Students Speak Out
### ON DRUG SCENE

"The drug scene is kind of 'hush.' People don't walk around talking about it. If you use drugs, you won't have trouble finding them, but if you don't, you won't be surrounded by the drug culture."

Q "Lots of **drugs are available for those who want them**. However, TPD and FSUPD alike are completely unforgiving if you get busted."

Q "Lots of drugs are available locally, but I'm not sure if this is campus specific. That stuff is **available no matter where you go**. It's up to you whether you're going to do drugs or not."

Q "I can't really comment because I don't do drugs. But, if I said we were a completely drug-free campus, I'd be lying. It's around, but it's **not like people are getting wasted in the hallways** or anything."

Q "I'd say that **more students abuse alcohol than drugs**. Heavy drinking can be a problem, but I don't hear much about drug problems."

## Drug Counseling Programs

### Students Teaching Alcohol & Other Drug Education
(850) 644-8871

Services: Provides information and services to educate students on the responsibilities and risks associated with drinking and the dangers of drug use.

### Student Counseling Center
2nd Floor, Student Life Building
(850) 644-2003
Services: Counseling, crisis intervention, referrals, workshops and presentations.

For a detailed listing of all drug and alcohol counseling sessions on campus, check out the complete College Prowler book on FSU available at www.collegeprowler.com.

## The College Prowler Take
**ON DRUG SCENE**

While illegal drugs are present on campus, they aren't highly visible, and most students don't pay much attention to them. Alcohol and marijuana are the drugs of choice, although harder stuff like ecstasy and methamphetamines are available if you know where to look. FSU has a very strict drug policy. However, the users and abusers tend to stay off the radar, so you won't hear much about arrests and expulsions. For the most part, the drug culture is quiet and secretive. People who want to be involved in it can find it on their own, while those who prefer to stay clean won't be tempted.

**C+**

**The College Prowler™ Grade on**
## Drug Scene: C+

A high grade on Drug Scene indicates that drugs are not a noticeable part of campus life; drug use is not visible, and no pressure to use them seems to exist.

# Overall Experience

## Students Speak Out
**ON OVERALL EXPERIENCE**

"In the fall, I'll be starting my sophomore year. I relished in all the experiences I've had so far, and I look forward to next year. I wouldn't trade Florida State for anything."

"FSU is a quality school. They put **a little too much emphasis on the football team**, but, other than that, I think they have their priorities in line. They are building a solid reputation as a research university, and, as a science major, that means more opportunities for me to pursue. I highly recommend coming here."

"I haven't met that many people that were disappointing. Sometimes I feel like I'm still in high school, but that may be because I still live at home. And I didn't do as well academically [as I hoped I would]. Overall, I would like to build a time machine and do it over—maybe at a nice school up North. But FSU seems to be **a great place to go for most people**."

"I love my experiences at FSU. I honestly **wouldn't change anything about my college experience**. This school is awesome, and I recommend that you come here!"

> "I love Florida State—so much that I'm thinking about living here and going to law school. I like Florida, and being up in the panhandle is **a great way to avoid some heat and still have no snow**."

## The College Prowler Take
### ON OVERALL EXPERIENCE

You would be hard-pressed to find a graduate of Florida State University who doesn't have fond memories of the years they spent on campus, and current students will also agree that they are happy with their decision to attend school here. There is something for everyone here, from athletics to academics, and you'd have a hard time finding a more comfortable setting than Tallahassee.

Although it has a reputation as a party school, FSU also has a growing reputation for turning out some of the best and brightest graduates in the entire nation. The school is now turning its focus toward research, which should appeal to those who are interested in science and mathematics. But, never fear, FSU also emphasizes the arts, through their award-winning film and theatre departments. Choosing which college to attend is not an easy decision, but if you're looking for the perfect combination of a good education and a good time, you can't do much better than Florida State University.

# Georgia Tech

225 North Avenue NW, Atlanta, GA 30332
www.admission.gatech.edu    (404) 894-4154

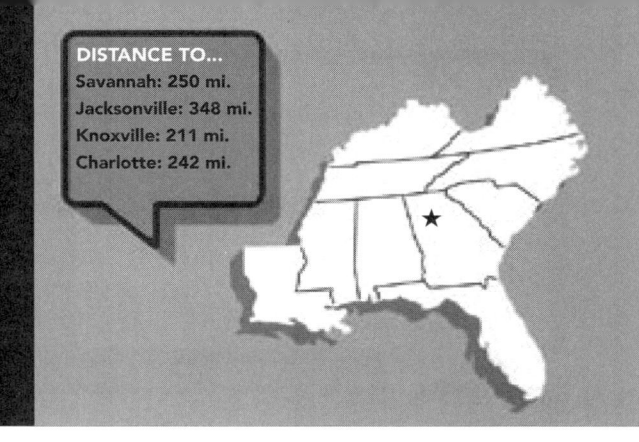

**DISTANCE TO...**
Savannah: 250 mi.
Jacksonville: 348 mi.
Knoxville: 211 mi.
Charlotte: 242 mi.

"The city's phenomenal growth and the Institute's traditions and academic reputation have been mutually beneficial to each other."

**Total Enrollment:**
10,367

**Top 10% of High School Class:**
58%

**Average GPA:**
3.7

**Acceptance Rate:**
63%

**Tuition:**
$4,278 in-state, $17,558 out-of-state

**SAT Range (25th-75th Percentile):**
Verbal     Math       Total
600 – 690  650 – 740  1250 – 1430

**ACT Range (25th-75th Percentile):**
Verbal   Math    Total
25-30    27-32   26-30

**Most Popular Majors:**
53% Engineering
15% Business
13% Computer Sciences
4%  Architecture and Related Services
3%  Biological and Biomedical Sciences

**Students also applied to:***
Duke University, MIT, University of Florida, University of Georgia, Virginia Tech

*For more school info check out www.collegeprowler.com

## Table of Contents

| | |
|---|---|
| Academics | 140 |
| Local Atmosphere | 142 |
| Safety & Security | 144 |
| Facilities | 145 |
| Campus Dining | 147 |
| Campus Housing | 149 |
| Diversity | 150 |
| Guys & Girls | 152 |
| Athletics | 153 |
| Greek Life | 155 |
| Drug Scene | 156 |
| Overall Experience | 158 |

## College Prowler Report Card

| | |
|---|---|
| Academics | B+ |
| Local Atmosphere | A- |
| Safety & Security | B+ |
| Facilities | B |
| Campus Dining | C- |
| Campus Housing | D |
| Diversity | B- |
| Guys | B |
| Girls | C |
| Athletics | A |
| Greek Life | B+ |
| Drug Scene | A- |

# Academics

**Special Degree Options**
Pre-professional programs: pre-health and pre-law, teacher certification program, dual degrees available

**Sample Academic Clubs**
Academic Quizbowl Team, Freshman Council, Indonesian Student Association, National Society of Black Engineers, National Society of Collegiate Scholars, Phi Mu, Semper Fi Society, Society of Physics Students, SPAARC

## The Lowdown
ON ACADEMICS

**Degrees Awarded:**
Bachelor of Science (B.S.), Master of Science (M.S.), Doctor of Philosophy (Ph. D.)

**Undergraduate Schools:**
College of Architecture, College of Computing, DuPree College of Management, College of Engineering, Ivan Allen College, College of Sciences

**Full-time Faculty**:
746

**Faculty with Terminal Degree**:
95%

**Student-to-Faculty Ratio**:
14:1

**Average Course Load**:
15 or 16 credits

**AP Test Score Requirements**
Possible credit for scores of 4 or 5

**IB Test Score Requirements:**
Possible credit for scores of 4 to 7

### Did You Know?

Georgia Tech is consistently ranked one of the top 10 public universities by several national academic publications.

Every freshman dorm has a Learning Center, which offers tutoring to new students as they adjust to college life and its academic rigors.

**Best Places to Study:**
The library

## Students Speak Out
### ON ACADEMICS

"Most of my classes are small, and my professors and I are on a first-name basis. I enjoy my classes, for the most part, and find them challenging."

Q "**Teachers are a real mix**. Some really care to help students, while others are disinterested and care only for the research."

Q "**Most of the teachers are foreign**. Sometimes they can be hard to understand, but they are all really nice and always willing to take time out of their day to help you."

Q "Teachers are great. If you make an honest effort to succeed in their class, then **they will do their absolute best to help you out**. I've only had two teachers in the past three years at Tech that I really didn't like. The rest have been really great."

Q "I would say that 70 percent of the teachers are only there to teach because they are told to. **They have more important things on their mind**, such as their own research. They will not help that much, so you are basically learning the material yourself. But, you can choose the professors you want based on past grade distributions posted on the 'net."

## The College Prowler Take
### ON ACADEMICS

If you choose to matriculate at Georgia Tech, it can be expected that your professors in any given course of study will be among the most recognized and respected names in their fields. Doctorates from Princeton, MIT, Stanford, CalTech, and Georgia Tech roam the halls, instructing the next generation's leading scientists and engineers. Having come from demanding academic backgrounds themselves, Georgia Tech professors are notorious for being stingy with grades. Do not expect to receive exemplary grades at Georgia Tech unless you are willing to put in the time and effort required. With that said, the vast majority of these professors will do their best to accommodate difficulties and problems, if they are informed of them. Most large classes consist of one professor that oversees several teaching assistants (or TAs). The professor is obligated to carry on the regular lectures and the general administration of the class, but each TA is given charge over a small subset of students. Most of the interaction that takes place in the course is experienced between the students and TAs.

More specifically, different fields of study usually beget different breeds of professors. Overall, you will be expected to learn things without supervision and will be held to very high standards. Of course, the harshness is not without reason, and Tech graduates are generally very well-trained and sought after in their various fields.

**B+**

**The College Prowler™ Grade on**
## Academics: B+

A high Academics grade generally indicates that professors are knowledgeable, accessible, and genuinely interested in their students' welfare. Other determining factors include class size, how well professors communicate, and whether or not classes are engaging.

# Local Atmosphere

**City Websites**

http://www.atlanta.com

http://www.creativeloafing.com

http://www.accessatlanta.com

http://www.ajc.com

http://www.bestofatlanta.com

## The Lowdown
ON LOCAL ATMOSPHERE

### Did You Know?
Centennial Olympic Park was built for the 1996 Olympic Games. It is now a 21 acre park with fountains, outdoor concerts, and events enjoyed by students, locals, and tourists.

**Region:**
Southeast

**City, State:**
Atlanta, Georgia

**Setting:**
Big City

**Distance from Destin, FL:**
7 hours

**Distance from Nashville, TN:**
4 hours

**Distance from Savannah, GA:**
4 hours, 30 minutes

**Points of Interest:**
Atlanta Botanical Garden, Centennial Olympic Park, CNN Center, Coca-Cola Museum, Fernbank Museum, Fox Theatre, High Museum of Art, Lake Lanier Islands & Water Park, Piedmont Park, Shakespeare's Tavern, Six Flags Over Georgia, Stone Mountain Park, Zoo Atlanta

**Major Sports Teams:**
Braves (baseball), Hawks (basketball), Falcons (football), Thrashers (hockey)

## Students Speak Out
ON LOCAL ATMOSPHERE

"**The atmosphere in Atlanta is diverse. There are many local communities within the downtown area, some of which should be frequented, and some of which should be avoided.**"

"**Atlanta is a great city to be a part of.** Stay away from some of the shady places, and definitely travel in a big group at night. There is a lot to do and see in Atlanta, especially Centennial Olympic Park, Underground Atlanta, CNN Building, SciTrack, Buckhead, the different malls, and many other things."

"Atlanta is huge and still growing. **A lot of people are moving to Atlanta** from all over. There are a lot of universities and colleges here: Emory University, Georgia State University, Agnes Scott College, Spelman College, and Morehouse College are just a few. Definitely visit Six Flags, White Water—one of the nation's top ten water parks—and go see a play at the Fox Theater."

"**There is a ton of cool stuff to see in town**. Georgia State University is literally across the street, but it stays that way. We don't mix, but we don't stay away, you know? Emory is also about 10 minutes away. Their parties are way better. I highly recommend going."

"**Stay away from anything more south than our school**. Northern adventures are okay. The Fox Theater around the corner has awesome operas, symphony, plays, etc. Tons of concerts come through Atlanta."

"Atlanta is pretty fun. It has most **anything you could want in a big city**—restaurants, museums, symphony, theater, movies, bars, dance clubs, music, you name it. There are also a lot of things like running and biking clubs. Just down the street from Tech is Piedmont Park, which is a huge park that has running and biking trails, lots of green space, and places to rent in-line skates."

"**There really aren't areas that are so bad** you will be shot at if you turn down the wrong road or anything. As for the places that are 'rough' areas, you really wouldn't have any reason to go there anyway. There are some fun things like the Coca-Cola museum, where they have a laser show every night in the summer, and there are tons of malls and stuff. Plus, we have professional baseball, football, basketball, hockey, women's soccer, and some other minor league sports. Most major concerts come to Atlanta too, and radio stations do outdoor concerts on Fridays during the summer."

# The College Prowler Take
## ON LOCAL ATMOSPHERE

Georgia Tech is in the heart of midtown Atlanta, which provides a very urban environment for students. Along with all of the amenities and luxuries that Atlanta city life provides, there are also a few drawbacks. For instance, city life in general can sometimes be dangerous. Caution is a virtue. However, Atlanta is an exciting city with a vibrant local music scene (which has produced the likes of John Mayer, Collective Soul, and Outkast), as well as four major professional sports teams, and numerous other attractions. Atlanta is the biggest and fastest growing city in the Southeast, and students will always be provided with a wealth of options for entertainment.

**A-**

The College Prowler™ Grade on
## Local Atmosphere: A-

A high Local Atmosphere grade indicates that the area surrounding campus is safe and scenic. Other factors include nearby attractions, proximity to other schools, and the town's attitude toward students.

# Safety & Security

## Students Speak Out
### ON SAFETY & SECURITY

"Security and safety on campus are high given its neighborhood. Although there have been some robberies and car thefts, campus is very safe for the most part."

## The Lowdown
### ON SAFETY & SECURITY

**Number of GT Police:**
46

**Number of Emergency Phones:**
76

**Phone:**
(404) 894-2500

**Health Center Office Hours:**
Monday-Friday 8 a.m.-4:30 p.m.

**Safety Services:**
Escort Services, Stingerette Shuttle Service, Stinger Bus Service

Q "We have **a police station right on campus**, so they can respond pretty quickly to things. Tech is in midtown Atlanta, so you have to be alert and not do dumb things like walking alone at 2 a.m. I wouldn't say that I feel unsafe on campus. There is an escort service that tends to take a while to get to you sometimes, but it is better than walking by yourself in the middle of the night. During the day, though, I wouldn't hesitate to walk by myself on campus or in the areas surrounding the University."

Q "I would say that for a downtown campus, **it's very secure**. I rarely see any homeless people on campus, and you can always find a police car somewhere. Also, there are emergency call boxes all over school in case you need to call the police. There are vans that you can call at night to take you places; they run until 3 a.m., and after that, you can call campus police to escort you anywhere. West Campus is quieter than East, with less homeless people, because East Campus is right next to the interstate. I lived on East Campus my freshman year, and I never felt unsafe."

Q "Security is pretty good. They have nighttime patrolling and shuttles at night that will **escort you home late**—great for heading home from nearby bars. They run like a cab service. Tech is in downtown Atlanta, but I never felt unsafe. I walk around at night a lot on campus."

Q "I know two people that have had their car broken into and **one person had their car stolen** right out of the Curran parking deck."

## The College Prowler Take
### ON SAFETY & SECURITY

Georgia Tech has a good campus police force, which patrols the campus extensively at night. Campus police officers are just as competent as Atlanta city police, and they have every intention of protecting you, the student. In addition to offering a good police force, Georgia Tech also offers a shuttle service that can take you to and from surrounding locations during the night hours. It is very convenient, and can be reached 24 hours a day through an 800 number.

With all of that said, one must still remember that Atlanta has routinely ranked among the most dangerous cities in the country over the last twenty years. Students should avoid traveling alone on foot during the evening and early morning hours, no matter if they are on campus, or in the middle of downtown. The reality of the big city will not forgive any naïveté on your part. Get informed about city life, and use common sense. Travel with friends and stay in crowded areas.

**B+**

### The College Prowler™ Grade on
### Safety & Security: B+

A high grade in Safety & Security means that students generally feel safe, campus police are visible, blue-light phones and escort services are readily available, and safety precautions are not overly necessary.

# Facilities

## The Lowdown
### ON FACILITIES

**Student Center:**
Yes, the Student Center

**Athletic Center:**
Student Athletic Center
Campus Recreation Center

**Libraries:**
1

**Movie Theatre on Campus?**
No, although organizations do show movies in the Student Center Theater.

**Bowling on Campus?**
Yes

**Bar on Campus?**
No

**Coffeehouse on Campus?**
Yes, the WestSide Coffeehouse

**Popular Places to Chill:**
The Student Center
Music Listening Room

## Favorite Things to Do

Students can head over to the Music Listening Room or the outdoor Basketball Courts. They might also check out the Arcade/Entertainment Center, which is on the first floor of the Student Center.

### Computers

**High-Speed Network?** Yes
**Wireless Network?** Yes
**Number of Labs:** 7
**Charge to Print?** No
**24-Hour Labs:**
Student Center Computer Lab

### COLLEGE PROWLER™

Need help finding certain buildings on campus? For a detailed listing of all campus facilities and their whereabouts, check out the complete College Prowler book on Georgia Tech available at *www.collegeprowler.com*.

## Students Speak Out
### ON FACILITIES

"GT has done some things to make campus nicer, but it's not one of those campuses that people would describe as beautiful."

Q "Some of the facilities are nice and some are not so nice. There is a **brand-new athletic center being built**, but the Student Center is who knows how old. Georgia Tech is doing quite a bit to improve the quality of its student facilities, though, and is in the process of renovating the Student Center as well."

Q "Facilities are extraordinary! When the Olympics came, they built new, very nice dorms and athletic facilities. I've visited many campuses, and **Tech has the best dorms, classrooms, and student areas**. All the facilities are just phenomenal."

Q "The facilities on campus are really nice. Everything is pretty new and **very technologically advanced**. Our facilities are much better than any other university I've ever visited."

Q "The Student Center is nice. There are lots of couches and chairs to lounge around on. There is also a bowling alley, pool, and an arcade room. The post office is there; and **there's also a theater where they show free movies** before they come out in the theater. There's a music listening room, which I recommend visiting as much as you can. It is peaceful and comfortable, and you can totally relax or study. There is also a big screen for watching TV."

## The College Prowler Take
### ON FACILITIES

The Student Center is the hub of student activity on campus. Located squarely in the middle of campus, it houses a computer cluster, a music listening room, a food court, a ballroom and a theater. Many functions are held in the ballroom, and the theater regularly holds free screenings of popular movies, along with occasional concerts.

The Student Center is also slated for a makeover next year, which will integrate the facility more completely with the adjacent Houston Mall and Bookstore area. The campus post office, located on the ground floor of the Student Center, will be moved to a more accessible location in the facility, and the existing market and clothes store will be expanded to better serve the students. In addition to all of this, Bobby Dodd Stadium is nearing completion, and will soon hold upwards of 60,000 people. The new Bobby Dodd will have a old-fashioned brick look, and Tech students will finally have the "bowl" stadium that they've always wanted.

## Campus Dining

### The Lowdown
### ON CAMPUS DINING

**Freshman Meal Plan Requirement?**
No

**24-Hour On-Campus Eating?**
No

**Student Favorites:**
Chick-fil-A, Pizza Hut

**Meal Plan Average Cost:**
$499-$1,284

**B**

The College Prowler™ Grade on
### Facilities: B

A high Facilities grade indicates that the campus is aesthetically pleasing and well-maintained; facilities are state-of-the-art, and libraries are exceptional. Other determining factors include the quality of both athletic and student centers and an abundance of things to do on campus.

**COLLEGE PROWLER™**

Need help finding the best on-campus food? For a detailed listing on all eateries on campus, check out the College Prowler book on Georgia Tech available at *www.collegeprowler.com*.

## Students Speak Out
### ON CAMPUS DINING

> "The food in dining halls is notoriously horrible, but there are other options. The Student Center has a myriad of food choices, and there are many places in walking distance of campus."

Q "On-campus food is all right, but isn't all campus food kind of yucky? There are **two dining halls where you'll eat everyday** as a freshman. They have a salad bar, sandwich bar, cereal bar, and ice cream bar everyday. There are also hot foods that change everyday, and a hot sandwich line, where they make chicken sandwiches, hamburgers, etc. They also serve a good breakfast, but I haven't known any place to mess up a breakfast."

Q "The food in the dining halls is pretty crappy. You'll probably do the Freshman Experience program; if you do, **you'll be required to have a dining hall meal plan**. I recommend the 10 meal-per-week plan, as I found myself only eating there six or seven times a week. On campus, there is a food court in a central area, so you can hit that between classes. There's also a place called Junior's, which has awesome chicken fingers and breakfasts."

Q "Junior's, which is the oldest restaurant on campus, is pretty cool. It's a tradition to go there before football games or after staying up all night—they open at 6 a.m. The French toast special is awesome! Also, **the Student Center has a food court with gyros, smoothies**, Chick-fil-A, and Taco Bell."

Q "**I enjoy food from the dining hall** and from the Student Center. There's Burger King, Chick-fil-A, sandwiches, and Mexican."

## The College Prowler Take
### ON CAMPUS DINING

Georgia Tech has two dining halls, Brittain and Woodruff, located at opposite ends of the campus. While they are definitely no place to take a date—or anyone, for that matter—to have a nice meal, they are adequate for everyday use.

The quality of the food has improved steadily over the last five years. Breakfast food is always your best bet at these dining halls, and students are free to make their own sandwiches and salads at the salad bar, if they choose to do so. For a satisfying lunch or breakfast with a professor, friend, co-worker, or anyone else, there are two other choices on campus: Junior's Grill and the Student Center food court. The Student Center offers an exceptional variety of choices for lunch, including Chick-fil-A, Burger King, and even a salad bar.

**The College Prowler™ Grade on**
## Campus Dining: C-

Our grade on Campus Dining addresses the quality of both school-owned dining halls and independent on-campus restaurants as well as the price, availability, and variety of food.

# Campus Housing

## The Lowdown
ON CAMPUS HOUSING

**Undergrads on Campus:**
58%

**Number of Dormitories:**
23

**Number of University-Owned Apartments:**
8

**Room Types:**
Traditional—double room with a central bathroom facility
Suite—two double rooms with a connecting bathroom

**Cleaning Service?**
Public areas are cleaned once a week.

**You Get:**
Usually, you get an extra-long twin bed, desk, carrel, desk chair, lockable footlocker, wardrobe and dresser, but it depends on the dorm.

**Bed Type:**
Extra-long twin, which can be bunked

**Also Available:**
Learning Communities, which are groups of people with the same academic interests that live in the same dorm.

## Students Speak Out
ON CAMPUS HOUSING

"The dorms are small. The Freshman Experience is a good program, and I would definitely recommend it. You should upgrade to on-campus apartments after your first year."

Q "As a freshman, **you'll want to live anywhere on East Campus**, but they fill up fast. I really hated the dorms. I had awesome roommates, but sharing a bathroom with 50 other people sucks. The housing repair team fixes your stuff, but you usually have to wait several days—sometimes a week or two—and they'll show up without warning. If you aren't there, they'll leave a note saying they'll come back at a certain time. If you can get into a suite, that would be your best bet, but most freshmen can't; choose a Freshman Experience dorm instead. The best thing I can say is that you'll most likely make a ton of friends from living in the dorm. My roommates and the guys on my floor were awesome, so I can't complain too much."

Q "The dorms are okay, but Tech does a Freshman Experience program that you can do where everyone in those dorms are freshman. I did that, and it worked out well. **Cloudman was the best girls' Freshman Experience dorm** last year."

Q "Housing is limited, and **you're only guaranteed housing for the first two years**. They're all pretty nice because the older ones have all been renovated, and all the apartments were built for the Olympics when they were in Atlanta, so they're pretty nice, too."

Q "The dorms are, well, dorms. Nothing too extravagant, but they are lots of fun. They are located on East and West Campus. **East Campus is where all the Greeks are** and where the football stadium is, so during football season East Campus is lots of fun. That's also where most freshmen live because there are six huge dorms. West Campus is the nicer side of campus. It is where almost all of the upperclassmen housing. There are five smaller dorms. If you are really into fitness and playing sports, I'd recommend West Campus because it's by the athletic complex and the big turf field."

## The College Prowler Take
### ON CAMPUS HOUSING

Dorms on campus are notoriously expensive, and accommodations leave something to be desired. Freshman dorms on East Campus are mostly small, two-person rooms about 12 feet by 14 feet in size. Sections of eight to ten rooms share a common bathroom with multiple open showers. These bathroom facilities are located at the ends of each hall. But some buildings have common bathroom facilities for every four to five rooms. Woodruff houses one bathroom with two showers between every pair of rooms. 6th Street Apartments, 8th Street Apartments, and Hemphill Apartments all house four-, five-, and six-person apartments, each with a kitchen, living area and two full bathrooms.

**The College Prowler™ Grade on**
### Campus Housing: D

A high Campus Housing grade indicates that dorms are clean, well-maintained, and spacious. Other determining factors include variety of dorms, proximity to classes, and social atmosphere.

# Diversity

## The Lowdown
### ON DIVERSITY

**Native American:** 0.2%

**Asian American:** 17.2%

**African American:** 8.2%

**Hispanic:** 3.2%

**White:** 70.2%

**International:** 5.1%

**Unknown:** 1.1%

**Out-of-State:** 35.9%

### Minority Clubs
Pride Alliance, National Society of Black Engineers, African American Student Union, African Students Association, Minority Recruitment Team, Asian Christian Fellowship, Asian Student Interest Association, Society of Women in Business, Society of Women Engineers, India Club

### Political Activity
There are students from all political affiliations on campus. There is a student organization on campus for Democrats, Republicans, and Libertarians.

## Most Popular Religions
Christianity, Muslim

## Gay Tolerance
Historically, Georgia Tech has not been particularly accepting of the GLBTQ community, but, in the past 15 years, organizations like Gay and Lesbian Alliance and Safe Space have developed and the campus has become much more accepting of the gay community, although there are still some students who are more accepting than others.

## Economic Status
The majority of students are middle- to upper-class.

## Students Speak Out
ON DIVERSITY

"It's pretty diverse, with students from over a hundred countries and almost all 50 states. Many of these groups are not large, though."

Q "Campus is really diverse! I don't know the exact statistics, but there is definitely a **good mix of nationalities on campus**. I am Indian, and have never felt out of place, by any means."

Q "People-wise, we have a lot of Asian Americans, but there are also plenty of Caucasian people, too. There **aren't very many Hispanic or black students**, though. There are plenty of foreign people from European countries and other places, as well."

Q "Tech is pretty diverse. I'm African American, and there are a lot of Asians, quite a few Indians, and a lot of Middle Easterners. I think there is a **pretty good representation of ethnicities and races here**. That's saying a lot, coming from a minority."

Q "It seems like there are a lot of foreign students on campus. I know there are things like the **India club and the Muslim group**, as well as a couple of things like the Black Graduate Student Association."

## The College Prowler Take
ON DIVERSITY

The Tech campus and the city of Atlanta are both quite diverse areas, but most students find that the two are diverse in very different ways. Atlanta has a very large African American population, although the school itself does not. Georgia Tech's campus possesses a truly international diversity, with student groups for every ethnicity and country imaginable. More than one-sixth of the undergraduate student body is of Asian decent, and most of the international students are from East Asia and the Middle East.

The Tech environment offers many community connections for international students and students of all other ethnic backgrounds. Even though many different ethnicities and countries are represented on campus, often times the groups of people don't mix. It is not unusual for the people from a particular country to hang out only with each other, but the University does attempt to have everyone interact through different student organizations and campus events.

### The College Prowler™ Grade on
## Diversity: B-

A high grade in Diversity indicates that ethnic minorities and international students have a notable presence on campus and that students of different economic backgrounds, religious beliefs, and sexual preferences are well-represented.

# Guys & Girls

## Students Speak Out
### ON GUYS & GIRLS

"Well, there are a lot of dorky people at Tech, but no matter what you are like, you'll find your group of people. Tech has a ton of different kinds of people. There is a good bit of really hot guys, but not many pretty girls."

"What girls? The ratio at Tech is about four to one, so there are lots of guys. The guys are all really sweet, though. Although women are a serious minority in engineering, I've never met a guy that has ever doubted my capabilities. The girls on campus are incredibly inspirational. They are definitely **some of the most capable, enthusiastic and motivated people** I've ever met in my life! Since there aren't many girls, most guys will do anything to hang out with a female, even if it means helping her out with her schoolwork."

"The guys range through the spectrum. At a school that is like 75 percent guys, I'm sure you can find whatever you're looking for. There are big **dumb jocks, smart geeky nerds, and mixes of both**, whatever it is that you are interested in. The girls are a little different. A lot of the ones I've met from sororities seem to be really fake. A lot of the girls on campus aren't too attractive. There are some hot ones here, but most of them know they're hot."

"Most of the girls are not all that, and the ones that are have attitudes. I have found a few that were enjoyable to talk to. Fifty percent of the guys are really nerdy and have nothing else to their personality. It depends on the major. Look for guys in non-engineering majors. **The girls are just ugly**. Let's put it that way."

"I'm not into the southern vibe; it's just not my deal. The **students are kind of dorky**, as tech nerds would be expected [to be]. If you're looking for hot, check out Georgia State."

## The Lowdown
### ON GUYS & GIRLS

**Women Undergrads:** 29%

**Men Undergrads:** 71%

### Birth Control Available?
Yes. The Women's Clinic offers birth control, emergency contraception, pregnancy tests, exams and STD testing.

## The College Prowler Take
### ON GUYS & GIRLS

Typical Tech students are very hardworking and highly motivated, regardless of their gender. Georgia Tech has a small contingent of stereotypical, laid-back, party-animal guys and girls. However, many guys tend to embrace more of an academic lifestyle, and are not as interested in large social events. It is possible that many of the guys consider themselves "loners." Guys at Georgia Tech outnumber girls by almost three-to-one.

Girls at Georgia Tech are usually exceptionally intelligent and enthusiastic about their course of study, but are generally more socially inclined. Sorority girls are very social, generally without exception, which works well for like-minded guys. Fraternity guys are not all so socially minded, as fraternities exist for many different reasons. Some fraternities are oriented around business, some around ethnicity, and some around academics.

**The College Prowler™ Grade on**
## Guys: B

A high grade for Guys indicates that the male population on campus is attractive, smart, friendly, and engaging, and that the school has a decent ratio of guys to girls.

**The College Prowler™ Grade on**
## Girls: C

A high grade for Girls not only implies that the women on campus are attractive, smart, friendly, and engaging, but also that there is a fair ratio of girls to guys.

# Athletics

## The Lowdown
### ON ATHLETICS

**Men's Varsity Teams:**
Football
Basketball
Baseball
Cross Country
Golf
Swimming and Diving
Tennis
Track and Field

**Women's Varsity Teams:**
Basketball
Cross Country
Softball
Swimming and Diving
Tennis
Track and Field
Volleyball

### Intramurals (IMs)
Sports offered depend on the semester. This summer: softball, 3-on-3 basketball, sand volleyball, kickball

### Club Sports
Baseball, Bowling, Crew, Cricket, Cycling, Equestrian, Golf, Gymnastics, Ice Hockey, In-line Hockey, Kayaking, Men's Lacrosse, Women's Lacrosse, Parachute, Rugby, Sailing, Men's Soccer, Women's, Soccer, Squash, Swimming, Tennis, Triathlon, Men's Ultimate Frisbee, Women's Ultimate, Frisbee, Women's Volleyball, Men's Volleyball, Water Polo, Water Skiing, and Wrestling

### Getting Tickets
You will needs tickets for games. They are pretty easy to get, but kind of pricey. For football, season tickets are $195 and a single game is $28. Order tickets online at *ramblinwreck.collegesports.com*.

**Athletic Division:**
NCAA Division I-A

**Conference:**
Atlantic Coast Conference

**School Mascot:**
Yellow Jacket

## Students Speak Out
ON ATHLETICS

> "Varsity sports are really big on campus, especially the football games. As a student, you can go to any game for free, as long as you get a ticket."

Q "Sports are not a big concern of the majority of the campus, but for those like me, it is a really big deal, and we really get into it. **IM sports are always going on**, and you can find many others on your playing level."

Q "Football is really big. Everyone goes to the games. It's a big drink fest, and everyone dresses nice. Baseball is kind of big. **Our baseball team is highly ranked,** and the men are hot! Basketball is good, but we are going through a new coach transition and our team isn't very good. Tech also has a swimming team, water polo team, lacrosse, rugby, tennis, track, etc. Intramural sports are the best! Even if you suck at a sport but want to play, you can! I played softball. They also have ultimate Frisbee, touch football, soccer, basketball, and lots of other things."

Q "**You will learn the joys of tailgating**, which is a huge deal in the South. There are lots of cool traditions here mixed with lots of great parties, too."

## The College Prowler Take
ON ATHLETICS

It is highly recommended that all students attend the home football games, and also the basketball and baseball games when possible. Tech consistently fields one of the country's best baseball teams, and has garnered four national college football championships, the last of which came in 1990. Sporting events are always great fun for students to attend, and really complete the college experience for the Tech student.

In addition to varsity sports, intramural sports are made available for all students, and offer great social opportunities for fun and games. IM sports are very popular among the students, and include basketball, ultimate Frisbee, racquetball, and flag football. Club sports are also made available. These are sports teams that do not have enough support to achieve varsity status, but are still funded by the Student Government Association. Club teams travel to other colleges and play against other club teams in their respective sports. Club sports at Georgia Tech include rugby, rowing, lacrosse, and wrestling.

**The College Prowler™ Grade on**
## Athletics: A

A high grade in Athletics indicates that students have school spirit, that sports programs are respected, that games are well-attended, and that intramurals are a prominent part of student life.

# Greek Life

### Did You Know?

In addition to social fraternities and sororities, there are also dozens of academic Greek organizations on campus.

## The Lowdown
ON GREEK LIFE

**Number of Fraternities:**
6

**Number of Sororities:**
10

**Undergrad Men in Fraternities:**
29%

**Undergrad Women in Sororities:**
20%

**Multicultural Colonies:**
Alpha Sigma Rho, Alpha Phi Alpha

**Other Greek Organizations:**
Greek Council, Greek Peer Advisors, InterFraternity Council, Order of Omega, Panhellenic Council, Hellenic Society, Rho Lambda Panhellenic Honor Society

## Students Speak Out
ON GREEK LIFE

"**Greek life is pretty big on campus, and most people think that you have to join a sorority or fraternity to have fun. You can definitely have fun without it.**"

Q "I only rushed a few places and didn't go Greek. It just wasn't for me. But a lot of my friends got involved and loved it. I had a few friends in sororities, and they seemed to love it. **It didn't really dominate their lives**, unless they wanted it to."

Q "Greek life doesn't dominate the social scene at all. **Tech won't allow it**. Greeks used to get an unfair advantage by saving old tests and passing them on to future Greeks, so now all professors are required to keep old tests online for everyone."

Q "I'm African American, so it's a little different, as far as the historically black Greek fraternities and sororities are concerned. But there is rush for everyone else, and all the Greeks get along, as far as I know. **A few of the fraternities throw great parties**."

Q "I would say that Greek life **has a larger influence here than at most schools**, since the ratio of guys to girls is so skewed. I also think Greek life is bigger on southern campuses, but this is just my image."

## The College Prowler Take
### ON GREEK LIFE

Tech's Greek system is relatively small, especially when compared to other larger state schools. Fraternities and sororities promote themselves as campus organizations that enhance student life academically, as well as socially. They supply members with Word, notes and tests from past years, and provide invaluable connections both on campus, and, later, in professional life. However, many Tech students do not have the time or the funds that are required to be involved in the Greek system. Fraternities and sororities charge dues that finance their houses and parties, and the act of joining such an organization is a long process that lasts for an entire semester. Most Tech students choose to skip the whole Greek experience altogether.

# Drug Scene

## The Lowdown
### ON DRUG SCENE

**Most Prevalent Drugs on Campus:**
Alcohol, Marijuana

**Liquor-Related Referrals:**
26

**Liquor-Related Arrests:**
67

**Drug-Related Referrals:**
4

**Drug-Related Arrests:**
16

**Drug Counseling Programs:**
Georgia Tech Counseling Center
(404) 894-2575
Hours: Monday-Friday 8 a.m.-5 p.m.

**B+**

The College Prowler™ Grade on
## Greek Life: B+

A high grade in Greek Life indicates that sororities and fraternities are not only present, but also active on campus. Other determining factors include the variety of houses available and the respect the Greek community receives from the rest of the campus.

## Students Speak Out
**ON DRUG SCENE**

"There aren't too many drugs apparent on campus. If you don't want to see drugs, they won't be there. No pressure whatsoever, but they are out there."

Q "**Hard drugs are not that popular**, but drugs such as marijuana are readily accessible, but that does not mean that they pose a threat to those who wish not to partake."

Q "The drug scene is not bad. **I have a few friends who smoke pot**. From what I've heard, there are hard drugs on campus, but I've never seen them or even heard people who've said they've seen them."

Q "I'm sure there are some drugs, but Tech does a really good job of **keeping them low**."

Q "After three years at Tech, I've never been asked for any drug. **I know some people that like to get high on the weekends**, but they never pressure anyone else. It's totally an independent decision."

## The College Prowler Take
**ON DRUG SCENE**

Georgia Tech's academic rigor is most likely a deterrent as far as widespread drug use is concerned. The drug scene is not overly visible on campus, so many parents and students might be completely unaware of its existence. However, do not be fooled. Drugs are available on campus and are used heavily in some communities of students. But, doing so does not enhance your chances for involvement in campus activities, and will most likely compound any problems that you might face academically.

**The College Prowler™ Grade on**
## Drug Scene: A-

A high grade on Drug Scene indicates that drugs are not a noticeable part of campus life; drug use is not visible, and no pressure to use them seems to exist.

# Overall Experience

## Students Speak Out
### ON OVERALL EXPERIENCE

Q "I would not trade my time here at school for anywhere else. I've loved every minute of it, no matter how stressful or hard it can be. I know coming out of school that **I'll be able to find a great job** and they help you with that. I am going to miss school when I graduate. I don't think there is another school in the country that can compare with Tech."

Q "Tech is quite possibly the best school I could've found. I looked around a lot, but nothing is quite like it. **I love living in the middle of the city**, and campus really is in the heart of downtown Atlanta. There is more to do than most have time for, including on-campus activities. As for school life, during the week it is pretty strenuous work; but on the weekends, I would have to say that Tech is one of the greatest schools in the Southeast, if not the country."

{ "Tech is great school to get an education, but not the best place to get the whole college experience. Atlanta is all right, but I don't plan to stay here after graduation."

Q "Some parts are tough, and you have to work through. Overall, I enjoyed the experience and **I am glad God put me here**. I have met some awesome people, and I value the relationships I have made here."

Q "Sometimes I wish I was somewhere a little academically easier with a better social scene, but overall, I really like Tech. **I wish there were more girls, but I've adjusted to the fact that they just aren't around**. The classes are hard. If you came here, prepare to work hard, even on weekends. Overall, I think Tech is an awesome place, but I know a lot of people who don't enjoy it."

Q "If you choose to go to Tech, **you really have to know how to budget your time**. Studying used to come second to everything. But you definitely have to have your priorities straight when it comes to Tech or any school. It's all about time management. I need to focus on raising my GPA."

## The College Prowler Take
### ON OVERALL EXPERIENCE

It is true that many Tech students might sometimes wish that they had chosen another, less-demanding school for college. Georgia Tech is very academically rigorous, to an extreme degree that alienates many students and parents. But, many see the school as a sort of "proving ground" for professional life.

**The size of the student body is not too large, and it is easy for one to get involved socially and academically without straining one's GPA. The difficulty of academic life at Georgia Tech instills a rare motivation in students here, which prepares them well for professional life. Most students feel that an education at Tech is well worth all the work that goes into it.**

# James Madison University

800 S. Main Street, Harrisonburg, VA 22807
www.jmu.edu          (540) 568-5681

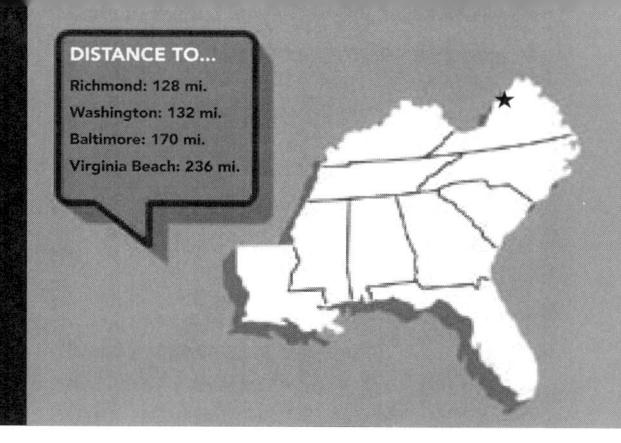

**DISTANCE TO...**
Richmond: 128 mi.
Washington: 132 mi.
Baltimore: 170 mi.
Virginia Beach: 236 mi.

*"JMU has grown from a small, all-women's college to a blossoming university and continues to be more competitive every year."*

**Total Enrollment:**
14,354

**Top 10% of High School Class:**
30%

**Average GPA:**
3.7

**Acceptance Rate:**
62%

**Tuition:**
$5,476 in-state, $14,420 out-of-state

**SAT Range (25th-75th Percentile):**
Verbal          Math            Total
540 – 620       540 – 630       1080 – 1250

**ACT Range (25th-75th Percentile):**
Verbal          Math            Total
N/A             N/A             22-26

**Most Popular Majors:**
20%  Business
12%  Social Sciences
9%   Health Professions
8%   Communications
8%   Computer and Information Sciences

**Students also applied to:***
College of William and Mary
George Mason University
University of Virginia
Virginia Tech
Mary Washington College

*For more school info check out www.collegeprowler.com*

### Table of Contents

| | |
|---|---|
| Academics | 160 |
| Local Atmosphere | 162 |
| Safety & Security | 163 |
| Facilities | 165 |
| Campus Dining | 167 |
| Campus Housing | 168 |
| Diversity | 170 |
| Guys & Girls | 171 |
| Athletics | 173 |
| Greek Life | 175 |
| Drug Scene | 176 |
| Overall Experience | 178 |

### College Prowler Report Card

| | |
|---|---|
| Academics | B |
| Local Atmosphere | B- |
| Safety & Security | A |
| Facilities | A |
| Campus Dining | B+ |
| Campus Housing | B+ |
| Diversity | D- |
| Guys | B |
| Girls | A- |
| Athletics | B- |
| Greek Life | B+ |
| Drug Scene | B- |

# Academics

## Sample Academic Clubs
Getting involved with clubs or activities at JMU is one of the best ways to meet people, and learn about yourself and your school. For example, you could write for JMU's school newspaper, *The Breeze*, sing in an a cappella group like the Blues Tones or Low Key, enjoy the outdoors with the Mountain Biking Club, or lend a helping hand with Habitat For Humanity.

## Did You Know?
James Madison University was originally a state normal and industrial school for women. The first male students tread upon school grounds in 1946 under President Duke.

**Best Places to Study:**
Taylor Down Under (TDU), Carrier Library, the Loft (in the 4th floor of Warren), the Quad (in sunny weather)

## The Lowdown
### ON ACADEMICS

**Degrees Awarded:**
Certificate, Bachelor, Master, Post-Master Certificate, Doctorate

**Undergraduate Schools:**
College of Arts and Letters, College of Business, College of Science and Mathematics, College of Integrated Science and Technology, College of Education

**Full-time Faculty:**
721

**Faculty with Terminal Degree:**
84%

**Student-to-Faculty Ratio:**
17:1

**Average Course Load:**
5 courses

**Special Degree Options:**
Combined-degree programs: Physics and Engineering, 3-2; Forestry, 3-2; non-degree seeking tracks

**AP Test Score Requirements:**
Possible credit for scores 3, 4, or 5

**IB Test Score Requirements:**
Possible credit for scores of 5, 6, or 7

## Students Speak Out
### ON ACADEMICS

"The teachers here are amazing. They know so much about the subjects that they teach and are willing to help you whenever you need it. Most of the time the classes are interesting In general, I enjoy my classes."

Q "Every teacher I've had here, no matter whether they were exciting or boring, good at teaching or just good at their subject, **they all seem to be really interested in the students** and the students' well being. Sometimes it just takes a little effort on the students' behalf to realize that most of these teachers really do care. How interesting the classes are really depends on the teacher, the subject and the student's interest level."

💬 "**I did not enjoy the general education classes** that I had to take as requirements. I found that they were boring, and the teachers were just as uninterested in them as the students were. However, now that I am in my major classes, I find that I am having more fun. Clearly, it is because I am learning about things that I am interested in, but the teachers seem to be more excited to teach the information as well."

💬 "In my experience so far, the teachers have been either very passionate and interesting, or quite boring. Mostly, it's been the former. The general education classes here are pretty tough, in comparison to other schools. JMU seems to be really serious about their education system. The key to finding a good teacher, though, is to **ask an upperclassman or an older sibling who's good.** Some of the best classes I have taken have been ones that other people told me were awesome."

💬 "I'm taking mostly general education classes this semester, and on the whole, these professors could be summarized in a word as 'liberal.' They are very opinionated, and vocal about current events and historical interpretation, and often add a liberal slant when teaching their course. As far as proficiency, **they teach and present the information effectively.** This style is new to me, as I'm an ISAT major, and my professors more often lean towards an engineering or logical style of thinking. And though often still liberal, the material is usually presented devoid of the professor's opinion or beliefs."

## The College Prowler Take
### ON ACADEMICS

At JMU, education is like a piggy bank. You get out of your education what you put into it. Not every class will come as naturally as breathing, and sometimes it takes a little extra oomph on the part of the student. On the plus side, the majority of JMU professors genuinely care for their pupils. Most professors are not only knowledgeable about their various subjects, but enthusiastic about them as well. James Madison takes pride in its curriculum and is rigid in its efforts to "round out" its student body. One prominent example is its detailed freshman curriculum. In 1997, the University switched to a new set of general education requirements. The new guidelines require students spend 41 to 43 hours taking courses in five clusters, covering all the basics. This academic quintuplet is the building block of the curriculum.

Experience is the real meat and potatoes at James Madison. Generous servings of innovative internships, extensive lab work and research in and out of the classroom, peer discussions, and hands-on homework combine to make a full meal. Students can take their pick of 77 different academic programs, covering such diverse areas as Hospitality Tourism Management, Writing and Rhetoric, Women's Studies, Geology, Communication Sciences, Disorders and Psychology, and much more. Competent and interesting programs like these, along with an equally qualified faculty, have helped JMU gain national recognition as one of the finest institutions of its kind.

**B**

The College Prowler™ Grade on
## Academics: B

A high Academics grade generally indicates that professors are knowledgeable, accessible, and genuinely interested in their students' welfare. Other determining factors include class size, how well professors communicate, and whether or not classes are engaging.

# Local Atmosphere

## City Websites

http://www.ci.harrisonburg.va.us/
http://www.hometownusa.com/va/Harrisonburg.html
http://www.city-data.com/city/Harrisonburg-Virginia.html

## The Lowdown
ON LOCAL ATMOSPHERE

**Region:**
Northern

**City, State:**
Harrisonburg, Virginia

**Setting:**
Small city in a rural setting

**Distance from Washington, DC:**
2 hours

**Distance from West Virginia:**
45 minutes to 1 hour

**Points of Interest:**
Fort Harrison, Shenandoah Valley Folk Art & Heritage Center, Harrisonburg and Dayton Farmer's Markets, Virginia Quilt Museum, Campus Art Galleries (JMU, EMU), D. Ralph Hostetter Museum of Natural History (EMU), M. T. Brackbill Planetarium (EMU), Stonewall Jackson Inn Bed & Breakfast, By the Side Of the Road Bed & Breakfast, the Joshua Wilton House

**The Great Outdoors:**
Blue Ridge Parkway, 3.0 Miles NW
Endless Caverns, 13.0 Miles N
Massanutten Resort, 10.0 Miles E
Natural Chimneys, 2.0 Miles S
Shenandoah National Park, 3.0 miles E
Civil War Battlefield, 10.0 Miles N

## Students Speak Out
ON LOCAL ATMOSPHERE

"**The atmosphere here is pretty chill, on campus and off. Harrisonburg isn't really the most exciting town to live in, but I wouldn't say there's anything to stay away from either.**"

Q "There are townies and some weird people, but there's also a lot of people who are just friendly locals. EMU is fairly close, but I have never been. There are a few areas of Harrisonburg [that] I probably wouldn't want to go in at night by myself, but overall I'd say **it's a pretty nice place to visit and explore**. Klein's is great for ice cream; there's even a place where you can paint your own pottery. Coffee shops like the Daily Grind and Artful Dodger are there."

Q "Harrisonburg is unlike any other town! **It's a small college town with not much in it**, considering that one-third of its population is college students. However, there are other universities that are very close to JMU: Bridgewater, EMU, and UVA. But, because we are in the mountains, there is hiking, and Massanutten is only a 30 minute drive away."

Q "The town is full of welcoming people. Many of them have lived here most of their lives, and they are really sweet. There is always something to do, and the mountains are close enough to go on hikes and even skiing. **I would definitely stay away from certain places in downtown Harrisonburg**. Some good places to visit are Shenandoah National Park, Kline's Ice Cream, Massanutten, Dave's Taverna, and even Luray Caverns."

> "Harrisonburg is **going through a huge transition right now** from a small town to a larger suburb, so it gives off this vibe that's a mixture of southern country life and the more fast-paced, suburban lifestyle."

> "Downtown Harrisonburg has remained charming despite the city's growth. A lot of the store owners down there have a small-town mentality that makes them personable and friendly. **There are a few vegetarian restaurants downtown**, such as 14 Carrots and the Little Grill, which I've never been to, but are supposed to be very good."

# Safety & Security

## The College Prowler Take
### ON LOCAL ATMOSPHERE

If you are looking for a thriving, exciting metropolis, like Miami or New York, you might want to think twice about making JMU your four or five year abode. However, if a medium-sized city in a country setting is what gets you going, you should be drawn here like a moth to a flame. Harrisonburg's humble charms are its natural ones: the Shenandoah Valley is a nesting place for magnificent views, breathtaking sunsets, and a plethora of outdoorsy activities. Although it's a town of only around 35,000, Harrisonburg is the commercial and agricultural center for the surrounding areas. (You'll notice immediately the numerous fields dotting the hillsides and the factories with facilities throughout town.) Harrisonburg may lack huge shopping malls, rambunctious dance clubs, and big-city thrills, but as far as historic setting, local dives, and all the necessities go, the town suffices nicely.

## The Lowdown
### ON SAFETY & SECURITY

**Number of JMU Police:**
22 full-time, 45 cadets

**Phone:**
(540) 568 - 6911 (on campus, 6911)

**Safety Services:**
(RAD) Rape Aggression Defense, emergency phones, cadet patrols/escorts, university safety engineer, four marked police cars, JMU Safety Committee

**Health Center Office Hours:**
Monday-Friday 8 a.m.-5 p.m., Saturday 8 a.m.-12 p.m., closed Sunday, open at 9 a.m. first and third Thursdays of every month

## B-

**The College Prowler™ Grade on**
### Local Atmosphere: B-

A high Local Atmosphere grade indicates that the area surrounding campus is safe and scenic. Other factors include nearby attractions, proximity to other schools, and the town's attitude toward students.

### Did You Know?
The Silent Witness Form, located online on the Public Safety Website, allows students to anonymously and confidentially report incidents of crime.

## Students Speak Out
### ON SAFETY & SECURITY

"I feel very safe off campus. You can always see policemen around. Campus cadets are around at night, and they are more than happy to escort you back to your room."

Q "Campus, itself, I feel is very safe. Personally **I've never felt threatened or in danger**, but I also try to avoid stupid situations. Don't be that girl who walks home alone at three in the morning; it's just not a good idea anywhere."

Q **"Security is tight on campus**. I always see at least two police cars during the day patrolling the campus, and even more during the weekend. The blue telephone setups around campus are there in case of any emergencies. I feel really safe when I walk around on campus, even at night."

Q "I've always felt very safe and secure on campus, even walking around by myself at four in the morning. However, **there have been incidents of stalkers and 'peeping Toms,'** which are probably typical though of a school with this many girls."

Q "I never lived on campus, but when I am there at night and in the daytime, I feel very secure. There are always police cars patrolling campus, and cadets patrolling around where the cars can't go. **Even off campus, I feel safe**. On the weekends when everyone is partying, no one really bothers you if you're walking alone. They'll just say 'hey,' and go on their merry way. Walking alone down dark alleys, or in places that are unlit or deserted, is really stupid, and I think that would be dangerous anywhere."

## The College Prowler Take
### ON SAFETY & SECURITY

As with any college, especially one where the females dominate the scene, there is bound to be the occasional peeping Tom, aggressive drunk frat boy, or lewd bathroom graffiti artist. However, students agree that generally they feel snug as a bug in a rug walking around campus, day or night. Campus police make regular visits to the scene, visibly patrolling the sidewalks on foot and the roads by car. The consistently perceptible police force, along with the emergency-phone boxes, create a feeling of safety on campus. It goes without saying, however (although we're going to say it), that common sense is the best precaution. Don't let the relative safety of JMU and Harrisonburg make you feel invincible.

**The College Prowler™ Grade on**
## Safety & Security: A

A high grade in Safety & Security means that students generally feel safe, campus police are visible, blue-light phones and escort services are readily available, and safety precautions are not overly necessary.

# Facilities

## The Lowdown ON FACILITIES

**Student Center:**
The University Center is comprised of four buildings: Taylor, Warren, Grafton-Stovall, and Phillip's Hall.

**Athletic Center:**
There is the UREC, Marilyn Crawford Fitness Center in Godwin, and a new athletic center (the Robert & Frances Plecker Athletic Performance Center) is under construction.

**Libraries:**
4; Carrier Library, Music Library, CISAT Library, Educational & Technology Media Center

**Movie Theater on Campus?**
Yes, Grafton Stovall Theater is behind Taylor and Warren.

**Coffeehouse on Campus?**
Yes, TDU and the College Center both sport a Java City.

**Popular Places to Chill:**
TDU, the quad (when it's sunny), the APL, or Barnes & Noble

## Computers

**High-Speed Network?** Yes
**Wireless Network?** Yes
**Number of Labs:** 14 labs
**Numbers of Computers:** 370
**24-Hour Labs:** Hillside Basement PC Lab
**Charge to Print?** Yes (cost is $.05 per page)
**Operating Systems:** PC, Mac

## Favorite Things to Do

On a weekend, check out Grafton-Stovall Theater to find out what's on screen. Regardless, you can watch it for $2.50. Any day of the week, hit up the gym for some racquetball, swimming, weight lifting, running, or kick boxing. Grab a cup of Joe at Java City in TDU, where you can also kick back and watch local poetry readings or bands, or play pool. Students also dig the APL on the fourth floor of Warren. Or, listen to guest lectures or concerts at Wilson Auditorium or the Convocation Center. Catch a basketball game in the spring, or a football game in the fall. Just keep in mind that there's more to life than winning!

## Did You Know?

JMU offers CMIB (CampusNet Move-In Bonanza), a special service available during the fall to help students configure their computers to the JMU network.

## Students Speak Out ON FACILITIES

"The facilities on campus are really great, especially the athletic ones. It seems as though they are always trying to improve and add field and athletic areas. Even UREC by itself is impressive enough."

> "The facilities are awesome! The athletic center is huge and has tons of equipment to use. There are lots of places to eat, and they are really clean. You always have tons of choices for food. The student resource center is also fantastic. **You can go there to learn how to do a résumé**, look for internships, and even try and figure out what type of career is best suited for you."

> "The Reading and Writing Resource Center is great. There are some really helpful people there who are willing to read your papers and critique them. It's hard to make an appointment sometimes, though, so **you have to plan ahead**."

> "The facilities are super nice! The recreational center is one of the best things about JMU. The campus also has a lot of areas where students can just chill out or do some homework. **Taylor Down Under has to be my favorite spot** because it's colorful and comfortable. I go there to do everything from sleep to eat to cram for tests."

> "I really like the campus, because it's really pretty, and it has character. The quad is the best when it's hot outside because everyone comes out to be social. We also have a really great library, dining hall, gym and all sorts of other cool places to go. **TDU is really good for commuters**, and for anyone who needs a quick nap in between classes."

> "Computer accessibility and networking is excellent. **Food is incredible** and easily accessible. UREC is an amazing recreation facility, rivaling even 'big business gyms.'"

## The College Prowler Take
### ON FACILITIES

In the mid-nineties, JMU entered in a landscaping contest; when the results were in, JMU placed high among competitors that included the White House and Disney World. On a summer day, when the sun shines down on the expansive, grassy, tree-framed quad, it's easy to see why. On one of those same warm, summer days, the quad, and just about every other spot of available grass, will be plastered with readers, sleepers, Frisbee players, trombone players, dog walkers, sunbathers, and faculty members. Although most of the campus consists of the original buildings, with their aged beauty, the newer part of campus is splendid as well. ISAT and HHS, College Center and Skyline Area residence halls (Rockingham, Blue Ridge, Chesapeake, and Potomac) are great examples of modern architecture on campus. Equipped with state-of-the-art computer labs, air-conditioning, beautiful lighting, and expert interior and exterior design, their only downside is proximity to main campus. However, the addition of these facilities only serves to enhance the appeal of James Madison as a whole.

The College Prowler™ Grade on
### Facilities: A

A high Facilities grade indicates that the campus is aesthetically pleasing and well-maintained; facilities are state-of-the-art, and libraries are exceptional. Other determining factors include the quality of both athletic and student centers and an abundance of things to do on campus.

# Campus Dining

## The Lowdown
ON CAMPUS DINING

**Freshman Meal Plan Requirement?**
Yes

**24-Hour On-Campus Eating?**
No

**Student Favorites:**
Let's Go, PC Dukes, Festival, Mrs. Green's

**Meal Plan Average Cost:**
$1,054

### Did You Know?

Punches are an integral part of every JMU meal plan, big or small. Meal Punches are exchanged at many dining locations for entry, and others for pre-ordained meal combinations. Students generally can only use one meal punch per meal period. To use up extra punches on their meal plans, students often double punch, or use both lunch and dinner punches at the same time. Just be aware that you can only double punch Monday through Thursday after 11 a.m. So much for late-night, weekend munchies!

## Students Speak Out
ON CAMPUS DINING

"As far as campus food goes, JMU's is pretty good. There is a wide variety of thigns to eat on campus, from Sbarro, to Mexican, or Italian, to delis and turkey dinners."

Q "Personally, I like the food on campus. **There are a ton of different places to eat**, and as long as you don't let yourself go to the same place all the time, you won't get sick of what's around. Everyone must try Door 4 Subs. Even though they don't take punches, those sandwiches make me happy."

Q "The food on campus is amazing. **You have a wide selection of food**, ranging from the typical pizza to sushi. There are tons of places to satisfy your appetite and they are located at different places on campus. Some good places to eat are D Hall, or the main dining hall, Let's Go, Mrs. Green's, and Festival. The main dining hall has anything you want depending on the day you go. They have everything from salad to cheeseburgers."

Q "The food is, overall, pretty good. Although, sometimes you feel like **you get stuck in a rut of eating pizza or sandwiches all the time**. My favorite places to eat are Sbarro in Market One and Cranberry Farms in Festival, which has Thanksgiving dinner type foods."

Q "JMU is ranked nationally among public universities in America for great food. **Fresh Food Company runs the dining services on campus**, and there are numerous locations to eat out. The best of these is Festival."

Q "D Hall is always good because it's **all-you-can-eat**, as is Mrs. Green's, which is a salad bar."

## The College Prowler Take
### ON CAMPUS DINING

A plethora of dining choices are available to students and faculty at JMU, regardless of the size of your stomach or appetite. Whether you feel like you could eat a rhino or merely a small salad, you will be able to find whatever you desire. Fortunately for JMUers, the food available isn't shabby either. From do-it-yourself, carry-out salad bars, to buffet-style eating, to pizza and pasta, to home-cooked turkey and mashed potatoes, it is inevitable that no stomach will leave unfilled. Students agree almost unanimously that JMU's food is wonderful—even amazing.

**B+**

The College Prowler™ Grade on
### Campus Dining: B+

Our grade on Campus Dining addresses the quality of both school-owned dining halls and independent on-campus restaurants as well as the price, availability, and variety of food.

**COLLEGE PROWLER™**

Want to know more about on-campus dining? For a detailed listing of all dining facilities on campus, check out the College Prowler book on James Madison available at *www.collegeprowler.com*.

## Campus Housing

## The Lowdown
### ON CAMPUS HOUSING

**Undergrads on Campus:**
42%

**Number of Dormitories:**
37%

**Number of University-Owned Apartments:**
1; reserved for grad students

**Room Types:**
JMU residence halls include suites, quads, triples, singles and doubles. Suites are two or three rooms; these rooms share a common lounge and sometimes a bathroom.

**Available for Rent:**
Refrigerators and carpets

**Cleaning Service?**
Community baths and lounges cleaned on a regular basis by residence staff.

**You Get:**
Single bed, individual desk with chair, built-in closet, chests of drawer, ceiling lighting, mini-blinds, telephone, TV cable hookup, Ethernet, free local/campus phone calls

**Bed Type:**
Bunk beds, some lofts, all are twin-sized extra-long beds (36 x 80 inches)

**Also Available:**
Hardwood or tile floors, carpeted rooms, AC, smoke-free housing; some suites share lounges with a small sofa, end table and two chairs.

### Did You Know?

Water beds are prohibited in all JMU residence halls due to their excessive weight and the possibility of water leakage.

### Students Speak Out
ON CAMPUS HOUSING

"There are a lot of different kinds, from the suites in the Village, to just regular halls. Where you want to live really depends on you. You'll meet more people in a hall dorm, yet a suite gives you extra room and more privacy."

"All of the dorms have their ups and downs. I have lived in the Village for two years, and it's nice because **it's so central to everything on campus**, [like] the quad and ISAT. However, it doesn't have air-conditioning. It definitely feels more like a community here. Logan and Gifford are the nicest dorms because they have just been recently renovated."

"The dorms are pretty nice, but some of the newer ones are all the way across campus, which is very inconvenient. **They have nice accommodations**, and most of them are strategically located, so food and other resources are easy to walk to."

"There are lots of different styles of dorms. I lived in 'the Village,' which has suites. I really liked that because three rooms share a sort of living room that comes furnished, so it was really nice when you had company. However, **the Village doesn't have air-conditioning**, which sounds more horrible than it really is."

"One of the things I think are cool are the suites, because **they each have four rooms that share a 'living room' area**. And they all share a bathroom, which is much better than sharing a bathroom with a whole hall."

### The College Prowler Take
ON CAMPUS HOUSING

An integral part of a typical college student's experience includes living in a dorm, or more officially, a residence hall. Students at JMU have plenty to choose from: 37 residence halls house nearly half of the undergraduate student body. The most popular dorms, hands down, are those with air-conditioning. Those dorms are Potamac and Chesapeake, which also are two of the newest additions to campus. Dorms give students a place to chill, sleep, and sometimes get busy—with homework, of course! The dorms at JMU offer scenery, community, or commodity, depending on what strikes your fancy—it's all up to you.

**B+**

**The College Prowler™ Grade on**
### Campus Housing: B+

A high Campus Housing grade indicates that dorms are clean, well-maintained, and spacious. Other determining factors include variety of dorms, proximity to classes, and social atmosphere.

# Diversity

## The Lowdown
ON DIVERSITY

### Minority Clubs
Diversity on campus may be low, but JMU seems to embrace the meager amount of diversity that is there. Hundreds of clubs on campus are available for minority students, including, but not limited to, the Asian Student Union, the Italian Cultural Society, the Middle Eastern Club, Women of Color, and Latino Student Alliance.

### Gay Tolerance
In general, Madison students are accepting, and even supportive, of the various sexual orientations present on campus. Clubs like Harmony promote awareness, tolerance, and equality.

### Economic Status
Although JMU students come from various social and economic backgrounds, the majority are from middle-class or upper-middle-class families.

**Native American:** 0%

**Asian American:** 5%

**African American:** 4%

**Hispanic:** 2%

**White:** 88%

**International:** 1%

**Out-of-State:** 29%

### Political Activity
JMU is the sixth most politically active school, according to *Mother Earth*. Clubs and organizations like Orange Band, the College Democrats, the College Republicans, EARTH, and EQUAL contribute to the atmosphere at JMU. Although the campus is not as ethnically or racially diverse as others in the country, it is diverse in belief and outlook. Madison students are relatively involved in their campus, community and nation.

### Most Popular Religions
The most prominent religions on campus are Christianity and Catholicism. Religious houses and organizations, such as the Canterbury Episcopalian house and the Catholic Campus Ministry house, can be found in areas surrounding campus and religious services, and groups meet weekly on campus.

## Students Speak Out
ON DIVERSITY

"I don't think the campus is very diverse on a superficial level, but if you look around, you'll find diversity in people from all sorts of backgrounds and life experiences."

Q "Unfortunately, **the campus is not diverse**. Most of the students here come from white, middle-class backgrounds. However, there are programs in place to diversify the campus."

Q **"The campus is extremely diverse.** There are people who are artistic, involved in sorority or fraternity life, and also people who are just here to study and learn more about themselves."

Q "Unfortunately, ethnically and racially speaking, the campus isn't too diverse. Most everyone at JMU is white, middle-class, American, and, if they're female, blonde. The good thing about JMU is that **it does embrace the minimal diversity that is around**. I am good friends with some people from other backgrounds and races, and I find them to be some of the most amazing people here!"

> "I have seen, and heard of a lot more diversity on other campuses than there is here. It's kind of pathetic, I think. People say that admissions is trying to recruit more people of different races and walks of life, which is good. I hope it works, because I think it's more fun to have people around with different viewpoints. **I really miss learning about other cultures** from the people who live in them. So hopefully that will change."

## The College Prowler Take
### ON DIVERSITY

**At first glance, JMU may seem to be about as diverse as homogenized milk. On a second glance, you still might not notice any more variety—until you realize that, at JMU, diversity runs beneath the skin. Taking beliefs, hobbies, and outlooks into consideration, students note that the campus becomes a little less clone-like. Students have commented that minorities tend to stick together, but others stand by the belief that all students at Madison freely and frequently interact. Regardless, many students express complaints about the lack of actual diversity on campus, but also realize that the miniscule amount present should be cultivated.**

The College Prowler™ Grade on
## Diversity: D-

A high grade in Diversity indicates that ethnic minorities and international students have a notable presence on campus and that students of different economic backgrounds, religious beliefs, and sexual preferences are well-represented.

# Guys & Girls

## The Lowdown
### ON GUYS & GIRLS

Women Undergrads: 60%

Men Undergrads: 40%

### Birth Control Available?
Yes. The Health Center provides contraceptives to female students through the Choices program. In addition, condoms are provided free of charge at the Health Center.

### Social Scene
Social is James Madison's middle name (the school, not the dead President). It's impossible not to find yourself at, or at least invited to, a party at JMU on a weekend or weeknight. On a Friday night, it's definitely easier to locate someone decked out and ready to rumble than someone who's chillin' at his or her pad. Although nearly extinct, rare species of non-partiers do exist, although their habitats have been greatly compromised by settlers of the rather intoxicated sort.

### Hookups or Relationships?
The nature of JMU (overpopulation of gals, deficiency of guys) creates a scene that tends to embrace random hookups. Many of the folks who are couples have been couples for a long time, some still sticking it out in relationships that started in high school. Many of the girls are together with a fellow from a different school; Bridgewater, UVA, and Virginia Tech, which are all relatively nearby, making long distance relationships equally promising.

## Dress Code

Although JMU kids tend to dress a little on the preppy side, hair tied back with ribbons, decked out in khaki pants and polo shirts with the collars turned up, there is no real dress code on campus. Some students create their own fashion with a wardrobe from vintage and thrift stores, garage sales, and random sale racks. Others go for the baggy pants and skater shoes. Finally, some go for the casual, un-showered look, which is best completed with sweat pants and a T-shirt. The best-dressed award, however, definitely goes to our future CEOs and investment bankers from the CoB (College of Business). You can spot a business major a mile away, with their pinstriped pants suits and/or nylons, and flawlessly gelled, blow-dried, and curled hair, which cannot be found in great numbers anywhere else.

## Students Speak Out
### ON GUYS & GIRLS

"There are a lot of stereotypical guys you want to avoid; then there are a lot of really great ones, too. The girls are the same way. There are a lot of great people here; sometimes you just have to weed through a bit."

Q "JMU has a reputation for having pretty girls, especially since there are more girls than guys. **There are not as many guys**, but you can find some cuties! There are a wide variety of different types of people."

Q "The guys are all jerks that just want a piece, except for a few. Generally they are good-looking. **The girls all seem the same** and the majority are self-centered. There are a few groups of people that are very nice, but they are very hard to find."

Q "There's a lot more girls than guys, which makes things interesting. **The girls here are generally very pretty**, and I'd say a good 80 percent color their hair. They have a reputation for being blonde and slim. The guys are harder to stereotype; there are all kinds."

Q "**Guys here are pretty chill**. They like to party, and they love JMU because the ratio here is 60:40. The girls here are mad hot, and there are so many of them. Most of them love to party too, so that's cool."

## The College Prowler Take
### ON GUYS & GIRLS

For the guys at JMU, it takes a glance or two to find some eye candy; for the girls, it may take some serious elbow grease and/or hiring of private detectives to find a decent male prospect, but female students will admit they do exist. Although JMU guys are harder to lump into one category, female students lament that all the hot ones are taken, and that all the rest either like their own gender or are jerks that just want a piece. JMU ladies, on the other hand, seem to be largely blonde, tan, and beautiful. These female hordes can be intimidating at times, especially in the party scene. The lack of males on campus does account for a certain amount of cattiness and competition, both of which alcohol can augment.

**The College Prowler™ Grade on**
## Guys: B

A high grade for Guys indicates that the male population on campus is attractive, smart, friendly, and engaging, and that the school has a decent ratio of guys to girls.

**The College Prowler™ Grade on**
## Girls: A-

A high grade for Girls not only implies that the women on campus are attractive, smart, friendly, and engaging, but also that there is a fair ratio of girls to guys.

# Athletics

## Club Sports
All-Girl Cheerleading, Baseball, Men's Basketball, Women's Basketball, Bowling, Caving, Equestrian, Fencing, Field Hockey, Gymnastics, Men's Lacrosse, Women's Lacrosse, Outing Club, Roller Hockey, Men's Rugby, Women's Rugby, Ski Racing, Men's Soccer, Women's Soccer, Softball, Swimming, Table Tennis, Tae Kwon Do, Tennis, Triathlon, Men's Ultimate Frisbee, Women's Ultimate Frisbee, Men's Volleyball, Women's Volleyball, Men's Water Polo, Women's Water Polo

## Intramurals
Racquetball singles, Sand Volleyball, Indoor Soccer, Bowling, Table Tennis, Walley Ball, Softball, Ultimate Frisbee, Basketball

## The Lowdown
### ON ATHLETICS

**Men's Varsity Teams:**
- Basketball
- Cross Country
- Golf
- Gymnastics
- Football
- Soccer
- Swimming and Diving
- Tennis
- Wrestling
- Track and Field

**Women's Varsity Teams:**
- Basketball
- Cross Country
- Soccer
- Swimming and Diving
- Fencing
- Golf
- Lacrosse
- Soccer
- Tennis
- Volleyball
- Softball
- Archery
- Field Hockey
- Gymnastics
- Track and Field

**Athletic Division:**
NCAA Division I (Division I-AA for football)

**Conference:**
Atlantic 10 Conference, Colonial Athletic Association, Eastern College Athletic Conference

**School Mascot:**
The Dukes

**Fields:**
Long Field, Mavck Stadium, Soccer and Lacrosse Fields, JMU Field Hockey, Track & Field Complex

## Getting Tickets
Hop over to the Athletic Ticket Office tc snag tickets for your favorite JMU sports. The ticket office is located at the D entrance of the JMU Convocation Center, and is open Monday through Friday from 9 a.m. until 5 p.m.. Worry, but not too much, about getting tickets for football, men's basketball, women's basketball, baseball, or soccer. Admission to all other home sporting events is free.

## Students Speak Out
ON ATHLETICS

## The College Prowler Take
ON ATHLETICS

"Varsity sports aren't very big, however, many people participate in IM sports. JMU has a pretty big IM program. You can do anything from water polo to ultimate Frisbee."

"Varsity sports are around, but I don't think any of them are exceptionally good or highly ranked. However, **there's a lot of school spirit** anyway. Intramural sports are really popular, and they are a lot of fun. Since you can pick co-ed and the level, you can be as serious or as laid-back as you want with it."

"Varsity sports aren't really that big. The best teams are girl's lacrosse and field hockey, which don't really even yield that big of a crowd. Even though we're not that great, there's still a relatively good turnout for football. I think **intramurals are really popular**. Most JMU students are really into keeping fit and are athletic."

"Unfortunately, the sporting events that most people think to go to are not the ones that JMU excels at. **Our football team is terrible** and out basketball team isn't that much better. However, our archery team and water polo teams are very good."

"I was kind of disappointed when I moved here because the JMU football team really isn't that great. My school freshman year had a decent football team, and **I miss the unity that a winning team can bring to a school**. However, JMU kids still have school spirit without a football team to rally behind. Everybody loves the purple and gold! And there are other varsity teams like field hockey, soccer, and archery that are really good. Intramural sports seem to be almost more popular than the varsity ones."

JMU athletic teams aren't known worldwide for their talent or success. However, students agree that they can still pimp school spirit without a winning team. Homecoming at JMU is still a riot, and a source of plenty of purple and gold pride, even if the home football team may score more bruises than points. For the athletically minded, there are plenty of events on campus, both to watch and to participate in. Teams like archery and women's hockey are quite talented and successful, although largely unnoticed by the majority of the student body. Many students do note, however, that intramural sports have garnered quite a following.

**B-**

The College Prowler™ Grade on
## Athletics: B-

A high grade in Athletics indicates that students have school spirit, that sports programs are respected, that games are well-attended, and that intramurals are a prominent part of student life.

# Greek Life

## Students Speak Out
### ON GREEK LIFE

*"Greek life doesn't take over JMU socially. I think it involves a really low percentage of students. So if you're in it, cool, if not, that's cool too. It won't hurt your social life if you're not involved."*

Q "It is said that Greek life is 12 percent of the campus. However, there are times when it feels more like 50 percent, seeing all the letters around campus. But **I do not feel that it dominates the social scene**. There are so many more opportunities for students to get involved in clubs and organizations, and most of the time, you hang out with those people."

Q "There is a noticeable interest in sorority and fraternity life on campus. **There are lots of people who are involved**, but it doesn't dominate the social scene at all. People accept the fact that there are people in Greek life and those who aren't."

Q "It's big enough that if you're into that sort of thing then you can get really involved, but if you're not then it doesn't matter. **I haven't gone to a frat party all year**. If you want to be a part of Greek life, be ready to give it a big chunk of your life; it takes a lot of time, energy and money."

Q "I don't really know much about the Greek life on campus. Sometimes it seems like there are a lot of Greeks because **you see so many T-shirts with letters** when you walk around campus. It doesn't dominate the scene at all, which is nice. The only frat parties I have been to have been really loud, crowded, and dirty. And they all have steep steps!"

## The Lowdown
### ON GREEK LIFE

**Number of Fraternities:**
15

**Number of Sororities:**
8

**Undergrad Men in Fraternities:**
18%

**Undergrad Women in Sororities:**
19%

**Multicultural Colonies:**
Hermandad de Sigma Iota Alpha
Los Latinos Unidos

### Did You Know?

On-campus sorority houses and fraternity houses have a living capacity of 28 people.

A total of 280 Greek men and women live in on-campus houses.

## The College Prowler Take
### ON GREEK LIFE

Greek life at JMU is really only prominent if you make it that way. Students agree that Greek life doesn't dominate the scene. If fraternities and sororities are your piece of pizza, there is a buffet to choose from. If not, that's cool, too. On weekends, frat houses are great, although crowded—it's the place to be for the social butterfly. Although beer prices are never steep, the stairs are! It's just something to watch out for, if you venture in that direction. Many students don't really know much about the Greek scene, but that doesn't mean it doesn't exist. In fact, there are 2,069 Greek people, of which 1,286 are sorority women and 783 are fraternity men. Driving down Main Street, you might notice letters on some of the huge, formidable buildings on either side of the street. That is about all the Greekness you will be subjected to, unless you choose to attend a Greek function, get drunk at a Greek house, or become a Greek yourself.

## Drug Scene

## The Lowdown
### ON DRUG SCENE

**Most Prevalent Drugs on Campus:**
Marijuana, Alcohol, and Caffeine

**Liquor-Related Referrals:**
356

**Liquor-Related Arrests:**
47

**Drug-Related Referrals:**
31

**Drug-Related Arrests:**
78

## B+

**The College Prowler™ Grade on**
### Greek Life: B+

A high grade in Greek Life indicates that sororities and fraternities are not only present, but also active on campus. Other determining factors include the variety of houses available and the respect the Greek community receives from the rest of the campus.

## Drug Counseling Programs
**Counseling and Student Development Center**
*http://www.jmu.edu/cousnelingctr/*
Phone: (540) 568-6552

Services: substance abuse consultation, education, screening, assessment, referrals, and individual and group counseling

### JMU Health Center
*http://www.jmu.edu/healthctr/*
Phone: (540) 568-6177

Services: alcohol and drug peer education programs, educational brochures, and health screenings

## Students Speak Out
### ON DRUG SCENE

> "There are drugs, but if you don't want to see them or be around them, then you can make it so you're not."

Q "It is present, just like on every other campus. However, **it's not something that you will see unless it's something that you are looking for**. I have never done drugs, and I have never found that I was in a situation that I didn't want to be in concerning them."

Q "People smoke pot on occasion and tons of people smoke. **Alcohol is always abused**, and the majority of the people here definitely take part in it."

Q "A good number of people smoke weed, and there are all different types of people too. If people are doing it at parties, **they're almost always very secretive about it**, and do it in a bedroom, because it's still not universally accepted. Heavier drugs aren't really talked about, and I haven't really seen a lot of drug activity, other than weed."

Q "Lots and lots of people drink, and lots and lots of people smoke pot. At almost any given party, you can find some room where the door is closed and there are four or five people smoking up behind it, having a good old time. Other than pot and drinking, I don't hear about too many other drugs being used. **The majority of students at JMU are hardcore partiers**, and the minority doesn't drink at all. There isn't really an in-between."

## The College Prowler Take
### ON DRUG SCENE

The drug of choice at JMU is alcohol. Many students don't consider alcohol to be a drug, but also seem to depend on it as if it were one. Students have taken note of the large amount of partying that goes on around the Harrisonburg vicinity. They also note that the majority of people at JMU seem to be involved, at some level, in the party scene. Of course, not everyone is, but the people who get smashed get more attention. After all, sober people don't push people through screen doors, get in loud, rowdy fights, drive drunk, pass out in strange places, or have cops surrounding their houses. In addition to alcohol, marijuana is used on a regular basis. Hardcore drugs are seldom spoken of, but like in any other college community, are doubtlessly present. At JMU, if and how much they are used is kept very hush-hush. Alcohol and marijuana use definitely outshine any other drug use around the 'Burg.

**B-**

**The College Prowler™ Grade on**
## Drug Scene: B-

A high grade on Drug Scene indicates that drugs are not a noticeable part of campus life; drug use is not visible, and no pressure to use them seems to exist.

# Overall Experience

## Students Speak Out
### ON OVERALL EXPERIENCE

Q "JMU is such a cool place to go to school. I think the teachers really are pretty good on the whole, and the people are so fun. **The girls are so hot**, too. There is a lot to do around here, if you are into being outdoors."

Q "I love JMU, and I've learned a lot since I've been at college. Sometimes, I've wondered if I'd be happier at a bigger school where sports were more important, and the school was better known, but **I can't imagine feeling more at ease than I do here**. The campus is beautiful, the people are nice, the teachers are great, and I really can't complain."

{ **"Overall, I have had a great experience here at JMU. It's something so different than I have ever experienced. The people here are so friendly, and they want to make sure that you have a good time and enjoy yourself."**

Q "The professors and administration are top-notch. The faculty is really here to help you learn, and cares more about an individual's learning experience than most colleges, I think. They dedicate themselves to each and every person. Overall, it's okay. The social scene is definitely not for people who don't drink or don't like parties. **I do wish I had chosen another college** because the majority of the people I have met care only about getting drunk and letting loose, rather then their education."

Q "I feel like I have finally found a place that I belong. JMU is home to me. The people are absolutely amazing, and most of the teachers are wonderful individuals with an incredible amount of knowledge to share. **I love the outdoorsy environment**, and the view of the mountains absolutely makes me smile every time. I am so excited to come back next year, and this year isn't even over yet! This is a truly unique school, filled with a healthy and contagious energy."

## The College Prowler Take
### ON OVERALL EXPERIENCE

Students note that Harrisonburg is a few beans short of a burrito as far as bars and nightclubs go. As a result, apartments and houses have become the main squeeze as far as parties go. Some students complain about the fact that most of JMU's students are heavily involved in the party scene. On Monday morning, as you dodge empty kegs and red plastic cups on your walk from the apartments to campus, it's hard to believe that not everyone takes part in the weekly hullabaloo. However, if you choose to abstain, even the most dedicated of drinkers will most likely respect your choice.

Although students will lodge some minor complaints about the floundering festivities, the whimsical weather, the perpetual parking pitfalls, and the lack of notable nightlife, the overall consensus is that JMU is a lovely location to live. With JMU's beautifully landscaped campus, the close proximity of the luscious Shenandoah Valley, the knowledgeable professors, friendly staff, and warm-hearted student body, it's not a huge surprise that students spend four or more very happy years at James Madison University. Freshman, upperclassmen, graduates, and transfers agree that Madison is a unique place to receive an education. The amorous attitude around town and campus has created a truly welcoming environment at James Madison University, and helped Harrisonburg live up to its nickname, "The Friendly City."

# University of Alabama

**DISTANCE TO...**
Atlanta: 202 mi.
New Orleans: 293 mi.
Panama City: 321 mi.
Memphis: 239 mi.

Box 870100 Tuscaloosa, AL 35487-0100
www.ua.edu          (205) 348-5666

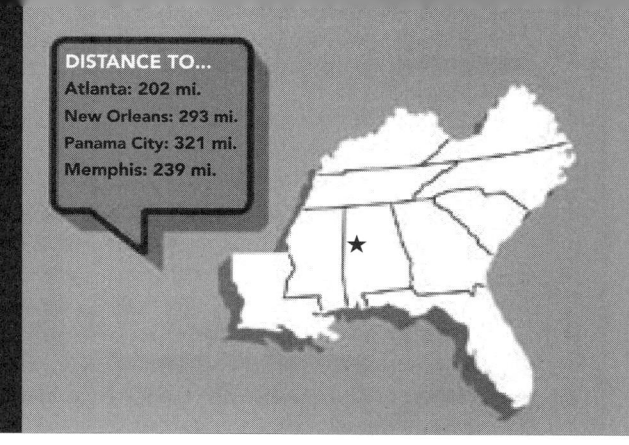

"With the growing academic programs and the comfortable, yet eclectic, environment, more and more students are coming to find Tuscaloosa as their home away from home."

**Total Enrollment:**
14,270

**Top 10% of High School Class:**
24%

**Average GPA:**
3.3

**Acceptance Rate:**
87%

**Tuition:**
$4,630 in-state, $12,664 out-of-state

**SAT Range (25th-75th Percentile):**
| Verbal | Math | Total |
|---|---|---|
| 490 – 610 | 500 – 610 | 990-1220 |

**ACT Range (25th-75th Percentile):**
| Verbal | Math | Total |
|---|---|---|
| 21-28 | 19-26 | 21-26 |

**Most Popular Majors:**
8% Finance
8% Marketing/Marketing Management
6% Business Administration and Management
4% Accounting
4% Mass Communication/Media Studies

**Students also applied to:***
Auburn University
University of Alabama-Birmingham
University of Georgia
University of Mississippi

*For more school info check out www.collegeprowler.com

## Table of Contents

| | |
|---|---|
| Academics | 180 |
| Local Atmosphere | 182 |
| Safety & Security | 183 |
| Facilities | 185 |
| Campus Dining | 186 |
| Campus Housing | 188 |
| Diversity | 189 |
| Guys & Girls | 191 |
| Athletics | 193 |
| Greek Life | 195 |
| Drug Scene | 196 |
| Overall Experience | 198 |

## College Prowler Report Card

| | |
|---|---|
| Academics | B- |
| Local Atmosphere | B |
| Safety & Security | A- |
| Facilities | A- |
| Campus Dining | B |
| Campus Housing | B- |
| Diversity | D+ |
| Guys | B+ |
| Girls | A |
| Athletics | A+ |
| Greek Life | A |
| Drug Scene | B- |

# Academics

## The Lowdown
### ON ACADEMICS

**Special Academics Programs**
Academic Common Market, Blount Undergraduate Initiative, Capstone International, English Language Institute, Freshman Seminars, Fulbright Programs, Interim Program, Mallet Assembly, McNair Scholars Program, New College, Parker-Adams Year Program

**Sample Academic Clubs**
The Academy, Alabama Student Society for Communication Arts, Alpha Kappa Psi, Ambassadors of the College of Engineering, American Choral Directors Association, American Institute of Aeronautics and Astronautics (AIAA), American Marketing Association, Executive Engineering Council, Modern Languages and Classics Graduate Student Association, New College, Philosophy Club, Sigma Alpha Iota, Society of Physics Students, Student Dietetic Association

**Degrees Awarded:**
Bachelor, Master, Doctorate

**Undergraduate Schools:**
College of Arts & Sciences, College of Commerce and Business Administration, College of Communication and Information Sciences, College of Community Health Sciences, College of Education, College of Engineering, College of Human Environmental Sciences, Capstone College of Nursing, School of Social Work

**Full-time Faculty:**
864

**Faculty with Terminal Degree:**
89%

**Student-to-Faculty Ratio:**
19:1

**Average Course Load:**
15 hours

**Did You Know?**
Need a tutor? The Center for Teaching and Learning, located in 124 Osband Hall, offers tutorial services in math, writing, reading, and other subjects.

Want to get one of those boring core classes out of the way without leaving your house? Try one of UA's on-line courses.

**Best Places to Study:**
Any of the UA libraries
The Ferguson Center

## Students Speak Out
ON ACADEMICS

> "Your academic experience here depends on the department you're in. They range in quality from 'stunning' to 'where the hell did you graduate from? Auburn?!'"

Q "Grad students are the best teachers. They're more understanding, and they know what it's like to be **loaded down with work**."

Q "Teachers are great once you start taking the classes specific to your major. The core classes are better than you might expect, but sometimes **big classes might make you feel left out**, just like at almost any major university. But, many teachers are making efforts to eliminate that feeling from their classes. Overall, the professors here are all above average and very helpful if you seek help from them."

Q "Most **teachers I've encountered are excellent**. There are, however, a few teachers I wish I had never encountered. The classes seem interesting based on the skill and likability of the teacher."

Q "Most of the teachers are helpful and generally care about their students. However, some are stuck on the Ph.D. and they don't care whether you pass or fail or what problems or concerns you have about the class. My classes are interesting for the most part, but sometimes I feel like I'm on a merry-go-round, having the **same information thrown at me over and over**."

## The College Prowler Take
ON ACADEMICS

At the University of Alabama, the quality of the teachers and classes are, overall, exceptional. However, like at all universities, there are always a few bad seeds. Students usually find the classes for their major to be the most interesting, since this is what they have chosen to do with their lives. But, don't worry, students have ways of finding out which core classes are taught by the best teachers. It's good to do a little research about your teacher before picking their class. Just ask around, because students love talking about teachers that made their learning experiences either better or worse. If you do find yourself in a class that has you bored or confused, contact your teacher through e-mail, during office hours, or by phone. If students talk to their teachers about problems they are having, the problems can usually be fixed.

**B-**

**The College Prowler™ Grade on**
## Academics: B-

A high Academics grade generally indicates that professors are knowledgeable, accessible, and genuinely interested in their students' welfare. Other determining factors include class size, how well professors communicate, and whether or not classes are engaging.

# Local Atmosphere

**City Websites**
http://www.tuscaloosa-alabama.com/
http://www.ci.tuscaloosa.al.us/

## Students Speak Out
ON LOCAL ATMOSPHERE

## The Lowdown
ON LOCAL ATMOSPHERE

"Tuscaloosa is a mid-sized town. A black college [Stillman] and a junior college [Shelton] are in the area, but nothing big. It gets crazy during football season."

Q "There are two junior colleges within 15 minutes of UA. We have two malls in town, and there is also **lots of historic stuff that you can visit**. Three of the buildings on campus were here during the Civil War and are still in use."

Q "A popular T-shirt slogan in Tuscaloosa is, 'A drinking town with a football problem.' **You've got to love football** or at least be willing to love it if you're going to fit in here. In Alabama, there are several smaller colleges, but when it comes down to it, there is pretty much just the University and that other school [Auburn University]. But there's also a pretty big junior college here in Tuscaloosa."

Q "The atmosphere in Tuscaloosa is a **perfect example of the common college town stereotype**. There's all-night partying, long nights at the bars on the strip, and of course Alabama football games in the fall. Although partying and having fun with your friends is part of Tuscaloosa's nightlife for students, so is spending long hours in the University's libraries."

**Region:**
South

**City, State:**
Tuscaloosa, Alabama

**Setting:**
Small town

**Distance from Atlanta, GA:**
3 hours, 20 minutes

**Distance from New Orleans, LA:**
4 hours, 45 minutes

**Points of Interest:**
Paul W. Bryant Museum, Denny Chimes, Bama Theatre, Mercedes-Benz Visitor Center & Museum, Lake Tuscaloosa, the Cliffs, Hurricane Creek, the Strip, Bryant Denny Stadium, Alabama Museum of Natural History

**Closest Shopping Malls or Plazas:**
University Mall, University Town Center, McFarland Mall, Downtown Plaza

Q "The atmosphere in Tuscaloosa is **full of all different kinds of people, which makes it unique**. The atmosphere during the fall is full of school spirit, tradition, and memories that will last a lifetime. The spring is laid-back, relaxed, and beautiful in nature. A college nearby is Shelton, a community college. However, UA is in its own world, which is nice: you feel like you're in a crimson bubble."

## The College Prowler Take
ON LOCAL ATMOSPHERE

Tuscaloosa is a typical southern college town, with a lot of its attention spent on football. To live in this town, you must be able to accept that in the fall 'Bama football takes over. The whole town celebrates game days and school spirit is everywhere, but don't think that the excitement stops there. When football season is over, there are still tons of things to do in this town. On "the Strip," you can always find good food, your favorite bands, and unique shopping. With all that's offered in Tuscaloosa, many students say that there's never a dull moment. Those who love hiking, camping, and water sports will find a veritable heaven-on-earth in Tuscaloosa.

# Safety & Security

## The Lowdown
ON SAFETY & SECURITY

**Number of UA Police Officers:**
40+

**Phone:**
(205) 348-5454

**Website:**
*http://www.cofc.edu/publicsafety*

**Health Center Office Hours:**
Monday – Friday 8 a.m. – 6 p.m.
Saturday – Sunday 1 p.m. – 4 p.m.

**Website:**
*http://www.wellness.cofc.edu/health.htm*

**Safety Services:**
Escort Service, Emergency Phones, Trolley

**B**

The College Prowler™ Grade on
## Local Atmosphere: B
A high Local Atmosphere grade indicates that the area surrounding campus is safe and scenic. Other factors include nearby attractions, proximity to other schools, and the town's attitude toward students.

### Did You Know?

Leaving the bars and can't drive home? Then don't. Take advantage of the Tuscaloosa Trolley.

Out after-hours and stuck without a ride? Try a free ride! The Bama Escort Service, a program of the UA police, will give you a free car ride between locations on campus. Call 348-RIDE.

"I would say that safety and security are above average. Crime is not bad, and the police are always pretty much on top of things. **The dorms are patrolled well**, and most all-girls dorms even have parking lot escorts. Also, the most commonly frequented areas are well-lit and have emergency phones installed nearby."

## The College Prowler Take
### ON SAFETY & SECURITY

## Students Speak Out
### ON SAFETY & SECURITY

"There are lots of telephones for security, but light is scarce on some parts of campus."

"Security is pretty good. When it's lacking, it's usually because students haven't taken the necessary precautions. Don't walk alone at night, because you never have to. The campus police offer **escort services to drive you at night**."

"To the best of my knowledge, safety and security aren't really a big problem on campus. Of course, you have to be smart about things—don't do anything like wander around campus by yourself late at night; although, plenty of people do and don't generally have a problem, but it's best to be careful. The campus police are great. There are **emergency phones all over campus** in case you ever have a problem. The police also offer an escort service that will take you to and from places on campus, such as the dorms, the computer labs, or the recreation center, late at night or any time that you don't feel comfortable driving or walking somewhere alone."

"I haven't had much of a problem with the security on campus. Now, I have heard **stories of a few bad things happening** over the past couple of years, but any university will have isolated occurrences."

For the most part, students agree that the UA police do their job. Although some students can recall a few problems in the past, they believe that no school is completely safe. At UA, there's no reason to walk alone at night since the school offers a free escort service, the Bama Escort Service, which provides students with free rides between campus locations. There are also plenty of emergency (blue) phones located all around campus for students to use if they have any problems. And there's no worry when it comes to the dorms. UA police patrol the dorm areas and there are RAs in all of the dorms. Although they do feel safe, students still express how important it is to be smart while on campus, and off campus as well.

**A-**

### The College Prowler™ Grade on
## Safety & Security: A-

A high grade in Safety & Security means that students generally feel safe, campus police are visible, blue-light phones and escort services are readily available, and safety precautions are not overly necessary.

# Facilities

## Favorite Things to Do
Besides attending Bama athletic events, students enjoy floating down the Lazy River or going down water slides at the Rec Center. After taking a dip in the pool, you can enjoy a movie at the Ferguson Center for only $1. While at the Ferg, grab a bite to eat, or play a game of pool with your friends in the Ferguson Center Pool Hall. Check out the Crimson Calendar, *http://events.ua.edu/*, often to find out what events are going on each month on campus.

## The Lowdown
### ON FACILITIES

## Computers
**High-Speed Network?** Yes
**Wireless Network?** Yes
**Number of Labs:** 60+
**Number of Computers:** About 2,000
**24-Hour Labs:** 127 Gordon Palmer Hall
**Charge to Print:** Yes

**Student Center:**
The Ferguson Center (the Ferg)

**Libraries:**
9

**Athletic Center:**
The Student Recreational Center (the Rec)

**Movie Theater on Campus?**
Yes, the Ferguson Center

**Bar on Campus?**
No, but the Strip is within walking distance of UA.

**Coffee on Campus?**
Starbucks in the Ferguson Center and Java City in the Gorgas Library

**Popular Places to Chill:**
The Ferg, the quad, the Rec pool

## Students Speak Out
### ON FACILITIES

"Our rec center is great. We just got a new pool, and it's lots of fun. Pretty much whatever you want to do on campus, you can."

Q "The facilities are average. The Ferguson Student Center is nice. It has a large dining area, a 24-hour post office, a huge game room, a ballroom, a theater where free movies are shown year-round, and a supply store. Most of the **buildings on campus are old and very historic-looking**. That's not to say that they aren't good, but they aren't new. They are all designed in a Greek or Victorian architectural style. They are very beautiful, and the quad is very scenic. The athletic facilities are great."

Q "Most buildings are nice, and with **all the renovations**, I believe this campus is moving up."

Q "Most of the **facilities are clean and spacious**. It's evident that the University devotes a lot of time and money to making the environment here very comfortable."

Q "The on-campus facilities are very clean and **accessible to all students**. Many of the buildings on campus are older, allowing all the history that they possess to shine through."

# Campus Dining

## The College Prowler Take
ON FACILITIES

UA students don't only enjoy using the facilities on campus, but they also take pride in them. The Ferguson Center is one of the most visited facilities on campus. It offers students numerous places to eat, a post office, a supply store, and even pool tables. The Ferg is a great place to go between classes. You can always find students there reading, studying, or hanging out around Starbucks. The Student Recreational Center (the Rec) is another widely used facility at UA. It offers plenty of exercise equipment for various needs and several workout classes. Overall, students enjoy the facilities on campus and think that the University successfully strives to keep them clean and comfortable.

## The Lowdown
ON CAMPUS DINING

**Freshman Meal Plan Requirement?**
No

**24-Hour On-Campus Eating?**
Paty's 24 Hour Diner is open all night and Wing's stays open until 2 a.m.

**Student Favorites:**
The Ferguson Center Food Court, the Freshfood Company, Buffalo Phil's, Blimpie

**Meal Plan Average Cost:**
There are eight different meal plans that students can choose from. The costs range from $600 to $1,200 per semester, depending on how many meals students want per week.

### Did you know?
There are 100 vending machines on campus that accept Bama Cash.

Bama Dining allows parents to send birthday cakes to let their students know they care. There are two different size cakes. Both include paper plates, napkins, and forks.

## A-

### The College Prowler™ Grade on
**Facilities: A-**

A high Facilities grade indicates that the campus is aesthetically pleasing and well-maintained; facilities are state-of-the-art, and libraries are exceptional. Other determining factors include the quality of both athletic and student centers and an abundance of things to do on campus.

## Students Speak Out
ON CAMPUS DINING

"The food isn't too bad. I recommend a meal plan for your first year, or at least your first semester, because eating in the dining halls is a good way to meet people."

Q "At the student center there are **two large food courts for all the students' cravings**. Also within all the campus dorms there are multiple food places, like Julia's and Paty's 24 Hour Diner, to grab a bite to eat for students on the run."

Q "The **food on campus is actually pretty good!** You have to try the Fresh Food Company at the Ferg—it's awesome!"

Q "Food on campus is good, but the prices are high. Burke cooks the down-home food, while **the Fresh Food Company has a healthier selection**."

Q "Food is pretty decent. Over the span of all the campus-dining establishments, there is a pretty good variety of good choices. Fresh Food Company offers a unique selection and the Ferguson Center provides **many great choices**. Food at Home Zone is usually good if you need some home cooking."

## The College Prowler Take
ON CAMPUS DINING

Students enjoy the wide variety of food that UA's campus offers. When living on campus, meal plans are said to be the way to go. However, they are not mandatory. If students need to grab a bite on the go, the Ferg offers many fast food restaurants, including Chick-fil-A, Burger King, and many others. If in a real rush, grab a snack from one of the many vending machines on campus and use your Action Card. If it is late, students can enjoy Paty's 24 Hour Diner or Wing's. Also, many of the dorms have buffet-style restaurants that offer the students all they can eat for a set price. Students say the food on campus can be pricey, but with Bama Cash and Dining Dollars students can enjoy campus food without using their own money.

**B**

For more info on what Campus Dining has to offer, check out the full-length guide on the University of Alabama, available at www.collegeprowler.com.

The College Prowler™ Grade on
## Campus Dining: B

Our grade on Campus Dining addresses the quality of both school-owned dining halls and independent on-campus restaurants as well as the price, availability, and variety of food.

# Campus Housing

**Did you know?**

All campus residents have access to UA's movie channel, which plays different movies every week.

## The Lowdown
ON CAMPUS HOUSING

## Students Speak Out
ON CAMPUS HOUSING

**Undergrads on Campus:**
25%

**Number of Dormitories:**
15

**Number of College-Owned Apartments:**
3

**Room Types:**
Single – rooms which only include one person, but are the same size as a double
Double – rooms which include two people
Suites – the biggest dorm rooms available

**Cleaning Service?**
Common areas are cleaned in each hall every day during the week. This includes hallways, lobbies, study rooms, and bathrooms. Students in apartments are responsible for cleaning their own rooms.

**You Get:**
Bed, desk and chair, dresser, closet, free campus and local phone calls, basic cable

**Bed-Type:**
Standard twin beds are available in each room.

**Also Available:**
Long distance phone calls, extra cable channels, ResNet Internet connections

"The dorms are great. They're not necessarily 'tidy,' but they're a great way to meet people from all over the place—especially freshmen girls, like in Tutwiler."

"The dorms on campus aren't bad at all. I lived in **Rose Towers, which is an apartment-style co-ed dorm**. We had three people sharing a two bedroom, one bathroom, furnished apartment."

"**I don't think there's such a thing as a 'nice' dorm** at UA, but none of them are too bad either."

"**You either love the dorms or you hate them**. If you're the type of person who likes to be around others then the dorms are for you. But, even if you need your own space, Alabama has individual rooms too. It all depends on what you like."

"Its college! Every student has to, and should, experience dorm life! **Tutwiler is the popular girls dorm**, which is fun because most of your friends will be living in there, just on different floors. That's the nice part—you don't have to drive to see them. You can just take the stairs or elevator. Small rooms and community bathrooms; it's up to you to make the most out of it."

## The College Prowler Take
### ON CAMPUS HOUSING

It all depends on what type of living environment students are familiar with and can adjust to. If you are the type that needs your own space, then a place like Rose Towers may be best for you. Most students that live or lived in a dorm recommend living in one for at least the first year at UA. The social environment that the dorms offer helps students make friends and adjust to the campus easier. Students say checking out all the dorms before deciding which one to live in is the best way to find where you belong. Dorm life is a part of college, and students at UA say the experience is what makes living in them fun. Although some are nicer than others, students feel that it's all about the friends you make while living there.

## Diversity

### The Lowdown
### ON DIVERSITY

**Native American:** 1%

**Asian American:** 1%

**African American:** 15%

**Hispanic:** 1%

**White:** 81%

**International:** 1%

**Unknown:** 0%

**Out-of-State:** 21%

### Minority Clubs
UA has over 200 student organizations, so there are clubs for everyone. At UA there are many minority clubs that sponsor events and throw parties. There are a number of African American fraternities and sororities on campus, along with multicultural organizations. There are also many international clubs offered since UA's international program is so popular.

## B-

**The College Prowler™ Grade on**
### Campus Housing: B-

A high Campus Housing grade indicates that dorms are clean, well-maintained, and spacious. Other determining factors include variety of dorms, proximity to classes, and social atmosphere.

## Most Popular Religions

There are about 20 religious organizations at UA, and they are very active on campus. Most of the groups chalk the quad to let students know about events that they are holding.

## Political Activity

UA has five political organizations on campus, and the College Democrats and the College Republicans are among the most popular of them. During any state or national election these organizations can usually be found handing out stickers and encouraging students to vote.

## Gay Tolerance

The Queer-Straight Alliance organization is widely known around campus. However, the gay community is rather small and mostly quiet.

## Economic Status

At UA there are students from all economic backgrounds. Most of the students refer to the Greeks as "the rich kids."

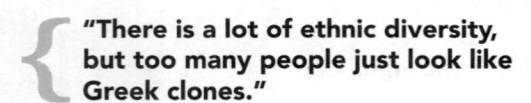

## Students Speak Out
### ON DIVERSITY

{ "There is a lot of ethnic diversity, but too many people just look like Greek clones."

Q "The campus has a **high percentage of diversity on it**. People from all over the United States and the world come to Alabama to learn and to be part of the university. With all the different types of ethnic groups and people on campus, there's bound to be a lot of diversity."

Q "There is an even distribution of guys and girls. I don't know what the statistics are, but there is a relatively **fair distribution of black and white students** as well. There are more white students than black students, though. There are also some foreign students, but most of them are graduate students. Racial issues are not as big a deal as they were 20 years ago. People are raised differently these days and are taught to accept everyone."

Q "We have a sizable population of international students; especially in the Engineering department—my major is Chemical Engineering. **The whole Civil Rights thing was big here** on campus during its time, but we're still a pretty diverse school. I've visited schools that were much worse—Mississippi, for example—but I've also visited schools that were better."

Q "I would say that the campus is fairly diverse. It's obviously comprised **mostly of white males and females**, but there are a good number of African Americans as well as students from all the corners of the globe."

## The College Prowler Take
### ON DIVERSITY

UA's student body is overwhelmingly white. If you're from a small town, UA may seem pretty diverse, but people from big cities will find it decidedly homogenous. But, the students here are always willing to learn and are open to meeting new people and experiencing new things, even if those people are few and far between. Students today feel that racial and ethnic differences are not the problem that they once were. UA is not separated by how much money students have, their color, or their beliefs. For the most part, the students are accepting of others and have the opportunity to meet different kinds of people while being on this campus, although not nearly to the extent as at many other colleges.

**D+**

The College Prowler™ Grade on
### Diversity: D+

A high grade in Diversity indicates that ethnic minorities and international students have a notable presence on campus and that students of different economic backgrounds, religious beliefs, and sexual preferences are well-represented.

# Guys & Girls

## The Lowdown
ON GUYS & GIRLS

**Women Undergrads:** 53%

**Men Undergrads:** 47%

## Hookups or Relationships?
There are as many students in relationships as there are that aren't. Usually the younger students are not as involved in serious relationships as the older ones. The younger students are generally wrapped up in the overwhelming social scene and are too busy meeting people to settle down, although this is not true for everyone. Most UA students recommend spending your first year on campus meeting other students and developing friendships.

## Dress Code
The dress code on campus is usually the same for everyone—laid-back. Most of the students come to class in jeans and T-shirts. But, going out on the town entails a whole different wardrobe. For social events, most students dress up according to the occasion.

At UA, there's a stereotypical dress code for the Greek students. Students believe you can tell who is Greek by what they wear. Chances are, if they're wearing a button-down Polo, a Northface jacket, or sunglasses around their neck, they're considered to be "fratastic," another word for being Greek.

## Birth Control Available?
Yes, female students who have had an exam with their doctor or have had an exam with the Russell Student Health Center can have their birth control prescriptions filled.

## Social Scene
UA is full of southern hospitality. The students are very interactive and usually very outspoken. If freshmen are ever lost around campus, they shouldn't be afraid to ask someone for help, and if you missed a day of class then just ask someone near you for notes. Don't be scared of this campus; the students are very friendly and willing to help. Outside of class, most students are busy participating in organizations or hanging out on the Strip. If you want to become more social at UA, join a club or an intramural sport. These are great ways to meet new people.

## Students Speak Out
ON GUYS & GIRLS

"If you are looking for hot guys with lots of ambition, check out the business school. Sorority girls have a reputation for being snotty, but I've found that's not always the case."

Q "From what I hear, the guys here are hotties. They all usually have **shaggy 'Greek' haircuts and wear short shorts**. There is also an abundance of beautiful females here. I guess there aren't many unattractive people in Tuscaloosa in general."

Q "Just like everybody else, but I will say girls here are **beautiful southern girls**, and everybody dresses up to go out so we always look nice. Guys are shaggy-haired, laid-back guys, and most of them always look really nice as well."

Q "The frat guys all look alike. They wear a T-shirt from some Greek party and their New Balances or Birks and an old nasty hat, and **they all drive some sort of big 4x4 truck** that has their Greek letters on the back. The other guys on campus are just your average guys with a southern accent. Girls are very cliquish, especially if they are in a sorority. They follow certain guidelines of whom they can and cannot associate with."

Q "There are plenty of guys and girls on this campus. Like anywhere else you might go, there will be **some hot people and some not-so-hot people,** some nice people and some not-so-nice people, but around here there do seem to be more nice people than usual."

## The College Prowler Take
### ON GUYS & GIRLS

Southern gentlemen and southern belles swarm around this campus like bees around a hive. There are more girls than guys at UA, and the guys say they're in heaven—but the girls aren't complaining either. Like at all schools, you won't find everyone you meet to be a supermodel, but don't fret if that's what you're into. There's plenty of eye candy to go around. With so many hot students roaming about, students find it easy to hook up. Walk to class or take a walk around the quad and check out all the hotties that Bama has to offer. According to the students, they're everywhere! The guys at the business school seem to enjoy the best reputation for hotness among the guys on campus, and the girls are thought to be gorgeous in general.

**COLLEGE PROWLER™**

Wanna know more about UA hotties? Check out the College Prowler book on the University of Alabama available at *www.collegeprowler.com.*

**B+**

**A**

The College Prowler™ Grade on
### Guys: B+

A high grade for Guys indicates that the male population on campus is attractive, smart, friendly, and engaging, and that the school has a decent ratio of guys to girls.

The College Prowler™ Grade on
### Girls: A

A high grade for Girls not only implies that the women on campus are attractive, smart, friendly, and engaging, but also that there is a fair ratio of girls to guys.

# Athletics

**Athletic Division:**
NCAA Division I

**Conference:**
Southeastern Conference

**School Mascot:**
An elephant named Big Al

## The Lowdown
ON ATHLETICS

### Most Popular Sports
Football is by far the most popular sport at UA. It's not only a popular sport, it's a tradition. All other sports take a back seat to football, but basketball and gymnastics gather a pretty big crowd as well.

### Overlooked Teams
The women's golf team has received a large number of awards over the years, but if you ask UA students what they know about the women's golf program, most won't have too much to say.

**Men's Varsity Teams:**
Basketball
Swimming
Baseball
Football
Cross Country
Diving
Golf
Tennis
Track & Field

**Women's Varsity Teams:**
Basketball
Volleyball
Gymnastics
Swimming
Soccer
Softball
Cross Country
Diving
Golf
Tennis
Track & Field

### Did You Know?
**How Crimson Tide Got Its Name:**

In the early newspapers Alabama's football team was listed as the "varsity" or the "Crimson White" after the school colors. The "Thin Red Line" was the first nickname that became popular and was used by numerous headline writers. This nickname was used until 1906. The name "Crimson Tide" is said to have been first used by Hugh Roberts, a former sports editor of the Birmingham Age-Herald. He used "Crimson Tide" in describing an Alabama-Auburn game played in Birmingham in 1907. The game was played in a sea of red mud and it looked as Auburn was going to win. But the "Thin Red Line" turned the game around and held Auburn to a 6-6 tie. This game is where the name "Crimson Tide" came from.

## Club Sports
Bama Ultimate Frisbee, Lacrosse, Rugby, Water Skiing, Crew, Soccer, Volleyball, Team, Handball, Cricket, Equestrian, Cycling

## Intramurals
Badminton, Basketball, Bowling, Football, Golf, Horseshoes, Inner-Tube Water Polo, Racquetball, Soccer, Softball, Swimming, Table Tennis, Track and Field, Volleyball, Wiffleball, Wrestling

## Fields
Bryant-Denny Stadium, Sam Bailey Stadium, Sewell-Thomas Stadium, Soccer Field, Softball Stadium, The Rec (IM) fields, Varsity Tennis Courts

## Getting Tickets

Getting student tickets for UA athletic events are probably the easiest thing to do on this campus. Students can get into any event by just showing their Action Card, except for football games. Getting football tickets consists of a little more. All students have to do is sign up for football tickets online (*www.rolltide.com*). The student package consists of one ticket for every home football game, and it costs $35. This is a great deal since these tickets are usually sold around campus at much higher prices.

## Students Speak Out
### ON ATHLETICS

> "Football, football, and football. In the fall, Tide fans are full of spirit and tradition. Mark your calendar—every Saturday will be booked for Alabama football. Roll Tide!"

Q "Varsity sports, and especially football, are the major focus of the entire University. Sports provide a social environment more than anything. Everyone goes to football games whether they like football or not because it's 'the thing to do.' I'm a huge Bama fan, and to me, there's **nothing better than 85,000 people going nuts at a Bama football game**. Our basketball and baseball teams were both nationally ranked this season, and our gymnastics team won the national gymnastics championship."

Q "Football is a religion. Tuscaloosa is known as 'a drinking town with a football problem.' We take great **pride in all of our varsity sports,** and IM sports are popular year round. I hear a lot of people participate in things like ultimate Frisbee, soccer, softball, flag football, and other IMs."

Q "There is a great student recreation center, called 'the Rec,' and there are intramural sports practically all year round. Just about **every sport known to man is available** as an intramural sport, and it's all free."

Q "There are plenty of athletic activities on campus! We have a huge recreational center where you can work out and sign up to participate in IM sports. I am sure that you have heard of our football tradition, but the basketball games are also a lot of fun. There is **always something going on with University of Alabama athletics!**"

## The College Prowler Take
### ON ATHLETICS

Football is almost a religion in Alabama. It's a tradition that takes over the school, and even the surrounding town. Students count down the days until the fall in anticipation of the start of football frenzy. The town, the campus, and people from all over pack into the Bryant-Denny Stadium for every home game to show their Crimson Pride. Football game days are a statewide holiday in Alabama. If you're not a football fan, don't fret. All you have to do is experience just one Bama game in the student section and you will be changed into a fan.

# A+

### The College Prowler™ Grade on
## Athletics: A+

A high grade in Athletics indicates that students have school spirit, that sports programs are respected, that games are well-attended, and that intramurals are a prominent part of student life.

# Greek Life

## The Lowdown
ON GREEK LIFE

**Number of Fraternities:**
26

**Number of Sororities:**
20

**Undergrad Men in Fraternities:**
19%

**Undergrad Women in Sororities:**
26%

**Multicultural Colonies:**
Delta Xi Phi, Alpha Delta Sigma

**Other Greek Organizations:**
Greek Council, Greek Peer Advisors, Interfraternity Council, Order of Omega, Panhellenic Council

## Did You Know?

During Homecoming Week, the sororities battle against each other to win the Spirit Cup. All of the girls spend hours decorating the front of their house with chicken wire and colored pomps. It turns out to look like a huge picture the size of the sorority house.

Every fall, each fraternity has their big party that lasts all weekend, and sometimes all week. Each fraternity has the same theme every year, and they usually have cookouts during the days and the best bands at night. Everyone is welcomed to these events.

## Students Speak Out
ON GREEK LIFE

"**Greek life dominates campus life; avoid it if you don't think that it's for you.**"

Q "Alabama has what some consider the **largest Old South Greek system in the country**. Ole Miss is the only school that compares with Bama. If you're into that sort of thing then go for it, but if you aren't, then they aren't going to stop you or anything if you don't want to get involved."

Q "Only about 20 percent of the students here join Greek organizations, but **Greeks pretty much run the political bodies** and are quite outspoken. I'm not anti-Greek or anything, and I actually think that they're given a really hard time about racial issues and such, but while it's certainly something to consider as a way to make friends, there are numerous other opportunities to do the same like clubs, sports, and other campus organizations."

💬 "The Greek scene at Bama is very big. **Their presence is sometimes a little too influential**, but they throw great parties and most of them are cool to be around."

💬 "If you are a Greek, then yes, it dominates your social scene. If you're not, then it doesn't. Your **social scene is yours and it can be dominated by whatever you choose**—Greeks, chasing bands, church, athletics, drugs, clubs—whatever you choose, it is purely up to you."

## The College Prowler Take
### ON GREEK LIFE

Students say the Greeks are easy to point out since the have a certain look to them. This look is considered to be on the preppy side. It is said that the Greeks always come into class wearing T-shirts with their letters on them, and their cars have stickers revealing which Greek organization they are apart of. The fraternity houses are always throwing parties and all students are usually welcome, so many independent students attend these parties as well. The Greek stereotype is that they are rich, stuck-up, and that they don't care to be your friend unless you, too, are a part of the Greek system. There are plenty of students who chose not to go Greek, but they say they still have many good friends that are.

**A**

The College Prowler™ Grade on
## Greek Life: A

A high grade in Greek Life indicates that sororities and fraternities are not only present, but also active on campus. Other determining factors include the variety of houses available and the respect the Greek community receives from the rest of the campus.

# Drug Scene

## The Lowdown
### ON DRUG SCENE

**Most Prevalent Drugs on Campus:**
Marijuana and prescription drugs

**Liquor-Related Referrals:**
181

**Liquor-Related Arrests:**
53

**Drug-Related Referrals:**
18

**Drug-Related Arrests:**
16

**Drug Counseling Programs:**
The Counseling Center often conducts screenings. They offer individual therapy to students, and they also offer three support groups. The Counseling Center gives prevention lectures on campus to inform students of drug and alcohol abuse.

## Students Speak Out
ON DRUG SCENE

## The College Prowler Take
ON DRUG SCENE

> "People are always looking for Adderall during exams, and it is easy to get. During midterms and final exam time, it is everywhere."

Q "The University has always been known for its **never-ending presence of drugs, particularly cocaine**. But, being a student here for three years now, I can vouch for the University by saying that I have never seen cocaine. When it comes to seeing and using drugs on campus, it really depends all on you, and the situations you allow yourself to be in. If you go to a place you know that drugs will be, then, of course you will be around it. But, if you stay away from those places, then, most likely you will not see it."

Q "Every college has drugs present, but I haven't encountered it too much. It all **depends on the people you become friends with**."

Q "I don't know anything about the drug scene here. I know it's out there, and **I've heard people talking about marijuana** and once even cocaine, but I've never seen it. I tend to stay away from people who are a part of it, and places where it would probably be found."

Q "The **entire drug scene pretty much exists in my apartment**. No, but seriously, if I were to be a connoisseur of drugs, hypothetically speaking, of course, it wouldn't take much work for me to track down whatever my drug of choice might be, unless it's heroin. I haven't seen any of that down here, yet."

As far as drugs go at UA, students say if you want it then you can get it, and if you don't then you won't see it. Students think that drugs are present at every school, and it is up to the individual to decide if they want to be around it or not. There is a rumor that cocaine is big at UA, however most students say they have never seen it. The most commonly used drug among UA students is Adderall. Students use this to stay up late at night cramming for exams. One thing that is for sure is that this town is definitely a drinking town. Even if you are not 21, students say getting alcohol is no problem. Although drugs are around, students say they do not feel pressure to do them.

**B-**

The College Prowler™ Grade on
## Drug Scene: B-

A high grade on Drug Scene indicates that drugs are not a noticeable part of campus life; drug use is not visible, and no pressure to use them seems to exist.

# Overall Experience

## Students Speak Out
ON OVERALL EXPERIENCE

{ "I couldn't be any happier. I went to a small private school freshman year, and by October, I was ready to split. I wanted the big football games, Greek life, the night life on the Strip, and the diversity of the many students."

Q "I just graduated and I am quite thankful that I chose UA. **The school's traditions drew me in**, and even now I take pride in having been a part of them. There is no doubt in my mind that I received a top education and an excellent college experience overall."

Q "UA has been a great experience for me so far. I have met so many wonderful people from all different backgrounds. I also have learned so much from the people I have met. From my two years at UA so far, I am more mature, responsible, and determined. At times I wish I was not in the South because I think it is conservative, but overall UA is a **great university filled with amazing people and opportunities**."

Q "My overall experience at Alabama has been **the best experience of my life**. I have met so many great people and made friendships for a lifetime. The education is great and the campus is absolutely beautiful. I would never choose to go to another school."

Q "I love everything about the University of Alabama, **its traditions, its sports, and its activities. It feels like home**. The minute you set foot on the quad, or whenever you hear the fight song being played after one of the best college football teams in history scores a touchdown, you get chills. Game day is one of the best experiences of your life."

## The College Prowler Take
ON OVERALL EXPERIENCE

The University of Alabama students constantly brag about their school's traditions and spirit, and their pride is shown throughout the town. Some say it's the incredible education that drew them here, and others say it's Bama football that brought them to this school. But, no matter the reason they chose to come here, most believe that it was the best choice they could have made.

After graduation, some students go straight to getting a job, some further their education by going to UA's grad school, and some even go to UA's law school. No matter what the students decide to do with their future, they believe that Bama has prepared them for it. Students advise upcoming freshmen to walk around the quad, visit the Strip, or watch a football game to understand why they "love UA."

**COLLEGE PROWLER**

Read more students' opinions on their overall experience in the College Prowler guidebook on the University of Alabama, available at www.collegeprowler.com.

# University of Central Florida

4000 Central Florida Boulevard, Orlando, FL 32816
www.ucf.edu          (407) 823-3000

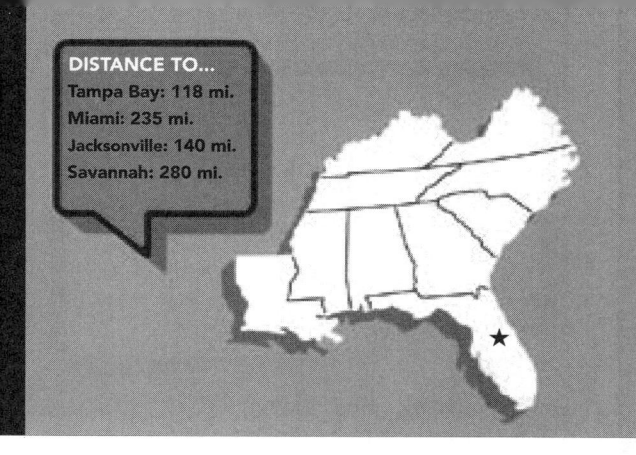

**DISTANCE TO...**
Tampa Bay: 118 mi.
Miami: 235 mi.
Jacksonville: 140 mi.
Savannah: 280 mi.

*"UCF has the means to be a powerhouse one day ... not only in athletics, but in research and academics, as well."*

**Total Enrollment:**
25,757

**Average GPA:**
3.8

**Top 10% of High School Class:**
35%

**Acceptance Rate:**
60%

**Tuition:**
$3,180 in-state, $15,686 out-of-state

**SAT Range (25th-75th Percentile)**
| Verbal | Math | Total |
|---|---|---|
| 520 – 610 | 530 – 220 | 1050 – 1230 |

**ACT Range (25th-75th Percentile)**
| Verbal | Math | Total |
|---|---|---|
| 20-24 | 20-27 | 22-27 |

**Most Popular Majors:**
29% Business Management
10% Education
 9% Health Professions and Related Sciences
 9% Psychology
 6% Engineering

*For more school info check out www.collegeprowler.com

**Table of Contents**

| | |
|---|---|
| Academics | 200 |
| Local Atmosphere | 202 |
| Safety & Security | 203 |
| Facilities | 205 |
| Campus Dining | 206 |
| Campus Housing | 208 |
| Diversity | 209 |
| Guys & Girls | 211 |
| Athletics | 212 |
| Greek Life | 214 |
| Drug Scene | 215 |
| Overall Experience | 216 |

**College Prowler Report Card**

| | |
|---|---|
| Academics | B- |
| Local Atmosphere | A |
| Safety & Security | A- |
| Facilities | A |
| Campus Dining | B |
| Campus Housing | B- |
| Diversity | B- |
| Guys | B+ |
| Girls | A+ |
| Athletics | B- |
| Greek Life | B |
| Drug Scene | C |

# Academics

**Full-time Faculty:**
1,158

**Faculty with Doctoral Degree:**
803 or 69%

**Student-to-Faculty Ratio:**
18.6:1

**Special Degree Options**
Accelerated Undergraduate Program and Study Abroad
Phone: (407) 882- 2300
www.international.ucf.edu

## The Lowdown
ON ACADEMICS

**Degrees Awarded:**
Bachelor, Master, Specialist, Doctorate

**Undergraduate Schools:**
College of Arts and Sciences, Burnett Honors College, College of Business Administration, College of Education, College of Engineering and Computer Science, College of Health and Public Affairs, Rosen School of Hospitality Management

**Academic Programs** (as of 06/2003):
84 Baccalaureate Programs
64 Master Programs
3 Specialist Programs
23 Doctoral Programs

**SACS:**
Level 6 Institution

**SREB Classification:**
Four-Year II Institution

**Carnegie Classification:**
Doctoral/Reasearch Universities-Intensive

**Average Course Load:**
12 credit hours (4 courses at 3 credits each)

### AP Test Score Requirements
There is possible credit for scores of students who participated in the Advanced Placement program in high school, and receive a score of 3, 4, or 5 on the national examinations.

### IB Test Score Requirements
Students who have participated in the International Baccalaureate program in high school may receive a maximum of 30 hours of credit for a score of 4 or higher on the subsidiary or higher level exams.

Students must fill out a form telling the University they are planning on transferring the credits online at *www.sarc.sdes.ucf.edu/acceleratedcredit.html*.

### Did You Know?

UCF is one of the fastest growing metropolitan research universities in the country.

**Best Places to Study:**
Library, Student Union, Bookstore Café

## Students Speak Out
### ON ACADEMICS

> "Most general education courses tend to be large and boring, but once you are in your core track, the subject material is much more interesting."

Q "I think the teachers are ridiculous. Throughout my UCF four-year experience **I have encountered about three good professors**."

Q "**Some classes are interesting**, but most are boring."

Q "**Very few classes held my attention**. I guess it's a good thing that most of them didn't have attendance policies."

Q "A lot of teachers here really care about educating their students, and really helping them get the most out of their classes. Then there are a few **bad apples that always take attendance**, and lecture word for word out of the book."

Q "Most of the teachers are accommodating and flexible with their schedules. My teachers have gone out of their way to make sure **the students are really learning the material**."

Q "The teachers range **from boring to awesome** and inspirational."

Q "I find that **most teachers are passionate** about what they teach."

## The College Prowler Take
### ON ACADEMICS

UCF seems to offer a good learning environment for students. Many professors are passionate and genuinely interested in their students learning. Like anywhere else, you have your bad seeds thrown into the mix. Most teachers will assist you any way that they can, and are there to work with you and your needs.

Students seem to be torn down the middle whether they find classes boring or interesting, with upper-level classes receiving better reviews. Once you get here, it is advised that you ask around to see what professors are well-liked and which classes are most interesting. Just think of the student body as a fountain of knowledge when it comes to recommending professors and courses.

**B-**

**The College Prowler™ Grade on**
### Academics: B-

A high Academics grade generally indicates that professors are knowledgeable, accessible, and genuinely interested in their students' welfare. Other determining factors include class size, how well professors communicate, and whether or not classes are engaging.

# Local Atmosphere

## Points of Interest

Thornton Park Shopping Center; here you will find unique stores, including a trendy bookstore, coffee shops, hip restaurants, hair salons, clothing and trinkets. Lake Eola is within a mile of Thornton Park, surrounded by a large sidewalk with a playground and swan boat rentals available. Thornton Park is located right beside downtown Orlando off of Expressway 408.

Pointe Orlando is an outdoor shopping, dining, and entertainment complex, with over sixty retail stores and seven restaurants. There is also a movie theater that shows IMAX movies, and club Matrix for the late-night partygoers. Pointe Orlando is located on International Drive and only a short drive away from Orlando's theme parks.

Downtown Disney has it all: Cirque du Soleil, the House of Blues, Pleasure Island, ESPN Zone, the largest Disney character store, many restaurants, a movie theater and tons of shops. Downtown Disney is located on Disney property in the Disney resort area in Lake Buena Vista.

Waterford Lakes is approximately five miles from the UCF campus. Waterford lakes has an assortment of restaurants, stores, and businesses. There is something here for everyone, ranging from Chucky Cheese to upscale hair salons, dentist's offices, Kinko's office supply store, and Super Target.

## The Lowdown
**ON LOCAL ATMOSPHERE**

**Region**:
Southeast, Central Florida

**City, State**:
Orlando, Florida

**Setting**:
Metropolitan area/big city

**Distance from Miami, Florida**:
3 hours, 45 minutes

**Distance from Atlanta, Georgia**:
5 hours, 45 minutes

**Major Sports Teams**:
The Orlando Magic (NBA)

**City Websites**
www.cityoforlando.net
www.orlandosentinel.com

## Students Speak Out
**ON LOCAL ATMOSPHERE**

"I like the atmosphere because it is a place where you get the experience of college life and also life in a big city."

Q "There are plenty of downtown areas catering to all different interests, such as **dance clubs, bars, unique shops and bookstores**, and scenic parks."

Q "UCF is about an hour from **Disney World** and 30 minutes from Universal."

- "**Rollins is the only other university**, and it is a private school."
- "Orlando has a **fun, relaxing atmosphere**; its as fast or as slow-paced as you like it to be."

## The College Prowler Take
### ON LOCAL ATMOSPHERE

It's safe to assume that you will never be bored in Orlando, Florida, as long as you take advantage of what the city has to offer. There is something for everyone in Orlando, whether you favor a fast and upbeat tempo or a slow, relaxing day enjoying the outdoors. Orlando's vast amount of theme parks and resort areas make it the number one vacation destination in the United States. The weather is beautiful year-round and the people are mostly friendly (whether they're tourists or residents).

# Safety & Security

## The Lowdown
### ON SAFETY & SECURITY

**Number of UCF Police**:
47

**Phone:**
(407) 823-5555

**Health Center Office Hours**:
Monday-Thursday 8 a.m.-8 p.m.
Friday 8 a.m.-6 p.m.
Saturday (Acute care only) 10 a.m.-2 p.m.

### Safety & Security Tips

There are blue-light phones located throughout campus. Just press the red button and talk into box for help. The blue light will flash and alert police of your location.

S.E.P.S. (Safety Escort Patrol Service): A free service, where patrol students ride around on golf carts and pick pedestrians up and drop them off at their destination. You can call S.E.P.S. for free from any campus pay phone. This is a number to keep handy in your phone: (407) 823-2424. Hours: 7 p.m.-1 a.m. Sunday-Thursday.

UCF offers self-defense classes every semester and safety seminars throughout the year.

The College Prowler™ Grade on
## Local Atmosphere: A

A high Local Atmosphere grade indicates that the area surrounding campus is safe and scenic. Other factors include nearby attractions, proximity to other schools, and the town's attitude toward students.

### Did You Know?

If you call and make an appointment with Student Health Services, even the day of, you will usually get one. To make an appointment call (407) 823-3850.

### The College Prowler Take
**ON SAFETY & SECURITY**

If you are considering doing something illegal on campus, don't do it—you will most likely be caught. UCF has its own police station located on campus with many police officers patrolling the campus. Always drive with caution on campus and obey the speed limits. Don't hesitate to call for a safe ride if you are on campus after dusk. This is an excellent service that UCF provides so that you will arrive safely at your destination, whether it's the parking garage or your dorm room.

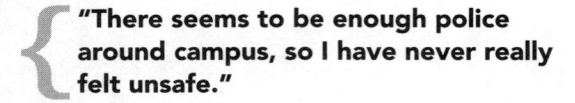

### Students Speak Out
**ON SAFETY & SECURITY**

"There seems to be enough police around campus, so I have never really felt unsafe."

Q "Security is okay; **I never have had any concerns**. Orlando is still an urban area though, and crime does occur on a regular basis."

Q "I feel safe because there are emergency posts on campus and UCF police are everywhere. If something were to happen, I'm sure the **evildoers would be quickly apprehended**."

Q "I often see security walking around. I personally have felt safe and fortunately **never needed security** aid for any reason."

Q "Security on campus seems to be very **strict and clean-cut**. Officers take care of situations in a professional manner."

**A-**

The College Prowler™ Grade on
### Safety & Security: A-

A high grade in Safety & Security means that students generally feel safe, campus police are visible, blue-light phones and escort services are readily available, and safety precautions are not overly necessary.

# Facilities

**Computers**

**High-Speed Network:** Yes

**Wireless Network:**
Yes, in the library, student union, and bookstore.

**Charge to Print:**
Most labs charge five cents for black and white printed pages. The library charges 10 cents.

## The Lowdown
ON FACILITIES

**Student Center:**
The Student Union provides meeting spaces, offices, programs and services.

**Athletic Center:**
Recreation and Wellness Center

**Libraries:**
The UCF library

**Movie Theatre on Campus?**
No

**Bowling on Campus?**
No

**Bar on Campus?**
Yes, Wackadoo's

**Coffeehouse on Campus?**
Yes

**Favorite Things to Do:**
Feed the squirrels, even though it is discouraged, attend a group workout class, get an hour massage for $30, visit the UCF Robinson Observatory

**Popular Places to Chill:**
Student Union, the Bookstore Café, the Business Administration Building, or the grass area around the fountain

## Students Speak Out
ON FACILITIES

"Facilities are extremely nice and well-kept. So much money has been spent on state-of-the-art technology and equipment in every building."

Q "Everything at UCF is pretty new and still very nice; even **the bathrooms are usually very clean**."

Q "The facilities on campus are **nice and reliable**. Most of the facilities on campus have been built recently. Some complain that some of the larger buildings are gaudy and take up too much space, but I don't think that's something to really complain about—these are glass-half-empty kind of people."

Q "**The gym is top-notch**; you should work out in the morning, or you will be waiting in line for everything. There's a lot of eye candy to help motivate your workout, as well."

> "The gym is beautiful, as is the student center; **the computers are okay**, but they seem a little slow—there are tons of them, though."

## The College Prowler Take
### ON FACILITIES

By popular vote the UCF gym has received good reviews. The gym itself (let alone the entire UCF campus) is definitely worth checking out. Not only can you work out there, but you can partake in the wellness center programs, such as the biofeedback programs and massage therapy sessions. Aside from the gym, the facilities at UCF are new and usually clean. This should be expected, however, because UCF hasn't really been around long enough to have deteriorated or aged just yet. When the time comes for renovations, the administration will likely keep everything up-to-par in a tidy manner (keeping with the Orlando tradition).

# Campus Dining

## The Lowdown
### ON CAMPUS DINING

**Freshman Meal Plan Requirement?**
There is no requirement.

**Meal Plan Average Cost**:
The average cost for a meal plan dining in the Marketplace dining hall (with unlimited meals in one day) per semester is $1,538, and per year the average cost is $3,000.

**24-Hour On-Campus Eating?**
Nope

**Student Favorites:**
Wackadoos, Chick-fil-A, Subway

**Did You Know?**

UCF can cater any event, from coffee-breaks to black-tie galas.

Catering Services Office Location:
Student Resource Center- Building 7
Monday - Friday 8 a.m.-5 p.m.
Phone: (407) 823-2494

### The College Prowler™ Grade on
## Facilities: A

A high Facilities grade indicates that the campus is aesthetically pleasing and well-maintained; facilities are state-of-the-art, and libraries are exceptional. Other determining factors include the quality of both athletic and student centers and an abundance of things to do on campus.

## Students Speak Out
ON CAMPUS DINING

"The meal plan has such a variety; I never get tired of the assortment. I love how the chef makes your food to order."

"There is **so much to pick from** as far as food on campus. My favorite spot is Wackadoo's."

"Wackadoo's is the place to go and is the social spot on campus. It serves great food and cold beers. **Not too many college campuses offer a spot as good as this**."

"The dining hall is great because it's all you can eat, and you can't beat that. The **variety of food accommodates everybody**—even the pickiest eaters."

"I worked for two months with dining services, so first hand **the food is pretty good**. Don't walk back to the meal plan kitchen—it might change your mind. Bad smell."

## The College Prowler Take
ON CAMPUS DINING

You will never go hungry while living on, or visiting, the UCF campus, as there is enough variety for everyone. Conveniently, you can find tons of fast food all over the campus. There really is every type of food, ranging from hotdogs to Mexican to Greek. The dining hall certainly holds its own and receives praise from most students. Although it doesn't seem to be a place to eat three meals a day, it provides students with easy eating and a huge variety every day. If you live on campus, getting a meal plan is a good way to go.

**B+**

Still hungry? Pick up the UCF guidebook from www.collegeprowler.com to find out the best eateries, on and off campus.

The College Prowler™ Grade on
### Campus Dining: B+

Our grade on Campus Dining addresses the quality of both school-owned dining halls and independent on-campus restaurants as well as the price, availability, and variety of food.

# Campus Housing

### Did You Know?
Each room is furnished with a bed, mattress, dresser, desk, and chair. Apartment living rooms are furnished with a love seat, two side chairs, and a small dining table with four chairs.

## The Lowdown
ON CAMPUS HOUSING

**Undergrads on Campus**:
3,759

**Number of Dormitories**:
5

**Number of University-Owned Apartments**:
4 buildings in Hercules; 4 buildings in Nike; 15 buildings in Lake Claire-12 apartments each

**Room Types**:
Residence halls and apartments

**Cleaning Service?**
Yes, the Custodial Staff Service cleans the bathrooms, and the carpet is vacuumed once a week.

**Bed Type**:
Extra-long twin (80")

**Also Available**:
Community Living Guide with all the information you need to live on campus is provided when you move in.

## Students Speak Out
ON CAMPUS HOUSING

"**When you live in the dorms, you never have to worry about parking. I roll out of bed and walk to class.**"

Q "Old dorms closest to campus are old and dirty. **Academic Village** is really nice, though."

Q "I am very **happy with my decision to live in the dorms**. The social experience alone is worth it."

Q "Why would you live on campus when there are so many **off-campus apartments right around the corner**? They provide more freedom with a similar atmosphere."

Q "Academic Village is pretty nice, but the other dorms are dumps. **They are all way over-priced**, and you can find much better places for $100; it's sometimes $200 cheaper [to live] off-campus. Avoid Pegasus Landing at all costs. It's dirty, and there have been numerous robberies and car thefts."

## The College Prowler Take
### ON CAMPUS HOUSING

There are many options available for all types of students, whether you are an incoming freshman or an upperclassman. They have something to satisfy everyone. If you are planning to live on campus, Academic Village is the way to go. These dorms are new and set up as apartment-style housing. Check out the other dorms before signing up for them, as you never know how you will feel about someplace until you see it in person.

## Diversity

### The Lowdown
### ON DIVERSITY

**Native American:** 0.5%

**Asian American:** 4.9%

**African American:** 8.4%

**White:** 71.2%

**Hispanic:** 11.6%

**Out-of-State:** 8%

**Unknown:** 3%

### Most Popular Religions
Christianity, Judaism, and Catholicism are the most popular religions at UCF. There is no formal religious affiliation, and there is no place on the application form for religion.

### Political Activity
There are many political-social activism groups on campus: American Civil Liberties Union, Body of Animal Rights Campaigners, and Campus Peace Action to name a few.

**B-**

### The College Prowler™ Grade on
## Campus Housing: B-

A high Campus Housing grade indicates that dorms are clean, well-maintained, and spacious. Other determining factors include variety of dorms, proximity to classes, and social atmosphere.

### Gay Tolerance

There are many sexual orientations on UCF's campus; there are diversity videos available at the UCF library upon request.

### Economic Status

UCF is a state school. Therefore, it receives tons of financial aid from the state for the students. Students vary from underprivileged to upper-class. The majority of students on campus come from middle-class families.

## The College Prowler Take
### ON DIVERSITY

Orlando seems to be the melting pot of Florida, and UCF's location makes it a prime spot for a diverse campus. The campus is relatively diverse, with most students' ethnicity being white. UCF's campus is not restricted to one way of thinking; there are many religions represented, a lot of political activities going on, and a club for everyone. The campus does not discriminate, and all students are free to openly believe and practice whatever they choose.

## Students Speak Out
### ON DIVERSITY

"**UCF is pretty diverse;** I would say it is above average. There are a lot of ethnicities and all aspects of life."

"**There is a good mix** of Asians, Hispanics, African Americans, and Caucasians. We're a state school, so we're more diverse than your average university."

"UCF is an extremely diverse campus, which makes for a better learning environment. There are **groups for everything from religion and culture to sexual orientation**."

"At UCF, [students are] mostly white **middle-class** with spatters of minorities every few feet."

"UCF is probably **just as diverse** as any other school in Florida."

# B-

The College Prowler™ Grade on
## Diversity: B-

A high grade in Diversity indicates that ethnic minorities and international students have a notable presence on campus and that students of different economic backgrounds, religious beliefs, and sexual preferences are well-represented.

# Guys & Girls

## The Lowdown
### ON GUYS & GIRLS

**Women Undergrads**: 55%

**Men Undergrads**: 45%

### Birth Control Available?
Yes. You can obtain a prescription for birth control from Student Health Services at (407) 823-2701.

### Social Scene
UCF is notorious for its happening social scene. Students on campus are there to learn and to socialize. UCF students are extremely friendly and outgoing. There are plenty of hot spots on campus to relax and people watch, as well as socialize. Many students enjoy the bar type scene of Wackadoo's in the student union to hang out and meet people. Even in class, there is always a student who wants to make friends, and maybe more.

### Hookups or Relationships?
Hookups, hookups, and more hookups. Most relationships here at UCF don't seem to last very long. With all the hot ladies on campus, the men seem to stray every now and again. However, stranger things have happened and some people do fall in love and have long lasting, meaningful relationships. Have fun, and be safe! You are only an undergraduate once.

### Dress Code
The hot weather requires minimal clothing. The girls wear short skirts, tank tops, and flip-flops. The guys are usually clad in Abercrombie T-shirts, shorts, and flip-flops. When the weather cools off, the clothes come back on. Girls wear jeans, pullovers, sweaters, and tennis shoes. Guys wear jeans, sweatshirts, and athletic shoes. The school style is more relaxed and laid-back than the going out style. A night out on the town usually requires high heels, a short dress or skirt, and a sexy top for girls. Guys should wear buttoned-up, collared shirts, nice pants, and dress shoes to go out in. No matter what, though, be sure to remember your accessories. Whether it is a nice watch, a designer bag, or chandelier earrings, be sure to add something to your outfit that makes it stand out—in a good way, of course.

## Students Speak Out
### ON GUYS & GIRLS

"**Everywhere you look on campus there are young beautiful people. Hugh Hefner should just set up a booth on campus!**"

Q "By majority vote, I have to say, **girls are a lot more attractive at UCF than the boys** are."

Q "At UCF, **male pickings are slim**. There are lots of skinny, pretty girls."

Q "Boys are boys anywhere you go, and UCF is no exception. You got hot ones and not-so-hot ones. Look out for the **not-so-hot guys posing as hot ones**."

Q "A lot of the guys look like they are on steroids and are superficial. There are **more cool and pretty girls** than guys."

Q "There are hot girls and guys everywhere. **Everyone is nice and friendly**, and it is really easy to make friends. Just be careful, a lot of the guys are players."

## The College Prowler Take
### ON GUYS & GIRLS

Make no mistake about it, UCF has plenty of guys and girls to choose from. However, it does seem that the guys have the advantage. There are more girls than guys in general, so the guys have the upper hand. Not to worry though, because UCF's social scene makes it easy to meet people, no matter what. The student body enjoys their mating and dating. Regardless of what your parents tell you, it is an important part of many undergraduate students' lives. The campus seems to be fairly promiscuous. Not too many students are into relationships at UCF, most just want to explore (and conquer) all their options.

# Athletics

## The Lowdown
### ON ATHLETICS

**Men's Varsity Teams:**
Football
Basketball
Soccer
Baseball
Cross Country
Golf
Tennis

**Women's Varsity Teams:**
Basketball
Cross Country
Softball
Track & Field
Rowing
Volleyball
Tennis
Golf
Soccer

### The College Prowler™ Grade on
## Guys: B+

A high grade for Guys indicates that the male population on campus is attractive, smart, friendly, and engaging, and that the school has a decent ratio of guys to girls.

### The College Prowler™ Grade on
## Girls: A+

A high grade for Girls not only implies that the women on campus are attractive, smart, friendly, and engaging, but also that there is a fair ratio of girls to guys.

## Club Sports
Women's Rugby, Baseball, Billiards, Brazilian Jujitsu, Cricket, Men's Crew, Dive Club, Ice Hockey, Karate, Kite Surfing, Roller Hockey, Soccer, Surfing, Snowboarding, Table Tennis, Volleyball, Water Polo, Water Skiing

## Intramurals (IMs)
Ultimate Frisbee, Bowling, Dodgeball, Tennis, Soccer (coed also), 4-on-4 Flag Football, Football, Floor Hockey, Disc Golf, Softball, Volleyball, Football, Baseball, Basketball

**School Mascot:**
Nitro (male) Glycerin (female). They are knights.

**Athletic Division:**
NCAA Division I

**Conference:**
USA

## Most Popular Sports
Baseball, Basketball, Football

## Overlooked Teams
IM Ultimate Frisbee; Men's Crew Club—won more state championships then any other UCF team; Women's Rugby, Cheerleading

## Getting Tickets
All UCF students get in for free with their school ID. For non-students, there is a Ticketmaster on campus or you can order them online from the UCF Website. They are reasonably priced from $5-$15.

"Our sports teams are getting better each year. As for intramurals, it's **run by uptight officials** who look for ways to take all the fun out of IM as much as they can. Duante Culpepper went here!"

## The College Prowler Take
### ON ATHLETICS

While most students couldn't tell you a thing about the athletes at UCF, they definitely could talk your ear off about tailgating. Students anticipate the football season and the tailgating that accompanies the games. The drinking and partying that takes place on the field outside of the stadium prevents students from actually attending the football game itself. This is a problem that officials and administration are trying to fix. The attendance at games is poor for most sports; UCF lacks spirit probably due to the fact that the school isn't really that competitive yet in popular sports such as basketball and football.

## Students Speaks Out
### ON ATHLETICS

"Most people tailgate and go to the football games. Some people go to the basketball games."

"**I really enjoy IM sports** at UCF. This program has also allowed me to continue being a referee official while getting paid a minimal amount."

"The tailgating during varsity football games probably gets more attention than the game itself. **Our basketball team made the NCAA tournament** last year!"

"**Sports suck, period** at UCF, but IM sports are fun."

**The College Prowler™ Grade on**
## Athletics: B-

A high grade in Athletics indicates that students have school spirit, that sports programs are respected, that games are well-attended, and that intramurals are a prominent part of student life.

# Greek Life

## The Lowdown
ON GREEK LIFE

**Number of Fraternities:**
24

**Number of Sororities:**
22

**Multicultural Fraternities:**
Lambda Sigma Upsilon (Latin), Czar Lambda Theta Phi (Latin), Alpha Alpha, Sigma Lambda Beta (Latin/colony)

**Multicultural Sororities:**
Sigma Lambda Gamma (Latin), Iota Beta, Lambda Theta (Latin), Beta Theta

**Did You Know?**

Last year, the Greeks at UCF spent over 16,000 hours performing various community service projects.

## Students Speak Out
ON GREEK LIFE

"**Greek life dominates the bars and clubs around school. After freshmen year, you really don't notice though.**"

"Greek organizations **provide a calendar of social events** including formals, homecoming, skit nights, mixers, singing competitions, and other special events. Sororities and fraternities can offer more of a family atmosphere and go beyond ordinary friendships, often lasting a lifetime."

"Greek life is huge, but then it gets **repetitive and boring**; it does not dominate."

"Greek life is fun, if that's your bag. **It doesn't dominate the social scene**; it adds to it."

"I wouldn't say that Greek life is dominant on the social scene, per se. It is if you would like it to be. This **depends on the activities you choose** to partake in."

### College Prowler

Planning to go Greek? Visit *www.collegeprowler.com* to compare Greek life on different college campuses across the South.

## The College Prowler Take
### ON GREEK LIFE

The UCF Greek life is very enthusiastic; it is also has a very visible presence on campus. Members of fraternities and sororities provide the majority of school spirit at UCF. It is also safe to say that no other segment of the student population has dedicated more time and resources, or has raised more money for charities than the members of the UCF Greek community. Students who join fraternities and sororities seem happy with their decision. It is a social and active way to be involved, while making lasting friendships. For the most part, students are involved in Greek life for their freshmen and sophomore years, with their participation and dedication trickling off after that. Many students don't feel that joining a fraternity or a sorority is right for them. They do not feel alienated or overlooked due to this decision.

**B**

### The College Prowler™ Grade on
### Greek Life: B

A high grade in Greek Life indicates that sororities and fraternities are not only present, but also active on campus. Other determining factors include the variety of houses available and the respect the Greek community receives from the rest of the campus.

## Drug Scene

### The Lowdown
### ON DRUG SCENE

**Most Prevalent Drugs on Campus**: Marijuana, Cocaine, Ecstasy, Prescription Medicine (Xanax, pain killers, Darvocets, Vicadin, Oxycotton, Valium, Adderall, anything they can get their hands on)

**Liquor-Related Referrals**:
95

**Liquor-Related Arrests**:
7

**Drug-Related Referrals**:
66

**Drug-Related Arrests**:
29

### Drug Counseling Programs

The Alcohol and Other Drug Programming Office
(407) 823-0879

Alcoholics Anonymous
(407) 521-0012

Alanon/Alateen Information Line
(407) 291-1900

Narcotics Anonymous
(407) 425-5157

## Students Speak Out
**ON DRUG SCENE**

"No one sells drugs on campus. Many students smoke marijuana and drink alcohol outside of campus events."

Q "You can get **whatever you want, when you want it**. Whatever you want; they got it."

Q "There are **too many drugs, and too many victims and users** here. I hate to see people just throwing caution to the wind."

Q "There are **very few drugs on campus**. Many students smoke marijuana and drink alcohol off campus, though."

Q "It's not hard to get drugs, just like anywhere else, its no worse or better. **It's not like they're selling crack in the library**."

## The College Prowler Take
**ON DRUG SCENE**

UCF students study hard and play hard. Marijuana is used by many students. Pills, such as Adderall, are also popular among students to assist them in concentration while studying. The school offers many counseling and educational programs about both drugs and alcohol. UCF provides a wealth of knowledge and advice on drugs and alcohol, giving its students the best information to make intelligent, thought out choices.

**The College Prowler™ Grade on**
## Drug Scene: C+

A high grade on Drug Scene indicates that drugs are not a noticeable part of campus life; drug use is not visible, and no pressure to use them seems to exist.

# Overall Experience

## Students Speak Out
**ON OVERALL EXPERIENCE**

"I do wish I was somewhere else. I wish I was in a more cultured town with less of corporate America."

Q "I like the school a lot. I wish I was at a smaller school. There are **too many students**, and UCF needs to cut down on freshmen admissions—please."

Q "UCF is a good school that is improving every year. This **could be a great place to get an education** in years to come."

Q "**I am so happy that I chose UCF** for my college career! And, I would never change it, even if I had the opportunity to. I chose UCF over the University of Hawaii at Manoa, and am extraordinarily happy that I picked Orlando."

Q "I have had an **overall good experience** so far. I kind of wish I went to a school with more of a college town atmosphere, though."

## The College Prowler Take
ON OVERALL EXPERIENCE

This college is growing by leaps and bounds. The students love to hang out, and they all know how to have a good time. There is so much to do, and something for everyone. Come on, do you really need any more reasons to go to college in Florida?

Orlando is an exciting city with tons of attractions and activities available to all. In many ways, going to school at UCF resembles a four-year vacation (Disney on Sunday, classes on Monday!). Downtown Orlando on a Friday night can, at times, seem like Mardi Gras, and City Walk on a Saturday night is not to be missed. Also, Floridians are welcoming and friendly and most students at UCF make friends quickly and easily. Friendly faces and sunny skies; what more could a college student ask for? The stellar academics, up-and-coming sports teams, and state-of-the-art facilities are reason enough to spend the next four years of your life at UCF; the city of Orlando is just one big fringe benefit. Come join us!

# University of Florida

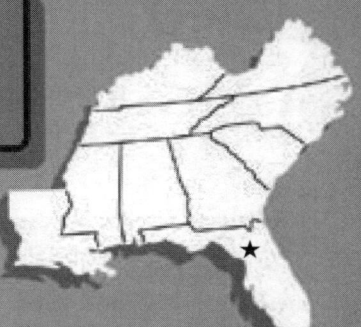

201 Criser Hall, Gainesville, FL 32611
www.ufl.edu          (352) 392-1365

**DISTANCE TO...**
Atlanta: 322 mi.
Orlando: 113 mi.
Miami: 338 mi.
Savannah: 209 mi.

*"UF supporters come from every county in Florida, every state in the Union, and over 100 countries."*

**Total Enrollment:**
31, 217

**Top 10% of High School Class:**
79%

**Average GPA:**
3.9

**Acceptance Rate:**
52%

**Tuition:**
$2,780 in-state, $13,283 out-of-state

**SAT Range (25th-75th Percentile):**
| Verbal | Math | Total |
|---|---|---|
| 560 – 660 | 580 – 680 | 1140 – 1340 |

**ACT Range (25th-75th Percentile):**
| Verbal | Math | Total |
|---|---|---|
| 22-30 | 25-31 | 24-29 |

**Most Popular Majors:**
23% Business
12% Social Sciences
12% Engineering
10% Communications
6% Health Professions

**Students also applied to:***
Florida State University
University of Virginia
University of Georgia
Rollins College

*For more school info check out www.collegeprowler.com

### Table of Contents

| | |
|---|---|
| Academics | 219 |
| Local Atmosphere | 221 |
| Safety & Security | 222 |
| Facilities | 224 |
| Campus Dining | 226 |
| Campus Housing | 227 |
| Diversity | 229 |
| Guys & Girls | 230 |
| Athletics | 232 |
| Greek Life | 234 |
| Drug Scene | 235 |
| Overall Experience | 237 |

### College Prowler Report Card

| | |
|---|---|
| Academics | B |
| Local Atmosphere | B+ |
| Safety & Security | A |
| Facilities | A |
| Campus Dining | B- |
| Campus Housing | B- |
| Diversity | C+ |
| Guys | A |
| Girls | A |
| Athletics | A+ |
| Greek Life | A |
| Drug Scene | B |

# Academics

## The Lowdown
ON ACADEMICS

**Degrees Awarded:**
Bachelor, Master, Specialist, Engineer, Doctorate, and Professional

**Undergraduate Schools:**
College of Agricultural and Life Sciences; School of Forest Resources and Conservation; College of Business Administration; Fisher School of Accounting; College of Design, Construction, and Planning; School of Architecture; School of Building Construction; College of Dentistry; College of Education; School of Teaching and Learning; College of Engineering; College of Fine Arts; School of Art and Art History; School of Music; College of Health Professions; College of Journalism and Communications; Levin College of Law; College of Liberal Arts and Sciences; College of Medicine; College of Natural Resources and Environment; College of Nursing; College of Pharmacy; College of Veterinary Medicine; the Graduate School

**Full-time Faculty:**
1,723

**Faculty with Terminal Degree:**
93.8%

**Student-to-Faculty Ratio:**
21:1

**Average Course Load:**
15 credits (5 courses)

## Special Degree Options
There are combined bachelor/master programs in which students can complete 12 hours of the master degree during the bachelor degree, with the credits counting for both degrees. These programs exist in almost every college and in many majors, with more being developed all the time. Contact your department advisor for more information, or visit www.isis.ufl.edu/cdp1.html.

## AP Test Score Requirements
Credit for scores of 3, 4, or 5 in a variety of courses

## IB Test Score Requirements
Credit for scores of 4 (with IB diploma), 5, 6, or 7 (only in higher-level exam areas without IB diploma, either level with IB diploma) in a variety of courses

## Sample Academic Clubs
American Marketing Association, Benton Engineering Council, Christians in Construction, Design Club, English Society, Florida Undergraduate Film, German Club, Honors Ambassadors, Internet and Computer Law Association, John Marshall Bar Association, Khmer Student Organization, Law College Council, Minority Business Society, National Association of Future Doctors of Audiology, Order of the Engineer, Pre-Professional Service Organization, Rho Chi (Pharmacy), Student Society of News Design, Tau Beta Pi (Engineering), Undergraduate Economics Society, Volunteers for International Student Affairs, Zoology Club

### Did You Know?

The University is among the nation's top three schools in terms of number of majors offered on a single campus.

Only about 10 percent of 2,890 undergraduate course sections offered in fall 2002 had more than 100 people signed up for a class.

**Best Places to Study:**
Library West, Smathers Library (it's silent!), Reitz Union, Plaza of the Americas

## Students Speak Out
### ON ACADEMICS

{ "Almost all of my professors were very interesting and willing to help outside of class. Although some of my [general education] classes weren't my favorites, I loved the classes in my major."

Q "Most of the **teachers are really accessible and check their e-mail** all day long, which is very convenient. It's always good when you go out of your way to meet with them or talk to them, because then you are more than just a face in a chair in a lecture hall."

Q "You will get good and bad [instructors] just like any other school, but **I haven't had a totally bad experience**, yet. Most of my teachers have been totally awesome and made the class more fun."

Q "I feel that I have had the opportunity to take a wide variety of classes. I have done multimedia projects for visual anthropology, taken pictures for an ecology course in Mexico, learned about black holes in astronomy, and read interesting short stories in Caribbean literature. The **exposure to new ideas and information has been very exciting**. I was able to take these classes because I didn't just take what everyone else was taking. I did a little reading in the course catalog, asked older students, and sat in in a class to decide if it was the class for me."

Q "I think everyone has different experiences with classes and professors depending on what type of student they are, what major they've chosen, and whether or not the major they've chosen is the right one for them. I was lucky enough to find my passions and pursue them at UF. The majority of my classes were great. The ones that were less than stimulating and led by readers rather than teachers were easily compensated for by those that taught me more than I could have hoped for and **provided wonderful mentoring relationships**."

## The College Prowler Take
### ON ACADEMICS

With about 1,700 professors here, it can be difficult to characterize them as a single group. For the most part, though, they are extremely interested in their subjects and in sharing with whoever will listen, which can sometimes mean that you get your ear talked off. But usually, it just means that they're really easy to approach and totally interested in helping you get everything you can out of their classes. UF does not have its reputation as one of the top universities in the Southeast for nothing, and the intensity of the schoolwork here can be a real surprise for the whiz kids who show up in August having gotten As all through high school without a whole lot of studying.

At some schools, you can have either breadth or depth: a lot of majors with only a few faculty and classes in each, or a more restrictive choice of majors with tons of professors and plenty of courses. UF, however, is a place with both. What's more, most Gators don't take academic life so seriously that it's irritating; people (including professors) know how to be not just smart but cool. All of these positive aspects won't just fall in your lap, of course—this is too big a place for anyone to hold your hand for four years—but if you take some responsibility for your own education, all your academic dreams can be met at the University of Florida.

**B**

**The College Prowler™ Grade on**
## Academics: B

A high Academics grade generally indicates that professors are knowledgeable, accessible, and genuinely interested in their students' welfare. Other determining factors include class size, how well professors communicate, and whether or not classes are engaging.

# Local Atmosphere

**City Websites**
www.cityofgainesville.org
www.visitgainesville.net
www.gvlculturalaffairs.org

## Students Speak Out
ON LOCAL ATMOSPHERE

## The Lowdown
ON LOCAL ATMOSPHERE

"Every type of student can find something to do in this town. Whether you're into the club scene, alternative music, or sporting events, your needs will be met."

Q "Some find Gainesville too small, while others think it's just right. Gainesville is not an Orlando or a Tampa, though both are within two to three hours' drive. Gainesville has a decent-sized mall and an active downtown for going out. There are also **lots of restaurants and bars dispersed throughout the city**."

Q "Well, the city is pretty much the college. It's a little strange because you have very little connection with people out of your age range. FSU, UNF, and UCF are about two hours away each in their respective directions, so it's a good spot. The **beach is also about two hours away, or less**, depending on where you go."

Q "Gainesville is a **quintessential college town**. There's no question as to what fuels the city: the University and its students. I would suggest exploring every corner of town whenever you have the opportunity. The little restaurants and stores, especially along University Avenue, have so much character, and there are some beautiful parks and gardens. There's a treasure on every corner if you take the time to find it."

Q "Gainesville is the prototypical college town. It is **vibrant and alive in the fall during football season**, and relaxed and casual year-round. Most of the roads around the University are canopied by the branches of trees on either side, which further gives it a collegiate feel."

**Region:**
Southeast (North Central Florida)

**City, State:**
Gainesville, Florida

**Setting:**
Suburban college town

**Distance from Orlando:**
2 hours

**Distance from Jacksonville:**
1 hour, 30 minutes

**Points of Interest:**
Gainesville-Hawthorne State Rail-Trail (for biking and walking), Devil's Millhopper (giant sinkhole you can walk down into), Kanapaha Botanical Gardens, Lake Wauburg, Payne's Prairie State Preserve (where the buffalo roam), Harn Museum of Art, Florida Museum of Natural History, Hoggetowne Medieval Faire (February), Downtown Art Festival (early March and early November)

**Major Sports Teams:**
Tampa Bay Buccaneers and Jacksonville Jaguars (football), Orlando Magic (basketball), Tampa Bay Lightning (hockey), Florida Marlins (baseball)

## The College Prowler Take
### ON LOCAL ATMOSPHERE

Gainesville could be an absolute prototype for the college town. UF is the only university here, and although there is also a huge, high-quality community college (Santa Fe C.C.) in our fair village, this place is pretty much centered on being the Land of the Gator. There's not much scary about G'ville, but it isn't a good idea to walk around alone late at night, especially in the woods or on the eastern side of town (don't worry; UF is on the west side). That's not really a problem, though; you'll still find everything you could wish for on a Friday night (and plenty of things to tell your parents you're busy with as well).

Of course, this town is neither New York City nor the backwoods of Alaska, so if you're looking for the extremes in population, setting, or events that go with those kinds of places, Gainesville may not be the ideal location for you.

## B+

**The College Prowler™ Grade on**
### Local Atmosphere: B+

A high Local Atmosphere grade indicates that the area surrounding campus is safe and scenic. Other factors include nearby attractions, proximity to other schools, and the town's attitude toward students.

## Safety & Security

### The Lowdown
### ON SAFETY & SECURITY

**Number of UF Police:**
89

**Phone:**
(352) 392-1111 or 911
(352) 392-1409 for Community Services

**Health Care Center Hours:**
Monday-Friday, 8 a.m.-6:30 p.m.
Saturday-Sunday, 12 p.m.-4 p.m.
Closed some holidays

### Safety Service

Blue-light phones – found all around campus; pick one up in an emergency or for an escort.

Student Nighttime Auxiliary Patrol (SNAP) – call 392-SNAP (7627) after 6:30 nightly for an on-campus van or walking escort by student employees carefully chosen by the police department.

Rape Aggression Defense (RAD) – free course offered by Community Services to help students learn self-defense methods.

Bicycle/property registration – fill out the appropriate form by going to www.police.ufl.edu and clicking at the top of the orange menu on the left.

Office of Victim Services – provides a civilian support person for anyone who may become a victim of crime while on UF's campus. A victim advocate is available 24 hours a day, seven days a week.

## Students Speak Out
### ON SAFETY & SECURITY

"I feel very safe here. The University has its own police force that responds to calls. In the residence halls there are also nighttime security assistants who patrol the area."

Q "Security is pretty good on campus. We have **lighted emergency call boxes all over campus**. We also have SNAP, which is a van, car, or person that takes you home to make sure you are safe at night."

Q "There are **campus cops that go around on bike, foot, and car**. The University has a program implemented to give rides to people who are on campus late or after dark. All you have to do is call them on one of the many free-use phones on campus."

Q "UF has done a **great job of lighting the campus**—which is beautiful, by the way—with antique-styled path lamps, which provide plenty of light for walking at night without washing out the campus with artificial light. As well, student government and UPD have a system called SNAP which offers rides to those who do not wish to walk at night—free of charge."

Q "I would say that security and safety are comparable to most colleges. But **people do run into danger here**. For the most part, a little common sense will keep you safe and out of jail in Gainesville."

## The College Prowler Take
### ON SAFETY & SECURITY

UF's state- and nationally-accredited police department is not just some lame rent-a-cop force. They keep an eye on the campus 24 hours a day, 365 days a year, in patrol cars, on motorcycles and bicycles, and by foot. In an emergency, they can be just about anywhere on campus in what seems like an instant. In fact, you might be a little dismayed with how fast they'll be there at just the moment you decide to put the pedal to the metal and zoom past 20 mph on your speedometer.

However, the noticeable police presence on campus makes anyone who remembers the UF tragedies of the early nineties feel better, and anyway, most of them are really nice people who genuinely want to help students feel safe at school. Like dealing with academics at such a big school, the thing to remember is to take a little personal responsibility, and it shouldn't be an issue.

**The College Prowler™ Grade on**
## Safety & Security: A

A high grade in Safety & Security means that students generally feel safe, campus police are visible, blue-light phones and escort services are readily available, and safety precautions are not overly necessary.

# Facilities

## The Lowdown
ON FACILITIES

**Student Center:**
J. Wayne Reitz Union, better known as "the Reitz" or "the Union"

**Libraries:**
14

**Athletic Center:**
The Southwest Recreation Center ("Southwest Rec") is enormous. The Student Recreation and Fitness Center ("Student Rec," or "SRFC") is slightly less enormous but still extremely functional. The O'Connell Center Weight Room ("O'Dome Weight Room") is exactly what it sounds like—a place to lift weights.

**Movie Theater on Campus?**
Yes, in the Reitz Union: no regular schedule

**Bowling on Campus?**
Yes, in the game room on the ground floor of the Reitz Union

**Bar on Campus?**
The Orange and Brew in the Reitz Union courtyard serves beer, but it's not exactly the stereotypical bar.

**Coffee on Campus?**
There are Java City stores in the Reitz Union food court and in the HUB.

## Computers

**High-Speed Network?**
Yes

**Wireless Network?**
In many campus locations

**Number of Labs:**
5 for general student use; some departments have labs restricted to their own students.

**24-Hour Labs:**
Architecture 118, near Broward Hall and Burger King

**Charge to Print:**
Dot-matrix printers: free; black-and-white laser printers: $.10 per page; color laser printers: $.75 per page. (Actually getting your paper finished and printed out on time: priceless.)

## Did You Know?

UF dorms have this fabulous invention called DHNet, which is the Division of Housing's name for Ethernet. There are two DHNet jacks in every dorm room, and the connection is super fast.

One warning: you can't run Kazaa or Morpheus or any other P2P programs from computers on campus, so you might be hitting Best Buy to get your tunes the old-fashioned way.

## Students Speak Out
### ON FACILITIES

"The facilities on campus are, bar none, the best in the country. The gyms available to students can get a little crowded with over 40,000 students, but they are very nice and have new equipment."

Q "**We have excellent facilities**. We have a number of gyms to work out at. You can also run around the football stadium, or walk or run up and down the football bleachers."

Q "This may sound dorky, but I always thought the libraries were really nice. Assuming you know which library you need to be in to find what you are looking for, the staff there is always helpful, and I love the little window seats where you can sit quietly and **read while watching the bustling campus below you**."

Q "Another benefit of attending a big school is that the **University has the resources to provide great facilities**. UF has a very strong athletic program, from club sports to the University's teams. Whether you want to participate in a sport, work out at a gym, or watch the Gators play, you have the facilities waiting for you. Inside [the Reitz Union] you'll find places to eat, a movie theater, a game room, and student government offices, and the list goes on."

Q "The Reitz has morphed since I have been here. They just built a large new ballroom and **now they built a new bookstore** which is also houses a welcome center and a new parking garage. The Reitz is also home to a bowling alley, pool tables, and air hockey table. It's a really nice place to hang out for some cheap, yet valuable, fun—especially if you're not 'of age' yet for some of the other Gainesville entertainment. Most of these facilities are kept open most of the day and into the night, which makes them very convenient for students."

## The College Prowler Take
### ON FACILITIES

You know the phrase "the natives are getting restless?" Well, the administration must have been afraid of what 48,000 restless UF natives might do if they got bored, because they've really planned for satisfying the whims of every Gator. With all the things going on at the Reitz, it's an ideal place to hang out if you don't know what you want to do—a strawberry smoothie from Freshens on the ground floor will never fail to make you feel better. And if it's not just substance you're looking for; if you want a pretty face to go with it as well—UF has that, too. Basically, keep your feet moving and your eyes open, because there's plenty to do on campus and plenty to look at while you do it.

The College Prowler™ Grade on
### Facilities: A

A high Facilities grade indicates that the campus is aesthetically pleasing and well-maintained; facilities are state-of-the-art, and libraries are exceptional. Other determining factors include the quality of both athletic and student centers and an abundance of things to do on campus.

# Campus Dining

## Students Speak Out
### ON CAMPUS DINING

"To be honest, the on-campus food isn't that great. I got a meal plan, but I won't recommend it unless you really can't cook. I ended up eating out a lot and cooking although I had a meal plan. There are a ton of restaurants."

## The Lowdown
### ON CAMPUS DINING

Q "The food on campus is very good for cafeteria food. There are also **many well-known restaurants like Wendy's and Chick-fil-A** on campus. Students have many options when it comes to a food plan. You can choose a certain number of meals a week, a declining balance, or keep food in your dorm room."

Q "On-campus food sucks ... but **it probably does everywhere**. Get the meal plan if you live on campus, though."

**Freshman Meal Plan Requirement?**
No

**Meal Plan Average Cost:**
19 meals/week: $1,370-1,450
14 meals/week: $1,256
10 meals/week: $1,151

**24-Hour On-Campus Eating?**
Only in your dorm room, my friend.

**Student Favorites:**
Wendy's, Subway, Chick-fil-A

Q "The food on campus is food on campus. **Don't expect it to be something it's not**. If it's not fast food, and there is plenty of that at various places, it's cafeteria food. There are a couple of all-you-can-eat places, however, that offer a good variety for about six dollars."

Q "The dining halls aren't bad. I wouldn't recommend going there every night, but there are plenty of people who do. The cool thing about that is you can get a **good, balanced, hot dinner every night of the week**, and make a few friends with the staff—they will recognize you after awhile—while you're at it. It does get old after awhile for most people, though."

### Did you know?

If you want to split hairs, the "all-you-can-eat" description of Broward Dining and Gator Corner should say "all-you-can-eat-in-this-building," since you're really not supposed to take food out of there. However, doing so is not a difficult proposition.

You can visit Broward Dining and Gator Corner even if you don't have a meal plan.

## The College Prowler Take
### ON CAMPUS DINING

There are two kinds of on-campus food: the kind that uses up a meal block (Gator Corner and Fresh Food Company/Broward Dining) and the kind that uses up a declining balance (everything else). The meal-block variety is pretty cheap, very filling, and easy to get to, and it'll prevent you from lying to your mom when you tell her you've been eating your veggies. After a couple of semesters, you'll probably get tired of it, and it's not really anything to write home about to start with. Besides, there's actually a third kind of on-campus food: the type that comes from the supermarket and is located in your dorm room—this is often the tastiest and most convenient route to go.

**B-**

### The College Prowler™ Grade on
### Campus Dining: B-

Our grade on Campus Dining addresses the quality of both school-owned dining halls and independent on-campus restaurants as well as the price, availability, and variety of food.

# Campus Housing

## The Lowdown
### ON CAMPUS HOUSING

**Undergrads on Campus:**
22%

**Freshmen on Campus:**
71%

**Number of Dormitories:**
24

**Room Types**
Singles, Doubles, Triples – one, two, or three students to a room, bathroom shared with the rest of the floor

Suites – usually four people in two bedrooms, a living area, and a bathroom

**Available for Rent**
Mini-fridge with microwave

**Cleaning Service?**
Hallways and bathrooms except in co-ops; bathrooms in suite-style areas.

**You Get**
Bed, desk, chair, dresser, closet/wardrobe, wastebasket, window coverings, cable TV jack, Ethernet, free campus and local calls

**Bed Type**
Bunk-able extra-long twins. Mattresses are 80" by 36" and 7" thick, except in the Springs Complex where they are 80" long by 39" wide by 7" thick.

## Students Speak Out
### ON CAMPUS HOUSING

{ "Dorms are a lot of fun. You meet so many people and have a great time. You can check online; some don't have A/C. Avoid those. Some are suites, like apartments, and others are normal dorms, depending on preference."

Q "One awesome thing is the cable. If you live on campus, you get great channels, and, in addition, **there is a movie channel that shows Pay-Per-View-type movies** all month. It's great because you get to watch newer movies all the time. I think it's great to live on campus at least one year."

Q "The dorms are all very different. If you like communal living—much more social, but you share hall bathrooms—the Tolbert area is fun and close to classes. Springs, Keys, Lakeside, and Hume are newer, more expensive, and a little less social. Your chances for fewer roommates and a bathroom shared with only a few people increase in these halls. **East and Springs were my favorite places to live**."

Q "Most of the dorms on campus are at least decent. I would **avoid the dorms without air conditioning** because it gets very hot! Of course, the newer and more expensive the dorm, the nicer it is."

Q "There's no more fulfilling experience in your first year of college than spending your nights at Murphree Hall, where the **lack of air conditioning invites the town's most social cockroaches**."

## The College Prowler Take
### ON CAMPUS HOUSING

The most important thing to remember is that dorms are dorms: they all involve nasty linoleum or industrial-strength carpeting, cinder block walls, possibly irritating neighbors, a lack of automatic dishwashers, and a bathroom to be shared with as many as 50 other kids. On the other hand, you are offered all kinds of practice with choosing carpet remnants, applying posters in an artistic and wall-obscuring fashion, getting along with your fellow (wo)man, and achieving parent-surprising levels of immodesty. UF's "residence facilities" (for some reason, they are not officially called dormitories) are about as good as those in most other places for figuring it all out.

**B-**

**The College Prowler™ Grade on**
### Campus Housing: B-

A high Campus Housing grade indicates that dorms are clean, well-maintained, and spacious. Other determining factors include variety of dorms, proximity to classes, and social atmosphere.

**COLLEGE PROWLER™**

Need help choosing a dorm? For a detailed listing on all dorms on campus, check out the College Prowler book on University of Florida available at *www.collegeprowler.com.*

# Diversity

## The Lowdown
ON DIVERSITY

- **Native American:** 1%
- **Asian American:** 7%
- **African American:** 8%
- **White:** 70%
- **Hispanic:** 11%
- **International:** 1%
- **Unknown:** 2%
- **Out-of-State:** 18%
  (includes graduate students)

### Minority Clubs
In all seriousness, UF has practically any ethnicity- or religion-based club you could name, and if it's not here, you can start it. There are quite a few fraternities and sororities with members mostly of one ethnicity or religion, as well.

### Most Popular Religions
UF is home to one of the world's largest Jewish student populations, and there is also a variety of active Christian and Muslim groups.

### Political Activity
It's not exactly Berkeley in the sixties, but with so many students here you know there's more than a few who are really into their causes, which run the whole spectrum.

### Gay Tolerance
Reasonably high; there are some fairly active lesbian/gay/bisexual/transgender groups on campus.

### Economic Status
Largely middle-class, although there seems to be a fair-sized group of the extremely well-off and a slightly smaller group of those who aren't. It can be harder to tell the differences here than it was in high school, though.

## Students Speak Out
ON DIVERSITY

"It's quite diverse. There is a blend of people here, but we are all Gator; we all get along well, and everyone seems to look past differences. I am very impressed by the diversity."

"Campus is probably **not that diverse compared to others**. They are trying to attract more minorities. Most minority students here go to the smaller schools for some reason—the directional schools like West Florida, South Florida, and North Florida."

"UF is quite diverse, but it **definitely has its cliques based on race**. Ever see the scene in "Higher Learning" where the quad is divided by races? It gets that way around Turlington Plaza."

"The campus is not as diverse at some campuses in major metro areas. The racial make-up is not as diverse as some places. As a minority, I don't think there are as many people here like me as at some other schools. That is okay for me because **I have met people from Brazil, Taiwan, Florida, Haiti, Ohio, etc.**, and I have learned words in new languages, eaten new foods, and developed an appreciation for different kinds of music."

## The College Prowler Take
### ON DIVERSITY

Diversity is possibly—no, definitely—this campus's favorite buzzword. You hear it absolutely everywhere, which is fine as long as the people saying it mean it. Fortunately, in most places here they do, and all kinds of people—not just different races, but different religions, backgrounds, nationalities, sexual orientations, political inclinations, and so on—live and study here together pretty darn peacefully.

There are students from every state in the union and more than 100 countries, and groups, observances, and events to celebrate every single one. This does not mean, of course, that people don't rally for even greater diversity, and regardless of the fact that Florida has abolished affirmative action in state universities, it seems like things are getting more diverse all the time.

**The College Prowler™ Grade on**
## Diversity: C+

A high grade in Diversity indicates that ethnic minorities and international students have a notable presence on campus and that students of different economic backgrounds, religious beliefs, and sexual preferences are well-represented.

# Guys & Girls

## The Lowdown
### ON GUYS & GIRLS

**Women Undergrads:** 54%

**Men Undergrads:** 46%

### Birth Control Available?
Yes, the infirmary offers a variety of oral contraceptives, emergency contraceptives, and free condoms.

### Social Scene
It's almost completely impossible to characterize the entire student body's social attitudes, but, in general, people are very outgoing—to an extent. There aren't that many kids who will just walk up to unknown classmates and introduce themselves, but, then again, anyone who does will probably be pretty well received. And, of course, within their own more familiar groups, Gators are usually quite gregarious.

### Hookups or Relationships?
At a campus this big, there's plenty of both. You'll hear a lot of people talk about significant others, but in most circles here there isn't exactly a prejudice against more random hookups.

## Dress Code

For the most part, people dress comfortably but nicely—Abercrombie and Fitch, American Eagle, and Hollister are big favorites, but for class you can never go wrong with a Gator shirt of some sort (school spirit is definitely cool here), khaki shorts, and sandals. And plenty of people head to school in basketball shorts and tank tops as well. But if that's not enough guidance, just lean toward the preppy side. Oh, and girls, especially freshmen, often seem to think the smaller the clothing, the better—but taking this concept too far will actually get you more withering stares than admiring glances; it's best to wear whole garments when you go to class and save the barely-there for clubbing.

## Students Speak Out
**ON GUYS & GIRLS**

"You have so many different types of people here that it's not even funny. You're sure to find someone to get along with. In my opinion, there are a lot of really hot guys. There are also good-looking girls, too."

Q "There were 46,000 students last year, and the vast majority was quite attractive. But it's diversified; there is a **grand array of different cultures, peoples, looks, and everything**. However, everyone I've met was nice, even complete strangers. They're all in the same situation you're in, and always looking for another friend, or at least a party mate."

Q "Most people are really nice. I would say UF is a mixture of thin and not so thin, cute and not so cute, etc. There are **quite a few good-looking guys**, not to mention some Abercrombie models, so you don't have to worry so much about looking for eye candy!"

Q "Mostly I'd say the 'preppy type,' but there are 'hippie-ish' types if you like those kinds of people. Girls are hot! I **can't really put the attitudes of everyone in one word or phrase**. College isn't like high school, there are different groups of people, and people find their niches."

Q "The guys are hot. I guess the girls are hot too. Appearance seems like a pretty big issue here. When I was a freshman, people used to joke and call the school Club UF, because **freshman girls always dress like they are going clubbing** to go to class—cute little tops and skirts with the latest shoes everywhere. As you get older though, it becomes more about comfort and less about looks. On the whole, I'd say we are a pretty good-looking crowd, all sun-tanned and in sandals."

## The College Prowler Take
**ON GUYS & GIRLS**

Well, the first thing to remember is that even though we're a good hour from the nearest beach, this is Florida we're talking about, so you'll find a lot of people with tans and sun-streaked hair. As much as the human scenery may seem to indicate it, though, UF's admissions committee is not exactly worried about getting hot students; Gators are here because they have talents you don't practice in front of a mirror. The vast majority of your classmates will be smart or really smart, and a nice personality usually finds its way in there, too. With more than 40,000 students, of course, you're going to come across people who don't add a whole lot to the room. But here's the bottom line: most kids at UF are pretty cool, and an awful lot of them are nice to look at.

The College Prowler™ Grade on
### Guys: A

A high grade for Guys indicates that the male population on campus is attractive, smart, friendly, and engaging, and that the school has a decent ratio of guys to girls.

The College Prowler™ Grade on
### Girls: A

A high grade for Girls not only implies that the women on campus are attractive, smart, friendly, and engaging, but also that there is a fair ratio of girls to guys.

# Athletics

## The Lowdown
ON ATHLETICS

**Men's Varsity Teams:**
Baseball
Basketball
Cross Country
Football
Golf
Swimming and Diving
Tennis
Track and Field

**Women's Varsity Teams:**
Basketball
Cross Country
Golf
Gymnastics
Soccer
Softball
Swimming and Diving
Tennis
Track and Field
Volleyball

## Club Sports
Aikido, Badminton, Break Dancing, Bujutsu, Butokukan Karate, Canoe and Raft, Crew, Cuong Nhu, Cycling, Equestrian, Fencing, Men's Ice Hockey, International Folk Dancing, Isshinryu Karate, Judo, Karate, Kendo, Kodenkan Jiu-Jitsu, Men's Lacrosse, Women's Lacrosse, Motorsports, Outdoor Club, Racquetball, Men's Roller Hockey, Women's Roller Hockey, Men's Rugby, Women's Rugby, Running, Sailing, SCUBA, Skateboarding, Men's Soccer, Women's Soccer, Surfing, Synchronized Swimming, Table Tennis, Tae Kwon Do, Tennis, Triathlon, Men's Ultimate Frisbee, Women's Ultimate Frisbee, Men's Volleyball, Women's Volleyball, Men's Water Polo, Women's Water Polo, Water skiing, Wrestling

## Intramurals (IMs)
Basketball, Bowling, Flag Football, Golf, Indoor Soccer, Kickball, Racquetball, Sand Volleyball, Softball, Swimming, Tennis, Track, Ultimate Frisbee, Volleyball

## Getting Tickets
The athletic tickets people worry most about are the prized spaces in the student section of the football stadium. They're quite inexpensive—about $42 for six games—and downright cheap when you consider how badly people want the tickets and how much non-students pay for them (alumni season tickets require chilling on a wait list for a few years and then shelling out over a grand). You almost make up for all the money you save when it comes time to buy the tickets, though—you have to keep calling and, finally, most people who really dedicate the necessary day or day-and-a-half to dialing the 800 number will end up with a set of tickets.

Football is the only sport for which this process is so difficult; men's basketball sees people camping out a few days in advance for big games, but that's because there are no season tickets and there is no charge for students. Ticket-acquiring is not the slightest issue for any other sport.

**School Mascot:**
Albert the Alligator
(he has a girlfriend named Alberta)

**Athletic Division:**
NCAA Division I

**Conference:**
Southeastern Conference (SEC)

## Students Speak Out
### ON ATHLETICS

{ "Varsity sports are very big—they dominate life. I haven't played IMs, but they're fun and easy to sign up for—a great way to meet people!"

Q "It's UF! Sports are huge. Football season is the most fun in the world. Everyone has parties and stuff and has **ridiculous amounts of school pride**. It's honestly the best part of UF. Other sports are pretty big, too. Of course, basketball and baseball are big as well. I know a lot of people who did IM sports, too. They have every type of sport to do and a lot of people play them. Sports at UF are a lot of fun."

Q "As you may know, Gator football is huge. We have **awesome football and basketball teams**. You should see this place on game day. I absolutely love it!"

Q "The two big varsity sports are football and basketball ... and obviously they are really big because we are really good. **IM sports are only good if you choose to participate**. I think they are run well but if you don't attempt to do them, you don't really know much about them. I play IM basketball ... really fun!"

Q "Sports are huge at UF. I think we have **one of the biggest intramural and club sports programs in the country**. And, of course, who hasn't heard of the Gators? Football games are definitely a huge part of the UF experience and a lot of fun for everyone."

## The College Prowler Take
### ON ATHLETICS

Even if you come here knowing nothing about it and try hard never to think about it once, it is still guaranteed that you will be very familiar with football by the time you leave. If this doesn't already sound like the unbelievable blast that it is, you are urged—nay, implored—to find out for yourself what it feels like to bop on out of the stadium after a home victory, with you and 83,000 of your closest friends all chanting, "It's great ... to be ... a Florida Gator!" so loudly your ears buzz. If you're not converted after that, well, you can always head for the hills on game day and come back when it's all clear—don't worry, the people on University Avenue will be too tipsy to spit at you retreating back.

**The College Prowler™ Grade on**
## Athletics: A+

A high grade in Athletics indicates that students have school spirit, that sports programs are respected, that games are well-attended, and that intramurals are a prominent part of student life.

# Greek Life

## The Lowdown
### ON GREEK LIFE

**Number of Fraternities:**
31

**Number of Sororities:**
23

**Undergrad Men in Fraternities:**
14%

**Undergrad Women in Sororities:**
15%

### Multicultural Greek Council Fraternities (culturally-based)
Lambda Theta Phi
Sigma Lambda Beta
Lambda Alpha Upsilon
Sigma Beta Rho

### Multicultural Greek Council Sororities (culturally-based)
Lambda Theta Alpha
Sigma Lambda Gamma
Gamma Eta

## Students Speak Out
### ON GREEK LIFE

"Greek life is fairly large but by no means dominates the social scene. There are 45,000 students here and about 4,000 are Greek."

Q "This depends on you. I was in a sorority but found out it wasn't my thing. It doesn't dominate the social scene, but **if you are in it, it becomes your life**. Between school, parties, and volunteering, it can get overwhelming. It might be different for you if you are interested and find one you fit into."

Q "Greeks make up 15 percent of the school but they **seem to dominate the Student Senate and politics at UF**, which I think is bad for the school. I don't think that an 'aristocracy' should be running things, and I think they're out of touch with the average student."

Q "I didn't rush my freshman year and met tons of people on my floor in my dorm and was fine. I had tons of fun. I rushed a sorority my sophomore year because I was interested in it and wanted to check it out. **Rush sucks, it's such a fake process**, but I'm really happy now that I am in a house. The campus is so big that sororities don't dominate the social scene."

Q "It dominates the social scene if you are in a fraternity or sorority. If you pledge, that's great, if you don't, like me, it's also not a big deal. You still have just as much fun and meet just as many people. **Parties are everywhere and people are everywhere**, no matter if you pledge or not."

## The College Prowler Take
### ON GREEK LIFE

Greek life is pretty big here. Only about 15 percent of students belong to social fraternities and sororities, but, for one thing, 15 percent of 48,000 is a lot. For another, Greeks tend to be very active in student government, the Student Alumni Association, and other campus organizations, which means you see and hear them pretty frequently. On the other hand, 85 percent of 48,000 constitutes an even larger bunch—definitely enough to ensure that those outside the Greek system have plenty of company.

By no means is it necessary to join up in order to have a good time during your stay in Gainesville; there are a million other ways to get involved with the university and have a good time.

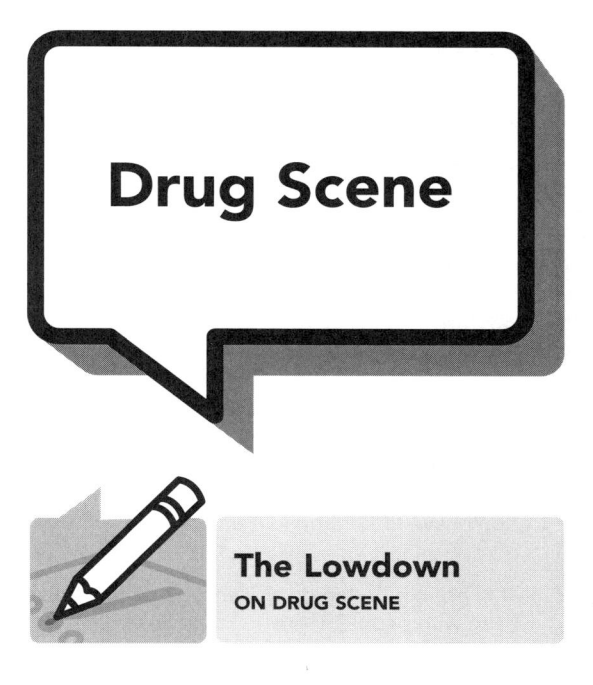

## Drug Scene

### The Lowdown
### ON DRUG SCENE

**Most Prevalent Drugs on Campus:**
Tobacco, Alcohol, Marijuana, Ecstasy

**Liquor-Related Referrals:**
10

**Liquor-Related Arrests:**
11

**Drug-Related Referrals:**
4

**Drug-Related Arrests:**
8

**Drug Counseling Programs:**
Talk with someone in the Mental Health Clinic, (352) 392-1171

The College Prowler™ Grade on
## Greek Life: A

A high grade in Greek Life indicates that sororities and fraternities are not only present, but also active on campus. Other determining factors include the variety of houses available and the respect the Greek community receives from the rest of the campus.

## Students Speak Out
### ON DRUG SCENE

"A lot of weed, little bit of X, not too much in the range of coke or heroin, at least from what I've seen."

"If you want drugs, **I'm sure you could find whatever you want**. If you want to stay away from them, you have no problem doing that. Just like any college town, it's done, but you don't have to be around it unless you want to."

"I'm not big on the drug scene, so I don't really hang with people who are. From what I know, weed is the drug of choice for anyone who does drugs, but it's normally select groups, so it can be available if you want it. If you aren't into that, **it's not something you have to deal with**."

"There are drugs around, I won't lie, and you hear about it, but it's not a huge problem or anything. **It's about the same as every other university** in this country. It's not hard to stay away from it if you want."

"I know that a number of students do use drugs, but the **drug scene is something that is easily avoided**."

## The College Prowler Take
### ON DRUG SCENE

Most hard drugs, it seems, are not particularly popular on campus. Pot has something of a following (for better or for worse, this town is famous for its "Gainesville Gold"). Ecstasy, Rohypnol ("roofies"), and a few others have shown themselves in some places. Beer and hard liquor are the usual limits for most people here, with pot coming in at a popular but not all-pervasive second place.

**Of course, there are students at UF with bigger, more expensive, more dangerous drug habits, but it's not hard to steer clear of them or the people they buy from; in fact, you'd have to do a little work to steer into it.** Well, except maybe at night in the scarier parts of east Gainesville—it's not baseball cards they're trading down there!

**The College Prowler™ Grade on**
## Drug Scene: B

A high grade on Drug Scene indicates that drugs are not a noticeable part of campus life; drug use is not visible, and no pressure to use them seems to exist.

# Overall Experience

## Students Speak Out
**ON OVERALL EXPERIENCE**

"It's been a great experience, and I don't wish I went anywhere else. Whatever you are looking for in a college experience, I have no doubt you can find it here."

Q "I love UF. I think everything about it is great. The faculty is nice and helpful; students are friendly; the school overall is awesome. **I wouldn't go anywhere else**. I think you should give UF a chance because it really is an amazing school."

Q "I like going to school at UF. The people are nice. The town is kind of small, but it's filled with college students. There are lots of people your own age. The classes aren't too bad, just **keep up with the work and pay attention**."

Q "I am from New Jersey, and I decided to come here not knowing anyone. Well, that was the best decision I ever made. I love it here in Florida. I have met amazing people and just love everything about being here, from the big-time sports, to the location, to **being able to go to every big city and beach in Florida**, to going out on the town here, which I am big on and think is great. Well, as you can see, I love it here, and I don't want to leave ever. I don't think I will ever go back to New Jersey, at least. Everything I ever wanted in a college, this place has. The campus is beautiful and so much better than any other campus I've seen."

Q "At first, when I chose UF, I was wondering if I made the right choice. Sometime around the beginning of my freshman year, I pretty much had a feeling like I did make the correct choice. **I like the whole 'spirit' of the school** and how everyone supports the Gators. I think UF is pretty diverse and has every kind of group that any school would have. Let me warn you about one thing—UF is run like a government bureaucracy. That's one big complaint I have about the school. You're a number to them. Their academic counseling has improved since I was a freshman. In 2000, I would have to wait 30 to 45 minutes to see someone, now I wait 15 minutes at most. Consider that there are 46,000 people here."

## The College Prowler Take
**ON OVERALL EXPERIENCE**

The University of Florida is a huge school, and that is putting it mildly. With that come tremendous resources and facilities: we have all the libraries, dorms, athletics, courses, clubs, and services you could want—at a good price. But, that is not all. If you make the effort, you'll find that we also have the professors, staff, and students to make those otherwise inert resources and facilities alive and worthwhile. There are so many people here that sometimes things take a little time—for instance, you can't just waltz into the dean's office and expect to see him instantly, as some folks seem to expect. But, the overwhelming majority of students will tell you that that is patently irrelevant, especially considering that you are meeting more people, doing more things, going more places, learning more about life, and having more fun than you ever have in your life. That, my orange-and-blue friends, is why they call them "bright college days," and, like so many other things, they don't get any brighter than here at UF.

# University of Georgia

DISTANCE TO...
Atlanta: 72 mi.
Columbia: 164 mi.
Charlotte: 200 mi.
Savannah: 239 mi.

212 Terrell Hall, Athens, GA 30602
www.uga.edu    (706) 542-8776

*"Everyone I knew at UGA seemed to be having a blast."*

**Total Enrollment:**
22, 971

**Top 10% of High School Class:**
43%

**Average GPA:**
3.6

**Acceptance Rate:**
75%

**Tuition:**
$4,272 in-state, $15,588 out-of-state

**SAT Range (25th-75th Percentile)**
| Verbal | Math | Total |
|---|---|---|
| 560 – 660 | 560 – 660 | 1120 – 1300 |

**ACT Range (25th-75th Percentile)**
| Verbal | Math | Total |
|---|---|---|
| 24-29 | 23-28 | 24-28 |

**Most Popular Majors:**
6% Marketing/Marketing Management
5% Psychology
4% Biology/Biological Sciences
4% Political Science and Government
4% Management Information Systems

**Students also applied to:***
Auburn University
Emory University
Georgia Institute of Technology
University of North Carolina
Vanderbilt University

*For more school info check out www.collegeprowler.com

## Table of Contents

| | |
|---|---|
| Academics | 239 |
| Local Atmosphere | 241 |
| Safety & Security | 242 |
| Facilities | 243 |
| Campus Dining | 245 |
| Campus Housing | 247 |
| Diversity | 248 |
| Guys & Girls | 250 |
| Athletics | 251 |
| Greek Life | 253 |
| Drug Scene | 255 |
| Overall Experience | 257 |

## College Prowler Report Card

| | |
|---|---|
| Academics | B- |
| Local Atmosphere | A- |
| Safety & Security | B+ |
| Facilities | A- |
| Campus Dining | B |
| Campus Housing | B- |
| Diversity | D- |
| Guys | A |
| Girls | A+ |
| Athletics | A |
| Greek Life | A |
| Drug Scene | B- |

# Academics

## The Lowdown
ON ACADEMICS

**Degrees Awarded:**
Associate, Bachelor, Master, Doctorate

**Undergraduate Schools:**
College of Agricultural and Environmental Sciences, Franklin College of Arts and Sciences, Terry College of Business, College of Education, College of Environment and Design, the School of Environmental Design, the Institute of Ecology, College of Family and Consumer Sciences, Warnell School of Forest Resources, Grady College of Journalism and Mass Communication, School of Law, College of Pharmacy, School of Public and International Affairs, School of Social Work, College of Veterinary Medicine, Department of Aerospace Studies, Military Science Department

**Full-time Faculty:**
1,722

**Faculty with Terminal Degree:**
94%

**Student-to-Faculty Ratio:**
13:1

**Average Course Load:**
15 hours

## Special Degree Options
Pre-professional programs: pre-law, pre-medicine, pre-veterinary science, pre-pharmacy, pre-dentistry, pre-theology, pre-optometry, forest resources, journalism, landscape architecture, medical technology, nursing

Combined-degree programs: five-year landscape architecture program, bachelor's/master's degree honors programs, dentistry program with Medical College of Georgia

Cooperative education programs: agriculture, art, business, computer science, education, engineering, health professions, home economics, humanities, natural science, social/behavioral science, technologies, vocational arts

## AP Test Score Requirements
Acceptable scores vary depending on the test

## IB Test Score Requirements
Acceptable scores vary depending on the test

## Sample Academic Clubs
Demosthenian Society, Phi Kappa Literary Society, the UGA Block and Bridle Club, American Society of Agricultural Engineers, National Association of Black Journalists, Red and Black newspaper, American Association of Textile Chemists and Colorists

### Did You Know?
Forty-three percent of freshmen will graduate in four years.

**Best Places to Study:**
Student Learning Center (SLC), Main Library, Science Library, Law Library, on North Campus under a tree, Starbucks

## Students Speak Out
ON ACADEMICS

"I found that there was a general apathy towards classes that I thought I had left behind in high school. Since I am motivated mostly to perform well academically, I hated this aspect of UGA."

Q "Most of the professors I have had are **very eccentric and more lively than high school teachers**. My professors hold a broad knowledge of their material, and present it with enthusiasm and a blend of personal background."

Q "Since **most of my classes are huge lecture classes**, I didn't really get to know any of the teachers personally, but I think, at the very least, all of my teachers have been very fair in their policies. In all the office hours I have been to, they have been extremely willing to help in any way. As for the classes, some are interesting and some you just have to take to graduate. I think the interest factor mostly depends on the teacher anyway."

Q "The teachers I have had here are a mixed bag. I've had some very interesting ones, and some who made class last forever. **It really all depends on the subject** you're learning, and whether they can make you excited about the topic."

Q "If a student takes the time to get to know the teacher, **the teacher makes the effort to get to know the student**. I have had teachers that have genuinely taken the time to help out when needed. Several of my teachers have made the content of their courses apply to my life and interests. There are lecture classes, as well as small intimate classes available for students."

## The College Prowler Take
ON ACADEMICS

UGA attracts students who want to learn and students who want to party, and often students who possess both desires. UGA gets a bad reputation for being a "party school," but you cannot come here and be a complete joke, and expect to pass. Don't get the wrong impression though: having fun is extremely important to most students on campus, but eventually you'll have to put in the study time, or you won't pass. Some classes, especially freshman classes, are very big, filling up auditoriums that hold a couple hundred, but the professors really try to make themselves accessible for the most part. They always encourage students to stop by their offices for help or for study reviews. Most large classes will break down into discussion groups once a week with a teaching assistant, who is a graduate student. Labs are taught by TAs most of the time. The TAs are very helpful, and they relate extremely well with the students. It is, however, not uncommon to have teachers that speak poor or no English.

There is a major for everyone at UGA, and many people pursue double-majors or minors. Some of the more atypical majors include Agricultural Business Operations, Landscaping, Plant Pathology, etc. What's more, our Honors Program has been compared to an Ivy League education. The students in the Honors Program love it because classes are smaller, and they register ahead of everyone else; they also involve more open discussion and a greater emphasis on self-expression.

**B-**

**The College Prowler™ Grade on**
## Academics: B-

A high Academics grade generally indicates that professors are knowledgeable, accessible, and genuinely interested in their students' welfare. Other determining factors include class size, how well professors communicate, and whether or not classes are engaging.

# Local Atmosphere

## The Lowdown
ON LOCAL ATMOSPHERE

**Region:**
South

**City, State:**
Athens, Georgia

**Setting:**
College town

**Distance from Atlanta:**
1 hour

**Points of Interest:**
Georgia State Botanical Gardens, downtown Athens, the Arch

**City Websites:**
http://www.uga.edu/uga/Athens.html
http://www.visitathensga.com/

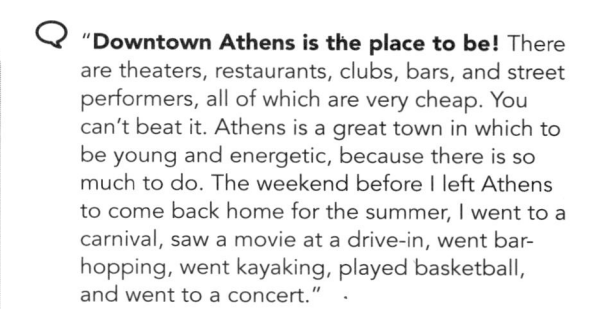

---

Q "**Downtown Athens is the place to be!** There are theaters, restaurants, clubs, bars, and street performers, all of which are very cheap. You can't beat it. Athens is a great town in which to be young and energetic, because there is so much to do. The weekend before I left Athens to come back home for the summer, I went to a carnival, saw a movie at a drive-in, went bar-hopping, went kayaking, played basketball, and went to a concert."

Q "Athens is a small town when you take out the student population, and **if you're here over the summer it can be really boring**, but once the students get back in the fall there's lots to do—definitely more than any other small town in Georgia."

## The College Prowler Take
ON LOCAL ATMOSPHERE

**Athens, "the Classic City," is the perfect college town. Downtown offers amazing nightlife, with numerous clubs, bars, cafés, restaurants, and shops. Music is a cornerstone of downtown Athens, with plenty of opportunities for students to see local and sometimes famous bands, as well as opportunities to join one of their own. Unlike some towns, Athens actually has enough bars to accommodate the number of partygoers living here. Downtown is located within walking distance from the dorms, so walking to and from parties is not a problem, and no one has to drive. Taxis and student-sponsored organizations also provide transportation.**

## Students Speak Out
ON LOCAL ATMOSPHERE

"Athens is what I had always imagined a college town would be like. The school's campus is gorgeous, and UGA is located in a large town that revolves around the University. There are tons of things to do."

The College Prowler™ Grade on

## Local Atmosphere: A-

A high Local Atmosphere grade indicates that the area surrounding campus is safe and scenic. Other factors include nearby attractions, proximity to other schools, and the town's attitude toward students.

# Safety & Security

## The Lowdown
### ON SAFETY & SECURITY

**Number of Police:**
71

**Phone:**
(706) 542-2200 for emergencies
(706) 542-0097 for non-emergencies

**Health Center Office Hours:**
Fall and Spring Semesters: Monday-Friday 8 a.m.-8 p.m., Saturday-Sunday 10 a.m.-5 p.m. Summer: Monday-Friday 8 a.m.-5 p.m., Saturday 9 a.m.-12 p.m.

**Safety Services:**
Escort services, emergency phones, self-defense classes, Watchdawgs, hand-scanning Identification system in dorms

### Did You Know?

There are 25 call-boxes sprinkled throughout the UGA campus.

All UGA police officers are college educated; many are attending graduate programs.

## Students Speak Out
### ON SAFETY & SECURITY

"The campus is an overall safe place. Obviously, common sense is a critical virtue to possess in a campus environment that includes over 30,000 different people."

Q "I wouldn't suggest walking alone at night in Athens. **There have been a few rapes** of girls who were drunk and walking home alone on campus at night. Don't do that! That's the same thing that would happen anywhere."

Q "Security on campus has been quite a problem for the past few years. There have been several rapes and a number of attacks on students. However, most of these attacks could have been avoided. **Having some street smarts would prevent a lot of those attacks**."

Q "The campus seems pretty secure. **I've never really felt unsafe on campus**. It is a little eerie at night, but that's the way things always are. All in all, I would say it's very safe here."

Q "The only time I ever felt unsafe was when **there were bomb threats called in last semester**. They had to clear out some buildings, and the buses stopped running and everything. That was kind of scary, but I think they got it under control pretty fast."

Q "Some of the services that the University provides are emergency call-boxes, hand scan stations for entering dorms, and an **organization called Watchdawgs** that provides students with free rides home from downtown after a night at the bars. Overall, UGA provides a safe environment."

## The College Prowler Take
### ON SAFETY & SECURITY

Students feel safe on campus probably 99 percent of the time. Walking home from downtown can potentially be dangerous, especially if you are alone—some people have been mugged, and even raped, doing so. Students should always go out in groups. If you are going downtown, make sure someone is sober enough to keep you from being unsafe. The downtown cops are mainly there to bust underage drinkers, but they are usually out in droves should you need them for something else. Security at major events was noticeably increased after September 11th; students and other fans can expect their purses and cargo pant pockets to be searched at the entrance to every football game and at most other sporting events. The cops are pretty lax on drinking laws during game days, allowing open containers and drunk minors to slide by.

**B+**

### The College Prowler™ Grade on
## Safety & Security: B+

A high grade in Safety & Security means that students generally feel safe, campus police are visible, blue-light phones and escort services are readily available, and safety precautions are not overly necessary.

# Facilities

## The Lowdown
### ON FACILITIES

**Student Center:**
The Tate Student Center

**Athletic Center:**
The Ramsey Center

**Libraries:**
4

**Movie Theater on Campus?**
Yes, there is a movie theater in the Tate Center.

**Bowling on Campus?**
No

**Bar on Campus?**
No, but downtown is literally across the street from North Campus.

**Coffeehouse on Campus?**
Jittery Joe's is in the Student Learning Center.

## Computers

**High-Speed Network?** Yes
**Wireless Network?** Yes
**Number of Labs:** 9
**Numbers of Computers:** 849
**24-Hour Labs:** Yes
**Operating Systems:** PC, Mac, and UNIX
**Charge to Print?**
Yes, usually six or seven cents per page.

## Favorite Things to Do

Students meet friends for lunch at Bulldog Café or hang out at the Student Learning Center (which has become the place to see and be seen), play ultimate Frisbee on the Myers quad, nap on North Campus, head downtown for lunch or a coffee, and work out at Ramsey Center.

## Popular Places to Chill

North Campus, Starbucks downtown, Blue Sky Coffee downtown, the Tate Center, Ramsey, the Student Learning Center

## Did You Know?

Soccer, volleyball, and rhythmic gymnastics events for the 1996 Centennial Olympic Games in Atlanta were held in UGA's Stegeman Coliseum and Sanford Stadium.

## Students Speak Out
### ON FACILITIES

"Some of the classrooms are really old, and the ones in Park Hall smell like a sweaty gym. The new rooms in the SLC are really nice though, with comfy chairs and lots of leg room."

Q "**Our student center has a movie theater** that runs new movies, classic movies, and sneak previews of upcoming movies—I saw "Road Trip" two months before it came out in theaters—as well as the Bulldog Café, study rooms, art galleries, the bookstore, and many advertisements and offices that can help get you involved in the thousands of activities that take place at UGA."

Q "The Student Learning Center and the Ramsey Center are probably the most popular places on campus, and they are always filled with students because they're good places to get work done or work out, as well as good places to meet people and hang out. **The SLC is also really nice**, and the coffee shop is conducive to hanging out."

Q "**The workout center is endless with available equipment** and venues to meet everyone's interests. You name it, it's there—from swimming, to racquetball, to weight lifting, to Pilates. There is a brand new student center equipped with Internet access, where many students go to study individually, as well as in groups. There are designated quiet areas, but also rooms that are appropriate for discussions. Students love it!"

Q "The athletic facilities are impressive, probably the most impressive aspect of campus. We have an **83-million-dollar student fitness center** that houses an indoor track, indoor Olympic-sized pool complete with diving, numerous dance and aerobic studios, eight basketball courts, a gymnastics area, two volleyball courts, two separate weight training facilities, and more."

## The College Prowler Take
### ON FACILITIES

UGA's facilities are pretty impressive overall. The Student Learning Center has been a major addition to campus. Aside from computers, the Student Learning Center boasts 26 brand-new state-of-the-art classrooms, 96 private group study rooms with marker boards, wireless Internet access, and the much-anticipated coffee shop. The interior of the Student Learning Center is surprisingly elegant, with cherry wood furnishings and marble bathroom counter tops, among other features. The libraries are extremely large, and have many floors and areas to study. The main library also has small theaters, where students watch cultural films and that sort of thing. There are many private study rooms as well. There are student lounges in the libraries where students can talk louder than in normal study areas, which make them a popular place for group project meetings. Facilities in general are good, but many buildings are in need of renovation, including many of the science facilities and some dorms.

**A-**

### The College Prowler™ Grade on
### Facilities: A-

A high Facilities grade indicates that the campus is aesthetically pleasing and well-maintained; facilities are state-of-the-art, and libraries are exceptional. Other determining factors include the quality of both athletic and student centers and an abundance of things to do on campus.

# Campus Dining

## The Lowdown
### ON CAMPUS DINING

**Freshman Meal Plan Requirement?**
No

**Meal Plan Average Cost:**
$2,192 for five-day plan
$2,394 for seven-day plan

**24-Hour On-Campus Eating?**
No

**Student Favorites:**
Pizza, cheese sticks, Philly cheese steak sandwiches, cheeseburgers, burritos, chicken fingers

### Did You Know?

The dining halls have a day at the end of the year when they request that students return all stolen silverware. This event is always a huge success.

UGA Food Services has received 52 national awards for their excellence in student meal plans.

## Students Speak Out
### ON CAMPUS DINING

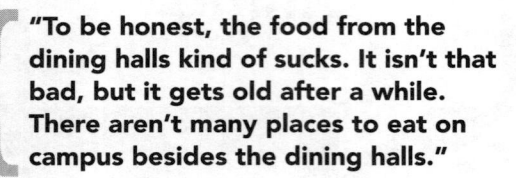

"To be honest, the food from the dining halls kind of sucks. It isn't that bad, but it gets old after a while. There aren't many places to eat on campus besides the dining halls."

Q "**The food on campus is very good**, but like any kind of food, eating it can get old after months and months of the same thing. If you eat there a good bit, and mix in the local food sometimes; it should not be a problem."

Q "The on-campus food is very good. I lived in the dorms for two years and, therefore, have a lot of experience in this area. There are three main dining halls, with one more under construction. Snelling is the best one, offering made-to-order sandwiches of every kind. Bolton and Oglethorpe are the other two, and both provide full course meals and salad bars. The **dining halls occasionally offer theme nights** where shrimp kabobs and luau-type foods are served."

Q "The food on campus is amazing. **There is something for everyone**, including foods such as tofu pizza, Philly cheese steak sandwiches, salad bars, omelet stations, and ice cream tables with every topping imaginable. Whether you are in the mood to eat healthy or not, there is always something for you. Another nice feature is that the nutritional information of all the foods is available for you, so you can know exactly what you're eating. The dining halls also have specialty days, on which the dining hall is specially decorated with themes like 'Beach Party,' 'Under the Big Top,' 'Tastes From Around the World,' and 'Silver Platter Night.'"

Q "Personally **I find the food a bit bland**, and sometimes, they mix leftovers with other leftovers and call it a new dish. I don't feel like the meal plan saves much money on food or is a very healthy option. The highlight of the meal plan is Sunday brunch, especially the French toast sticks and the amazing desserts."

## The College Prowler Take
### ON CAMPUS DINING

Most freshmen will live in a high-rise dorm, and therefore be eating at Bolton a lot. Bolton has a great salad bar, and if grilled cheese and tomato soup is your thing, you can find it there every day. There are literally about a dozen cereals to choose from all day long, which is awesome. However, the variety gets very old by second semester and strange options, such as cod fillets, show up now and then.

**The College Prowler™ Grade on**
### Campus Dining: B

Our grade on Campus Dining addresses the quality of both school-owned dining halls and independent on-campus restaurants as well as the price, availability, and variety of food.

# Campus Housing

## The Lowdown
ON CAMPUS HOUSING

**Undergrads on Campus:**
17%

**Number of Dormitories:**
17

**Available for Rent:**
Mini-Fridge, microwaves, lofts

**Available for Purchase:**
Dorm-size carpet, lofts (can even be set up for you), posters

**Bed Type:**
Twin extra-long (39"x80") Most beds are bunkable, all beds can be lofted.

## Room Types
Most rooms are double occupancy with bathrooms at the end of the hall. Older dorms have suite-style rooms with four to six people sharing a bathroom connecting two rooms. O-House has doubles with a bathroom for every two rooms.

## Cleaning Service?
Yes, in public areas. Staff cleans community and semi-private bathrooms several times a week. Halls and student lounges are regularly vacuumed.

## You Get
Rooms come with a bed, desk and chair, bookshelf, dresser, closet or wardrobe, window blinds, cable TV jack, Ethernet or broadband Internet connections, free campus and local phone service

## Did You Know?
All rooms are non-smoking.

Bunking beds is free.

## Students Speak Out
ON CAMPUS HOUSING

"The dorms at UGA are definitely a good way to start off your college career. They are a great way to meet people and get used to your new college environment."

Q "The dorms are decent, but the **social life there is incredible**. For freshmen, I recommend Russell. It is a co-ed dorm that houses around 1,000 students. The rooms are small but you can loft the beds and do other things to make more space. You will meet amazing people there, though. For all-female living, Brumby is located next to Russell and houses around 900 girls. The only dorm I would avoid is Creswell. It is older and just not as nice as the others."

Q "The dorm life is a must for upcoming freshmen. It is the best way to meet people and get settled into a new life in Athens. You meet people that are going through the same things you are: leaving your family, deciding a major, the anxiety of meeting new people, and so on. There are also some disadvantages of dorm life though, like **sharing bathrooms, less privacy, small rooms, waiting for elevators**, and central air."

> "**The dorms are all right, but not that great**. They're pretty small but you can make do. Russell, Creswell, and Brumby are the ones most freshman live in, so any of those would be good for a new student."

> "The dorms are a lot of fun, but **you lose a lot of privacy**, which I thought was kind of hard to deal with. You'll meet lots of people, though. It's almost impossible not to."

## The College Prowler Take
### ON CAMPUS HOUSING

Each hall has an RA who will answer any questions you have and try to keep order. Each hall has its own parties and socials every so often, and there is definitely a sense of community within every dorm. The bathrooms are usually very clean, though they sometimes get pretty gross over the weekend—especially football game weekends!—and aren't cleaned until Monday. All the dorms now have air conditioning. If you are lucky enough to have an individual unit in your room, as Creswell residents do, count your blessings. The dorms with central air are usually on the warm side. You can open your windows, but this does not always help.

### B-

**The College Prowler™ Grade on**
## Campus Housing: B-

A high Campus Housing grade indicates that dorms are clean, well-maintained, and spacious. Other determining factors include variety of dorms, proximity to classes, and social atmosphere.

# Diversity

## The Lowdown
### ON DIVERSITY

Native American: 0%

Asian American: 4%

African American: 5%

Hispanic: 2%

White: 88%

International: 1%

Out-of-State: 9%

### Minority Clubs
UGA has African American and Asian sororities and fraternities. UGA also offers minority students the opportunity to join the Abeneefoo Kuo Honor Society, Black Affairs Council, Black Educational Support Team, Hispanic Student Association, Indian Cultural Exchange, and Pamoja Dance Company.

### Most Popular Religions
There are a lot of very active Christian groups. Baptist groups probably have the largest numbers. Catholics are the smallest Christian group. There are a significant number of Jewish students. There is a Jewish student center, as well as predominantly Jewish sororities/fraternities for students to join.

## Political Activity

The College Republicans and Young Democrats both have large followings. Both Republicans and Democrats are very active, with both sides hosting lectures, participating in anti- or pro-war demonstrations, and speaking out to newspapers and students.

## Gay Tolerance

The campus is not terribly tolerant toward gays and lesbians. Like any place, there are some students who are supportive of the gay community, and others who are not. There have been several demonstrations at the Tate Center about this issue.

## Economic Status

UGA has students from diverse economic backgrounds, but there seems to be a predominant amount with wealthy parents. However, HOPE scholarship has changed the composition of UGA for the better, allowing large numbers of middle and lower income students the opportunity to come here.

## Students Speak Out
### ON DIVERSITY

"The campus is actually not that diverse. There are some minority groups at UGA, but very few of them. Most of the people here are white."

Q "I'm not going to lie to you. It's not very diverse. **Most of the kids are upper-middle class and white**. UGA is quite lacking in diversity. A whole lot of the kids are from the Atlanta area and are in-state students, mostly because of the HOPE scholarship that is given to Georgia high school students who maintain a GPA of 3.0 or higher. The HOPE pays for a student's in-state tuition."

Q "The minorities that go here are generally accepted and **looked upon as equals**. If you've heard that the South can be very racist, don't be worried about that. Although there are occasionally people who are racist, most of the people who I've met are not."

Q "Racially, the campus isn't as diverse as others, though it seems like it's pretty diverse to me. **It seems like it's more diverse** when you're walking around on campus. Everyone seems to get along, and there are also events organized all the time by certain minority groups."

Q "**Most of my TAs were Asian**, and I know a few African American students here, but there's definitely a white majority. I've heard racist comments on campus and downtown a couple of times, and there is definitely the 'Old South' mind-set in some students, but, being white, I guess I don't know exactly how big of a problem that is."

## The College Prowler Take
### ON DIVERSITY

For a state that is 29 percent black, the fact that only five percent of UGA's student population is African American is pretty pitiful. There are a noteworthy number of Asian and Indian students on campus. Many TAs and professors are Asian or Indian as well. There is a lot of Old South spirit alive at UGA. Many fraternities still fly the Confederate flag every now and again. Because UGA is so predominantly white, this is a fairly common theme. People are not usually openly racist or critical to one's race, but the undercurrent is still there. The good news is that the minority students and clubs on campus seem to be very involved and close-knit. If you can find your niche, you'll probably make friends for life.

**The College Prowler™ Grade on**
## Diversity: D-

A high grade in Diversity indicates that ethnic minorities and international students have a notable presence on campus and that students of different economic backgrounds, religious beliefs, and sexual preferences are well-represented.

# Guys & Girls

## The Lowdown
**ON GUYS & GIRLS**

Women Undergrads: 56%

Men Undergrads: 44%

### Birth Control Available?
Yes, at the University Health Center, birth control prices vary depending on the type and quantity of birth control purchased. For some prescriptions, purchasing a three month supply is cheaper than purchasing one month. Also, costs from the pharmacy do not include a physical exam that may be required for the prescription.

At the pharmacy, birth control pills range in price from $14 to $38 per month depending on the type of pill. OthoEvra (patch) is $22/month, if you buy a three-month supply. Nuvaring (vaginal ring) is $22/month, if you buy a three-month supply. Depo-provera is $49 per shot, which is needed every three months, plus the injection fee. Diaphragms are $34. Condoms are between $5 and $6 for a pack of twelve.

### Social Scene
There are unlimited opportunities to meet people at UGA: on the bus, at the Student Learning Center, in any class, in group projects, in Greek organizations, in clubs, in the library, at sporting events, at coffee shops, and, of course, downtown.

### Hookups or Relationships?
Many people are in stable relationships, but there is a huge pool of singles out there. Hookups are rampant downtown and at football games. Because alcohol is so popular, morning-after experiences and walks of shame are pretty common for many students. Almost everyone is looking for "romance" in some capacity.

### Dress Code
During the week, people wear shorts, tank tops, flip-flops, and T-shirts to class. Some people even wear pajamas. It gets really hot outside, especially if you have to walk fast up a hill to class, so minimal clothing is really a good idea. On game days, its all red and black everywhere you look. Red pants are extremely popular for guys and girls, and you'll find that most of the stores in Athens stock red and black clothing for game days. To go out, most people get dressed up. Many girls will wear designer clothing and stiletto heels downtown. Skimpy little skirts and dresses are always popular. Guys get dressed up too, but in more of an Abercrombie sort of way.

## Students Speak Out
**ON GUYS & GIRLS**

"The guys here are hot, but it seems like they're all taken by the beautiful girls here. A guy once said that if you threw a rock into a crowd, you would hit a hot girl."

Q "The girls on this campus are **the most gorgeous girls that a man will ever encounter** in his life. I can make this claim after having visiting a lot of different schools."

Q "**Most of the guys are gentlemen**, but there are those who think that they're God's gift to women. I've met too many of those."

Q "The girls here are amazing. I'll be honest with you. One of the main reasons I came to school here is because **the girls here are hotter than anything I've ever seen**, and I'm coming from Atlanta. You will not find hotter girls anywhere else, trust me. Not only are they hot, but a lot of them are really easy!"

> "I would have to say **most people here are very good-looking**. There are a lot of fake tans on guys and girls alike and a lot of highlights around campus, and there are definitely girls that go overboard on makeup, but there are a lot of girls who are just naturally beautiful walking around."

# Athletics

## The College Prowler Take
### ON GUYS & GIRLS

Most people at UGA are very good-looking and friendly. There are a lot of tan, toned bodies walking around campus and downtown. Students are often easygoing and looking for a good time, making it at least fairly easy to talk to people. Downtown is always a fashion show, since everyone usually looks their best when they go out. Sometime last year, some of the guys here began wearing short shorts. There is definitely a classic frat boy look involving the short shorts, Rainbow flip-flops, and collared, brightly colored golf shirts. This, coupled with hair that has not been cut since they left home, is pretty standard for many guys. As many students noted, there is also an abundance of ridiculously hot young women on this campus as well—some say the hottest you'll find anywhere!

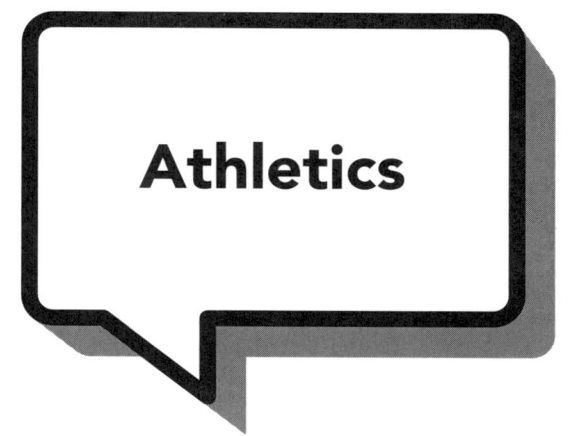

## The Lowdown
### ON ATHLETICS

**Men's Varsity Teams:**
Football
Soccer
Basketball
Cross Country
Track
Golf
Swimming/Diving
Tennis
Cheerleading
Baseball

**Women's Varsity Teams:**
Soccer
Basketball
Cross Country
Track
Swimming
Tennis
Volleyball
Cheerleading
Gymnastics
Golf
Equestrian
Softball

### A

### A+

**The College Prowler™ Grade on Guys: A**

A high grade for Guys indicates that the male population on campus is attractive, smart, friendly, and engaging, and that the school has a decent ratio of guys to girls.

**The College Prowler™ Grade on Girls: A+**

A high grade for Girls not only implies that the women on campus are attractive, smart, friendly, and engaging, but also that there is a fair ratio of girls to guys.

## Intramurals (IMs)
Arena Football, Basketball, Dodge Ball Tournament, Final's 5K Race, Flag Football, Free Throw Contest, Golf Tournament, Indoor Soccer, Outdoor Soccer, Racquetball Tournament, Slam Dunk Contest, Softball, Squash Tournament, Team Tennis, Tennis Tournament, (Doubles, Singles) Three Point Contest, Ultimate Frisbee, Volleyball, Wiffleball

## Club Sports
Aikido, Badminton, Baseball, Chinese Shao-Lin, Crew, Cricket, Cycling, Dodgeball, Equestrian, Fencing, Ice Hockey, Integrated Fighting, Judo, Kali, Karate (Bu Do Kai), Karate (Tae Kwon Do), Kashima Shin Ryu, Lacrosse, Power Lifting, Racquetball, Rugby, Sailing, Soccer, Table Tennis, Tai Chi, Team Handball, Ultimate Frisbee, Volleyball, Water Polo, Water Skiing, White Water Rafting, Wrestling

**Athletic Division:**
NCAA Division I

**Conference:**
SEC

**School Mascot:**
Bulldog

**Fields:**
Intramural Fields off College Station Road

## Most Popular Sports
On the varsity level, the football and basketball teams have the largest presence on campus. All of the IM sports are also very popular. Soccer and basketball draw large numbers, and ultimate Frisbee has a cult following.

## Overlooked Teams
Baseball, hockey, swimming, tennis, soccer, volleyball—basically everything, except football and basketball, is overlooked. With the exception of gymnastics, women's teams don't receive a lot of attention.

## Getting Tickets
Football tickets are complicated. For season tickets, students scan their student IDs and pay for the tickets in the spring, but don't pick up the actual tickets until the fall. For away tickets, students have their IDs scanned and are put into a lottery for each game. E-mails are then sent out to tell you which tickets, if any, you've won. You pay for and receive the away tickets in the fall. Freshmen have their own lottery for home games—some get all the home games and others get only three. Tickets to any other event are under five dollars per event, often free, and shouldn't be a problem to get at the gate.

## Students Speak Out
### ON ATHLETICS

"Varsity sports are huge on campus. UGA wins the most national championships out of any school, except Stanford."

Q "This is UGA! **It's Bulldawg country!** You better get out of town on football weekends if you don't like football. It's a way of life. The games are so much fun. I didn't like football, until I started going to school at UGA. It's awesome, and is always such a great experience!"

Q "**Intramural sports are huge at UGA**. I play basketball and soccer. We have everything here: softball, flag football, indoor and outdoor soccer, swimming, volleyball, ultimate Frisbee, basketball, racquetball, and every IM sport imaginable. The Ramsey Center, which is the student workout center, features two weight rooms, aerobics and gymnastics studios, yoga classes, six basketball courts, racquetball and squash courts, an indoor soccer gym, table tennis, volleyball, swimming pools, and an indoor track. Our intramural fields are also close to Lake Herrick and offer such activities as canoeing, rowing, and fishing. Surrounding the lake are miles of off-road trails and dozens of softball, soccer, rugby, and football fields."

Q "I have lived in Athens my whole life, and **I have grown to hate football season**. You can't go anywhere or do anything on game weekends. Everyone is drunk and obnoxious!"

Q "Our tennis, gymnastics, and swimming and diving teams are national champions every year. However, the lifeblood of the sports program is the football team. Our football team is usually one of the best teams in the country, and you would be **hard-pressed to find someone at UGA who doesn't love the Bulldogs**. Football season is one of the times at UGA when the most partying occurs. Downtown Athens after a home football game is incredible. Intramural sports are also very popular. You can find any sport that you could possibly want."

Q "My friends and I played intramural softball, basketball, and volleyball and we had a blast doing it. **It was a great way for us to hang out and do something different, besides drink**. We were not very good, but it was definitely worth doing."

## The College Prowler Take
ON ATHLETICS

Football is God for many people at UGA. The alumni support for our Dawgs is tremendous. They show up in their RVs and trailers on Thursdays for a Saturday game. Alumni settle all over campus and you will pass many of them grilling and drinking on your way to Friday classes—should you actually choose to go. There is an overwhelming feeling of pride for our Dawgs on game days, especially from the alumni who were around for the low points. Intramural sports are really popular for fitness and recreation. Some of the teams are really good, and others are just horrible. So, at any level, you'll find your niche if you are interested.

**A**

The College Prowler™ Grade on
## Athletics: A

A high grade in Athletics indicates that students have school spirit, that sports programs are respected, that games are well-attended, and that intramurals are a prominent part of student life.

# Greek Life

## The Lowdown
ON GREEK LIFE

**Number of Fraternities:**
28

**Number of Sororities:**
22

**Undergrad Men in Fraternities:**
16%

**Undergrad Women in Sororities:**
20%

### Did You Know?

UGA offers professional fraternities in every college.

The all-fraternity average GPA is 3.07. The average for all male students is 2.96.

The all-sorority average GPA is 3.33. The average for all female students is 3.22.

## Students Speak Out
ON GREEK LIFE

"I think that this is one of the most disappointing aspects of UGA: the Greeks rule. I went through rush, but never pledged. The Greeks definitely dominate the social scene."

"**Greek life is not as big as I thought it would be**. I went through rush last year, but it was just not for me. UGA Greek organizations sponsor one of the most serious rush programs in the South, but if you really want to be in a sorority or a fraternity, I would go through with it. You will meet a lot of new people that way, but if you definitely know that you don't want to be in a sorority or a fraternity, you will not feel left out."

"I think something like 22 percent of the campus is involved in social sororities and fraternities. I am in a professional fraternity and there are many of those that you can join, but none of the Greek organizations dominate the social scene. UGA is a place where **you will not ever feel pressured by the Greeks**, but there is an adequate Greek scene if you decide to join an organization. Either way, you won't lack social opportunities! Trust me!"

"Greek life is pretty big. **Lots of girls rush sororities their freshman year, and some guys rush fraternities**. They mostly mingle with each other, but it's easy to have a great time while not being a member of one."

"Sometimes I feel like there is actually **a lot of animosity between Greeks and non-Greeks**. Any time one Greek person does something wrong, people are so quick to write off the rest of us as drunken party-crazy people. There are way more Greeks who contribute to charities, have good GPAs and are upstanding people than there are screw-ups."

## The College Prowler Take
ON GREEK LIFE

Every night of the week there is some Greek social or party going on, and the themes are really creative. If you have trouble meeting people and making friends on your own, you might want to consider rushing. In a Greek organization, you will meet hundreds of people, both males and females, and there is great camaraderie within the Greek community. The Greeks can tend to dominate social life on campus at times, and if you live in an all-female dorm, there really is no escaping the incessant sorority news and gossip. Some of the Greeks are very stuck-up and snobby, and will not pay any attention to non-Greeks, but of course this does not apply to everyone. Many Greeks comment that while they love being a part of their brotherhood or sisterhood, being Greek involves a lot of time and a lot of money, and can be very stressful at times.

The College Prowler™ Grade on
### Greek Life: A

A high grade in Greek Life indicates that sororities and fraternities are not only present, but also active on campus. Other determining factors include the variety of houses available and the respect the Greek community receives from the rest of the campus.

# Drug Scene

## The Lowdown
ON DRUG SCENE

**Most Prevalent Drugs on Campus:**
Alcohol, Marijuana

**Liquor-Related Arrests:**
433

**Drug-Related Arrests:**
20

## Drug Counseling Programs at the University Health Center

### Health Promotion Department
Phone: (706) 542-8690

The Health Promotion Department focuses on prevention and education. There are courses available concerning alcohol, tobacco, and drugs. Students can find support groups, counseling, intervention information, and there is also a health resource library available.

### Counseling & Psychological Services (CAPS)
Phone: (706) 542-2273

Psychologists team up to work with students suffering from alcohol or drug related issues. Individual therapy sessions are also available if you make an appointment.

### Medical Clinic
Phone: (706) 542-8666

The Medical Clinic conducts drug testing and offers counseling for smokers trying to quit.

### Advantage Behavior Health Systems
Phone: (706) 369-5745

Advantage Behavior Health Systems offers alcohol assessments, a risk reduction course for students, and treatment options.

### Alcoholics Anonymous
Phone: (706) 543-0436

AA is a self-help group for students struggling with alcoholism and their peers.

### Commencement Center
Phone: (706) 475-5797

The Commencement Center has many treatments available for students suffering from alcohol and drug related addictions.

## Students Speak Out
ON DRUG SCENE

"The drug scene is just like that of any other large campus. Pot is popular, and if you do it, that's cool, but if you don't, that's cool, too. I have friends who smoke pot, and friends who don't."

Q "Drugs are present, but it's up to you to decide how close you get to them. I mean **alcohol is obviously prevalent**. I haven't seen much else, though, aside from marijuana. Stuff is available if you ask around, but if you don't want to see anything, you won't."

Q "Cocaine is actually pretty prevalent, but it's kept kind of quiet. I know a few people who do it, but I myself would never get involved in that stuff for obvious reasons. I've **never felt pressured to use it**, and it's not something to be worried about. You just have to think for yourself."

> "I don't know much about the drug scene on campus. There's the occasional marijuana bust in a dorm room, and I think **a girl died at a club last year doing too much ecstasy**. Otherwise, there isn't much of anything at all on campus."

> "The drug scene here at UGA is pretty prevalent. I've heard that one of our dorms actually is **rumored to be one of the top 10 pot-smoking dorms in the nation**. Alcohol is also a very big deal here. Athens has been called a 'drinking town with a football problem' to poke fun at the extreme amounts of alcohol consumed by students."

> "I know people that do drugs, but I would say alcohol is a much bigger problem than, like, cocaine or pot or anything. If you get caught with drugs, especially in the dorms, **you obviously get into a lot of trouble**, and the penalties for alcohol are not as bad."

## The College Prowler Take
### ON DRUG SCENE

Alcohol is definitely the most abused substance on campus. There are a lot of students, especially guys, who drink all the time. Drinking is one of the most popular pastimes at UGA. Alcohol is pretty easy to get, no matter what age you are, and the excitement of downtown just encourages more drinking.

Smoking pot is pretty popular too, but if someone is smoking in a dorm, he or she is usually caught pretty quickly. Creswell Hall is rumored to be one of the most common places people obtain and smoke pot. Cocaine is apparently fairly common on campus, as is ecstasy. There was also a recent story circulating about police finding Oxycontin in someone's dorm. But, none of these are a big problem for UGA. You might hear a handful of stories involving these drugs in a whole year.

Find out more info on counseling programs at UGA by picking up the College Prowler book available on *www.collegeprowler.com.*

**B-**

The College Prowler™ Grade on
### Drug Scene: B-

A high grade on Drug Scene indicates that drugs are not a noticeable part of campus life; drug use is not visible, and no pressure to use them seems to exist.

# Overall Experience

## Students Speak Out
**ON OVERALL EXPERIENCE**

"Sometimes I wish that I had chosen a smaller school, but overall I'm happy that I'm here. After my first year, I found myself feeling more like a number than an actual student. I love this school, but you should consider the size in making your decision."

Q "I had the choice of going to a small private college, and I am so glad that I chose UGA instead. **The trick to succeeding at a big university is to find your niche**. I suggest getting involved. Whether it's in a Greek society or in any of our hundreds of student organizations, you can meet people with similar beliefs and interests, while also being exposed to tons others!"

Q "I absolutely love UGA! If I had the opportunity to go back and do it all over again, I wouldn't change a thing. I have enjoyed my stay here, and I can't wait for the new semester to begin. **Athens is pretty quiet in the summer**, but it's pretty rocking in the fall and spring. I would never go to another college. UGA has more than met my expectations. It gets better and better as each day goes by."

Q "My overall experience has been amazing. **I love it here and am so glad I came**. I have had so much fun these past few years while also getting a great education. In town, there is always something going on, and there are always a ton of people around. It just makes for a great college experience. I wouldn't trade my experience for anything in the world."

Q "**UGA is a lot like a big family**. There are people that annoy you, and people you don't want to see, but overall, you have an overwhelming fondness for people because you know you are all sharing something in common that you can be proud of."

## The College Prowler Take
**ON OVERALL EXPERIENCE**

One of the most amazing things about students at UGA is that you will never hear even one person say they don't like being here. UGA and Athens have so much to offer, in so many different categories, that there really is something for everyone. The positive energy of 30,000 people who are happy to be here is captivating, and something you will instantly want to be a part of. It will not take long before you regard Athens as your second home, and, after about a week, you'll forget how big a school it is.

It's exciting to be in Athens because there is always something going on, whether it is entertainment, a demonstration, job fairs, or just a chance to hang out with people you just met who are now your best friends. Students are encouraged to explore their talents and make the most of their four years here, and most students are able to achieve their ultimate "college experience." Sometimes it seems like we are all characters in some cheesy teen movie because college life in Athens is so classic, but academically, socially, and personally, this school seems to have changed most of us for the better.

# University of Kentucky

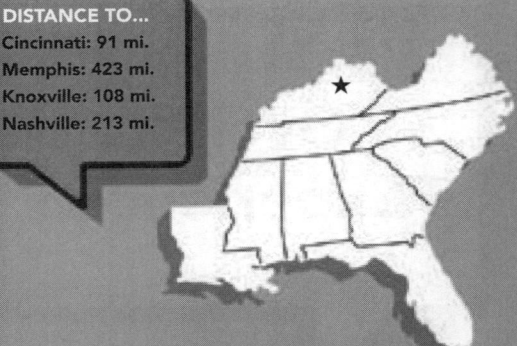

101 Gillis Building, Lexington, KY 40506
www.uky.edu          (800) 432-0967

**DISTANCE TO...**
Cincinnati: 91 mi.
Memphis: 423 mi.
Knoxville: 108 mi.
Nashville: 213 mi.

*"There are many 'true blue' fans out there that can't see UK past its famous football program."*

**Total Enrollment:**
16,274

**Top 10% of High School Class:**
28%

**Average GPA:**
3.6

**Acceptance Rate:**
81%

**Tuition:**
$5,315 in-state, $12,095 out-of-state

**SAT Range (25th-75th Percentile):**

| Verbal | Math | Total |
|---|---|---|
| 510 – 620 | 510 – 630 | 1020 – 1250 |

**ACT Range (25th-75th Percentile):**

| Verbal | Math | Total |
|---|---|---|
| 21-28 | 21-27 | 22-27 |

**Most Popular Majors:**
6% Marketing
6% Finance
5% Psychology
5% Accounting
5% Business

**Students also applied to:***
University of Louisville
Miami University of Ohio
Ohio State University
University of Tennessee

*For more school info check out www.collegeprowler.com

## Table of Contents

| | |
|---|---|
| Academics | 259 |
| Local Atmosphere | 261 |
| Safety & Security | 262 |
| Facilities | 264 |
| Campus Dining | 266 |
| Campus Housing | 267 |
| Diversity | 269 |
| Guys & Girls | 270 |
| Athletics | 272 |
| Greek Life | 273 |
| Drug Scene | 275 |
| Overall Experience | 276 |

## College Prowler Report Card

| | |
|---|---|
| Academics | B- |
| Local Atmosphere | B+ |
| Safety & Security | B- |
| Facilities | B |
| Campus Dining | B- |
| Campus Housing | C+ |
| Diversity | D- |
| Guys | A- |
| Girls | A |
| Athletics | A |
| Greek Life | B+ |
| Drug Scene | B- |

# Academics

**AP Test Score Requirements**
Possible credit for scores of 4 or 5

**IB Test Score Requirements**
Possible credit for scores of 5, 6, or 7

**Sample Academic Clubs**
Academic Team, Accounting Team, Clinical Neurosciences Club, and various honor societies separated by major and class ranking.

## The Lowdown
### ON ACADEMICS

**Degrees Awarded:**
Bachelor, Master, Post-Master Certificate, Doctoral, First Professional

**Undergraduate Schools:**
Agriculture, Architecture, Arts & Sciences, Business & Economics, Communications & Information Studies, Dentistry, Design, Education, Engineering, Fine Arts, Health Sciences, Law, Medicine, Nursing, Pharmacy, Public Health, Social Work

**Full-time Faculty:**
1,800

**Part-time Faculty:**
499

**Faculty with Terminal Degree:**
86%

**Student-to-Faculty Ratio:**
16:1

**Average Course Load:**
Most students take 15 or 18 credit hours

**Special Degree Options:**
Honors Program, Interdisciplinary, Distance Learning, Study Abroad

### Did You Know?
Students looking for peace and quiet should head to the library or either the third or fourth floor of the Stern Center.

**Best Places to Study:**
William T. Young Library or any of the other libraries and labs around campus stay relatively quiet, unless midterm or final exams are approaching.

**COLLEGE PROWLER**

Need help choosing a major? For a detailed listing on all fields of study, check out the College Prowler book on University of Kentucky available at *www.collegeprowler.com*.

## Students Speak Out
### ON ACADEMICS

> "The higher the course number you are in, the more likely the professors will take a personal interest in you. This is especially true for University Studies Program [USP] courses."

Q "I hated every professor I had during my first two years of college, but I began to form better relationships with my professors during my last two years of college. **I have found the majority of my classes to be interesting**. Most of my first year classes weren't as beneficial as they could have been. The professors didn't care if you were there or not, because they will get paid regardless."

Q "For the most part, **teachers are very enthusiastic and helpful**. In high school, they always tell you that college professors won't care to help you or give extra credit, but the teachers at UK actually are really concerned about how students are doing, and most do give extra credit at some point. Not all classes are interesting, but a lot of them are. It's up to students to make an effort to engage themselves in the class."

Q "Most of the teachers are good at what they do, but one **big problem is their availability**. They are not really personable, so as a student, you are expected to find out info yourself, and get things done that way. Sometimes, they are not much help."

Q "The teachers are what can be expected of a university. You've got your arrogant teachers who think they're teaching at Harvard, and then you have your friendly ones who sit there and tell you about their weekend. The main thing is just getting to know the teacher, going to office hours, and e-mailing them. My strategy is to basically be a pest so that they know my name, recognize my face, and realize that I'm one of their students. Those are just the professors. You will also have your typical teaching assistants [TAs] that are foreign, and you won't be able to understand a word they are saying. **UK offers a lot of tutoring for the main courses**; it definitely comes in handy!"

## The College Prowler Take
### ON ACADEMICS

As with most large state schools, students can feel a bit overwhelmed by the undergraduate class sizes during their first few semesters at the University of Kentucky. It may be a bit intimidating to be in a class with 200 or more people, and very tempting to not attend every lecture if attendance is not taken. Although some TAs are foreign and hard to understand, that is true of almost any school. Those freshman 101 classes may seem trivial and pesky, but every school has them and Kentucky is no exception. In the end, once you get into the swing of things, you'll be happier that you went to even the largest, seemingly most insignificant class. With a little self-discipline and dedication, students can make it past those enormous first-year classes and onto smaller more personalized ones.

Getting to know your professors can be a very wise decision to set yourself apart in large introductory classes. It can also be helpful to team up with other students in large classes and form study groups to help everyone keep up with the course load. Chances are, if you're confused, someone in the group can help clear things up, and you can do the same for another student. Not to mention, it is absolutely necessary to know at least a few people in class, just in case you miss the lecture and need to borrow notes or find out what was discussed. The University of Kentucky can seem like a large place until you make friends, and getting to know professors might seem like a task, but it is one that is well worth the effort. It's all about carving a comfortable place for yourself.

**B-**

The College Prowler™ Grade on
## Academics: B-

A high Academics grade generally indicates that professors are knowledgeable, accessible, and genuinely interested in their students' welfare. Other determining factors include class size, how well professors communicate, and whether or not classes are engaging.

# Local Atmosphere

**Did you know?**

Lexington is known for its "bluegrass," which thrives on the limestone beneath the soil. Hence, the state slogan, "The Bluegrass State."

## The Lowdown
ON LOCAL ATMOSPHERE

**Region:**
Southeast

**City, State:**
Lexington, Kentucky

**Setting:**
Small city

**Distance from Louisville:**
1 hour

**Distance from Cincinnati:**
1 hour, 15 minutes

**Points of Interest:**
The Kentucky Horse Park, Victorian Square, the Arboredum, Shakervillage of Pleasant Hill, Keeneland Race Course, Saddle-bred Museum, the Henry Clay Estate, Mary Todd Lincoln House

**Sports Teams:**
The Lexington Legends (minor league baseball)
The Horsemen (indoor football)

**City Website:**
www.visitlex.com

## Students Speak Out
ON LOCAL ATMOSPHERE

"Lexington is a multi-college town. With UK, Lexington Community College, Eastern Kentucky University, Centre, and Transylvania all nearby, there are a bunch of college students running around."

Q "I've lived here my whole life and I like it. Its got things to do ... bowling, clubs, and bars. For the most part, I just hang out at friends' houses. I get a little annoyed that they taking away farm lands, and making more places to shop. They **keep taking away from the beauty of Lexington** just for the sake of expansion."

Q "Transy [Transylvania] is in town, but it is very different from UK. Lexington is kind of a college town, but it seems like **Lexington exploits the University and its tradition**. There is not much diversity of things to do, but I have had a blast with places like Pazzo's and McCarthy's."

Q "Lexington is a nice average size city; we're not too far from other cities, but there are fun things to do in town. The **surroundings are generally pretty**; Lexington is a very clean city. The Fayette County area is very serene, because it surrounds Lexington with countryside and horse farms that provide a great escape from the city."

# Safety & Security

> "The **atmosphere is kind of old-fashioned and not very progressive**. Lexington was once a pretty small town so it still holds those conservative ideals and ways of thinking. However, there are so many people in Lex because of UK, so there are a lot of liberal views, as well. There are some universities close by, such as Transylvania and Georgetown, but I wouldn't say that they really have much of an impact on UK. Keeneland is definitely a good place to visit, as well as the horse park. Nicholasville Road may be a good place to stay away from if you're new in town because traffic there can be overwhelming."

## The College Prowler Take
### ON LOCAL ATMOSPHERE

Lexington is a town rich in the history of horse racing and the Old South. Many historic homes and tourism opportunities make for great weekend trips out into the country. Horse races allow for a reason to get dressed up and spend a day at the track. As home to several other universities, Lexington also provides various other colleges for students to mingle with. Lexington is a fairly traditional city with down-home values and the mentality of a much smaller town. Possibly the best part of Lexington is that it is so close to Cincinnati, Louisville, and several state parks. Students get the best of both worlds—city living and enough outdoor adventure to get away from the exhaust of cars and the stress of schoolwork.

**B+**

The College Prowler™ Grade on
## Local Atmosphere: B+

A high Local Atmosphere grade indicates that the area surrounding campus is safe and scenic. Other factors include nearby attractions, proximity to other schools, and the town's attitude toward students.

## The Lowdown
### ON SAFETY & SECURITY

**Number of UK Police Officers:**
About 40 officers

**Phone:**
Emergency: 911
Non-emergency: (859) 257-5770

**Security Updates Infoline:**
(859) 257-5684

**Health Center Office Hours:**
Fall and Spring Semesters: Mon.- Fri., 8 a.m.-6 p.m., Saturday, 9 a.m.-11 a.m.
Summer Hours: Mon.-Fri, 8 a.m.-4:30 p.m.

**Safety Services:**
Catwalk escort service, blue-light phones, well-lit walkways, shuttle services

### Did You Know?
UK Health Services provides eating disorder information, sleeping disorder tests, and suggestions for different remedies.

## Students Speak Out
### ON SAFETY & SECURITY

> "Security is in numbers at UK. The police do what they can, but things still happen. Students should take advantage of escort services when walking late at night. Police are generally friendly and helpful."

Q "**We have had a few instances** where people have been robbed on campus, however this has generally occurred at night. UK is big campus with a lot of people. Just like being in any big city, I wouldn't walk anywhere alone at night on campus. I usually try to have a guy walk with me, or be with a bunch of people."

Q "They seem to be trying to improve it, but **I keep hearing about different things late at night**; attacks near the library that have been going on for a while now. They don't seem to be able to control that."

Q "There have been quite a few attacks on campus lately, but I've never really felt particularly unsafe. **Campus police take all attacks really seriously**, and always make a big effort to keep students informed so that they can take the necessary precautions. You'll always see a lot of cops around campus, and I think you'd be safe at night, as long as you're not walking alone."

Q "In the past. there were a bunch of incidents right on the outskirts of campus, but UK police did a good job of going door-to-door handing out fliers of wanted persons. Basically, just like any other place, **don't walk alone at night**—there are SafeCats to escort you anywhere on campus at night."

## The College Prowler Take
### ON SAFETY & SECURITY

The Kentucky campus has been featured in several crime reports over the last year, especially crimes against women. However, drastic measures have been instilled to ensure student safety: a large number of officers patrol on bike, foot, and car, and safety buttons have been installed all over campus; just pressing them guarantees a response. Unfortunately, services like Catwalk have been handed over from organization to organization in a bidding war, leaving the service underfunded, and all but abandoned. The best way to stay safe on campus is to store the campus police phone number in your cell phone and always travel with other students if you have to walk on campus at night. There really is safety in numbers! With a good measure of common sense, students should be safe on campus.

**B-**

**The College Prowler™ Grade on**
## Safety & Security: B-

A high grade in Safety & Security means that students generally feel safe, campus police are visible, blue-light phones and escort services are readily available, and safety precautions are not overly necessary.

# Facilities

## The Lowdown
### ON FACILITIES

**Student Center:**
It features a Starbucks, Kentucky Fried Chicken, Long John Silver's, pizza, sub, and smoothie shops. It houses the campus radio station, WRFL, as well as Student Government, Student Activities Board, and clubs. There is also a bookstore located in the Student Center addition.

**Libraries:**
William T. Young, Margaret I. King, and several other smaller libraries

**Athletic Center:**
The Johnson Center is open to all UK students and offers free classes, machines, free weights, racquetball courts, basketball courts, an indoor track and locker rooms.

**Aquatic Center:**
Lancaster Aquatic Center offers recreational swimming hours that change weekly, depending on swim meets, etc. It's free to swim but bring your own towel, unless you want to rent one. Lockers are also available to rent while you swim!

**Popular Places to Chill:**
Common Grounds Coffee House, Tolly-Ho, K-Lair, Jimmy John's, Kirklevington Park, The Arboretum, Jacobson Park

## Favorite Things to Do

Greek events are popular with students. Just before the Kentucky versus Florida football game, the Student Activities Board sponsors a "Gator Roast" where they block off a section of the Avenue of Champions to traffic and have a live band play. The Mr. UK Pageant has become a favorite event, as well as Greek Sing.

Football games in the fall are a tradition even stronger than the Kentucky's poor football record. Fans tailgate around Commonwealth Stadium for hours, or even days, before kickoff and share food and school pride. The UK men's basketball team is the pride of the school, and many students spend evenings in the winter and spring studying at ticket lotteries hoping to get good seats to a basketball game. The UK Cool Cats hockey team has a loyal following, and the games make the perfect weekend activity, as they start at midnight.

## Computers

**High-Speed Network?** Yes

**Wireless Network?** Yes

**Number of Labs:** 21

**24-Hour Labs:**
There are two located at Boyd Hall and the Commons.

**Charge to Print:**
Typically 10 cents for black and white and 50 cents for color, deducted from a Wildcard account

## Students Speak Out
### ON FACILITIES

"The facilities are state-of-the-art. The library is really big, and we just got a brand-new athletics facility that is free for students to work out at."

Q "There are free workout facilities and a pool; there's an **outdoor center where you can rent camping equipment**; the computers are updated regularly. As far as the student center is concerned, no one hangs out there, except to wait for their next class or to eat lunch. There's a game room, but there's never anyone there."

Q "The athletic facilities are top-notch because they are brand-new. **Athletics are very important to UK**. I don't like the student center because it is on the northwestern part of campus, away from the athletic facilities and the largest part of campus housing."

Q "**UK's student center has improved since we got a Starbucks**. They've tried to clean it up and modernize it. They are trying to give it a new look. It seems to be pretty popular, because there are always people there to meet for coffee between classes. It's quite small and there isn't really enough room for people to sit and stay in there for any length of time."

Q "The **Johnson Center is great to work out in**, brand-new and has easy to use machines, if you go at certain times. The student center is a little outdated, but nice if you have a dining card and can eat on campus, because it's close to the buildings."

## The College Prowler Take
### ON FACILITIES

By far the largest monetary commitment the University makes besides education is athletics (a close second). With the opening of the Johnson Center, students have a state-of-the-art workout facility where they can climb, run, swim, play, and take classes on fitness. Don't expect much elbow room just after New Year's or before spring break. After a few nights of working out during the busiest time, you'll develop a schedule to work around the masses.

The student center, however, is anything but state-of-the-art. Unattractive architecturally, it seems to be an afterthought to some of the more attractive and historical buildings on campus. Perhaps Kentucky just needs a little face-lift to take care of some of those concrete monsters from the sixties they like to hold classes in. However, the Johnson Center alone merits a high rank in this category.

**B**

**The College Prowler™ Grade on**
## Facilities: B

A high Facilities grade indicates that the campus is aesthetically pleasing and well-maintained; facilities are state-of-the-art, and libraries are exceptional. Other determining factors include the quality of both athletic and student centers and an abundance of things to do on campus.

# Campus Dining

## Students Speak Out
### ON CAMPUS DINING

"The food on campus is fine, but not great. Avoid the fast food places in the student center—grease, grease, and more grease. K-Lair serves good hangover food."

Q "**Campus food sucks and costs more**. Pazzos, Jimmy John's, Kashmir, and Qdoba are all around campus, so you'll never go hungry."

Q "**Food on campus is pretty good**. There's Starbucks and KFC and more cafeteria-like food. Ovid's in the library is really good, and so is Intermezzo."

Q "The food court in the **student center seems to have a good variety** of places; there is LJS, pizza, KFC, sub sandwiches, Mexican, burgers, etc. It seems that many people go there to eat. South Campus offers the Commons dining hall with nearly the same food options."

Q "Commons is on South Campus and has about everything you could ask for, even hand-dipped ice cream! **The best place, by far, on campus is Ovid's**. It's in the same building as the library. They have good salads, wraps, sandwiches, and awesome desserts. They are a little expensive, but I would rather pay the extra money to eat there."

Q "Food on campus is pretty good. The biggest place is the Commons Market on South Campus where the two dorm towers are located. They have sandwich places, stir-fry, grills, pasta, **baked potato bars and salad bars**—lots of goodies. There are your usual grease pits or the fancy Ovid's Cafe in our monstrous library."

## The Lowdown
### ON CAMPUS DINING

**Freshman Meal Plan Requirement?**
Yes

**24-Hour On-Campus Eating?**
No, but Tolly-Ho is close-by and always open.

**Student Favorites:**
Cafe, the Commons, K-Lair, Blazer Courtyard

---

**COLLEGE PROWLER**

Hungry? For a detailed listing on all eateries on and off campus, check out the College Prowler book on UK available at www.collegeprowler.com.

## The College Prowler Take
ON CAMPUS DINING

Don't be surprised when halfway through your freshman year you have become too wide for your twin extra-long dorm bed. Kentucky offers a variety of food that will more than double you in size, if you aren't careful. Most students seem to feel that it is overpriced because of the convenience, and nobody seems satisfied with the campus dining plan for the Wildcat Card. There are great places on campus to get a cup of coffee and slice of cheesecake for late-night studying. If you live on Central Campus, definitely plan on spending some time in the legendary K-Lair Grill. You might also want to spend some time working out afterward, to keep from getting too pudgy.

**B-**

The College Prowler™ Grade on
## Campus Dining: B-
Our grade on Campus Dining addresses the quality of both school-owned dining halls and independent on-campus restaurants as well as the price, availability, and variety of food.

# Campus Housing

## The Lowdown
ON CAMPUS HOUSING

**Undergrads on Campus:**
25%

**Number of Residence Halls/Houses:**
19

**Number of College-Owned Apartments:**
Paige Apartments; 25 buildings, each with 8 two-bedroom apartments

**Room Types:**
Singles, Doubles, and Suites

**Cleaning Service?**
Common bathrooms are attended to by staff, but rooms are the occupants' responsibility.

**You Get:**
Each dorm room offers Internet access, phone lines, desk, bed, and a closet.

### Did You Know?

Haggin Hall is referred to as "the Dungeon" by students.

Donovan Hall is known as "the Virgin Vault."

## Students Speak Out
### ON CAMPUS HOUSING

"The North Campus dorms are old, but not so bad. The Kirwan and Blanding dorms are okay, too, but the towers have bars on the windows and feel like prisons. Haggin Hall is like a nightmare."

"**I would go with South Campus dorms**. That's where the majority of freshmen live. They're small and compact, but accessible to the Johnson Center and the football stadium. Lots of the South Campus dorms became 24 hour visitation this year. North Campus is for academics, usually quiet. Donovan and Haggin are strict … Haggin is the nastiest dorm on campus."

"I lived in the Wesley Foundation for Methodist students. Other denominations live there, but they want Christian people there. The one thing that I did like is that we had our own kitchen, so we could cook and not eat out all the time. Some of the dorms have one kitchen for several hundred people. We shared it between 50. The Wesley Foundation had visitation hours and an **open door policy if you had a visitor of the opposite sex**. Many people didn't like that. It is important to choose your housing carefully based on your own personal beliefs and comfort levels."

"I lived in Kirwan and it was one of the nicest dorms on campus. Usually the whole Kirwan-Blanding complex is a nicer option for campus housing. **I would never live in Haggin Hall** or any of the dorms on North Campus because they lack air conditioning."

## The College Prowler Take
### ON CAMPUS HOUSING

An integral part of college life for any student is the journey of self-discovery. The best way to learn about your own personal limitations as a human being is to live in a dormitory at Kentucky. You will learn what true compromise is, and maybe even come out of it all with a few good friends. Most students live in the dorms for at least one year and hate it the entire time because the rooms are so old and small. Ask them a few years later though and they will tell you they had the time of their life.

**The College Prowler™ Grade on**
## Campus Housing: C+

A high Campus Housing grade indicates that dorms are clean, well-maintained, and spacious. Other determining factors include variety of dorms, proximity to classes, and social atmosphere.

# Diversity

## The Lowdown ON DIVERSITY

**Native American:** 0%

**African American:** 5%

**Asian American:** 2%

**White:** 91%

**Hispanic:** 1%

**International:** 1%

**Out-of-State:** 14%

**Most Popular Religions**
Christianity (Protestant and Catholic) is, by far, the most represented religion on campus.

**Political Activity**
UK offers clubs of various party affiliations, but it tends to maintain a conservative air.

**Economic Status**
The University of Kentucky tends to attract students from middle-class backgrounds whose parents are helping pay for their educations.

**Minority Clubs**
There are a few African American fraternities and sororities on campus.

**Gay Tolerance**
The Lavender Society and Lambda Lambda Lambda offer activities and support for gay students.

## Students Speak Out ON DIVERSITY

"I think campus could be more diverse, but I've met people from all walks of life."

"Most of the international students tend to stay with people of their nationality. **There isn't a lot of race intermingling at UK**. This is especially evident in dining halls and large campus functions where a lot of people would be gathered. UK is predominantly voluntarily segregated."

"UK is not as diverse as it should be for a school of its size. When you walk into the student center, there are two distinct sides divided by color. The black students keep themselves, and they are in a stark minority. I don't always see a lot of diversity at UK; **people tend to stick with people that look like them**, unless they are in a major with people from other backgrounds."

"In ethnicity, the campus isn't very diverse; **it's mostly white, some black, and Asian**. However, in interests and stuff like that it is very diverse; you can join a group or club for any interest."

"Diversity is a problem at UK; **it is basically all white here**."

"**There's a little bit of everything on campus**, which is really cool. I've met so many different people, and I've learned so much from my new friendships."

## The College Prowler Take
### ON DIVERSITY

If you are a white, middle-class suburbanite, be prepared to be surrounded by thousands of people just like you. It is a strange occasion to hear anyone refer to the University of Kentucky as diverse, and if they do, nobody takes them seriously. When you consider the variety of ethnicities in the state, it is actually quite shocking that UK has maintained such a homogenous population. A quick stroll through the student center during lunch time will give you an idea of what a black and white campus it is: there is a perfect division that is seldom crossed between students of different races. The lack of diversity is one of UK's setbacks and seems to be one of the limitations of the old-fashioned values the school is known for. If diversity is number one on the list of things you're looking for in a school, you should know that UK is not the place that you are going to find it.

## Guys & Girls

### The Lowdown
### ON GUYS & GIRLS

**Women Undergrads:** 52%

**Men Undergrads:** 48%

## D-

The College Prowler™ Grade on
### Diversity: D-

A high grade in Diversity indicates that ethnic minorities and international students have a notable presence on campus and that students of different economic backgrounds, religious beliefs, and sexual preferences are well-represented.

### Birth Control Available?
Yes, its available through University Health Services.

### Social Scene
Most students are either in relationships or aren't dating. Very few people casually date.

### Hookups or Relationships?
Many students are in committed relationships, but hookups do occur. If students hook up, they are likely to start dating.

### Dress Code
Students wear a wide variety of clothing to classes, everything from the "just rolled out of bed" pajamas look to the "ultra prim and proper" Greek look. For going out, most students dress up a bit more than they would for class, especially if they are going dancing.

## Students Speak Out
### ON GUYS & GIRLS

"Guys are laid-back; girls are blonde. Girls ... many are high maintenance. Guys are usually former athletes. Sorority girls think the campus is theirs, but guys get sick of them after the first year."

Q "The men at UK seem to be a mixture of different types of guys. It really depends on where you are. We have super preppy geeks, a few punk rockers, and a lot of country boys around the engineering building. For the most part, they are gentlemen. They will hold doors open for you and offer you their seat. **There are always a few rotten apples.**"

Q "**Some guys on campus are gentlemen**, others are better to avoid. Greek guys tend to be full of themselves. Most of the girls at UK are attractive, friendly and intelligent, however a few that choose to go the sorority route tend to lack the common knowledge imparted upon their far superior, independent counterparts."

Q "Most of the guys are okay, pretty nice to get along with. **There are lots of hot girls**, too."

Q "**All 12,000 guys rock**. The same sweeping generalization holds true for the ladies."

Q "The **girls at UK are just as diverse as the men**; they seem to be friendly for the most part. Sometimes it takes them a little while to open up to you, but they will smile and be friendly when you walk by."

## The College Prowler Take
### ON GUYS & GIRLS

Attractive people are never in short supply at Kentucky. After being chosen as having the most attractive girls in the SEC by *Playboy* magazine several years running, UK has quite a reputation. You'll find everyone at UK, from farm kids to upper-crust country club types with old family money. There are plenty of opportunities to meet people at parties and in class. A social life is not hard to come by at Kentucky. Just make sure that you are studying as much astronomy as you are heavenly bodies. All in all, Kentucky has some very stunning eye candy for a walk to class.

**The College Prowler™ Grade on**
### Guys: A-

A high grade for Guys indicates that the male population on campus is attractive, smart, friendly, and engaging, and that the school has a decent ratio of guys to girls.

**The College Prowler™ Grade on**
### Girls: A

A high grade for Girls not only implies that the women on campus are attractive, smart, friendly, and engaging, but also that there is a fair ratio of girls to guys.

# Athletics

## The Lowdown
### ON ATHLETICS

**Athletic Division:**
NCAA Division I

**Conference:**
Southeastern Conference and Mid-American Conference (soccer)

**School Mascot:**
The Wildcat

**Getting Tickets:**
Basketball tickets are hard to get unless you're a student or very wealthy; football tickets are easier.

**Men's Varsity Teams:**
Baseball
Basketball
Cross Country
Football
Golf
Riflery
Soccer
Swimming and Diving
Tennis
Track (indoor and outdoor)

**Women's Teams:**
Basketball
Cross Country
Golf
Gymnastics
Riflery
Soccer
Softball
Swimming and Diving
Tennis
Track (indoor and outdoor)
Volleyball

**Number of Club Sports:**
27

**Number of Intramurals (IMs):**
20 and constantly growing

**Most Popular Sports:**
Basketball, Football

**Overlooked Teams:**
Hockey

**Fields:**
Seton Center fields, Haggin Field, Stoll Field

## Students Speak Out
### ON ATHLETICS

"**UK basketball is bigger than Godzilla on a bender, while football is getting some steam. IM sports are fun, and people like to get involved.**"

"**Basketball and football dominate the sports scene.** But, club sports like hockey can have a cult following. IMs are great to play, as well."

"**Greek IM sports are a good way to socialize** with other members of the Greek community. There are various sports and leagues available; they provide a great way to meet people, and it's always important to uphold the tradition of winning certain events that your fraternity or sorority wins year after year."

"Varsity sports at UK are huge, especially basketball. UK basketball is life. Our football team, well, we enjoy rooting for the underdog. A lot of people get season tickets, and **enjoy the tailgating before games**. It often becomes a bigger event than the actual game."

> "**Football and basketball bring in the money** for our athletic program. They get the most publicity. There has been an effort to publicize more women's sports like basketball and gymnastics. They buy billboards, commercials, and offer prizes for attendance. I've got friends that play IM softball and flag football. Students form independent leagues and compete against each other's dorms, clubs, or majors."

## The College Prowler Take
ON ATHLETICS

The truly wonderful thing about Kentucky athletics is the opportunity to watch basketball, or to actually play in an intramural sport. Kentucky basketball is infectious. It will bring you to your feet, and give you some great memories of your college years, if you let it. The football team doesn't exactly have a winning record, but the fans are die hard, loyal, and don't ever seem to care about what the actual score was. Greek sports and intramurals are a great way to get involved and make some friends while staying in shape. Leagues are easy to form and join and most schools or organizations have some sort of opportunity, for sport. Be ready to wear blue constantly and have your life be dictated by Big Blue Fever during basketball season, if you attend Kentucky.

### The College Prowler™ Grade on
## Athletics: A

A high grade in Athletics indicates that students have school spirit, that sports programs are respected, that games are well-attended, and that intramurals are a prominent part of student life.

# Greek Life

## The Lowdown
ON GREEK LIFE

**Number of Fraternities:**
23, 15 have houses

**Number of Sororities:**
16, 14 have houses

**Undergrad Men in Fraternities:**
18%

**Undergrad Women in Sororities:**
22%

**Other Greek Organizations:**
Greek Council, Greek Peer Advisors, Interfraternity Council, Order of Omega, Panhellenic Council

### Did You Know?

With approximately 20 percent of students involved in a Greek organization, Greeks control student government and many leadership positions.

## Students Speak Out
### ON GREEK LIFE

> "Greek life is huge. I think they have like 1,500 girls rush every year. After the first two years, the Greeks finally realize there are other people outside their circle and relax a little."

Q "It sort of creeps me out a little, but I have friends who are Greek and **they throw decent parties**."

Q "Greek life dominates UK's social scene because most Greek organizations host events together, and this creates a large intermingling of people. A large amount of UK's population, is Greek. **Greek life is fun and outgoing** and provides an easy avenue to meeting new people and forming lasting friendships, not only with people your age, but people older and younger than you. Greek life is good, however, getting involved in other campus organizations, like Campus Crusade for Christ, or something else, can create just as many possibilities for socializing."

Q "With student government elections, there are cliques that give you a better chance of getting into office. They control student government, and are, by far, the loudest voices on campus. **Many of the independent students feel underrepresented**, and that their voices are not heard, because they don't have that kind of support. Greeks at UK love to be loud and proud, often in an obnoxious way."

## The College Prowler Take
### ON GREEK LIFE

Most students at Kentucky that go Greek do so at the demand of their parents, or because they are looking for a way to make friends quickly, and have people to party with. Luckily, most students at UK are not Greek, and enjoy mixing with the rest of campus. Greeks seem to be a dying breed at UK, especially after they have completed their freshman year rush; few people that rush stay in for more than two years. If you are interested in Greek life or wish to run for student government—an institution that is completely controlled by Greeks—be prepared to drop a few hundred dollars each semester buying clothes to impress people you barely know. Rush is the first week of school, and you'll have hundreds of "best friends" at the end of the week.

**B+**

### COLLEGE PROWLER

Find out which house is best for you. Check out the College Prowler book on UK available at www.collegeprowler.com.

**The College Prowler™ Grade on Greek Life: B+**

A high grade in Greek Life indicates that sororities and fraternities are not only present, but also active on campus. Other determining factors include the variety of houses available and the respect the Greek community receives from the rest of the campus.

# Drug Scene

## The Lowdown
ON DRUG SCENE

**Most Prevalent Drugs on Campus:**
Marijuana, Caffeine

**Liquor-Related Referrals:**
373

**Drug-Related Referrals:**
91

**Drug Counseling Programs:**
Higher Education Center for Alcohol and Other Drug Prevention, Alanon, Alcoholics Anonymous and Adult Children of Alcoholics

Bluegrass Area Central Offices
(859) 276-2917

Narcotics Anonymous, Lexington
(859) 253-4673

## Students Speak Out
ON DRUG SCENE

"People who aren't serious about school or their grades smoke marijuana. They usually end up spending an extra year or two in college. It's your call."

Q "**Drugs are all over the place**, but kept under raps, normally."

Q "**Lots of people smoke pot**, and the majority drink on the weekends. That's about all I know."

Q "I've seem people smoking marijuana in houses around campus. It goes on all the time. **Security is pretty lax about it**."

Q "**It is definitely here**, but I am not sure how big or small the scene is."

Q "Yeah they are there, but how much, I don't know. I hung out with **some people in the dorms who smoked weed every day**, but that was the extent of the drugs I saw. I know there are others, though."

Q "As far as drugs are concerned, **marijuana is a cash crop in Kentucky**, and you won't have trouble finding anything else you could want. But, if you're not into drugs, you'll never have to see them. And unless you try to get caught, you probably won't."

Q "It's there I guess, but it's not by any means in your face. **Drinking is just more common here**. I know that if you wanted drugs, you probably wouldn't have any trouble finding them, but really, you just don't see it a lot, and you rarely hear of drug busts."

## The College Prowler Take
### ON DRUG SCENE

Just as in high school, there will be people at Kentucky who are interested in drugs and not in school. They will, however, probably be in college for the better part of a decade. Drugs are available depending on the sort of people you socialize with. For the most part, there are so many activities that don't involve drugs that you may never notice them.

There is no peer pressure involved with the drug scene on campus, but you may want to keep a close eye on your drink at parties, as people have been known to wake up the next morning not knowing where they are. Use good judgment, and watch who you hang out with.

**B-**

The College Prowler™ Grade on
### Drug Scene: B-

A high grade on Drug Scene indicates that drugs are not a noticeable part of campus life; drug use is not visible, and no pressure to use them seems to exist.

## Overall Experience

### Students Speak Out
### ON OVERALL EXPERIENCE

"UK is a great school, and I'll be proud to have a degree on my wall that says I went to school here."

Q "I'm glad I stayed somewhat close to home. **I like the big school and the atmosphere**. I've done well in school and will be graduating in four years. Plus, it's still really affordable compared to other colleges."

Q "I love UK. I love the School of Journalism. And I'm going to enjoy my senior year, because I'll sure miss it and the people once I'm gone. I'm glad I didn't transfer, which earlier in my career, I gave serious consideration to. I'm a Kentucky boy, and **I don't want to be anywhere else**."

Q "I've actually really enjoyed my experience at UK very much. It's been great to be able to be near my family, and make so many friends in my program and form close friendships. **My overall experience has been great**."

Q "My experience at UK has been very interesting, to say the least. I don't regret the parties I've been to, all the women I've hooked up with, skipping classes. I've enjoyed every minute of my five years here and would do it all over again. I wouldn't want to be anywhere else, because **UK feels like home to me**."

# The College Prowler Take
## ON OVERALL EXPERIENCE

Kentucky students bleed blue and take any chance they get to display their spirit. Some students can feel overwhelmed when they first come to campus by all the organizations and people. It takes about a year to really settle in and find a group or niche on campus that makes you feel like you belong.

Kentucky offers a well-rounded education and opportunities for networking and making friends while staying in a mid-sized city with traditional values. With the exception of the parking problem, the lack of diversity, and the sometimes annoying Greek population, Kentucky provides students with a great education and a great experience, both in and out of the classroom.

Read more students' opinions on their overall experience in the College Prowler book on the University of Kentucky available at www.collegeprowler.com.

# University of Mississippi

**DISTANCE TO...**
Atlanta: 335 mi.
New Orleans: 354 mi.
Memphis: 81 mi.
Nashville: 286 mi.

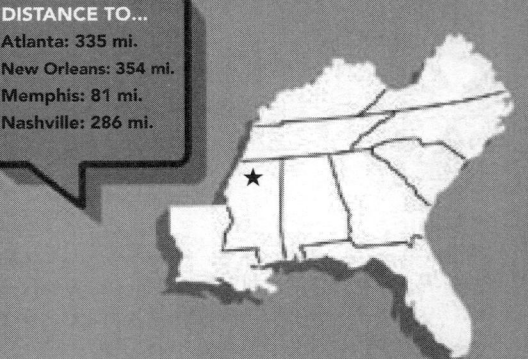

PO Box 1848 University, MS 38677-1848
www.olemiss.edu       (662) 915-7226

*"Attending a Southern university has many stigmas that Northern universities and their students don't know about."*

**Total Enrollment:**
10,079

**Top 10% of High School Class:**
35%

**Average GPA:**
3.4

**Acceptance Rate:**
80%

**Tuition:**
$4,110 in-state, $9,264 out-of-state

**ACT Range (25th-75th Percentile)**
| Verbal | Math | Total |
|---|---|---|
| 20-27 | 18-25 | 20-26 |

**Most Popular Majors:**
8% Elementary Education and Teaching
7% Marketing/Marketing Management
6% English Language and Literature
6% Accounting
5% Business/Commerce

**Students also applied to:***
Mississippi State University
Auburn University
University of Alabama
Jackson State University

*For more school info check out www.collegeprowler.com

## Table of Contents

| | |
|---|---|
| Academics | 279 |
| Local Atmosphere | 281 |
| Safety & Security | 282 |
| Facilities | 284 |
| Campus Dining | 285 |
| Campus Housing | 287 |
| Diversity | 288 |
| Guys & Girls | 290 |
| Athletics | 291 |
| Greek Life | 293 |
| Drug Scene | 294 |
| Overall Experience | 296 |

## College Prowler Report Card

| | |
|---|---|
| Academics | B- |
| Local Atmosphere | A- |
| Safety & Security | A- |
| Facilities | B |
| Campus Dining | C- |
| Campus Housing | C+ |
| Diversity | D |
| Guys | B- |
| Girls | A |
| Athletics | A |
| Greek Life | A |
| Drug Scene | B- |

278 | UNIVERSITY OF MISSISSIPPI

# Academics

## The Lowdown
ON ACADEMICS

**Degrees Awarded**:
Bachelor, Master, and Doctorate

**Undergraduate Schools**:
College of Liberal Arts, School of Accountancy, School of Business Administration, School of Education, School of Engineering, School of Pharmacy and School of Applied Sciences

**Full-time Faculty**:
550

**Faculty with Terminal Degree**:
83%

**Student-to-Faculty Ratio**:
21:1

**Average Course Load**:
5 courses/15 hours

## AP Test Score Requirements
There is possible credit for scores of 3, 4, or 5, depending on your school.

## IB Test Score Requirements
There is possible credit for scores of 5 or higher in the higher level. Once the admissions office receives your transcripts they will cart them off to your respective schools where the department will decide what classes you will receive credit for.

## Sample Academic Clubs
Academy of Student Pharmacists, Air Force Reserve Officer Training Corps (AFROTC), American Indian Science and Engineering Society, American Marketing Association, American Society of Civil Engineering, American Society of Mechanical Engineers, Black Law Student Association, Institute of Electrical and Electronics Engineers, Kappa Psi, Mississippi Association of Physicists, Mississippi Law Journal, National Association of Black Journalists

## Special Degree Options
Dual-Degrees: Bachelor of Accountancy; Bachelor of Arts in Liberal Arts; Bachelor of Arts in Education: Elementary Education, English, Mathematics, Social Studies; Bachelor of Science in Criminal Justice; Bachelor of Science in Nursing; Bachelor of Science in Paralegal Studies

One-year Master degree available for a general Master in Business Administration (MBA)

## Did You Know?
There are fewer than 20 students in 40 percent of classes at Ole Miss.

Among other things, the J.D. Williams Library features the Hall of Mississippi Writers, the William Faulkner Room, and the world-famous Music/Blues Archive.

## Students Speak Out
ON ACADEMICS

"**The teachers here really take an interest in their students. They care about more than just lecturing; they want their students to succeed in class and in life.**"

"I loved my history classes, especially the Civil War and Civil Rights Movement classes. Since the University is home to a Civil War cemetery and was the site of important Civil Rights protests, it **made the classes come alive**."

> "My teachers were extremely personable. I felt as though I could go to them at any time, and talk about anything. When it came time for me to apply to graduate schools, they went to unbelievable extremes to help me gather information, as well as write recommendations. My teachers seemed **enthusiastic about the subjects** they taught and very educated!"

> "The majority of **my teachers at Ole Miss were outstanding**. I developed friendships with many of them that I will keep for the rest of my life. I felt that most of them really cared about the students and were very passionate about their area of expertise."

> "For the most part, the teachers don't care about the students. They are **underpaid and more interested in their research**. They will tell you that their job does not revolve around the students."

> "The teachers and classes at Ole Miss are like pretty much everything else. Some are great, with the ability to inspire students, and some are not so great. Many schools have restructured their schedules and programs so that a majority of the classes, even entry level ones, are **taught by tenured professors** assisted by graduate assistants, rather than the other way around."

## The College Prowler Take
### ON ACADEMICS

As an out-of-state student, many people may ask you, "Why would you go to Mississippi to get an education?" Well, there are plenty of reasons! One of them is that you get a great education at a reasonable price. If you ask any student, you will probably hear that most entry level and required classes are boring. The basic, 100-level classes are "weed-out" classes. They're not fun in any way, shape, or form, but the great thing about Ole Miss is that the school has made sure to keep the professors, not graduate students, in charge of these classes. Once you make it past those 100-level classes, it's smooth sailing.

Since teachers at Ole Miss have the luxury of teaching small classes, they are able to make time for each individual student. At large universities, you may become just a number, but at Ole Miss you are a person with a name, a face, and individual needs. Because of the small class sizes, students are less intimidated to ask questions or to see their teachers outside of class. As you progress into the upper-level classes, you will meet students who are in the same field as you. In some cases, Ole Miss teachers become lifelong friends who can help students achieve their goals and assist them when you apply for law school, graduate school, or a job.

**B-**

The College Prowler™ Grade on
## Academics: B-

A high Academics grade generally indicates that professors are knowledgeable, accessible, and genuinely interested in their students' welfare. Other determining factors include class size, how well professors communicate, and whether or not classes are engaging.

# Local Atmosphere

## The Lowdown
### ON LOCAL ATMOSPHERE

**Region**:
South

**City, State**:
Oxford, Mississippi

**Setting**:
Small city of about 10,000 residents

**Distance from Tupelo**:
50 minutes

**Distance from Memphis**:
1 hour, 15 minutes

**Points of Interest**:
The largest Cedar Bucket in the world, John Grisham's home on Highway 6, Rowan Oak (William Faulkner's home), the Confederate graveyard, Doorknob to the Universe, and Sardis Lake

**Major Sports Teams**:
Memphis Grizzlies—NBA Basketball
Memphis River Kings—Minor-league (CHL) professional hockey

**City Websites**:
www.oxfordms.com
www.oxfordarts.com

## Students Speak Out
### ON LOCAL ATMOSPHERE

"The atmosphere at Oxford is unique. During the famous football months, the tiny, unique town of Oxford is so full of energy and school spirit that you can literally feel it in the air."

Q "The downtown square is famous for **Square Books**, where you can see tons of famous authors' autographs and enjoy coffee or ice cream while sitting up on the balcony that overlooks the Square. The dining experience is incredible in Oxford, with places such as Bottletree Bakery, City Grocery, and the Downtown Grill."

Q "Oxford is a true college town—small and focused on the University. **Oxonians are warm and eager to build relationships with the student body**. Many of the University's service projects and traditions overlap with those of the Oxford-Lafayette community. Visit Graceland Too in Holly Springs; it's an Ole Miss tradition. Late on Friday and Saturday nights, carloads of students make the 40-minute drive to see 'Elvis.'"

Q "The town of Oxford is amazing!!! It may seem like a small place, but once you actually start meeting people and going out, it will seem like the best place for any university to be. There's a junior college in Oxford—Northwest Community College. The town is so small and compact, but there is so much to visit. **You must drive to Graceland, too** before you leave Oxford—you'll be talking about it for ages! The Square is a wonderful place to shop, eat, and to just hang out."

Q "The atmosphere at Ole Miss is definitely a warm one. Everyone is friendly. The town and University represent the idea of southern hospitality. No other major universities are present and the town is small, but the **nightlife is great.** There are many bars to go to, and you'll more than likely see many people you know when you go out."

Q "The atmosphere of the town centers around the University. During the summer months, Oxford gets a little bit of a breather before it springs back into action with the arrival of a new school year. If you're coming to the University as a graduate student or for law school, you'll quickly learn which local hangouts are known as '**kiddie bars**.' Avoid these 'kiddie bars' like the plague if you are over 21. The Square is loaded with great shopping and great food, so start working your way around."

## Safety & Security

## The College Prowler Take
ON LOCAL ATMOSPHERE

## The Lowdown
ON SAFETY & SECURITY

**Oxford is like no other place on earth. It doesn't have that "Mississippi redneck" feel that one might expect. Oxford is a very artsy, intelligent town with a huge music and literary scene. Every spring, there's the William Faulkner Conference of the Book, which brings in Faulkner scholars from all over the world and provides students a great opportunity to gain knowledge outside of the classroom. Oxford may be located in a state typically thought of as backwoods and uneducated, but when you enter the city limits, you will feel its rich history, and be eager to experience all the literature, films, and music you can in the four or five years that you are lucky enough to reside in this little haven of a city. You will find at least as many options for entertainment as cities much bigger than Oxford offer.**

**Number of UPD Police**: Around 25

**Phone**: (662) 915-7234

**Website**: www.olemiss.edu/depts/u_police/

**Health Center Office Hours**: Monday-Friday, 8:00 a.m. - 5 p.m.

**Student Health Services phone**: (662) 915-7275

**Wellness Center (counseling) phone**: (662) 915-3784

**Safety Services**: 24-hour patrols, HEAT unit (housing enhancement awareness team, assigned in and around residence halls from 10 p.m. to 6 a.m.), escort service (Rebel Patrol) in evening hours, Code Blue emergency telephone system for immediate assistance—dial 9-411 for a police emergency; 9-911 for fire dept. and ambulance; dial 9-232-1439 for Crisis Intervention, and enter your phone number for an immediate call back.

## A-

The College Prowler™ Grade on
## Local Atmosphere: A-

A high Local Atmosphere grade indicates that the area surrounding campus is safe and scenic. Other factors include nearby attractions, proximity to other schools, and the town's attitude toward students.

## Students Speak Out
### ON SAFETY & SECURITY

"I have never felt unsafe walking at night anywhere on campus. I know that if there ever was a problem, there are emergency phones located all over campus."

Q "I feel **extremely safe on and off campus**. Oxford is a small community, so you always feel safe. The campus police make themselves very visible and are willing to come pick you up at any point on campus. Since Ole Miss has a large majority of students living on campus, I felt as though I was always surrounded by other students."

Q "Oxford is the safest place I have ever lived. No one ever locked their door or was afraid to walk around at night, and you often saw cars with the keys in them and running, with no owner in sight. In fact, the campus crime report was one of the best parts of the *Daily Mississippian*. It was always amazing to see how many freshmen got arrested for public intoxication, or that unattended backpacks were stolen. These **criminal masterminds** were a force not to be reckoned with."

Q "There are definitely places on campus that you should avoid at night by yourself, but luckily you never have to do so. There's security at the library to walk you to your car if you need it. You can also **call the University Police Department to take you where you need to go** if you feel unsafe. This isn't to say that the campus is unsafe, but there are certainly measures in place to help keep you safe. The police cars patrol campus throughout the day looking for suspicious behavior and essentially making their presence known."

Q "I felt that the campus was very secure and although I never walked alone at night, I never felt threatened or scared to be out past dark. People are always willing to make sure that you get back home safely, and, if needed, you can utilize the **Rebel Ride** to get back to your house in one piece."

## The College Prowler Take
### ON SAFETY & SECURITY

Students at Ole Miss are thankful that they are able to go to a school where there is very little to worry about, as far as safety is concerned. It seems that anyone can go out at any time of night and go for a walk, or walk to their car at night from a building on campus, and not worry about whether they are going to be abducted, mugged, or injured in any way. Even though walking around alone at night, no matter where you are, is not the brightest idea, there are always times when you have no option other than to be alone, and it's during those times that being in a small town like Oxford is very comforting.

**A-**

**The College Prowler™ Grade on**
### Safety & Security: A-

A high grade in Safety & Security means that students generally feel safe, campus police are visible, blue-light phones and escort services are readily available, and safety precautions are not overly necessary.

# Facilities

## The Lowdown
### ON FACILITIES

**Student Center**:
The Student Union

**Athletic Center**:
The Turner Center (day phone: 662-915-7275; night: 662-915-5597), features swimming pools, various courts, weight lifting and exercise equipment, a suspended running track, and more.

**Libraries**:
1; (662) 915-7091

**Movie Theater on Campus?**
Yes, in the Turner Center on Friday nights. One of the rooms has been converted into a theater where students and faculty can see films for $1.

**Bowling on Campus?**
No

**Bar on Campus?**
No

**Coffeehouse on Campus?**
Yes, two; one in Weir Hall and one in the Union.

**Popular Places to Chill:**
The Union, the Grove

### Computers
**High-Speed Network?** Yes

**Wireless Network?** Yes

**Charge to Print?** Yes

**24-Hour Labs**: Weir Hall (662-915-7396)

**IT Helpdesk**: 100 Weir Hall (662-915-5222)

**Numbers of Computers**: 3,500

**Number of Labs**:
One public lab and many more available through individual departments and residents halls.

### Favorite Things to Do
There are a ton of different things to do off campus, but what some students don't take advantage of are the opportunities on campus. Recently, students have caught the fever and often play a pick-up game of ultimate Frisbee in the Grove. There's always an exhibit to check out on display in the School of Southern Studies in Barnard Observatory. Or, you can go to the J.D. Williams Library's blues archive to learn more about famous musicians—while listening to the collections they've donated.

## Students Speak Out
### ON FACILITIES

"Ole Miss has excellent facilities. They have a state-of-the-art workout center. Alumni continuously pour money into the school, so buildings are constantly being renovated. The student union could use some improvement."

Q "The facilities on campus are kept very nice, indeed. Equipment is usually kept in good working order and is of **the latest technology**."

Q "The school is in the process of updating many of the old buildings on campus. If a building is falling apart, it's either being worked on, or will be very soon. **Get used to construction tape and temporary walls**."

> "Even though some buildings might look a little old from the outside, most facilities on campus are fairly nice on the inside. The computer labs are very up-to-date, and have a lot of new computers to work on. The union looks like a building from the 1970s, but you can find everything you need inside. The Union takes on a kind of comfortable character that grows on you. The **Turner Center is very modern and new**; all the workout equipment, basketball courts, and racquetball courts are in great shape and are a pleasure to use."

# Campus Dining

## The College Prowler Take
### ON FACILITIES

"CAUTION ... Men at Work." This is the current theme on campus, as for the past three years the university has been working on a master plan that has become fondly known as the Phoenix Plan. The plan has been broken down into several sections. They say that they broke it up so that the expenses can be split up and taken on a little at a time, but students think it's so the University can keep them constantly guessing as to which yellow-taped path might actually get them to their desired locations. But it's really not that bad, and it's going to look great when they're finally done. The most popular facility, in terms of looks and functionality, is the Turner Center, which many students feel is a great athletic facility—it has everything from swimming pools to ping-pong tables.

## The Lowdown
### ON CAMPUS DINING

**Freshman Meal Plan Requirement?**
Yes

**24-Hour On-Campus Eating?**
No

**Student Favorites:**
Pan Asia, Chick-fil-A, Grille Works for breakfast

**Meal Plan Average Cost:**
Ranging in price from $540-$900

### Did You Know?

There are some local clothing shops in Oxford that have begun to accept the Ole Miss Express as a form of payment.

There's a meal plan designed specifically for those students who plan to go through rush and join the Greek system. It allows you to only buy a mean plan for one semester, because most fraternities and sororities require you to pay for their own meal plans, which include breakfast, lunch, and dinner.

**B**

The College Prowler™ Grade on
## Facilities: B

A high Facilities grade indicates that the campus is aesthetically pleasing and well-maintained; facilities are state-of-the-art, and libraries are exceptional. Other determining factors include the quality of both athletic and student centers and an abundance of things to do on campus.

## Students Speak Out
### ON CAMPUS DINING

"The food on campus leaves a lot to be desired. The Union has a Chick-fil-A and excellent sushi, but most of the other dining areas aren't very good. Most students eat at fraternity or sorority houses on a regular basis."

Q "The food has improved on campus but still doesn't compare to that of the surrounding restaurants or a home cooked meal. The sushi bar in the Union isn't half bad—sounds scary but isn't too bad. **Johnson Commons** is where you can get the most out of your buck. The Union tends to be overpriced for certain items."

Q "The food is okay, but I mainly stick with fast food places off campus, or, if I want to eat somewhere nice, I would **go to the Square**."

Q "The food on campus is great and can be a **great way to gain the infamous freshman 15**. They have Chick-fil-A, pizza, salads, sushi...."

Q "The Union offers a wide selection of food. Many students enjoy one of the new additions of fresh sushi. There's a deli, a Chick-fil-A, and an area that serves hot plates of breakfast, lunch and dinner. The student union also contains a Barnes and Noble that has a coffee shop in it where you can get the usual drinks. **The Colonel Store** also carries all your essentials: candy bars, chips, and drinks. Best of all, they all take the Ole Miss Express. Johnson Commons also provides a good cafeteria-style food option where you can find everything from pizza and hamburgers to pasta and salads, though it does have limited serving hours."

## The College Prowler Take
### ON CAMPUS DINING

It's a good thing that the meal plan is only required during your freshman year, because, for many students at Ole Miss, it's a total waste. Johnson Commons is only open at strange hours, and it's all the way across campus from most of the dorms. This is really inconvenient if you're hurrying to class and want to grab a quick bite to eat. The great thing, though, is the Ole Miss Express, which was implemented during the 2003 school year. That was when the Associate Student Body and the leaders of the school got together to formulate a program that off-campus food venders would accept and use, making the Flex Dollars capable of more than they had been before. Also, if you're looking for a good food choice on campus that's different, many students swear up and down that the sushi in the Union is the best they've ever had. Others are not so brave! If you're into it, check it out, and decide for yourself.

**C-**

The College Prowler™ Grade on
## Campus Dining: C-

Our grade on Campus Dining addresses the quality of both school-owned dining halls and independent on-campus restaurants as well as the price, availability, and variety of food.

# Campus Housing

**Also Available**
The Honors College has special floors available to those students who are in it.

**Did You Know?**
Ole Miss is a dry campus. No alcohol is allowed on campus, especially in the dorms.

## The Lowdown
ON CAMPUS HOUSING

**Undergrads on Campus**: Approximately 4,500

**Number of Dormitories**: 16 (7 male, 9 female)

**Number of University-Owned Apartments**: 2

### Room Types
Private, double, deluxe, and suites. deluxes and Suites are shared by two roommates. They are usually corner rooms and slightly larger than a double.

### Available for Rent
Microwaves and refrigerators

### Cleaning Service?
No, but there are cleaning services for the community areas, including the bathroom and TV rooms.

### You Get
All rooms include a bed, window coverings, phone jack, Ethernet hook-up, cable jack, a closet and a set of drawers, a desk, and a bookshelf

### Bed Type
Twin extra-long mattresses; the beds are bunkable to add extra space to your room, and lofts are available for purchase at the beginning of each semester.

## Students Speak Out
ON CAMPUS HOUSING

**"The dorms are fun. Everyone lives there their freshman year. By sophomore year, only girls tend to still be on campus. I don't really know what dorms to stay away from considering I only lived in Crosby."**

Q "I was actually a transfer student, so I didn't experience the dorm life at Ole Miss, and I'm glad, because the **dorm life isn't for everybody**, okay!"

Q "I lived in Stewart my freshman year and loved it. It had plenty of storage and was close to everything. My second year, I lived in Crosby; still nice and the bathrooms were larger, but not as much storage as Stewart. **All of my friends that lived in the Twin Towers [Martin] hated it**. I couldn't see how they kept all of their stuff there. Martin is out on the edge of campus, and it really sucked for them when it rained or was bitter cold. Most of them had outrageous parking tickets due to that. The upside is that they could keep the freshman 15 at bay with all of the walking."

Q "Dorm life was okay. Stewart Hall was fine for me; a little outdated, but since I lived there they've renovated it, and it looks nice. I always heard you wanted to **avoid all-guy dorms**, especially the older ones, and if you don't like to party and stay up late, don't go to Martin."

💬 "Dorms are dorms. **The Phoenix Project** in the housing department has done much to improve the dorms in the past few years and is still working. This has entailed renovations of bathroom facilities, common areas, and room furnishings. The University has done away with all-freshman dorms, which is sad because it did provide an excellent way for freshman to bond. However, this does mean that there are more dorm options for everyone."

## The College Prowler Take
### ON CAMPUS HOUSING

It's required at Ole Miss that all freshmen live on campus, but living in the dorms isn't all bad. For those of you who are from out-of-state and don't know anybody at Ole Miss, living in the dorms is a great experience that will allow you to meet lots of new people. Before you leave home, buy a special pair of flip-flops for the showers and the bathrooms. Bathrooms are communal and not likely to be as clean as the one you're used to at home. They're usually cleaned about once a week by the custodial staff, but what that really means is that they hook up a hose to the water faucets and spray the bathroom down. It's pretty gross, but you get used to it and it makes you even more appreciative of clean bathrooms when you move out.

### The College Prowler™ Grade on
## Campus Housing: C+

A high Campus Housing grade indicates that dorms are clean, well-maintained, and spacious. Other determining factors include variety of dorms, proximity to classes, and social atmosphere.

# Diversity

## The Lowdown
### ON DIVERSITY

**Native American:** 0%

**Asian American:** 1%

**African American:** 13%

**White:** 84%

**Hispanic:** 0%

**International:** 1%

**Unknown:** 1%

**Out-of-State:** 32%

## Minority Clubs

There are many minority clubs. The most popular ones are the African American clubs that are available for almost every different career path at Ole Miss.

## Political Activity

Most students are pretty conservative and would probably label themselves Republicans. Around election time, you'll see lots of cars with the Republican candidate's stickers. Most students aren't outspoken about their political views, though.

## Most Popular Religions

On campus, most students are Christian. It would not be impossible, however, to find those who hold various beliefs on religion.

## Gay Tolerance

Even though Mississippi is a very conservative state, and the Republican Party dominates Oxford, Ole Miss tends to be pretty tolerant of homosexuality. There are a couple of organizations that support the gay population, such as ALLIES, which is well-known all over the United States. Although there's a sizable gay community on campus, they're relatively quiet and don't always make their sexual preferences known.

## Economic Status

Ole Miss ranges in economic status from very poor to the very wealthy. Most of the campus is probably high-middle to upper-class, since the tuition is rather high, especially for out-of-state students. Even though a lot of people have a lot of family money, the campus isn't one that you would label as "stuck-up."

## Students Speak Out
### ON DIVERSITY

"The school is trying to become more diverse, but it doesn't seem to be having huge success—probably because of its history."

"Campus is very Greek-oriented. There's diversity, but **most people try to conform**."

"The campus is surprisingly diverse. Despite the University's **less than perfect history in regard to race**, the school has a nice, eclectic group of students. There are a lot of international students, and African American enrollment is up."

"Some students from India and Pakistan attend the University. **Events celebrating the cultures** of Ole Miss's diverse populations, like India Night, have grown in popularity in the past few years."

"Uncle Bob tries hard, but there's **not a lot of diversity**. We do have black athletes."

"No matter what your interests are at Ole Miss, there's a place for you. While Ole Miss may not sport the most diverse-looking student population statistically, the diversity is there. You just have to look around. The University will be a great resource in helping you to meet a diverse crowd. They organize events such as dinner nights with the faculty, and **international nights** where students from other countries present elements of their culture such as food, dance, and history."

## The College Prowler Take
### ON DIVERSITY

The University attained notoriety in 1962 when it refused to enroll James Meredith because of his skin color. Meredith won his court case against the school, and was allowed to enroll. However, then-State Attorney, General Robert F. Kennedy, had to call out the state national guard to ensure Meredith's safety, and two people were killed in the riots that ensued afterwards. Meredith went on to become the first African American graduate of Ole Miss, and things are much different now. While celebrating "Forty years of Open Doors at Ole Miss" last year, the school made new commitments to expanding itself and also to increasing minority enrollment. So, even though the numbers don't show that it's diverse, Ole Miss is working on it.

**The College Prowler™ Grade on**
## Diversity: D

A high grade in Diversity indicates that ethnic minorities and international students have a notable presence on campus and that students of different economic backgrounds, religious beliefs, and sexual preferences are well-represented.

# Guys & Girls

## The Lowdown
ON GUYS & GIRLS

**Women Undergrads**: 53%

**Men Undergrads**: 47%

### Birth Control Available?
Yes, its available from the health center, after an exam by a doctor.

### Social Scene
When freshmen arrive on campus, some know about 20 or 30 people they went to high school with and expect to just hang with them most of the time. News Flash: no one wants to go to college and hang out with just the people that they knew in high school. Step out of your shell and meet new people.

### Dress Code
Different groups have their own styles. The preppy group is mostly made up of Greek students who get all decked out to go to class. The art kids wear baggy clothing, ragged with wear, and covered in whatever medium they prefer. The newest trend is the outdoorsy look. These are the people who love to camp, hike and mountain climb. Well, most of the people who dress this way probably don't actually do those things, but they've realized how comfortable the clothes are. These folks choose to wear North Face, Patagonia, and Columbia jackets, boots, pants, and messenger bags.

### Hookups or Relationships?
As it is just about anywhere, the girls are typically looking for relationships while the guys are usually into playing the field. Usually, by their junior or senior year, the guys are ready to settle down and the girls have found the right guy for them and both end up in committed relationships.

## Students Speak Out
ON GUYS & GIRLS

"You can find a little of everything, but during football weekends everyone seems to turn into clones. The guys all dress in ties, and the girls all wear their best new outfit and heels."

"There tends to be mouth-watering guys around every corner and enough cute girls to make everyone want to **hit the gyms and tanning booths more often**."

"Well, the **girls out number the boys**, majorly! But there are some hot guys on campus and, trust me, they're not all in fraternities, either."

"Most of the **boys seem to be short**. They get a reputation for being gentlemen, but some don't live up to the title. The girls get a reputation for being snobs, but again, most don't live up to that description either."

"**Girls are pretty; the boys are lacking**."

"The majority of guys are the **classic 'good ol' boys' who love huntin' and drinkin'**. But then there are others who are really different. The girls, in general, have blonde hair and wear lots of makeup. They live for their sorority sisters. But, there are others who are really different and break the mold. There are a lot of pretty girls at Ole Miss. And every now and then, you'll see a beautiful boy. Just check out the men's tennis team, for example."

## The College Prowler Take
**ON GUYS & GIRLS**

As the numbers show, the girls outnumber the guys by a great deal. This is great for the guys, but it pretty much sucks for the girls. But, even though the guys are so outnumbered, it seems that there's never a shortage of guys to go on dates with. The girls are lucky due to the fact that we're in the South, and Ole Miss has some true southern gentlemen who open doors, pay for meals, make the right phone calls, and edit their language around the fairer sex. Chivalry is not dead in the South—most of the time, girls can expect to be treated with courtesy and respect. The general consensus is that the girls are much better-looking than the guys here, though. Guys are much better off, because the women at Ole Miss are hotties. They're well-bred, well-spoken, and drop-dead gorgeous. Ole Miss has produced more Miss America's than any other school in the nation.

**B-**

**A**

The College Prowler™ Grade on
### Guys: B-

A high grade for Guys indicates that the male population on campus is attractive, smart, friendly, and engaging, and that the school has a decent ratio of guys to girls.

The College Prowler™ Grade on
### Girls: A

A high grade for Girls not only implies that the women on campus are attractive, smart, friendly, and engaging, but also that there is a fair ratio of girls to guys.

# Athletics

## The Lowdown
**ON ATHLETICS**

**Men's Varsity Teams:**
Baseball
Basketball
Cross Country
Football
Golf
Tennis
Track and Field (indoor)
Track and Field (outdoor)

**Women's Varsity Teams:**
Basketball
Cross Country
Golf
Shooting (Rifle)
Soccer
Softball
Tennis
Track and Field (indoor)
Track and Field (outdoor)
Volleyball

### Club Sports
Fencing, Tae Kwon Do, Hapkido. Soccer, Men's Volleyball, Rugby, Iaido, Triathlon, Karate, Badminton

### Intramurals (IMs)
Soccer, Flag Football, Softball, Basketball, Bowling, Ultimate Frisbee, Kickball, Wiffleball, Volleyball, Racquetball, Tennis, Table Tennis, Poker, X-box

### Fields
Oxford University Swayze Field— Baseball
Vaught-Hemingway Hollingsworth Field—Football
Tad Smith Coliseum—Basketball

**Athletic Division**:
NCAA Division I

**Conference**:
Southeastern Conference (SEC)

**School Mascot**:
Colonel Reb

## Most Popular Sports
At Ole Miss, football is the number one sport. Students cheer on the team, and use games as a major social event.

## Overlooked Teams
The men's tennis team has been ranked in the top ten of the SEC for ten out of the past 11 years. In 2004, the men's tennis team was ranked number five in the nation. But, since matches are often on the same day as Ole Miss baseball games, tennis doesn't get much of a crowd.

## Getting Tickets
Getting tickets to varsity sporting events early is a must for football and men's basketball. You can either go to the Ole Miss Ticket Office, located in front of the football stadium, or you can get tickets online at www.olemissticketoffice.com.

Athletic Dept. Ticket Office: (662) 915-7167

## Students Speak Out
### ON ATHLETICS

"Sports on campus are good. There's a lot of support for athletics from the students. I don't know much about IM sports."

"**Sports are part of life at Ole Miss** and the school takes its sports teams very seriously. Whether it's soccer, basketball, football, or baseball, you'll always find a large crowd of students enjoying the game. IMs are a big part of life on campus, and it gives people the opportunity to participate in friendly games for fun."

"**Football time and the Grove are the best part of Ole Miss**. It's a tradition, and no one will understand it until they are actually a student. If you're not born a Rebel, you soon will be one!"

"Football is huge, no matter what. Basketball and baseball are big, if they're having a winning season. Most people seem to **get involved in an intramural sport at least once** while they're there."

"Varsity sports are an enormous part of life on the Ole Miss campus. Students and fans alike follow SEC sports from one season to the next. They provide social events for those who love mingling, and are **spectacular events** for those who have a love of the game."

## The College Prowler Take
### ON ATHLETICS

Ole Miss is all about football and its traditions. There's a canopy of trees covering a grassy area near the stadium called the Grove where families, fraternities, sororities, and fans set up tents. Some families have been "Groving" in the same patch for more than 30 years. The tables in the tents are piled high with food and beverages, and an occasional flower arrangement. Some of the tents actually have candle chandeliers. If you're worrying that you won't have a tent, don't. You'll either join an organization that does, or make friends with family tents. And if you feel like you are intruding, don't!—people in the South, especially Mississippi, are hospitable and friendly and want to have all the friends that they can, especially when it comes to cheering for Ole Miss football!

The College Prowler™ Grade on
## Athletics: A

A high grade in Athletics indicates that students have school spirit, that sports programs are respected, that games are well-attended, and that intramurals are a prominent part of student life.

# Greek Life

## The Lowdown
ON GREEK LIFE

**Number of Fraternities:**
19

**Number of Sororities:**
13

**Undergrad Men in Fraternities:**
33%

**Undergrad Women in Sororities:**
33%

### Did You Know?

The first Greek organization on the Ole Miss campus was Delta Psi fraternity/St. Anthony's Hall, in 1854.

Every fraternity and sorority has their own philanthropy project which raises money to help with a charity that their nationals have chosen.

## Students Speak Out
ON GREEK LIFE

"Greek life is great for the younger crowd, but once you get established in Oxford, it no longer dominates your social calendar."

Q "Yes, it dominates the frat parties, Grove, sometimes, etc. It's great! It was **the best thing for me** and I made so many friends through it, especially girls. But, even *I* made guy friends because I was Greek, which was always a good thing. I even met my fiancé because I was Greek!"

Q "Greek is chic. But, a lot of people do it and complain about it the whole time. If you're not familiar with the system, **I would recommend giving it a year**, and then making the decision to join or not."

Q "Greek life can be obnoxious, and if you live on campus, **it dominates the social scene**. Once I moved off campus, I realized that most people are not actually Greek. And the older the Greeks get, the more they realize how silly it is."

Q "While you don't have to be Greek to have fun, there are advantages to belonging to a Greek organization. There are those who take being Greek very seriously, and those who are in it to have fun, but, either way, I'd recommend joining one because I made some of my best friends of my life through my organization. It's very nice to come in freshman year with a place to go and belong, and being Greek **taught me a lot about responsibility and friendship**."

## The College Prowler Take
### ON GREEK LIFE

Greek life at Ole Miss isn't just another organization you join. It's a way of life. And, the Greeks on campus aren't just partiers who go out all the time. They're the ones who run ASB, and they're in all the clubs, involved in religious organizations, on the Student Programming Board, and volunteering and conducting fund-raisers for charities. They're basically everywhere, and are involved all over campus and the city. Most Greek organizations require each member to get a certain amount of points each semester through service hours and attendance at campus-wide lectures. Each fraternity and sorority has different rules to abide by, but almost all have some sort of academic policy that you must sign and agree too. If you're even remotely thinking that you'd like to be in a Greek organization and about going through rush, Ole Miss is a great place to do it; it is fun and you'll meet tons of people. If you decide you're not sure you want to commit to something that serious and time consuming, wait a year. You can always rush as a sophomore.

### The College Prowler™ Grade on
## Greek Life: A

A high grade in Greek Life indicates that sororities and fraternities are not only present, but also active on campus. Other determining factors include the variety of houses available and the respect the Greek community receives from the rest of the campus.

# Drug Scene

## The Lowdown
### ON DRUG SCENE

**Most Prevalent Drugs on Campus:**
Alcohol, Marijuana, Adderall, Ritalin

**Liquor-Related Referrals:**
101

**Liquor-Related Arrests:**
123

**Drug-Related Referrals:**
1

**Drug-Related Arrests:**
67

## Drug Counseling Programs
### Psychological Counseling and Crisis Intervention
Phone: (662) 915-3784

Services: They assist with day-to-day problems like depression, anxiety, family and relationship problems, alcohol and drug abuse, and identity and trauma issues.

### The Bessie S. Speed Alcohol and Drug Education Program
Phone: (662) 915-3784

Services: Counselors conduct workshops on a variety of health education topics in classes, dorms, Greek houses, and other campus locations.

## Students Speak Out
ON DRUG SCENE

> "Though I have seen people using drugs, I think drug use is less prevalent on the Ole Miss campus than other major universities."

Q "Drugs really are everywhere on campus, and in Oxford, from the 4.0 engineering student, to the typical-looking druggie hippie. **Pot, pills, and cocaine dominate** the scene in Oxford. You'd really be surprised at the amount of people that use, and who's using it."

Q "Well, I know it's alive, and occurs more often than we actually see. I know it's **in frat houses, and probably even sororities**, but then we don't really know for fact, now do we?"

Q "There's certainly a drug scene on campus. Primarily, drug use tends to lean towards **alcohol and marijuana**, though the harder stuff is present, also. Many more people deal and use than meets the eye, but the use is there if you know where to look."

Q "While I know there are people on campus who use drugs, I never came in contact with any myself, except for the ever-popular alcohol and cigarettes. I think it depends on the type of person you are, and who you hang out with, as to the prevalence of drugs in your campus life, because **you could make it as big or little a part of your life** as you want. I choose little."

## The College Prowler Take
ON DRUG SCENE

Like many things on the campus of Ole Miss, what you see isn't always what you get. Outwardly, Ole Miss appears to have no sort of drug problem, but inwardly, there are some groups that do partake in drug use, whether prescription or illegal. If that is your scene, you can find what you want. It just takes knowing the right contacts, which is true in most towns. But be careful, the cops on campus, here might shrug off beer in a cup during football games, but they will not overlook any illegal drugs, under any circumstances. They have a very strict drug policy in Mississippi, and Oxford is very much in step with the state on that issue. The fines are heavy, and the jail time is worse, so if you do choose to do drugs, be careful, and not just because you can get in trouble from the authorities.

**B-**

**The College Prowler™ Grade on**
### Drug Scene: B-

A high grade on Drug Scene indicates that drugs are not a noticeable part of campus life; drug use is not visible, and no pressure to use them seems to exist.

# Overall Experience

## Students Speak Out
### ON OVERALL EXPERIENCE

"I love the Ole Miss experience and consider myself extremely fortunate for having the opportunity to meet the professors I did and live in such a unique location as Oxford."

"I like Ole Miss. **I have learned a lot of valuable things here, and met a lot of good friends** that I will never forget. However, sometimes, I wonder what it would have been like to attend the University of Alabama."

"Ole Miss is great. It may not have the attention of other places, but with the **SEC-school atmosphere in a smaller setting**, I would not have wanted to go anywhere else."

"My overall experience at Ole Miss was amazing. I just graduated in May, and I miss it incredibly. The friends I made there, and things I learned there will forever be a part of me. Willie Morris once wrote that you never actually leave your past; it becomes a part of who you are. This is how I feel about Ole Miss. It has **made me the person I am today**."

"Although the academic demands are not equivalent to Harvard, **I got a great education** from Ole Miss by forcing myself to take harder classes with more demanding teachers. You will get out what you put in."

## The College Prowler Take
### ON OVERALL EXPERIENCE

Overall, students don't want to leave Ole Miss or Oxford even after they graduate. There are many students at school who choose to get additional degrees just so they don't have to leave. The University provides almost everything one could want in a college experience. There are great sporting events that are heavily attended by the student body. There's a hopping nightlife. There are many religions and church denominations available. There's a supportive faculty, a beautiful campus, and interesting classes. The job rate for recent graduates is very high, and has competitive salaries with other SEC schools with the same majors. If there's something that students complain about and say that they would change about their college experience, it's typically that Oxford doesn't have some of the conveniences, such as a nice movie theater, or a mall, that other campuses in larger cities have. For most, this minor inconvenience is counteracted by Memphis being so close by.

Many students credit Ole Miss with making them a better all around person, and say that they have fond memories that will last a lifetime about a place that will be with them forever.

# University of North Carolina

CB 9100, 103 South Building, Chapel Hill, NC 27599
www.unc.edu					(919) 966-3621

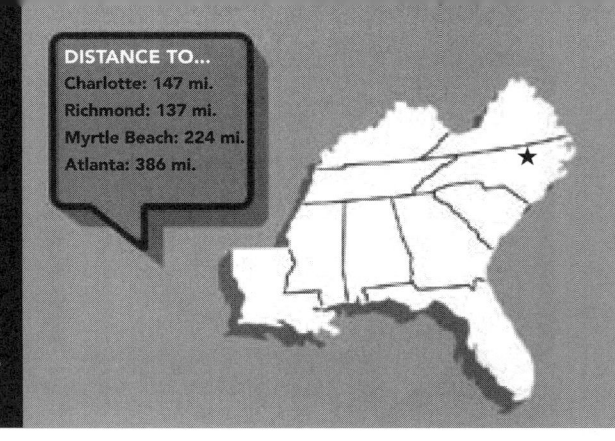

**DISTANCE TO...**
Charlotte: 147 mi.
Richmond: 137 mi.
Myrtle Beach: 224 mi.
Atlanta: 386 mi.

*"UNC at Chapel Hill is one of the most competitive and prestigious public universities in the nation."*

**Total Enrollment:**
15,355
**Top 10% of High School Class:**
70%
**Average GPA:**
4.0
**Acceptance Rate:**
37%
**Tuition:**
$3,205 in-state, $16,303 out-of-state
**SAT Range (25th-75th Percentile):**
| Verbal | Math | Total |
| --- | --- | --- |
| 590 – 690 | 600 – 700 | 1190 – 1390 |

**ACT Range (25th-75th Percentile):**
| Verbal | Math | Total |
| --- | --- | --- |
| 24-30 | 25-30 | 25-30 |

**Most Popular Majors:**
18% Communication and Journalism
18% Social Sciences
11% Business
10% Psychology
8% Biological and Biomedical Sciences

**Students also applied to:***
Duke University
East Carolina University
North Carolina State University–Raleigh
University of Virginia
Wake Forest University

*For more school info check out www.collegeprowler.com

## Table of Contents

| | |
| --- | --- |
| Academics | 298 |
| Local Atmosphere | 300 |
| Safety & Security | 301 |
| Facilities | 303 |
| Campus Dining | 305 |
| Campus Housing | 306 |
| Diversity | 308 |
| Guys & Girls | 309 |
| Athletics | 311 |
| Greek Life | 313 |
| Drug Scene | 315 |
| Overall Experience | 316 |

## College Prowler Report Card

| | |
| --- | --- |
| Academics | B+ |
| Local Atmosphere | B+ |
| Safety & Security | A- |
| Facilities | A |
| Campus Dining | C+ |
| Campus Housing | B+ |
| Diversity | C+ |
| Guys | B+ |
| Girls | A- |
| Athletics | A+ |
| Greek Life | A |
| Drug Scene | B+ |

# Academics

## The Lowdown
ON ACADEMICS

**Special Degree Options:**
Double-Majors

**AP Test Score Requirements:**
Possible credit for scores of 3 or higher

**IB Test Score Requirements:**
Possible credit for scores of 5 or higher

**Sample Academic Clubs**
American Medical Women's Association, Black Business Student Alliance, Carolina Economics Club, Phi Alpha Delta Law Fraternity, UNC-CH Undergraduate Investment Club

**Degrees Awarded:**
Bachelor, Master, Doctorate

**Undergraduate Schools:**
College of Arts and Sciences, General College, Kenan-Flagler Business School, School of Education, School of Government, School of Information and Library Science, School of Journalism and Mass Communication, School of Law, School of Medicine, School of Nursing, School of Pharmacy, School of Public Health, School of Social Work

**Full-time Faculty:**
1,203

**Faculty with Terminal Degree:**
86%

**Student-to-Faculty Ratio:**
14:1

**Average Course Load:**
15 credit hours

## Did You Know?

*Kiplinger's Personal Finance* noted UNC-CH as one of the "Best Value" schools.

Several national academic syndicates ranked UNC-CH 28th overall among national universities, fifth among public national universities, fourth for having the "least student indebtedness" among national universities, and fifth for having the "best undergraduate business program."

**Best Places to Study:**
Undergraduate Library, Student Union

## Students Speak Out
ON ACADEMICS

"Some teachers are great; some are horrible. Ask the upperclassmen which professors to take and which ones to avoid. This will make your academic life at UNC so much easier."

Q "Most **teachers are great, and will work with you**. I've had only two bad experiences. Also, if you are taking AP credit or any college-bridge program classes, UNC accepts almost all of them! I came in with 27 credits, so I'm a year ahead in school. It's nice to skip over those intro classes!"

Q "The teachers at UNC vary. Some teachers are interesting and **make the subjects they teach fun**, while others are dry and uninspiring. Fortunately, at UNC, the former definitely represents a higher percentage than the latter."

Q "Here at Carolina, we have **professors who are very experienced and resourceful**. Professors make sure that they are up-to-date with all the latest information and theories. I value each of my professor's expertise and knowledge of the world in accordance to their particular field. Yes, I personally find the majority of my classes very interesting; however, the enthusiasm comes from my professors and the amount of excitement and interest they have in the subject matter, which is reflected onto the students."

Q "Many professors seemed to be as uninterested in teaching as they were **preoccupied with professional standards**—retaining tenure, being published, research, and personal interviews. This is the primary reason that the classes were less than interesting."

## The College Prowler Take
ON ACADEMICS

UNC boasts one of the most accomplished faculties on the East Coast. A large percentage of Carolina's professors have received awards for their research, and many were inducted into national programs based on their respective fields. Take for instance Dr. Oliver Smithies, a professor of pathology and laboratory medicine. In 2001, he received the **Albert Lasker Award for Basic Medical Research. Those who receive the Lasker award have often been called "America's Nobels," as 63 scientists who've received the award have later received the Nobel Prize. The faculty, like the student body, is diverse: UNC has over 100 African American faculty members. All professors are required to have office hours, and many professors will arrange to meet with students by appointment, if their office hours conflict with the student's schedule. Some have even been known to set up professor-student appointments at their private residences.**

Freshman students and some sophomore students are likely to have mostly TAs for their prerequisite courses. Some teachers are less approachable than others, grade unfairly, and test rather hard. Other teachers are friendlier and easier to associate with than others.

**B+**

The College Prowler™ Grade on
## Academics: B+

A high Academics grade generally indicates that professors are knowledgeable, accessible, and genuinely interested in their students' welfare. Other determining factors include class size, how well professors communicate, and whether or not classes are engaging.

# Local Atmosphere

**City Websites**
http://www.ci.chapel-hill.nc.us
http://www.chocvb.org

## Students Speak Out
ON LOCAL ATMOSPHERE

## The Lowdown
ON LOCAL ATMOSPHERE

"There are six colleges within 31 miles, so it's a great area for young people. We're eight miles from Duke, about 20 from NC State, and one hour away from Greensboro."

"Chapel Hill is in a good spot: it's two hours from the beach and two from the mountains. There are several other known universities in the area, such as Duke, NC State, and Wake Forest. **The area is absolutely gorgeous**. I transferred from the University of Hawaii, and I think that this campus is every bit as beautiful as the campus at UH."

"Chapel Hill has to be the best college town in America. We're always winning awards for just that. Durham and Raleigh are both good mid-sized cities with a fair amount to do. Together with Chapel Hill, they form what amounts to one big urban area called the Triangle. **We've got lots of good venues that have good concerts**, and Raleigh has a NHL team."

"Chapel Hill's campus is beautiful, or at least the surrounding area [is]. I definitely didn't want to be in a big city when I went to college, but I still wanted to have a nightlife. I wanted to be able to go hiking, and have a lot of nature around me, but still be able to go out at night and have a few options. UNC is **perfect for anyone who enjoys the outdoors**."

**Region:**
Southeast

**City, State:**
Chapel Hill, North Carolina

**Setting:**
Suburban

**Distance from Duke:**
15 minutes

**Distance from the Beach:**
2 hours

**Points of Interest:**
Lost Colony at the Outer Banks, TopSail Beach, Kitty Hawk, Linville Caverns, Myrtle Beach

**Sports Teams:**
Carolina Cobras (AFL), Carolina Hurricanes (NHL), Carolina Panthers (NFL), Charlotte Sting (WNBA)

> "Chapel Hill is a typical small town. There's **not very much to do around here** unless a group or organization throws a party. In Raleigh, there is North Carolina State University; in the town over, Durham, there is Duke. It's nice to go check out other schools in the area, and see what they have available."

## The College Prowler Take
ON LOCAL ATMOSPHERE

Chapel Hill is the epitome of a college town, and has everything a college student could ask for. If you like to salsa dance into the wee hours of the morning, you can. If you and your friends want to grab a beer and watch sporting events with hundreds of fellow students and friends, go right ahead. Hungry at three o'clock in the morning after hours of studying and/or partying?—by all means eat! Everything you need is at most a 15 minute walk from campus—just head to Franklin Street. Franklin Street, or simply "Franklin" to UNC students, borders the University and offers an array of clothing boutiques, thrift stores, music stores, coffeehouses, cafés, restaurants, nightclubs, movie theaters, and churches. It's no wonder that several publications, including *Sports Illustrated*, have dubbed Chapel Hill "the ideal college town."

**B+**

The College Prowler™ Grade on
## Local Atmosphere: B+

A high Local Atmosphere grade indicates that the area surrounding campus is safe and scenic. Other factors include nearby attractions, proximity to other schools, and the town's attitude toward students.

# Safety & Security

## The Lowdown
ON SAFETY & SECURITY

**Number of UNC Police Officers:**
86

**Phone:**
911 (emergencies)
(919) 962-8100 (non-emergencies)
(919) 967-7273, Rape Crisis Center 24 Hour Crisis Line
(919) 966-4721, UNC-CH Hospital emergency room
(919) 966-2281, Student Health Services

**Health Center Office Hours:**
Monday – Friday, 7 a.m. – 11 p.m.;
Saturday – Sunday, 8 a.m. – 5 p.m.

## Safety Services

Bike registration, fingerprinting, building access, patch information, Project ID, (COP) Community Oriented Policing, (RAD) Rape Aggression Defense, self defense training, emergency blue-light phones, P2P shuttle, the Safe Shuttle, Safe Ride

### Did You Know?

Campus police always warn students to keep their possessions in their sight. Larceny is the most common crime on campus.

## Students Speak Out
ON SAFETY & SECURITY

"You can call the P2P service to pick you up at any hour of the night. I feel safe on campus, but it is common sense to lock your doors and not carry large amounts of money on you."

"Security and safety at UNC are decent. We have late-night escorts who will pick you up anywhere on campus, if you want someone to walk home with. But, then again, **we've had some problems with assaults on campus** the past two semesters. They were nothing major, but they still happened. I heard through the grapevine that security will be beefed up next year."

"**Security here is fantastic, especially for women**. I walk home at all hours, and I always feel safe. There are call boxes, buses that run from 7 a.m. to 3 a.m., and golf carts that transport students from the library; and the best part is that these are all free! There is very little crime, but crime does exist."

"Security and safety is definitely an area that UNC **seems to take seriously**. Because of the amount of women enrolled, as well as for the concern of all students' well-being, UNC has incorporated security posts every couple yards where, at the touch of a button, campus security will arrive in a few minutes. P2P, the transportation system after 7 p.m., is also a reliable source that aids considerably in the safety of UNC students. Not only do the P2P buses run until 3 a.m., but, if you need a safe ride home later, a personal P2P van will arrive."

"The security is very good here. **All the paths and greenways are lit up**, and have emergency boxes everywhere. The main library has a shuttle service at night to take you back to your dorm instead of walking alone. There is also a shuttle service to get uptown where all the restaurants and bars are that runs until 3 a.m.."

## The College Prowler Take
ON SAFETY & SECURITY

The safety and security of its students is a top priority for UNC officials. The Department of Public Safety at UNC-Chapel Hill heads a first-rate division of police, security, and emergency services, ensuring that students live in a safe and secure environment. The Department of Public Safety exercises Community Oriented Policing (COP)—by combining the efforts of UNC Public Safety and the University community to keep Chapel Hill safe, COP keeps UNC-Chapel under a warm and cozy protective blanket. Security guards and campus police patrol the campus and streets 24 hours a day. In case of an emergency, "blue lights" are located all over the campus: simply find the nearest blue light, press the button, tell the operator your emergency, and wait a minute or two for police to arrive. With UNC Public Safety, personal responsibility, and a little student vigilance, the greatest danger to UNC students is that they might take for granted their college years.

**A-**

The College Prowler™ Grade on
### Safety & Security: A-

A high grade in Safety & Security means that students generally feel safe, campus police are visible, blue-light phones and escort services are readily available, and safety precautions are not overly necessary.

# Facilities

## Computers
**High-Speed Network?** Yes
**Wireless Network?** Yes
**Number of Labs:** 8
**Number of Computers:** 318
**24-Hour Labs:** Undergraduate Library
**Charge to Print:**
Yes (at some terminals it's 10 cents)

## The Lowdown
ON FACILITIES

### Favorite Things to Do
The Student Recreation Center (SRC) has the latest exercise equipment and offers exercise classes taught by certified aerobics instructors. After winter break and before spring break, the gym is packed with people trying to look their best for their spring break vacations.

**Student Center:**
The Student Union

**Libraries:**
17

**Athletic Center:**
The Student Recreation Center, Woolen Gymnasium, Fetzer Gymnasium

**Popular Places to Chill:**
The Wall, the Yard, the Pit, the Quad, the Student Union

**Movie Theater on Campus?**
Yes, there is one in the Student Union.

**Bar on Campus?**
No. Although the Coffee House and the Library are just two of the several bars that are located on nearby Franklin Street.

**Coffeehouse on Campus?**
Yes, there is Java City (located in several places on campus) and the Daily Grind, in the Pit.

### COLLEGE PROWLER
Want to hear more about campus facilities? For more info and student quotes, check out the book on UNC available at *www.collegeprowler.com*.

## Students Speak Out
### ON FACILITIES

{ "Some facilities, such as the classrooms and dorms, are in need of some renovation. However, the SRC and computer labs are in pristine condition."

Q "UNC just received a 500-million-dollar grant to redo some of the main lecture buildings and update them with the **newest high tech teaching materials**, such as projector screens and Internet drop down screens."

Q "Most facilities here are very good. We have some buildings that are in bad shape, but NC just passed a huge bond referendum that has sent construction workers around campus into renovation frenzy. It's like a bunch of Bob Vilas running around here! So, be prepared for even **more construction on our campus than normal** for the next few years. But, it's worth it."

Q "The facilities on campus are beautiful. The Student Recreation Center [the gym] is **well-equipped with a wide variety of machines** that function properly on a regular basis. The computers in the newly renovated library [the undergraduate library] are really nice and work pretty well. The new addition to the Student Union has plenty of room for studying; the Student Union will be better when the renovations of the older part are finished. However, as of right now, the Student Union is only average."

Q "The facilities on campus are pretty impressive. The Dean Dome, where all the basketball games are, is **nothing short of immaculate**. The libraries, especially the newly renovated undergraduate library, provide comfortable, spacious and, for the most part, quiet places to study."

## The College Prowler Take
### ON FACILITIES

The UNC Student Union now offers several conference rooms, study rooms, lounges, and a large computer lab, open for student and faculty use. During finals, the Union allows students to reserve conference rooms for study groups. Student clubs often use the Union to hold their meetings, events, and parties. The Union also has a large gallery for student artwork. Playmakers' Theater invites directors, producers, and actors from across the nation to perform for UNC students and other guests. The Student Recreation Center (SRC) has the latest exercise equipment, and offers exercise classes taught by certified aerobics instructors. If you are interested in taking a different approach to getting in shape, or if you just want to have fun, Fetzer and Woolen gyms have Olympic-sized swimming pools (one indoor and outdoor) and several full-size basketball courts, among other things. UNC is dedicated to keeping its facilities up-to-date with the latest equipment.

**The College Prowler™ Grade on**
### Facilities: A

A high Facilities grade indicates that the campus is aesthetically pleasing and well-maintained; facilities are state-of-the-art, and libraries are exceptional. Other determining factors include the quality of both athletic and student centers and an abundance of things to do on campus.

# Campus Dining

## Students Speak Out
ON CAMPUS DINING

"The food on campus it isn't all that healthy, especially in the dining halls. The only good spots to eat at are at the bottom of Lenoir because of the fast food chains available."

Q "The food is actually pretty good, when I think about it. We have Lenoir and Chase dining halls and we have places like Subway, Burger King, Chick-fil-A, a Mexican place, a smoothie place, and a pizza place. You can also choose 'Tar Heel Express,' which allows you to have **food delivered to your dorm from over 40 restaurants** around the University. The good spots, in my opinion, are Subway, Burger King, and the Union café, which is like a mini convenience store."

Q "We have two dining halls: Lenoir and Chase. Chase is on South Campus, which is where most freshmen live. It gets criticized a lot, but the food there is surely better than high school food. During the day, when you're further up campus, or anytime you want to make the walk from South Campus, you've got Lenoir as an option. Downstairs, it has fast food places, and upstairs is the cafeteria. **The atmosphere in Lenoir is great**—it's a historic building that has been recently renovated. It's really modern inside and the food and overall variety is really good. Your meal plan is such that you buy a certain number of meals per week at the dining halls, and then get Flex dollars for the fast food joints if you choose."

Q "The food on campus is okay. Don't be fooled by the great food during the first week of class, because it isn't always that tasty. If I had to choose between dining halls, I would eat at Lenoir over Chase. If you eat at Chase, you always leave having an odd smell on your clothes—any person who goes to Carolina and smells your clothes will know where you've been. Lenoir has other **options like Chick-fil-A, Subway, and Burger King**, so that's your best bet."

## The Lowdown
ON CAMPUS DINING

**Freshman Meal Plan Requirement?**
No

**24-Hour On-Campus Eating?**
No

**Student Favorites:**
Subway, Chick-fil-A, Burger King

**Meal Plan Average Cost:**
Between $1,297 and $1,315

**Did you know?**
Every semester, before finals, UNC's cafeteria holds a "Midnight Breakfast" to fuel everyone's study habits.

Q "The main dining hall, Lenoir, has very good food for a dining hall. However, sometimes eating at Lenoir is pretty time consuming because of the buffet style setup, especially when it's **crowded at certain times during the day** [11:30 a.m. to 1:00 p.m., 4:00 to 5:30 p.m.]. The other dining hall, Chase, isn't the greatest. The á la carte places in downstairs Lenoir, however, are less time consuming and very tasty."

# Campus Housing

## The College Prowler Take
ON CAMPUS DINING

Just about every student agrees that all UNC dining options are a step above repetitive high-school cafeteria food. Also UNC's dining halls have fast food options, and the cafeterias are arranged in an all-you-can-eat buffet style. Carolina has two dining halls: the top of Lenoir, located on Main Campus, and Chase Dining Hall, located on South Campus (a little more convenient for students). Students are given the option of constructing their own meal plan. This can be quite advantageous for both students who cook for themselves on a regular basis and students who have a hard time boiling water on a stove. With all the options available for UNC students, the "Freshman 15" can very easily turn into the "Freshman 30" if you're not careful.

## The Lowdown
ON CAMPUS HOUSING

**Undergrads on Campus:**
79.5%

**Number of Dormitories:**
33

**Number of College-Owned Apartments:**
0

**You Get:**
Bed, dresser, desk and chair, closet or wardrobe, window coverings, cable TV jack, Ethernet Internet connections, free campus and local telephone calls

**Cleaning Service?**
Yes, in public areas. Community and suite-style bathrooms in all dormitories, except Craige-North, Morrison-South, Erhinghaus-South, and Hinton-James North.

**Bed-Type:**
Twin extra-long (36" wide x 80" long x 6" deep); Students are able to bunk or loft beds.

**Also Available:**
Smoke-free living, theme housing

## C+

The College Prowler™ Grade on
### Campus Dining: C+

Our grade on Campus Dining addresses the quality of both school-owned dining halls and independent on-campus restaurants as well as the price, availability, and variety of food.

## Room Types

Residence rooms in campus housing include standard and suite-style units.

Standard—students share a large, central bathroom facility (most first-year students are assigned to these rooms).

Suite-style—students share a semi-private bathroom.

### Did you know?

Students can get HBO for $10 per month.

Roommates can purchase the option to have a separate number with a distinct ring tone.

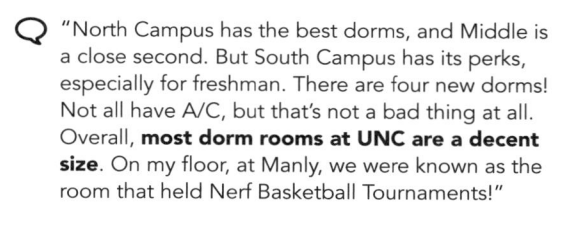

## Students Speak Out
ON CAMPUS HOUSING

"All of the residential buildings on campus are pretty nice. However, some are nicer than others. I would say avoid Whitehead because it is so far from campus."

Q "The dorms here need renovation and they need it soon. I don't like it in Craige or Morrison. The only dorms you'd want to live in are the new dorms and Hinton-James. I do prefer the older South Campus dorms because they are like a hotel and not enclosed, so **visitation is never a problem**."

Q "I recommend requesting North Campus. It's much bigger and nicer. These are easier to get as a girl, because most of these are all-girl dorms. South Campus has huge nine-story dorms that they just renovated. The only real advantage of living here is that **you will meet a ton of people living in the larger dorms**."

Q "North Campus has the best dorms, and Middle is a close second. But South Campus has its perks, especially for freshman. There are four new dorms! Not all have A/C, but that's not a bad thing at all. Overall, **most dorm rooms at UNC are a decent size**. On my floor, at Manly, we were known as the room that held Nerf Basketball Tournaments!"

Q "I lived in Carmichael for two years and loved it! The **South Campus dorms are where all the incoming freshmen live**. The freshmen dorms are Morrison, Ehringhaus, Craige, and Hinton-James. You will meet many interesting people if you live in one of these four dorms. They are decent in size, and the community of the dorms is incredible."

## The College Prowler Take
ON CAMPUS HOUSING

Overall, students at UNC seem happy with their current living arrangements, even though a few residents of the old South Campus dorms complain of too much noise, outdated rooms, and the lack of A/C. However, a good majority of upperclassmen do recommend South Campus for the dynamic social life. Also, the Department of Housing offers theme housing. This allows students to interact with their hallmates who share similar interests. Currently there are eight themes: Academic Enhancement Program, First Year Initiative, Business Global Scholars Program, Health Sciences, Language Houses, Living Well, UNITAS, and Women's Perspective. There's a dorm that will suit any of your needs. The perfect roommate ... well, that's another story.

**B+**

The College Prowler™ Grade on
### Campus Housing: B+

A high Campus Housing grade indicates that dorms are clean, well-maintained, and spacious. Other determining factors include variety of dorms, proximity to classes, and social atmosphere.

# Diversity

## The Lowdown
ON DIVERSITY

**Native American:** 0.8%

**Asian American:** 5.6%

**African American:** 11.1%

**Hispanic:** 1.9%

**White:** 77.8%

**International:** 1.2%

**Unknown:** 1.7%

**Out-of-State:** 18.6%

### Political Activity
UNC is a very politically involved school. There are Democratic, Republican, and independent groups present on campus. However, Carolina is known as a fairly liberal school, as indicated by the national controversy sparked by the summer reading books assigned to incoming freshmen for the past two years.

### Minority Clubs
There are dozens of minority clubs at UNC, as well as several shows that support and celebrate the different ethnicities on campus.

### Most Popular Religions
Because UNC is located in the southern Bible belt, most students are Christian, specifically southern Baptist or Catholic.

### Gay Tolerance
UNC has a sizable gay population. Students are accepting of the gay population, and there are several clubs and organizations that provide support for gay students, such as SafeZone and LBGT.

### Economic Status
Students from diverse economic backgrounds come to UNC. However, most students would say that Carolina consists mainly of students from the upper-class, wealthier economic segment of the population.

## Students Speak Out
ON DIVERSITY

"There is very little diversity around here. That is a reflection of the world we live in, however. Also, the Hispanic population on campus is very small."

Q "Coming from a town that is extremely non-diverse, I think Carolina is quite diverse. However, your **opinion on overall diversity definitely depends on where you're from**. If you're from New York City, then you probably won't find UNC that diverse. However, if you come from Fargo, North Dakota, then you'll think you just stepped off of a boat to another continent."

Q "The campus is diverse, offering a student group or club for almost every race on campus. While the **student population is still predominantly Caucasian**, the numbers of racially diverse individuals definitely seem to increase every year."

Q "Well, North Carolina law says that enrollment has to be at least 80 percent in-state, so we aren't too diverse in that sense. Our **racial diversity is getting better every year**. UNC has a really tolerant, liberal outlook on religion and sexual orientation. Still, most of us around here are middle-class white kids."

## The College Prowler Take
**ON GUYS & GIRLS**

Last year, Carolina enrolled students from all 50 states, and over 100 countries. At a campus as diverse as Carolina's, students are bound to experience, accept, and appreciate other cultures and backgrounds. UNC is one of the most racially and ethnically diverse campuses in the nation. At 22.3 percent, it has one of the highest minority rates among public and private universities. African American, Asian American, Native American, and Hispanic students are all currently at an all-time high at UNC. Therefore, even if UNC isn't as diverse as some schools on the East or West Coasts, at least we're moving in the right direction.

**C+**

The College Prowler™ Grade on
## Diversity: C+

A high grade in Diversity indicates that ethnic minorities and international students have a notable presence on campus and that students of different economic backgrounds, religious beliefs, and sexual preferences are well-represented.

# Guys & Girls

## The Lowdown
**ON GUYS & GIRLS**

Women Undergrads: 59.6%

Men Undergrads: 40.4%

### Birth Control Available?
Yes, female students are required to have a pap smear before they receive birth control pills from Student Health Services, and they must have an annual pap smear to renew their prescription. Student Health Services offers other kinds of birth control, as well.

### Social Scene
It is quite easy to meet people at UNC. Since several dorms are co-ed, you have to run into someone of the opposite sex sooner or later. It is up to you to interact with them, however. Granted, because UNC's gender ratio has a disproportionate number of females, it is slightly easier for men to date and interact with females than the other way around. However, because there are so many schools in the area, females have a prime selection to choose from, also.

## Hookups or Relationships?

There is a sizable amount of students who are in relationships either with other UNC students or with students from another college in the area (NC State, Duke, Wake Forest). On the whole, most girls at UNC are in relationships, some more serious than others. However, with a little under 16,000 undergrads, there is still a sizable singles pool currently available for hookups, friendships, or whatever you choose.

## Dress Code

There is no dress code at UNC. Some students dress to impress everyday, while other students dress in whatever they could find that morning that was not curled up into a ball. During the spring and summer seasons, most everyone is in short sleeves or sleeveless shirts, shorts, skirts, and sandals (typically the rainbow flip-flops). There are a variety of styles, ranging from Abercrombie & Fitch, EckoRed, Gap, or a UNC sweatshirt, T-shirt, or jeans. Also, when it's time to dress for a night on the town, Carolina students can certainly clean up real nice!

Want more info on guys and girls at UNC? Check out www.collegeprowler.com for the full-length guide on the University of North Carolina.

## Students Speak Out
### ON GUYS & GIRLS

*"A lot of girls complain that finding a good guy is tough. Most people on campus are very nice and very attractive. Everyone here seems to be very image and fashion conscious."*

Q "UNC is a great place to meet that special someone. We have **lots of preps, quite a few nerds**, a lot of preppy white guys who try to act like they're from the ghetto, a few that are truly ghetto, a few surfers, skaters, and hippies. It's a great place, and most of us love it."

Q "Well, there are so many girls around here. I believe it's 60 percent girls and 40 percent guys. It's not too fun to be a girl around here, but if you're a guy, you're almost guaranteed a girlfriend. **I go to other schools to find guys**, and there are plenty other schools around here; I personally believe that the guys are okay around here ... but not enough for everyone though."

Q "The guys on campus are pretty hot. Also, most guys here are **extremely focused and motivated,** and pretty friendly too. But, they are limited! The females on campus are nice, come from a good background, are looking to prosper, and are focused as well."

Q "Everyone at UNC is very cliquish. **Hot is a perceived adjective**."

## The College Prowler Take
### ON GUYS & GIRLS

At UNC there is definitely no shortage of places to meet people of the opposite sex, and doing so is usually not a problem—especially if you're a guy. This is largely due to the 60:40 girl-to-guy ratio. Sustaining a relationship is also quite possible here. You have the southern belles, the preppies, the classic frat boys, the hip-hop lovers, the rockers, the quiet ones, the loud ones, the wannabes, and the ambitious types who are involved in everything. That's what makes Carolina guys and girls cream of the crop.

# Athletics

## The Lowdown
### ON ATHLETICS

**Men's Varsity Teams:**
Baseball
Basketball
Cross Country
Football
Golf
Lacrosse
Soccer
Swimming & Diving
Tennis
Track & Field
Wrestling

**Women's Varsity Teams:**
Basketball
Cross Country
Field Hockey
Golf
Gymnastics
Lacrosse
Rowing
Soccer
Softball
Swimming & Diving
Tennis
Track & Field
Volleyball

## B+

**The College Prowler™ Grade on**
### Guys: B+

A high grade for Guys indicates that the male population on campus is attractive, smart, friendly, and engaging, and that the school has a decent ratio of guys to girls.

## A-

**The College Prowler™ Grade on**
### Girls: A-

A high grade for Girls not only implies that the women on campus are attractive, smart, friendly, and engaging, but also that there is a fair ratio of girls to guys.

## Club Sports
Adventure Racing, Aussie Rules Football, Baseball, Basketball, Cheerleading, Crew, Equestrian, Field Hockey, Football, Golf, Gymnastics, Ice Hockey, Judo, Lacrosse, Roller Hockey, Rugby, Sailing, Scuba, Ski, Soccer, Softball, Squash, Swimming, Track & Field, Ultimate Frisbee, Volleyball, Water Polo, Water Skiing

## Intramurals (IMs)
Arena Football, Basketball, Flag Football, Golf, Indoor Soccer, Inner Tube Water Polo, Kickball, Sand Volleyball, Soccer, Softball, Sports Trivia, Street Hockey, Racquetball, Ultimate Disc, Volleyball, Whiffleball

### Most Popular Sports
Basketball, football, soccer, and track and field. Club sports are popular and most IM sports are popular, as well.

### Overlooked Teams
Women's basketball, women's soccer, and baseball

### Fields
Carmichael Field, Kenan Stadium, Henry Stadium, Dean Smith Center

### Getting Tickets
Your student ID will get you admission to most varsity sports competitions. For basketball games, students are often required to stand in line and receive a wristband the week of the game. A couple of days before the game, those students with wristbands will receive tickets for the upcoming game and possibly the next few games. However, for the big rivalry games, students will often camp out the night before the wristband distribution. After the wristband distribution, two random numbers are picked and those with numbers on their wristband that fall into that range will receive a ticket.

## Students Speak Out
### ON ATHLETICS

"All sports at UNC are fantastic! Tickets are free, and there's always a sport to watch. My friends adored IMs. We wear more school apparel than at most universities. Even my Dockers have a UNC emblem!"

"Varsity sports are a huge part of college life at UNC. **People will line up for basketball tickets early in the morning,** or even the night before the ticket distribution. IM sports are pretty big, as the majority of people on campus are interested in athletics, though not on a varsity level."

"Varsity sports at Carolina are huge! We **consistently have one of the best college basketball teams**, year after year. Football games are a great experience—I've rushed the field twice! There are also many other sporting events to attend, such as soccer, women's basketball, and baseball."

"All sporting events on campus are free for students, but the number of basketball tickets is limited because of the high demand. We take pride in the Carolina tradition of collegiate basketball, with **names such as Michael Jordan, James Worthy, Jerry Stackhouse, Rasheed Wallace, and Vince Carter**. IM sports are abundant, and are fun on campus. We also have many sports clubs on campus, such as the ski and snowboard team, which I am a member of! Overall, the sports scene here at Carolina is awesome! Go Tar Heels baby!"

"Sports are huge here! I'm sure you know about our basketball dynasty already. Our football team is getting good again, and we just won the NCAA championship in men's soccer. We also were runner-up in women's soccer. Our women's team has won something like 16 championships since women's soccer was introduced by the NCAA over 20 years ago. **Nearly all of our varsity sports post winning records** and we usually finish in the top five in the Sears Cup standings [that cup is given to the best overall Division I sports program, based on points earned in every sport]. IM sports are also big and offered in a lot of different sports."

"Athletics is a very big deal at Carolina because there is so much tradition involved. Of course, varsity athletics are a big deal, but there are many, many levels of athletics that are available to everyone. Participating in athletics, on any level, is a **great way to get involved and meet people with similar interests**. I met my boyfriend through co-ed volleyball intramurals."

## The College Prowler Take
ON ATHLETICS

If you are an athlete, a sports fan, or both, UNC is your paradise. Everyone is familiar with UNC's storied basketball program—we won another national championship in 2005!—and many directly associate the color powder-blue with our basketball team. Football, men's and women's basketball, and soccer are three of the more competitive and popular varsity sports at UNC. However, if you don't make the team, or if you're simply not interested in playing on the varsity level, you can join a club sport or an intramural sport. Club and intramural sports provide a high degree of competition, without the time commitment and pressure that varsity sports demand. Overall, you'll be hard-pressed to find a school with more pride and respect for its athletic programs than UNC.

# Greek Life

## The Lowdown
ON GREEK LIFE

**Number of Fraternities:**
29

**Number of Sororities:**
20

**Undergrad Men in Fraternities:**
5%

**Undergrad Women in Sororities:**
7%

**Multicultural Colonies:**
Theta Nu Xi Multicultural Sorority, Inc.

### Did You Know?
The average GPA for Greeks is 3.302. The average GPA for non-Greeks is 2.989.

**A+**

The College Prowler™ Grade on
## Athletics: A+

A high grade in Athletics indicates that students have school spirit, that sports programs are respected, that games are well-attended, and that intramurals are a prominent part of student life.

## Students Speak Out
### ON GREEK LIFE

> "Greek life is a big thing at UNC, but there are many other types of social groups to get involved in. The nightlife and frat parties are always fun. I swim at UNC, and the swim team was almost a fraternity in itself."

Q "Greek life? What's that? We have a lot of frats and sororities, but I don't really take part in that. There are **a lot of cool frat brothers and sorority sisters** at UNC, but the majority of them are immature. They think you can just buy popularity, and that money makes you a better person."

Q **"Greek life will only dominate the social scene if you let it** and are involved in an organization. There are plenty of other types of groups and clubs to join. You can eventually find a group of people that you fit in with and feel comfortable with. If you complain about being bored and having no one to hang out with, you must not be leaving your room and being proactive about it."

Q "Fraternities and sororities **definitely make their mark on campus**, offering great parties for the masses every weekend. During rush week, there is practically a party every day somewhere in Frat Court. However, during the rest of the year, the Greek presence on campus, while alive, is not as dominant."

Q "Greek life doesn't mean much at Carolina, like it did in the past. I'm not sure why, but **people don't seem to care whether you're Greek or not**. However, large numbers of people do gather around when Greeks are stepping, pledging, and just acting like fools!"

## The College Prowler Take
### ON GREEK LIFE

If going Greek is something that interests you, UNC has 22 fraternities that comprise the Interfraternity Council (IFC), 10 Panhellenic sororities, eight historically black fraternities and sororities, nine fraternities and sororities in the Greek Alliance Council, two honors fraternities, and several professional fraternities. However, don't expect to rush a fraternity or sorority and immediately start getting hammered off of rum and cokes ... it just doesn't work that way. Greeks are required to devote a certain amount of time to their organization, volunteer around the area, and sponsor activities for non-Greek students. Only a little under 12 percent of UNC students are Greeks, so if going Greek is not for you, 88 percent of the student population feels the same way. If you are not Greek, that does not mean that you cannot attend a sorority or fraternity party, it just means that you are not committing yourself to a group. Greek or not Greek, Greek life does not define or rule the social scene.

**The College Prowler™ Grade on**
### Greek Life: A

A high grade in Greek Life indicates that sororities and fraternities are not only present, but also active on campus. Other determining factors include the variety of houses available and the respect the Greek community receives from the rest of the campus.

# Drug Scene

## The Lowdown
ON DRUG SCENE

**Most Prevalent Drugs on Campus:**
Alcohol

**Liquor-Related Referrals:**
0

**Liquor-Related Arrests:**
47

**Drug-Related Referrals:**
18

**Drug-Related Arrests:**
23

### Drug Counseling Programs

**Student Health Services Center for Healthy Student Behaviors**

Phone: (919) 966-6586

Services: Alcohol & Drug Counseling, Alcohol Education Classes, Driving While Impaired Treatment, Drug & Alcohol Assessments, Tobacco Use & Smoking Cessation, Outreach & Education, In-House Education Resources

### Had Enough.org

www.cspinet.org/booze/hadenough/index1.html

Services: one-on-one counseling, and report a friend for alcohol abuse counseling

## Students Speak Out
ON DRUG SCENE

"**It depends on who you're hanging out with, but cocaine and ecstasy are big in the sorority, fraternity, and athletic scenes.**"

Q "The only drugs that I have run into at parties are alcohol and weed. The **harder stuff is rarely heard of at UNC**. The occasional ecstasy pill will pop up, but that's about the extent of it."

Q "The drug scene is not bad here. **There is some pot around**. I'm sure if you wanted drugs, someone from that kind of crowd would tell you how to go about getting them. There's enough natural high in Chapel Hill to go around."

Q "I drink, but that's about it, and I only do that maybe once a month. I don't do drugs and neither do my friends, so I don't know much about the drug scene. **I don't think it is really widespread or a problem** on our campus. Binge drinking will be the only real drug related problem you'll encounter with any frequency."

Q "There are drugs here, but **they're very avoidable**. There's really nothing to worry about."

## The College Prowler Take
ON DRUG SCENE

UNC security does a good job of warning students of the dangers of taking drugs, and getting carried away with alcohol consumption. However, for those students who do get caught up in the drug scene, Student Health Services provides plenty of aid and advice on how students can control their partying lifestyle. Unfortunately, many students fail to take these services seriously. Drug prevalence at UNC-CH is relatively small. Of course, if you are looking to do drugs, you will probably be able to find some rather easily. You will, by no means, be considered uncool for not doing drugs. People at UNC respect each other's lifestyles and decisions. The most prevalent drug at UNC, like most other college campuses, is alcohol. Although drugs are more than likely available to any UNC student, they definitely do not dominate the social scene or UNC culture in any way.

**B+**

The College Prowler™ Grade on
### Drug Scene: B+

A high grade on Drug Scene indicates that drugs are not a noticeable part of campus life; drug use is not visible, and no pressure to use them seems to exist.

# Overall Experience

## The Lowdown
ON OVERALL EXPERIENCE

"I couldn't have picked a better, more well-rounded school. Academically, it's really challenging. Socially, there's always something to do. Diversity is something that's really embraced, and we're the Tar Heels; sports are great!"

Q "Overall, I am happy to be here at Carolina. I transferred here from the University of Georgia, where people are more laid-back and less stuck-up. That is my main complaint about Carolina. However, I stress, there are **many really cool people here**, but you just have to look a bit harder."

Q "My overall experience here at UNC is one that I will always remember. There are great people, teachers, and students all around. **I have found lifelong, strong friendships here**, as well as the one girl, who I feel is my true love. Point being, UNC has a lot to offer. I suggest not missing out!"

Q "I absolutely love Carolina. It was the best decision I ever made to go here, and I wouldn't trade it for anything. **UNC is truly the complete package**. It's one of the best public schools in the nation, has a great location, superb athletics, amazing tradition, good weather, and great school colors. Once you enroll, your blood will run Carolina blue forever."

"Overall, I am glad I attend UNC-Chapel Hill because it's a well-known school throughout the nation. However, I do at times wish I were somewhere else, because **the social life for blacks is not that great**. Academics can be threatening, too, when you walk into a class and you're the only black person or minority. Your success at Carolina will depend on how focused you are and on your goals. My only advice is not to get caught up in the party scene your first year."

To find out more about life at UNC, look for the College Prowler guidebook available at www.collegeprowler.com.

## The College Prowler Take
### ON OVERALL EXPERIENCE

Students who attend Carolina are often happy with their choice—even if it wasn't their first. Carolina is surrounded by a great college town, is one of the most prestigious public schools in the nation, and is one of the most diverse schools in the nation. The list goes on and on. What more could a college student ask for? At times, yes, Carolina, like any college, can seem a little redundant and repetitious. However, if you find a good group of friends and find your niche at Carolina, you'll always find something new around the corner.

At Carolina, your good experiences will outweigh your negative experiences by a ton. Yes, there will be run-ins with teachers, failed midterms, pop-quizzes, parking catastrophes, shallow people, and messy and annoying roommates. However, that's a part of college life at any school. It doesn't take long to adjust to Carolina. It's mainly common sense—hang out with old friends, make new friends, party, take a weekend trip or two (but don't forget to bring along your books!). Students who attend UNC realize that they are receiving a great college education and an even better college experience.

# University of South Carolina

Columbia, SC 29208
www.sc.edu
(800) 868-5872

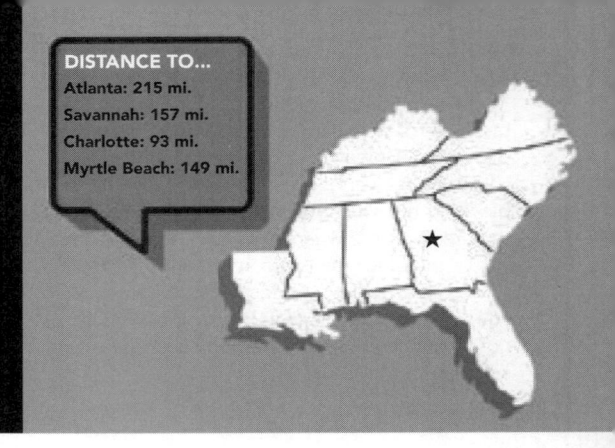

**DISTANCE TO...**
Atlanta: 215 mi.
Savannah: 157 mi.
Charlotte: 93 mi.
Myrtle Beach: 149 mi.

*"USC is committed to ensuring the future success of their students at a reasonable price."*

**Total Enrollment:**
14,884

**Top 10% of High School Class:**
26%

**Average GPA:**
3.8

**Acceptance Rate:**
64%

**Tuition:**
$6,356 in-state, $16,724 out-of-state

**SAT Range (25th-75th Percentile):**
| Verbal | Math | Total |
|---|---|---|
| 510 – 620 | 520 – 630 | 1030 – 1250 |

**ACT Range (25th-75th Percentile):**
| Verbal | Math | Total |
|---|---|---|
| N/A | N/A | 22-27 |

**Most Popular Majors:**
- 7% Experimental Psychology
- 6% Financial Management Services
- 5% Marketing
- 5% Business
- 5% Biology

**Students also applied to:***
Clemson University
College of Charleston
University of North Carolina
University of Georgia

*For more school info check out www.collegeprowler.com

## Table of Contents

| | |
|---|---|
| Academics | 319 |
| Local Atmosphere | 321 |
| Safety & Security | 322 |
| Facilities | 324 |
| Campus Dining | 326 |
| Campus Housing | 327 |
| Diversity | 329 |
| Guys & Girls | 331 |
| Athletics | 332 |
| Greek Life | 334 |
| Drug Scene | 336 |
| Overall Experience | 337 |

## College Prowler Report Card

| | |
|---|---|
| Academics | B- |
| Local Atmosphere | B+ |
| Safety & Security | B+ |
| Facilities | A- |
| Campus Dining | A- |
| Campus Housing | C+ |
| Diversity | C- |
| Guys | A- |
| Girls | A |
| Athletics | A |
| Greek Life | A- |
| Drug Scene | B+ |

# Academics

## The Lowdown
### ON ACADEMICS

**Degrees Awarded:**
Associate, Bachelor, Master, Doctorate, First-Professional

**Undergraduate Schools:**
Moore School of Business; College of Education; College of Engineering and Information Technology; School of the Environment; College of Hospitality, Retail, and Sports Administration; College of Liberal Arts; College of Mass Communications and Information Studies; School of Music; College of Nursing; College of Pharmacy; Arnold School of Public Health; College of Science and Mathematics; College of Social Work; South Carolina Honors College

**Full-time Faculty:**
1,431

**Faculty with Terminal Degree:**
85.5%

**Student-to-Faculty Ratio:**
14:1

**Average Course Load:**
15 hours

**Special Degree Options:**
Interdisciplinary Studies Program: College of Hospitality, Retail, and Sports Management

**AP Test Score Requirements:**
Possible credit for scores of 3, 4, or 5

**Sample Academic Clubs**
Academic Team, American Chemical Society, Anthropology Student Association, Carolina Debate, Criminal Justice Association, DMSB Doctoral Student Association, Geography Club, Geology Club, Marine Science Society, Mock Trial Team, Psychology Graduate Student Association

**Did You Know?**
White House Chief of Staff Andrew Card, Jr., Pulitzer Prize-winner Jim Hoagland, and Grammy Award-winning musicians Hootie and the Blowfish are among some of the University of South Carolina's most notable alumni.

**Best Places to Study:**
Thomas Cooper Library, Horseshoe, dorm study rooms

## Students Speak Out
### ON ACADEMICS

"All of the teachers that I've had have been tremendous. They are willing to meet with you and give you as much help as you need. They all have really seemed to care."

Q "**Some teachers are fantastic, and a few are terrible**. Many are extremely intelligent and knowledgeable, but just not very interesting. The key is to do your research before signing up for classes. Ask people from your major; they will tell you who to take, and who not to take. That is always key. For your first semester, it won't make that much of a difference, but as you get deeper into your specific major, you'll really want to get into the best classes."

Q "I really like the professors; **they're just fine here**. You can always find the type of professor you want, but keep in mind it's not high school anymore. They treat you fairly in my opinion. USC is a big school, though, so there isn't always a lot of personal help unless your classes have a graduate student teaching assistant [TA]."

Q "Teachers are normal. **You get the stuffy old professors who have been lecturing the same way for years**, and you get the new ones that are willing to try new things. Classes are all right; however, I haven't really begun any classes related to my major, so I'm not too interested in the general classes I'm taking."

Q "I find most classes interesting, but there are a few that just go on and on. I also find that, in some classes, rather than being taught new things, I feel like the **professors are just using their position to enforce their opinions** on their students."

## The College Prowler Take
### ON ACADEMICS

Unfortunately, it seems impossible for students to categorize the teachers at the University of South Carolina as "good" or "bad." Students find all kinds of teachers at the University of South Carolina, with varying teaching methods and varying levels of personal involvement with the students. Academic advisers are often helpful when trying to find out information about particular teachers, but sometimes students are forced to rely on word of mouth to find out which teachers will best meet their needs.

As far as academics in general go, the University of South Carolina isn't exactly Ivy League, although it does have potential. Efforts are being made to bring academics to the next level of excellence. Students wanting to take advantage of some of the best facilities, courses, and professors should consider applying for the Honors College. Or, students can choose to be a part of one of the University of South Carolina's nationally ranked programs. With the University president making unprecedented changes, this is an exciting time to be attending the University of South Carolina, and taking advantages of the new opportunities being provided. Ultimately, the education you receive at the University of South Carolina depends on the effort you put forth, but the means of obtaining an excellent education are definitely there for those who desire to do so.

**B-**

The College Prowler™ Grade on
## Academics: B-

A high Academics grade generally indicates that professors are knowledgeable, accessible, and genuinely interested in their students' welfare. Other determining factors include class size, how well professors communicate, and whether or not classes are engaging.

# Local Atmosphere

**City Websites**
http://www.columbiasc.net/
http://www.columbiasouthcarolina.com/

## Students Speak Out
ON LOCAL ATMOSPHERE

## The Lowdown
ON LOCAL ATMOSPHERE

"This is the South. The biggest adjustment is a cultural one. The people are incredibly warm and friendly—almost suspiciously so to an outsider."

Q "Columbia is a medium-sized city with well over 200,000 in the metro area. There is a women's college—Columbia College—and two small African American colleges in town. Clemson University, our bitter rival, is about 100 miles northwest of us in a tiny little town. The College of Charleston, another large university, is 90 miles to the east. **Charlotte, North Carolina is 70 miles north on the freeway**, and Atlanta is a three-hour drive. Charleston, South Carolina may be the most beautiful and historic town in the country and well worth many trips."

Q "**If you like city life, this is the university for you**. If not, go somewhere out in the country. It is a busy campus. There are relaxing locations on the campus, such as the Horseshoe, but other than that, it is a 'go, go, go' atmosphere. Columbia is very open and spread out. There are lots of things to do during the day. Visit are the state museum and Riverbank Zoo."

Q "The atmosphere in Columbia is very laid-back and kind. **People aren't in a hurry here**. Everything moves pretty slowly. I'd definitely visit the museum, Lake Murray, and the zoo. The zoo here is very neat, and is one of the nicest in the United States. I can't really think of anything to stay away from, except for the neighborhood called Olympia."

**Region**:
Southeast

**City, State**:
Columbia, South Carolina

**Setting**:
Mid-Sized City

**Distance from Myrtle Beach**:
3 hours

**Distance from Charleston**:
2 hours

**Distance from Atlanta**:
3 hours, 30 minutes

**Points of Interest**:
Downtown, Lake Murray, Riverbanks Zoo, South Carolina State Museum (Gervais St.), Finlay Park (Assembly St.), Sesquicentennial State Park (Two Notch Rd.), McKissick Museum (Horseshoe), Koger Center for the Performing Arts (Assembly St.), Columbia Museum of Art (Main St.), Frankie's Fun Park (Parkridge Dr.)

**Major Sports Teams:**
Inferno (hockey)
Bombers (baseball)

> "I love Columbia! It's a great place, and **we are only two hours from the mountains and two hours from the beach**! Charleston is a great place to go—the College of Charleston is a huge party school. And the Citadel, a military type school with hot guys, is about two hours away! There aren't any other big universities around except Clemson, which is about two and a half hours away from here."

## The College Prowler Take
ON LOCAL ATMOSPHERE

Located in the heart of Columbia, many students are delighted by the mix of southern charm on campus and the fast pace of the urban setting. The campus grounds are scattered with gorgeous greenery and tons of secluded gardens that make great places to study or get a breath of fresh air. Columbia also harbors a vast array of historical treasures, which are an attraction to many students. On campus, students are able to visit McKissick Museum on the Horseshoe, which hosts art shows and collections generally featuring southern culture. If you're willing to travel a bit, Charleston, Myrtle Beach, Atlanta, and the Blue Ridge Mountains are all within a few hours of Columbia. The southern atmosphere, the urban setting, and the variety of activities in the area combine to make the atmosphere at the University of South Carolina ideal for many students.

# Safety & Security

## The Lowdown
ON SAFETY & SECURITY

**Number of USC Police**: 32

**Phone**: (803) 777-4215

**Health Center Office Hours**: Monday-Friday 8 a.m.-5 p.m.; Sundays for urgent conditions only 4 p.m.-8 p.m.

**Safety Services**: Emergency call-boxes, escort services, shuttle system, Rape Aggression Defense System, 24-Hour Help Line

### Did You Know?
Once the button on an emergency call-box has been pushed, the USC Police Department typically has an officer on the scene in less than one minute.

## B+

**The College Prowler™ Grade on**
## Local Atmosphere: B+

A high Local Atmosphere grade indicates that the area surrounding campus is safe and scenic. Other factors include nearby attractions, proximity to other schools, and the town's attitude toward students.

## Students Speak Out
### ON SAFETY & SECURITY

*"While at USC, common sense needs to be used. What I mean is, you can't expect to go walking alone at 3 a.m. and expect to be as safe as you would be earlier in the evening."*

Q "Security is a big issue, since **the University is located in the middle of a big city**. At every location on campus, there is a call-box within view. If anything ever happens, you run to one and hit a button. A big, blue light starts flashing soon after that, and the police are there within minutes."

Q "I've never had any problems, but **there are some incidents that occur every once in a while**. Mostly everything is pretty well-lit. The dorms are also pretty safe, although some of the freshman ones are pretty slack on who can come in and whatnot."

Q "USC has its own private police force, the USCPD, which is very good—except when they're pulling you over to give you a speeding ticket. **There are usually patrol cars driving around everywhere**, and if you are walking around at night, because it is a pretty big campus, you can call campus security and they will drive you around."

Q "Security on campus is pretty good. We have campus police, and you see them riding around on their bikes or in the cars, but unfortunately, **there is crime everywhere**. I think that the security does all that they possibly can. Most of the dorms have security officers at the desk, and you have to sign your male guest in; female guests have to be signed in after 8 p.m.."

Q "**Security is fine**; just don't be stupid and think you're invincible just because you're in college and on your own—stay in groups after dark. Use your intuition and common sense. If something doesn't feel right, it usually isn't. And there are these call boxes all around campus that you can call, even if it's not an emergency. They'll send an escort over."

## The College Prowler Take
### ON SAFETY & SECURITY

Safety is an issue that students should be concerned about in Columbia. Being in the middle of a city, there are dangerous people, and if students are not careful, they can find themselves in dangerous situations. However, with that being said, the University of South Carolina does provide a number of services to ensure the safety of the students. In addition to the city police force, students have access to the services of the USC Police Department (USCPD), which patrols campus 24 hours a day. The call-boxes placed throughout campus allow the students fast access to the USCPD in emergency situations; at the push of a button, a police officer is guaranteed to be there within minutes. There is also an escort service that operates five nights a week between 8 p.m. and 12 a.m., allowing students to call for an escort if they feel that they are in an unsafe situation.

**B+**

**The College Prowler™ Grade on**
### Safety & Security: B+

A high grade in Safety & Security means that students generally feel safe, campus police are visible, blue-light phones and escort services are readily available, and safety precautions are not overly necessary.

# Facilities

## The Lowdown
ON FACILITIES

**Student Center:**
The Russell House University Union

**Athletic Center:**
Blatt PE Center, Strom Thurmond Wellness and Fitness Center

**Libraries**:
8

**Movie Theater on Campus?**
Yes, the Russell House University Union has one on the second floor.

**Bowling on Campus?**
No

**Bar on Campus?**
No

**Coffeehouse on Campus?**
No. Although, Cool Beans is less than a block from the Horseshoe on College Street.

**Popular Places to Chill:**
The Horseshoe (in the middle of campus on Sumter Street), the Russell House University Union, Cool Beans coffee shop

**Computers**

**High-Speed Network?** Yes

**Wireless Network?** Yes

**Charge to Print?** Varies

**Number of Labs:** 8

**Numbers of Computers:**
16 in each dorm lab; more than 200 in Thomas Cooper Library

**24-Hour Labs:**
Bates, Patterson, the Towers, Columbia Hall

## Favorite Things to Do

Many students enjoy going to see flicks for free at the Russell House, which are usually playing several nights a week. Similarly, there is almost always a theatrical production showing at Longstreet Theater or Drayton Hall, which draws rather large crowds. The University also hosts "Late Night Carolina" every semester, where students can get free food, watch movies, and participate in games and other activities (in the past students have been able to make their own music videos, make arts and crafts, etc.). Or, if music is your thing, the Koger Center often hosts band and orchestra concerts, as well as dance and theatrical performances. The new gym has also given students more incentive to get in shape, so there is almost a big crowd there. Whether in the mood for burning some energy, or getting some rest and relaxation, the facilities at the USC provide several options for students when they want to get out of their dorms.

**COLLEGE PROWLER**

Looking for things to do on campus? Check out the College Prowler book on USC at *www.collegeprowler.com*.

## Students Speak Out
### ON FACILITIES

"The University held a huge fund-raising drive in order to make the facilities here top-notch. The computer centers here are excellent, and the athletic facilities are top-of-the-line."

"The campus is really nice. **They built a Greek village** [fraternity and sorority houses], and they just finished a new sports arena for the basketball team—the hockey team gets the old one—a new student and intramural sports facility, and two new apartment-style upperclassman dorms."

"I think that **the new gym is the largest workout gym in the whole state**; it also has an Olympic-sized pool! The student center has restaurants, and lots of people are always there. We have a great football stadium. A Greek village is being built, and we also have a new basketball arena."

"**Campus facilities at USC are amazing**. The recreational center is a phenomenon; its up-to-date equipment and technology make it easy for any student to come and go at their own convenience. Academic tutoring is another one of USC's perks. There you can find a variety of 'free help' whether it's with the writing center or math labs that are open at a variety of times."

"I would have to rate the facilities average; **they aren't that bad**. There could be improvements, but I think you are going to find room for improvement at any university."

## The College Prowler Take
### ON FACILITIES

With all of the improvements that have been made to the on-campus facilities during the past year, students overall seem to be very satisfied. Recent improvements include the building of the Strom Thurmond Wellness and Fitness Center, which houses five basketball courts, an indoor and outdoor pool, an indoor track, a climbing wall, as well as strength training equipment, among other amenities. Students really enjoy taking advantage of the long hours and brand-new equipment in this multi-million-dollar facility. Not too far from the newly opened Wellness and Fitness Center is the Carolina Center, which also opened this past school year and is where USC now holds many of its sporting events. Although some of USC's facilities have room for improvement, the recent opening of the Wellness and Fitness Center and the Carolina Center make USC's facilities among some of the best in the state.

**A-**

The College Prowler™ Grade on
### Facilities: A-

A high Facilities grade indicates that the campus is aesthetically pleasing and well-maintained; facilities are state-of-the-art, and libraries are exceptional. Other determining factors include the quality of both athletic and student centers and an abundance of things to do on campus.

# Campus Dining

## The Lowdown
### ON CAMPUS DINING

**Freshman Meal Plan Requirement?**
Yes

**24-Hour On-Campus Eating?**
No

**Student Favorites:**
Pandini's, Taco Bell, the GMP

**Meal Plan Average Cost:**
$1,000 per semester

### Did You Know?

The University of South Carolina offers a Five Points Meal Plan, which allows students to eat at many of their favorite restaurants off campus. It acts like a debit card so that you only pay for what you eat.

## Students Speak Out
### ON CAMPUS DINING

"I think the food on campus is above-average. I don't mind it at all, but like everything else in life, you sometimes get tired of it and need a change."

Q "The best places to eat on campus, I think, are the Roost and the Gimp. **The Roost is where most of the athletes live, and you can eat all you want there**. The Gimp is located inside our student union. There you have a variety of choices from salads to something similar to a home cooked meal. The only problem with the Gimp is that they sometimes like to rip you off on prices. Upstairs in the Russell House [student union] you also have Taco Bell, Chick-fil-A, and Pizza Hut. There are also some more restaurants downstairs in the Russell House. A lot of people like Patterson, which is located inside one of the freshman girl dorms, but I only ate there once this past year, and it was okay."

Q "**Food on campus isn't that great**. It's probably just because I'm so sick of it. The Grand Market Place [GMP] is where most people eat on campus, but the meal plans are pretty much a rip-off. You should definitely get a cash card."

Q "**I love the food**! There are, like, 20 different places to eat on campus. You hardly ever get tired of it, and they have this thing where you can eat at a bunch of off-campus restaurants as well, like Groucho's—my personal favorite—Zorba's, Pita Pit, Subway, Wendy's, Burger King, Hardee's, Andy's Deli, and many sit-down type restaurants."

Q "Food on campus ranges from average to good. **It's not fantastic, but it's not bad either**. The main student union in the middle of campus contains everything from greasy fast food to a better-than-average cafeteria, a good sub shop and an average veggie place. There are several other good places on campus, including a good all-you-can-eat buffet at the Roost."

> "If you want variety, then USC has it. **A meal plan can provide a lot for any student**. From the buffet style at the Patio, to the Italian cuisine in Capstone, USC offers a variety of quality food."

## The College Prowler Take
ON CAMPUS DINING

The Russell House University Union has the biggest variety of food options, as it houses an Italian cuisine restaurant, a sub place, a juice bar, several fast food restaurants, and the Grand Market Place (the GMP, affectionately called "the Gimp"), which offers salads, sandwiches, stir-fry, and homestyle meals. Some of the dorm buildings, such as Capstone, Patterson, and Bates have their own cafeterias. On top of this, there are several grab-and-go places around campus, where students can grab a bite on their way to or from class. Students generally seem to rate the food on campus anywhere from average to good. The main complaint is that the food gets old after a while, which is understandable, when you're eating campus food anywhere from 10 to 21 times a week.

# Campus Housing

## The Lowdown
ON CAMPUS HOUSING

**Undergrads on Campus:**
47%

**Number of Dormitories:**
26

**Number of University-Owned Apartments:**
11

**You Get:**
Air conditioning; voice, cable and data connections; twin bed; dresser; desk and chair; closet

**Available for Rent:**
Micro-fridge

**Cleaning Service?**
Cleaning services provided for all hall/community bathrooms

**Bed Type:**
Twin extra-long

**Also Available:**
Special-interest housing; wellness housing; no-visitation housing; quiet floors in certain dorms

## A-

The College Prowler™ Grade on
### Campus Dining: A-

Our grade on Campus Dining addresses the quality of both school-owned dining halls and independent on-campus restaurants as well as the price, availability, and variety of food.

## Room Types

Residence rooms include traditional, suite-style, and apartment buildings.

Traditional: Community bathrooms and two students to a room; most first-year students are assigned to these kinds of rooms.

Suite-style: One semi-private bathroom adjoins two rooms, with two students to a room.

Apartment: Two, three, or four students share a common living area, kitchen area, and bathroom, and each student has his or her own room.

### Did You Know?

Special-interest housing includes Maxcy Honors Hall, Bates Engineering Community, Moore's Wellness Community, and Moore's Pre-Medical Community.

Room inspections take place periodically to ensure that students are meeting campus regulations.

## Students Speak Out
### ON CAMPUS HOUSING

"Most of the dorms are okay. You'll have a bed, a dresser, and plenty of space. I would live on campus for freshman year, but then I recommend moving off campus sophomore or junior year for more freedom."

Q "**I would advise against Bates** [freshman only], Bates West, and the Roost [both upperclassmen]. I don't recommend them—not because they are bad, but because unless you have a car and unless you want to take the shuttles all of the time, it is a long walk. These dorms are also far away from Five Points, and shuttles don't run past 5:30 p.m.."

Q "**You get what you pay for**. You could pay for an elegant room in the South or East Quad and live like a queen, or you could opt to live in one of the Towers buildings and gag whenever someone uses the restroom, in the large communal bathroom/shower area, but you'd save money. If you want to strike a nice balance, the dorm rooms in Capstone aren't all that bad, really. They're not huge, but they're not microscopic. There is enough space, so you're not in your roommate's face, and there is decent closet space. If you want a balance, I'd go there."

Q "I'd recommend either Patterson Hall, McClintock, or Wade Hampton. **If you happen to be a freshman girl, you will definitely want to try and get Patterson**. This is where you will meet the most girls. Stay away from the Towers. McClintock and Wade Hampton are also for freshman girls, but aren't as large as Patterson. Patterson also has a place to eat downstairs. When you become an upperclassman, I'd recommend East Quad, South Quad, or anything on the Horseshoe—it's probably the prettiest place on campus."

Q "I hated Patterson—it has nine floors, and **the fire alarms and laundry facilities are awful**. But, other than that, it's not too bad. It has a dining area in the basement, and it is easy to meet a lot of different people since it's so big. The Towers are co-ed, and those are the less strict ones, but they aren't as nice. Wade Hampton and McClintock aren't too bad, but they are kind of strict and stuck-up."

### COLLEGE PROWLER

Need help choosing a dorm? For a detailed listing on all dorms on campus, check out the College Prowler book on USC available at www.collegeprowler.com

## The College Prowler Take
### ON CAMPUS HOUSING

There are advantages and disadvantages to living on campus. Most students find that living on campus their freshman year is beneficial because it allows them the opportunity to interact with students outside of class and get involved in a lot of activities around campus without having to worry about commuting. If you live on campus, you've got the convenience of being able to roll out of bed 15 minutes before class starts and still make it on time, and you've also got the convenience of being surrounded by hundreds of students in the same boat that you're in, which can sometimes make the transition a whole lot easier.

**C+**

The College Prowler™ Grade on
## Campus Housing: C+

A high Campus Housing grade indicates that dorms are clean, well-maintained, and spacious. Other determining factors include variety of dorms, proximity to classes, and social atmosphere.

# Diversity

## The Lowdown
### ON DIVERSITY

**Native American**: 0%

**Asian American**: 3%

**African American**: 18%

**Hispanic**: 1%

**White**: 76%

**International**: 2%

**Out-of-State**: 13%

### Most Popular Religions

Christianity is by far the most prominent religion on campus. There are a lot of religious clubs and organizations, most of which are Christian-oriented.

### Political Activity

USC is located in a very conservative area of the country, but students of all political opinions find ways to express their views. Politically involved students really have the chance to make an impact, especially because USC is in the middle of South Carolina's capital, and only a few blocks away from the state house.

### Gay Tolerance

Anti-gay sentiments are not expressed very visibly at USC, but this may be in part because the gay population remains relatively quiet.

### Economic Status

The majority of USC students are middle- to upper-class in terms economic status. You will see a few cruising around in a new Mercedes their parents bought them, but, for the most part, the students here are not incredibly wealthy.

### Minority Clubs

There are a total of 13 minority clubs on campus, but they are generally unseen and unheard.

## Students Speak Out
### ON DIVERSITY

"I feel that the USC campus is very diverse, but we still have a long way to go."

Q "I don't know about specifics, but **different groups are represented on campus** through things like the Association of African American Students, Brothers of Nubian Decent, Filipino Association, Bisexual Gay Lesbian Association, and a lot more."

Q "The campus is **not as diverse as most places** I would expect, but there are no problems."

Q "The campus is pretty diverse. There are different racial and religious groups all over the campus. **Everyone celebrates in his or her own way**, and that hasn't caused a problem for anyone."

Q "USC is not very diverse. **Many people are still stuck in a narrow-minded perspective**. Even though USC is located in Columbia, there are still many people who live out in the country, isolated from people and retaining the ideals of their parents and grandparents. And we all know how times change."

## The College Prowler Take
### ON DIVERSITY

While many USC students claim that campus is very diverse, the statistics indicate otherwise. The campus is 76 percent Caucasian and 18 percent African American, leaving only six percent for other nationalities. One reason that students may be under the impression that the campus is more diverse than it is in reality, is that there are a number of organizations that cater to individual ethnic groups, such as the Filipino American Student Association, the Hindu Students Council, the Students Association for Latin America, and about 10 other such organizations that increase students' awareness of ethnic groups on campus. And the truth of the matter is that many students do not come from an incredibly diverse background, so the presence of a small number of international students or persons of a different ethnic background makes the campus "diverse" to them. The fact of the matter is that, in general, colleges across the nation are not incredibly diverse. While USC has a long way to go before it may be considered truly diverse, in relation to other universities, it is better than average.

**C-**

The College Prowler™ Grade on
## Diversity: C-

A high grade in Diversity indicates that ethnic minorities and international students have a notable presence on campus and that students of different economic backgrounds, religious beliefs, and sexual preferences are well-represented.

# Guys & Girls

## The Lowdown
### ON GUYS & GIRLS

**Women Undergrads:** 54%

**Men Undergrads:** 46%

### Birth Control Available?
Yes; free condoms are available to all students. At the Women's Care Clinic, students can also purchase birth control pills, Depo-Provera injections (every three months), Lunelle monthly injections, vaginal contraceptive rings, Ortho Evra contraceptive skin patch, and diaphragms.

### Social Scene
The social scene at USC is always bustling. Because the campus is so big and because there is such a big student body, the parties are plentiful, and students generally enjoy taking the opportunity to get away from their studies. But, not everyone at Carolina is a social butterfly. On the contrary, you will find many different kinds of people: some who don't care to socialize at all and others who can't seem to stop. However, students in general are quite amiable and it's not hard at all to find friends, whether it's in class, at the dorm, or out and about around campus. The abundance of social activity at USC is one of the things that makes it such an exciting place to live and learn.

### Hookups or Relationships?
The odds of finding a significant other at USC are really good, just because there are so many options. There are slightly more females than males on campus, but you wouldn't even be able to tell just by walking around campus. While many students date or hook up, the majority of students are not involved in serious, long-term relationships.

### Dress Code
At USC, pretty much anything goes in terms of clothing. Most people tend to dress casually, in whatever keeps them cool and comfortable; some students don't even bother getting out of their pajamas before going to class. But, there are also some people who don't go out in public without wearing a dress or tie. Punky, preppy, messy, artsy—whatever your style, you will undoubtedly find your niche here at USC. Even though shorts or jeans and T-shirts are the norm, it generally doesn't attract too much attention if someone is wearing something completely out of the ordinary.

## Students Speak Out
### ON GUYS & GIRLS

"Guys are really southern and base themselves on southern pride, especially the fraternity guys. The best frats are part of the Southern Triad, i.e. KA, ATO, and SAE."

Q "The **guys from up north are rude**. The guys from the south are usually pretty generous and courteous. The girls from up north are usually pretty nice, but they can also be kind of rude. Girls from the south are nice and sweet. I'd say there are attractive guys on campus. The girls on campus are attractive as well."

Q "There are definitely a lot of hot guys, if you like southern boys, and **most of the girls look alike**—blonde, southern girls. If you look a little different, I think the guys take it as a plus. The guys are outnumbered by the girls, though, so that sucks."

> "As far as the girls go, **there's a lot of eye candy**. If you're into girls, there's a whole lot of them. There's a big stigma here against homosexuals, though, except in three cities: Columbia, Greenville, and Charleston. They are like the oasis spots in a region filled with prejudice. Also, if you are for gay rights, there's a group here called the GBLA [Gay Bisexual and Lesbian Association]. It's a student group that advocates for equal treatment. They're actually getting a pretty big following at USC."

# Athletics

## The College Prowler Take
### ON GUYS & GIRLS

It's true that down here in South Carolina the weather is sweltering, but the guys and girls are even hotter! According to students, the guys tend to be more chivalrous and charming than average, and the girls are beautiful, even if many of them may fall into the typical "southern belle" category. They are the blonde and the beautiful, and the package generally comes with a distinctive southern drawl and, of course, that perfect golden-brown tan from hours out in the hot Carolina sun. This is not to say that all of the girls and guys are good-looking. It just depends on what you find attractive.

## The Lowdown
### ON ATHLETICS

**Men's Varsity Teams:**
Baseball
Basketball
Football
Golf
Soccer
Swimming
Tennis
Track (indoor)
Track (outdoor)
Track and Field (indoor)
Track and Field (outdoor)

**Women's Varsity Teams:**
Basketball
Cross Country
Golf
Soccer
Softball
Swimming
Tennis
Track (indoor)
Track (outdoor)
Track and Field (indoor)
Track and Field (outdoor)
Volleyball

### The College Prowler™ Grade on
## Guys: A-

A high grade for Guys indicates that the male population on campus is attractive, smart, friendly, and engaging, and that the school has a decent ratio of guys to girls.

### The College Prowler™ Grade on
## Girls: A

A high grade for Girls not only implies that the women on campus are attractive, smart, friendly, and engaging, but also that there is a fair ratio of girls to guys.

## Club Sports

Bowling, Equestrian Sports, Fencing (men's), Frisbee (women's), Karate (women's), Lacrosse, Martial Arts, Mountaineering (women's), Racquetball (men's), Rugby (women's)

## Intramurals (IMs)

Basketball, Bowling, Field Hockey, Flag Football, Frisbee, Indoor Soccer, Racquetball, Soccer, Softball, Tennis, Volleyball, Water Polo

**Athletic Division:**
NCAA Division I

**Conference:**
Southeastern (SEC)

**School Mascot:**
Gamecock

**Fields:**
Williams Brice Stadium, Fields at the Blatt PE Center

## Students Speak Out
### ON ATHLETICS

"USC is in the biggest sports conference in the nation. Gamecock football is absolutely huge at USC. We have one of the most dominant sports programs in the country. Intramural [IM] sports are big as well."

Q "**Varsity sports are huge here**. Our football team is really getting good. We have gone to a New Year's Day bowl, and we have a great coach who is well-known around the country. Our basketball team is also on the rise. We made it to the semifinals in the SEC tournament, and then made it to the finals of the NIT championship in New York City. We should have a great chance at making it to the NCAA tournament next year. IM sports are also big; they have a ton of sports to play. They are competitive and fun at the same time."

Q "**Varsity sports are very big**. The football team is especially big. Football games are like one huge party. Before the games, people will tailgate for hours, and eat and drink. The football games average about 82,000 people per game."

Q "Football dominates the varsity sports, but **the basketball teams are also very good**. A new arena opened last fall for the basketball teams, and it seats about 18,000 people. IM sports on campus are also pretty good. They have everything—flag football, soccer, softball, basketball, volleyball, tennis, golf, racquetball, ultimate Frisbee, badminton, bowling, floor hockey, and sand volleyball. Last spring, the new PE facility was made available for students, and it is absolutely gorgeous. It has six basketball courts, indoor and outdoor pools, and an indoor rock climbing wall."

Q "Sports are very popular on campus, both IM and varsity. I think that **if you like football you would love our games**. There are 80,000 plus people in our stadium during the games and over 100,000 people that tailgate. It's a blast, even if you aren't a big football fan. Most of our teams do really, really well! My friend plays IM soccer, and she loves it."

## Most Popular Sports
Football is, by far, the most popular sport, not necessarily because the team is incredibly great, but because USC has got some die-hard football fans, and coach Lou Holtz also helps bring the crowds. Baseball and basketball also draw pretty big crowds, with the baseball team making it to the College World Series in 2003, and the basketball team hosting games in the brand-new, state-of-the-art Carolina Center.

## Overlooked Teams
Students don't generally hear a lot about the women's track team, which was the NCAA champion in 2002. However, with so many athletic activities going on all the time, there are many teams that are overlooked by the general public.

## Getting Tickets
Tickets for sporting events are available to students for free at the Russell House and are usually easy to obtain as long as its not a huge game. For example, students usually have to win a drawing in order to get tickets to the USC/Clemson football game because there are not enough tickets to go around.

Q "**Intramurals at USC seem to be pretty common among sororities and fraternities**, church organizations, and other extracurricular clubs. Sports seem to play a large part in these particular organizations. So, if you're interested in intramurals, I recommend you join a club of some sort that would provide an organized team."

## The College Prowler Take
### ON ATHLETICS

In case you haven't noticed from the student responses, football is pretty much the focus of the sports calendar for USC students. Students really make a big deal out of tailgating and attending the games, even if they just do it for the social aspect, rather than to actually watch the game. Intramural sports, on the other hand, experience minimal fan turnout, but are still a great way for students to get together and have fun. Anyone can join an intramural team, and there are several to choose from. There are actually more intramural sports teams than there are varsity sports teams. Lots of students create intramural teams through a club or organization, but any individual can sign up to be on a team. Students can choose from sports such as rugby, tennis, soccer, crew, track and field, and many more. Whether it's high athletic participation or great school spirit you're looking for, USC athletics have the best of both worlds.

**A**

### The College Prowler™ Grade on
## Athletics: A

A high grade in Athletics indicates that students have school spirit, that sports programs are respected, that games are well-attended, and that intramurals are a prominent part of student life.

# Greek Life

## The Lowdown
### ON GREEK LIFE

**Number of Fraternities:**
18

**Number of Sororities:**
12

**Undergrad Men in Fraternities:**
17%

**Undergrad Women in Sororities:**
17%

### Did You Know?

Once a year, Greeks team up with the local Red Cross Chapter to sponsor a week-long competition against arch-rival Clemson University to see which school can collect the most blood from its students.

## Students Speak Out
### ON GREEK LIFE

"I would say that Greek life has a big part in the social scene; most people are a part of Greek life—Go Tri Delt!"

"**Greek life here is vibrant, but not that dominating**. I have a lot of friends in frats and sororities and they enjoy it, but I also have many other friends who are not Greek. I am not in a fraternity, and do not feel like I am missing out on anything. I have many friends and an active social life. Up until now, there has not been any Greek housing on campus, so Greeks have not been as dominant here as they are some places. They are building five Greek houses right now on the periphery of campus, which seems to be best for everyone. They have their life, which seems to be pretty positive, without infringing on those who maybe have differing values."

"I think that the sororities are definitely dominating. **They were really bad in my dorm**—Patterson—but, I don't like sororities. Greek life is pretty big on campus. I was one of the few girls who didn't rush my freshman year, but there are plenty of other things to do. The fraternities aren't too bad, though. There are a lot of cliques, at least in my class, but you can still have a great social life without joining."

"I do not think that Greek life dominates the social scene at all. I am in a Greek service sorority, and I just love it. **We aren't the type that goes out and parties all the time**, but we are awesome friends, all of us, and we know how to have a good time. We know the times when we need to do our service work, as well. But anyway, there are a lot of sororities and fraternities if you are interested, but it isn't like you have to be in one to fit in."

"**Greek life does dominate the social scene**, especially your freshman year. I did not go Greek, however, I am very close with a fraternity, and all my friends are in sororities. I still have a blast and don't pay a dime. If you join, Greek life will run you about $1,000 in dues alone."

## The College Prowler Take
### ON GREEK LIFE

Greeks are the minority at USC, with less than 20 percent of the student body participating, but the people who are involved are very vocal and visible on campus about their organization, so Greek life seems a lot more prominent on campus than it really is. Most students agree that Greek life is a major part of the social scene on campus, but it does not dominate. So, when it comes to Greek life, the average USC student can take it or leave it.

**A-**

### The College Prowler™ Grade on
### Greek Life: A-

A high grade in Greek Life indicates that sororities and fraternities are not only present, but also active on campus. Other determining factors include the variety of houses available and the respect the Greek community receives from the rest of the campus.

# Drug Scene

## Students Speak Out
### ON DRUG SCENE

"The only illegal drug you see on campus is weed; a lot of people smoke. It's not hard to find. There are a lot of other drugs used, but people usually keep it on the DL."

Q "Honestly, I don't do drugs, and I have no idea about the drug scene. **I know people do them here** just like at every other university around the United States, but that is really all I know about the drug scene."

Q "I have never been offered drugs, but it might be because I don't hang out with that crowd. I'm sure that you can get them, but I would say they are **much less prevalent** here than in more liberal areas of the country."

Q "Of course, like any large university, drugs are around if you want them, but **I've never seen them pressured on anyone**. Pretty much, if you want them you can get them, but it's possible to stay away from it all."

Q "As far as drugs go, **Columbia, in general, has a pretty big coke problem**. Many of the club and bar owners deal the stuff out the back door, but I have not seen any violence erupt as a result of drugs being dealt. There is definitely a coke problem though."

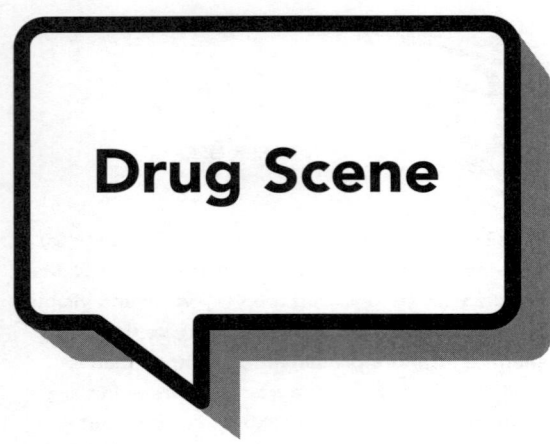

## The Lowdown
### ON DRUG SCENE

**Most Prevalent Drugs on Campus:**
Alcohol, Marijuana, Ecstasy

**Liquor-Related Referrals**:
357

**Liquor-Related Arrests**:
24

**Drug-Related Referrals**:
100

**Drug-Related Arrests**:
46

## Drug Counseling Programs

**Counseling and Human Development Center**
Phone: 777-5223

Services: There is a substance use workshop, which increases students' personal awareness of their relationship with drugs and helps them make healthier lifestyle choices.

**Thomson Student Health Center**
Phone: 777-3957

Services: Smoking cessation programs

For a detailed listing of all counseling sessions on campus, check out the College Prowler book on USC available at www.collegeprowler.com.

## The College Prowler Take
### ON DRUG SCENE

The drug scene at USC is not highly visible, but it is there nonetheless. Marijuana is the most common drug of choice, but ecstasy and cocaine are available as well. The prominence of the drug scene depends on the crowd with which a student chooses to associate him or herself. When students do choose to get high, they usually do it in private, with their circle of friends, or at parties. You will not see anyone trying to pressure anyone into doing drugs, as people on campus are usually more concerned about using drugs for their own entertainment than about making money by pressuring people into buying them. But, if a student wants drugs, they are there for the taking.

Alcohol is used more and is easier to obtain than anything else. But, the extent of a student's exposure to drugs in general really just depends on their friends, and the atmosphere in which they live on campus.

**B+**

### The College Prowler™ Grade on
### Drug Scene: B+

A high grade on Drug Scene indicates that drugs are not a noticeable part of campus life; drug use is not visible, and no pressure to use them seems to exist.

# Overall Experience

## Students Speak Out
### ON OVERALL EXPERIENCE

"I actually wish I would have gone somewhere else. Columbia is a lot of fun for the first couple of years because football is really fun and the weather is nice most of the time. However, now I am tired of it."

Q "I have had a really good experience here, but it seems to me that the most important element that decides your happiness at college is **the friends you make**. I have met freshman who think this is the most fantastic place on earth, and others who can't wait to transfer. This is a good school. I have met some great people, built lifelong friendships, and I've also learned a lot of cool stuff, as well."

Q "I am going to be a senior, and **I sometimes wish I would have chosen a different school**, but overall, I love it. I have had some of the best memories here, and I don't think I would want to be anywhere else. But, we always say that when it comes to Carolina, you either hate it, or you love it."

Q "I've really enjoyed my transition to South Carolina. **There is a lot of school spirit and plenty of nice people** on campus to help you with problems or whatever the case may be. It's a really nice place to be. I guess I haven't heard any bad comments from anyone, and I think that I am going to an awesome and very unique school. I have really enjoyed my time here."

Q "I would never consider going anywhere but USC. **I love it with all my heart.** People in South Carolina are really kind. The campus is beautiful with oaks, ponds, palmettos, and gardens. It is truly a special place. USC has over 20,000 students, but you cannot go two feet without seeing someone you know. I would highly recommend that you become a Gamecock and come to USC. With all the new buildings and developments that are going on, it is an exciting time to be a Gamecock."

## The College Prowler Take
ON OVERALL EXPERIENCE

If there is one word to describe the experiences you will have at USC, it would have to be "unforgettable." Being away from home for the first time is one of the things that makes it so exciting, and even at times a bit scary. But the freedom you get when you come here just feels so natural that it makes you wonder why they don't send people to college sooner! Academically, there are courses and teachers here who can make you look at things in ways you've never considered before, and can literally change your outlook. The professors will fill you with facts and figures, but some of them can teach you a lot about life as well. And, on top of this, with such a large student population, you will inevitably form new relationships, some that will last a lifetime.

As at any college, the quality of the experience depends on what you put into it. There are thousands of new people to meet, and there are constantly activities going on, and constantly things to be learned both in class and outside of class, but those who don't take advantage of these opportunities will not get a lot out of their experience here. Some students do get tired of being at USC after a while, and some hate it from the start for whatever reason. USC is not the place for everyone. But, overall, students seem to be thoroughly enamored with Carolina and wouldn't trade their title of Gamecock for anything in the world.

# University of South Florida

**DISTANCE TO...**
Orlando: 82 mi.
Jacksonville: 197 mi.
Miami: 283 mi.
Panama City: 380 mi.

4202 E. Fowler Avenue Tampa, FL 33620-9951
www.usf.edu          (813) 974-3350

*"The school has a diverse student population, tons of special events, and aims for the success of each individual student."*

**Total Enrollment:**
21,604

**Top 10% of High School Class:**
21%

**Average GPA:**
3.6

**Acceptance Rate:**
62%

**Tuition:**
$3,166 in-state, $16,040 out-of-state

**SAT Range (25th-75th Percentile)**
| Verbal | Math | Total |
|---|---|---|
| 490 – 590 | 490 – 600 | 980 – 1190 |

**ACT Range (25th-75th Percentile)**
| Verbal | Math | Total |
|---|---|---|
| 20-23 | 22-27 | 20-25 |

**Most Popular Majors:**
8% Elementary Education and Teaching
7% Information Science/Studies
7% Psychology
5% Criminal Justice/Safety Studies
5% Marketing/Marketing Management

**Students also applied to:***
University of Central Florida
University of Florida
University of Georgia
Florida State University

*For more school info check out www.collegeprowler.com

## Table of Contents

| | |
|---|---|
| Academics | 340 |
| Local Atmosphere | 342 |
| Safety & Security | 343 |
| Facilities | 345 |
| Campus Dining | 346 |
| Campus Housing | 348 |
| Diversity | 349 |
| Guys & Girls | 351 |
| Athletics | 352 |
| Greek Life | 354 |
| Drug Scene | 355 |
| Overall Experience | 356 |

## College Prowler Report Card

| | |
|---|---|
| Academics | B- |
| Local Atmosphere | A- |
| Safety & Security | B- |
| Facilities | B+ |
| Campus Dining | B- |
| Campus Housing | C- |
| Diversity | B- |
| Guys | A- |
| Girls | A |
| Athletics | B |
| Greek Life | B+ |
| Drug Scene | B- |

# Academics

**Sample Academic Clubs**
Society of Professional Journalists, Community of Future Physicians and Natural Scientists, International Health Interest Group, American Medical Association, Society of Women Engineers, Anthropology Club

## The Lowdown
ON ACADEMICS

**Degrees Awarded:**
Bachelor, Master, Specialist, and Doctorate

**Undergraduate Schools:**
College of Arts and Sciences, College of Business, College of Education, College of Engineering, College of Visual and Performing Arts, College of Nursing, College of Marine Science (St. Petersburg campus), New College of USF, College of Public Health, School of Architecture, Center for Aging Studies, College of Medicine, Honors College

**Full-time Faculty:**
1,834

**Student-to-Faculty Ratio:**
16:1

**Average Course Load:**
24 credits per year

**AP Test Score Requirements:**
Possible credit for scores of 3, 4, or 5

**IB Test Score Requirements:**
Possible credit for scores of 4, 5, 6, or 7

### Did You Know?

The Carnegie Foundation ranks USF in the top national classification for its research.

USF received more than $200 million in sponsored research and grants a few years ago. Money was donated for research into issues critical for Floridians, including homeland defense, education, children's services, health care, bioengineering, and life sciences.

**Best Places to Study:**
The reading room at the library or the fish tank room at the Marshall Center

## Students Speak Out
ON ACADEMICS

"The teachers here are quite good. On occasion, you get a teacher who is there to just make your life difficult, but everyone will leave USF with one teacher in mind who left a great impression."

Q "Freshman year, I was stuck with a teacher that did not need to teach at this school at all. From what I have experienced, **teachers in the science department are not all bad**, but the majority of them stink."

Q "For the most part, teachers are good. The problem is when you get a bad one **they're normally really, really bad**."

Q "Most of my professors have been excellent, but I have had some very **lousy graduate student professors** who should not be teaching just yet."

Q "The teachers are great teachers. They really know the material, and during their office hours, they do what they can to help the students understand. The **classes are, for the most part, very interesting**; otherwise, I would not be taking them. There are some classes that have to be taken because the major requires them. Some of these classes can be very boring."

## COLLEGE PROWLER™

Find out all you need to know about the University's courses and professors, by picking up the USF guidebook from www.colllegeprowler.com.

## The College Prowler Take
### ON ACADEMICS

Professors at USF are generally knowledgeable about the subject matter, willing to work with students, and intent on helping students pass. However, there is always the chance that students will end up with a graduate student professor who can barely speak English, or an 80-year-old science professor that speaks in a monotone. While these kinds of classes can be unbearable, students must sometimes force themselves to suffer through them because the class with the horrible professor is also the only class that meets the credit requirement. On the other hand, most students will be lucky enough to come into contact with at least one professor during their time in school that will have an incredible impact on their life.

Because of recent budget cuts, classes are sometimes crowded and intimidating. USF is aiming to expand the University so that it may get more funding and offer more classes, but the school still has a long way to go. Some departments are faring better than others, but some have been seriously hurt by the cuts. It is a shame that students cannot opt to get a minor in art because the art department barely has enough finances to stay open for students pursuing a major. Although USF offers a variety of majors, clubs, and resources for students, the environment can sometimes make classes more difficult and confusing than they need to be.

**B-**

The College Prowler™ Grade on
## Academics: B-

A high Academics grade generally indicates that professors are knowledgeable, accessible, and genuinely interested in their students' welfare. Other determining factors include class size, how well professors communicate, and whether or not classes are engaging.

# Local Atmosphere

## Students Speak Out
### ON LOCAL ATMOSPHERE

"I would like to think that Tampa's a fast paced city. There is one university 15 minutes away and several community college campuses nearby. There's lots of stuff to do in the city."

Q "Tampa is a very interesting place, with **so many things to do**. You can go to the movies, go clubbing, go out to different dinner places, go bowling, and do all that good stuff. There are also many things that can get you in trouble in this city, if you hang out with the wrong crowd. In the town I lived in before I moved here, I had nothing to do."

Q "I think the atmosphere around here is **great, and it's getting better all the time**. I've been here for five years, and it has changed very much. When you go out to any store or restaurant, you know that you are near USF because they have all of the 'This is Bull Country' stuff around now, so it's definitely more of a USF feel. University of Tampa is another school in our area but you never really hear of it too much. Busch Gardens is probably the closest attraction to visit, but I'd rather drive to Orlando, which is not too far; its parks are better."

Q "Tampa is a borderline hick town. There is **Ybor City** where a lot of people ages 16 to 35 go clubbing. Tampa is only an hour away from some decent beaches."

Q "The atmosphere in Tampa is very inviting. There is not much to stay away from, except for the strip clubs. Busch Gardens and Adventure Island are the two main attractions in this city. There is also **Clearwater Beach** that is about one hour south of Tampa."

## The Lowdown
### ON LOCAL ATMOSPHERE

**Region**:
Southeast

**City, State**:
Tampa, Florida

**Setting**:
Medium-Sized City

**Distance from Orlando**:
1 hours, 30 minutes

**Distance from Miami**:
4 hours, 30 minutes

**Points of Interest**:
Busch Gardens, Adventure Island, Museum of Science and Industry, Tampa Bay Performing Arts Center, Ybor City, Florida Aquarium, Old Hyde Park Village, Riverfront Park, Lowry Park, Raymond James Stadium, Tropicana Field

**Major Sports Teams:**
Buccaneers (football), Devil Rays (baseball), Lightning (hockey)

**City Websites:**
http://www.tbo.com
http://www.tampabay.com

## The College Prowler Take
### ON LOCAL ATMOSPHERE

There are a plethora of attractions for students looking for something interesting to do in Tampa. The area surrounding the school is dotted with bars and restaurants, and there are two awesome amusement parks a short bus ride away from the school. Those interested in veering a little further from campus can visit Ybor City or Channelside, two large complexes that are excellent for shopping, dining, and watching movies. For students who wish to spend their days baking in the Florida sunshine, some of Florida's most beautiful beaches are less than an hour away from the Tampa campus.

# Safety & Security

## The Lowdown
### ON SAFETY & SECURITY

**Number of USF Police**:
49

**Phone**:
911 (emergencies)
(813) 974-2628 (non-emergencies)

**Health Center Office Hours**:
Monday – Friday 8:30 a.m.-5:00 p.m., closed on weekends.

**Safety Services**:
SAFE Team (974-SAFE) transportation service, crime prevention programs, Rape Aggression Defense (RAD), emergency call boxes

**A-**

### The College Prowler™ Grade on
## Local Atmosphere: A-

A high Local Atmosphere grade indicates that the area surrounding campus is safe and scenic. Other factors include nearby attractions, proximity to other schools, and the town's attitude toward students.

### Did You Know?

USF offers a number of crime prevention programs throughout the semester, free of charge.

USF's Tampa campus is ranked one of the safest college campuses in Florida.

## Students Speak Out
### ON SAFETY & SECURITY

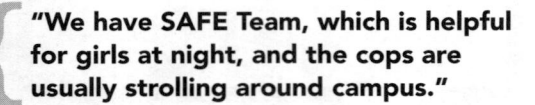

"We have SAFE Team, which is helpful for girls at night, and the cops are usually strolling around campus."

Q "There are those beacon things that someone can push in case of an emergency scattered all around campus. There are always police lurking around, and now there is an officer riding around on a motorcycle. **Theft is quite common in the dorms** because students often leave their rooms open or unlocked."

Q "**Security and safety are pretty good** on campus. I really haven't heard of anything too bad happening on campus."

Q "A few years ago you would always hear of **car break-ins** and stuff like that. I don't live on campus now, so I don't know what it's like for residents. As the campus has been growing, they've been putting in more of the emergency call-boxes, which are good for students."

Q "Security is pretty good on campus. Since I have been at this school I have **never had to worry about my safety**."

## The College Prowler Take
### ON SAFETY & SECURITY

Students at USF generally feel safe on campus. Most areas of the campus are lit up at night, so students need not fear that there is someone lurking in the shadows. However, for those who are afraid to walk alone late at night, the SAFE Team will transport students anywhere on campus in the late hours of the night. SAFE Team's presence also deters criminals from committing crimes because of the elevated possibility that their acts will be observed. There are also emergency call boxes located at crucial areas throughout campus. The University Police Department does an excellent job of making students feel safe during their time on campus.

**B-**

The College Prowler™ Grade on
### Safety & Security: B-

A high grade in Safety & Security means that students generally feel safe, campus police are visible, blue-light phones and escort services are readily available, and safety precautions are not overly necessary.

# Facilities

## The Lowdown
ON FACILITIES

**Student Center:**
The Marshall Center

**Athletic Center:**
Campus Recreation Center; there is also an Outdoor Recreation Center located at Riverfront Park.

**Libraries:**
Three, and the main library is six stories high

**Movie Theatre on Campus?**
No

**Bowling on Campus?**
No

**Bar on Campus?**
No, but the Greenery is located within walking distance of the campus.

**Coffeehouse on Campus?**
Yes, Starbucks is in the library.

**Popular Places to Chill:**
The Tampa Room at the Marshall Center, MLK Plaza, and in front of Cooper Hall

### Computers
**High-Speed Network?** Yes
**Wireless Network?** Yes
**Number of Labs**: 14
**Numbers of Computers**: 644
**24-Hour Labs**: No
**Charge to Print?**
USF students are offered 30 free prints per day, 10 of which may be in color. Prints are seven cents if money on a USF identification card is used.

### Favorite Things to Do
"Movies on the Lawn" (MOTL) is a weekly USF tradition, showing recently released movies that are free for students. Intramural sports are a great way for student groups to get involved with some recreational athletic activity. The Bull Market is a weekly marketplace where students can purchase second-hand books, jewelry, food, and learn about the diverse communities at USF. Students also enjoy basketball games, football games, and theater performances. The Marshall Center game room is open late and has pool, table tennis, and video games for students.

## Students Speak Out
ON FACILITIES

"The recreation center is very nice, and big, but usually gets crowded during peak hours. The school is building a new athletic center for the sports on campus."

"I like the different facilities on campus. **I especially like the gym**, and also the computers that are available for us to use and print with no cost. I know I have saved a lot of money on ink and paper this year."

💬 "The gym is okay, but it needs to be bigger. The computers in the **computer labs are okay, although they tend to have their issues** now and then, shutting down on people and what not. The Marshall Center, being the main student activities building, could be improved greatly. To have a nicer Marshall Center would definitely make coming on campus more fun, but, obviously, there is controversy on how to pay for a new one."

💬 "Most of the facilities are pretty decent. They are **not as great of some other campuses** around the state, but they do what they can for the students. The gym is one of the best facilities on campus. The computers are some of the best around."

## The College Prowler Take
### ON FACILITIES

Thousands of dollars are spent on the facilities at USF each year, and everything is getting bigger and better, as more students come to the school. While this is great for students, it also means added tuition costs and higher fees. Many of the facilities are crowded during peak hours, so be prepared to wait to use some of the exercise equipment at the gym or the pool tables in the games room. The variety of things to do on campus is superb, and most students can find something that suits their own personal interests. The school's facilities are kept clean, and most of them are open late. USF offers dozens of things for students to do, so those who are bored have no excuse.

## B+

**The College Prowler™ Grade on**
### Facilities: B+

A high Facilities grade indicates that the campus is aesthetically pleasing and well-maintained; facilities are state-of-the-art, and libraries are exceptional. Other determining factors include the quality of both athletic and student centers and an abundance of things to do on campus.

# Campus Dining

## The Lowdown
### ON CAMPUS DINING

**Freshman Meal Plan Requirement?**
Yes

**24-Hour On-Campus Eating?**
No

**Student Favorites:**
Starbucks, Bene Pizza and Pasta, Sushi

**Meal Plan Average Cost:**
$1,377.85 per semester

### Did You Know?

The Fresh Food Company is a buffet-style restaurant in the residence area, offering an array of dishes from around the world.

## Students Speak Out
### ON CAMPUS DINING

"The main dining hall is the Fresh Food Company, which has been remodeled and serves better food. There is also the Tampa Room located inside the Marshall Center, which has better food."

Q "The food is not very good compared to other schools. But it has gotten better in the past years. There are several fast food places and most are **good, but expensive**."

Q "I like the food at Einstein's. I think it is pretty decent, and some of the things on the menu are good and tasty. As far as food that comes with a meal plan, it sucks because the food is not tasty and gives **stomach problems**."

Q "I think the **food on campus is really, really good**, especially when it comes to variety, but not when it comes to price. It's so expensive that I never really eat there, unless I have extra cash."

Q "In the Tampa Room, the fact that you can have anything, from plain chicken nuggets to sushi, is good, and they have a lot of **good stuff for vegetarians**. I guess if you have Flex bucks or something from your meal plan, then you might not mind paying for it, but for the poor college student, I would recommend bringing your own lunch here. Sometimes the lines are really long and it costs a fortune. The eating areas are not all that great in the Marshall Center, but I hear the new dining halls for people on meal plans are really nice, like the Fresh Food Company."

Q "Most students are on a limited budget, and don't want to spend **$5 for a bagel**, but unfortunately that is how it is becoming. It is best to leave campus to get food. To prove my point, they are building a Starbucks inside the library, which pisses me off."

## The College Prowler Take
### ON CAMPUS DINING

The variety of food at USF has increased in recent years, reflecting the diverse tastes of USF students. While most students would consider this a good thing, others are upset with the influx of fast food restaurants making their way onto campus. The places to eat on campus are essentially an oligopoly, with most places having high prices for a small amount of food. USF is trying hard to keep the students content with their meals, but expensive food is making students upset. Of course, students who can't really afford to spend all of their money on food still end up eating on campus anyway because it beats the hassle of having to leave during the busiest parts of the day. Hopefully, the next few years will bring more diversity and cheaper prices to USF's dining facilities.

**B-**

The College Prowler™ Grade on
### Campus Dining: B-

Our grade on Campus Dining addresses the quality of both school-owned dining halls and independent on-campus restaurants as well as the price, availability, and variety of food.

# Campus Housing

## Did You Know?

National statistics show that students who live on campus are more involved in university life and have a higher rate of academic success.

In recent years, more than $120 million in residence hall renovations and new construction have taken place or are currently underway at USF.

## The Lowdown
### ON CAMPUS HOUSING

**Undergrads on Campus:**
3,798

**Number of Dormitories:**
12

**Number of University-Owned Apartments:**
3

**Room Types:**
Singles, doubles, traditional, suite, apartments, Greek housing facilities

**Cleaning Service?**
The bathrooms and common areas of the dorms are cleaned daily. Open kitchens in applicable dorms are also cleaned daily.

**You Get:**
Cable TV, late-night computer labs for residential students, Ethernet connection, local phone service and voicemail, mailbox, study lounges, employment opportunities, use of fitness center, laundry rooms

**Bed Type:**
Single

**Also Available:**
Eta is an all-female community for women pursuing majors in math, science, or engineering. Delta offers a residential learning program. Epsilon is a community specifically for international students and honor students. Magnolia is available to married students and students with dependent children.

## Students Speak Out
### ON CAMPUS HOUSING

"Most of the dorms aren't that great, but they're working towards building newer, nicer ones. New ones include Maple, Holly, and Castor."

Q "**Avoid all the old dorms like Zeta, Beta, and Kappa**, because they are so crappy. I don't think they are safe or clean, but the new dorms are nice, though."

Q "I lived in Gamma when it was old and crappy, and I liked it that way, so I recommend to any freshmen to **live in an old crappy dorm, because you meet the best down-to-earth friends** there. But since Gamma is new now, and renamed Castor, it must be nice to live in, with new bathrooms and other facilities. I also lived in Holly, the apartment-style dorms, and they are really nice too. I don't think there are really any to avoid."

Q "They have recently built some newer dorms in the past few years, but I have been in some of the older dorms, and they are **the size of a bathroom stall**."

Q "The dorms are not very good. The worst ones are Epsilon, Beta, and Delta, although these are the same ones that are being renovated. The best places to live on campus are the **Holly Apartments**."

## The College Prowler Take
### ON CAMPUS HOUSING

The USF community can expect two things once the on-campus renovation project begins to wind down: 1) Complaints about the dorms' drudgery and miniscule size will gradually fade away, and 2) on-campus life will become much more social due to the fact that students will more likely want to live in apartment-style and suite-style dorms, like Castor, Maple, or Holly, rather than Zeta, Kappa, or Theta, which all kind of resemble 1950s army-style barracks. Although, many USF students will vehemently argue that the current social activity on campus is nowhere near lacking. Small parties and get-togethers do go on, and there is a sense of camaraderie amongst each dorm and its members.

**C-**

### The College Prowler™ Grade on
### Campus Housing: C-

A high Campus Housing grade indicates that dorms are clean, well-maintained, and spacious. Other determining factors include variety of dorms, proximity to classes, and social atmosphere.

# Diversity

## The Lowdown
### ON DIVERSITY

**Native American:** Less than 1%

**Asian American:** 5%

**African American:** 11%

**White:** 71%

**Hispanic:** 9%

**International:** 3%

**Unknown:** Less than 1%

**Out-of-State:** 5%

### Political Activity

Students at USF openly share their political views all over campus. With buttons, T-shirts, and an endless stream of free information, the political unions at USF make their voices heard. WBUL listeners can tune in to hear the most liberal-minded students at USF voice their opinions. Last spring, dozens of USF students chartered a bus and traveled to Washington, D.C. to protest the war in Iraq.

## Minority Clubs

The Black Student Union has a huge presence at USF. The BSU constantly has parties and fund-raising events that are open to everyone, regardless of skin color. There are also several honors societies that are enacted specifically for minorities, and there are plenty of clubs for minority professionals on campus.

## Most Popular Religions

There are several social clubs for Christians at USF, but Judaism and Islam are popular with students on campus as well.

## Gay Tolerance

USF is welcoming to all students, regardless of sexual orientation. The PRIDE Alliance often holds special events to promote awareness about homosexuality, and last year Delta Lambda Phi, a gay fraternity, organized on campus.

## Economic Status

There are people from all economic backgrounds on campus, but it seems that wealthier students haven't chosen to attend USF. Many students have scholarships and financial aid, allowing them to attend school cheaply. People from lower-class backgrounds interact with people from higher-class backgrounds on a regular basis, inside and outside of school.

"USF is **extremely diverse**, especially for being in a southern state."

"Campus is pretty diverse. I see **people from all over the world** on a day-to-day basis."

## The College Prowler Take
### ON DIVERSITY

With the only African Studies department in the state of Florida, Latin fraternities and sororities, and an active PRIDE Alliance, USF tops the chart in diversity. The "minorities" on campus don't seem like minorities at all. The statistics show that the majority of USF students are white, but judging from the activity in the Marshall Center, MLK Plaza, and Cooper Hall, most people would guess otherwise. Minority groups have made their presence known and will continue to be the leaders of minority students. The school offers countless clubs, associations, and alliances for students to join, which form the collective identity that is USF. USF holds its diverse student body in high esteem, representing those of different ethnicities, races, religious affiliations, and sexual orientations to the fullest extent possible.

## Students Speak Out
### ON DIVERSITY

"I think we have an extremely diverse campus. There are a lot of clubs for diverse groups of people."

"The campus is very diverse. **Every walk of life** is on this campus."

"I think the campus is very diverse. **I just love when people are talking in a foreign language** and I hear them. I think it is a good sign. I love it."

**B-**

The College Prowler™ Grade on
## Diversity: B-

A high grade in Diversity indicates that ethnic minorities and international students have a notable presence on campus and that students of different economic backgrounds, religious beliefs, and sexual preferences are well-represented.

# Guys & Girls

## The Lowdown
ON GUYS & GIRLS

**Women Undergrads**: 58%

**Men Undergrads**: 42%

### Birth Control Available?
Yes. Female birth control is available in pill form ($14 per pack or $35 for 3 packs), patches ($20 for a one-month supply), or the shot ($60 for 3 months). Students who wish to get birth control on campus must have a recent exam with their home provider or with Student Health Services on record. Student Health Services also allows students five free condoms per day, five days per week.

### Social Scene
With so many things going on at USF, students who seek the attention of the opposite sex should have no problem doing so. Men have the advantage, because there are more women than men at USF. This is especially true on campus, where some of the dorms are designed specifically for women. People at USF interact all of the time, making it so that even the shyest students have the opportunity to meet new people.

### Hookups or Relationships?
It depends on how much alcohol is involved when potential partners meet. Random hookups are common with those involved in fraternities or sororities and those who are constantly partying, but the more mild students at USF prefer long-term, serious relationships.

### Dress Code
Visitors to USF will find most students wearing jeans, even in the hottest days of summer. The screen printed USF logo is popular among athletes at USF, and the recognizable "A&F" of Abercrombie & Fitch is popular with those who like to show that they can afford it. Most students wear whatever they can find after rolling out of bed in the morning, but there are a few students who settle only for Burberry and DKNY. One thing is for sure at USF ... an outfit from Diesel will get more double takes than an outfit from Neiman Marcus.

## Students Speak Out
ON GUYS & GIRLS

> "There are plenty of hot women wearing next to nothing in the Florida sun ... need I say more?"

> "The guys, for the most part, are hot, well, some of them anyway. Some of these **guys are a little bold for me**, asking me if I have a boyfriend, and when I say yes, they still say, 'Would you like to go out to dinner with me?' The girls I have met are nice. Some of them are plain rude, thinking that they are 'Ms. Thang,' and that all must bow down to them. I think it is funny when I meet those kinds of people."

> "I heard that for every guy on campus there are three or four girls, or something like that. There are definitely **more girls on campus than guys**, unfortunately. Choosing from the guys that are here can be a little difficult because most of them have girlfriends."

> "There are **some very fine girls**, but on average, I would have to say the girls at University of Central Florida are better. That's just my opinion. There are always the good girls with the bad."

> "Both the **girls and guys are pretty attractive**. I met my boyfriend here, as a matter of fact."

## The College Prowler Take
### ON GUYS & GIRLS

It's not difficult to find attractive members of the opposite sex around campus. Girls can spot some incredible eye candy in the weight room as the football players pump iron. Guys can catch USF's loveliest ladies basking in the summer sun in tank tops, shorts, and summer dresses. The more academically-minded students at USF are able to find at least a few hotties in their classes, and these sexy guys and girls might actually even have more than half of a brain! Even the University's most picky students find someone to crush on by the end of the semester. Whether it is a serious relationship or a not-so-serious hookup that students are looking for, USF has something for both the guys and the girls.

**A-**

**A**

**The College Prowler™ Grade on**
## Guys: A-

A high grade for Guys indicates that the male population on campus is attractive, smart, friendly, and engaging, and that the school has a decent ratio of guys to girls.

**The College Prowler™ Grade on**
## Girls: A

A high grade for Girls not only implies that the women on campus are attractive, smart, friendly, and engaging, but also that there is a fair ratio of girls to guys.

# Athletics

## The Lowdown
### ON ATHLETICS

**Men's Varsity Teams:**
Baseball
Basketball
Cross Country
Football
Golf
Soccer
Tennis
Track & Field

**Women's Varsity Teams:**
Basketball
Cross Country
Golf
Soccer
Softball
Tennis
Track & Field
Volleyball

### Club Sports
Aikido, Badminton, Bowling, Boxing Club, Crew Team, Ice Hockey, Lacrosse, Rugby Football, Scuba Diving, Surfing, Tae Kwon Do, Volleyball, Water Skiing, Women's Rugby

### Intramurals (IMs)
Flag Football, Disc Golf, Badminton, Whiffle Ball, Table Tennis, Volleyball, Soccer, Ultimate Frisbee, Golf, Track & Field, Basketball, Softball, Sand Volleyball, Swimming, Racquetball, Wrestling

**Athletic Division:**
NCAA Division I-A

**Conference:**
Conference USA

**School Mascot:**
Rocky the Bull

**Fields:**
Intramural football field, rugby field, soccer fields, lacrosse field, Fowler fields

## Most Popular Sports

Football is huge at USF, largely because there is no other college in the Tampa Bay area that has a football team. Basketball is also a popular sport, although the turnout for basketball games isn't nearly as huge as it is for football games. The men's and women's rugby teams are increasing in popularity, but it's rumored that most of the sport's participants have never actually watched a rugby game in their entire lives.

## Overlooked Teams

The women's golf team has done well in recent years, but the team's achievements have been overlooked by the USF student body, a group that is impressed with more fast-paced sports.

## Getting Tickets

Admission is free to all athletic games for USF students. For those who are not USF students, tickets are generally cheap and easy to obtain.

# Students Speak Out
## ON ATHLETICS

"**Varsity sports are very big on campus, especially basketball and football.** They're not as big as other schools' sports but it's getting better each year."

Q "**Varsity sports are not really that big** on campus, but they are growing. IM sports and club sports are very big."

Q "I think freshman year, especially when you live on campus, it's easier and more fun to become involved with intramural sports because you have to get a team together. A lot of the sororities and fraternities have their own teams. Overall, the biggest varsity sport is football and that's because **the games are really fun**. It seems like no one really shows up to the baseball games or anything."

Q "**IM sports are a lot bigger than varsity sports**. Our football team has started to get bigger and our basketball team is still doing well."

Q "IM sports are very big and there's a big turnout for most games. **Greeks participate in most sports,** as well."

### COLLEGE PROWLER™

Read more student quotes about USF sports in the College Prowler guidebook, available at *www.collegeprowler.com*.

### The College Prowler Take
**ON ATHLETICS**

Students are steadily becoming more involved with the athletics at USF. Several of the Bulls' football games were broadcast on ESPN, and they will soon join the Big East Conference. While these are awesome feats for the athletic department and for USF, the students have yet to catch on to the hype surrounding USF football. Although varsity sports have become more popular with students in recent years, game turnouts are not nearly as large as they should be. However, the tradition seems to be rising. Each year, more and more students have come out to show their support for the Bulls.

**The College Prowler™ Grade on**
## Athletics: B

A high grade in Athletics indicates that students have school spirit, that sports programs are respected, that games are well-attended, and that intramurals are a prominent part of student life.

# Greek Life

### The Lowdown
**ON GREEK LIFE**

**Number of Fraternities**:
19

**Number of Sororities**:
14

**Undergrad Men in Fraternities**:
7%

**Undergrad Women in Sororities**:
8%

## Multicultural Colonies
Alpha Kappa Alpha, Alpha Phi Alpha, Delta Sigma Theta, Lambda Psi Delta, Lambda Theta Alpha, Lambda Theta Phi, Phi Beta Sigma, Sigma Gamma Rho Sigma Lambda Beta, Sigma Lambda Gamma

### Did You Know?
In 2003, students at USF joined together to form a local chapter of Delta Lambda Phi, a traditionally gay fraternity.

## Students Speak Out
ON GREEK LIFE

"I think Greek life is getting bigger by the year. It does dominate a lot of the social scene around here."

Q "I think **it does dominate the social scene** because everywhere you go you see people wearing Greek letters."

Q "I definitely do not think that Greek life dominates the social scene; it **can contribute to your social scene**, if you choose to be in a sorority or fraternity. If you are a fun person anyway, and have some friends, you don't really need to go Greek to make your life more fun."

Q "**Greek life on campus does dominate** the social scene. Like most campuses, everywhere you turn you'll see someone in letters. Going Greek makes it easier for people from out of town to feel as if they belong."

## The College Prowler Take
ON GREEK LIFE

If students are willing to invest the time and money that it takes to go Greek, then joining can be a great option for making friends on campus. Students should know that the Greek lifestyle is consuming. Students must attend various social events throughout the year, participate in community events, and pay dues regularly. It can be a huge time investment, but most fraternity and sorority members would argue that it is worth it to rush.

**B+**

The College Prowler™ Grade on
## Greek Life: B+

A high grade in Greek Life indicates that sororities and fraternities are not only present, but also active on campus. Other determining factors include the variety of houses available and the respect the Greek community receives from the rest of the campus.

# Drug Scene

## The Lowdown
ON DRUG SCENE

**Most Prevalent Drugs on Campus:**
Alcohol, Marijuana, Xanax

**Liquor-Related Referrals:**
10

**Liquor-Related Arrests:**
23

**Drug-Related Referrals:**
1

**Drug-Related Arrests:**
23

### Drug Counseling Programs

**The Counseling Center for Human Development**
Phone: (813) 974-2831
Services: Literature, psychological assessment screenings, short-term treatment, and referral to other treatment resources as needed

**Student Health Services**
Phone: (813) 974-2331
Services: Health care, literature, and referral services

## Students Speak Out
### ON DRUG SCENE

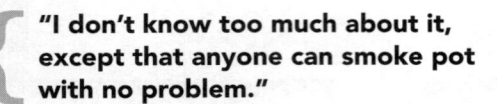

> "I don't know too much about it, except that anyone can smoke pot with no problem."

Q "I think I used to hear a lot more about drug use on campus my freshman year, because I was around a lot more people who were doing drugs. You have to know someone who is going to hook you up with drugs, because apparently they are **not as easy to get as you might think** they are. I don't think it is an extremely bad problem."

Q "It's always best to do all your business off campus. If a student is caught with drugs or alcohol twice, they can **possibly be expelled** from not just USF, but all Florida universities."

Q "Although harmless in the hands of responsible people, marijuana is not the best thing to use while trying to study. It makes things a lot more difficult to remember. Marijuana is the only drug which I condone, and a **surprisingly large amount of students use it**."

Q "Drugs are **there if you want them to be**. If not, they might as well not exist."

## The College Prowler Take
### ON DRUG SCENE

Although alcohol is consumed just about every place on campus where the residents are old enough to drink, drugs and alcohol are much more prevalent off campus than on campus. Marijuana is sometimes found in the dorms, but most students weigh the use of marijuana against the consequences and decide that it is safest to take their recreational drug use off campus. The penalties for all drugs on campus are serious, and can get students expelled from the school. The drug scene outside of campus is pretty big. College students have been known to use cocaine, smoke pot, take pills, and get drunk, all in one night. This type of drug use is extremely dangerous, and has had some serious consequences in the past, but it seems that most USF students know their limits.

**B-**

**The College Prowler™ Grade on**
## Drug Scene: B-

A high grade on Drug Scene indicates that drugs are not a noticeable part of campus life; drug use is not visible, and no pressure to use them seems to exist.

# Overall Experience

## Students Speak Out
ON OVERALL EXPERIENCE

> "I love this place, but I wish it was a little more of a college town, where the town revolves around campus."

Q "I enjoy it here. I got involved my second year, moved off campus with friends and I absolutely love it. It's a different experience then a college that is in the middle of nowhere and in a 'college town.' So, it really **depends on what you want to experience**. It took me awhile to get adjusted, but now I love it. The beach is only 15 minutes away. What more could you ask for? While my friends from back home are walking in the snow, I am laying out!"

Q "Sometimes, I wish I were somewhere else, but I like it here. **It has grown on me**. With every school there is always a good and bad, so you just have to make the best of the situation. That is what I have done, and it is just wonderful."

Q "In the beginning of my time here, I wanted to leave, because I was going through the homesickness thing, but now **I love it, and I know I wouldn't want to leave**."

Q "This was not my first choice of colleges. **I wish I were up in UF [University of Florida]**, but, for family reasons, I had to stay here at this school. The education, I believe, is the same, but the student body is not as great as it is in UF. They have better social events up there."

## The College Prowler Take
ON OVERALL EXPERIENCE

Most students sincerely enjoy USF. Students can look forward to meeting many people from diverse backgrounds, and the teachers here are strong role models for students. While sometimes classes are stressful and unbearable, the lessons taught outside of school are invaluable. Sometimes classes can be difficult, but the school offers students numerous ways to relieve their stress and anxiety. With the various facilities on campus, nighttime activities, dining out, or just laying around in the sun, USF has much more to offer than just academics. Even students who find venturing off to a new school hard on them at first, quickly grow to like USF.

Of course, college is what you make of it. Students who spend their time in their dorm rooms miss out on opportunities to make friends and grow as people. Those who get involved in student activities seem to enjoy their college experience much more than those who don't get involved. That's why it is important to take advantage of the opportunities that USF presents to its students. Overall, most students who come to USF enjoy their time here, even if this university was not their first choice of schools.

# University of Tennessee

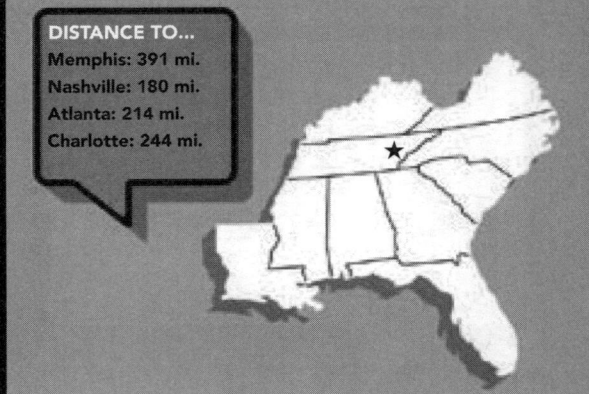

**DISTANCE TO...**
Memphis: 391 mi.
Nashville: 180 mi.
Atlanta: 214 mi.
Charlotte: 244 mi.

800 Andy Holt Tower, Knoxville, TN 37996
www.tennessee.edu          (800) 221-8657

*"I love UT! I am a die-hard Vols fan and wouldn't want to go anywhere else."*

**Total Enrollment:**
17,513

**Top 10% of High School Class:**
26%

**Average GPA:**
2.4

**Acceptance Rate:**
71%

**Tuition:**
$4,748 in-state, $14,528 out-of-state

**SAT Range (25th-75th Percentile):**

| Verbal | Math | Total |
|---|---|---|
| 500 – 610 | 500 – 620 | 1000 – 1230 |

**ACT Range (25th-75th Percentile):**

| Verbal | Math | Total |
|---|---|---|
| 21-28 | 20-26 | 21-26 |

**Most Popular Majors:**
10%  Psychology
4%   Accounting
4%   Journalism
4%   Logistics and Materials Management
4%   Political Science

**Students also applied to:***
Middle Tennessee State University
Auburn University
University of Memphis
University of Georgia

*For more school info check out www.collegeprowler.com

## Table of Contents

| | |
|---|---|
| Academics | 359 |
| Local Atmosphere | 361 |
| Safety & Security | 362 |
| Facilities | 364 |
| Campus Dining | 366 |
| Campus Housing | 367 |
| Diversity | 369 |
| Guys & Girls | 370 |
| Athletics | 372 |
| Greek Life | 374 |
| Drug Scene | 375 |
| Overall Experience | 377 |

## College Prowler Report Card

| | |
|---|---|
| Academics | B- |
| Local Atmosphere | B |
| Safety & Security | B |
| Facilities | B+ |
| Campus Dining | B |
| Campus Housing | B- |
| Diversity | D |
| Guys | A- |
| Girls | A |
| Athletics | A+ |
| Greek Life | A- |
| Drug Scene | B- |

# Academics

**Special Degree Options**
Student-Designed Majors, Double-Majors, Dual-Degrees, Independent Study, Honors Program, Phi Beta Kappa, Pass/Fail Grading Option, Internships, Distance Learning

**Sample Academic Clubs**
Alpha Kappa Psi Professional Business Fraternity, American Society of Civil Engineers, German Club, Geography Club, the Society of Physics Students, and Spanish Club

## The Lowdown
ON ACADEMICS

**Degrees Awarded:**
Bachelor, Master, Doctorate

**Undergraduate Schools:**
Agricultural Sciences and Natural Resources, Architecture and Design, Arts and Sciences, Business Administration, Communications, Education, Engineering, Human Ecology, Music, Nursing, Social Work

**Full-time Faculty:**
1,398

**Faculty with Terminal Degree:**
88%

**Student-to-Faculty Ratio:**
18:1

**Average Course Load:**
13 hours

**AP Test Score Requirements:**
Possible credit for scores of 3 or higher on most subjects

**IB Test Score Requirements:**
Possible credit for scores of 5 or higher on most subjects

### Did You Know?
Top "feeder" high schools for UT include Farragut, Bearden, Red Bank, Houston, Germantown, Ooltewah, Brentwood, Centennial, Knox West, and Soddy Daisy.

**Best Places to Study:**
Hodges Library is the most productive work area, but it gets busy around examinations. Other options include dorms or home, if travel is possible.

## Students Speak Out
ON ACADEMICS

"Teachers range from highly effective to highly useless. Teachers for most of the more popular majors have their TAs do a considerable portion of the coursework."

"It all depends on your learning style and what type of teacher you like. There are many teachers for each subject and class, and there are many sections for each class and level. **You can choose your professor**, rather instead than living with a professor you despise. UT is pretty good about weeding out the bad seeds in teaching. They don't keep professors if students don't give them good ratings."

## The College Prowler Take
### ON ACADEMICS

Q "For the most part, teachers are easygoing and really helpful. I've never had a teacher who refused to help in any way he could. College is very different from high school though, so be forewarned that teachers will not remind you when something is due. **You get a syllabus at the beginning of the year** and it becomes your bible—do not lose it! Many teachers get really peeved if you ask for another one. Make sure you stay on top of the readings and assignments, because there is no break-in time. You will have reading homework on the first day for every class. I guarantee it."

Q "**Teaching assistants often get a bad reputation** here at UT, but many of the best teachers I have had were TAs. They often have a sense of humor, and are more laid-back than professors. They seem to identify more with the students, and will go the extra mile to teach them something. Others, however, are out to prove themselves, and may try to make things difficult."

Q "**Some professors play games with students**, which sometimes includes handing out study guide sheets that suggest spending time on things that will not be on the test, requiring expensive books that are rarely or never used, and giving vague answers to questions asked during pre-test classes. Don't be surprised if they take attendance on days that students like to skip, such as those right before spring break, and they pretty much give out test questions on those days."

After the first day of classes, you may feel that UT is a large school with cold and hard professors. As time passes, however, you will learn that they are human, and want you to learn the material and develop as a student. Most professors really do want you to visit them during office hours, so don't be afraid to ask for extra help!

Some professors may be difficult to understand, but you will be surprised how easily you pick up on their lingual nuances. Teaching assistants will often make you laugh with clever explanations and witty responses to questions. You will encounter a bad seed from time to time, though. Whether it is a professor who is too wrapped up in his research, impossible to understand, or generally lousy at lecturing, chances are strong that you will have no choice but to endure a few bad profs. Every professor has quirks and pet peeves, such as late students, absent students, cell phones, lack of class participation, sleeping, or the mandatory squirming and packing up by students around the class's ending time. Tennessee 101 is a useful tool to check out professors while scheduling classes.

**B-**

The College Prowler™ Grade on
### Academics: B-

A high Academics grade generally indicates that professors are knowledgeable, accessible, and genuinely interested in their students' welfare. Other determining factors include class size, how well professors communicate, and whether or not classes are engaging.

# Local Atmosphere

## The Lowdown
ON LOCAL ATMOSPHERE

**Region:**
South

**City, State:**
Knoxville, Tennessee

**Setting:**
Medium-sized college town

**Distance from Atlanta:**
2 hours

**Distance from Knoxville:**
2 hours

**Points of Interest:**
The Great Smoky Mountains National Park, Pigeon Forge, Gatlinburg

**Major Sports Teams:**
Titans (football), Predators (hockey)

**City Websites:**
www.knoxville.com

## Students Speak Out
ON LOCAL ATMOSPHERE

"**Knoxville may seem like a big town trapped in a small town mentality. The people here cling to small town values and traditions.**"

Q "Knoxville is a great city. **The campus is a major part of the city**, but they have a historic downtown and two decent malls. You can always find something to do, and you are only 30 minutes away from the Smoky Mountains."

Q "Knoxville is highly influenced by college football. If you are not a football fan or you despise the color orange, you will be very unhappy being here, during football season or not. Except for houses, **orange is a highly accepted color for most everything** here."

Q "Knoxville might seem really boring, if you come from a big city. **We get a few good concerts in every year**, and the Women's Basketball Hall of Fame is here. Knoxville is very laid-back. Pellissippi State Technical Community College is the only other large college around here—it's a good school, with smaller classes and cheaper prices than UT."

Q "**The atmosphere of the town is a case of two extremes**. When things are going on, this town is so exciting. When things are not going on, this place is like the weather: dull and gray. There are no other universities in Knoxville. You should visit events that go on in the downtown area, but other than that, you are visiting each other in the dorms or apartments."

## The College Prowler Take
### ON LOCAL ATMOSPHERE

Knoxville truly serves as a happy medium between a large city and a small town. It is an easy transition for students coming from either extreme. In a way, Knoxville can be as large as you want it to be, depending on how willing you are to travel and explore.

The people of Knoxville are rather relaxed (except on game day!), and there are plenty of places to go to enjoy leisurely activities. You will not feel trapped in Knoxville. Atlanta and Nashville are not too far away, and you can be in the mountains in even less time. While many consider Knoxville a "college town," not all of the exciting activities take place on campus. You may find that Knoxville is the ideal size for a college student.

# Safety & Security

## The Lowdown
### ON SAFETY & SECURITY

**Number of UT Police:**
77 security personnel

**Phone:**
(865) 974-3114, or 4-3114 from an on-campus phone

**Health Center Office Hours:**
Monday – Friday 8 a.m. to 4:30 p.m.

**Safety Services:**
Multiple van services, blue-light phones, security in select buildings

**Did You Know?**
Eight full-time physicians, one full-time psychiatrist, and 13 full-time nurses work at the health center, and all are board-certified.

**B**

The College Prowler™ Grade on
## Local Atmosphere: B

A high Local Atmosphere grade indicates that the area surrounding campus is safe and scenic. Other factors include nearby attractions, proximity to other schools, and the town's attitude toward students.

## Students Speak Out
### ON SAFETY & SECURITY

"UT has a new late-night van service. My experience has been that it responds very quickly, usually in two to three minutes."

"**Security on campus is at a medium level**, not too loose and not strict. You feel safe in some places, and in others you feel threatened. Safety is just the same as security; the University tries to put on a good front, but sometimes events happen that soil that front."

"**The campus is about as safe as you make it**. Use common sense, and follow a few simple rules, and you will never be in danger. Avoid dark places where no other people are present. As soon as you arrive on campus, write down the van service number and put it in your pocket or save it in your cell phone. You never know when you'll need a ride."

"I think that the University is really safe, all things considered. The campus has a van service that runs a basic route around the campus at night, so you never have to walk alone. There's also an escort service. You can call and tell them your exact location, and they will pick you up or take you somewhere, depending on your distance from campus. The campus has more than 50 emergency phones located at various places around campus. The phones have buttons that will contact the police. **UT has its own police station and real police**, not just campus cops."

"**There are always cops out patrolling**; and UT has its own police department, which is nice. The only problems occur when people are stupid and walk alone late at night or something like that. Even then, there aren't many incidents, and I feel very safe."

## The College Prowler Take
### ON SAFETY & SECURITY

Most students' opinions on safety and security boil down to one thing: using your common sense. Even with all of the services the UTPD offers, none are a replacement for using your head. The UTPD officers take their jobs very seriously, and are always looking out for students' safety. For a school of UT's size, they are very successful, and the majority of students don't walk around with spray mace key rings tightly in hand. All of the services mentioned here are at your disposal, and are sure to make you feel safer. Make sure you know the numbers to call if need be, and if you don't already have one, a cell phone may be a good investment (sorry, mom and dad). By programming these numbers into your cell phone on your day of arrival, you may dodge a few uncomfortable moments.

The College Prowler™ Grade on
### Safety & Security: B

A high grade in Safety & Security means that students generally feel safe, campus pol ce are visible, blue-light phones and escort services are readily available, and safety precautions are not overly necessary.

# Facilities

**Computers**
**High-Speed Network?** Yes
**Wireless Network?** Yes
**Number of Labs:** 27
**24-Hour Labs:** No
**Charge to Print?** No

## The Lowdown
ON FACILITIES

**Student Center:**
The UC is centrally located on campus and houses several eateries, the bookstore, a gift shop, a software shop, a post office, etc.

**Athletic Center:**
The Student Aquatic Center, the HYPER Building, "the Bubble," the IM Field

**Libraries:**
John C. Hodges Main Library, James D. Hoskins Library, Webster Pendergrass Agricultural-Veterinary Medicine Library, George F. DeVine Music Library

**Movie Theater on Campus?**
Movies are periodically shown in the UC.

**Bowling on Campus?**
The bottom level of the UC, called "the Down Under," has bowling for under $3.

**Bar on Campus?**
No, there are no bars on the campus, per se, but there are many good bars on the Strip, such as Cool Beans, Hannah's, Charlie Pepper's, Henry's, and Liquid Knoxville.

**Coffeehouse on Campus?**
There is a Starbucks in the Hodges Library.

### Popular Places to Chill
You can chill out by the pool and study (but it is only fair to warn you, it can be a bit distracting on busy days!), or watch one of the many intramural games taking place throughout the year. There are also many places on the Strip to chill, but many are over 21 after a certain time. Hanging out with friends in dorms is also popular.

### Favorite Things to Do
Students play intramural flag football, soccer, softball, ultimate Frisbee, and basketball games, swim laps at the Student Aquatic Center pool, and work out at "The Bubble."

**COLLEGE PROWLER**

Visit www.collegeprowler.com and pick up the guidebook on UT. Inside, you'll find all the campus info you need to decide if UT is right for you.

## Students Speak Out
### ON FACILITIES

"The only facility that is current is the athletic facility, because it is always being remodeled or updated. The computer labs are fairly updated. The student center badly needs renovation to become somewhat modern."

"They really try to separate the athletes from regular students at UT. The athletes have one of just about everything to themselves, and what they have is all cutting-edge and modern. Many of the long overdue renovations to student facilities are now taking place, and they are worth a visit."

"The facilities are very nice. They are updating everything, so it's great! UT has the best workout facility in Tennessee, and it's open to all students. When it's warm, the pool is a great place to go and lay out, study, or swim."

"The UC has a basement where you can bowl or play pool, air hockey, or Ping-Pong. You can even take bowling as a class!"

"My biggest complaint with the older buildings is air conditioning. There is no rhyme or reason as to when UT turns heating on and off. During an unusually warm spring semester day, the heat will be blowing at full blast while it's 70 degrees outside. The recently finished Alumni Memorial Building has a reputation for being frigidly cold year-round. You will be very uncomfortable in either situation, so dress accordingly."

## The College Prowler Take
### ON FACILITIES

The crème de la crème of UT's facilities are still reserved for athletes. Most students have a mild abhorrence for athletes, due to the pampering they receive by the University, and feel like athletes are provided with their own large campus "country club." The University does spend a few of the leftover dollars on facilities for the other students, and most of the students that use them are satisfied with their accessibility and quality. Most of the academic buildings are rather old, but many have been renovated and brought up to some semblance of modernity. A university of this size suffers a lot of wear and tear. Anything new does not stay new for long, and no matter how hard they try to maintain facilities, some get worn and dirty quickly. UT is eternally a "work in progress," but it is certain athletics will remain top priority.

**B+**

The College Prowler™ Grade on
## Facilities: B+

A high Facilities grade indicates that the campus is aesthetically pleasing and well-maintained; facilities are state-of-the-art, and libraries are exceptional. Other determining factors include the quality of both athletic and student centers and an abundance of things to do on campus.

# Campus Dining

## The Lowdown
ON CAMPUS DINING

**Freshman Meal Plan Requirement?**
Yes

**24-Hour On-Campus Eating?**
No

**Student Favorites:**
Smokey's in the UC for lunch, breakfast at any of the cafeterias

**Meal Plan Average Cost:**
Plans range from $1,110 to $1,310

### Did You Know?
Pay close attention to the meal plan rules. There are only certain hours you can use your daily allowance for meals. Meals not within certain hours are deducted from "bonus bucks." Prices of goods in the small snack shops in and around dorms are highly inflated.

## Students Speak Out
ON CAMPUS DINING

"The food on campus is on both sides of the spectrum. The student center is where you can get the best food, and Presidential Court is a close second. Other than that, the other food places are either horrible or average."

"**I eat my meals in Gibbs Hall.** A lot of the football players live in Gibbs, and since Tennessee cares so much about football, this cafeteria has the best food by far. I'm not sure if non-resident, non-athletes can eat there, though. I ate in the other dining hall last year, and the food was pretty good, though it was what you would expect in a college dining hall."

"As a freshman, you will love eating the fast food in Presidential. **It's quick, and tastes pretty good**, but I promise you will miss home cooking after a few weeks. Be forewarned, eating this stuff every day can really pack on the pounds!"

"**Dining in the UC has gotten much better over the last few years**. The food is near restaurant quality, with great recipes and variety. As expected, with all the renovations and new offerings, price has also gone up. You almost can't get a decent, filling meal at the UC for less than six dollars."

"I think that **the food on campus is pretty decent**. There are a variety of cafeterias located around campus with buffet-style food. Every cafeteria has a salad bar and a sandwich bar, and one section that offers food made to your preference, like pasta or sandwich wraps. There is always a vegetarian option, too, if that is something you need."

"At UT, **there are cafeterias that resemble mini food courts**, with options like Chick-fil-A, Pizza Hut, home-cooked food, and Starbucks. You just need to make sure that you look at the different meal plan options. There are also bonus bucks, which are great, and act like a debit card on your student ID. The bonus bucks allow you to shop at the on-campus grocery stores and eat over your daily allowance."

## The College Prowler Take
### ON CAMPUS DINING

If you live in a dorm as a freshman, which is required for non-commuters, you are more or less required to purchase a meal plan. Students' opinions vary on the quality and selection of food, but most are satisfied with what UT offers. When you have had your fill of cafeteria food, there are many fast food options. One thing is for certain, you will gain a whole new appreciation for your mother's cooking that you had taken for granted so many years. You will clean your plate, and possibly the rest of the family's plates, during each visit. Since you will be stuck with the UT Dining Services meal plan, why not make the most of it? The key is to read and understand the meal plan rules. Keep track of your Bonus Bucks, and eat during allotted dining hours. Also, bear in mind that the money you don't use is not donated to charity and is not tax deductible, so if you don't use it, you have essentially thrown it away.

## B

The College Prowler™ Grade on
### Campus Dining: B

Our grade on Campus Dining addresses the quality of both school-owned dining halls and independent on-campus restaurants as well as the price, availability, and variety of food.

# Campus Housing

## The Lowdown
### ON CAMPUS HOUSING

**Undergrads on Campus:**
34%

**Number of Dormitories:**
13

**Number of University-Owned Apartments:**
4

**Room Types:**
Single and double occupancy, community bathrooms, suite-style bathrooms, and apartments

**Cleaning Service?**
The double occupancy rooms have a maid service that performs light cleaning of bathrooms.

**You Get:**
All residents are provided with cable and computer connections, a desk, desk chair, dresser, closet, mattress pad, trash can, micro-fridge (combination refrigerator/freezer/microwave), and a telephone (with free local calling).

**Bed Type:**
Twin extra-long

### Did You Know?

Gibbs Hall is required by NCAA regulations to house a minimum of 51 percent non-athletes. It is still, however, very difficult for freshman non-athletes to get a room assignment there.

### Students Speak Out
ON CAMPUS HOUSING

"For freshman, Humes, South Carrick, and Morrill are all great. Avoid Clement if you aren't into the old building feel, and know that Humes has the best staff."

"The **dorms are generally rundown**, and need a lot of remodeling to become modern looking and accommodating. The most popular dorms are around the Presidential Court area [Humes, North and South Carrick, and Reese]. The dorms to run away from are Clement and Hess. If you like the tight-knit community opportunity, Hess and Morrill are your best bets."

"The dorms are fairly nice. **Hess is the freshmen dorm, and people there are generally crazy**, earning it the nickname 'the Zoo.' Other dorms are a little nicer, but nowhere near as fun."

"Girls who are considering joining a sorority should consider moving into Humes, which always **seems to be Greek dominated**. The same is true for guys planning to join a fraternity with Reese, but not as dominant. The RAs in these two dorms are also thought to be the best."

"The dorms provide a good experience. **If you like to be more social, try South Carrick or Humes**. Morrill is too far away. Hess and Melrose are the closest to classes. It seems like residents in any dorm always rave about how it's the best, but I would avoid the ones across the street, like Clement, because they're too far."

### The College Prowler Take
ON CAMPUS HOUSING

There are positive and negative aspects to each dorm. You must make a decision based upon your preferences and priorities. Your academic and social life will not be solely determined by which dorm you are assigned to, and you will be able to make friends no matter where you go. Make sure you understand the rules and regulations of living in each dorm before you arrive. Some of them are rather strict and may catch you off guard. The dorms have improved somewhat over the last several years. Air conditioning seemed to be one of the biggest complaints, but now many of the dorms have working air conditioners, as well as new windows, which will pay off from August until the middle of October. Since there is no perfect dorm, and none that can really be a huge pain, try to make the most of whatever situation you have and make new friends.

**B-**

The College Prowler™ Grade on
### Campus Housing: B-

A high Campus Housing grade indicates that dorms are clean, well-maintained, and spacious. Other determining factors include variety of dorms, proximity to classes, and social atmosphere.

# Diversity

**Political Activity**
College Republicans, College Democrats

**Economic Status**
The students at UT run across the board as far as economic status is concerned. Of course, on a college campus, everyone is going to try to convey the impression that they have a bit of money with more expensive clothes and accessories. The economic diversity on campus, however, is very wide ranging.

## The Lowdown
ON DIVERSITY

**Native American:** 0%

**Asian American:** 2%

**African American:** 7%

**Hispanic:** 1%

**White:** 89%

**International:** 1%

**Out-of-State:** 14%

**Minority Clubs**
Black Cultural Programming Club, Association of Black Communicators, NAACP, National Society of Black Engineers

**Most Popular Religions**
Baptist, Methodist

**Gay Tolerance**
The campus is accepting of its gay and lesbian students, and has groups such as the Gay and Straight Political Network and the Lambda Student Union.

## Students Speak Out
ON DIVERSITY

"The campus is not as diverse as the administration would like it to be. There are many cultures represented, but not in many numbers, just small pockets of culture."

"Knoxville is in eastern Tennessee, which is much more predominantly white than middle and western Tennessee, but I think the campus is still about 15 percent African American. **There are a lot of smaller ethnic groups represented**, too."

"Diversity is one of the main reasons I wanted to come to UT. I went to an all-white high school and was never exposed to other races, but now **I have friends from all over**, and it's awesome."

"The new school president made campus diversity a top priority. He implemented a new way of attracting minority students to the school, and I think **there is already a very diverse crowd here**."

"What's diverse here? This is the South! **It is all 'white-bread' folk**, with the occasional exchange student to provide what little culture there is here."

"All I see is a bunch of white folks with an **occasional sprinkling of black**."

## The College Prowler Take
### ON DIVERSITY

Most students will probably agree that UT is much more diverse than the high school they attended, regardless of their background. Many high schools in Tennessee are rather homogeneous, regardless of their size. While an individual's perception of UT's level of diversity may vary, UT does make many efforts to accommodate minority students and make their college experience rewarding. UT has attempted to attract more minority students through various programs and offerings. UT attracts a wide array of international students, and chances are very likely you will share a class with one. While UT's level of diversity may be considered less than ideal by many students, students of all backgrounds are comfortable at UT.

**The College Prowler™ Grade on**
## Diversity: D

A high grade in Diversity indicates that ethnic minorities and international students have a notable presence on campus and that students of different economic backgrounds, religious beliefs, and sexual preferences are well-represented.

# Guys & Girls

## The Lowdown
### ON GUYS & GIRLS

**Women Undergrads:** 52.5%

**Men Undergrads:** 47.5%

### Birth Control Available?
Yes, the Knox County Health Department offers birth control to students in the form of condoms, birth control pills, and Depo-Provera shots. For female students who would like pills or the Depo-Provera shot, an appointment and initial exam is required. The initial exam is $137, but is on a sliding scale according to income. Refills are also offered. The Family Planning Clinic is located in the basement of the UT Student Health Services Building. For more information, call (865) 215-5320.

### Social Scene
Social interaction is somewhat dependent on football season, but it's very active throughout the year.

### Hookups or Relationships?
Hookups are slightly more prominent, but if you're looking for a relationship, you can find others that are like-minded, at least in the realm of upperclassmen.

## Dress Code

Popular brands and stores are where students derive the UT dress code. For girls, it's Banana Republic, J. Crew, Express, Ann Taylor, North Face, and Kate Spade. Guys wear a lot of Polo, Brooks Brothers, Lacoste, North Face, and New Balance.

## Students Speak Out
### ON GUYS & GIRLS

> "You have your hot ones and you have your not-so-hot ones, but they are all pretty good. Some girls are rather intimidating at first, but most are just afraid of what the other girls are thinking about them."

Q "If you are a guy that prefers the blonde-haired, blue-eyed, classy and posh southern belle, UT could be considered their capital. **You will not be disappointed**."

Q "Honestly, **we have one of the best looking campuses around**! Everyone is classy, too. You don't have little hoochie girls walking around without any clothes on. Most everybody dresses in nice looking, preppy, name brand clothing."

Q "Gorgeous girls and attractive guys are a dime a dozen here. The only thing that really determines their date-ability is their attitudes. **Many of them know they've got 'it' and act like it**."

Q "If you are from another part of the country that doesn't practice chivalry, you better learn as quickly as possible. **Women here will expect doors to be held** and chairs to be pulled. If you cannot learn to be a gentleman, you will be at a great social disadvantage."

## The College Prowler Take
### ON GUYS & GIRLS

A walk around campus on a warm September afternoon says it all: unless you remain confined within dorm walls, you will meet more members of the opposite sex than you could ever hope to remember. Don't worry, though, you'll remember the important ones! Your selection is extremely wide. If a particular guy or girl makes you yawn—next! Great looks, a fancy car, and impeccable clothing do not always guarantee success with the opposite sex at UT. The common denominator among those truly successful with the opposite sex is a positive attitude and confidence. The outside appearance will only get you so far, especially if you are in it for more than mere casual encounters. There are huge amounts of different types of guys and girls to choose from, so whether you seek a friend, a date, a hookup, or a relationship, there are unlimited choices. You will enjoy meeting the friendly and laid-back students of UT.

**The College Prowler™ Grade on**
## Guys: A-

A high grade for Guys indicates that the male population on campus is attractive, smart, friendly, and engaging, and that the school has a decent ratio of guys to girls.

**The College Prowler™ Grade on**
## Girls: A

A high grade for Girls not only implies that the women on campus are attractive, smart, friendly, and engaging, but also that there is a fair ratio of girls to guys.

# Athletics

**Athletic Division:**
NCAA Division I

**Conference:**
SEC

**School Mascot:**
Volunteers; "Smokey," a Blue Tick Coon Hound

**Fields:**
Lindsey Nelson Baseball Stadium, Fulton Bottoms Field, Intramural Fields, Neyland Stadium, Soccer Complex, Softball Stadium

## The Lowdown
ON ATHLETICS

**Men's Varsity Teams:**
Baseball
Basketball
Cross Country
Football
Golf
Swimming & Diving
Tennis
Track & Field

**Women's Varsity Teams:**
Basketball
Cross Country
Golf
Rowing
Soccer
Softball
Swimming & Diving
Tennis
Track & Field
Volleyball
Cheerleading

## Most Popular Sports
On the varsity level, football is the most popular sport by far, but women's basketball is also very popular with the UT crowd. As far as intramurals are concerned, you can find people that are interested in everything.

## Overlooked Teams
The men's baseball team does consistently well, but they definitely walk in the shadow of the more popular sports.

## Getting Tickets
The ticket office will announce a weekly schedule where students can scan for tickets. Ticket fees are included in their UT bill as an "activity fee." If you wait until the last minute, you will most likely be issued a "standing-room only" ticket.

## Club Sports
Alpine Skiing, Bowling, Canoeing & Hiking, Equestrian, Ice Hockey, Lacrosse, Martial Arts, Racquetball, Rowing, Rugby, Snow Ski, Soccer, Tennis, Ultimate Frisbee, Volleyball, Water Polo

## Intramurals (IMs)
Soccer, Sand Volleyball, Golf, Tennis, Billiards, Volleyball, Table Tennis, Flag Football, Bowling, Basketball, Ultimate Frisbee, Softball

**COLLEGE PROWLER**

Wanna know more about club sports or IMs? For a detailed listing of all on-campus athletic organizations, check out the College Prowler book on Tennessee available at *www.collegeprowler.com*.

## Students Speak Out
### ON ATHLETICS

> "Everybody in Tennessee is a dedicated Tennessee football fan. I don't think there's a school around that can muster up a better crowd than our 107,000 screaming fans."

Q "The intensity you will experience at a classic Tennessee football game is incredible. **It is almost like a European soccer match**, except without all the violence."

Q "**You will know when it is football time in Tennessee**. The tailgaters start showing up mid-week, and the campus will be packed way before the game starts. You will wake up to the sound of the Pride of the Southland Band practicing across the street from the dorms, and you will almost smell the barbecue and Jack Daniels whiskey as soon as you set foot outside. I guarantee that you have never seen so much orange in your life."

Q "Varsity sports are a huge part of this campus. We live and experience every twist and turn of most of the sports teams. **IM sports are moderate**: football, soccer, basketball, ultimate Frisbee, softball, and golf are the huge sports. There are also club teams and other various sports that you can join."

Q "**The campus is really active in the fall**, with football games and basketball games. I mean, it is UT football—no explanation should be needed for that. Everyone looks forward to football season because it's so much fun! Going to a UT football game is an experience in itself."

## The College Prowler Take
### ON ATHLETICS

If you hail from Tennessee, you may be aware of the Vol craze, but you have only heard and seen a small part of what UT athletics is about. If you are from out-of-state, even in an area with a collegiate football team, you will still be surprised by how seriously the Volunteers take football. Even if you are not a huge sports fan, you will enjoy the excitement and tradition that goes along with a football game. It is only fair to warn you that if you dislike sports, you may want to vacate Knoxville in the event of a football game. You will probably have to go pretty far away, though. Also, IM sports are popular, both to play and to watch. There are great chances to play sports, whether it is something you participated in during high school, or you just want to make friends, or you just want to learn. In many IM sports, the playoffs draw a pretty big crowd, so you may have an audience when you score—or when you drop the ball.

**A+**

The College Prowler™ Grade on
### Athletics: A+

A high grade in Athletics indicates that students have school spirit, that sports programs are respected, that games are well-attended, and that intramurals are a prominent part of student life.

# Greek Life

## Students Speak Out
ON GREEK LIFE

*"Greek life is definitely the place to be if you want to get into activities right away. The first pledge semester in Greek organizations is the busiest. It really helped me to know what things were like right away."*

Q *"For me, **I made a lot of friends in the dorm my freshman year**. After that, they all went their separate ways to different places, and I never heard from or saw much of them again. It seems this is less likely to happen if you are Greek, because they tend to stick together more."*

Q *"Being Greek is pretty big on campus, but that doesn't mean it segregates people. **I'm Greek, but a lot of my best friends are not**. It just depends on how open-minded you are about people and things—you can control how much it dominates your life."*

Q *"If you do not go Greek, it does not mean that you will have an unhappy time at UT. The school is so big that **everyone has plenty of opportunities**, if they are willing to work, regardless if they are Greek or not."*

Q *"Greek life encompasses 10 percent of the campus. To those 10 percent that live and breathe it, **they are a fairly tight-knit group** that generally stays within its own ranks. Greek life throws most of the parties, and does a majority of the philanthropic work around campus. They attempt to dominate, but this campus does not care."*

## The Lowdown
ON GREEK LIFE

**Number of Fraternities:**
22

**Number of Sororities:**
18

**Undergrads in Fraternities:**
15%

**Undergrads in Sororities:**
19%

### Did You Know?

Fraternities at the University of Tennessee report that an average of 53 percent of Greeks are involved in some kind of campus leadership activity outside of the fraternity.

## The College Prowler Take
### ON GREEK LIFE

If going Greek is something that interests you, going through rush is definitely something to consider. At the very least, you will meet people that you will see again and again throughout your college career. Through a Greek organization, you will be able to participate in philanthropies, parties, formals, and the many Greek events that happen throughout the year. If you choose not to do so, you will still have many opportunities at UT to keep busy, and you will still be able to make many friends. On paper, it may seem that the number of Greeks is relatively small, and that they may not have that much impact on campus, but they do make their presence felt. Learn as much as you can about the individual chapters, and Greek life in general. Talk with those who have chosen the Greek life, and ask plenty of questions. There is a lot you can do before going through rush to determine if it is for you.

### The College Prowler™ Grade on
## Greek Life: A-

A high grade in Greek Life indicates that sororities and fraternities are not only present, but also active on campus. Other determining factors include the variety of houses available and the respect the Greek community receives from the rest of the campus.

## Drug Scene

### The Lowdown
### ON DRUG SCENE

**Most Prevalent Drugs on Campus:**
Marijuana, Alcohol

**Liquor-Related Referrals:**
283

**Drug-Related Referrals:**
70

### Drug Counseling Programs

Alcoholics Anonymous
(865) 522-9667 or (800) 841-2319

Alanon/Alateen
(865) 525-9040

Narcotics Anonymous
(865) 521-1989 or (800) 249-0012

Lighthouse Alcohol and Drug Treatment Center (residential, private)
(865) 558-8880

Centerpointe (residential and outpatient, state-supported)
(865) 523-4704

## Students Speak Out
### ON DRUG SCENE

"People will not try to shove it in your face and won't put pressure on you to do it. People who do drugs are somewhat discreet about it; they slip away, do their thing, and come back."

Q "**The drug scene on campus has leveled off** in recent years since I came here. I remember seeing it all over the place. But, since that time, the drugs have decreased in use. The people who use drugs, however, use them more extensively now, while numbers have dropped."

Q "**Weed is the main drug in the area**. Crystal meth is on the rise, but the cops are really cracking down on it. The part of town you're in determines the type of drugs you run into. X is also very big here. Typical drugs like crack, coke, and heroin are present but very underground. You really have to go looking for those, and run in those crowds to find them."

Q "Depending on the circle of friends you spend your time with, **drugs can either be very prominent or nonexistent**. It seems like there is not an overwhelming pressure to do drugs, but if you are someone that is against it, you would do best to keep those who do at a distance."

Q "If you want them, you do not have to search a whole lot to find them if you know a lot of people. **Marijuana is by far the most prominent drug**, but for many it is just a stepping stone to harder drugs."

## The College Prowler Take
### ON DRUG SCENE

Most students agree that there is not a lot of pressure to do drugs at UT. For someone who wants drugs, however, they are not impossible to find. You will probably know people that do it, but they probably will never pressure you to do it. Most students agree that the people who choose to do drugs keep it to themselves and their close friends. Marijuana is the number one cash crop in the state of Tennessee, and it is easily the cheapest and most readily available drug. A lot of drug users limit their use to marijuana alone and do not use any harder drugs. With drugs in general, it is easy to maintain your stance once it is made.

**B-**

The College Prowler™ Grade on
### Drug Scene: B-

A high grade on Drug Scene indicates that drugs are not a noticeable part of campus life; drug use is not visible, and no pressure to use them seems to exist.

# Overall Experience

Q "I'm a very picky person and I had a list of eight schools I was going to apply to, but after visiting UT, it was the only school I applied to. **I'm not trying to beef up UT**, because I know how stressful it is to have to decide on a school, but I like it a lot."

Q "My experience in school has been **a mixture of positives and negatives**. The positives have been my social life, experience in the classroom, and overall outcome in life. The negatives revolve around how the administration treats me as a number rather than a person."

## Students Speak Out
ON OVERALL EXPERIENCE

> "If you are looking for a place to have fun and still get some studying done, UT is definitely the place to go."

Q "For the most part, I like UT. I've learned it is what you make it, and you really have to just find your own niche. I go part-time now, and I wish I could be on campus all the time because that is the best way to really get involved and learn about the stuff you will like. Some people don't have that luxury, though, so you have to find other ways to get involved. It really is a good place. **Campus is really pretty**, and for the most part the people are really nice. The teachers are helpful, and you just have to remember why you are there in the first place. Don't get too wrapped up in having fun and forget about your education. You will regret it. I've seen it happen."

Q "My experience at UT has been good, but Tennessee is suffering because they don't have an income tax, so **many programs are being cut at UT and tuition is on the rise**. It'll be interesting to see how the state legislature deals with the funding problem."

## The College Prowler Take
ON OVERALL EXPERIENCE

UT draws students from all over, and it is little wonder why. UT has a personality all its own. The level of pride and tradition here is among the strongest in the country, and the amount of support Knoxville has for UT is amazing, especially with sports. You will love the laid-back southern style UT has to offer, and you will enjoy spending time with the people you meet here. Ask any UT alumni about their most positive life experiences, and most of those experiences will have occurred at UT.

It is understandable that UT can appear intimidating on paper, especially to those coming from a small town. But, there are many different activities to become involved in, and they are yours for the taking, if you are willing to make the effort and work hard. The key to success at UT, as well as any college, is to learn to manage your time properly. As long as you remember that education is the main reason for coming to UT, and prioritize accordingly, you will be very happy during your college days.

# University of Virginia

PO Box 400160, Charlottesville, VA 22904
www.virginia.edu      (434) 982-3200

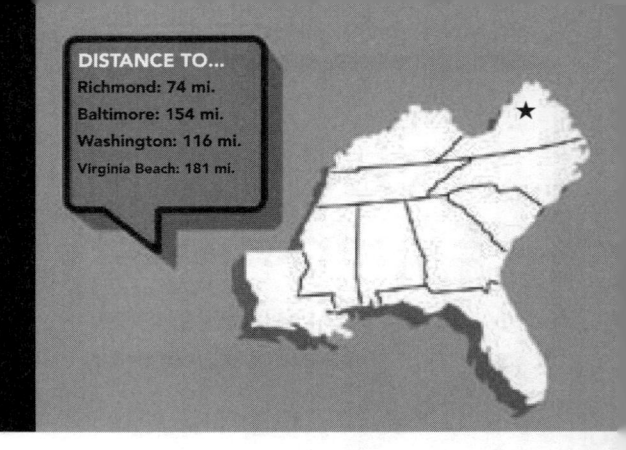

**DISTANCE TO...**
Richmond: 74 mi.
Baltimore: 154 mi.
Washington: 116 mi.
Virginia Beach: 181 mi.

*"UVA is growing at the pace of the world around it, while still trying to keep a connection to its past traditions."*

**Total Enrollment:**
13,050

**Top 10% of High School Class:**
85%

**Average GPA:**
4.0

**Acceptance Rate:**
39%

**Tuition:**
$6,600 in-state, $22,700 out-of-state

**SAT Range (25th-75th Percentile):**

| Verbal | Math | Total |
|---|---|---|
| 600 – 710 | 630 – 720 | 1230 – 1430 |

**ACT Range (25th-75th Percentile):**

| Verbal | Math | Total |
|---|---|---|
| 25-31 | 26-31 | 26-31 |

**Most Popular Majors:**
13%  Economics
10%  Business
9%   Psychology
8%   English
7%   International Relations

**Students also applied to:***
College of William and Mary
Cornell University
Duke University
University of North Carolina–Chapel Hill
Virginia Tech

*For more school info check out www.collegeprowler.com

## Table of Contents

| | |
|---|---|
| Academics | 379 |
| Local Atmosphere | 381 |
| Safety & Security | 382 |
| Facilities | 384 |
| Campus Dining | 385 |
| Campus Housing | 386 |
| Diversity | 388 |
| Guys & Girls | 390 |
| Athletics | 391 |
| Greek Life | 393 |
| Drug Scene | 395 |
| Overall Experience | 396 |

## College Prowler Report Card

| | |
|---|---|
| Academics | A- |
| Local Atmosphere | B |
| Safety & Security | B+ |
| Facilities | B |
| Campus Dining | C- |
| Campus Housing | B- |
| Diversity | C |
| Guys | B+ |
| Girls | A- |
| Athletics | A |
| Greek Life | A |
| Drug Scene | B |

# Academics

## Did You Know?

UVA has the highest graduation and retention rate of any public college or university.

**Best Places to Study:**
Alderman or Clemons libraries, coffee shops on The Corner

## The Lowdown
ON ACADEMICS

**Sample Academic Clubs**
Virginia Math Team, Technology Club, McIntire Entrepreneur's Group, Sigma Theta Delta International

**Degrees Awarded:**
Bachelor, Master, and Doctorate

**Undergraduate Schools:**
Arts and Sciences, Architecture, Commerce, Education, Engineering, Nursing

**Full-time Faculty:**
2,005

**Faculty with Terminal Degree:**
92%

**Student-to-Faculty Ratio:**
16:1

**Average Course Load:**
15 credits per semester

**Special Programs:**
Double-Major, Double-Minor, Interdisciplinary Studies (create your own major)

**AP Test Score Requirements:**
Possible credit for scores of 4 or 5

**IB Test Score Requirements:**
Possible credit for scores of 6 or 7

## Students Speak Out
ON ACADEMICS

"**During my time at UVA, I had a handful of the best, as well as some of the most disinterested, teachers I've ever had.**"

"**You have to go out of your way** to make sure your professors know you."

"Most of the classes I took at UVA were very interesting. The professors were enthusiastic and really knew their stuff. My e-school classes, on the other hand, were almost always boring and badly taught. The **professors did not seem to be in touch with the students at all**—they were impossible to reach outside of class. Many of them did not know the subject matter of the class at all. One professor rarely even showed up for class."

Q "At UVA, I found that the greatest challenge was the way the courses were structured, and more specifically, the class size of most of the courses. For courses within my majors, it was not until my final year that I had a class where the professor was close enough to me that I did not need my glasses to make out their face. I suppose that in short, **I found most of my college experience rather impersonal**. In order to overcome the large class sizes and truly get to know a professor, one had to expend a good deal of energy going to extra office hours, staying after class, etc. As a result of this dynamic, some of my more influential teacher-student relationships at UVA were with TAs."

Q "There are bad and there are good teachers. The majority of teachers I have interacted with are **friendly, and do care whether or not you are actually learning**. You get to know them better in smaller classes; however, many smaller classes are taught by grad students. Those classes are less desirable. I've heard horror stories of grad student teachers who spoke very little English, but I never had the misfortune of being in one of their classes."

Q "The teachers are good and bad. It depends what school you are applying to. They have **more excellent teachers than bad teachers**. Usually, you will get a professor, but in some classes, you end up with a graduate assistant or teaching assistant."

## The College Prowler Take
### ON ACADEMICS

Most students agree that the professors at UVA are outstanding, qualified, brilliant, passionate men and women. As expected, there are occasional complaints about class structure, material, and size, as well as the unfortunate case of a disinterested teacher. The quality and interest level of classes and professors varies throughout the different schools and departments at UVA. For the most part, students find that classes and professors in the College of Arts and Sciences (particularly the English, Drama, History, and Psychology departments) are more liberal and interesting. Some of the more technical, scientific courses and schools (Biology or Engineering, for example) can be a necessary burden.

Perhaps the most common complaint is the frustrating nature of the professor-student relationship. There are some of the more popular, busy professors, whose main priorities are often research/writing projects and graduate level courses. Other students are frustrated when, instead of being taught by their professors, courses are led by TAs (teaching assistants); teaching assistants are not much older than undergraduate students, and occasionally you'll run into one who can barely speak English.

Unfortunately, some of the best classes and professors teach mainly upperclassmen, leaving the younger students waiting for the full academic experience of UVA. In the meantime, learn from your TA. Remember that TAs are more accessible, younger, and often very enthusiastic about the classes they're working with.

**The College Prowler™ Grade on**
### Academics: A-

A high Academics grade generally indicates that professors are knowledgeable, accessible, and genuinely interested in their students' welfare. Other determining factors include class size, how well professors communicate, and whether or not classes are engaging.

# Local Atmosphere

## Students Speak Out
### ON LOCAL ATMOSPHERE

"Charlottesville is a much divided community. Students think they're in their own little world. But, there is a lot here. Go to events that aren't alcohol-related: Fridays at Five, anything on the Downtown Mall."

Q "Charlottesville has a **small-town feel, which at times is wonderful and relaxing**, and at other times, stifling and insulating. There is a community college nearby, called Piedmont, although I wouldn't say this has a huge impact on the University community. Overall, I always thought of Charlottesville as made up of college kids—mostly affluent and from other cities—the professors and their families, the ex-hippies who landed in Charlottesville because it has a liberal-friendly feel, and all the other people affectionately referred to by the college kids as 'townies.' Definitely find time to visit the Downtown Mall. There is a free trolley from the Corner and Grounds. The Downtown Mall is a great place to see a movie, eat, or just walk around."

Q "There are no other universities really, although some commute to Piedmont. The town is really nice in areas that are **generally populated with University students**, such as the Corner, Barracks Road, Downtown Mall. However, there are some sections of town that you definitely want to stay away from. So, if you are wandering around and all of a sudden it looks like you are in Compton, turn around and go back the way you came."

Q "Townies don't like us. We don't like townies. **There's a big rivalry**."

Q "It's a great social scene. **Everyone is always finding fun and new things to do** in Charlottesville. There are outdoor activities at your fingertips, and you can always run to the mall if you are desperate for the newest thing at Express. People are always going out, making new friends, and visiting pubs on The Corner."

## The Lowdown
### ON LOCAL ATMOSPHERE

**Region:**
Central, Southeast

**City, State:**
Charlottesville, Virginia

**Setting:**
A small city in a rural area

**Distance from Washington, DC:**
2 hours, 30 minutes

**Distance from Richmond:**
1 hour, 30 minutes

**Points of Interest:**
The Blue Ridge Mountains, the James River, Mince Springs, Beaver Creek, the Downtown Mall, Monticello, all sorts of vineyards, Fridays after Five, the Farmer's Market (every Saturday morning, during the summer months), the Virginia Film Festival (every year, for a weekend in October), the Virginia Festival of the Book (every year, for a week in March), Star Hill (a music club supposedly owned by Faulkner's grandsons)

**City Websites:**
www.charlottesville.org

**Major Sports Teams:**
Mainly the UVA sports teams

## The College Prowler Take
### ON LOCAL ATMOSPHERE

Charlottesville has a unique, artistic, natural feel to it. It is surrounded by the beautiful hills and mountains of the Blue Ridge, which have much to offer—from hiking and picnicking to a simple stroll along Skyline Drive. There are plenty of lakes and ponds just outside of town, where students like to lay-out and cool-off in the summer and spring. The real cultural centers of Charlottesville are mainly in and around the Downtown Mall. There are art galleries, music clubs, bookstores, and theaters. There is a great artistic tradition in Charlottesville. Many writers, musicians, and artists reside and work in town. Although it can seem stifling at times, the area has more than enough to occupy students over four years of college, and if you're willing to be creative and explore new places, there's a lot to be discovered.

# Safety & Security

## The Lowdown
### ON SAFETY & SECURITY

**Number of UVA Police:**
190 (60 UVA police, 130 security staff)

**Phone:**
911 (emergencies)
(434) 924-7166 (administrative calls)

**Health Center Office Hours:**
Mon.-Fri. 8 a.m.-5 p.m.
Sat. 8:30 a.m.-12 p.m.

**Safety Services:**
Escort service (Shuttle runs from 8 p.m.-7 a.m., 434-242-1122), blue-light phones, Lighted Pathway System (emergency phones, video cameras, well-lit paths), self-defense classes, safety information

**B**

**The College Prowler™ Grade on**
## Local Atmosphere: B

A high Local Atmosphere grade indicates that the area surrounding campus is safe and scenic. Other factors include nearby attractions, proximity to other schools, and the town's attitude toward students.

## Students Speak Out
### ON SAFETY & SECURITY

> "I always felt very safe when I was at UVA—too safe. I became naive almost, like nothing could ever happen to me. I always see cops around and blue-light emergency phones are all over."

💬 "I usually feel safe on campus, because there are generally lots of other students nearby. However, after working as a volunteer with a rape crisis hotline, I know there are many incidents that occur, even on what feels like a safe campus. **Caution and clear thinking are always in order**."

💬 "Coming from a guy, **I've never had any problems walking alone** at night. But the recent assault and battery incidents have caused me to worry about my female friends. I always make sure after parties that they have an escort home."

💬 "You can check out cell phones from the library. They have a link to 911 on them, and you can use them if you're going to walk home and either don't feel safe, or want to call an escort. All of the **University's police officers carry guns and are fully trained**—they're not just security guards. Personally, I have never ever felt scared here, and many girls walk around by themselves at all hours of the night. There is very little crime, most likely due to our honor system, which holds much water here."

## The College Prowler Take
### ON SAFETY & SECURITY

Most students at UVA feel pretty safe overall. The UVA police and security system is quite a noticeable presence on the grounds. In addition to the school's 90 police officers, there is a staff of about 130 security workers. Standard campus security services are offered at UVA (blue-light phones, escort services, etc.), but the best safety tool has been an increase in awareness among the student body. If there's one flaw in the security at UVA, it's students not understanding the importance of looking out for safety. As one student said, it's easy to feel "almost too safe." On campus, and in parts of Charlottesville, life can seem over-insulated at times, and when tragedies happen, it comes as a shock to many. Students are advised to simply use common sense, and stay informed of what's going on around campus.

**B+**

**The College Prowler™ Grade on**
### Safety & Security: B+

A high grade in Safety & Security means that students generally feel safe, campus police are visible, blue-light phones and escort services are readily available, and safety precautions are not overly necessary.

# Facilities

## Computers
**High-Speed Network?** Yes
**Wireless Network?** Yes
**Number of Labs:** 11
**24-Hour Labs:** Yes, several
**Charge to Print?**
Yes – $0.08/sheet for black and white, $0.60/sheet for color; printing can only be done using your Cavalier Advantage account (with your UVA student ID).

## The Lowdown
ON FACILITIES

**Favorite Things to Do**
Work out, lie on the lawn, grab a meal with friends, walk to a bar off-campus, see a movie in Newcomb

**Popular Places to Chill**
The Lawn (during nice weather), on the Corner, the fourth floor of Clemons Library

**Student Center:**
Newcomb Hall, 2nd floor

**Athletic Center:**
UVA has multiple gyms and athletic facilities, including the Aquatic and Fitness Center (AFC), Memorial Gym, North Grounds, and Slaughter Gym

**Libraries:**
Alderman, Clemons, Music Library (Old Cabell Hall), Environmental Science Library (Clark Hall), Psychology Library (Gilmer Hall), and the Fine Arts Library (Campbell Hall)

**Movie Theater on Campus?**
Yes—Newcomb Hall Theater (the basement of Newcomb Hall)

**Bowling on Campus?**
No

**Bar on Campus?**
No—but, there are bars just off the Grounds.

**Coffeehouse on Campus?**
Yes—there's a Greenberry's in Alderman Library and the bookstore. There are also several snack places that are sure to have coffee: the PAV, the Bakery, and the Castle.

## Students Speak Out
ON FACILITIES

"The AFC is great—though I wish the pool was open more. I constantly wanted to swim when the pool wasn't open. In terms of fitness equipment, UVA is great."

Q "**Right now the facilities are adequate,** but in the next few years you're basically gonna have a whole new UVA. The school is implementing a wide range of new construction, additions, and renovations, which will make the school even better than it is."

Q "The facilities depend on which school you are in. The engineering school's facilities, such as the library and computer labs, are **old, dirty, uncomfortable, and falling apart**. Most of the classrooms are in the basement with no windows, and students must sit in cramped seating. They are currently building a new library though, and it's supposed to be very high-tech and comfortable for students to use. The law school facilities, on the other hand, are awesome—very high-tech, clean, and comfortable."

Q "UVA really cares about its athletes and sports fan ticket-holders. The **athletic facilities are top-notch**, and I understand that a new basketball arena is even in the works. The computers in the labs are also nice. While all these facilities are nice, the administration shows its favoring of the athletics at UVA as students watch privileges—like free and unlimited printing in the computer labs—go down the tubes in the same year in which ground is broken for the new basketball arena."

Q "Facilities are nice, and **new buildings are being built**, including a new student center in a couple years, new parking garage, new basketball stadium, and another library."

## The College Prowler Take
### ON FACILITIES

Students agree that the athletic facilities (especially the Aquatic and Fitness Center) are superb. There always seem to be some sort of renovations going on—for example, currently they are working on a new parking garage and admissions building. However, despite the excellent gyms and new projects, UVA sometimes neglects other parts of the campus. Students generally don't feel that they have a "student center" to hang out at, and some will complain about the condition of labs and classrooms within the various colleges. For the most part, computer labs and classrooms are well-equipped, and the constant construction around campus shows signs of progress for the future.

**B**

The College Prowler™ Grade on
## Facilities: B

A high Facilities grade indicates that the campus is aesthetically pleasing and well-maintained; facilities are state-of-the-art, and libraries are exceptional. Other determining factors include the quality of both athletic and student centers and an abundance of things to do on campus.

# Campus Dining

## The Lowdown
### ON CAMPUS DINING

**Freshman Meal Plan Requirement?**
Yes

**24-Hour On-Campus Eating?**
No

**Student Favorites:**
The PAV, the Bakery, Greenberry's (in Alderman Café)

**Meal Plan Average Cost:**
$1,390

## Students Speak Out
### ON CAMPUS DINING

"It's not horrible. You can find decent stuff. There's always salad stuff. The problem is they serve the same thing over and over again."

Q "UVA dining leaves a lot to be desired. Compared to other schools, UVA doesn't really have a wide assortment of choices. **UVA needs more fast-food chains** on Grounds."

> "Dining hall food is dining hall food, for the most part. **Some of the food they serve is really sub-par,** but the dining halls all now have some sort of ethnic or alternative meal station, which is usually pretty good."

> "Some days are definitely better than others, but I could always find something to eat, **maybe not the healthiest**. Chick-fil-A, located in the PAV on the ground floor of Newcomb Hall, was a godsend."

> "The food on campus is something you should get away from as soon as you possibly can. It doesn't seem bad at first, but night after night of eating the same generic food gets old fast. If you are a vegetarian or vegan, you are bound to have an even harder time. As a vegetarian, I often found myself **frustrated with the options and unable to put together a balanced meal.** Many nights I ended up with cereal for dinner."

## The College Prowler Take
### ON CAMPUS DINING

Most students find the on-campus dining to be pretty standard, as far as cafeteria food goes. Some say that they love the dining halls, but such students are few and far between. The salad, wrap, cereal, and ethnic and alternative food stations are normally pretty reliable, in that everyone can probably find something to eat there. The biggest complaint seems to be that the food is always the same. Another problem is that it is sometimes difficult for vegetarians and vegans to find something that suits their special diet needs. Despite the standard repetition, the dining hall does offer a good number of options, as well as the opportunity to chat with friends and have group meals.

### The College Prowler™ Grade on
## Campus Dining: C-

Our grade on Campus Dining addresses the quality of both school-owned dining halls and independent on-campus restaurants as well as the price, availability, and variety of food.

# Campus Housing

## The Lowdown
### ON CAMPUS HOUSING

**Undergrads on Campus:**
47%

**Number of Dormitories:**
5

**Number of University-Owned Apartments:**
None

**Room Types:**
Singles, Doubles

**Bed Type:**
Single

**Cleaning Service?**
Yes

**You Get:**
Ethernet connection, laundry facilities, mailroom, AC (Hereford and Brown only), snack bars, vending machines, residential advisors, faculty advisors (Brown and Hereford only), study lounges, TV lounges, bathrooms, computer labs, kitchens (International Residential College only)

**Also Available:**
After first year, the following dorms are offered: Language Houses, Lambeth Field Dorms, Bice Dorm, Gooch & Dillard Dorm, Faulkner Dorm, Copeley Dorm, and Lawn and Range Rooms (must apply separately).

## Students Speak Out
### ON CAMPUS HOUSING

"I think it's good to live on Grounds your first two years and then live in an apartment off Grounds. It's a good taste of the real world—dealing with landlords and bills and all."

Q "**New dorms are nicer but farther away**. Typically, they don't create such a close-knit community with lots of people, just because you're in a suite with 10 people as opposed to a hall with 30, like the old dorms. If you're a transfer student, you should definitely try to get into Lambeth—it's more part of the party scene."

Q "Do not live in Hereford, ever. **Old dorms are the place to live, to meet people** and have fun, but the dorms are crap. But, at least that way you have something to complain about together!"

Q "For the first year, there seems to be a big split between new dorms and old dorms people. New dorms have several rooms off of a common area and a shared bathroom, while old dorms have a hall-style arrangement. **New dorms tend to be more diverse**; old dorms tend to be more social. I lived in new dorms, and if I had to do it again, I might choose old dorms just because I think there is greater potential for meeting people with the hall-style living."

Q "Dorms are very nice. I would choose McCormick Road dorms; they are doubles, hallway-style. **Alderman is suite-style with five doubles**, all attached to a large common room. They are all good; I like McCormick Road best, because that's where I lived."

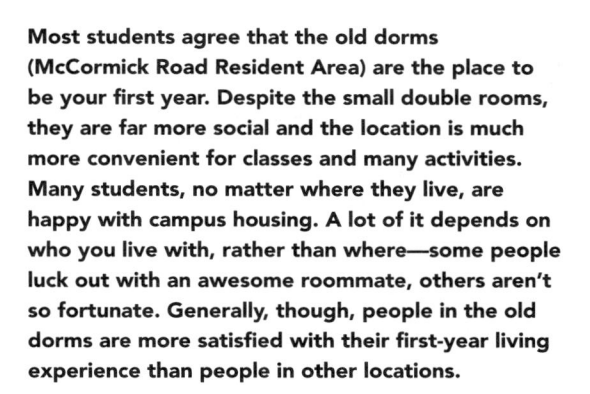

## The College Prowler Take
### ON CAMPUS HOUSING

Most students agree that the old dorms (McCormick Road Resident Area) are the place to be your first year. Despite the small double rooms, they are far more social and the location is much more convenient for classes and many activities. Many students, no matter where they live, are happy with campus housing. A lot of it depends on who you live with, rather than where—some people luck out with an awesome roommate, others aren't so fortunate. Generally, though, people in the old dorms are more satisfied with their first-year living experience than people in other locations.

**B-**

**The College Prowler™ Grade on**
### Campus Housing: B-

A high Campus Housing grade indicates that dorms are clean, well-maintained, and spacious. Other determining factors include variety of dorms, proximity to classes, and social atmosphere.

**COLLEGE PROWLER™**

Need help choosing a dorm? For a detailed listing on all dorms on campus, check out the College Prowler book on UVA available at *www.collegeprowler.com*

# Diversity

## The Lowdown
ON DIVERSITY

**Native American:** 0.3%

**Asian American:** 10.9%

**African American:** 9%

**Hispanic:** 3%

**White:** 69.6%

**International:** 4.5%

**Unknown:** 2.6%

**Out-of-State:** 25-30%

## Gay Tolerance
UVA is becoming increasingly accepting of its gay and lesbian population. There are various active organizations at the University promoting gay awareness (Gay and Lesbian Christian Students Association, the Missionary, Out on Rugby, the Queer Student Union, etc.). It took a while for UVA to get to this stage, though, and there is still evidence of intolerance in many places.

## Minority Clubs
There are many minority clubs at UVA, including: Black Student Union; Afghan Student Organization; Arab Student Organization; Asian Student Union; Black Student Alliance; Graduate Women in Business; Lesbian, Gay, Bisexual, Transgender Union; Latin American Students Association; National Organization for Women at UVA; Society of the Virginia Irish; Society of Women Engineers; Society for the Promotion of Indian Classical Music and Culture Among Youth (SPIC-MACAY); UniTE; Zeta Phi Beta Sorority; etc. Some of these groups have a much bigger presence on Grounds than others (i.e. Black Student Union and the National Organization for Women at UVA).

## Most Popular Religions
There are a few prominent Christian groups within the University that have meetings and houses together. There are also groups representing many other religions (Baha'i Association, Baptist Student Union, Buddhist Meditation Society, Campus Crusade for Christ, Chabad Jewish Heritage Student Association, Korean Catholic Student Ministry, Muslim Students Association, Quaker Worship Group, etc.). However, keeping true to Jefferson's ideal of the separation of church and state, there is no one religious affiliation associated with the University. In fact, the school chapel stands noticeably separate from the rest of the Grounds.

## Political Activity
Charlottesville, while being a wonderful place to spend four years of college, can be too sheltered from what's going on in the world. Obviously, some events (like the war in Iraq) bring out a lot of passion within the student population, and there are plenty of active organizations that feed this political passion among those students (Critical Mass, Take Back the Night, Amnesty International, Children of War, European Society, the Declaration, Republican and Democrat Organizations, etc.). Overall, however, the UVA student body can seem very apathetic toward political matters.

## Economic Status
UVA students come off as pretty wealthy—with the cars and clothes and drinking habits, it would seem one would have to be. In fact, however, there are plenty of students on financial aid, student loans, scholarships, etc. While many are from the upper/middle-class, there is a diversity of economic backgrounds.

## Students Speak Out
### ON DIVERSITY

> "The campus is very diverse. There are more minorities going to Virginia now than ever."

Q "There's a lot of diversity, but **there's also some self-segregation**. We're trying to work on that. Like, my sorority is maybe going to try to have a party with one of the fraternities from the black fraternal council. I know it sounds normal, but, at Virginia, it's kind of a new concept. I'm excited—that would be fun."

Q "**UVA has its share of ethnic diversity**, however blending to achieve a functional diversity seems more of a challenge. The African American students have been accused of self-segregation, which I found during my time at UVA to be a huge social force. Of course, there is likely self-segregation on the part of the white students from northern Virginia as well."

Q "Diversity on campus sucks. There are diverse ethnicities, but they don't intermingle so much. African Americans tend to stick together, and the Black Student Alliance has this philosophy about bonding within their own little community and helping each other out. I'm sure they would readily disagree with me, but it is true that **black-white relations at UVA suck**."

Q "I like that UVA has a diverse crowd. But, because UVA is so diverse **there are some tensions that come to the surface** sometimes."

## The College Prowler Take
### ON DIVERSITY

Student opinion varies a great deal on diversity issues. Some believe that diversity at UVA is good and getting better, while others see the University as primarily a rich, white man's school. Much of this depends on personal experience, and experience tends to be what you make of it among UVA's student body. Many students have encountered self-segregation among the various campus groups, and feel this is one of the biggest barriers to achieving functional diversity. The best way to experience diversity at Virginia is to seek it out for yourself—there are many different people at the school, once you get past social cliques. Overall, UVA could do better with diversity. At least the administration recognizes this and is trying to promote a new look for the school.

The College Prowler™ Grade on
### Diversity: C

A high grade in Diversity indicates that ethnic minorities and international students have a notable presence on campus and that students of different economic backgrounds, religious beliefs, and sexual preferences are well-represented.

# Guys & Girls

## The Lowdown
**ON GUYS & GIRLS**

Women Undergrads: 55%

Men Undergrads: 45%

### Birth Control Available?
Yes. The pill, the patch, the ring, the shot—basically everything is offered. Call a few weeks in advance to schedule an appointment (434-924-2773); sometimes they get really backed up, so the earlier you call the better. Sometimes, it is also helpful and less intimidating to talk with a PHE (Peer Health Educator) about these sorts of things, in addition to a gynecologist. The Peer Health Educator is usually an upperclassman who is fully trained and has all sorts of important information about women's health; for this service, call (434) 924-2773.

### Social Scene
The UVA social scene is difficult to define. Certainly Greek life makes up a lot of it, though definitely not as much as it used to. But, while the school holds tight to many of its traditions—Greek life included—UVA is expanding to include a variety of different social scenes as more and more different kinds of people join the community. Students are generally outgoing, friendly, and interested in what they do; the social scene is a huge part of student life.

### Hookups or Relationships?
UVA can be odd, and sometimes frustrating, in terms of relationships, dating, and hookups. Often you'll find two types of people: those who randomly hook up at frat parties and bars, and those who are in extremely serious relationships that will probably culminate in marriage. There is very little of the casual dating that comes in between.

### Dress Code
UVA's social dress code is quite distinct, but easily followed:

Guys—polo shirt with the collar flipped up, khakis or jeans, flip-flops or Reefs, orange visor or baseball hat, and sometimes the fratty pants (all plaid, sort of ridiculous looking)

Girls—tiny skirt or capri pants, button-down pink blouse or extra tight tank top, pearls, flip-flops, lots of makeup

## Students Speak Out
**ON GUYS & GIRLS**

"There are lots of good-looking people on campus. Virginia has a reputation for having hot guys, so that's such a bonus. The girls here are mixed, but there are plenty of guys to choose from."

Q "At UVA, there are two dominant subtypes. The guy: dressed in khakis, flip-flops even in the winter, polo shirt with the collar turned up making him look something like a confused magician, and bag slung over his shoulder. The girl: **spent hours on her hair this morning to impress the polo boy**, carrying the latest Kate Spade bag over one shoulder, no matter how heavy her books are, wearing a tank top and skirt, even as it becomes too cold to be comfortable, and either Reef flip-flops or a higher-heeled version."

Q "Both guys and girls seem ridiculous. I suppose **we have a reputation for being good-looking**, but I think that comes with a healthy dose of snottiness. Just my opinion."

# Athletics

> "**They are hot guys, and they know it**, which defeats the purpose of them being hot. There are a lot of girls I can't stand here."

> "The guys are mostly shaggy-haired preppy boys, but if you like more northern boys, there are some of them too. The girls are pretty much the same, just pretty preppy. **Everyone is preppy, smart, and mostly in shape.** Most of the people at the school are very attractive. It's like a little utopia."

> "There are **some really hot girls here**. If you are looking for guys, there are a lot of us, too."

## The College Prowler Take
### ON GUYS & GIRLS

UVA students have a very refined look. Most really care about appearances, so you will certainly see a lot of dressing up for class, as well as a lot of jogging around Grounds and working out at the gym. Some find this to be a cute and distinctive feature of UVA, while others find it really obnoxious and superficial. Most students agree the girls are way hotter than the guys. It is remarkable how similar people look at UVA, in their clothes and actions. While this probably isn't true when you get down to the deeper levels, superficially, there is a lot of the same thing. In general, people are very friendly and outgoing, with a wonderful laid-back sense of humor. There is certainly a degree of snobbishness, but you can get past this without too much trouble.

## The Lowdown
### ON ATHLETICS

**Men's Varsity Teams:**
Baseball
Basketball
Cross Country
Football
Golf
Lacrosse
Soccer
Swimming and Diving
Tennis
Track and Field
Wrestling

**Women's Varsity Teams:**
Basketball
Cross Country
Field Hockey
Golf
Lacrosse
Rowing
Soccer
Softball
Swimming and Diving
Tennis
Track and Field
Volleyball

---

**B+**

The College Prowler™ Grade on
## Guys: B+

A high grade for Guys indicates that the male population on campus is attractive, smart, friendly, and engaging, and that the school has a decent ratio of guys to girls.

**A-**

The College Prowler™ Grade on
## Girls: A-

A high grade for Girls not only implies that the women on campus are attractive, smart, friendly, and engaging, but also that there is a fair ratio of girls to guys.

**Athletic Division:**
NCAA Division I

**Conference:**
Atlantic Coast

**School Mascot:**
The Cavalier or the Wahoo (a fish that can drink twice its weight—what do you think that suggests?)

## Club Sports

Archery, Badminton, Belly Dance Club, Ballroom Dance, Brazilian Jiu-Jitsu, Capoeira, Cavalier Road Runners, Cricket, Cycling, Diving, Etcetera Winterguard, Fencing, Field Hockey, ISKF Karate, Judo, Mahogany Dance Troupe, Men's Ice Hockey, Men's Lacrosse, Men's Soccer, Men's Tennis, Men's Rugby, Men's Squash, Men's Ultimate Frisbee, Men's Volleyball, Men's Water Polo, Myo Sim Karate, Rhapsody Dance Ensemble, Sailing, Shotokan Karate, Taekwondo, Uechi-Ryu Karate, University Dance Club, Virginia Alpine Ski Team, Virginia Dance Company, Virginia Golf Club, Virginia Swim Club, Virginia Rowing Association, Virginia Soccer League, Women's Basketball, Women's Ice Hockey, Women's Lacrosse, Women's Rugby Football, Women's Soccer, Women's Softball, Women's Tennis, Women's Ultimate Frisbee, Women's Volleyball, Women's Water Polo, Wushu (Kung Fu) Kumdo, Swing Dance, Snowboarding, Golf, Gymnastics, Baseball, Riding

## Intramurals (IMs)

Flag Football, Soccer, Softball, Basketball, Field Hockey, Inner Tube Water Polo, Volleyball, Tennis

## Most Popular Sports

Football, Basketball, Soccer, Lacrosse

## Getting Tickets

The Virginia Athletic Ticket Office is located in Bryant Hall at the Carl Smith Center (off Stadium Road).

Address: Virginia Athletic Ticket Office
P.O. Box 400826
Charlottesville, VA 22904-4826

Hours: 9:00 a.m. to 5:00 p.m. Monday through Friday.

Phone: 800-542-UVA1 (8821) or 434-924-UVA1 (8821)

Fax Number: 434-243-3571

Students can get into any athletic event for free with their student ID. Everyone else must purchase tickets for the following sports during regular season: Football, Basketball (Men's and Women's), Baseball, Soccer (Men's and Women's), and Lacrosse (Men's and Women's). There is also an admission charge for any ACC or NCAA championship events.

## Students Speak Out
### ON ATHLETICS

{ *"IM sports aren't that big—I never really heard about them. Obviously, basketball and football are huge. It is a big tradition to go to the football games, but it's not for everyone."*

Q *"Tons of people participate in IMs. There are dorm leagues, frat leagues, co-ed leagues, independent leagues ... **tons of leagues and tons of IMs.** Varsity sports are also big, especially football and basketball."*

Q *"Basketball is big here—some of the crazier fans, like me, are known to **camp out for weeks before big games** in snow and rain, just to get the closest seats to the floor—it's ACC basketball, need I say more? Our football team is getting a lot stronger, too, and more popular, of course."*

Q *"Things are big for different people. **Varsity football is huge**, and soccer and lacrosse have decent followings, as well. IM sports are a great time, but they require some initiative—as in, you have to go sign up for them. Usually dorms or fraternities or other organizations put together little teams to compete in flag football, Frisbee, soccer, etc. Pretty fun."*

Q *"IMs are great. I played football, basketball, soccer, softball, and floor hockey. **Virginia football dominates weekends**. There are pre-games everywhere, at the lawn or at frats, or at people's apartments. Virginia basketball is nuts; people camp out for weeks to go to the games."*

## The College Prowler Take
### ON ATHLETICS

Athletics at UVA have always been huge, and most everyone recognizes this coming into the school. Basketball and football in particular are very big sports here, no matter the quality of the team from season to season. Going to home football games is definitely a tradition at UVA; students get all dressed up (pearls for the ladies, orange-striped bow ties and neckties for the guys), go to tailgates beforehand, and sing the "Good Ole Song" at every touchdown. In many ways, it's true that you don't get the full experience at Virginia until you've been to a sporting event. Intramurals and club sports also have a pretty big presence on Grounds. Almost any sport you can think of is offered. UVA students enjoy watching sports and enjoy being active.

## Greek Life

### The Lowdown
### ON GREEK LIFE

**Number of Fraternities:**
32

**Number of Sororities:**
16

**Men in Fraternities:**
30%

**Women in Sororities:**
30%

### Multicultural Colonies

Omega Phi Beta Sorority, Inc. (dormant), Alpha Kappa Delta Phi Sorority, Inc., Lambda Upsilon Lambda Fraternity, Inc., Phi Delta Alpha Fraternity, Lambda Theta Alpha Latin Sorority, Inc., Sigma Psi Zeta Sorority, Inc., Lambda Phi Epsilon Fraternity, Inc., Theta Nu Xi Sorority, Inc.

### Other Greek Organizations

Greek Council, Greek Peer Advisors, Interfraternity Council, Order of Omega, Panhellenic Council

**A**

The College Prowler™ Grade on
## Athletics: A

A high grade in Athletics indicates that students have school spirit, that sports programs are respected, that games are well-attended, and that intramurals are a prominent part of student life.

## Students Speak Out
### ON GREEK LIFE

> "The Greek life is very popular here, and it dominates the social scene, especially for first-years."

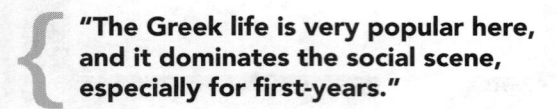

"Greek life does dominate the social scene, which doesn't mean there aren't other options, but it definitely dominates. I think, personally, that **it's very superficial**."

"There are plenty of frats here, but it doesn't dominate the social scene. You will see **a ton of people heading to the frats on Thursday and Friday nights**, but if you aren't into the Greek life, you will still have a blast. I didn't rush, but only about 40 percent of first-year girls do. If you are into the Greek life, by all means, go for it! You'll have a blast and form great relationships."

"**It's all frats and sororities**. After a while, you want to shoot someone, because all you see are SUVs. You have to look hard to find people that aren't like this, and then when you do, it's often just people who are consciously trying to be the opposite of a prep, so they aren't really that interesting."

"Greek life is a big part of Virginia social life. However, I'm not Greek, and **one doesn't have to become Greek in order to have a good time**. Make sure that, if you want to go Greek, that it is for you, because Greek life isn't for everybody."

## The College Prowler Take
### ON GREEK LIFE

Most students feel that Greek life dominates the social scene at UVA. Many are bitter about this, and find it superficial, costly, obnoxious, and over-prevalent. Those involved in Greek life, however, love the people they have met and the relationships they have formed. All sorts of people are involved in the Greek scene, as well as in the non-Greek scene—at UVA, students need to be a bit more open-minded both ways. There are plenty of other groups to join (literary magazines, a cappella groups, theatrical groups, athletic groups, community service organizations, etc.). In any case, even if you don't consider the Greek option, at least go to a frat party at some point—they really can be a fun time, or at least an interesting experience.

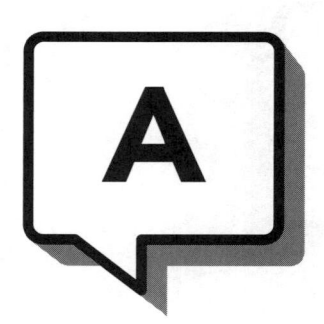

### The College Prowler™ Grade on
### Greek Life: A

A high grade in Greek Life indicates that sororities and fraternities are not only present, but also active on campus. Other determining factors include the variety of houses available and the respect the Greek community receives from the rest of the campus.

# Drug Scene

## The Lowdown
### ON DRUG SCENE

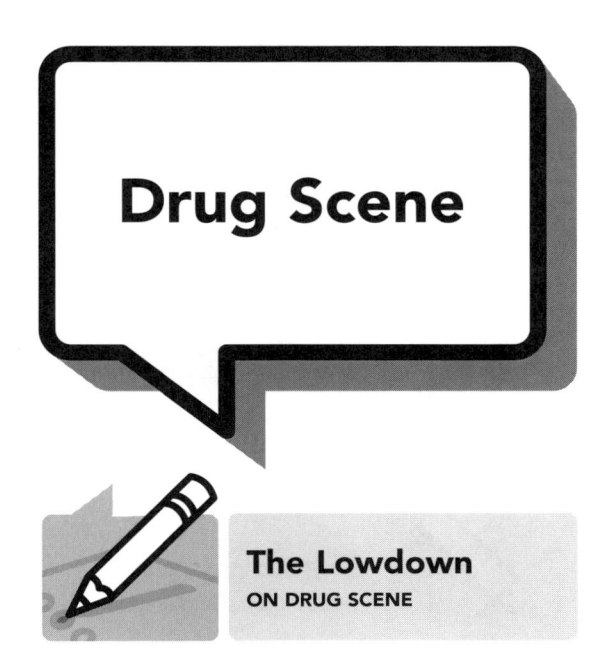

**Most Prevalent Drugs on Campus:**
Alcohol, Tobacco, Marijuana

**Liquor-Related Referrals:**
309

**Liquor-Related Arrests:**
1

**Drug-Related Referrals:**
51

**Drug-Related Arrests:**
7

## Drug Counseling Programs/Substance Abuse Resources

### Educational Programming

- Institute for Substance Abuse Studies – the coordinating body for substance abuse prevention, education, treatment and research at the University (434) 924-5276

- Peer Health Educators – a peer group trained in substance abuse information providing informal educational sessions (434) 924-1509

- University Police Department – officers providing information and seminars in the legal aspects of areas related to substance abuse (434) 924-7166

### Consultation and Treatment

- Addiction Science Center – outpatient treatment program with free initial evaluation and consultation (434) 924-0399

- Addiction Treatment Program – inpatient treatment program at Blue Ridge Hospital (434) 924-5555

- Student Health – Alcohol and Substance Abuse Counseling is available from Counseling and Psychological Services for confidential evaluation and treatment of students with substance abuse concerns. Family and group sessions, including groups for ACOAs and recovering students, are also available. (434) 924-5556

- Aid to Impaired Medical Students – information, consultation, intervention and referrals for medical students (434) 924-9130

- Aid to Impaired Residents – information, consultation, intervention and referrals for Health Sciences Center residents (434) 924-2047

- Assistance on Substance Abuse for Professional Nurses – information, consultation, intervention and referrals for licensed professional nurses (434) 924-5555

- Employee Assistance Program – information, consultation, intervention and referrals for faculty and staff (434) 982-1665

## Students Speak Out
### ON DRUG SCENE

"I don't think UVA has a drug problem. Of course college is a time of experimenting, but I don't think it's overindulged at this school."

Q "If you don't know about the drug scene, you'll never see it at all. There are certain **sororities and fraternities known for certain drugs**, particularly coke and weed. But, that's anywhere you go."

Q "I don't know much about the drug scene. I guess if you want to do drugs bad enough you can, but **no one pushes it on you.** To me, it seems nonexistent."

Q "I think it isn't as prevalent as it is at the schools my friends go to, but it is there. Fraternities often times have a good amount of drug use, but it isn't anything that makes me uncomfortable. **I'd say it is average, maybe less**."

Q "There's **a lot of alcohol use and abuse**, but other drugs aren't as popular. I think 30 percent of students smoke. In my substance abuse class, we learned that marijuana was the number one illicit drug used—of course, it is college, right?"

## The College Prowler Take
### ON DRUG SCENE

Most students don't think of UVA as a drug school. The biggest drug used among students is alcohol, by far. Generally, if you don't know about drugs or aren't interested in knowing about them, you'll never see the scene around Charlottesville. Some students feel as though marijuana and cocaine are a problem, but for the most part no one sees heavy drug use. Some sororities and fraternities are known for certain drugs, but, again, if you don't know about it, you don't see it. While there definitely are drugs around UVA, the actual scene is a relatively small problem. UVA loses points for the sheer volume of alcohol that flows through it every week, but, in the end, this school has a pretty safe drug scene.

**B**

The College Prowler™ Grade on
### Drug Scene: B

A high grade on Drug Scene indicates that drugs are not a noticeable part of campus life; drug use is not visible, and no pressure to use them seems to exist.

# Overall Experience

## The Lowdown
### ON OVERALL EXPERIENCE

"Because I didn't fit in well with the social scene at UVA—Greek-influenced, pretentious ... shall I go on?—I often thought I would be better suited elsewhere. But if you're in-state, it's a great deal for the money."

Q "I did wish I was somewhere else some of the time. The best time that I had in college was when I was studying abroad in Spain on the UVA program. **UVA is so big it was hard to connect with a lot of people** when there. I recognize that my experience at UVA was not like most. But now that I've graduated, I'm glad I went to UVA. The degree means something—it's a really good school."

Q "UVA is really big into tradition. I love the feeling that the University tries to **preserve some of the best parts of its past while opening the door to new things every day**. I do not know what else I can say about UVA, other than the fact that it was truly the best four years of my life, and I will be back for many years to come. UVA has one of the world's largest endowments—UVA alumni give back more money than most schools, which I think is a testament to how much they loved their time here!"

Q "I personally love UVA. The thing to remember is that you will meet people who will one day become **the political, business, and social leaders of the country**. When you graduate from UVA, it's like graduating from an Ivy League school, because it feels Ivy League, and there are numerous alumni who are currently CEOs who love to hire UVA students."

Q "Although I am transferring, I think that UVA is a very good school. **I had a lot of fun there**, and I did not wish that I was anywhere else this past year. The only reason that I am transferring is because I am getting more scholarship money."

## The College Prowler Take
### ON OVERALL EXPERIENCE

Most students talk about the enjoyable experiences and positive feelings they associate with UVA; the University has some of the most devoted alumni in the nation. Of course, there are those who wish they had gone somewhere else, who are turned off by things such as the lack of diversity, the prominence of Greek life, and student naivete and pretentiousness, which are more noticeable at some times than others. Those who really like UVA appreciate its traditions, the friendly and outgoing atmosphere, the beautiful setting, and the outstanding academic environment. If you come to UVA, be prepared to take both the good and the bad. In the end, for most, the positive aspects of the University outweigh the negative, and the environment is as vibrant and academic as it was when Thomas Jefferson founded it, well over a century ago.

**COLLEGE PROWLER™**

Want to read more students' quotes on their experiences at UVA? Check out the complete College Prowler book on the University of Virginia available at *www.collegeprowler.com.*

# Virginia Tech

201 Burruss Hall, Blacksburg, VA 24061
www.vt.edu          (540) 231-6267

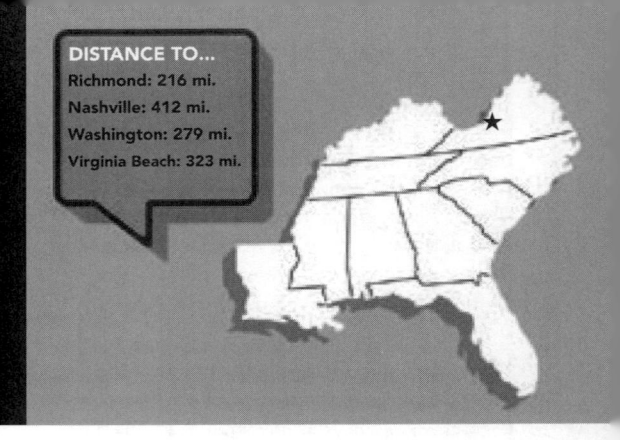

**DISTANCE TO...**
Richmond: 216 mi.
Nashville: 412 mi.
Washington: 279 mi.
Virginia Beach: 323 mi.

*"As a state university, Virginia Tech offers majors in many different academic fields."*

**Total Enrollment:**
20,730

**Top 10% of High School Class:**
40%

**Average GPA:**
3.6

**Acceptance Rate:**
69%

**Tuition:**
$5,838 in-state, $16,531 out-of-state

**SAT Range (25th-75th Percentile):**

| Verbal | Math | Total |
|---|---|---|
| 550 – 630 | 570 – 650 | 1120 – 1280 |

**SAT II Requirements:**
Virginia Tech requests that all incoming freshman take the SAT II Subject Writing Test by January of their senior year in high school. This test is not required for admissions, but is used for placement in freshman English classes.

**Most Popular Majors:**
24%  Business
19%  Engineering
4%   Biology
4%   Psychology
4%   Computer Science

**Students also applied to:***
University of Virginia
James Madison University
College of William and Mary
George Mason University
Radford University

*For more school info check out www.collegeprowler.com

## Table of Contents

| | |
|---|---|
| Academics | 399 |
| Local Atmosphere | 401 |
| Safety & Security | 402 |
| Facilities | 404 |
| Campus Dining | 406 |
| Campus Housing | 407 |
| Diversity | 409 |
| Guys & Girls | 411 |
| Athletics | 412 |
| Greek Life | 414 |
| Drug Scene | 416 |
| Overall Experience | 417 |

## College Prowler Report Card

| | |
|---|---|
| Academics | B |
| Local Atmosphere | B- |
| Safety & Security | A- |
| Facilities | B+ |
| Campus Dining | B+ |
| Campus Housing | C+ |
| Diversity | D+ |
| Guys | B+ |
| Girls | B |
| Athletics | A |
| Greek Life | B+ |
| Drug Scene | B- |

# Academics

## The Lowdown
ON ACADEMICS

**Special Degree Options**
Dual-Degree Programs: Students can get dual-degrees in any of the majors available at Tech. For instance, a student can major in engineering and English, or in psychology and philosophy. However, in order to earn two degrees, students have to take 30 more hours of classes than what is required for their first degree. Most degrees require a completion of about 120 credit hours. For a student to get a dual-degree, they would need to complete around 150 hours of classes.

**Sample Academic Clubs**
Alpha Chi Sigma (Professional Chemistry Fraternity), Alpha Epsilon Delta (Pre-Med Honor Society), Biology Club, English Students' Society, Business Information Technology Club, Dairy Club at Virginia Tech, Economics Club, Philosophy Club

**Degrees Awarded**:
Associate, Bachelor, Master, Doctorate

**Undergraduate Schools**:
Agriculture and Life Sciences, Architecture and Urban Sciences, Pamplin College of Business, Engineering, Liberal Arts and Human Sciences, Natural Resources, Science

**Full-time Faculty**:
1,251

**Faculty with Terminal Degree**:
90%

**Student-to-Faculty Ratio**:
17:1

**Average Course Load**:
5 courses

**AP Test Score Requirements:**
Possible credit for scores of 3, 4, or 5

**IB Test Score Requirements:**
Possible credit for scores of 4, 5, 6, or 7

**Did You Know?**
The undergraduate program at Virginia Tech is ranked 26th in the nation when compared to other public universities. Tech is also ranked as the 46th best value nationally.

You can go to *http://www.ratevtteachers.com* to see student evaluations of every teacher at Tech. This website is very helpful when you are deciding what classes to take.

**Best Places to Study:**
Math Emporium, Library, Torgersen Crossover

Need help choosing a major? For a detailed listing on various courses and professors on campus, check out the College Prowler book on Virginia Tech available at *www.collegeprowler.com*.

## Students Speak Out
### ON ACADEMICS

> "For the most part, my professors have been great. They are often passionate about their subject, and, since this is a research university, it is nice to work with professors who work in their fields."

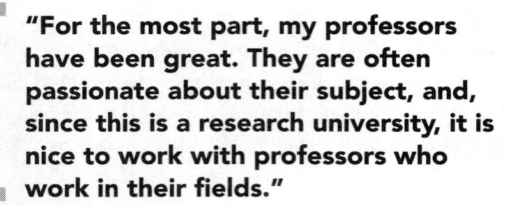

Q "Teachers suck over here because they can't teach. Almost all of the professors here have some kind of research that they are doing, so **teaching is not the main focus**. The good news is that they are willing to help you in any way they can. All the professors have office hours where you can go and talk or get help. If you can't go during office hours, you can make an appointment. You can also e-mail the professors for help. They are pretty good about answering e-mails."

Q "I have had a great variety of teachers here at Tech, from teachers that are so busy with research that they usually weren't at class, to teachers that slept three hours a night because **they spent all their time grading and preparing lectures**. I have noticed that the dispositions of the lower-level teachers in the math and science departments are generally worse. I theorize that this is because their brains quickly become bored with teaching easy introductory classes. Most engineering courses I find interesting, by nature if nothing else, but this also has a lot to do with the professors."

Q "For the most part, **all of the teachers are fair and respectful**. You really do learn a lot more than in high school. I took mostly AP classes in high school and didn't think I would learn a lot of new stuff in college, but I was wrong."

Q "VT has a ton of good majors. **Business is great here**. Engineering is great, and all the other majors are reputable. I like the faculty, and I am friends with a few of my teachers, as well as the dean of Pamplin College of Business. The faculty is always there for you, and will help you a lot if you need them to."

## The College Prowler Take
### ON ACADEMICS

Everyone knows Virginia Tech for its engineering department. While Tech does have an excellent engineering program, there are other programs at the University that shouldn't be overlooked. The Pamplin College of Business offers degrees in accounting, business, information technology, economics, finance, and more. Business management is one of the most popular majors at Tech, along with engineering, biology, psychology, and computer science. Besides sciences and business, Tech offers many liberal arts majors. In the English department, students have the opportunity to take classes with poet Nikki Giovanni. Virginia Tech students in all kinds of majors have the advantage of taking classes with professors who are active in their fields. Some students do worry that professors get more wrapped up in research than in teaching, especially since Virginia Tech wants to become a top 30 research institution, but even these students will admit that professors are usually willing to take time to meet with students on an individual basis to provide extra help.

At the beginning of a student's time at Tech, classes are large (often 300 students or more), and are often taught by graduate students. It can be easy for freshmen to feel a little lost within a University so large, but classes do get smaller as students get more involved in their majors. Picking a major can be a hard decision, but advisers are available to help. Advisors will even sit down with students to help them make decisions on individual classes.

**B**

The College Prowler™ Grade on
### Academics: B

A high Academics grade generally indicates that professors are knowledgeable, accessible, and genuinely interested in their students' welfare. Other determining factors include class size, how well professors communicate, and whether or not classes are engaging.

# Local Atmosphere

## The Lowdown
ON LOCAL ATMOSPHERE

**Region:**
Southeast

**City, State:**
Blacksburg, Virginia

**Setting:**
Rural

**Distance from Washington DC:**
4 hours

**Distance from Richmond:**
3 hours, 30 minutes

**Points of Interest:**
Roanoke, Radford University, New River, Cascades, Appalachian Trail, Huckleberry Trail, Chateau Morrissette

**City Websites:**
http://www.blacksburg.gov

## Students Speak Out
ON LOCAL ATMOSPHERE

"Students make up the surrounding area. The college town is awesome because when you go downtown, it's filled with people your age."

Q "**The atmosphere is very college oriented**. There is not much else around, but that does not make it lacking. Blacksburg, and the surrounding area, can provide you with all that you desire, as well as offer something unique. The Blue Ridge and Shenandoah Mountains are right at our doorstep, and they provide endless beauty and entertainment."

Q "I love Blacksburg! Since Blacksburg is a relatively small town, **it feels like Tech is the center**. As a freshman, the campus felt like a town within the town. I was so scared because Tech is so huge, but as I learned where the buildings were, and the hangouts, and met more people, the campus became smaller. I see familiar faces on practically every inch of the campus."

Q "In downtown Blacksburg, right off campus, there are some neat little shops, yummy restaurants, and great night life. **There is a handful of fun bars and places to hang out** and maybe play some pool or darts. And within 30 minutes of this place, there are so many outdoor things to do, like go to the New River and go tubing, or hike up the Cascades, or go camping or rock climbing. Radford University is 20 minutes away, too, and lots of people go there to visit and party."

Q "Virginia Tech makes Blacksburg **a small town wearing a big town's clothes**. There are so many people going to Virginia Tech that on the way home, you might think you are in a New York City rush-hour traffic jam—if it wasn't for the cow pastures. There are a few beautiful scenic locations near Blacksburg that are must-sees. The Cascades are beautiful in the summer, and when they freeze over in the winter. Also, Tech campus is about 20 minutes away from a great place on the river to go tubing or climbing."

## The College Prowler Take
### ON LOCAL ATMOSPHERE

Blacksburg is a little town, known only because it is home to Virginia Tech. Living in Blacksburg combines the convenience of being able to walk everywhere with the familiarity of knowing most of the shops and restaurants in town. The town's size and location do leave some students feeling like they're in the middle of nowhere. Students who come to Virginia Tech from big cities may miss the hustle and bustle, diversity, and range of experiences available to city dwellers. But, on the plus side, there is a downtown area that caters to college student tastes. Also, a variety of restaurants surround the campus, many of which are priced to fit a student budget. Blacksburg is mostly self-sufficient with numerous grocery stores, restaurants, shops, and services. While Blacksburg tries to offer Virginia Tech students an assortment of places to eat and things to do, there is a limit to how much such a small town can offer. By a student's fourth year of school, they may be ready to get out of Blacksburg and see something new.

**B-**

The College Prowler™ Grade on
### Local Atmosphere: B-

A high Local Atmosphere grade indicates that the area surrounding campus is safe and scenic. Other factors include nearby attractions, proximity to other schools, and the town's attitude toward students.

# Safety & Security

## The Lowdown
### ON SAFETY & SECURITY

**Number of Tech Police:**
39

**Phone:**
231-6411 (non-emergency)
911 (emergency)

**Health Center Office Hours:**
Monday, Tuesday, and Friday: 8 a.m.-5 p.m.
Wednesday and Thursday: 9 a.m.-5 p.m.
Saturday: 9 a.m.-12 p.m.

**Safety Services:**
Blue-phones, Safe Ride, escort service (231-SAFE), Rape Aggression Defense (RAD)

### Did You Know?

The police department in Blacksburg has created the Adopt-A-Hall program for Tech. Police officers visit dorms to get to know students in a positive way.

While various types of crimes do occur in Blacksburg, the crime rate here is below both the national average and the average for universities in Virginia.

## Students Speak Out
### ON SAFETY & SECURITY

"I've never felt threatened or unsafe, even when walking home alone at night from another dorm. The sidewalks and streets are well-lit."

Q "Blacksburg is one of the safest places that I have ever lived. I love the fact that I can leave my car unlocked at my apartment complex, and no one will bother it. The campus itself has **security guards that walk around throughout the night**. This, plus the campus emergency phones, gives a good sense of security for the entire campus."

Q "If you're smart, **you'll be safe every day of your four years at Tech**. For me, the most dangerous place is crossing this one street; since you sometimes can't see cars until they are really close to you, but this isn't a problem, if you're careful. Sometimes girls go to parties, get really drunk, and then trust some complete stranger to take them home—that's never a good idea. Ninety percent of assaults are alcohol-related, so, basically, as long as you're responsible you'll probably be fine. There are blue-phones located all over campus that are connected to the campus police, so you could use one and have someone come get you quickly if you were ever in trouble."

Q "**Campus is very secure**. We have our own police department, and throughout campus, there are emergency stations [where] one can get help if needed. I've never had the need to, or seen anyone, use them, though."

Q "Campus feels safe for the most part. **You do hear about things, though**. I have known people who have had things stolen. You also hear about the occasional rape, which is scary, but there are measures taken to make sure we are safe, such as night shuttles from parking to the dorms and emergency phones canvassing campus."

## The College Prowler Take
### ON SAFETY & SECURITY

Students who live on and off campus feel pretty safe in Blacksburg. Whether walking to class, going downtown, getting home at night, or going out to party, most students feel secure. Blue lights and good lighting add to security around the campus grounds, and police officers are a constant presence downtown. The police can be reassuring when you're alone at night, but intimidating if you're going out to party. At night, dorms are only accessible if you have a Hokie Passport (Virginia Tech student ID). Getting to parties is pretty safe as well. Most fraternity parties have designated drivers who take students to and from campus. The Blacksburg Transit bus system also goes to many apartment complexes, but only runs until about two in the morning on the weekends.

Blacksburg has a low crime rate, though missing bikes tend to be a common occurrence on campus. The best way to stay safe in Blacksburg is to avoid risky situations. If you're careful and use the services Tech offers, you'll probably have no problem with safety.

**A-**

**The College Prowler™ Grade on**
### Safety & Security: A-

A high grade in Safety & Security means that students generally feel safe, campus police are visible, blue-light phones and escort services are readily available, and safety precautions are not overly necessary.

# Facilities

**Favorite Things to Do**
Deet's Place, a coffee shop on campus, is a great place to study and regularly holds open mic nights. Squires Student Center is the home of the BreakZONE, where you can find pool tables, bowling, table tennis, and arcade games. Squires also has two-dollar movies on the weekends and houses Haymarket Theater, where students can catch plays. Burrus Hall brings in big-name bands, as well as major productions, like the musical "Rent." Even the drill field has events for students. The drill field regularly showcases fireworks, bands, and fairs.

## The Lowdown
ON FACILITIES

**Student Center**:
Squires Student Center

**Athletic Center**:
McComas Hall, War Memorial Hall, Cassell Coliseum, Lane Stadium/Worsham Field, Merryman Center

**Libraries**:
Carol M. Newman Library, Art and Architecture Library, Veterinary Medicine Library

**Movie Theater on Campus?**
No, but sometimes the Squires Student Center shows two-dollar movies in Colonial Hall (an auditorium-like classroom).

**Bowling on Campus?**
Yes, the BreakZONE is in Squires Student Center.

**Bar on Campus?**
No

**Coffeehouse on Campus?**
Deet's in Dietrick Dining Hall, GBJ café in Burke Johnston Student Center, Au Bon Pain in Squires Student Center

**Popular Places to Chill**:
Deet's, GBJ, Squires Student Center

## Computers
**High-Speed Network**? Yes
**Wireless Network**? Yes
**Number of Labs**: 18
**Numbers of Computers**: More than 846
**24-Hour Labs**: The Math Emporium
**Charge to Print**? Yes

## Students Speak Out
ON FACILITIES

"The facilities vary greatly in how nice they are, because some buildings on campus were built in the 1800s, and some were built just a few years back."

Q "The gyms on campus are very nice. **They have outstanding equipment**, but most of the time they are packed, and you have to wait in line to use them. There are plenty of opportunities to take up a sport that doesn't require waiting time. For example, I play racquetball and tennis, and I rarely have to wait on a court. If you can find yourself an apartment with a nice gym, like I have, then you never have to wait on weights."

Q "Tech spends a lot of money on **keeping the facilities looking new and clean**—i.e. the bathrooms are never gross. There are two gyms with pretty much every workout machine offered; there are pools, volleyball, basketball, and tennis courts, too. The buildings are nice and well-kept."

Q "Squires Student Center is very nice, complete with the media company offices, a major auditorium, a bank and ATMs, and excellent food at Au Bon Pain and Sbarro. The gym is nice, but **there are not nearly enough machines to accommodate all the students**, especially at the beginning of second semester when people are trying to enforce New Year's resolutions."

Q "The athletic facilities on campus are great. We have two gyms, and **one has a basketball court and swimming pool**. There are plenty of outdoor tracks and tennis courts. There's even a street hockey court. You name the sport, and you can probably play it here. The student centers are decent. You'll mostly go there for food or classes, though. Squires Student Center has pool tables, bowling lanes, and an arcade; however, the student centers are usually very crowded, so I wouldn't recommend studying in them."

Q "**The student center is very nice**. It has a lot of things to offer, but I rarely hang out there, other than to pick up a meal."

For further information on the facilities on campus, check out the College Prowler book on Virginia Tech available at www.collegeprowler.com.

## The College Prowler Take
### ON FACILITIES

"These buildings look like castles," one student remarked on his first visit to Tech. Indeed some of the buildings at Virginia Tech do look a little like castles, with their limestone exterior and unique architecture. However, some of the most ancient-looking buildings have some of the most state-of-the-art setups inside. Tech does a great job of keeping up with repairs and renovations, improving old structures, while building new ones as well. As for dorms though, the majority could use some work (of the facilities on campus, the dorms are the least impressive). Tech's campus does have a neat, unified look because the stone on the exterior of all the buildings matches. While the stone doesn't affect much on the inside of the buildings, it does make the campus attractive.

**B+**

The College Prowler™ Grade on
### Facilities: B+

A high Facilities grade indicates that the campus is aesthetically pleasing and well-maintained; facilities are state-of-the-art, and libraries are exceptional. Other determining factors include the quality of both athletic and student centers and an abundance of things to do on campus.

# Campus Dining

## The Lowdown
ON CAMPUS DINING

**Freshman Meal Plan Requirement?**
Yes

**24-Hour On-Campus Eating?**
No, but Dietrick Express is open till 2 a.m.

**Student Favorites:**
West End, Hokie Grill, Au Bon Pain

**Meal Plan Average Cost:**
$1,021

### Did You Know?
You can get lobster with your meal plan at West End. West End earned the title "Best College Specialty Restaurant in the United States" in 1999.

## Students Speak Out
ON CAMPUS DINING

"You will never go hungry at Tech. There is a lot to eat! Try West End and D2 for some good dishes!"

Q "Food is decent. There is a lot of variety, and the **atmospheres of the dining centers are all very interesting**. Sometimes the food can get old because, although there are many dining centers, they offer most of the same food every day."

Q "The food on campus is great. **The dining halls offer a lot of variety**, from gourmet and high-class—fresh Maine lobster!—to the everyday salad bar and the overcooked, undersized burgers. Really, Tech has some of the best food of any campus I have been to."

Q "The food on campus is pretty good, it's **overpriced, but good**. Portions go down, and prices go up every year. If you work out, Dietrick is the place to go, because it's cafeteria-style and all-you-can-eat. West End Market has great food, but it's usually very crowded. In fact, crowding is a problem with all the dining halls on campus. You'll learn to stay away during peak times. On top of that, there are a few chain places like Chick-fil-A, Pizza Hut Express, and Sbarro."

Q "**Food on campus is exquisite**! There isn't one place I don't like to eat. I lived in Thomas Hall my freshman year, so I keep Schultz Dining Center close to my heart, but I am up for eating anywhere. I like Schultz and D2 the best because of balanced meal you can fix for yourself. I am one of the few people I know who still uses a full meal plan, being a senior and living off campus."

## The College Prowler Take
ON CAMPUS DINING

All college students love to eat, and there seems to be something for everyone when it comes to food on Tech's campus. If you're super hungry, Schultz Dining Hall and D2 offer the all-you-can-eat option. D2 is also a good place to find meals specially prepared for vegetarian and vegan students. For a wider variety of foods there is Owen's Food Court, which features international foods, deli sandwiches, smoothies, a salad bar, Philly cheese steaks, burgers, and desserts. It's easy to find healthy choices in each dining hall, and students can go online to find out nutritional information for all the dishes served around Tech. Eating on campus is very popular at Tech, so sometimes dining halls get very crowded during the lunch and dinner rush. With 11 dining halls to choose from and hundreds of different dishes, it takes a while to try it all. Even though freshmen are required to purchase a meal plan, most don't mind, and some students enjoy Tech food so much that they continue to get meal plans for the rest of their years as students.

## B+

**The College Prowler™ Grade on**
## Campus Dining: B+

Our grade on Campus Dining addresses the quality of both school-owned dining halls and independent on-campus restaurants as well as the price, availability, and variety of food.

# Campus Housing

## The Lowdown
ON CAMPUS HOUSING

**Undergrads on Campus:**
44%

**Number of Dormitories:**
26

**Number of University-Owned Apartments:**
None

**Number of University-Owned Greek Houses:**
18

### Room Types
Tech offers two room types, though the majority of on-campus housing consists of traditional rooms. In traditional rooms, students share a room and have their own sink. Bathrooms are shared by the hall. In suites, rooms are centered on a shared living room and bathrooms are shared by 10 or fewer people.

### Available for Rent
Mini-fridge with microwave

### Cleaning Service?
Yes, public areas (lounges, halls, kitchens) and shared bathrooms are taken care of by the cleaning staff.

## You Get
Bed, desk, chair, closet, dresser, mirror or medicine cabinet, sink, cable TV outlet, Ethernet connection, phone, local phone service, answering service

## Bed Type
Twin extra-long (80"x36" or 84"x36"); loft and bunk bed options depending on dorm

## Also Available
Substance-free living, First-Year Experience Program, International Community, Leadership Community, Honors Community, Biological and Life Sciences Learning Community, Hypatia (Women in Engineering Learning Community), Corps of Cadets

## Did You Know?
Pritchard Hall is the biggest all-male dorm on the East Coast. Sometimes, when they have fire drills late at night, you can hear them from across campus!

Freshmen make up 58.2 percent of students living on campus.

When the weather gets warm, head out to "Slusher Beach," the grassy area behind Slusher Tower and Slusher Wing. Why is it called the beach? Because that's where everyone goes to get sun!

### COLLEGE PROWLER™

Looking for the best dorm on campus? For a detailed listing of all dorms, check out the College Prowler book on Virginia Tech at www.collegeprowler.com.

## Students Speak Out
ON CAMPUS HOUSING

{ "Pritchard is a dorm that should be avoided if possible; there is something wrong about having a thousand guys in one building. The new residence halls are pretty nice."

Q "**Living in a dorm stinks**, I don't care how nice, or clean, or big, or small it is. There are too many people in one enclosed environment for it to be enjoyable. The biggest problem is that the rooms are really small—especially for two people. What should get you through your dormitory experience in your freshmen year is knowing that you can live off campus for the next three years."

Q "The **dorms are dorms**. There are some nicer ones that have air conditioning. I always hear good things about New Residential and Harper."

Q "Dorm life here can either suck or rock depending on what you're like. **They're generally small and loud**, and you have to share showers with the whole hall. If you get along with your roommate, and have a decent pair of headphones, and aren't bothered by someone taking a shower next to you, you'll probably like it. The close quarters make it easy to meet your neighbors. Stay away from Thomas Hall. It's way on the edge of campus, away from everything, and it's right next to the power plant."

Q "**Dorms are a wonderful way to live your freshmen year**. You meet amazing people, and it makes everything on campus very accessible. If you have an 8 a.m. class, you don't have to wake up extra early to drive over to campus, and you don't have to deal with the atrocious parking on campus—or lack thereof."

## The College Prowler Take
### ON CAMPUS HOUSING

Virginia Tech has 26 dorms and 18 Greek houses for students. Freshmen are required to live on campus their first year, but many choose to make that their one and only year in a dorm. A lottery system is used to pick who gets to stay on campus past freshmen year, and space is limited, so getting a spot can be a challenge. The majority of dorms are large with small rooms, no air conditioning, and hall bathrooms. The few dorms that are suite-style, carpeted, and air-conditioned are reserved for upperclassmen or leadership students. While dorms may be lacking in style and comfort, living in them does have its advantages. If you live on campus, you can head back to you room for a quick nap between classes. Dorm living is also a great way to get to know people your first year at school. The dorms also offer extras, like shared kitchens, laundry rooms, and study lounges. Being on campus does make it easier to get to the dining halls and class, but the price is your comfort.

**The College Prowler™ Grade on**
## Campus Housing: C+

A high Campus Housing grade indicates that dorms are clean, well-maintained, and spacious. Other determining factors include variety of dorms, proximity to classes, and social atmosphere.

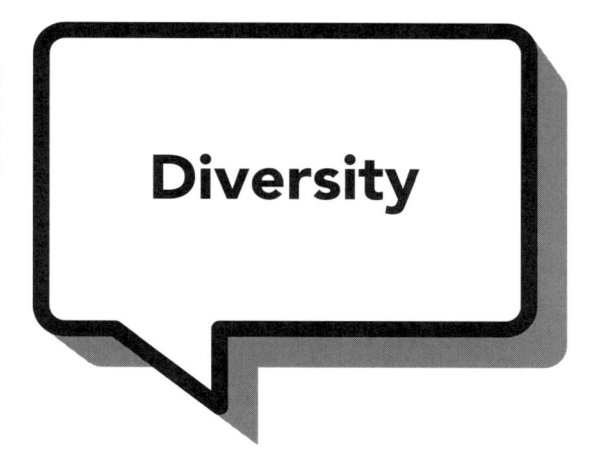

# Diversity

## The Lowdown
### ON DIVERSITY

**Native American:** 1%

**Asian American:** 7%

**African American:** 6%

**Hispanic:** 2%

**White:** 77%

**International:** 3%

**Unknown:** 4%

**Out-of-State:** 27%

### Minority Clubs

There are a number of active minority clubs on campus. To name a few: the Black Student Alliance, NAACP, and the Indian Students Association.

### Most Popular Religions

There are about 30 Christian student groups on campus, making Christianity the most represented religion at Tech. However, there are also students who are Muslim, Jewish, Unitarian, Buddhist, Jehovah's Witnesses, and members of other religions.

## Political Activity

While the campus is generally thought of as quite liberal, the student Republicans definitely have a voice. The Republicans and the Young Democrats often meet for lively political debates.

## Gay Tolerance

Students at Tech are generally open and accepting of their gay peers. SafeZone stickers around campus encourage students to feel comfortable being themselves.

## Economic Status

Students from many economic backgrounds go to Tech. Tuition here is lower than some other Virginia schools and financial aid is available, so Tech is able to meet the needs of those with lower economic status.

# The College Prowler Take
## ON DIVERSITY

Tech students come from many backgrounds, and have many perceptions of the world, but in terms of race, there is less variety. The student body is 77 percent white, with most other ethnicities represented in single digit percentages. In fact, some groups are even less represented; Native Americans make up only a quarter of a percent of the students at Tech. Diversity and discrimination are topics at Tech that have received much attention over the past few years. Tech students look around and appreciate the different backgrounds, cultures, religions, and sexual orientations of the students around them. However, students also realize that diversity is lacking at Virginia Tech.

# Students Speak Out
## ON DIVERSITY

{ "There isn't a lot of diversity. You have to go out of your way to find it sometimes."

Q "There is a lot of diversity and acceptance here. There are a lot of students from other countries and students of different races and backgrounds, sexual orientation, and interests. **Diversity is celebrated and encouraged** through organizations and activities."

Q "**Overall, it's not that diverse**. There are more international students here than minorities, or at least that is how it appears."

Q "Honestly, the campus is not very diverse, especially if you are from a bigger city. It is not uncommon to see different races or people of different cultures, but **you do not get a lot of exposure to those cultures** either."

Q "**It's becoming increasingly diverse**. People of many backgrounds populate the campus. There is an international dorm for international students, and it's cool to talk to them and learn what their home country is like."

**The College Prowler™ Grade on**
## Diversity: D+

A high grade in Diversity indicates that ethnic minorities and international students have a notable presence on campus and that students of different economic backgrounds, religious beliefs, and sexual preferences are well-represented.

# Guys & Girls

## Hookups or Relationships?
Partying on the weekends, and going downtown leads to many hookups. Occasionally, a random hookup even leads to a relationship. There are lots of couples at Tech, but probably just as many students who are only looking to hook up.

## Dress Code
The dress code at Tech is definitely casual. Jeans and a T-shirt are almost a uniform when it comes to dressing for class. Students also wear pajamas, workout clothes, dresses, and suits to class. However, if you're dressed up, you definitely stand out more.

### The Lowdown
ON GUYS & GIRLS

Women Undergrads: 41.1%

Men Undergrads: 58.9%

### Students Speak Out
ON GUYS & GIRLS

"Well, the guys vary a lot. We are a technical school, which means there are a lot of geeky-looking guys, but some of them are cute in their geekiness."

## Birth Control Available?
Yes. Schiffert Health Center provides multiple forms of birth control at cheaper prices than local pharmacies. Birth control that is available: pill, patch, injection, and ring. Condoms are sold in packs of 24 and cost five dollars. Female students who have a prescription from their doctor at home can purchase their birth control at the health center, and the health center can prescribe birth control, after students go through a contraception class. The morning-after pill and pregnancy tests are also available at the health center.

## Social Scene
Students at Tech like to get out and meet people, and there are plenty of opportunities to do so. Many times just going to class can lead to new friends. Working in a group for an assignment can be followed up by hanging out at a party. Most of the clubs at Tech, including the academic ones, have some sort of social component. It's possible to be a loner at Tech, but most students find it easier, and more fun, to be a part of the social scene.

"I don't know about the guys, but **there are a lot of good-looking girls** here. I didn't know what to do my freshmen year. I couldn't concentrate. I have learned to live with it now."

"Being a guy, I guess I could say most of the girls here are hot. **Okay, they're really hot**, and they're usually open to talking. It's different from high school. They're more mature, and they actually respond to respect. Nice guys don't always finish last."

"The girls are smoking hot and seem to be getting better-looking with each incoming freshmen class. Once known as a bad school to find good-looking girls, I'm certain the near future will bring descriptions of Tech as **one of the best schools to meet pretty girls**."

"The campus is diverse, so **there are plenty of different types** that should satisfy anybody's taste—i.e., there are jocks, brainy types, hippies, thespians, frat boys and sorority girls."

💬 "Honestly, I think that **Tech has some good-looking people**—boys and girls. The level of hotness varies, obviously, but there is a ton of the opposite sex to choose from."

## The College Prowler Take
### ON GUYS & GIRLS

With around 20,000 undergraduates at Tech, there are bound to be at least a few hotties wandering around campus. But, Tech students will tell you that there are a disproportionately large number of good-looking students, and they're distributed across all academic interests. As for the numbers of females and males at Tech, it's pretty even, though some individual departments and majors tend to have more of one sex than the other. Luckily, students tend to hang out across majors, so the male-female ratio evens out. Overall, the ratio of males to females isn't too bad, with 41 percent of undergrads being female, and 58 percent being male. And, with more and more females taking up technical careers, this ratio should only improve further in coming years (for the guys, that is!). Most times, Tech students don't notice the ratio; there always seems to be plenty of the opposite (or same) sex to go around.

**B+**

**B**

**The College Prowler™ Grade on**
## Guys: B+

A high grade for Guys indicates that the male population on campus is attractive, smart, friendly, and engaging, and that the school has a decent ratio of guys to girls.

**The College Prowler™ Grade on**
## Girls: B

A high grade for Girls not only implies that the women on campus are attractive, smart, friendly, and engaging, but also that there is a fair ratio of girls to guys.

# Athletics

## The Lowdown
### ON ATHLETICS

**Men's Varsity Teams:**
Baseball
Basketball
Cross Country
Football
Golf
Soccer
Swimming and Diving
Tennis
Track and Field
Wrestling

**Women's Varsity Teams:**
Basketball
Cross Country
Lacrosse
Soccer
Softball
Swimming and Diving
Tennis
Track and Field
Volleyball

## Club Sports

Baseball, Basketball, Bowling, Clay Target, Crew, Cricket, Cycling, Fencing, Field Hockey, Gymnastics, Ice Hockey, Lacrosse, Rugby, Soccer, Softball, Snow Skiing, Triathlon, Volleyball, Water Polo, Water Skiing

## Intramurals (IMs)

Golf, Soccer, Tennis, Home Run Derby, Putt-Putt, Softball, Racquetball, Bowling, Billiards, Volleyball, Flag Football, Basketball, 3-on-3 Basketball, Swimming, Dodgeball, Fantasy Football, Bowl Pick-em Contest, Table Tennis, Hearts, Inner Tube Water Polo, Wiffleball, Darts, 3-Point Shooting Contest, Slam Dunk Contest, Ultimate Frisbee, Sports Trivia, Chess Tournament

**Athletic Division**:
NCAA Division I

**Conference**:
ACC

**School Mascot**:
Hokie Bird

**Fields**:
English Baseball Field, Johnson/Miller Track/Soccer Complex, Rector Field House, Tech Soccer/Lacrosse Stadium, Tech Softball Park, Worsham Field

## Most Popular Sports

Football is, by far, the most popular sport at Tech. Hokie fans come decked out in their brightest maroon and orange and are always ready to yell. The stands are packed and wild. Basketball also draws a crowd, and now that Tech is in the ACC, basketball games may gather even more attention. Intramurals are lots of fun, and many students participate in them. Inner Tube Water Polo is a great IM sport to watch; spectators don't know whether to pay attention to the score or to whose inner tube is going to flip next.

## Overlooked Teams

Many sports teams here at Tech are overlooked because of the school's love affair with its football team. The men's and women's basketball teams are definitely worth checking out. The soccer teams also don't draw a huge crowd, but are great to watch.

## Getting Tickets

The days of camping out in front of Cassell Coliseum in order to get football tickets are now gone. An online lottery system has been set up to save students time and to make the whole ticket-getting process a little bit easier. Students submit their number online, and are notified later as to whether they've been picked to receive tickets. Some students question the fairness of the lottery system though, and are concerned that getting tickets is left up to too much chance. There is the option of buying season tickets for around 40 bucks, if you don't want to chance it.

## Students Speak Out
### ON ATHLETICS

"Both varsity sports and IM sports are popular. Football and basketball games are great, and the organization of IM sports is excellent."

"Obviously, **football dominates the varsity sports scene at Tech**, but now that Tech is in the ACC, there will be some stiff competition in other sports. For instance, basketball interest and support will surely increase when schools like Duke, UVA, and UNC begin coming to play Tech this year."

"**Sports are huge here**, especially ACC football and NCAA women's basketball. There is always a sport event happening, and they are always fun to watch. There is such Hokie pride; it is glorious. If we win we celebrate, if we lose we celebrate—because I mean, come on, I'm sure we didn't lose that badly."

"If you want to get involved in IM sports, you can. **They don't draw a big crowd** or anything, but they are fun."

"IM sports are an excellent way to play your favorite sports, and there are **several leagues that cater to different levels of play**."

## The College Prowler Take
### ON ATHLETICS

Football games draw students, alumni, friends, and family to Lane Stadium, leaving downtown Blacksburg silent when football games are going on. Even students who come to Tech with no interest in sports become drawn into the fierce loyalty that students have for their football team. Now that Virginia Tech has joined the ACC, the excitement has gone up a notch. Basketball is getting more attention because of the conference change. Most of Virginia Tech's sports are Division I, and the students are proud of this fact, and make it out to lots of sporting events. Football is the hardest sport to get tickets for at VT. Last fall, Virginia Tech began a new system for handing out student tickets. Now, instead of waiting in line for hours or even days for tickets, students have to enter a lottery system and cross their fingers, hoping to get a ticket. Students also get involved with intramural sports. Student organizations will set up their own teams, but individual students can get groups of friends together as well. These games are usually pretty lighthearted, but sometimes the competitive spirit kicks in and a fierce battle ensues.

# Greek Life

## The Lowdown
### ON GREEK LIFE

**Number of Fraternities:**
40

**Number of Sororities:**
19

**Undergrad Men in Fraternities:**
13%

**Undergrad Women in Sororities:**
15%

**A**

### The College Prowler™ Grade on
## Athletics: A

A high grade in Athletics indicates that students have school spirit, that sports programs are respected, that games are well-attended, and that intramurals are a prominent part of student life.

### Did You Know?

Fraternities and sororities can be seen around the campus and Blacksburg raising money for worthy causes and participating in service projects.

The Greek system at Virginia Tech is ranked 19th-largest in the nation.

## Students Speak Out
ON GREEK LIFE

"A lot of kids are in sororities and fraternities, but there's not an overwhelming influence of Greek life because the campus has so many other students [who are] not Greek."

"I wouldn't come close to saying that Greek life dominates the social scene, because **under 20 percent of Tech students are in a fraternity or sorority**, but I would say it is its own social scene. While you don't have to be Greek to have a good time or know where the party is, from what I notice, Greeks tend to hang out amongst themselves, and non-Greeks likewise. There's not much mixture between the two."

"**Greek life absolutely does not dominate the social scene**, just TOTS [Top of the Stairs Bar]—kidding, kidding. There is a good chunk of people involved in the Greek societies, but there is no status quo for how many students should be in a fraternity or sorority on campus, and students hardly feel pressured to join one or be forever doomed as a VT outcast."

"The nice thing about Tech is they offer more options than just cut-and-dry sororities or fraternities. **You have business and honor fraternities to get involved with as well**. I am in Phi Sigma Pi National, a co-ed honors fraternity, and I absolutely love the people and what we are involved with, but I do not by any means get caught up in the Greek scene."

"Tech has one of the largest Greek systems, but **the environment here is definitely not dominated by Greek life**, including the social scene. There are thousands of other organizations, and thousands of non-Greeks. Downtown, you'll find a balance between the Greeks and non-Greeks—and there really isn't much stress on that divide either."

"**You can't avoid seeing Greek life**, but there are plenty of other social opportunities to take advantage of."

## The College Prowler Take
ON GREEK LIFE

There are 38 fraternities and 18 sororities at Virginia Tech for students to choose from. While many students find Greek life to be fulfilling and fun, there's no need to join a fraternity or sorority in order to fit in. Fraternities and sororities do throw lots of parties, but these are usually open to everyone on campus. Greek members hang out together, throw parties together, and generally know each other better than they know non-Greek students. Non-Greek students are by no means excluded or treated differently by Greek-affiliated students, but there is some separation between the two groups. Though many Tech students embrace the Greek life, fraternities and sororities don't dominate the social scene. Just getting involved in student organizations can provide some of the same social opportunities and networking that are available through Greek organizations.

**B+**

**The College Prowler™ Grade on**
## Greek Life: B+

A high grade in Greek Life indicates that sororities and fraternities are not only present, but also active on campus. Other determining factors include the variety of houses available and the respect the Greek community receives from the rest of the campus.

# Drug Scene

**Alcohol Abuse Prevention at Virginia Tech**

http://www.alcohol.vt.edu

Services: Provides facts, statistics, and information about student drinking at Virginia Tech, including the consequences of drinking and getting in trouble

**Alcoholics Anonymous**

(540) 231-6557

Services: Meetings twice a week at Virginia Tech's Counseling Center and other locations

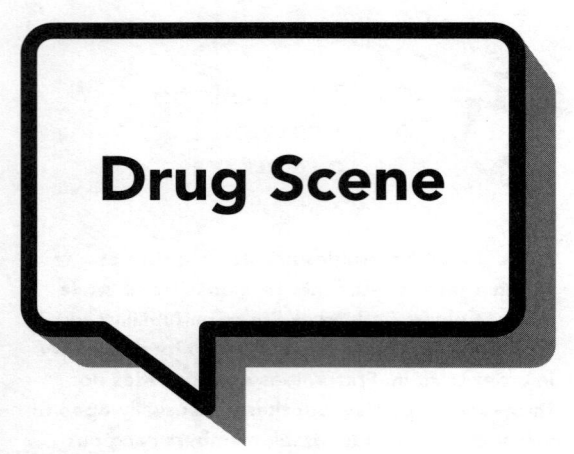

## The Lowdown
ON DRUG SCENE

**Most Prevalent Drugs on Campus:**
Alcohol, Marijuana

**Liquor-Related Referrals:**
776

**Liquor-Related Arrests:**
217

**Drug-Related Referrals:**
16

**Drug-Related Arrests:**
55

## Students Speak Out
ON DRUG SCENE

"Like any university, if you want to be involved with drugs, it isn't hard, but if you want to avoid them, that's easy, too."

"**The drug scene's going strong**, but only on more low-key drugs like pot."

"I haven't heard or seen much of anyone doing more than alcohol and marijuana. It's going to be there, but **no one will pressure you into doing it**. If you're uncomfortable with people doing it around you, there is plenty of stuff to do that doesn't involve drugs or alcohol."

"**I have a drug dealer in my dorm**. If you want drugs, they're pretty easy to find."

"What do you need drugs for? **Drinking is enough**. Drugs are not a very big thing here."

## Drug Counseling Programs

**Thomas E. Cook Counseling Center**

(540) 231-6557

Services: Online assessment tests for depression, alcohol dependency, eating disorders, and anxiety, group and individual counseling for students, and referrals for students to other counselors or programs

## The College Prowler Take
ON DRUG SCENE

According to VT students, in order to find people using drugs on or around campus, you have to go looking for them. While drug use does happen, it's not very visible around campus. If students are going to use a substance, it's usually alcohol or caffeine. The other most commonly-used substance around campus is marijuana. But, most students at Tech don't encounter any drug use at parties or on campus. Students say that if you want to avoid drugs, it is very easy to do—it is as simple as picking who you want to hang out with. Virginia Tech has a "zero tolerance" rule when it comes to drugs, so if you are caught using drugs it is almost guaranteed you'll be suspended, if not expelled.

**B-**

The College Prowler™ Grade on
## Drug Scene: B-

A high grade on Drug Scene indicates that drugs are not a noticeable part of campus life; drug use is not visible, and no pressure to use them seems to exist.

## Overall Experience

### Students Speak Out
ON OVERALL EXPERIENCE

"I do indeed wish I was in a town with something to offer everyone, not just the freshmen trying to sneak into bars."

Q "**I enjoy Tech**, but I honestly wish I was somewhere with more diversity and parking."

Q "I love Virginia Tech. Bottom line: **I could not ask for a better school**. It has everything I could ever want; the people, athletics, and organizations are amazing. But, you get out of it what you put in it. The one thing I can recommend is get involved. No matter what it is—just find something you like and do it. If VT doesn't have a group or organization you want to join, then find two other people and create your own group."

Q "Virginia Tech is worth the cost, and I love my department. There are countless opportunities here, and the people make it worth it. Everyone is so outgoing and nice that **you feel like you have 10 thousand friends**."

> "I have been here for four years and am now a graduate student here. I enjoy it. I am from Connecticut, in a town about an hour outside of NYC, so at times **I feel very isolated here**. Especially since Roanoke is considered the 'big city.' Who are they kidding?"

# The College Prowler Take
## ON OVERALL EXPERIENCE

Overall, Virginia Tech students have strong school spirit and value the education their university provides. In fact, many students have such a great time as undergraduates that they stay at Tech for graduate work. The academics have been improving each year, and admission into the University is becoming more selective. Each freshmen class comes in with higher high school GPAs and SAT scores than the last. Unfortunately, statistics also show that minority enrollment has been going down at Tech, and more students are choosing to not list their race.

The rural setting of Blacksburg, Virginia, is enjoyable for some students and frustrating for others. Even though Tech is home to more than 20,000 undergraduates, Blacksburg is still a small town. The area surrounding the town provides all kinds of outdoor activities. For students who come from more urban settings, Virginia Tech's small downtown and limited number of restaurants can be exasperating. But, even city students can appreciate how easy it is to walk from campus to town, and how safe the town is. When it comes to nightlife, students have all kinds of options. Downtown offers a number of bars and clubs, while parties can be found at Greek houses and apartment complexes. For students who are looking for alcohol-free fun, there is always something happening on campus.

Virginia Tech is a large school, so some students initially feel lost in the crowd. But, there are benefits to being at a large school. Tech has many resources and can offer all kinds of opportunities to its students. Opportunities come in the form of professors who are very involved in their fields, internships, jobs found by the Career Center, and classes that use the latest technology. Students who have the best experience at Tech find a major that they love, and then get involved. Virginia Tech has a lot to offer its students, as long as students make the effort to take advantage of all that is available.

# Davidson College

209 Ridge Road Davidson, NC 28035
www.davidson.edu          (800) 768-0380

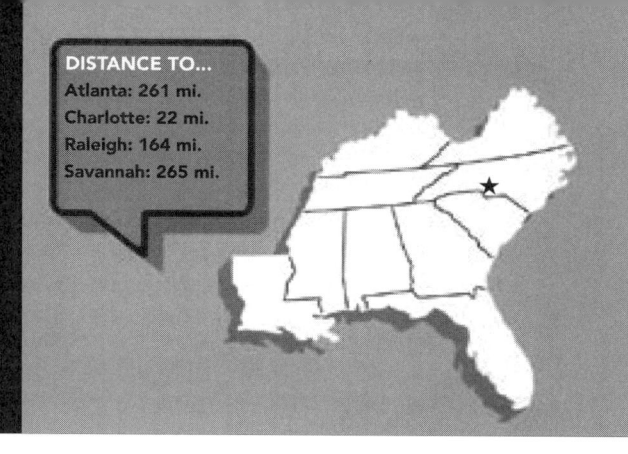

**DISTANCE TO...**
Atlanta: 261 mi.
Charlotte: 22 mi.
Raleigh: 164 mi.
Savannah: 265 mi.

*"The school is set up in a cozy little town, yet it's just minutes away from a bustling, big city."*

**Total Enrollment:**
1,711

**Top 10% of High School Class:**
76%

**Average GPA:**
3.8

**Acceptance Rate:**
32%

**Tuition:**
$27,171

**SAT Range (25th-75th Percentile)**
| Verbal | Math | Total |
|---|---|---|
| 630 – 720 | 640 – 720 | 1270 – 1440 |

**ACT Range (25th-75th Percentile)**
| Verbal | Math | Total |
|---|---|---|
| 24-31 | 24-31 | 27-31 |

**Most Popular Majors:**
14% English Language and Literature
13% Political Science and Government
12% History
12% Biology/Biological Sciences
9% Economics

**Students also applied to:***
Duke University
Wake Forest University
University of North Carolina
University of Virginia
Vanderbilt University

*For more school info check out www.collegeprowler.com

**Table of Contents**

| | |
|---|---|
| Academics | 420 |
| Local Atmosphere | 422 |
| Safety & Security | 423 |
| Facilities | 425 |
| Campus Dining | 427 |
| Campus Housing | 428 |
| Diversity | 430 |
| Guys & Girls | 431 |
| Athletics | 433 |
| Greek Life | 435 |
| Drug Scene | 436 |
| Overall Experience | 438 |

**College Prowler Report Card**

| | |
|---|---|
| Academics | A- |
| Local Atmosphere | C+ |
| Safety & Security | A+ |
| Facilities | A- |
| Campus Dining | C |
| Campus Housing | A- |
| Diversity | D- |
| Guys | B+ |
| Girls | B |
| Athletics | B |
| Greek Life | B- |
| Drug Scene | A- |

# Academics

## The Lowdown
### ON ACADEMICS

**Degrees Awarded:**
Bachelor

**Full-time Faculty:**
159

**Faculty with Terminal Degree:**
97%

**Student-to-Faculty Ratio:**
10:1

**Average Course Load:**
4 courses (12 credits)

**Special Degree Options:**
3-2 Engineering Program

**AP Test Score Requirements:**
Possible credit for scores of 4 or 5

**IB Test Score Requirements:**
Possible credit for scores of 6 or 7 on the higher level (HL) exam

**Sample Academic Clubs:**
Pre-Law, Pre-Med, and Pre-Theological societies, Mock Trial, French Club

### Did You Know?

All exams at Davidson are self-scheduled and un-proctored thanks to an academic Honor Code.

You won't find a single TA in any Davidson classroom. All classes are taught by professors themselves.

In 2003, a national academic syndicate ranked Davidson the number one liberal arts school in the nation for Faculty Resources, a category assessing such factors as student-to-teacher ratio, the percentage of faculty with terminal degrees, the percentage of faculty who work full-time, and faculty salary. Overall, Davidson was ranked the seventh best liberal arts college nationwide.

**Best Places to Study:**

Second floor or basement of E.H. Little Library, Chambers (the main academic building), Students looking for peace and quiet should head to the library, or the third or fourth floor of the Stern Center.

Need help choosing a major? For more detailed info on all professors and courses to choose from, check out the College Prowler book on Davidson available at www.collegeprowler.com.

## Students Speak Out
### ON ACADEMICS

"The professors here are great. They are especially wonderful to talk to after class. I've had very few professors who I found intimidating or hard to relate to."

"I've had **few problems getting into classes that I wanted to take**. There's almost always room, though. In most cases, the prof is willing to work with you and grant special permission for you to join the class. Yeah, they have the power to do that."

"The teachers at Davidson make or break the classes. The student-teacher ratio is such that everyone has the potential to develop a personal relationship with a teacher. My **most interesting teachers have taught my most interesting classes**; the material shines through whatever lens the teacher wants to show it through."

"I absolutely adore my professors. All of them are **completely devoted to their students**. Professors invite students to their houses for discussions, dinners, and even parties. I even had a professor go around to the admissions directors from visiting grad schools that I was interested in and tell them that I am the kind of student they want at their schools. Also, all of my professors were willing to go over my grad school admission essays with me."

"What they say about Davidson professors is right: they are **unbelievably brilliant, and their classes are endlessly fascinating**. I have enjoyed and learned many things from classes outside my English major interests, like astronomy, and other sciences."

"My experience has shown professors to be **warm, engaging, and very open to fostering friendships** that often transcend the hierarchical dualism of teacher versus student. Instead, many seem to view the classroom as a space in which learning takes place, not by simply relaying statistics to students, but through the interactive and dynamic process of dialogue between teacher and student."

## The College Prowler Take
### ON ACADEMICS

Students make it clear: academics at Davidson are some of the strongest the liberal arts community has to offer. Praise runs especially high for the low student-to-teacher ratio as well as the accessible, dedicated, and brilliant faculty. Complaints are mostly related to the relatively small number of majors offered and, more universally, the workload. Davidson is notorious for its hefty workload and less-than-generous grade inflation (it's more like grade deflation).

It's true that Davidson's excellent academic reputation is what attracts most students to the school in the first place. Students come here with the expectation that they will work hard, and find it's virtually impossible to 'slide by' academically once they're in. At the same time, many professors do go out of their way to make the mammoth workload less imposing. Profs here are almost always willing to negotiate due dates if you're in a bind, or simply to cut you a break when you're excessively stressed out. Overall, the professors at Davidson serve not only as teachers, but also as mentors. Professors are willing to form relationships with students outside of the classroom, give detailed recommendations, and are even willing to have students over for dinner. If this isn't grounds for a positive learning environment, I don't know what is. Now, please pass the stuffing.

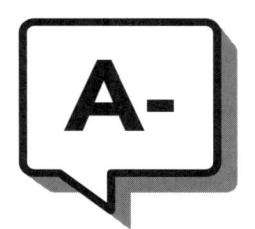

**The College Prowler™ Grade on**
## Academics: A-

A high Academics grade generally indicates that professors are knowledgeable, accessible, and genuinely interested in their students' welfare. Other determining factors include class size, how well professors communicate, and whether or not classes are engaging.

# Local Atmosphere

## City Websites

www.charlotte.com
www.charlottecvb.org
www.charlottechamber.com

## Students Speak Out
### ON LOCAL ATMOSPHERE

## The Lowdown
### ON LOCAL ATMOSPHERE

**Region:**
Southeast

**City, State:**
Davidson, North Carolina

**Setting:**
Small town on outskirts of medium-sized city

**Distance from Charlotte:**
20 minutes

**Distance from Winston-Salem:**
1 hour

**Points of Interest:**
Carowinds Theme Park, Mint Museum of Art, Museum of the New South, Charlotte Museum of History, Charlotte Nature Museum, Discovery Place, Blumenthal Theatre, Charlotte Repertory Theatre, Bank of America Building, North Carolina Racing Hall of Fame (Mooresville)

**Sports Teams:**
Panthers (NFL), Sting (WNBA), Bobcats (NBA), Checkers (East Coast Hockey League), Eagles (USL soccer), Carolina Cobras (Arena Football), Charlotte Knights (AAA Baseball), Kannapolis Intimidators (A Baseball)

"The town is small, boring, and suburban. Nothing ever happens here. There is not much to do, either."

Q "The town of Davidson is a very small, but wealthy, town. I found the environment at Davidson shocking coming from Washington, D.C., a very diverse community. What struck me the most was the **racial divisions that are still very much present in Davidson**. Also, there is a part of Davidson that's on 'the other side of the tracks,' quite literally. I think this is one aspect of Davidson that prospective students should be aware of. While this does not play a huge role in life at Davidson, I feel it is still something that people are conscious of."

Q "In terms of places to visit, there aren't really any exciting ones. Charlotte is the closest city and it's about 25 minutes down Highway 77. I think the lack of stuff to visit contributes positively to Davidson's academic environment ... **not as many distractions** as people might have at other schools."

Q "Davidson is a **close-knit, small town where most of the residents know one another**. The professors are well-known throughout the community, so I have found it interesting to meet community members who ask me which professors I currently have. They then frequently share some information about the professor's life in the town, which relates the prof on a more personal level to me as a student."

Q "There aren't any other universities around, and the **downtown area consists of one block** of little boutiques, sandwich shops, two banks, a coffee shop, the town library, a CVS, and a Ben & Jerry's. Basically, that's all that a college student could ever need!"

> "The atmosphere in **town is quaint, friendly, and quiet**. There really isn't much to the town of Davidson except the soda shop, Ben and Jerry's, and CVS. Christmas in Davidson is well worth experiencing though, as are Concerts on the Green."

## The College Prowler Take
### ON LOCAL ATMOSPHERE

While prospective students are often worried by Davidson's small-town setting, which boasts a total population of only 7,100—and that's including 1,600 college students—any student here can tell you the real truth about living in Davidson. What it boils down to is this: Davidson's setting offers, in many ways, the best of both worlds—small town and big city. The town of Davidson is, in itself, a tiny and quiet place, with weekends that usually hold more funerals than parties. It is undeniably quaint. The commercial center is located on Main Street (yeah, small town), which features a selection of family-run shops and businesses. However, Davidson's location also provides access to all the benefits of big-city entertainment, without the noise and clutter of a big-city campus. You see, if the 400-acre campus of ancient trees and red brick paths is cramping your style, and you've been through all the milkshakes and funerals you can handle, you always have good ol' Charlotte at your fingertips.

**C+**

The College Prowler™ Grade on
## Local Atmosphere: C+

A high Local Atmosphere grade indicates that the area surrounding campus is safe and scenic. Other factors include nearby attractions, proximity to other schools, and the town's attitude toward students.

# Safety & Security

## The Lowdown
### ON SAFETY & SECURITY

**Number of Police Officers:**
Six full time officers, seven part-time officers

**Phone:**
Non-emergency (704) 894-2178
Emergency 9-911
Officer Cellular Phone (704) 609-0344

**Health Center Office Hours:**
8:30 a.m. to 5:00 p.m.
Nurse on duty 7:30 a.m. to 9:30 p.m.

**Safety Services:**
First Responders (sexual abuse hotline), Rape Awareness Committee, emergency blue-phones, Risk Managers (students on duty at Patterson Court)

### Did You Know?
A student health counselor is on-call, available by beeper, for phone or face-to-face consultation or counseling during evenings, weekends, and holidays.

## Students Speak Out
### ON SAFETY & SECURITY

"Davidson's campus is extremely safe. I never felt threatened walking home alone late at night, nor have I felt worried about leaving my book bag sitting on a step outside."

Q "There is a myth that Davidson is its own little bubble, but it still exists in the real world, and although students follow a pretty strict Honor Code, the rest of the world doesn't. It would be wrong to say that the atmosphere at Davidson is 100 percent secure, but, overall, it **provides a comfortable, friendly college setting**."

Q "In addition to the campus security and police officers, the students look out for the security of one another and would call attention to a situation wherein another student could be in harm's way. Additionally, we have the blue-light system, police officers on bicycles, a **strong Honor Code, and escort services** that all attribute to the sense of security of our campus."

Q "The campus is safe, although there have been some recent thefts. **Students leave their doors unlocked** because they feel too safe. Students here are gullible like that."

Q "We have an Honor Code that is taken very seriously by students and faculty, so most students leave their doors unlocked and feel free to just leave book bags and other things in public places, knowing that they'll be there when they come back. Most crime that does occur is **instigated by people not associated with the college**."

Q Overall, the **campus is very safe**. However, there are incidents that do occur."

## The College Prowler Take
### ON SAFETY & SECURITY

Students at Davidson almost unanimously feel completely safe on campus. Whether in the dorms, at parties, or even walking around alone at night, there is little cause to worry about one's safety here—except for the presence of the occasional townie in a pickup truck who thinks he's Al Unser Jr.. The college grounds are well-lit and are patrolled regularly by campus police. Also, there is an extensive network of blue emergency phones that can be seen on all areas of campus. Even so, students attribute the majority of the school's security to an active and respected Honor Code. A cornerstone of life at Davidson, the Code is an unspoken agreement that students here will not lie, cheat, or steal during their four years on campus. While the system might sound a bit like 'Big Brother,' it is in fact just the opposite, providing a feeling of respect as opposed to fear.

**A+**

The College Prowler™ Grade on
### Safety & Security: A+

A high grade in Safety & Security means that students generally feel safe, campus police are visible, blue-light phones and escort services are readily available, and safety precautions are not overly necessary.

# Facilities

## The Lowdown ON FACILITIES

**Student Center:**
Alvarez Student Union in the Knobloch Campus Center

**Libraries:**
3

**Athletic Center:**
Baker Sports Complex
Student Union has a 24-hour workout room and climbing wall.

**Movie Theater on Campus?**
No, but the Union runs frequent midnight showings.

**Bar on Campus?**
900 Room serves alcohol once a week and additionally for concerts.

**Coffee on Campus?**
Union Cafe

**Popular Places to Chill:**
Union Cafe, Summit Coffee, hall lounges, Union patio, and Chambers lawn in the warm weather

## Computers

**High-Speed Network?**
Yes

**Wireless Network?**
Vail Commons, Library, Union, Sloan music building, Chambers

**Number of Labs:**
Three main labs, plus three additional labs devoted to sciences.

**Numbers of Computers:**
180 public

**24-Hour Labs:**
Belk 24-Hour, Student Computing Center

**Charge to Print?**
None

## Favorite Things to Do

The student-run Union Board hosts constant events throughout the year, including concerts, dances, coffeehouses, films, speakers, and special events (from pottery workshops to foam parties). The Union Cafe is a favorite student hangout. The Union Cafe is also open late Wednesday through Saturday. Additionally, students will head across Main Street to the shops and coffeehouses, which provide an off-campus getaway within walking distance!

Need help locating specific buildings on campus? For a detailed listing of the campus layout, check out the College Prowler book on Davidson available at *www.collegeprowler.com*.

## Students Speak Out
### ON FACILITIES

"Campus is beautiful with top-notch facilities. The student center is new and the academic buildings are being renovated. The athletic facility was built in the last 15 years."

"**Facilities on campus are some of the nicest** I've seen anywhere. Cambers, the main class building is undergoing major renovations to make it technologically up-to-date, and Baker Sports Complex is incredible for a small school. But the crown jewel is the Student Union. With the bookstore, post office, Union Cafe, weight room, climbing wall, offices for student organizations, wireless Internet access, state-of-the-art theater, and quiet corners to study, this has become the center of student life. Never a day goes by when I don't stop into the Union."

"The most **glaring void at Davidson is a late-night, weekend spot** to get some good 'drunk food.' We used to have one, but it got shut down to attract people to the new Union in order to please the Union's financiers. When isn't it all about the money?!"

"Davidson **definitely shows a long term dedication to growth and improvement** in its facilities. At the same time, Davidson cannot offer the same facilities that bigger schools can. During busy exam time, public computer labs fill up, and while the workout rooms are adequate for most people, it is not uncommon to hear the most serious athletes pining for larger facilities."

"**Davidson is not afraid to spend money.** The school is committed to making sure we have the best facilities, given the size of the student body and the limited donor pool. As a result, a lot of the facilities here are new, renovated, or simply well-maintained. It seems like practically every building has undergone renovation while I've been here. The renovation to the main academic building looks great so far, and has that wonderful new carpet smell. Eating houses and fraternities are also currently undergoing renovation."

## The College Prowler Take
### ON FACILITIES

For a small school, Davidson boasts some big-time facilities, many of them built within the past few years. Students consistently rave about the new Student Union, which provides an array of pool tables, work spaces, and inviting couches in a four-story, atrium atmosphere. The Union also houses a full-service post office, 24 hour workout room, and the state-of-the-art Duke Performance Hall. In addition, a brand-new music building opened last year, and the main academic building is currently in the process of a two-year renovation project. All new classrooms are equipped with computers and advanced digital projection systems. Finally, Davidson's status as an NCAA Division I school allows students access to athletic facilities that simply can't be found at schools of similar size. If you're looking for a small school atmosphere with bigger than average facilities, Davidson should certainly be on your list.

**The College Prowler™ Grade on**
### Facilities: A-

A high Facilities grade indicates that the campus is aesthetically pleasing and well-maintained; facilities are state-of-the-art, and libraries are exceptional. Other determining factors include the quality of both athletic and student centers and an abundance of things to do on campus.

# Campus Dining

## Students Speak Out
ON CAMPUS DINING

"There are only two places to eat on campus: Vail Commons Cafeteria and the Student Union Cafe. The cafeteria has tried to improve its food since I started as a freshman."

## The Lowdown
ON CAMPUS DINING

**Freshman Meal Plan Requirement?**
Yes

**24-Hour On-Campus Eating?**
No

**Meal Plan Average Cost:**
$3,479 (full board—19 meals)

**Other Options:**
The Wildcat Den is located in Baker Sports Complex, and offers sandwiches and smoothies Monday through Friday, 11:45 a.m. to 1:45 p.m.

### Did you know?

Most meal plans come with several hundred dollars worth of "Bonus Bucks," extra money that can be used toward purchasing meals.

Dining services even offers $50 extra Bonus Bucks to all students who submit their meal plans for the next semester ahead of schedule.

Q "However much students sometimes complain, the food in Commons [the cafeteria] and in the Union Cafe is edible in every sense of the word, and a number of dishes—Commons' soup, for example—are very, very good. The Union Cafe's monopoly on campus results in their dishes being ridiculously overpriced, however. I will say, though, that having a Commons meal plan for almost two years now has successfully made me more of a plant eater than I ever thought I'd become. **One good thing about Commons is the variety it offers**: personalized sandwiches, pizzas, quesadillas, a well-stocked salad bar, as well as their main day-to-day entrees."

Q "**The food is very good here**. Commons is decent, there's a cafe in the Student Union that gets really creative and has good food, although it's sometimes pricey, and there's a lunch place called the WildCat Den in the sports complex that is pretty good for sandwiches, smoothies, soup, etc. A little under half of the guys and about 75 percent of the girls join Greek organizations and eating houses, which have their own cooks."

Q "The **food is one of my few significant complaints about Davidson**. When I ate at Commons last year, I was frustrated by the lack of traditional dishes that they replaced with a diverse ethnic food selection. Also, for the meals I did like, the food was often not cooked properly, and, one time, I even found a long hair in my plate of fried okra. Food at my eating house is not much better—most of the time it is poor quality or not cooked well. The Union does not have a very wide selection."

Q "If the dinner menu is unappealing, there is a huge salad bar, a pizza bar, and a sandwich bar. I think the quality of food in **Union Cafe is better than in the cafeteria**."

## The College Prowler Take
### ON CAMPUS DINING

There simply is not too much to choose from in terms of on-campus dining at Davidson, as a few students didn't hesitate to point out. Vail Commons is the single cafeteria on campus, and the main place to use your meal plan (all freshmen are, in fact, required to buy 19 meals a week). Aside from Commons, students can use their meal plan at the Union Café, which serves a number of deli and grill options. Many students will also forgo the meal plan entirely, opting instead to eat at their fraternities or eating houses, which all employ their own cooks. Here the food tends to be substantially better than at Commons or the Café, but the selection is reduced.

Overall, it's easy to complain about food on campus, although most try to appreciate the variety that exists, given the relatively small number of students eating here. It's not impossible to enjoy on-campus dining at Davidson, but to do so usually involves taking it with a grain of salt.

**The College Prowler™ Grade on**
## Campus Dining: C-

Our grade on Campus Dining addresses the quality of both school-owned dining halls and independent on-campus restaurants as well as the price, availability, and variety of food.

# Campus Housing

## The Lowdown
### ON CAMPUS HOUSING

**Undergrads on Campus:**
100%

**Number of Residence Halls/Houses:**
11

**Number of College-Owned Apartments:**
6

**Room Types:**
Single, Double, Triple, Suite (Duke: two adjoining rooms; Tomlinson: two rooms with common room and bathroom), Pod (eight singles with common room and two bathrooms), Apartment (four to five singles with living room, kitchen and bathroom)

**Available for Rent:**
Micro-fridge

**Cleaning Service?**
Public areas only

**You Get:**
Bed, dresser, desk, Internet access, phone line

**Bed-Type:**
Twin extra-long; most can be bunked

**Also Available:**
Smoke-free, substance-free

## Students Speak Out
### ON CAMPUS HOUSING

"Some dorms at Davidson are really cool. Sentelle and Duke offer spacious rooms for upperclassmen. And down the hill, dorms are noted for their close proximity to Patterson Court, which can be a good and bad thing."

Q "Dorms are in **pretty good shape, but they lack character and are overpriced**. You cannot paint the walls like you can at many schools even if you return it to its original color or pay a fee. You're not technically allowed to nail anything into the walls, but people do it anyway—with the unfortunate result that walls end up looking like look like a teenager with bad acne. Exteriorly, the buildings are red brick; structurally, they are generally rectangular. This means they are simple and certainly look nice, but perhaps lack the character of older buildings at other schools."

Q "The **dorms at Davidson are top-notch**. I avoided the sophomore apartments due to the walk and the noise, but know plenty of people who had a blast there. Now I'm completely thrilled with my senior apartment, and pretty convinced I never want to live anywhere else. We're located in the west side of Hart. We also have the best view on the entire campus from our third story porch. From here Davidson looks like a tiny little city at night."

Q "The better dorms are opened up to students after they have finished their freshman year. I lived in Richardson my freshman year and it was pretty crappy all around, but since then **I lived in Sentelle for two years, which was great**, and now I live in the senior apartments, also great."

## The College Prowler Take
### ON CAMPUS HOUSING

As over 90 percent of Davidson students live on campus all four years, dorm quality is a pretty important aspect of Davidson life to take into consideration. Fortunately, while complaining about dorms on any college campus is common, the majority of Davidson's accommodations make it difficult to do so with any real sincerity. After three years of dorm living, seniors are welcomed into the college-operated Senior Apartments, which are more than spacious, with **private living rooms, kitchens, and even porches**. While there are certainly downsides to dorms at Davidson, for many it's ultimately a matter of preference. Dorms at Davidson might not be palaces, but for small-school, campus-owned housing, you'll feel like a king on a throne.

**A-**

The College Prowler™ Grade on
## Campus Housing: A-

A high Campus Housing grade indicates that dorms are clean, well-maintained, and spacious. Other determining factors include variety of dorms, proximity to classes, and social atmosphere.

# Diversity

## The Lowdown ON DIVERSITY

**Native American:** 0%

**Asian American:** 2%

**African American:** 5%

**White:** 87%

**Hispanic:** 3%

**International:** 3%

**Unknown:** 0%

**Out-of-State:** 78%

### Minority Clubs
The Black Student Coalition is one of the largest minority organizations, as well as the International Student Association.

### Political Activity
Davidson provides an interesting blend of Bible-beating young Republicans with a large liberal minority. While political sentiment on campus is not overwhelming, campus political organizations and their ringleaders are certainly a visible force.

### Most Popular Religions
By far, most students are Christian (predominantly Protestant, some Catholic), although there is an active Jewish student organization and small Buddhist minority.

### Gay Tolerance
Davidson is not what you would call gay-friendly. There are a few openly gay students who get along fine, but it is not atypical for them to feel separated, and even ostracized from the straight community.

### Economic Status
While the stereotype that most kids at Davidson are upper-middle-class is generally true, there are also plenty of kids from various economic backgrounds, many paying their own way.

## Students Speak Out ON DIVERSITY

"**Davidson is a small, conservative, southern school. I think this probably deters a lot of students from visiting. The lack of diversity around here is definitely not exaggerated.**"

"Davidson is not visibly diverse. The campus has an overwhelmingly large white majority, though there are a good number of black students, some Hispanics, and some Asians. Also, **almost everyone is straight—we have very few openly gay students**. I would say that Davidson has a lot of intellectual diversity, though. People come from a variety of backgrounds and experiences. Also, it seems that everyone exercises."

"For a college of only 1,600 students, Davidson does have its share of diversity, but nothing outstanding. Although, for such a small school in such a small town, **I'm amazed at how many international students we have**. The majority of the students are white, middle-class Americans, but Davidson has clubs, accommodations, and resources for most religions, ethnicities, etc. I think Davidson does its best at trying to recruit and accept a diverse student body—it's just too small."

> "Davidson is relatively diverse. But, **within the diversity there is self-segregation**. If you need an example, just go and sit in Commons for a couple of meals—you will see all types of people there, as diverse as you could want, but they will all be sitting with each other. It is kind of ironic, actually."

## The College Prowler Take
**ON DIVERSITY**

If Davidson consistently fields one criticism as an institution, this is it. Diversity is as frequent a concern on campus as it is a hot topic, resurfacing in conversations among students and admissions officials alike. Each semester, *The Davidsonian*, the student-run newspaper, prints multiple articles addressing issues of diversity on campus, all proceeding from one basic conclusion: there simply isn't enough of it. The numbers, in fact, reflect this, with just above 12 percent of the student body composed of racial minorities each year. At a school of 1,600, that's a little fewer than 200 people. For many minorities on campus, the lack of diversity is an everyday challenge. Minority students continually express concerns that their sole purpose at Davidson is to make the school look good, or that they're only a number or a statistic. Others say that the school is not truly dedicated the issue, nor willing to shed its "white Christian male" foundations. However, the great variety of individuals and ideas present on campus makes Davidson seem a great deal more 'diverse' than the numbers might indicate.

**D-**

The College Prowler™ Grade on
## Diversity: D-
A high grade in Diversity indicates that ethnic minorities and international students have a notable presence on campus and that students of different economic backgrounds, religious beliefs, and sexual preferences are well-represented.

# Guys & Girls

## The Lowdown
**ON GUYS & GIRLS**

**Women Undergrads:** 50%

**Men Undergrads:** 50%

### Birth Control Available?
Yes, at Student Health Center. Condoms supplied free by Student Health are stocked in first aid cabinets in every hall on campus.

### Social Scene
The students at Davidson are, for the most part, very outgoing and friendly. Despite this, and perhaps because everyone is also so busy with school work, it's typical here to get sucked into a small group of friends and stop meeting people. Most remedy this situation with drunken encounters on Patterson Court, but there are also plenty of "alcohol-free" opportunities out there as well.

## Hookups or Relationships?

It's one or the other with very little in between—you'll likely hear many on campus complaining about the lack of casual dating here. It's pretty common to see couples who date exclusively all four years, and probably just as common to hear that a friend hooked up randomly last weekend. Casual dating is hard to find, and usually (unfortunately) when someone asks someone else out, people assume more of a long-term interest than is often possible at the college level. Needless to say, the whole phenomenon adds to the dating tension, and a lot of people opt to get together only for one night.

## Dress Code

While not excessively so, Davidson is a preppy school. Students, guys and girls alike, take pride in their appearance. Take a look around in any given class, and you'll most definitely see students who put some effort into looking their best that morning. Clean shirts, pressed pants, and decent shoes are par for the course. The fact that all Davidson students have their clothes washed free of charge, and as often as they want, at the college laundry tends to help. Davidson isn't the only school that does this; unfortunately, the other two happen to be military academies.

At the same time, this doesn't mean everyone on campus is a fashion snob. It is not uncommon for students to roll out of their beds and into class in their sandals and pajama bottoms. With the workload here, and the lack of sleep that comes along with it, you'll certainly understand why. In general though, Davidson students will make sure they leave enough time to iron their polo shirts and jeans between study breaks.

## Students Speak Out
### ON GUYS & GIRLS

"Overall, students are preppy, although some to a greater extent than others. There are definitely those who don't fit the mold. I would say that this is an attractive campus with people who care about their appearance."

"I frequently comment to my friends when I go home for the holidays that the world seems to get a lot more attractive as soon as I leave Davidson's campus. I don't think this is actually true, but because Davidson is so small, I am used to the overall appearance of the students at Davidson. In a sense, dating someone at Davidson would be like 'inbreeding.' Also, the close community of Davidson makes it seem that **everybody is in everybody else's business**."

"There are **two types of relationships at Davidson: 'the marriage' and the 'hookup.'** You're either in an ultra-serious relationship, or you prefer one-night stands. Either way, the dating scene at Davidson is practically non-existent. I have found dating people off-campus much easier and more practical."

"The guys here are pretty cool. I spend the majority of my time with the boys from upstairs, and I like hanging out with them. The girls on my hall are super sweet and the coolest people ever. So far, I have found that most of the people I have met are very friendly. And yes the **guys on our campus are very, very good-looking**."

"I think **Davidson girls fall into one of four categories**: first, there are girls who are not too attractive, but fun to hang out with. Second, you have your girls who are attractive in the 'girl next door' kind of way. Third, we have the southern-belle-type beauties—praise the Lord! Lastly, there is the rare beauty who could be a model on any runway, anywhere."

> "Overall, I would say that Davidson is a pretty good-looking campus, and a very fit campus. **I wouldn't use the word 'hot' for many of the students**, but there are the exceptions. The guys I do know are very friendly and sincere, and the girls are also. Davidson is not the hottest college campus in the United States, but in terms of outstanding and interesting people, it's full of them."

## The College Prowler Take
### ON GUYS & GIRLS

Here's an interesting phenomenon: Davidson students can never seem to decide whether the student body is hot or not. Even so, while many won't hesitate to point out that the selection here doesn't compare to bigger schools (UNC, NC State), most still feel students here are pretty attractive, considering the limited number of people of the opposite sex. Maybe it's the climate, maybe it's the easygoing southern atmosphere, but there is some merit to the old saying, "The girls are prettier down south." As it turns out, the boys aren't so bad either. In terms of dating these people, however, the consensus is largely that it's an all or nothing venture—either hook up once, or get married. So, if you're inspired by either one of those options, you shouldn't have too much trouble here.

# Athletics

## The Lowdown
### ON ATHLETICS

**Men's Varsity Teams:**
Baseball
Basketball
Cross Country
Football
Golf
Soccer
Swimming & Diving
Track & Field
Tennis
Wrestling

**Women's Teams:**
Basketball
Cross Country
Field Hockey
Lacrosse
Soccer
Swimming & Diving
Track & Field
Tennis
Volleyball

### Club Sports
Crew, Fencing, Field Hockey, Lacrosse, Rugby, Sailing, Men's Soccer, Women's Soccer, Tennis, Ultimate Frisbee, Water Skiing

### Intramurals
Flickerball, 3-on-3 Basketball, 5-on-5 Basketball, Indoor Soccer, Volleyball, Softball, Small Field Soccer

### Most Popular Sports
The biggest varsity sports are football and men's basketball, although men's soccer also receives praise and draws a decent crowd.

### Overlooked Teams
Swimming, Track & Field, Cross-Country

---

**B+**

**The College Prowler™ Grade on Guys: B+**

A high grade for Guys indicates that the male population on campus is attractive, smart, friendly, and engaging, and that the school has a decent ratio of guys to girls.

**B**

**The College Prowler™ Grade on Girls: B**

A high grade for Girls not only implies that the women on campus are attractive, smart, friendly, and engaging, but also that there is a fair ratio of girls to guys.

**Athletic Division:**
NCAA Division I (except football—I AA)

**Conference:**
Southern (predominantly)

**School Mascot:**
The Wildcat

**Fields:**
Richardson Stadium, Baseball field, Soccer field, Intramural fields, Field Hockey field, Football practice field, Soccer practice field, Lacrosse field

**Getting Tickets:**
Tickets are widely available and free for all Davidson students.

## Students Speak Out
### ON ATHLETICS

"While many people at Davidson play sports because the school is Division I, I'd say Davidson is much more academically focused."

Q "I have found athletics to be a large part of campus life. **Almost everyone is active athletically in some way** or another while at school. Whether they work out on their own, play IM sports, club sports, or varsity sports, the student body is very active. The student body is also very supportive of each other and of the athletes. I found that many of my friends played sports in high school or college and therefore understand the type of hard work and commitment I put into playing a D-I sport."

Q "Athletics is an area for improvement. **School support for most events is not spectacular**. While we tend to be very competitive in most of our sports, students find themselves too busy with school work or other activities to attend. However, our college president, Bobby Vagt, can always be counted on to be the most vocal fan around."

Q "A lot of people participate in intramural leagues. **Varsity sports are supported pretty enthusiastically**. The soccer team went to the NCAA tournament this year and draws a big crowd, as does basketball, which plays big names like Duke, UNC, and some others. Football varies from year to year. Davidson is one of the smallest schools playing in Division I, but our teams usually hold their own."

Q "As one of the smallest Division I schools, the popularity of varsity sports **varies from sport to sport**. Football is usually a popular means to procrastinate from work on Saturday afternoons, while recent successes in women's volleyball, men's basketball, and men's soccer have vied for large crowds as well. Intramural sports are nearly as popular as some varsity sports. Flickerball, the most popular of the IMs, is always being played around campus."

## The College Prowler Take
### ON ATHLETICS

As the student body has already mentioned, Davidson is unique in its position as one of the smallest schools participating in NCAA Division I sports—and the whole University takes pride in its "Davidson vs. Goliath" role. If students aren't among the 25 percent playing a varsity sport, chances are they're participating in club or intramural teams, or out in the stands rooting everyone else on. The quintessential student-athlete is in fact a Davidson student-athlete, and all athletes here are held very much to the same academic standards as any other student. If you're seeking a highly selective liberal arts college and the highest level of athletic competition around, you'll be hard-pressed to find a better option than Davidson.

**B**

The College Prowler™ Grade on
## Athletics: B

A high grade in Athletics indicates that students have school spirit, that sports programs are respected, that games are well-attended, and that intramurals are a prominent part of student life.

# Greek Life

## The Lowdown ON GREEK LIFE

**Number of Fraternities:**
8

**Number of Sororities:**
No sororities, but five "Eating Houses"

**Undergrad Men in Fraternities:**
37%

**Undergrad Women in Eating Houses:**
77%

**Multicultural Colonies:**
Black Student Coalition

**Other Greek Organizations:**
Patterson Court Council, Order of Omega

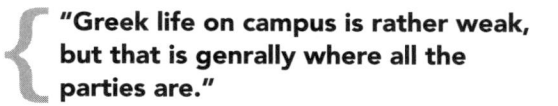

## Students Speak Out ON GREEK LIFE

"Greek life on campus is rather weak, but that is genrally where all the parties are."

Q "Greek life is good at Davidson. Although we don't have sororities, instead opting for the local eating house system, we do have fraternities. I wish that the system were equal, either frats and sororities, or eating houses for everyone. **I don't think it dominates the social scene**, however. Going out is just as much fun, whether you're a member of a house or not. Plus, restrictions on housing means that an entire hall won't be made up of people from a single house, which maintains inter-house relationships."

Q "What Greek life? We have some JV fraternities, true, but we all have friends at big schools, and we all know that frat life at Davidson is a far cry from the experience we hear about or have seen in movies [like] "Animal House", "Old School", [or] "PCU". We also have eating houses, not sororities, and they **really aren't that much like real sororities**."

Q "Davidson has fraternities for the men, and eating houses for the women. There are no sororities. The eating houses are exactly like sororities, but they are not nationally affiliated and they are self selected—the girls just choose their house. The **Greek life definitely does not dominate the social scene**. The close community of Davidson allows people who are not in an eating house or fraternity to participate in the parties that these organizations hold."

Q "The social and party life of Davidson revolves around Patterson Court. About half of the student body—maybe more—either belongs to a fraternity or an eating house. Lots of **people who aren't Patterson Court members attend their functions**. There is much more of a stigma towards males who don't join fraternities than towards females who don't join eating houses."

## The College Prowler Take
### ON GREEK LIFE

There's one motto that is extremely on-point when it comes to the social scene at Davidson College: we study hard and we play hard. Greek life provides a big part of the latter part of the phrase, with nearly 40 percent of males pledging fraternities, and 80 percent of women self-selecting into eating houses. Students are in agreement, however, that while Greek life is clearly present, it's not overwhelming, and affiliation is certainly not required if you want to have a good time on campus. There are plenty of other ways you'll have a good time on weekends while you're here. However, access to a car is essential in getting to many social events off-campus—but that's another story.

## Drug Scene

## The Lowdown
### ON DRUG SCENE

**B-**

**The College Prowler™ Grade on**
## Greek Life: B-

A high grade in Greek Life indicates that sororities and fraternities are not only present, but also active on campus. Other determining factors include the variety of houses available and the respect the Greek community receives from the rest of the campus.

**Most Prevalent Drugs on Campus:**
Marijuana

**Liquor-Related Referrals:**
121

**Liquor-Related Arrests:**
73

**Drug-Related Referrals:**
26

**Drug-Related Arrests:**
6

**Drug Counseling Programs:**
The College Health Center provides counseling.

## Students Speak Out
### ON DRUG SCENE

{ "Depending on the kind of narcotic, Davidson's drug scene is veiled very well. The chronic pot heads are fairly easy to weed out—no pun intended."

Q "I've heard rumors of a sizeable amount of cocaine users at Davidson, and many students are wealthy enough to be able to afford it. It is partly due to academic stress and the need to perform, but I don't know anyone who routinely uses cocaine or heavier drugs at school. **I've witnessed very little stigmatization in regards to drug use** on campus. In fact, I've witnessed more stigmatization toward smokers—I have experienced criticism myself—than I have seen people judge or criticize those who do drugs. 'Live and let live' seems to be most people's approach here."

Q "On campus, I never saw any drug use, but I assume certain kids were probably smoking pot. **I have not heard of the use of any harder drugs** at all."

Q "From what I've experienced, there isn't much of a drug scene on campus. I have never been offered marijuana at Davidson and have not even heard about the use of more hardcore drugs. **I was exposed to more drugs in high school** than I have been in college. I've talked to people who say they sometimes smoke weed, but I've never seen anyone doing it."

Q "I'm a bit naïve, so I didn't realize that there was a drug scene **until I spent time with some frat guys** last year."

Q "I have many friends who recreationally smoke marijuana, and a few who have done more heavy-duty drugs in the past, like Ecstasy, LSD, or cocaine, but they **keep their habits fairly quiet**."

## The College Prowler Take
### ON DRUG SCENE

While students realize drugs are available on campus, most agree that you won't hear much about them, unless you actively seek them out. Marijuana is most widely used, while harder drugs appear much more infrequently. Often students complain about the smell of reefer wafting through the halls of a few of the dorms (Richardson, Watts), but other than that, there's really not much of a problem.

Generally speaking, Davidson is much more of an alcohol campus than a drug campus, and most narcotics use takes place pretty discretely. Even so, it's not that infrequent to hear about kids getting busted in dorm rooms or basements of frat houses, usually for smoking weed. While drugs are available to those who want them, you definitely won't be bothered by any sort of drug culture on campus if you don't want to be.

**A-**

The College Prowler™ Grade on
### Drug Scene: A-

A high grade on Drug Scene indicates that drugs are not a noticeable part of campus life; drug use is not visible, and no pressure to use them seems to exist.

# Overall Experience

"In a way, **I do wish that I was somewhere else**—going to a college with less work, in a city with tons of people and many places to go on the weekend. But, if I had to do it again, I would still choose Davidson. The workload is really overwhelming, and it's easy to lose sight of the 'real world' apart from Davidson, but the friendships I have made and the opportunities that have stemmed from being a student here outweigh the stress of work—well, almost!"

## Students Speak Out
### ON OVERALL EXPERIENCE

"I don't think that I could have found a better place. Davidson offers everything a college should. With the support from the faculty, student body, and administration, it is easier to succeed here than at most places."

"I've had a fantastic experience at Davidson. I think it suits me perfectly. By Parents' Weekend of freshman year, I was so happy that I hadn't ended up at any of the Ivies that I'd applied to. **Davidson offers a wonderful, welcoming community, a fabulous education**, and a student body with the highest quality of personal character that I've seen anywhere."

"Davidson has certainly been a challenge. **I have frequently felt frustrated at the lack of a social scene**, and I have often found that many students lack open-mindedness. However, I also realize that the education my professors have given me is top-notch. I would not trade my experience at Davidson for anything. I think that experiences are made up of good and bad. The classroom experience has certainly been much more than I ever dreamed, but Davidson has also taught me a lot about myself. It represents what I believe in, and persuades me to stand up for what I think is right. I am proud of the person I have become, and I thank Davidson for making me this way."

## The College Prowler Take
### ON OVERALL EXPERIENCE

When assessing whether or not Davidson is a good school for you, it's important to determine how the pros and cons line up with your own expectations for your college experience. Don't come here expecting the endless beer-fests you'll find at larger state schools—there's not an endless stream of alcohol running through this place. Don't come here expecting a student body with great ethnic and socioeconomic diversity, as this isn't exactly New York City. Lastly, don't come here expecting enormous, big school athletics and athletic facilities, or a 70,000-seat stadium, because the sports teams just aren't as competitive here as they are at larger schools.

What you can expect at Davidson, however, is an outstanding community of students who respect and trust each other. You can expect a sprawling green campus, far disproportionate to the school's size. You can expect a good Division I athletic program, with a Division I caliber sports complex. You can expect a cozy, small town setting, and a sprawling neighboring city. You can expect to have a good time while drinking and partying. You can expect some good-looking guys and some good-looking gals. You can expect a lake. Most of all, you can expect top-notch academics, from top-notch professors taught in top-notch facilities, which all contribute to an interactive and personal learning experience that's simply unparalleled. There's a lot to look forward to at Davidson. And, you'll find when you graduate, even more to look back on.

# Duke University

**DISTANCE TO...**
Atlanta: 382 mi.
Raleigh: 30 mi.
Charlotte: 142 mi.
Richmond: 155 mi.

2138 Campus Drive, Box 90586, Durham, NC 27708
www.duke.edu  (919) 684-3214

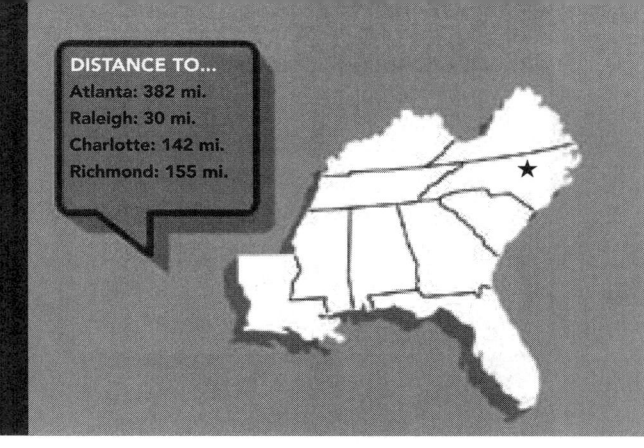

*"People should be informed that, at Duke, there is, in fact, life outside of March Madness."*

**Total Enrollment:**
6,169

**Top 10% of High School Class:**
88%

**Average GPA:**
3.9

**Acceptance Rate:**
25%

**Tuition:**
$30,720

**SAT Range (25th-75th Percentile)**
| Verbal | Math | Total |
|---|---|---|
| 660 – 770 | 670 – 750 | 1330 – 1520 |

**ACT Range (25th-75th Percentile)**
| Verbal | Math | Total |
|---|---|---|
| 28-33 | 29-34 | 29-34 |

**Most Popular Majors:**
18% Economics
9% Public Policy Analysis
8% Biology
8% Psychology
7% Political Science and Government

**Students also applied to:***
University of North Carolina
University of Virginia
University of Pennsylvania
Cornell University
Northwestern University

*For more school info check out www.collegeprowler.com

## Table of Contents

| | |
|---|---|
| Academics | 440 |
| Local Atmosphere | 442 |
| Safety & Security | 443 |
| Facilities | 445 |
| Campus Dining | 447 |
| Campus Housing | 448 |
| Diversity | 450 |
| Guys & Girls | 452 |
| Athletics | 454 |
| Greek Life | 456 |
| Drug Scene | 457 |
| Overall Experience | 458 |

## College Prowler Report Card

| | |
|---|---|
| Academics | A |
| Local Atmosphere | C |
| Safety & Security | C |
| Facilities | A- |
| Campus Dining | B+ |
| Campus Housing | B |
| Diversity | B+ |
| Guys | B+ |
| Girls | B |
| Athletics | A- |
| Greek Life | A |
| Drug Scene | B |

# Academics

## The Lowdown
### ON ACADEMICS

**Degrees Awarded:**
Bachelor, Master, Doctoral, Post Bachelor Certificate, First Professional

**Undergraduate Schools:**
Trinity College of Arts & Sciences, Pratt School of Engineering, School of Nursing

**Tenure/Tenure-track Faculty:**
1,498

**Other Faculty:**
866

**Faculty with Terminal Degree:**
93%

**Student-to-Faculty Ratio:**
9:1

**Average Course Load:**
12-15 credits (4-5 classes)

**AP Test Score Requirements:**
Possible credit for scores of 4 or 5

**IB Test Score Requirements:**
Possible credit for scores of 6 or 7

## Special Degree Options
Program II. Unlike Program I, which is the basic Trinity program, this is more of a create-your-own major. More information about this can be found at http://www.aas.duke.edu/trinity/program2/

## Sample Academic Clubs/Unions
American Society of Civil Engineers (ASCE): *http://www.duke.edu/web/ASCE/*

Biology Majors Union: *http://www.duke.edu/web/biomajors/*

PreMed Society: *http://www.duke.edu/web/premed/*

For a complete list of Duke clubs, and organizations, visit *http://www.duke.edu/org/org.html*

### Did You Know?
The Vice Provost for Interdisciplinary Studies works with faculty members and administrators across the University to support interdisciplinary research, collaboration, and instruction on Duke's Strategic Plan: "Building on Excellence."

**Best Places to Study:**
Your room, Lilly Library (East Campus), a comfy corner in the Bryan Center, the Sanford Building, Perkins Library (West Campus), your dorm bench, East or West Campus Quad

## Students Speak Out
### ON ACADEMICS

"My teachers have all seemed genuinely interested in teaching undergrads. Many of them have their own research going on the side, but I don't sense that it detracts from the quality of their classes."

"**The professors are, for the most part, amazing**. They know their subjects inside and out, but, better yet, are willing to help you understand, piece by piece, what they know. The classes don't just skim over things, but rather, make you go in-depth and have you learn things that you just wouldn't learn in a standard lecture."

"I found the professors to be very down-to-earth, and always willing to help. **They were all very accessible**, and seemed willing and able to do whatever it took in order for their students to succeed. I did find most of my classes interesting, even if it was in an area that I thought I had little interest. I think that's a tribute to the professors themselves; they have ways of making the material interesting."

"**The faculty at Duke is a mixed bag**. I've had great professors, and some that were really horrible. I guess it depends on your major, because most of the liberal arts people I know are happy with their teachers. I'm an economics and computer science major, and with two exceptions, all my professors have sucked royally."

"**The teachers are among the best I've encountered anywhere**. In my first year, many of my professors, especially in the science and engineering departments, seemed genuinely interested in fully enriching their students' academic experience at Duke. They tend to offer a very general, but intellectually challenging, presentation of the material. There are, of course, exceptions."

## The College Prowler Take
### ON ACADEMICS

Students at Duke seem to find the academic experience pretty satisfying on the whole, thanks in large part to their teachers. This is not to say that everything about Duke academics is peachy; some of the math and science teachers certainly sound like they could liven up a little. There is also the age-old problem of distinguished teachers who are there for the research facilities and not much else. However, these professors can be a remarkable asset if they choose to involve students in their research—which many are willing, able, and even thrilled to do. Even lecture classes need not be survival-only. Many lecturers take special care to get to know students one-on-one, and lectures will almost always have a lab or a discussion group taught by student TAs, where students get more personal attention.

Although all Duke professors are well-educated and established in their field, most students will tell you that the teachers here do their best to relay their knowledge to the students in a way that is easily comprehensible, yet challenging at the same time. With a few notable exceptions, teachers are excited about their subjects and, more importantly, about teaching what they know to their students. In general, Duke's professors play a vital role in the quality and success of its academics.

**The College Prowler™ Grade on**
### Academics: A

A high Academics grade generally indicates that professors are knowledgeable, accessible, and genuinely interested in their students' welfare. Other determining factors include class size, how well professors communicate, and whether or not classes are engaging.

# Local Atmosphere

## The Lowdown
ON LOCAL ATMOSPHERE

**Region:**
Southeast

**City, State:**
Durham, North Carolina

**Setting:**
Suburban

**Major Sports Teams:**
Durham Bulls (Minor League Baseball), Carolina Courage (Women's Soccer)

**City Websites:**
http://triangle.citysearch.com/
http://www.durham-nc.com

## Students Speak Out
ON LOCAL ATMOSPHERE

"Durham is one big bore. However, Chapel Hill is nice because it's a town built around a large university. Duke makes its own social scene since Durham doesn't provide one."

Q "There are two colleges near Durham. One is 15 minutes away in Chapel Hill [University of North Carolina], and the other is 20 minutes away in Raleigh [NC State]. Durham has the Durham Bulls baseball team, **the Carolina Hurricanes play nearby**, and all of the college basketball teams in the area are stellar, so sports are huge. There's also a cool museum in Raleigh. There's plenty to do in and around campus."

Q "**Duke and Durham are almost two completely separate worlds**. Durham is a rather small city, and it isn't a typical college town. Don't expect to find the same culture or entertainment options you'd see in New York or Boston. Wandering into the wrong sections of town will leave you in a high-crime, low-income area. I tend to spend most of my time on campus, unless I'm headed out for dinner and a movie."

Q "Durham is a friendly southern city with the **amenities of big-city living**. Some good places to go are Ninth Street, for shopping and dining, the new mall, and the streets at Southpoint. Seven miles west of Durham is Chapel Hill, which is more of a college town and has more things to do on Franklin Street."

Q "**The atmosphere is really cool and diverse**. Restaurants are great; there's a lot to do. You could have an awesome social life without ever leaving campus."

## The College Prowler Take
### ON LOCAL ATMOSPHERE

As much as the students love Duke, there are some shortcomings that simply cannot be overlooked. The atmosphere, or lack thereof, is at the top of the list. At the beginning of freshman year, student life officials herd all the first year students into the commons room, and do their best to scare everyone out of ever wandering around Durham alone. While East Campus is not situated near the nicest part of Durham, there are some nice, quiet little residential areas around East Campus, as well as some adequate shopping centers and restaurants within driving distance.

If you're looking for a college town, Chapel Hill is about 20 minutes away and really does live up to that description quite nicely. Duke and UNC provide a free bus back and forth everyday, which many students take advantage of. Honestly, other than Ninth Street, Durham has little in the way of atmosphere to offer the students. And that's no bull!

### The College Prowler™ Grade on
## Local Atmosphere: C

A high Local Atmosphere grade indicates that the area surrounding campus is safe and scenic. Other factors include nearby attractions, proximity to other schools, and the town's attitude toward students.

# Safety & Security

## The Lowdown
### ON SAFETY & SECURITY

**Number of Duke Police:**
51 sworn police officers, and 51 non-sworn security officers

**Police Phone:**
(919) 684-2444 (non-emergency)

**Police Website:**
http://www.duke.edu/web/police/

**Health Center Hours:**
By appointment Monday-Friday 8:30 a.m.-5:30 p.m.

**Health Center Phone:**
(919) 681-9355

### Safety Services
Card-only access to dorms, same-sex keyed bathrooms, Safe Rides (Dusk-to-Dawn Escort Service) (919) 684-7233, blue-light phones, safety lighting, self-defense classes

### Health Services
Allergy clinic, cold/flu/allergy self-help tables, gynecological services, health education, health exams, HIV counseling and testing, laboratory, medical care, nutritional counseling, pharmacy, physical therapy, substance abuse education, travel/immunization clinic, X-rays

## Students Speak Out
### ON SAFETY & SECURITY

"I got my car stolen sophomore year, but that's because I was an idiot. The guy got arrested before I even knew it was stolen. If you're on campus, you'll feel completely safe. The ghetto lingers, but it's not that bad."

Q "I've never really felt unsafe on campus. The University has its own campus police, and there are phones scattered across campus to call for help if you need it. You'll need a student ID in order to enter any of the dorms. **Most other buildings require ID on nights and weekends**. Unlike some schools, officers don't regularly guard campus or building entrances. We had a few sexual assault reports last year, but I don't know if it's higher than average or not."

Q "There are numerous problems with Duke Gardens at night—you'd walk through this area to cross from West Campus to Central Campus. Two of my friends got robbed at gunpoint twice doing just that. **More than a little caution is necessary**."

Q "I've never had a problem with feeling safe on campus. Although **Durham has a bad reputation for safety**, Duke has its own police force on campus, and I know they patrol frequently. I'd say that if someone uses common sense, he or she should generally be safe."

Q "**Security has beefed up a lot lately**, but there were some problems in the past. One student was attacked in a dorm bathroom, and another was attacked in a library bathroom. Cars are sometimes broken into, and there have been a few muggings at night when students have been walking alone. So just use common sense, and you should be safe."

## The College Prowler Take
### ON SAFETY & SECURITY

Most Duke students seem to feel pretty secure on campus, and Duke has worked hard to provide students with the utmost safety and comfort. They've taken many necessary steps that are now standard on many college campuses, like carded-entry to dorms and other facilities. Students are also briefed on methods for getting anyone out of the dorm who they don't think should be there. The bathrooms are also locked and the bathroom keys will open only the same-sex bathroom in your dorm. The campus itself almost always has people milling about at any time, and you don't have to feel uncomfortable walking on the main campuses late at night, but, as always, you should use the intelligence that God gave you. The administration also likes to keep students updated on safety and security measures. However, Duke is not in a very attractive area of Durham. Walking alone off campus is foolish, as there are occasionally thefts and robberies that occur in the area.

### The College Prowler™ Grade on
### Safety & Security: C

A high grade in Safety & Security means that students generally feel safe, campus police are visible, blue-light phones and escort services are readily available, and safety precautions are not overly necessary.

# Facilities

## The Lowdown
ON FACILITIES

**Student Center:**
The Bryan Center ("the BC")

**Athletic Centers:**
West Campus—Wilson Recreation Center
East Campus—Brodie Recreation Center

**Libraries:**
Perkins (West Campus), Lilly (East Campus), Music Library (East Campus), Vesic Library for Engineering, Math, and Physics (Science Drive), Biological and Environmental Sciences Library (Science Drive), Chemistry Library (Science Drive)

**Movie Theatre on Campus?**
Yes, Griffith Film Theater is in the BC.

**Bowling on Campus?**
No

**Billiards on Campus?**
Yes, there is one table in the BC lounge.

**Bar on Campus?**
No

**Coffeehouse on Campus?**
Yes, there are several around campus.

**Popular Places to Chill:**
Main quads, your dorm bench, BC couches

### Computers
**High-Speed Network?** Yes
**Wireless Network?** Yes
**Number of Labs:** 19
**Number of Computers:** 340
**24-Hour Labs:** All labs are open 24 hours
**Charge to Print?** No

### Favorite Things to Do
If you can find a DUI (Duke University Improv) performance, go to it! Duke's a cappella groups are also great, and there are some really amazing dance groups in a bunch of different styles. Local Colour, Duke's spoken word group, is also worth going to see. Plays can sometimes be an aesthetically rewarding experience. Movies in the Griffith Film Theater are either cheap or free, and they show some amazing films from time to time.

---

**COLLEGE PROWLER™**

Just how good are student facilities at Duke? Find out all you need to know about recreation centers on Duke's campus in the guidebook available at *www.collegeprowler.com*.

## Students Speak Out
### ON FACILITIES

"The recreation center is excellent, the computer labs are above average—they just renovated some of them—and the student center is okay."

"The gym on West Campus is extremely nice. **They have enough treadmills and elliptical machines to keep the cardio folks happy**, and the weight room is positively superb. Free weights, machines, whatever your pleasure is—it's available and in good condition. Throw in a few racquetball courts, basketball courts, a pool, and a juice bar, and you've got a very high-quality fitness center."

"The exterior of practically every building at Duke is breathtaking; old and Gothic, or Georgian, new and innovative. **The inside sometimes doesn't evoke the same pleasant adjectives**, particularly in the older buildings. The buildings on East Campus are nice, but the ones on West Campus are somewhat dark and cramped. All of the newer buildings I have seen are great, and the athletic buildings are made in the mode of shrines and palaces for kings."

"Every facility is at a different level of quality. As expected, the newer and recently renovated buildings are the nicest, while the **older buildings, with their grungy basements**, are the worst. The dining facilities are all excellent. The student center is great, but it's difficult to navigate."

"**All the facilities here are top-notch**. The gym on the East Campus is good; the gym on the West Campus is excellent. Lots of machines and free weights are always available, and we have an indoor pool and lots of tennis and basketball courts, both indoors and out."

## The College Prowler Take
### ON FACILITIES

Overall, Duke is a beautiful campus, and all the buildings are well-kept. The original buildings are just stunning—but, for reasons that baffle scientists and philosophers alike, they decided to build some of the newer ones in a neo-Gothic and neo-Georgian architectural style. Inside, though, the newer buildings are much nicer than the older buildings. Perkins, for example, could seriously use heavy renovation followed by some redecorating. The athletic centers are really quite pleasant and well-kept. Despite the griping and minor complaints, Duke students seem to be aware they have some nice facilities, and they try not to take them for granted.

**A-**

The College Prowler™ Grade on
### Facilities: A-

A high Facilities grade indicates that the campus is aesthetically pleasing and well-maintained; facilities are state-of-the-art, and libraries are exceptional. Other determining factors include the quality of both athletic and student centers and an abundance of things to do on campus.

# Campus Dining

## The Lowdown
ON CAMPUS DINING

**Duke University Dining Website:**
http://auxweb.duke.edu/Dining/

**Freshman Meal Plan Requirement?**
Yes

**24-Hour On-Campus Eating?**
Yes, Rick's Diner.

**Student Favorites:**
The Loop, The Great Hall, Armadillo Grill

**Meal Plan Average Cost:**
Freshman: $1,880-$2,015
Upper-Classmen: $1,315-$2,030

## Students Speak Out
ON CAMPUS HOUSING

Q "**Campus food tends to be decent**, but eating in the dining halls all the time will bore your taste buds after a while. Subway is popular for lunch. The Loop serves up pretty good pizza and burgers, and the milkshakes are quite enjoyable, too. If you're looking for greasy Mexican food, Armadillo Grill is the place to be. It'll destroy your arteries, but it's worth it. The more traditional dining halls are the Great Hall and the Marketplace. You'll have an all-you-can-eat meal plan at the Marketplace freshman year. Meals there are hit-or-miss. The fruit and the meat are a little shady, but the pasta is usually safe."

Q "The food is pretty good, and I think the meal plans cover almost all the places on campus. The Great Hall is a cafeteria with pretty good food and lots of variety, and the Loop has good sandwiches and pizza. **There is also a hot dog stand and a Breyer's ice cream shop**. Eating at the hospital is always a good choice, as it is cheap, and there are several places in the food court."

Q "I would give Duke's dining situation an 'A' compared to food options at other schools, but, I'll admit, **you get tired of it quickly**. Freshmen have a meal plan that offers all-you-can-eat from a dining hall called the Marketplace, but everyone is tired of it by the end of the year. Then, by senior year, all the upper-classmen come back to it on weekends because they miss it!"

Q "The cafeteria food is decent, though **it gets old after awhile**. The quality seems to rejuvenate itself around family and alumni weekends. The campus offers a million options with points that are initially delicious, but, frankly, going to the same restaurants all the time is boring. I need more variety."

{ "For the most part, I really like the food in the dining hall. It definitely doesn't compare to home-cooked meals, but there is a lot of variety."

## The College Prowler Take
### ON CAMPUS DINING

You'll hear plenty of complaints about the freshman meal plan, and many of them are justified. This meal plan requires freshmen to eat breakfast and dinner at the Marketplace every weekday (except Friday, when it's only breakfast), as well as brunch on Saturday and Sunday. On the one hand, this is very convenient: you eat dinner with your friends every night and don't have to worry about paying for overpriced fast food. On the other hand, although the food is really not nearly as bad as everyone will tell you, it really wears on you after a while. Duke's food service is known to be among the best in the nation, but students will complain anyway. If you can't find something you like on campus, you can use points to order from off campus. If you can't find something you like there, pack up and go home because you won't find better college food anywhere else.

**B+**

**The College Prowler™ Grade on**
### Campus Dining: B+

Our grade on Campus Dining addresses the quality of both school-owned dining halls and independent on-campus restaurants as well as the price, availability, and variety of food.

# Campus Housing

## The Lowdown
### ON CAMPUS HOUSING

**Undergrads on Campus:**
86%

**Number of Dormitories:**
13 residential halls on East Campus
6 residential quads on West Campus

**Number of University-Owned Apartments:**
407 apartment units for undergraduates and 117 for graduate students

**Available for Rent:**
Micro-fridges are available for rent. If you enroll at Duke, you will receive a brochure with all sorts of equipment available.

**Cleaning Service?**
Yes. Halls, commons rooms, and public bathrooms are cleaned daily. Your room, however, is up to you.

**You Get:**
Bed, desk, over-desk bookshelf, dresser, wardrobe or closet, phone and Internet jacks

**Bed Type:**
Twin extra-long (39"x80"); some beds can be bunked. Students build or buy their own lofts.

## Room Types

Duke offers single, double, and triple rooms in the residence halls, and one-, two-, and three-bedroom apartments on Central Campus. A few residence halls offer semi-private bathrooms.

## Also Available

All dorms are smoke-free. Substance-free housing is available for freshman year. Language dorms, special-interest housing, and selective living groups are available after freshman year.

### Did You Know?

Although West Campus is slowly getting air conditioning (only Craven and Kilgo quads now lack A/C), only the newer dorms on East have air conditioning.

Students are required to live on campus for three consecutive years. Study abroad, however, will count toward this requirement.

All residence halls are smoke-free. However, students in apartments on Central Campus may smoke with a roommate's permission.

## Students Speak Out
### ON CAMPUS HOUSING

"Most dorms on East are just about the same, aside from the newly air-conditioned Blackwell and Randolph and the remotely isolated Southgate. Everything on West is air-conditioned, except for Craven and Kilgo."

Q "I would advise new students to avoid Edens. It has the smallest rooms and the longest walk to the rest of campus. Double rooms are the most common, and they **average around 200 square feet**. If you're looking for the biggest rooms, you can find them in the WEL [West-Edens Link]."

Q "**Dorms at Duke are very nice**! We have new dorms on West Campus called the WEL [West-Edens Link]. They were built for sophomores and above. The rooms are huge! As a freshman, avoid Southgate and try to get a place at the main quad on East Campus—Brown, Pegram, Jiles, Wilson, and Bassett."

Q "The dorms are pretty nice at Duke. You're randomly assigned to a place for your freshman year. After that, there is a housing lottery in which **upperclassmen get the first shot at choosing rooms**. The air-conditioned rooms on East Campus are a bit smaller than the others, but beyond that trade-off, they're much the same. There's not really a dorm to avoid, even if you could."

Q "I find that the plan of having all first-year students on East Campus is a good idea, and it allows the new students to be together and share new experiences. **I didn't hear about any particularly terrible dorms**, except that Southgate is far from many facilities. On West, Edens is the trap to avoid, because it is miles away from any known civilization."

Q "The dorms at Duke are normal dorms. **They are not anything to get excited about**. Some of them have no A/C, which is bad. The dorms on the quad look really cool. It would be really neat to live in them for the first week, thinking to yourself, 'Wow! I can't believe I am living in this great, Gothic building in the heart of campus.' Then, in the second and all subsequent weeks, 'Wow, I can't believe how hot it is in this tiny #$@&!^ room!'"

Need help choosing a dorm? For a detailed listing on all Duke dorms, check out the College Prowler book on Duke available at www.collegeprowler.com.

## The College Prowler Take
### ON CAMPUS HOUSING

When all is said and done, Duke has some pretty nice housing. The view from the older dorms on the main quads is spectacular, and it's nice to be close to the action. The rooms are nice, but there is a difference between the older and newer dorms. In a lot of the new dorms, the floors are carpeted, but the walls are cinder block, and the rooms are pretty homogenous. The old dorms have hardwood floors and feature some pretty oddly shaped rooms (and for reasons no one can understand, no two rooms are shaped quite the same or have closets in the same place). Students agree that there are really very few dorms on Duke's campus that ought to be avoided. Some, granted, don't offer a good trade-off (usually it's either old-world beauty on main quad or air conditioning), but very few dorms indeed consist of a majority of truly miserable students. That is, at least living quarters aren't a primary reason for student bitterness.

**B**

The College Prowler™ Grade on
### Campus Housing: B

A high Campus Housing grade indicates that dorms are clean, well-maintained, and spacious. Other determining factors include variety of dorms, proximity to classes, and social atmosphere.

# Diversity

## The Lowdown
### ON DIVERSITY

**Native American:** 0%

**Asian American:** 12%

**African American:** 10%

**Hispanic:** 7%

**White:** 66%

**International:** 5%

### Regional Breakdown

**Carolinas:** 16%

**Northeast:** 15%

**Mid-Atlantic:** 20%

**Southeast:** 23%

**Midwest:** 12%

**West and Pacific:** 9%

**International:** 5%

## Minority Clubs

Duke has a number of thriving minority clubs, which put on astounding cultural programs each year. Perhaps one of the most active is SAASA, the South-Asian American Student Association, which involves most of the South-Asian Students on campus. The ASA (Asian Student Association) is also a vibrant part of the community, and you will find fraternities, clubs, and classes dedicated to different parts of the Duke community.

## Most Popular Religions

Duke is predominantly Christian, as might be guessed, with Duke Chapel dominating the West Campus scene. Duke Chapel does hold regular Protestant services each Sunday, and serves as a venue for memorials and various religious club meetings. However, most churches meet off campus, and there are vital members of other religious communities.

## Political Activity

Like many other college campuses, Duke has a very strong liberal streak, and conservatives are virtually unknown. Students have campaigned for Elizabeth Dole, staged multiple protests, sit-ins, rallies, and marches against the war in Iraq, distributed flyers and set up banners, demonstrations, etc., all to express their views. West Campus quad and bus stop seem to be the center of these demonstrations, and it is a rare week when you don't see someone sitting on a bus stop bench with a sheet draped over them and a poster explaining what they are protesting.

## Gay Tolerance

The gay scene is not very visible at Duke, but gays are not generally singled out for persecution. A recent campaign for gay acceptance handed out shirts reading "Gay? Fine by me." This was met with an enthusiastic response as students across campus lined up to get the shirts—the 2,000 they had ordered quickly ran out.

## Economic Status

Honestly, the Duke student body is astoundingly wealthy. Even those who are on financial aid usually manage to look, shop, and drive rich. There are, of course, people from a variety of economic backgrounds, but you wouldn't think it to look at the campus. Duke is remarkably image-conscious.

## Students Speak Out
### ON DIVERSITY

"The campus isn't really all that diverse, and everyone tends, initially, to stick to their own, which kind of sucks. It seems that rich, white kids are the norm, and there isn't much in the way of anyone else."

Q "**The campus is quite diverse** but people tend to self-segregate themselves. There has been a lot of work at the school to promote interracial relations, and there is definitely the option of meeting all sorts of people."

Q "If you desire diversity, you will have it, especially if you get involved in a sport or another activity. **I have made black friends, Asian friends, and white friends**. We also have students from other countries, including my friend's Pakistani resident assistant, and the cute Venezuelan girl in my French class. Aside from just the racial or ethnic standpoint, I think Duke students come from varied backgrounds and upbringings, and have a lot to share, even if it's just that South Dakota accent or an appreciation of grits with ketchup."

Q "Ethnically, I think Duke is very diverse. **Socioeconomically, I'm not so sure**."

Q "The school is very diverse. That is part of [the administration's] mission. **You'll find almost every race somewhere at Duke**. That's a good thing too, because everyone gets along really well."

## The College Prowler Take
### ON DIVERSITY

Though it may not be the most diverse campus in the world, Duke does have a thriving community of students from almost every ethnic background. However, Duke students do tend to segregate themselves, and hang out with their own ethnic group. This is not always the case, of course, but a number of students seem to have a group of friends of different races, and then another group of friends with only their own racial background. This is a little worrisome, but the administration's concern over the issue should prove that they're at least trying to remedy this. Most students agree that this issue will work itself out eventually.

## Guys & Girls

### The Lowdown
### ON GUYS & GIRLS

**Women Undergrads:** 49%

**Men Undergrads:** 51%

### Birth Control Available?
Yes. Duke Student Health offers a variety of contraceptive options, and condoms are available in all the dorm vending machines.

### Social Scene
It is a rare student who doesn't find Duke a bit cliquish. This is not to say that you can't make a lot of friends in a variety of groups, but sometimes Duke can feel like high school revisited. Students are fun, bright, and attractive, but tend to stay in small groups of fun, bright, and attractive people. It is easy to carry on a conversation with classmates on the bus, walking to or from a class, or anywhere on campus, but if you're from different groups, it is unlikely you will make many friends out of your casual acquaintances.

However, Duke can still be a lot of fun once you find your group of friends. Dorms, clubs, organizations, and projects—anything where you work with a lot with other people—can be great places to make strong friendships.

**B+**

**The College Prowler™ Grade on**
## Diversity: B+

A high grade in Diversity indicates that ethnic minorities and international students have a notable presence on campus and that students of different economic backgrounds, religious beliefs, and sexual preferences are well-represented.

## Hookups or Relationships?

Relationships seem to require a fair amount of effort to keep up, and when Duke students are working hard all day with their studies, there seems to be a limited amount of effort they're willing to give. So, although you will still find a number of students committed to each other and their relationships, hookups are the order of the weekend.

## Dress Code

There is no set dress code but, overall, students dress "preppy." A&F reigns supreme, with button-up shirts, logo T-shirts, khakis, and New Balances being a part of nearly every student's wardrobe. Duke students almost always look good, and you will find few who are willing to roll out of bed and go to class in their pajamas. Usually students are tastefully dressed, looking like they just stepped off the page of some magazine, although there is the occasional girl who doesn't seem to know how much is enough. Despite all the attractiveness, you may find yourself gazing longingly after the one or two people who have dared disapproval and bedecked their backpacks with pins, pierced an eyebrow, or let their hair grow out.

## Students Speak Out
### ON GUYS & GIRLS

"Well, I'm a guy, so I can tell you that the girls are mediocre. I find a lot of people at Duke to be a little introverted, so it's kind of hard to approach women, at least when sobriety is involved."

Q "The majority of people at Duke are **very attractive and very career-oriented**. There isn't much time or interest in starting serious relationships, so most don't make it past the weekend."

Q "Honestly, **there aren't enough good-looking girls at Duke**, so if you're hot, please, please come to Duke. My girlfriend has come up a few times and says the guys, in general, are pretty good-looking."

Q "**There are some good-looking gals**, but most of them know it, and are kind of stuck-up about it. The best girls are cute and down-to-earth. Most of the guys keep in pretty good shape; I see a whole bunch in the gym everyday. Almost everybody runs and takes care of themselves."

Q "Let's just say you will have **your choice of hot guys**."

## The College Prowler Take
### ON GUYS & GIRLS

Duke students are a pretty attractive bunch on the whole and go to great lengths to be viewed that way. Guys seem to get more praise than girls, at least in physical attractiveness. Girls, however, are not at all unattractive, and the main complaints seem to be about introverted, and sometimes shallow personalities. A lot of the students seem to have gotten a bit too caught up in their appearance to worry about personality and relationships though. This correlates to the dating scene at Duke. Students are much more likely to have a nice little Friday night hookup than to build a lasting relationship. After all, why put effort into finding something real and substantial, if you can have what you're looking for, with no strings attached?

**B+**

**B**

The College Prowler™ Grade on
### Guys: B+

A high grade for Guys indicates that the male population on campus is attractive, smart, friendly, and engaging, and that the school has a decent ratio of guys to girls.

The College Prowler™ Grade on
### Girls: B

A high grade for Girls not only implies that the women on campus are attractive, smart, friendly, and engaging, but also that there is a fair ratio of girls to guys.

# Athletics

**Athletic Division:**
Division I-A

**Conference:**
ACC (Atlantic Coast Conference)

**School Mascot:**
Blue Devil

## The Lowdown ON ATHLETICS

**Men's Varsity Teams:**
Baseball
Basketball
Cross Country
Fencing
Football
Golf
Lacrosse
Soccer
Swimming
Tennis
Track
Wrestling

**Women's Varsity Teams:**
Basketball
Cross Country
Fencing
Field Hockey
Golf
Lacrosse
Rowing
Soccer
Swimming
Tennis
Track
Volleyball

### Club Sports
Badminton, Ballroom Dance, Baseball, Women's Basketball, Men's Crew, Cycling, Dancing Devils, Equestrian, Field Hockey, Football, Golf, Hapkido, Ice Hockey, Judo, Women's Lacrosse, Outing, Road-runners, Roller Hockey, Men's Rugby, Women's Rugby, Sailing, Skating, Shooting, Ski, Men's Soccer, Women's Soccer, Softball, Squash, Swim, Table Tennis, Tae Kwon Do, Men's Tennis, Women's Tennis, Men's Ultimate, Women's Ultimate, Men's Volleyball, Women's Volleyball, Water Skiing

### Intramurals
First-year only: Six-a-Side Soccer, Flag Football, Basketball, Co-Rec Basketball, Volleyball, Softball

Regular: Flag Football, Soccer, Volleyball, Singles & Doubles Tennis, Golf, 5k Run, Basketball, Squash, Racquetball, Badminton, Co-Rec Basketball, Softball, Table Tennis

### Most Popular Sports
Men's basketball, obviously. Take a smart-kid school, add one really exceptional sports team, and it will become the Mecca around which we all flock.

### Overlooked Teams
Women's basketball is not necessarily overlooked, but it certainly doesn't get the attention it deserves, especially considering that Duke has some of the nation's top players.

### Athletic Facilities
Jack Coombs Field – Baseball
Cameron Indoor Stadium – Basketball
Schwartz-Butters Athletic Center
Wallace Wade Stadium – Football
The Duke Golf Club – Golf
Koskinen Stadium – Lacrosse and Soccer
Taishoff Aquatic Center – Swimming and Diving
Ambler Tennis Stadium/ Sheffield Indoor Tennis Center – Tennis
Wallace Wade Stadium – Track and Field
Memorial Gym – Volleyball

### Getting Tickets
Students get into Duke games for free, and getting in is usually not a problem—except for men's basketball. The stories you have heard about people camping out for months to get tickets are not the least bit exaggerated. Students form groups and plan schedules around being able to sleep in a tent from January to late February/early March.

## Students Speak Out
### ON ATHLETICS

> "Duke football is the worst, but people still go to games for school spirit and social activities. Basketball is, of course, the most popular."

Q "We're all nicknamed **'Cameron Crazies.'** Mostly everyone at Duke is crazy about b-ball. If you ever get the chance to go to a game, it's crazy. Nobody sits down. You stand the whole time. It's a great thing to experience. Women's golf is also a huge sport at Duke. I'm on the golf team. We are the ACC champs for the seventh year in a row, and the 1999 NCAA champs."

Q "Varsity sports are big here, of course, headlined by basketball. Students participate in bonfires on campus after big wins, and the basketball team is the rallying point for much school spirit. As freshmen, **many IM sports are organized by dorm**, contributing to a sense of unity, rather than anonymity. IM football, softball, volleyball, and basketball are the most prevalent. Duke also has club teams, which are relaxed teams for intercollegiate competition. Some examples include ultimate Frisbee, tennis, volleyball, and football."

Q "Duke has some of the top-ranked sports on campus. Being a basketball fanatic is key and even if you're not now, you'll eventually start seeing blue after a while. **It's hard not to catch the school's basketball fever**."

Q "**Duke oozes with school spirit**, especially during basketball season. If you're not a basketball fan before coming to Duke, you will be. Duke basketball will accelerate your interest to obsession status. Other teams do have a following on campus—lacrosse for example—but the big name sport on other campuses, football, is more than lacking at Duke. IM sports are widespread, though not publicized well."

## The College Prowler Take
### ON ATHLETICS

Have you ever heard of Duke basketball? If you haven't, then you must have been living under a rock for the last 20 years. Pulsating through everyone and everything at Duke is this current of basketball fanaticism. You see a ridiculously tall guy get on the bus, and the eyes of the students all around you light up, and you can see the strain on their faces as they try to hold themselves back from running up and asking for an autograph. This is not to say that you have to be a basketball fan before you come here—Duke will most definitely make one out of you. Ironically, the classic college sport, football, is just laughable at Duke. However, the other varsity and IM sports make a better-than-decent showing each year, and there's a good team for just about everyone out there. Mostly, though, there's basketball. Come, and let us make you a fan.

**A-**

The College Prowler™ Grade on
## Athletics: A-

A high grade in Athletics indicates that students have school spirit, that sports programs are respected, that games are well-attended, and that intramurals are a prominent part of student life.

# Greek Life

## The Lowdown
### ON GREEK LIFE

**Number of Fraternities:**
20

**Number of Sororities:**
17

**Undergrad Men in Fraternities:**
29%

**Undergrad Women in Sororities:**
42%

---

Q "Freshman year, I went to a lot of the rush parties for frats and found that **most frat brothers were jerks**, so I skipped that. However, the frats are good for throwing parties. Most parties are open, so there's no need to be affiliated with any one group. Most of the sorority girls I know only do it for the mixers with the frats, so judge accordingly."

Q "**Greek life here is actually fine**. I never thought I'd get involved in it, but I'm very glad I did. There are no closed parties, except for formals and semi-formals, and there's no such thing as a guest list for frat parties. I don't feel like it dominates the social scene, because you don't rush until second semester, so you have a chance to make friends before you're thrown into sorority life. I had friends ranging from all different types of sororities and independents."

Q "University officials are starting to crack down on certain frat behaviors that are deemed unsafe, such as some types of hazing, and have moved many from the main quad in order to **make room for guaranteed sophomore housing**."

Q "Yes, Greek life completely dominates the social scene, but you don't have to be involved in it to go to their parties. Personally, I don't drink, so I usually only go out to party on the weekend, but **some people here go to frat parties Thursday, Friday, and Saturday**. They can be really fun, if there's dancing and you're with fun people, or they can be boring; it just depends on which one and which night."

## Students Speak Out
### ON GREEK LIFE

"Greek life pretty much dominates the social life here. Half of the girls are in sororities, and about one third of the guys are in frats. The social life outside the houses is pretty much dead."

---

**COLLEGE PROWLER**

Need help finding the right sorority or fraternity for you? For a detailed listing of all Greek organizations on campus, check out the College Prowler book on Duke available at *www.collegeprowler.com*.

## The College Prowler Take
ON GREEK LIFE

Greek life at Duke is honestly huge; not as huge as its basketball following, but huge nonetheless. You can survive socially without being a member, but you won't get through Duke without being at least somewhat affected by Duke's Greek scene. The number of students in fraternities or sororities might be a bit overwhelming at first (almost half the girls and about a third of the guys are in a sorority or fraternity), but it's easy to understand after a bit. Although a social life is possible without paying dues to some group, when so many students have given in and signed up, you look around and realize that you, too, want to belong, and even if paying some dues is the way to do it, it might be worth trying.

# Drug Scene

## The Lowdown
ON DRUG SCENE

**Most Prevalent Drugs on Campus:**
Caffeine, Alcohol, Marijuana

**Liquor-Related Referrals:**
368

**Liquor-Related Arrests:**
339

**Drug-Related Referrals:**
43

**Drug-Related Arrests:**
48

## A

The College Prowler™ Grade on
### Greek Life: A
A high grade in Greek Life indicates that sororities and fraternities are not only present, but also active on campus. Other determining factors include the variety of houses available and the respect the Greek community receives from the rest of the campus.

## Students Speak Out
ON DRUG SCENE

"Whatever you want, you can get, but prices are a little high. The typical clientele are ignorant and have money to burn, so that kind of hurts everyone else."

- "Students can avoid it, but if you're looking for drugs, **you will be presented with a buffet**—if you know the right people. Marijuana is the most popular drug, and it can be found in most any social group."

- "Alcohol is by far the most common drug of choice, and **I think a lot of people take their drinking way too far**. A few people smoke, and every once in a while I hear about someone with marijuana or something in a dorm room."

- "Drugs are illegal. **Duke students are smart about their usage**; thus they participate in illegal activities behind closed doors."

## The College Prowler Take
### ON DRUG SCENE

The drug scene at Duke is pretty open, but not at all distracting. If you want them, you can find them. If you don't, you most likely won't ever have to worry about encountering an illegal substance. Student responses reflect that most students are aware that there are drugs on campus, but no one seems threatened or pressured by them. It's almost impossible to get through college without a whiff of something grassy, but at Duke you won't have to feel like you're endlessly rolling in the lawn—unless, of course, you want to. At Duke, it's not hard to drift through college innocently. This is something that can't be said at larger, more crime-infested universities. However, drugs do exist on the Duke campus, and that's something to bear in mind.

**B**

The College Prowler™ Grade on
### Drug Scene: B

A high grade on Drug Scene indicates that drugs are not a noticeable part of campus life; drug use is not visible, and no pressure to use them seems to exist.

# Overall Experience

## Students Speak Out
### ON OVERALL EXPERIENCE

"I, honestly, would not mind being somewhere else. There are other, cheaper, schools that are just as good, but I'm having a pretty good time anyway."

- "Since my freshman year, the University has progressively cared less about the social concerns and quality of life issues of its students, and more about catering to annual college ranking publications. Under the guise of providing students with a 'safe, diverse, and unique experience,' the University has succeeded only in driving the social scene in a more covert, exclusive, and potentially dangerous direction. By dressing in baggy attire and hiding behind tipped baseball caps, are undercover deans attending on-campus parties to protect students, or to single them out and punish them? By dissolving selective living groups for late paperwork during final exams, and by refusing to work toward compromise in the reinstatement and housing process, are University officials more concerned with maintaining campus diversity, or with permanently removing social organizations? **I'm not sure that this is a place you'll want to be in years to come**."

- "I would never go anywhere else after having been at Duke this past year. Though I had my gripes about not getting into Harvard or MIT, **I'm over that now**."

"**Duke offers a great educational opportunity**, especially for undergraduates, and if you can take advantage of the Freshman Focus program, do so. It's a great program for your first semester."

"I came into this experience with very high expectations, and even so, I've been completely blown away by this university. The Duke student philosophy is **'work hard, play hard,'** and we do. Duke offers students the chance to tailor their experience to whatever it is that they're looking for. Duke offers an environment where students are surrounded by success. The drive to succeed is key to Duke students' success."

## The College Prowler Take
### ON OVERALL EXPERIENCE

Duke students are generally happy with their experience, but it's not uncommon to find students who imagine they would be happier somewhere else. Academics, friendships, and even the beauty of the campus make this school an easy choice for many. However, a lot of students are concerned about the top-down social programming they see coming from Duke's administration. Rather than starting their own initiatives, Duke undergrads often seem apathetic, and the administration, frantic to see things not only progressing, but progressing in the direction they see fit, tries to shove social programming down students' throats. Students and administration are still trying to find a more level balance of power and, by doing so, are heading in a more unified direction. University politics have become a big concern, but the friendships students have forged seem to make up for whatever shortcomings they might perceive due to "the powers that be."

Duke is one of the top academic schools in the country, but that's not its hook. You'll never see Harvard's basketball team in the Final Four, or Yale students camping out for a week to get tickets to a sporting event. Obviously, basketball shouldn't be your major concern in choosing a college, but it is often used as an example because it typifies the difference between Duke and so many of the other top colleges. There's an emphasis on friends, social life, and fun here, and it's important to consider these aspects, as well as academics, when you're choosing a school. Remember, you're choosing the place you'll spend the next four years of your life, not just the name that shows up on your degree when all is said and done.

# Elon University

2700 Campus Box, Elon, NC 27244
www.elon.edu          (800) 334-8448

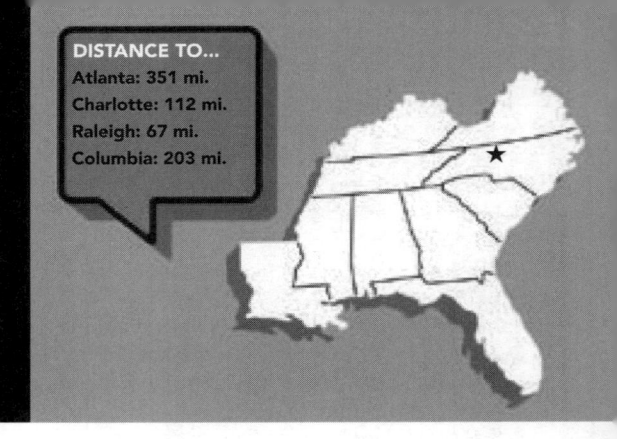

**DISTANCE TO...**
Atlanta: 351 mi.
Charlotte: 112 mi.
Raleigh: 67 mi.
Columbia: 203 mi.

---

*"A general belief held by faculty and staff is every student should get the help they need, when they need it."*

**Total Enrollment:**
4,309

**Top 10% of High School Class:**
24%

**Average GPA:**
3.6

**Acceptance Rate:**
45%

**Tuition:**
$17,555

**SAT Range (25th-75th Percentile)**
| Verbal | Math | Total |
|---|---|---|
| 530 – 620 | 540 – 630 | 1070 – 1250 |

**ACT Range (25th-75th Percentile)**
| Verbal | Math | Total |
|---|---|---|
| 23-30 | 24-30 | 23-29 |

**Most Popular Majors:**
- 9%  Economics
- 9%  Political Science and Government
- 8%  Psychology
- 7%  History
- 6%  Sociology

**Students also applied to:***
Furman University
James Madison University
North Carolina State University–Raleigh
University of North Carolina

*For more school info check out www.collegeprowler.com

## Table of Contents

| | |
|---|---|
| Academics | 461 |
| Local Atmosphere | 463 |
| Safety & Security | 464 |
| Facilities | 466 |
| Campus Dining | 468 |
| Campus Housing | 469 |
| Diversity | 471 |
| Guys & Girls | 472 |
| Athletics | 474 |
| Greek Life | 475 |
| Drug Scene | 477 |
| Overall Experience | 478 |

## College Prowler Report Card

| | |
|---|---|
| Academics | B+ |
| Local Atmosphere | D |
| Safety & Security | A- |
| Facilities | B+ |
| Campus Dining | B |
| Campus Housing | A- |
| Diversity | D- |
| Guys | B+ |
| Girls | A- |
| Athletics | B- |
| Greek Life | A |
| Drug Scene | A- |

# Academics

## Sample Academic Clubs
The Accounting Society, American Chemical Society, Beta Beta Beta (Honors Biology club), Crime Studies Club, Diverse Students of Science, Elon Engineers, Financial Management Association, Lincoln Pre-Med Society, Mathematics Association of America, Society of Physics Students, Society of Professional Journalists, Student NC Association of Educators

### Did You Know?
A recent national academic poll ranked three of Elon's academic programs among the best in the nation (First-Year Experiences, Service-Learning, and Learning Communities).

**Best Places to Study:**
Belk Library, Fireside Lounge in Student Center, dorm rooms

## The Lowdown
ON ACADEMICS

**Degrees Awarded:**
Bachelor, Master, Doctorate

**Undergraduate Schools:**
Martha and Spencer Love School of Business; Elon College, the College of Arts and Sciences; School of Education; School of Communications

**Full-time Faculty:**
252

**Faculty with Terminal Degree:**
213

**Student-to-Faculty Ratio:**
15:1

**AP Test Score Requirements:**
Possible credit for scores of 4 or 5

**IB Test Score Requirements:**
Possible credit for scores of 4 or higher on the Advanced exams, no credit for the Standard exams

## Students Speak Out
ON ACADEMICS

"My teachers are very unique individuals with an obvious passion for teaching. I feel the environment is such that I am free to express my beliefs and who I am in class."

"The teachers are great. They know a lot about the subjects in which they teach, and I am very impressed by the success they have had in their respective fields. The classes that interest me are the subjects I love. I have had a few other classes that aren't in my major, but **the teacher made all the difference**, allowing me to really understand the subject at hand."

"Like all schools, there are good and bad teachers. Fortunately, I have been able to have very good teachers my first year. **They're excited about the subject they're teaching**, and want to help you as much as possible so that you learn and understand the material."

Q "I have found plenty of professors very engaging in classes I never thought I would like. However, with some adjunct professors **I have had terrible experiences**. A majority of my classes have been interesting enough that I don't regret taking the class, especially if it isn't required for my major."

Q "The teachers at Elon are unique. They are very interested in their students, inside and outside of the classroom. I have had teachers ask me how other important things in my life are going, i.e. interviews or presentations in other classes. They are always willing to meet with you, for help in their class, or if you need help in another. My professors bring a light to the classroom, **I can tell they love their job**, and that directly affects how much I learn and how hard I work in their class."

Q "The classes are a lot different than the classes that I had in high school. You have a lot more freedom and responsibility for learning the material. **Most teachers incorporate other methods of teaching** than lecturing, so that makes the classes fun and entertaining, while also educational."

Need help choosing a major? For a detailed listing on all courses on campus, check out the College Prowler book on Elon available at www.collegeprowler.com

## The College Prowler Take
### ON ACADEMICS

Within the brick walls that make up Elon University, there is a fascinating world of information and knowledge. To prospective students, Elon looks exactly like what it is—a university that is trying to create a name and reputation for itself. From a student's standpoint, that image gets a little lost in the hectic schedule of going to classes, studying, having a job, and mostly trying to enjoy the college experience. However, we know we are a part of something that will eventually be bigger than what we are now. When we graduate, our degrees will tell employers that we've been through some of the toughest challenges students can face in today's world, and are trained and ready to take on more.

That being said, the academics at Elon are very rigorous. Each year, the admissions standards get increasingly harder, and each class is more intelligent. Despite that, we're still a very small school. Classes are small enough that you can ask lots of questions, professors get to know their students well, and there's never such a huge crowd that you have to fight to see your professor during office hours. If you want to succeed, Elon is the place to go. The school provides students with tremendous opportunity; it's really up to the student whether to make him or herself a leader or a follower. The opportunity to be a leader is there.

**B+**

**The College Prowler™ Grade on**
## Academics: B+

A high Academics grade generally indicates that professors are knowledgeable, accessible, and genuinely interested in their students' welfare. Other determining factors include class size, how well professors communicate, and whether or not classes are engaging.

# Local Atmosphere

## The Lowdown
ON LOCAL ATMOSPHERE

**Region:**
Southeast

**City, State:**
Elon, North Carolina

**Setting:**
Small town

**Distance from Raleigh:**
1 hour

**Distance from Durham:**
1 hour

**Points of Interest:**
Alamance Battleground State Historical Site, Firehouse Fine Arts Gallery, Alamance County Historical Museum, Tick's Driving Range, I-85 Golf & Baseball, Indian Valley Golf Course, Bass Mountain Music Park

**Major Sports Teams:**
None

**City Websites:**
http://www.ci.burlington.nc.us
http://www.burlington-area-nc.org

## Students Speak Out
ON LOCAL ATMOSPHERE

"Elon is a very quiet town, there aren't any other universities around that are close. It is a quaint town with not much to do, but there are a lot of service opportunities in Burlington."

Q "There is a very community-centered atmosphere that is always warm and welcoming. **Everything is mellow, and busy at the same time**. No other campuses are present. Watch the traffic in and out of campus, though, and be sure to visit the local restaurants and movie theater."

Q "Burlington is **the ugliest hick town ever**! It's drab, boring, and totally commercialized grossness. The only other universities around are 45 minutes away, but they've got much better stuff to do around their campuses."

Q "Well, **the town itself lacks in things to do**, but within Elon there is always something going on, so it's balanced out. We're in a good location as far as cities down the road from us. Chapel Hill, Durham, and Raleigh have good stores, restaurants and concerts. Greensboro is okay."

Q "Burlington isn't really that great, as far as being an active city. **There are other universities in reasonable distances from us**, but I don't really know anyone who leaves campus to hang out. Greensboro is about half an hour away, and Raleigh is only an hour, so if you really want to do something fun and interesting, it's highly possible."

## The College Prowler Take
### ON LOCAL ATMOSPHERE

Elon is in the middle of a ton of other universities: UNC Greensboro, UNC Chapel Hill, Duke, NC State, and Wake Forest. The town of Elon is really small, around 5,000-10,000 inhabitants (that includes University students and surrounding rural areas). The city of Burlington, which is about five minutes away, has a population of 44,917. Even though that may seem like a large number, the city of Burlington is probably as boring as they get. Many students complain about Burlington being too boring, but some like the quiet atmosphere. If you're looking for a city with buildings taller than three stories, buses, metros, and people always busy and going somewhere, Burlington is not the best area. One of the most fun things to do is go to Wal-Mart—that says a lot.

**D**

The College Prowler™ Grade on
## Local Atmosphere: D

A high Local Atmosphere grade indicates that the area surrounding campus is safe and scenic. Other factors include nearby attractions, proximity to other schools, and the town's attitude toward students.

# Safety & Security

## The Lowdown
### ON SAFETY & SECURITY

**Number of Elon Police:**
12 full-time police, 17 security personnel

**Phone:**
(336) 278-5555

**Health Center Office Hours:**
Monday-Thursday: 8:30 a.m.-6 p.m., Friday: 8:30 a.m.-4:30 p.m., Saturday: 11:30 a.m.-2:45 p.m.

**Safety Services:**
Bicycle registration; blue-phones; engraving of valuables; escort service; programs on: alcohol and drug awareness, fire safety, personal security, rape awareness, drug identification, self defense, van driver training

### Did You Know?

*The Elon Pendulum*, the school's newspaper, reports all students who are either arrested or given a referral, along with what crime they committed.

Elon offers a volunteer service called Safe Rides on Fridays and Saturdays from 10 p.m. to 2 a.m.

## Students Speak Out
### ON SAFETY & SECURITY

"Elon has its own police force that is always accessible to help students. It's never hard to find a police officer patrolling the campus or directing traffic. I feel very safe on our campus."

Q "**Elon is a very safe campus**, and any severe security incidents are reported to all students via e-mail. I have never felt unsafe on the campus, and if I ever did, I know security would gladly come walk with me, or check out the situation."

Q "**Security is very reliable and efficient** in providing the needs of safety and security for those who request it at Elon. One thing that caught my attention at Elon was the Safe Rides organization, run by students to help students get around to their destination and/or back to their dorm with no questions asked."

Q "Security is an extremely important issue. Although the campus itself is rather open, as soon as a crime or problems are reported, **police and campus security are on it**."

Q "The only avoidable issue would be that of bikes. If you have a bike, consider not bringing it on campus, as **there's a good chance it may be stolen**, or worse yet, vandalized."

## The College Prowler Take
### ON SAFETY & SECURITY

It's important to feel safe wherever you go to school, and environment plays a big role in this. Elon is located in a smaller area, so it's naturally going to be more secure than some city schools. However, the University still makes the safety of its students a priority. Elon has many programs that acquaint students with the security services offered on campus, and with what to do in dangerous situations. With Safe Rides, blue-lights, and escort services, students should feel pretty safe. Even in this cozy atmosphere, though, something bad can still happen, so students are constantly reminded to be safe rather than sorry.

**A-**

The College Prowler™ Grade on
### Safety & Security: A-

A high grade in Safety & Security means that students generally feel safe, campus police are visible, blue-light phones and escort services are readily available, and safety precautions are not overly necessary.

# Facilities

**Computers**
High-Speed Network? Yes
Wireless Network? Yes
Number of Labs: 18
Numbers of Computers: 580
24-Hour Labs: None
Charge to Print? No
Operating Systems: PC, Mac, Unix

## The Lowdown
ON FACILITIES

**Student Center:**
Moseley Center

**Athletic Center:**
Koury Athletic Center

**Libraries:**
1

**Movie Theatre on Campus?**
No

**Bowling on Campus?**
No

**Bar on Campus?**
No

**Coffeehouse on Campus?**
No

**Popular Places to Chill:**
The Zone, the Fireside Lounge, the Acorn Coffee Shop, first floor of Belk Library

### Favorite Things to Do
The Student Union Board often hosts concerts and fun activities in the Zone, McKinnon Hall, Alumni Gym, Fireside Lounge, or Cantina Roble. Racquetball is also quite popular on campus, as well as volleyball on any of the outdoor courts, or shooting hoops in Jordan Gym. Elon has a very active performing arts department, with shows in McCrary Theatre, Black Box Theatre, or Yeager Recital Hall. Iron Tree Blooming is a new, Zen-based meditation club that has drawn quite an interesting crowd of students.

**COLLEGE PROWLER**

Need help finding places to go on campus? Check out the College Prowler book full of Elon info available at www.collegeprowler.com.

## Students Speak Out
### ON FACILITIES

"The facilities are all renovated, extremely usable, and accessible. Some of the rooms don't have a digital projector or DVD drive, but that should be standard soon."

Q "Elon has done a wonderful job of 'keeping up with the times.' The computers have been updated multiple times. **Some of the facilities are still very new** because Elon has begun to grow recently, but they try their hardest to meet the needs of the students by constantly asking us to fill out evaluations or surveys."

Q "The facilities are exceptionally nice on the campus. Elon takes great pride in creating a welcoming, warm environment for the students in all different buildings. Each classroom has one wall painted a different color that helps brighten the room, and make it more interesting than a white box. **I have never seen trash around campus**; it is immaculate."

Q "Elon has fabulous facilities available for students. The library, fitness center, computer labs, and all the other functions are **constantly being evaluated and updated** so that the students have the best opportunities to do what interests them."

Q "The facilities are extremely nice. All the faculties are highly maintained, using all the latest stuff. Very swank, very nicely done. **I use the athletic center**, and it seems that as soon as something looks halfway worn out, they replace it with something sleeker and nicer."

## The College Prowler Take
### ON FACILITIES

All the facilities are state-of-the-art. For those into sports and fitness, we have two gyms, an indoor pool, and three aerobic studios, as well as soccer, baseball, and football fields. Our fitness center has cardiovascular equipment, as well as free weights. The school also offers 13 intramural sports. Our student center is beautiful; the marble floors, Elon spirit clothes and souvenirs, and the advertisements for cultural events and clubs all add to the feeling that there's something for everyone. We even have a fireside lounge where people can eat food from Octagon Café, or drink smoothies from Freshens. The second floor of the student center is home to a lot of the campus organizations' offices. While the University's entertainment facilities may be somewhat lacking compared to other schools, off-campus businesses have attempted to compensate. West End Cinemas is the closest movie theatre to campus, only five minutes away.

**B+**

The College Prowler™ Grade on
### Facilities: B+

A high Facilities grade indicates that the campus is aesthetically pleasing and well-maintained; facilities are state-of-the-art, and libraries are exceptional. Other determining factors include the quality of both athletic and student centers and an abundance of things to do on campus.

# Campus Dining

## Students Speak Out
### ON CAMPUS DINING

*"The dining halls on campus provide a good variety of different types of meals. Since there are a few different locations available for students, it's not hard to find what you are looking for."*

Q "**All of the dining halls are good.** I can honestly say that I've been to other schools and had their food, and it doesn't compare to ours. Harden dining hall has a variety of options, each day they change, and the menu is online, which is very nice. They began RFOC [Real Food on Campus] and it has made a difference. McEwen, Octagon, Acorn, Cantina, Varsity and Danieley Commons are all equally as good to eat at."

Q "The school has us fill out surveys, and from that **they have more vegetarian options,** soy milk, and healthier eating options. This lets me know that they are paying attention and have the students' interests at heart."

Q "I think the food isn't that great; however, I have been told it is much better than other schools. **It's hard to find meals that aren't just carbs,** because I don't eat meat."

Q "The food is all right; **it gets a little boring,** but I guess it would anywhere. Some of the meal plan rules are dumb."

Q "The food on this campus is good. We have good variety in where you can get food, but **the types of food are somewhat limited**—hamburgers are everywhere! There is no dining facility open before 11:00 a.m. on weekends, so whenever you are up early, you are not able to eat breakfast."

## The Lowdown
### ON CAMPUS DINING

**Freshman Meal Plan Requirement?**
Yes

**24-Hour On-Campus Eating?**
No

**Student Favorites:**
Octagon Café, the Acorn Coffee Shop, Harden Dining Hall

**Meal Plan Average Cost:**
$1,216

### Did You Know?

You can find out all the nutritional information you want at the Elon University Dining Services website. Visit http://www.ecampusservices.com/DiningWeb/ElonDining/Nutrition.html.

Want to see what's going on at one of the dining halls? Go to http://www.ecampusservices.com/Images/500076700/WebCams.htm and you can watch a live webcam video of what's going on at your favorite place to eat!

## The College Prowler Take
ON CAMPUS DINING

There tend to be jokes among college students that campus food is just plain awful, and one of the reasons why the "Freshman 15" exists is because everyone tends to eat at places on campus that serve fast food. Why are they eating fast food? Because it's the most edible stuff on campus! But, at Elon, this is not true. Yes, like any other college campus, there are negative rumors about the food quality, as well as a group of students who cannot find a single good thing to say about on-campus meals. But, on the whole, Elon has had a lot of success with their meal plan program and the food they serve. There is a variety of foods, so each student is accommodated, from the student with stomach problems to the pickiest vegetarian—all needs can be met. And, of course, if what's on the menu doesn't please you, there is always the fast food in Octagon Café.

### The College Prowler™ Grade on
## Campus Dining: B

Our grade on Campus Dining addresses the quality of both school-owned dining halls and independent on-campus restaurants as well as the price, availability, and variety of food.

# Campus Housing

## The Lowdown
ON CAMPUS HOUSING

**Number of Dormitories:**
17, but Danieley Center rooms are apartment/flat designs

**Number of University-Owned Apartments:**
6, and 13 Greek houses

**Room Types:**
Suite-style: five double rooms sharing a bathroom; or two double rooms connected by a bathroom
Standard: students assigned to a hall bathroom, living in double or single rooms

**Available for Rent:**
Micro-fridge

**Cleaning Service?**
Yes, cleaning is done twice a week in standard dorms.

**You Get:**
Beds (can be lofted or separated), desk, A/C, high-speed Internet wall jacks (cables available on move-in day)

**Bed Type:**
Twin extra-long; bunk-beds, lofts

### Also Available

Carpeting and bed/bath supplies can be ordered through the University. There are several Living and Learning communities, such as the Service Learning Community (3rd floor Chandler), Creative Arts, Math & Science, and Honors (1st, 2nd, and 3rd floors Virginia, respectively), as well as smoke-free and substance-free communities that students can elect to live in.

### Students Speak Out
ON CAMPUS HOUSING

{ "The dorms are pretty good; the buildings on the lake side of campus are not as nice, but have a great location for my major. Apparently, Sloan is the best dorm."

Q "The dorms are nice; **they all now have air conditioning**. I have lived in Chandler for two years, and it is wonderful to have a balcony to walk around on and sit outside on nice days. The campus is small, so anywhere is close to everything!"

Q "The dorms are well situated throughout campus and have great locations. **There are different styles of dorms** that you can choose from, so you can pick what's best for you. A dorm with a great location would be Chandler; especially the third floor!"

Q "The dorms are nice; there are some older ones and some newer ones. There are your typical hall dorms with hall bathrooms that are all one sex [Carolina and Smith]. Then there are hall dorms with bathrooms between two of the rooms where the 'suites,' meaning two rooms and a bathroom, are one sex but the hall is co-ed [Virginia and Moffitt]. **There are also suites that have five rooms** and nine people, with two bathrooms; these have a common living area [Chandler or Maynard]."

Q "The dorms are nice. There aren't too many bad places to live. **I like living in Chandler**, but I know people in other dorms who like where they live. If you want to be really close to the academic buildings, do not live in Chandler, Colclough, Maynard, Moffitt, or Staley."

### The College Prowler Take
ON CAMPUS HOUSING

Although no dorm could really ever have all the space most students crave, the rooms at Elon are big enough to fit most of your needs. In fact, on the whole, Elon has some pretty awesome dorms. You'll find that laundry facilities are almost always busy, but this is the case almost anywhere. The drawbacks are relatively minor, compared to the beautiful housing facilities Elon provides for its student body. Elon students can rest assured (in their extra-long twin beds) that they're getting one of the best deals around when it comes to campus housing.

**A-**

The College Prowler™ Grade on
### Campus Housing: A-

A high Campus Housing grade indicates that dorms are clean, well-maintained, and spacious. Other determining factors include variety of dorms, proximity to classes, and social atmosphere.

# Diversity

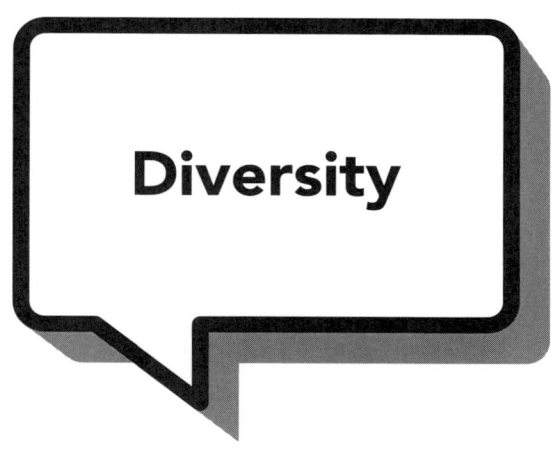

## The Lowdown
ON DIVERSITY

- **Native American:** 0.1%
- **Asian American:** 0.8%
- **African American:** 6.4%
- **Hispanic:** 0.8%
- **White:** 87.6%
- **International:** 1.1%
- **Unknown:** 3.2%
- **Out-of-State:** 71%

**Minority Clubs**
Black Cultural Society, Elon's Finest (dance organization that uses African-inspired movements), Elon Gospel Choir

**Most Popular Religions**
Catholic, Baptist, Episcopalian, Methodist

**Political Activity**
Political activity at Elon is moderate and largely encouraged by the University, which has made it a policy to get students involved in politics and their community.

**Gay Tolerance**
There is a high tolerance for homosexuals at Elon. The University not only has a policy of non-discrimination based on sexual orientation, but offers same-sex domestic partner benefits to staff members.

**Economic Status**
Elon is obviously a private school, and the majority of the students are upper-middle-class.

## Students Speak Out
ON DIVERSITY

"This is Elon's biggest downfall; admissions is really marketing the school so that we'll become more diverse, but this is a slow process that will take many more years."

Q "Our campus is **not very diverse**. I would like to see it become much more so in the next few years by drawing in more minority students."

Q "Elon's somewhat diverse, but **everyone segregates themselves**."

Q "Since the campus is so small, there is a lack of diversity. The school is trying to fix this, which will only come in time as the school grows. They try to bring culture into our lives as much as possible, so even though diversity is not in the classrooms everyday, **we still get exposed to different cultures** through events and at the dining halls on certain nights."

Q "I would like to think that the school is diverse. There are **students from everywhere imaginable**. Yes, there are a lot of white, preppy people, but they don't make up the entire school."

## The College Prowler Take
### ON DIVERSITY

One of Elon's definite weaknesses is the lack of diversity. However, both students and faculty are pressing for a more diverse school. Black students have voiced their concern about the small amount of African Americans at Elon, and how it affects them. And there are even fewer of the other minorities. Sometimes a student will see a Hispanic or Indian student, and make a joke like, "there walks diversity at Elon." Many students want higher diversity, and in the next few years, they might get it. Many students have voiced their opinion that admissions should try to go to areas that have diverse populations and promote Elon in the high schools there. Even though diversity is low, there is indeed hope for a more diverse campus in the coming years.

**The College Prowler™ Grade on**
## Diversity: D-

A high grade in Diversity indicates that ethnic minorities and international students have a notable presence on campus and that students of different economic backgrounds, religious beliefs, and sexual preferences are well-represented.

# Guys & Girls

## The Lowdown
### ON GUYS & GIRLS

**Women Undergrads:** 61%

**Men Undergrads:** 39%

### Birth Control Available?
Yes, it is at RN Ellington Health & Counseling Center.

### Social Scene
Students are very outgoing, and like to party at off-campus apartments, or any of the Greek houses on campus. There is a bowling alley that is particularly popular for group outings (especially student clubs), as well as a movie theatre. About 20 minutes away in Greensboro there are many nightclubs that students can get into at age 18.

### Hookups or Relationships?
Although random hookups do occur, a good amount of students are in serious relationships—some even engaged.

### Dress Code
Mostly preppy-casual, but completely laid-back. You usually see two different types of clothing styles on campus: jeans with a nice collared shirt, or sweatpants with an Elon sweatshirt. There's no pressure to dress up, and there's no shame in wearing your pajamas to class. Some girls walk around looking like Gap commercials; some look like they just got out of bed.

## Students Speak Out
**ON GUYS & GIRLS**

*"If a girl is going to college in search of a husband, Elon isn't the best place to go—the ratio is not in her favor! If a man is in search for a husband, Elon is a good choice for him!"*

"A lot of the girls are very nice, sincere people, but there are also those who are stuck-up snobs. **There are a lot of hot guys at Elon,** but then again, they are usually rude, taken, or gay. You wanted the truth, right? Since there is such a variety of people here though, it's not hard to find people with the same interests, and form great friendships."

"Guys are around, but relationship-wise, it's hard. Not everyone is looking for it at this point. But **everyone is super friendly** and fun to be around. The campus is full of beautiful and diverse people, in terms of thinking and backgrounds."

"The guys are all right; **they seem a little overbearing** on girls, and they think they can get away with anything. The girls are very cool; but some can come across as easy by the way they carry themselves at parties and with guys. The guys are definitely hot."

"Elon is considered one of the best-looking campuses for its grounds and its people. Greek life is huge so the people are really into that. And an important thing to remember is that **there are more girls than guys,** and the standard saying about guys is they are either gay, taken, or a player."

## The College Prowler Take
**ON GUYS & GIRLS**

You don't have to be dressed to impress all the time to meet or date people. Although it feels like you won't get the time of day unless you look like Carmen Electra or Brad Pitt, beneath the surface, students at Elon really appreciate a down-to-earth person who likes to put their best foot forward, even if it's just in jeans and a T-shirt, while maintaining an air of levelheadedness. For all this, however, the campus does seem very promiscuous at times. Some girls dress in ways that show exactly what their intent is; likewise, some guys obviously want to be "the big pimp." At any private school you're going to run into some social headaches, but Elon generally has an atmosphere of acceptance.

**B+**   **A-**

The College Prowler™ Grade on
### Guys: B+
A high grade for Guys indicates that the male population on campus is attractive, smart, friendly, and engaging, and that the school has a decent ratio of guys to girls.

The College Prowler™ Grade on
### Girls: A-
A high grade for Girls not only implies that the women on campus are attractive, smart, friendly, and engaging, but also that there is a fair ratio of girls to guys.

---

**COLLEGE PROWLER™**

Want to know more about Elon hotties? For more student quotes, check out the College Prowler book on Elon available at *www.collegeprowler.com*.

# Athletics

## The Lowdown
### ON ATHLETICS

**Athletic Division:**
NCAA Division I

**Conference:**
Southern Conference

**School Mascot:**
Phoenix

**Fields:**
Firehouse Field, Hunt Field, Intramural Fields, Ruud Field

**Most Popular Sports:**
Basketball, Intramural/Varsity Soccer

**Overlooked Teams:**
Women's Volleyball, Golf

**Getting Tickets:**
Students get in free with their Phoenix ID card. For non-students, tickets are easy to get as long as you visit the ticket office before any of the games.

**Men's Varsity Teams:**
Basketball
Baseball
Golf
Tennis
Cross Country
Cheerleading
Football

**Women's Varsity Teams:**
Basketball
Indoor Track
Cheerleading/Dance
Golf
Softball
Tennis
Track & Field
Cross Country
Soccer
Volleyball

### Club Sports
Field Hockey, Men's Lacrosse, Men's Rugby, Men's Soccer, Roller Hockey, Swimming, Volleyball, Ultimate Frisbee, Women's Lacrosse, Women's Rugby, Women's Soccer

### Intramurals (IMs)
Flag Football, Softball, Dodgeball, Water Polo, Ping-Pong, Soccer, Volleyball, Frisbee, and Basketball, and innovative programs like Arena Football, Wiffleball, and the 3-point Shootout

## Students Speak Out
### ON ATHLETICS

"Sports are pretty big, but sometimes there is trouble getting students to support them. Intramural sports, on the other hand, are huge. They're for fun and attract more of a crowd."

Q "Sports are pretty big, but **our sports teams kind of suck**. Intramural sports are well supported, but kind of a joke."

Q "Elon offers lots of sports for students to be involved with. If you're not on a varsity team, **there are lots of opportunities to be involved in intramural sports**. For those of us who played sports throughout our lives, and are not going to play varsity sports, intramural sports are fabulous because they allow you to keep playing."

Q "Sports are big; however, we suck, so there's not that much hype. **It isn't like going to a NCAA school;** it's a small school with not such a great team, but with spirit. Intramural seems to be pretty big."

Q "Varsity basketball is really a big draw, but most other sports are viewed as more of a novelty. IM sports have dedicated students who make sure the team trains and does well, but **they don't draw any kind of crowd**."

# Greek Life

## The College Prowler Take
ON ATHLETICS

Intramural sports are very big on campus, probably bigger than many varsity sports. Elon offers 17 varsity sports and 12 intramurals on campus. In the 2003-2004 academic year, the school was brand-new to a higher division—the Southern Conference. This advance has been very exciting for students and staff alike, and has helped our reputation grow. For anyone who doesn't feel like they are good enough for collegiate-level sports, or just wants to play for fun, Elon offers many intramural sports, including rugby, soccer, racquetball, and volleyball. A good percentage of students play either varsity or intramurals at some point in their college careers.

## The Lowdown
ON GREEK LIFE

**Number of Fraternities:**
10

**Number of Sororities:**
9

**Undergrad Men in Fraternities:**
9%

**Undergrad Women in Sororities:**
24%

**Multicultural Colonies:**
Alpha Kappa Alpha, Zeta Phi Beta, Sigma Gamma Rho, Omega Psi Phi, Alpha Phi Omega, Phi Beta Sigma

**B-**

The College Prowler™ Grade on
## Athletics: B-

A high grade in Athletics indicates that students have school spirit, that sports programs are respected, that games are well-attended, and that intramurals are a prominent part of student life.

### Did You Know?
Elon has what is called deferred rush, meaning all potential Greeks must have completed at least 12 Elon credit hours and have either a 2.35 minimum cumulative GPA for women, or 2.3 for men.

## Students Speak Out
### ON GREEK LIFE

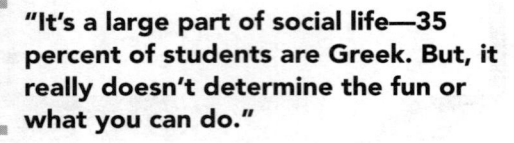

"It's a large part of social life—35 percent of students are Greek. But, it really doesn't determine the fun or what you can do."

Q "**Greek life is huge on campus**. Many people come just assuming they will join, others will end up joining because so many people do. This is one of the most prominent non-academic organizations on campus."

Q "Although the percentage of students in Greek life is not very high, it seems that **almost everyone is in a sorority or fraternity**. Greek life does host many of the social events on campus, but there are a lot of other organizations that provide great times to have fun."

Q "Although only about 35 percent of campus is Greek, **it's everywhere**. I'm not Greek, though, and life is still fun and exciting at Elon. It just depends on what type of social scene you want."

Q "Greek life dominates this school, but if you don't want to do it **there are other organizations**. There are Learning Communities that are very well-organized, and Elon Volunteers is a great way to learn about activities. Also, departments put together activities, such as learning how to do Spanish dances."

## The College Prowler Take
### ON GREEK LIFE

Elon has what we called a "deferred rush" meaning you cannot rush until at least the second semester of freshman year; also, you must have a minimum GPA of 2.35 for women and 2.3 for men before rushing. We have 23 social sororities/fraternities and 25 honors Greek societies, such as Phi Kappa Phi and Omicron Delta Kappa. Only officers live in houses, or some students with very high GPAs, and the rest of the members live either on or off campus (based on personal preference). Elon prohibits hazing, and prides itself on a Greek society that is very accepting of many different types of people. Also, you don't have to be Greek to go to the parties, you just have to be on the guest list. There is never a day that goes by where you will not see someone wearing some sort of T-shirt, pin, or carrying a bag with the name of their Greek organization on it.

Looking to go Greek? Pick up a College Prowler guidebook on Elon on www.collegeprowler.com and check out which house is right for you.

### The College Prowler™ Grade on
### Greek Life: A

A high grade in Greek Life indicates that sororities and fraternities are not only present, but also active on campus. Other determining factors include the variety of houses available and the respect the Greek community receives from the rest of the campus.

# Drug Scene

## The Lowdown
ON DRUG SCENE

**Liquor-Related Referrals:**
384

**Liquor-Related Arrests:**
1

**Drug-Related Referrals:**
26

**Drug-Related Arrests:**
20

### Drug Counseling Programs

Counseling Services, at the RN Ellington Health Center, provides referral recommendations and short-term counseling. Their phone number is (336) 278-7280. These services are free to students, faculty, and staff.

Rev. Richard McBride, the University chaplain, offers free referral recommendations, short-term counseling, and educational materials to faculty, staff, and students. His number is (336) 278-7729.

Ms. Resa E. Walch, director of substance education, offers free referral recommendations, short-term counseling, and educational materials to faculty, staff, and students. Her number is (336) 278-7209.

## Students Speak Out
ON DRUG SCENE

"The drug scene is pretty minimal. While a fair number of students smoke pot every now and then, other drugs are much rarer in terms of the overall student population."

Q "I don't know about drugs on campus. I've never heard of a problem. **It's mostly alcohol** that causes problems."

Q "**I've never had any encounters with drugs** or have heard of any since I arrived at Elon two years ago."

Q "There are always certain crowds that do drugs on campus, **nothing out of the normal**. It isn't a huge issue."

Q "If people do it, **they keep to themselves**; you can seriously go all four years and not see any of it."

### COLLEGE PROWLER

Visit www.collegeprowler.com and get the guidebook on Elon. You'll find all the info you need to decide if this school is right for you.

## The College Prowler Take
### ON DRUG SCENE

This is college, so, naturally, there is going to be a certain percentage of the population that chooses to use illegal drugs. However, this sort of thing isn't at all prevalent at Elon. Room checks are regularly conducted by RAs, so if anyone has drug paraphernalia they are immediately written up; there are different levels of punishments for different infractions, but the University won't go easy on those who break the law. On the whole, you can be confident that Elon students are level-headed, sober, drug-free students. As far as drinking is concerned—yes, it occurs, but everyone's pretty responsible. Students make it a point to have designated drivers, and, if not, there's always Safe Rides. Students say they never feel pressure to drink or do drugs at Elon.

**A-**

The College Prowler™ Grade on
### Drug Scene: A-

A high grade on Drug Scene indicates that drugs are not a noticeable part of campus life; drug use is not visible, and no pressure to use them seems to exist.

# Overall Experience

### Students Speak Out
### ON OVERALL EXPERIENCE

"It's been great overall. Sometimes I wish I were somewhere else, yes. I feel I can get more from other programs at other universities."

Q "I love it here. I'm becoming the person I'm meant to be, and growing as an individual through the organizations and classes I take. My collective experience is amazing. From Greek to organizations to studying abroad, I know, **I'll leave Elon with a strong sense of self**, and be equipped with what I need to live and function in our society."

Q "I couldn't imagine being anywhere else. I love Elon, and feel at home every time I come back from break. The atmosphere is very comfortable and easygoing. The administration takes care of their students and is always striving to accommodate to their needs. **They push the community feeling**, and it has worked. Elon has made this school more beautiful than the outside could ever show!"

Q "**I've had the best time in my life** because of Elon. They provide students opportunity, encouragement, and a starting path to a Bachelor or Master degree. I would not wish to be anywhere else other than Elon. As a matter of fact, I wish there were an Elon in Maryland, so I could go to school closer to home without sacrificing the wonderful opportunities and pleasures I get from Elon University."

> "I love Elon. There always certain drawbacks to any school, but **I can't imagine myself anywhere else**. I have been given great opportunity for leadership on campus, and have really come much closer to discovering my passions through a small university environment."

## The College Prowler Take
### ON OVERALL EXPERIENCE

Elon students enjoy the experience of attending the school, but, as with many things, there are a few drawbacks. For instance, the community is too small and quiet for some, and other schools are at least a half-hour away. The lack of diversity is also an issue for many. However, in spite of the drawbacks, most students here can't imagine being anywhere else. The school just offers so much. Socially there is a great Greek scene, and students also throw parties in their houses and/or apartments. There is also an abundance of nightlife in Greensboro, which is only a 20 to 30 minutes away, and well worth the trip. The academic curriculum can be rigorous at times, but the professors are willing to help in any way that they can. Elon's student body is great, even though some personalities can be a little difficult to deal with at times. There are not a lot of complaints about the University, other than its diversity issues and the size of the town. Don't be fooled by Elon's size—it may not be for everyone, but life at Elon can be a great experience.

# Emory University

1380 S. Oxford Road NE Atlanta, GA 30322
www.emory.edu          (404) 727-6036

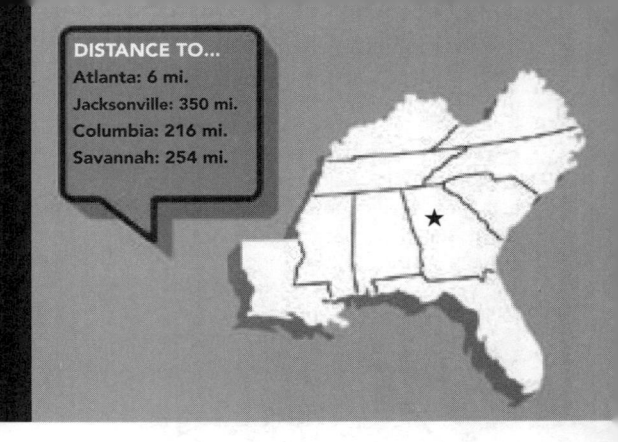

**DISTANCE TO...**
Atlanta: 6 mi.
Jacksonville: 350 mi.
Columbia: 216 mi.
Savannah: 254 mi.

*"A lot of what Emory has given me goes way beyond the simple realm of education."*

**Total Enrollment:**
6,193

**Top 10% of High School Class:**
90%

**Average GPA:**
3.8

**Acceptance Rate:**
42%

**Tuition:**
$29,322

**SAT Range (25th-75th Percentile)**

| Verbal | Math | Total |
|---|---|---|
| 640 – 720 | 660 – 740 | 1300 – 1460 |

**ACT Range (25th-75th Percentile)**

| Verbal | Math | Total |
|---|---|---|
| 27-32 | 29-33 | 29-33 |

**Most Popular Majors:**
20% History
18% Business Administration and Management
16% Biology/Biological Sciences
10% Psychology
7% English Language and Literature

**Students also applied to:***
Duke University
Georgetown University
University of Pennsylvania
Vanderbilt University
Washington University—St. Louis

*For more school info check out www.collegeprowler.com

**Table of Contents**

| | |
|---|---|
| Academics | 481 |
| Local Atmosphere | 483 |
| Safety & Security | 484 |
| Facilities | 486 |
| Campus Dining | 487 |
| Campus Housing | 489 |
| Diversity | 490 |
| Guys & Girls | 492 |
| Athletics | 493 |
| Greek Life | 495 |
| Drug Scene | 497 |
| Overall Experience | 498 |

**College Prowler Report Card**

| | |
|---|---|
| Academics | A- |
| Local Atmosphere | A- |
| Safety & Security | A |
| Facilities | A |
| Campus Dining | D+ |
| Campus Housing | B- |
| Diversity | C+ |
| Guys | B- |
| Girls | C |
| Athletics | C- |
| Greek Life | B+ |
| Drug Scene | C+ |

# Academics

## Special Degree Options
Dual-Degree Engineering Program with Georgia Tech; Accelerated four-year master's program in biology, chemistry, English, history, mathematics, mathematics and computer science, philosophy, political science, or sociology

## Sample Academic Clubs
Phi Beta Kappa, Phi Eta Sigma, Sigma Xi, DVS, the Senior Society, Ducemus, Mortar Board, Paladin Society

## The Lowdown
### ON ACADEMICS

**Degrees Awarded:**
Bachelor, Master, Doctorate

**Undergraduate Schools:**
Emory College, Goizueta Business School, Oxford College, School of Nursing

**Full-time Faculty:**
1,095

**Faculty with Terminal Degree:**
100%

**Student-to-Faculty Ratio:**
5:1

**Average Course Load:**
4 courses

**AP Test Score Requirements:**
Possible credit for scores of 4 or 5

**IB Test Score Requirements:**
Possible credit for scores of 5, 6, or 7

## Did You Know?
During Dooley's Week, if Dooley (a skeleton character that serves as Emory's other mascot) and his entourage come into your class and spray your teacher with a water gun, that class is dismissed.

**Best Places to Study:**
Cox Computer Lab, Woodruff Library, Law Library, Dental School Building, dormitories

## Students Speak Out
### ON ACADEMICS

"**The teachers are well-rounded and tend to be very passionate about their respective subjects, so it's not just about transferring facts to the students for them. This gives life to the classes.**"

Q "**There's good and bad.** I've had teachers say, 'If you have questions, come to office hours, stop by if I'm in my office, call, e-mail, stop me on campus and I'll help you right then and there,' and they will. Then there are the professors who don't get the point across and don't care. But, I've had more good than bad."

Q "Emory has a lot of requirements for the liberal arts degree, so you most likely will have to **take some classes that you really don't want to**."

Q "At Emory, **your grades hinge on class attendance**. If the teacher knows your face and you participate, it's a lot easier to work with them if you are having problems. Don't expect any teacher to help you if you never show up, though."

Q "Some teachers are amazing, and some are amazingly bad. **The best advice is to ask upperclassmen** to find out which teachers are best for you. Any senior can give you a great list of good and bad apples."

Q "Some teachers are **too interested in their own research** and writing to help the students, especially in the undergraduate business school. I had a teacher last year that basically made us do his research for him so that he could make money off it. I've also had teachers who make you buy their book for class, even when the book is horrible."

## The College Prowler Take
### ON ACADEMICS

Emory's small classes can be a real blessing for students, in terms of how much knowledge they get out of their classes. This small class size also means close interaction with teachers, so attendance is hugely important for a good grade. Being on a first name basis with your professor allows you some slack if you do miss a class or have trouble with an assignment. Many professors maintain a strange love/hate relationship with the school's administration, which can be endearing for students. Emory's e-mail system, LearnLink, serves as the perfect platform for online class discussions, assignments, and some private Q-and-A sessions with your teacher, if you like.

Academics are certainly Emory's strong suit, and the reason most students apply here in the first place. Many teachers and departments at Emory are nationally recognized, and some are award-winning. Numerous teachers are respected authors and researchers, and some are the authorities in their respective fields. The college is consistently ranked in the top 20 nationally, and nearly all of the graduate schools are highly respected, as well. Not all of the teachers are top-notch, but when you do find the great ones, you'll never forget them. As for majors, the humanities and undergraduate business school are well-funded and liked, while the performing arts are under-funded and ignored despite the new Donna & Marvin Schwartz Center for Performing Arts. Many students agree that Emory is not as hard as they had assumed, but that certainly doesn't mean that people looking for an easy four years should flock here.

**A-**

**The College Prowler™ Grade on**
## Academics: A-

A high Academics grade generally indicates that professors are knowledgeable, accessible, and genuinely interested in their students' welfare. Other determining factors include class size, how well professors communicate, and whether or not classes are engaging.

# Local Atmosphere

**City Websites**
http://www.atlanta.com
http://www.creativeloafing.com
http://www.accessatlanta.com
http://www.ajc.com

## The Lowdown
ON LOCAL ATMOSPHERE

**Region:**
Southeast

**City, State:**
Atlanta, Georgia

**Setting:**
Northeast Atlanta Suburb

**Distance from Metro Atlanta:**
15 minutes

**Distance from Athens (University of Georgia):**
1 hour, 30 minutes

**Distance from Florida:**
4 hours

**Distance from New Orleans:**
9 hours

**Points of Interest:**
CNN Center, Coca-Cola Museum, Little Five Points, Centennial Olympic Park, Buckhead, Virginia Highlands, Zoo Atlanta, High Museum of Art

**Major Sports Teams:**
Braves (baseball), Hawks (basketball), Falcons (football), Thrashers (hockey)

## Students Speak Out
ON LOCAL ATMOSPHERE

"There is nothing outside of Emory. People refer to it as a 'bubble' ... I prefer 'abyss.' You will never escape the clutches of the Emory social scene, so don't bother."

Q "**Everyone down here is so nice**, you really get a glimpse into southern culture and hospitality living in Atlanta. There are some places to avoid, like downtown and anyplace in southern Atlanta. I wouldn't recommend getting lost by yourself. It can be dangerous."

Q "Atlanta is a confusing city, both geographically and ideologically. There isn't a definite 'Atlanta' vibe or area; rather, **Atlanta is made of certain exclusive communities**, which are isolated from one another. The traffic in Atlanta is ridiculous and the city layout looks like Jackson Pollack threw it together, so you will definitely get lost every now and then."

Q "**The atmosphere is quite stimulating**, and there is much to be seen in the Atlanta area. There are numerous universities around including Georgia Tech, Georgia State, Oglethorpe, and more. One should stay away from the downtown areas, as they are sometimes unsafe. There are many things to visit, including the CNN center, Olympic Park, and the Cyclorama."

Q "Emory is in Atlanta, but **this is no college town**. In fact, it is nearly the opposite of a college town. You never really feel like you are going to college; it feels more like a country club outside of a major city."

## The College Prowler Take
### ON LOCAL ATMOSPHERE

Atlanta has tons of things to do for fun. Having a professional team in all four major sports means that you can enjoy pro sports year round. Atlanta has several great bohemian areas, like East Atlanta and Little Five Points, both full of cool shops and restaurants and exciting nightlife. Areas like Virginia Highlands, Buckhead, and Midtown also offer great nightlife and restaurants. Athens, where the University of Georgia is located, is just one hour away, and Savannah, a beautiful and fun place to visit, is about two hours away. Some students are bothered by Emory's distance from the major points of interest in Atlanta—indeed, the poor quality of transportation and Emory's isolation do sometimes restrict social life. While Atlanta may not be as rich in historical culture or artistic entertainment as larger, older cities, it is still easy to find fun things to do when you venture into this youthful metropolis.

## Safety & Security

## The Lowdown
### ON SAFETY & SECURITY

**Number of Emory Police:**
20+

**Phone:**
(404) 727-6111 or 911 (emergencies)
(404) 727-8005 (non-emergencies)

**Health Center Office Hours:**
Monday-Friday 8 a.m.-6 p.m., Saturday 10 a.m.-1 p.m.

**Safety Services:**
Security escorts, blue-light phones, police station located on campus

### A-

The College Prowler™ Grade on
**Local Atmosphere: A-**

A high Local Atmosphere grade indicates that the area surrounding campus is safe and scenic. Other factors include nearby attractions, proximity to other schools, and the town's attitude toward students.

### Did You Know?

Medical excuses are not issued by the Emory University Health Services except in the case of a serious, extended illness. Students are responsible for notifying their professors when they will be absent.

## Students Speak Out
**ON SAFETY & SECURITY**

"As far as safety, you've got the blue-light call-boxes positioned in various places in case you're ever in trouble, and they also have an escort service. You can walk across campus in the middle of the night and feel safe."

Q "**Campus is safe**, apart from random theft and break-ins. The blue-light system is around, even though I can't remember how it works, and I have never seen anyone use it."

Q "The only thing that ever makes me feel unsafe at Emory is the fact that the **Center for Disease Control and Prevention** is right next to campus. As long as that building doesn't blow up, you are always safe around here."

Q "Most students are **surprised at how bad some of the doctors are** in the Student Health Services. It seems like they really don't care about you sometimes. Still, I wouldn't want to be anywhere else if something bad happened to me, as Emory has an amazing hospital system."

Q "Emory is consistently one of the top hospital systems in the country, so you should never be worried if something bad happens to you. They have a **quick response time** since they are right on campus, and the doctors are world-class."

## The College Prowler Take
**ON SAFETY & SECURITY**

In a city with a sometimes disturbing crime rate, Emory could not be any safer. Situated in a suburban enclave more than 15 minutes from any high-crime area, Emory's few crimes are primarily committed by students themselves. Security is great; there is a fully functional police station directly on campus, and police patrol the area regularly. Other than the numerous petty thefts that occur each year, including some locker room wallet thefts, bike thefts, and dormitory laptop thefts, not much in the way of crime occurs on campus. Each dorm has locked doors that only residents have keys to, and a call-box is located outside of each dorm to limit non-Emory traffic. Regularly patrolling police, emergency call-boxes located all over campus, and campus escorts provide all of the security anyone could need here.

The College Prowler™ Grade on
### Safety & Security: A

A high grade in Safety & Security means that students generally feel safe, campus police are visible, blue-light phones and escort services are readily available, and safety precautions are not overly necessary.

# Facilities

**Computers**

**High-Speed Network?** Yes

**Wireless Network?** Yes

**Number of Labs**: 13

**Number of Computers**: 400+

**24-Hour Labs:** Woodruff Library

**Charge to Print?** $0.07 per page for students

## The Lowdown
### ON FACILITIES

**Student Center:**
The Dobbs University Center (DUC)

**Athletic Center:**
The Woodruff Physical Education Center (WoodPEC)

**Libraries:**
7

**Movie Theatre on Campus?**
Harland Cinema, but it only offers only one showing of one new movie per month.

**Bowling on Campus?**
No

**Bar on Campus?**
There is a bar in Emory Village, but not technically on campus.

**Coffeehouse on Campus?**
There are two coffeehouses in the Village, and you can get coffee at Dooley's Den at the Depot or Cox Hall.

**Popular Places to Chill:**
Dorm common areas, McDonough Field, Cox Hall, the DUC, Dooley's Den at the Depot

### Favorite Things to Do
Most students hang out in their dorms with others. Occasional fraternity parties are heavily attended. Trips to Emory Village are common. A lot of people play pickup basketball, soccer and football, and many people also throw Frisbee or sunbathe.

## Students Speak Out
### ON FACILITIES

"The new arts center is amazing, with lots of studios and space available to the artists; the athletic center appeals to just about everyone, especially if you play sports."

Q "Emory's facilities are very impressive, and when you look at them and use them, **you can really see where all of the money goes** here."

Q "All of the buildings are impressive, as most are made of marble or have beautiful copper fixtures adorning them. The gym, however, is in **dire need of new equipment**, and the roof leaks."

Q "Emory has a ridiculous endowment, so the facilities are really nice. The **constant remodeling and building** on campus creates a virtual obstacle course around construction, which is irritating."

> "This school's campus is so nice and perfect that they **filmed the movie "Road Trip" here** a few years back. There are constantly people working on the maintenance and upkeep of the campus, which is nice, but the construction can be overbearing sometimes. Overall, it looks like you go to school on a golf course or something."

## The College Prowler Take
### ON FACILITIES

Emory's facilities, as a whole, are very attractive and well-maintained. Nearly every building's exterior is made of marble, and most feature beautiful terra-cotta roofs and copper fixtures. This architectural bravado can alienate students, but it provides an impressive overall campus appearance. Acclaimed architect and Atlanta native, John Portman, famous for his innovative hotel designs, designed both the student center and gymnasium. Sometimes all of the construction can get in the way, but the beauty of the buildings tends to make you forgive this. The student center, known as the DUC (Dobbs University Center), is in the middle of campus and houses the bookstore, the mailroom, a video game room, a pool and foosball room, the freshman dining hall, and numerous administrative outlets for students, including the newspaper and the Office of Sorority and Fraternity Life. Emory's athletic facilities are some of the nicest in the entire Southeast.

The College Prowler™ Grade on
## Facilities: A

A high Facilities grade indicates that the campus is aesthetically pleasing and well-maintained; facilities are state-of-the-art, and libraries are exceptional. Other determining factors include the quality of both athletic and student centers and an abundance of things to do on campus.

# Campus Dining

## The Lowdown
### ON CAMPUS DINING

**Freshman Meal Plan Requirement?**
Yes

**24-Hour On-Campus Eating?**
Dooley's Den at the Depot

**Student Favorites:**
Cox Hall

**Meal Plan Average Cost:**
$400-$1,625 (choose wisely)

### Did You Know?

Emory's student government is in the process of expanding the EmoryCard's off-campus purchasing power, which will be a real blessing to students.

## Students Speak Out
### ON CAMPUS DINING

"The cafeteria has a lot to offer, and the food's pretty good for college, but after eating anything every day for a year, you get really sick of it."

Q "The food on campus is **just like any other college**. There is a good variety but you cannot expect much, as far as taste, considering the large amounts of food that have to be made."

Q "The main dining hall is located in the Dobbs University Center, and the quality of food is typical of most university dining halls; however, they offer a number of different options, and are **sensitive to the diversity of dietary lifestyles** on campus. Some people prefer Cox Hall because it operates like a mall food court, with chain-style dining, and has a regular crowd of Cox-rats, making it a social scene more than a dining facility. The restaurant Caffè Antico caters the museum café and a lot of faculty dine here, and the food is pretty good but overpriced. I rarely eat on campus because it is such an ordeal to avoid the scene."

Q "To put things simply, **the food could be better** here. The DUC is mediocre and Cox is too, and the other options are way overpriced."

Q "Picking the meal plan with the least DUC money and the most á la carte funds is the best idea. If you pick the unlimited meals at the DUC and least á la carte money, you will really regret it. **The DUC gets old**, and you'll spend all of the extra money way before the semester is over. A good middle-of-the-road plan is not a bad idea either; that way you don't have to eat alone at Cox or order Domino's while your friends eat at the DUC."

## The College Prowler Take
### ON CAMPUS DINING

The food on Emory's campus is so-so. At first, freshmen are excited by the idea of a food court featuring a Burger King and Chick-fil-A, but the excitement soon wears off when they realize that these are sub-par food court versions of their favorite fast food chains. The freshmen dining hall (there is only one) in the DUC features all types of food imaginable and serves food from early in the morning until late in the evening, but the food is far from amazing. It is easy to be fooled into thinking Emory has great food for the first few weeks of school, but the realization of its general blandness hits all freshmen around October.

**D+**

The College Prowler™ Grade on
### Campus Dining: D+

Our grade on Campus Dining addresses the quality of both school-owned dining halls and independent on-campus restaurants as well as the price, availability, and variety of food.

# Campus Housing

## The Lowdown
### ON CAMPUS HOUSING

**Undergrads on Campus:**
62%

**Number of Dormitories:**
20

**Number of University-Owned Apartments:**
0

**Room Types:**
Rooms vary widely depending on the dorm. Singles, doubles, triples, and apartments are all available.

**Available for Rent:**
Mini-refrigerators, laundry service, microwaves

**Cleaning Service?**
A cleaning crew works every weekday in every on-campus facility in all public areas.

**You Get:**
Bed, closet, desk, chair, Internet access, sinks in some rooms, dresser in some rooms

**Bed Type:**
Twin in most dorms, full in Clairmont Campus Apartments

**Also Available:**
Smoke-free areas, female-only dorms, special-interest housing

## Students Speak Out
### ON CAMPUS HOUSING

"The dorms are all relatively new, and all have air conditioning units that keep you cool during the hot spring and summer months."

Q "Freshman **dorms are pretty good**. I really don't know about upperclass dorms, although Clairmont Campus is getting pretty nice with the addition of a huge pool and activity area."

Q "The dorms are nice, although it would be wise to check ahead, because some are larger than others, and **location is key**—Turman is far from campus, and Dobbs has really small rooms. I lived in Harris, which is an exceptionally nice dorm—big room, newly remodeled."

Q "The dorms are pretty nice overall, and I can't think of anything too bad to say, except that Turman is far away and Dobbs has small rooms. Each floor [in first-year dorms] has an RA [resident advisor] and an SA [sophomore advisor]. The RA is supposed to be like your parent, while the SA is supposed to function as more of a sibling. Either way, you kind of feel like **they are out to get you** at first, but some of them end up being really cool. I still hang out with my SA, and it's been three years now."

Q "Some dorms, like Longstreet, have sinks in the rooms, which are nice for washing up, and others have cool amenities like big lawns or **workout and computer rooms**. If you know someone coming to school here, you can request them as a roommate, and you'll probably get them, and if you hate your roommate, you can always switch, which a lot of girls do."

## The College Prowler Take
### ON CAMPUS HOUSING

As a whole, the dorms on Emory's campus are nice, but there is nothing all that special about them. Each dorm has its differences from the next, and some are better than others in terms of location, etc. Each floor has both a sophomore advisor and a resident advisor, both there to help you out, and get you in trouble at the same time. Every dorm has a residence hall director, but this person is rarely seen unless you misbehave. Many students believe that the dorms could and should be nicer considering Emory's large endowment, but, alas, they are what they are, and students have to deal with that fact. The dorms on campus are some of the few Emory facilities that don't feel like a country club.

# Diversity

## The Lowdown
### ON DIVERSITY

**Native American:** 0%

**Asian American:** 15%

**African American:** 10%

**White:** 69%

**Hispanic:** 3%

**International:** 3%

**Out-of-State:** 71%

## B-

### The College Prowler™ Grade on
### Campus Housing: B-

A high Campus Housing grade indicates that dorms are clean, well-maintained, and spacious. Other determining factors include variety of dorms, proximity to classes, and social atmosphere.

### Minority Clubs

Emory's minority clubs are prevalent and vocal on campus. There are numerous African American, Asian, Indian, and Latino clubs that sponsor various events around campus constantly. There are two black fraternities and three sororities, one historically Jewish fraternity and two sororities, and an Asian sorority.

### Most Popular Religions
There are a lot of Jewish people at Emory, so there are also a lot of Jewish groups. The Jewish portion of Emory's students are very vocal, so much so that people outside of Emory joke that Emory, a Methodist school by nature, stands for "Early Methodist, Only Recently Yiddish."

### Political Activity
Emory is primarily a politically and socially liberal school. There were numerous well-attended protests during the recent Middle East action, and there have been other various liberal protests here before, as well. There are Young Republicans and Young Democrat clubs, but they are not especially vocal. Don't think that it is one-sided, however, as Emory students are known for some staunch political debates (they just happen to be in private).

### Gay Tolerance
This campus is very accepting of gay students and teachers alike.

### Economic Status
Emory is very expensive, yet most students do not have any trouble paying their tuition. There is some diversity within the economic backgrounds of students, but not nearly enough to quell complaints about all the "rich kids." It is not shocking at all to see five straight luxury cars drive past with students behind the wheel.

## Students Speak Out
### ON DIVERSITY

"Emory is a very diverse school, but at the same time there is a ridiculous amount of homogeneity. People from different ethnic and religious groups stick together ... a little too much."

Q "I was pleasantly surprised at the diversity on campus. You can find all groups and all races of people chatting around campus at any time. It makes for a pleasant environment, although **sometimes it seems a little fake**, especially when you go here and then look at Emory's brochures and pamphlets and see one person from each race with their arms around each other."

Q "This school **pretends to be diverse**, but hardly anyone mixes into other groups. If you are black, and you join a white sorority or fraternity, then the other black students will not respect you as much. There are all black fraternities and sororities, and there are Jewish frats and sororities."

Q "I have enjoyed the diversity at this school. There is **a great mix of all races, religions and people from all areas** of the country. I'm from Florida, but I have friends from New York, California, Illinois, and even South America."

Q "Emory offers a lot of racial diversity, but not many people indulge in the chance to learn about different cultures. There are a lot of Jewish people. The school is **not too economically diverse however**. Most people here come from families with a ton of money."

## The College Prowler Take
### ON DIVERSITY

As you walk around Emory's campus, you definitely notice the wide variety of skin tones that pepper the landscape here. Unfortunately for the students, the numbers do not accurately reflect the amount of intermingling that occurs on a daily basis. Most white students hang out together, as do most black and most Asian students, etc. If you wanted to, you could go to Emory for four years without ever really speaking to someone outside your own socioeconomic class or race. However, that certainly need not be the case. Most everyone appreciates the diversity of the campus, and certainly most people try to take advantage of it. Also, the amazing diversity of metropolitan Atlanta itself gives Emory an additional feeling of diversity.

**C+**

The College Prowler™ Grade on
### Diversity: C+

A high grade in Diversity indicates that ethnic minorities and international students have a notable presence on campus and that students of different economic backgrounds, religious beliefs, and sexual preferences are well-represented.

# Guys & Girls

## Dress Code

It's New York business casual mixed with bohemian rhapsody. Emory students seem to follow the latest trend like it's their job, and the abundance of New Yorkers who dress exactly alike doesn't skew this theory one bit. Thursday nights bring out guys in black shoes and dress shirts and slacks, and girls in their finest wears, as well. There is also a strong population of bohemian types that offset the more trendy dressers, but the often-audacious outfits some students choose almost always overshadow them. The weather allows for T-shirts and shorts for most of the year, which is always a comfortable way to get your learn on.

## The Lowdown
### ON GUYS & GIRLS

**Women Undergrads**: 55%

**Men Undergrads**: 45%

**Birth Control Available?**
Yes, it's available from Student Health Services.

**Social Scene**
The social scene on campus features many groups of students. There are people here heavily involved in the Greek system, and introverted people who are only here to study and get a 4.0. There are a great number of people who love to party and socialize. It is never hard to find someone to hang out with or party with, and it is also never a chore to find a study buddy or someone to fix your computer.

**Hookups or Relationships?**
A lot of people are in relationships, but there are ample amounts of people who only hook up. It's all about what you are looking for, but usually the people who primarily hook up hang out together, as do the people in relationships.

## Students Speak Out
### ON GUYS & GIRLS

> "There are definitely attractive people who go to Emory, guys and girls, however few are stunning, and even fewer are worth the effort."

> "The number of attractive people also varies widely each year—some classes are infinitely more attractive than others. Girls get fat after freshmen year—I gained almost 20 pounds—then they get **anorexic sophomore year** and round out in the last two years."

> "The guys are short and the girls are **pretentious and annoying**. Some are good-looking."

> "Beware of kids who come from very wealthy sheltered homes, and have no idea what goes on in the real world. Just as many, though, are down-to-earth. The girls get decent once you get your '**Emory goggles**.'"

> "The guys tend to be more easygoing, but with a large population from the north. The northern dominance is also present for the girls, who are less easygoing and, no, don't tend to be very attractive. Many of the students **come from a higher income family, and feel the need to show it**, which gets annoying."

## The College Prowler Take
### ON GUYS & GIRLS

The Emory student body rates at about a six. Not horrible, but certainly not great either. Fashion is very important to many students at Emory, and it is noticeable when a new dress trend hits the school. The amount of money girls and guys spend on clothes can get ridiculous, but also helps the campus to appear more attractive at face value. Fitness is also very important to Emory students. Although one could not classify this campus as a handsome or pretty one, the students here do maintain a high level of fitness, in part due to the great athletic facilities and dining options available. Don't be mistaken, though, as there are some very beautiful people on campus; you just have to find them. As a whole, this campus tends to be fairly sexually promiscuous, with many students engaging in multiple one-night stands and unattached hookups.

**B-**

**C**

**The College Prowler™ Grade on**
## Guys: B-

A high grade for Guys indicates that the male population on campus is attractive, smart, friendly, and engaging, and that the school has a decent ratio of guys to girls.

**The College Prowler™ Grade on**
## Girls: C

A high grade for Girls not only implies that the women on campus are attractive, smart, friendly, and engaging, but also that there is a fair ratio of girls to guys.

## Athletics

## The Lowdown
### ON ATHLETICS

**Men's Varsity Teams:**
Baseball
Basketball
Cross Country
Golf
Soccer
Swimming and Diving
Tennis
Track and Field

**Women's Varsity Teams:**
Basketball
Cross Country
Soccer
Softball
Swimming and Diving
Tennis
Track and Field
Volleyball

### Club Sports
Crew, Cycling and Triathlon, Equestrian, Fencing, Field Hockey, Gymnastics, Men's Lacrosse, Women's Lacrosse, Roller Hockey, Men's Rugby, Sailing Club, Table Tennis, Men's Ultimate Frisbee, Women's Ultimate Frisbee, Men's Water Polo, Women's Water Polo

### Intramurals (IMs)
Badminton, Basketball, 3-on-3 Basketball, Cross Country, Flag Football, Golf, Racquetball, Sand Volleyball, Soccer, Softball, Spring Holiday Run, Table Tennis Singles, Table Tennis Doubles, Tennis, Track and Field, Ultimate Frisbee, Volleyball, Wrestling

**Athletic Division:**
Division III

**Conference:**
University Athletic Association

**School Mascot:**
Eagle

**Fields:**
McDonough, Candler

**Most Popular Sports:**
Swimming and Soccer

**Overlooked Teams:**
Every team; athletics just aren't that big here.

**Getting Tickets:**
What tickets?

Pick up the Emory University guidebook from www.collegeprowler.com to hear what students have to say about the athletics on campus.

# Students Speak Out
## ON ATHLETICS

"Sports on campus are not a big part of Emory life. In fact, Emory varsity sports in particular draw fewer crowds than most IM games."

Q "School spirit is so poor that **I feel bad for anyone who plays a varsity sport**. There is no varsity football team, so in the fall when other schools have a unifying element on Saturdays, we have nothing. What we do have is a joke T-shirt that reads, 'Emory Football, Undefeated Since 1853.'"

Q "If you are looking for a great college sports environment, this is not the place for you. Emory has **no school spirit**, and people here complain about this a lot. I think that the lack of a football team, or any Division I team, for that matter, makes it boring here."

Q "Some of the teams are very successful here, yet no one seems to care. **IM sports garner more interest** than varsity. For instance, people read a weekly ranking of IM teams with more excitement than any report of varsity sports."

Q "IM sports are great because the fields are very nice, and it is run on a pretty well-organized system. **People take IM sports very seriously** here, even more seriously than the varsity sports sometimes."

Q Since we don't have football, or athletic scholarships, **we don't draw the most athletic group of people here**. School spirit is a joke here—I am not even sure what our mascot is."

## The College Prowler Take
### ON ATHLETICS

Varsity sports are all but nonexistent here, an aspect of Emory that many blame school-wide apathy on. The first and most important thing that should be mentioned is this: there is no football team at Emory. Not one. Not even D-III. That is a portion of Emory's overall college experience that is totally lacking. There is no unifying event that all students attend once a week. Basketball games are poorly attended, as are all other sports, despite Emory having some of the top D-III sports programs in the country. Simply put, not many people are interested in varsity sports at Emory. This is an aspect of the school that many students find disheartening. Intramural sports make up for some of the overall lack of school spirit, but, in general, sports are not at the forefront of anyone's mind here.

**C-**

### The College Prowler™ Grade on
### Athletics: C-

A high grade in Athletics indicates that students have school spirit, that sports programs are respected, that games are well-attended, and that intramurals are a prominent part of student life.

# Greek Life

## The Lowdown
### ON GREEK LIFE

**Number of Fraternities:**
15

**Number of Sororities:**
9

**Undergrad Men in Fraternities:**
22%

**Undergrad Women in Sororities:**
21%

### Did You Know?

Sororities on campus only have lodges in which their executive members live. Although a rumor exists that this is because of a Georgia law prohibiting more than four women from living in the same house, it is untrue, and sorority houses may be built sometime in the future.

## Students Speak Out
### ON GREEK LIFE

"During first and second semester of freshman year, rushing, and the thought of joining a frat or sorority, are very important things. It seems like everyone is talking about it."

Q "The Greek system here plays a big role on the campus. Sometimes **you just can't avoid it**. Plus, there really is not much to do on Friday and Saturday nights as a freshman, except to go to a frat party."

Q "Unfortunately, this school has **become really uptight** recently, with regard to fraternity parties. There are all sorts of stupid rules now that have taken a once flourishing system and turned it into a pretty boring time."

Q "Emory has systematically made **on-campus parties virtually nonexistent** because of all the regulations now in place—you have to show state ID and student ID and be on the guest list."

Q "**Greek life does dominate the social scene**, and provides a much-needed breath of fresh air to the University. Emory is a top-level school, and reflects this in its cutthroat competition. The fraternities and sororities offer students a chance to remember they are still young, and to enjoy their time among like-minded and motivated peers."

## The College Prowler Take
### ON GREEK LIFE

Ten years ago at Emory, Greek life clearly dominated the social scene. That line has certainly been blurred recently, and for the better. Nonetheless, Greek life is still a very dominant force on campus. Greeks make up about 30 percent of the student body, and there are many nationally recognized fraternities and sororities on campus. There is a strong group of people not in fraternities who also go out regularly, and the groups mix relatively well. Thus, fraternity row is a popular destination for many students on a Friday or Saturday night, Greek and non-Greek alike. There is also a strong group that opposes Greek life, though not very actively. All-in-all, the Greek community is very noticeable on campus, wearing letters or promoting philanthropic events they are sponsoring, rushing prospective new members, etc. Not as big as it once was, but still very visible.

**B+**

The College Prowler™ Grade on
### Greek Life: B+

A high grade in Greek Life indicates that sororities and fraternities are not only present, but also active on campus. Other determining factors include the variety of houses available and the respect the Greek community receives from the rest of the campus.

# Drug Scene

> "**Alcohol is king** at Emory. Pot is a distant second, but there are still a lot of smokers. This isn't like the University of Vermont or anything, but there is ample weed to be purchased. It is expensive though, because Emory kids only want the finest."

> "Lots of people smoke marijuana, and everyone drinks. Other than that, everything else is kept a secret. I'm sure there are some people doing hard drugs, but they keep that to themselves. Pot smokers and drinkers are very open about their use, and **pot in general seems to be accepted as a 'non-taboo'** on campus."

> "Since Emory kids have a lot of money, and this school can get socially boring sometimes, there are a lot of kids doing drugs here. And **not just smoking weed** either; I know a good amount that do coke, eat pills, and trip, also. I've heard also that Emory is a great campus to trip on because it is so beautiful."

## The Lowdown
ON DRUG SCENE

**Most Prevalent Drugs on Campus**:
Marijuana, Adderall, Ritalin

**Liquor-Related Referrals**:
43

**Liquor-Related Arrests**:
10

**Drug-Related Referrals**:
19

**Drug-Related Arrests**:
8

**Drug Counseling Programs**:
The Emory Clinic
Phone: (404) 778-5000
Services: Substance abuse counseling

## The College Prowler Take
ON DRUG SCENE

There is a surprising amount of marijuana smoked on campus. Many people openly discuss smoking pot in classes, and some teachers even occasionally mention it. There is also a relatively high amount of prescription drug use. Adderall and Ritalin are very commonly abused study drugs that are often used around midterms and finals. There is moderate hallucinogen use and a bit more noticeable cocaine use. There is a "scene" of drugs on campus, no doubt, but not one that evokes much pressure on students.

## Students Speak Out
ON DRUG SCENE

"Just like anywhere, if you want something, you can get it. Study drugs are much more popular than anything else. People are constantly taking drugs to study, and take tests."

The College Prowler™ Grade on
**Drug Scene: C+**

A high grade on Drug Scene indicates that drugs are not a noticeable part of campus life; drug use is not visible, and no pressure to use them seems to exist.

# Overall Experience

## Students Speak Out
### ON OVERALL EXPERIENCE

"My overall experience has been a good one. I went through my time of wanting to leave, or not feeling comfortable, but everyone has a niche to fill at Emory, and once I found mine, I never looked back."

Q "The only unity felt among students at Emory, besides those in student government, comes from the **general agreement that Emory sucks**, and we all wish we had gone somewhere else. I have threatened to transfer at least four times, and would like to be anywhere but here. But for some reason I stay, which says something about the school and the city."

Q "Emory is a great place because it offers a world-class education in a burgeoning major city. **Atlanta has great culture, and Emory does, too.** You can learn a lot from the top-notch professors or from the city itself. If you ever get tired of the same old Emory scene, you can venture out into Atlanta and be guaranteed of a good time."

Q "Emory, if you plan on being serious, can really hook you up. There is a great career center and also an alumni resource center where **you can easily find jobs**, and good ones at that. If you have drive here, you will succeed and come straight out of school with a great job waiting for you."

Q "My only problem with Emory has been the lack of true diversity on campus. This school puts itself out there as a very diverse school, but the truth is the school is full of cliques. The population of northeasterners is way **too noisy and snobbish**; there is a very high proportion of Jewish students, who primarily hang out only with other Jewish students; and any minority group only hangs out with themselves. The education is great, but the social scene is lacking."

## The College Prowler Take
### ON OVERALL EXPERIENCE

Overall, the Emory experience is a great, albeit interesting one. Emory can be trying at times, with its restrictive and sometimes uncooperative administration, but it can also be so rewarding. In evaluating the entire experience here at Emory, most students note the exceptional education they are receiving from world-class professors. Students who come here will never forget the amazing teachers they encounter, the friends they make, or the times that they spend here. Being confident is important at Emory, as it is a school full of cliques and social groups that seclude themselves from others, but if you can find your niche, you can easily have a good time.

Many students initially wonder if they would be better off somewhere else, a feeling that every college freshman has. Adapting to a new city, a new school, and new people can be hard. But most find, after four years here, that they are glad to have stayed, delighted to receive a diploma from such an acclaimed school, and happy to have lived in such a great city. The disappointment at the lack of a football team, or anger at a restrictive administration, fades after awhile, and it is replaced with a vigor for the city and for academics, and happiness that a school focused on academics still has numerous outlets for entertainment and fun. Emory students receive one of the best educations on one of the most beautiful campuses in the country, and, despite some students' grumblings, this is a great place to go to school.

# Furman University

3300 Poinsett Highway, Greenville, SC 29613
www.engagefurman.com          (864) 294-2034

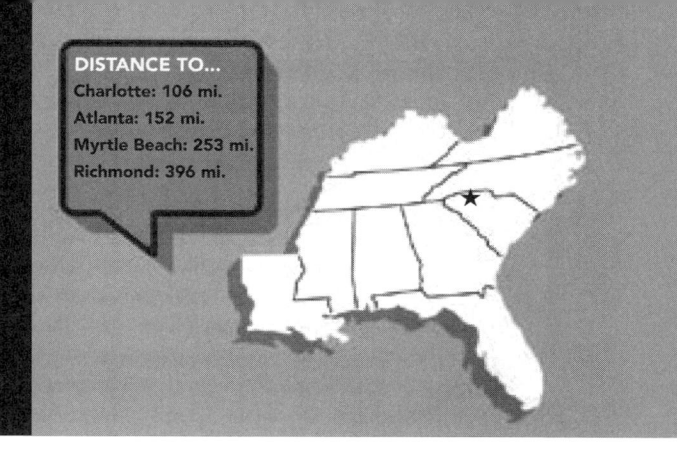

**DISTANCE TO...**
Charlotte: 106 mi.
Atlanta: 152 mi.
Myrtle Beach: 253 mi.
Richmond: 396 mi.

*"Furman is perpetually improving itself, and its national prestige is growing every year."*

**Total Enrollment:**
2,695

**Top 10% of High School Class:**
68%

**Average GPA:**
3.8

**Acceptance Rate:**
60%

**Tuition:**
$24,408

**SAT Range (25th-75th Percentile):**

| Verbal | Math | Total |
|---|---|---|
| 600 – 690 | 590 – 680 | 1190 – 1370 |

**ACT Range (25th-75th Percentile):**

| Verbal | Math | Total |
|---|---|---|
| 26-31 | 25-29 | 26-30 |

**Most Popular Majors:**
12% Political Science
11% Business
7% Health and Physical Education
7% History
6% English Language and Literature

**Students also applied to:***
Davidson College
Duke University
University of North Carolina–Chapel Hill
Vanderbilt University
Wake Forest University

*For more school info check out www.collegeprowler.com

### Table of Contents

| | |
|---|---|
| Academics | 500 |
| Local Atmosphere | 502 |
| Safety & Security | 503 |
| Facilities | 505 |
| Campus Dining | 506 |
| Campus Housing | 508 |
| Diversity | 509 |
| Guys & Girls | 511 |
| Athletics | 512 |
| Greek Life | 514 |
| Drug Scene | 515 |
| Overall Experience | 516 |

### College Prowler Report Card

| | |
|---|---|
| Academics | B- |
| Local Atmosphere | B+ |
| Safety & Security | A- |
| Facilities | B+ |
| Campus Dining | B |
| Campus Housing | A- |
| Diversity | D |
| Guys | B+ |
| Girls | A- |
| Athletics | B |
| Greek Life | A- |
| Drug Scene | A+ |

# Academics

## The Lowdown
ON ACADEMICS

**Degrees Awarded:**
Bachelor, Post-Bachelor Certificate, Master

**Undergraduate Departments:**
Art, Asian Studies, Biology, Chemistry, Classics, Communication Studies, Computer Science, Earth and Environmental Science, Economics and Business Administration, Education, English, Health and Exercise Science, History, Interdisciplinary Studies, Mathematics, Military Science, Modern Languages and Literatures, Music, Neuroscience, Philosophy, Physics, Political Science, Psychology, Religion, Sociology, Theater Arts, Urban Studies

**Full-time Faculty:**
211

**Faculty with Terminal Degree:**
98%

**Student-to-Faculty Ratio:**
11:1

**Average Course Load:**
3 courses in the fall and spring terms, and 2 during winter term

**Special Degree Options:**
Dual Degree Programs: Pre-Engineering, Forestry-Environmental Science
Pre-professional programs: Pre-Med, Pre-Law, Pre-Ministry

**AP Test Score Requirements:**
Possible credit for scores of 4 or 5

**IB Test Score Requirements:**
Possible credit for scores of 6 or 7

## Did You Know?

What are CLPs? CLP stands for Cultural Life Program, a program intended to supplement the educational experience of Furman students. Students must attend three sanctioned cultural events for every term they are at Furman before graduating (36 over four years). CLP events range from classical concerts, theater productions, political speeches, debates, and films.

Want to take fewer classes at a time? Furman's academic calendar is on a trimester system, meaning there is a fall, winter, and spring term. As a result, students generally only take three classes in the fall and spring, and two in the winter. Don't think this makes the academics a breeze, though! Completing two courses in less than eight weeks is difficult!

**Best Places to Study:**
Library, Academic Buildings

## Students Speak Out
### ON ACADEMICS

> "The teachers at Furman are generally helpful, attentive, and knowledgeable. The small classes are great; professors not only know students' individual scholastic abilities, but they can also know the students personally."

Q "Overall, I've found the professors to be extremely helpful and interested in their subjects. Of course, Furman is like any other school, in that there are those few professors who are mind-numbingly boring and their classes are soporific, but those are few and far between. This can be remedied by **taking GERs with professors who have good reputations** on campus, and by choosing electives that sound interesting to you."

Q "I have found most of my teachers to be very caring and concerned about the students' welfare. Almost all of them love to take one-on-one time with their students, and encourage visits to their offices. **I have been to one of my teacher's houses for dinner**, and I know that is not a rare occurrence at Furman. The teachers love to educate us and be involved in our lives."

Q "The classes I find most interesting are the ones for my major. I have had some teachers who were either really new or really old, and they were not very engaging in class, so it was pretty boring. **You get to fill out an evaluation form** at the end of every semester, so you can report any problems you have with teachers or classes."

Q "Most of the teachers at Furman are very engaged in the teaching process. They're willing to help students, meet with them personally, and go out of their way. Basically, **they care about the student more than your average professor**. I find the classes interesting, but also challenging and outright difficult."

## The College Prowler Take
### ON ACADEMICS

With an 11:1 student-teacher ratio, Furman prides itself on the high level of personal attention students receive from their professors. Many of the professors here chose to work at Furman over larger, more research-oriented schools because of their strong commitment to teaching undergraduates. While professors are required to hold office hours every day, most are frequently available whenever students decide to drop by to discuss a project or just to chat. It is not unusual for professors to invite the class over for dinner, or out to a downtown bar to celebrate the end of a term. The only downside to attending a school with such attentive professors is that those classes where you "only showed up for the final" don't really exist at Furman. Professors know when you are there, and expect you to be ready to participate in class discussion.

Furman has an excellent academic reputation in the Southeast, and its national prestige continues to grow. The academics are one of the primary reasons most students decide to attend Furman. While every professor may not be your favorite, nearly all of them are extremely dedicated to teaching. This consistent quality of educators makes for a broad base of strong academic departments in every field of study.

**B-**

The College Prowler™ Grade on
### Academics: B-

A high Academics grade generally indicates that professors are knowledgeable, accessible, and genuinely interested in their students' welfare. Other determining factors include class size, how well professors communicate, and whether or not classes are engaging.

# Local Atmosphere

## Students Speak Out
### ON LOCAL ATMOSPHERE

"I've really enjoyed going to school in Greenville. It's not huge, but it's not too small either. There are also lots of great bars and a few venues to visit for concerts and dancing."

Q "I absolutely love Greenville. There are two other colleges present, Bob Jones and Greenville Tech, but Furman is the premier university in the area. Greenville's downtown is my favorite thing about being a Furman student—**Main Street has hundreds of places to go** from restaurants to stores, and there are always concerts and other activities on Friday nights."

Q "The town has a southern feel, and everyone is pretty friendly. I see it as a mix of urban, suburban, and rural. Furman is close to downtown, local neighborhoods, and mountainous areas. **There are a few local schools close by**, and sometimes students from these schools come on campus to use the library or to just walk around. I've even had two guys from Greenville Tech knock on my apartment door and want to come in and visit. I think they were bored!"

Q "The atmosphere in Greenville is **'buckle of the Bible Belt' meets cosmopolitan downtown**. Although it seems somewhat schizophrenic, this duality is a nice balance that allows you to enjoy what both sides have to offer ... the county of Greenville is still run by racist fundamentalists, but the city of Greenville is run by a progressive, even-keeled city government."

## The Lowdown
### ON LOCAL ATMOSPHERE

**Region:**
Southeast

**City, State:**
Greenville, South Carolina

**Setting:**
Residential

**Distance from Atlanta:**
2 hours, 30 minutes

**Distance from Charlotte:**
1 hour, 45 minutes

**Distance from Ashville:**
1 hour

**Points of Interest:**
BMW Zentrum, Bi-Lo Center, Bob Jones University Museum and Gallery, The Peace Center for Performing Arts, Falls Park on the Reedy, Caesar's Head Overlook, Paris Mountain State Park, Greenville County Museum of Art, Main Street

**City Websites:**
http://www.Greenville.com
http://www.Greatergreenville.com

> "There is not as much stuff to do in Greenville as there is in Atlanta or Charlotte, but there is still plenty to do. It almost seems as though every month or so, something new is coming in and making a splash. There are a few other universities here but nothing that rivals Furman's prestige. **We're the big cats here** and the University gets a lot of attention from the community and media. It's great."

# Safety & Security

## The College Prowler Take
ON LOCAL ATMOSPHERE

For a city of its size, Greenville has much to offer. There are an array of restaurants and interesting cultural activities. The city is also on the national tour of many Broadway shows, and has several excellent music venues. Although Greenville does not have a college-town atmosphere, students don't really seem to mind. The friendly southern tone makes the town an inviting place to live. Of course, with southern hospitality comes southern conservatism, as well. While this is a draw for some students, others find it hard to digest the Bible Belt mentality. But, Greenville residents are not all Bible-thumping conservatives. The city has a diverse array of cultural and ideological perspectives, which many Furman students take in whole-heartedly.

## The Lowdown
ON SAFETY & SECURITY

**Number of Police:**
13

**Phone:**
(864) 294-2111

**Health Center Office Hours:**
24 hours a day, seven days a week.

**Safety Services:**
Emergency medical assistance, shuttle and escort services, 24-hour communication, investigative services, security alarm systems

# B+

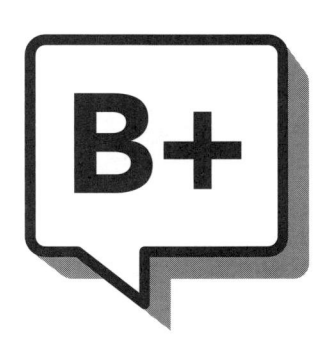

The College Prowler™ Grade on
## Local Atmosphere: B+

A high Local Atmosphere grade indicates that the area surrounding campus is safe and scenic. Other factors include nearby attractions, proximity to other schools, and the town's attitude toward students.

### Did You Know?

You can simply dial 2111 from any University phone to reach Public Safety immediately.

Furman offers a free 12-hour Women's Self Defense Course to students.

## Students Speak Out
### ON SAFETY & SECURITY

"The campus is very safe, especially compared to others, however, rapes and other crimes still happen, even in this idyllic college atmosphere."

Q "Everywhere you go on campus, there seems to be a Public Safety officer driving by. They're pretty vigilant, but there is a problem with security on campus. We don't have call-boxes like other colleges, so if you were being pursued by someone, you would have to get into a building to use a phone. **It's just not as safe as other places**, but on the other hand, I've never felt threatened or afraid to walk alone at night."

Q **"I never feel at risk** or in danger on Furman's campus. I would trust that if I left my wallet somewhere accidentally that it would be returned to me safely—you cannot find that everywhere nowadays."

Q "On the whole, the campus is pretty secure, and I don't have a lot of qualms about walking by myself at night. That doesn't mean incidents don't happen, but it's very rare. Unfortunately, **there are no emergency call-boxes around**, but it's such a small campus that Public Safety can intervene quickly should something happen. Still, it's good to exercise common sense about safety."

Q "I feel like **there's about as much security as there needs to be**. There are no metal detectors, and there aren't cops everywhere, but there are definitely cops around. There are also general precautionary measures, such as access cards to enter dorm buildings, on top of individual room keys. I have never felt unsafe."

## The College Prowler Take
### ON SAFETY & SECURITY

There is no question that Furman's campus feels extremely safe. About half of the students never lock the doors to their dorm rooms or apartments during the day or at night (although, Public Safety recommends always locking doors). Security may not be as tight as it is on other college campuses, but that's because there isn't really a need. Serious crimes occur very rarely on Furman's campus, and if a student doesn't feel safe walking alone at night, they can always call a Public Safety officer to escort them. Although not necessarily the wisest decision, students often feel that they don't have to exercise the same safety precautions they would in the "real world." Public Safety maintains a highly visible presence on campus, which contributes to the feeling of safety.

**A-**

The College Prowler™ Grade on
## Safety & Security: A-

A high grade in Safety & Security means that students generally feel safe, campus police are visible, blue-light phones and escort services are readily available, and safety precautions are not overly necessary.

# Facilities

## The Lowdown
ON FACILITIES

**Student Center:**
The University Center (The UC)

**Athletic Center:**
Personal Activities Center (The PAC)

**Libraries:**
James B. Duke Library, Maxwell Music Library, Ezel Science Reading Room

**Movie Theatre on Campus?**
Burgess Theater in the University Center

**Bowling on Campus?**
No

**Bar on Campus?**
No

**Coffeehouse on Campus?**
The Tower Cafe

**Popular Places to Chill:**
The Tower Cafe, the University Center, just about anywhere around the lake

**Favorite Things to Do**
Furman students tend to spend much of their free time outside, either jogging around the lake or playing a game of Frisbee golf. There is always something going on sponsored by FUSAB (Furman University Student Activities Board), such as a comedian, or concert. The Tower Café is the place most people go for a more social studying area.

**Computers**
**High-Speed Network?** Yes
**Wireless Network?** Yes
**Number of Labs:** 9
**Numbers of Computers:** About 330
**24-Hour Labs:** Plyler Hall
**Charge to Print:** None

## Students Speak Out
ON FACILITIES

"**The facilities and grounds are all very nice, with the exception being the PAC, which is truly the low point of campus and is in desperate need of replacement. Just last year, part of the ceiling caved in.**"

Q "**Nothing compares to the natural beauty of the lake and trees**, but the buildings are well-kept. The Physical Activity Center [PAC] is in the old gym, and it gets really hot in there, but they have machines for weights and cardio, and they just bought many new machines."

Q "Furman has great athletic facilities for a school of its size. Even the club teams have good fields to practice and play on. The computers offered are relatively new and fast, and **the student center is pretty modern**."

Q "Furman facilities are incredible when compared to other colleges. **The PAC is awesome;** there is a lot of equipment, but the atmosphere is still social. And, you don't feel like a wimp if you don't bench three times your body weight."

> "The best thing about campus facilities is that **you can walk or bike to almost all of them**. The student center is nice and has a decent variety of food, and a small movie theater where the student activities board hosts free movies. The PAC is also nice, and has a good selection of workout equipment and a pool."

## Campus Dining

### The College Prowler Take
ON FACILITIES

Furman's facilities offer a wide variety of services to students. The Physical Activities Center, or PAC, has a large gym with a climbing wall, indoor pool, and workout facility. While the workout facilities are in need of renovation, most of the equipment is new. The student center itself certainly perpetuates Furman's reputation of having the atmosphere of a southern country club. Picturesquely located at the banks of Furman's lake, the student center houses the bookstore, post office, copy center, and food court, as well as a movie theatre and coffee shop. Furman's campus is known for its beauty. Its lake, bell tower, rose garden, numerous fountains, and traditional architecture create a picturesque, idyllic setting.

### The Lowdown
ON CAMPUS DINING

**Freshman Meal Plan Requirement?**
Yes

**24-Hour On-Campus Eating?**
No

**Student Favorites:**
Pan Geos wraps, Chick-fil-A, and DH Chicken fingers

**Meal Plan Average Cost:**
$1,116

## B+

**The College Prowler™ Grade on**
**Facilities: B+**

A high Facilities grade indicates that the campus is aesthetically pleasing and well-maintained; facilities are state-of-the-art, and libraries are exceptional. Other determining factors include the quality of both athletic and student centers and an abundance of things to do on campus.

### Did You Know?
Every year before Thanksgiving and winter break, the dining hall serves huge holiday feasts. They decorate, play music, and serve an amazing meal with every possible holiday dish.

## Students Speak Out
### ON CAMPUS DINING

> "The food on campus is good. It just gets repetitive and boring after eating the same thing for a while."

Q "The food on campus isn't great, although it's better than other schools. **There's a good amount of variety**, and you can usually find something you like in the dining hall. If you aren't up for that, you can go to the PalaDen and use your food points to get sandwiches, ice cream, pizza, hamburgers, Chick-fil-A, wraps, or sushi. The only problem is that after about eight or nine at night, there is nowhere on campus to get a meal, although the Wendy's drive-thru is only about five minutes off campus."

Q "Don't let others mislead you: Furman's food is some of the best you will find in a university setting. Every college student complains about the food at their school, however, **students who complain at Furman should be ignored**. Furman's food is some of the most innovative and healthy I have ever experienced."

Q "I really like the on-campus food. In fact, I like it too much. The dining hall has a wide selection, and they have a salad bar, sandwich station, pizza, and cereal daily. You can always turn to one of these staples if the other choices are not your favorite. **The PalaDen has quality food**, but not a ton of choices. There are about six stations to choose from. My favorite food is the ice cream parfaits."

Q "The food on campus is not bad, but not great. The dining hall is a staple, but **that's all you'll get ... staple food**. It's good, but kind of bland. If they try to do too much, they usually screw it up. But they have their items that attract a lot of students—i.e., chicken fingers, black bean cakes, and fresh baked cookies."

## The College Prowler Take
### ON CAMPUS DINING

Eating anywhere every single day will get old, and the same is true with dining at Furman. There are really only two places to eat, the dining hall and the PalaDen food court, but each location offers a wide variety of food. There are some good healthy options in both places, but there is a time in every student's life when nothing looks worth eating but the cereal. Freshmen rarely use all of the dining hall meals they are required to pay for on their plans, and they often run out of points on their cards to use in the PalaDen. Dining Services truly tries to serve the students by giving them what they want. Dinner in the dining hall on weekend nights is, however, never a good idea. Another problem is that there are no places to get food on campus after 9 p.m., a pretty early hour in the life of a college student.

**B**

**The College Prowler™ Grade on**
### Campus Dining: B

Our grade on Campus Dining addresses the quality of both school-owned dining halls and independent on-campus restaurants as well as the price, availability, and variety of food.

# Campus Housing

## Students Speak Out
### ON CAMPUS HOUSING

"Avoid South Housing unless you like nasty communal bathrooms. Guys just became allowed to live in Lakeside Housing, and there you get private bathrooms for just you and three other people. It's really nice."

Q "I lived in Blackwell my freshman year, and I loved it, even though they do have the smallest rooms on campus. **Try to live on Southside**, and if you can't stand small rooms—although I'm telling you, especially if you are a girl, you will love Blackwell!—I would ask for Poteat."

Q "Compared to other schools the dorms are large and nice. There are two areas, South Housing and Lakeside Housing, and the rooms are bigger in South usually. **The smallest rooms are in Blackwell**, so if you can avoid that, you should. But, if you compare any room on campus to dorms at other schools, they will almost always be bigger."

Q "The dorms are fine—not outstanding, but not bad either. **Guys would probably prefer to live in South Housing**—it's closer to the gym and to the athletic fields—and so would girls who like those boys. Lakeside Housing is good for those who'd like to focus a little more on their studies, especially freshman year. Stay away from Blackwell because the rooms are tiny! Poteat and McGlothlin, both in South Housing, are good choices."

Q "The dorms are pretty nice. Lakeside housing sounds better than South Housing, but don't be fooled by the name like I was. Lakeside dorms are much smaller. The maids do a great job of cleaning everyday in the hallway, kitchen, and bathroom, but **I lived in a shoebox my freshman year** in Chiles."

## The Lowdown
### ON CAMPUS HOUSING

**Undergrads on Campus:**
95%

**Number of Dormitories:**
12

**University-Owned Apartments:**
11 buildings

**Room Types:**
Standard—students share large, central bathroom facility.
Suite—students share a semi-private bathroom with three other students.

**Bed Type:**
Twin (standard or extra-long) in dorms, and double beds in apartments

**Cleaning Service?**
In public communal areas, cleaning is provided daily. Suite and private bathrooms are not cleaned.

**You Get:**
Bed, desk and chair, dresser, closet, micro-fridge, window coverings, cable TV, Internet free campus and local phone calls

**Also Available:**
Theme housing such as language houses, living/learning communities, Greek halls, and environmentally friendly housing

## The College Prowler Take
### ON CAMPUS HOUSING

All freshmen and sophomores live in the dorms, and most students agree that this is a valuable part of connecting with other students. They generally have few complaints about Furman's dorms, although students almost universally agree that Blackwell is the worst residence hall. The social aspect of dorm life is a huge part of freshman year. Each freshmen hall has a theme, and halls compete against each other fiercely during orientation week. Many freshman form social groups from their hall and brother/sister halls that last all four years at Furman. RAs and freshman advisors, or "frads," that live in freshman halls are dedicated to adapting their hall to college life. The social atmosphere of dorm life seems to overshadow most shortcomings of the dorms themselves.

# Diversity

## The Lowdown
### ON DIVERSITY

**Native American:** 0.04%

**Asian American:** 1.5%

**African American:** 6.2%

**Hispanic:** 1.2%

**White:** 87.6%

**International:** 1%

**Unknown:** 3.16%

**Out-of-State:** 68%

### Minority Clubs
Furman has several minority organizations on campus. They achieve a fairly visible role on campus by sponsoring various events and parties.

### Political Activity
Although Furman has a reputation for having an extremely conservative student body, there is a healthy amount of ideological diversity. Many are outspoken about their political views, while a good portion seems to remain politically apathetic.

**A-**

The College Prowler™ Grade on
## Campus Housing: A-

A high Campus Housing grade indicates that dorms are clean, well-maintained, and spacious. Other determining factors include variety of dorms, proximity to classes, and social atmosphere.

**Economic Status**

True to its country club atmosphere, most students are upper-middle-class. Although many students help pay for their education through financial aid, most seem to easily support their "country club" lifestyles.

## Students Speak Out
### ON DIVERSITY

"This campus diverse? No way, not at all. But that is not a reason to hide from Furman—please, I beg of you minority students to embrace this upper-class, predominately white school. We need you!"

Q "This is one of the most homogeneous student populations you will find in the nation. It is filled with white, middle- or upper-class Christian Republicans from the south. Sadly, **most minorities are only here to play sports**, including international students, and consequently, isolate themselves in athletic cliques that prevent even a small amount of diversity to be fully felt."

Q "Diversity isn't exactly something Furman is known for. **The average student is white and of the upper-middle-class**, but there are minorities on campus. The administration is working hard to increase diversity and the incoming class for 2004 was the most diverse in Furman history."

Q "**There's very little diversity overall**. A good bit of the student body is very conservative and WASPy, and some don't have a lot of tolerance for people who are different, especially people of different religious faiths."

Q "The campus has people from many different states and countries, and it hosts a variety of different interests, religions, and opinions. Overall, though, I would have to say that **it isn't as diverse as most places** and that it leans a lot more toward the conservative side. No matter what your interest or belief, though, there will always be somewhere you will fit in."

## The College Prowler Take
### ON DIVERSITY

Clearly the numbers speak for themselves. Furman is not a diverse place. The administration would desperately like to attract a more diverse student body, and hopefully this will happen in the future. It is true that Furman is more diverse than it used to be, but the student population is still nearly 88 percent white. Of course, many of these students come from various geographical and ideological backgrounds, but whatever diversity Furman has is difficult to see just by looking.

**The College Prowler™ Grade on**
## Diversity: D

A high grade in Diversity indicates that ethnic minorities and international students have a notable presence on campus and that students of different economic backgrounds, religious beliefs, and sexual preferences are well-represented.

# Guys & Girls

## The Lowdown
ON GUYS & GIRLS

**Women Undergrads:** 56%

**Men Undergrads:** 44%

### Birth Control Available?
Student Health Services provides condoms.

### Social Scene
Furman is a very social place. Students are friendly and extremely involved in campus activities. It's probably hard to find a place where more people say "hi" or smile at you on the way to class. One of the benefits of going to a small school is that people's social groups seem to be very interconnected. Whenever you meet someone new, chances are one of your friends already knows them. The biggest complaint about the social scene is dating. Students tend to hang out in groups, instead of going on one-on-one dates.

### Hookups or Relationships?
Many students would say neither. Furman students are notoriously dissatisfied with the dating scene. Contrary to popular belief, however, Furman students do hook up with people and sustain dating relationships with other students. The problem is, there's not much in-between. People tend to be either practically engaged, or only occasionally hooking up with other people.

## Students Speak Out
ON GUYS & GIRLS

"Guys are either very academic and not very social, or fun and social while still being smart. They're definitely not all the same."

Q "Furman has an unusually attractive student body. **People work out all the time**, and generally dress rather well for classes. It's a preppy school, so if you like the country club, Lily Pulitzer, Ralph Lauren look then, yeah, I think you would think we are pretty hot!"

Q "I think that Furman students are overall very beautiful people. It almost seems like a requirement to get in, which can be intimidating a lot of times too. **The guys are, in general, preppy, outdoorsy, or sporty**. There are a few real nerds, but not a ton. The girls are pretty trendy and conservative for the most part. More girls dress up for class than I expected before I came here. PJ pants and T-shirts are a rarity in class."

Q "**The girls are mainly pretty, southern society girls** who don't get too wild or too booky. Other types can be found, but are usually outside of the Greek scene."

Q "Attentions ladies! **This school will ruin your love life**. The sex ratio is 60:40, female-to-male, and although that doesn't seem that skewed, girls in 'liberal arts' type majors will hardly ever meet many guys through classes. And since casual dating seems to be nonexistent, it's very hard to meet people for one-on-one dating, unless you're in a fraternity or sorority. If you don't meet someone orientation week, you're basically screwed. The guys don't really seem interested in dating, even though they have a plethora of lovely, smart, and attractive girls to choose from. I think they are intimidated since so many girls here are on the manhunt, looking to get their MRS. degree."

## The College Prowler Take
**ON GUYS & GIRLS**

Whether running around the lake or heading to the mall, Furman students work hard to keep up their appearances. But, even without all the work, Furman has attractive people. Of course, not everyone here could be on a magazine cover, but there are very few complaints about looks from guys or girls. Everyone seems to admire everyone else's polished conservative style, but girls are often left wondering why they can't get a date. Though the boyish "Abercrombie look" is prevalent on campus, many girls will complain about the high girl-to-guy ratio. Girls seem somewhat bitter about not being able to find their husband at Furman. Furman does have a reputation for having guys who are more attractive than the girls; however, things seem to be evening out some.

**B+**

**A-**

### The College Prowler™ Grade on
### Guys: B+

A high grade for Guys indicates that the male population on campus is attractive, smart, friendly, and engaging, and that the school has a decent ratio of guys to girls.

### The College Prowler™ Grade on
### Girls: A-

A high grade for Girls not only implies that the women on campus are attractive, smart, friendly, and engaging, but also that there is a fair ratio of girls to guys.

# Athletics

## The Lowdown
**ON ATHLETICS**

**Men's Varsity Teams:**
Baseball
Basketball
Cross Country
Football
Golf
Soccer
Tennis
Track and Field

**Women's Varsity Teams:**
Basketball
Cross Country
Golf
Soccer
Softball
Tennis
Track and Field
Volleyball
Cheerleading

**Club Sports:**
Baseball, Soccer, Tennis, Rugby, Handball, Lacrosse

**Intramurals:**
Volleyball, Soccer, Flag Football, Bowling, Basketball, Sand Volleyball, Softball, Tennis, Swimming

**Most Popular Sports:**
Football, Soccer, Baseball

**Overlooked Teams:**
Volleyball, Track & Field

**Getting Tickets:**
All sporting events are free with a Furman ID

**Athletic Division:**
NCAA I

**Conference:**
Southland Conference (Division I Football I-AA)

**School Mascot:**
Paladin

**Fields:**
Paladin Football Stadium, Stone Soccer Stadium, Furman Baseball Stadium, Pepsi Softball Stadium

## Students Speak Out
ON ATHLETICS

"Intramural sports at Furman are great. There are several levels of competition and a lot of good players."

Q "Lots of people go out to the football games and soccer games, but for some reason **no one is really a 'die-hard' fan** until they graduate and come back as alumni. The alumni come back and you see them all get really crazy and excited."

Q "Varsity sports are not as big as at large public universities, but the quality of our teams is incredible for the size of the student body. **There are lots of home games**, so if you want to be a fan, it's easy to get to the games! Intramural sports are mainly big with the frats and sororities."

Q "The sports events don't get a lot of student spectators, but they're fun when you decide to attend. **Football games get the largest attendance** and are social events on the weekends. Intramural sports are fun, and anyone can participate, regardless of athletic skill—or lack thereof. They're also fun to watch, if you aren't into playing."

Q "Intramurals are huge! Most of the **dorm halls create their own teams** and compete just as competitively as the fraternities and sororities. Lots of fun, and, surprisingly, they get lots of spectators."

## The College Prowler Take
ON ATHLETICS

Furman athletics are not nearly as big as they are at many larger institutions. However, Furman does have several very strong teams. Football gets the most attention on campus and has the best turnout, but the soccer and golf teams are also very competitive. Intramural and club sports have a strong presence on campus with a high level of participation. There seems to be something for everyone, whether they are serious about their sport, or they are trying it out for the first time. Students actually seem to get more excited and competitive about their intramural team than Furman's varsity sports. Besides football, the majority of students don't attend Furman athletic events. Furman's teams are great for such a small school; they just need more student support!

**The College Prowler™ Grade on**
## Athletics: B

A high grade in Athletics indicates that students have school spirit, that sports programs are respected, that games are well-attended, and that intramurals are a prominent part of student life.

# Greek Life

## The Lowdown
ON GREEK LIFE

**Number of Fraternities:**
7

**Number of Sororities:**
9

**Undergrad Men in Fraternities:**
30%

**Undergrad Women in Sororities:**
35%

### Did You Know?

Every year during homecoming week, each fraternity and sorority pairs up and competes in skits, banner decorating, float building, and spirit competitions all based on the homecoming theme. The winners are announced at half-time of the football game.

## Students Speak Out
ON GREEK LIFE

"Greek life is really nice. Only about half of the campus is in a frat or sorority so it does not dominate, and those who are not in one still hang out and go to parties with their buddies who are in one."

Q "Furman frats are probably like frats at most other colleges, but Furman sororities are definitely different. Since they don't have houses, there is much more emphasis on sorority involvement on campus, and as a result, there's not a whole lot of tension between the groups. Greek life doesn't dominate the social scene, but **if you are a really social type you will want to go Greek**."

Q "Greek life is incredibly fun! **It opens the door to meet lots of different people** and expands your social life. Because rush isn't until winter, most of my best friends are independent or belong to a different sorority than I do. We still go out together and spend just as much time together as we did before we went Greek."

Q "Greek life is a bigger part of campus than I had heard it was before I came. The frats and sororities have jersey days at least once a week and pin days, where they dress up, at least once a week, as well. Everyone knows who is in what group, and **it is a big part of your identity**. I would say that frats dominate the social scene. You pick which house you want to go to on Friday and Saturday nights."

Q "I have friends in all the sororities and a lot of independent friends. Your social circles are not dictated by what group you're a member of. **I love my sorority**, but I also have friends outside of it."

## The College Prowler Take
### ON GREEK LIFE

The Greek scene is a big part of life at Furman whether you are in a Greek organization or not. Most people have been to at least one fraternity party, or participated in a Greek-sponsored charity fund raiser. In addition, it is difficult to ignore the fraternity and sorority jerseys that students wear to class, and each Greek organization has an unofficially designated table in the dining hall. People seem to have lots of pride for their organization, but they don't let it take over their life. Students in fraternities and sororities are usually involved in other student organizations, as well. Girls seem more likely than guys to have friends who don't wear the same Greek letters, but there are also a large amount of guys who aren't in a fraternity at all. Overall, the most social people at Furman are Greek, but there are still lots of other ways to meet people and make friends if Greek organizations are not your thing.

**A-**

The College Prowler™ Grade on
## Greek Life: A-

A high grade in Greek Life indicates that sororities and fraternities are not only present, but also active on campus. Other determining factors include the variety of houses available and the respect the Greek community receives from the rest of the campus.

## Drug Scene

### The Lowdown
### ON DRUG SCENE

**Most Prevalent Drugs on Campus:**
Alcohol, Marijuana

**Liquor-Related Referrals:**
85

**Liquor-Related Arrests:**
1

**Drug-Related Referrals:**
16

**Drug-Related Arrests:**
1

### Drug Counseling Programs
**The Counseling Center**
Phone: (864) 294-3031
Services: free one-on-one counseling

**Health Services**
Phone: (864) 294-2180
Services: alcohol assessment service, educational programming for groups/organizations

## Students Speak Out
### ON DRUG SCENE

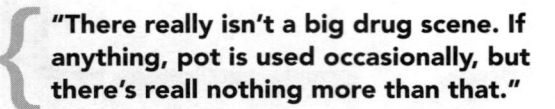

> "There really isn't a big drug scene. If anything, pot is used occasionally, but there's reall nothing more than that."

Q "To say it's not there would be a lie, because drugs are at every school. However, the only drug I'm aware of at Furman is marijuana. I would guess that **about seven to eight percent of students use the drug**."

Q "**The drug scene on campus is remarkably small**, although one can easily find pot, and sometimes cocaine, at off-campus parties or residences."

Q "The drug scene is pretty underground, but it's definitely there. I only have one close friend who regularly does drugs, but **I know it goes on** more than that."

Q "There are drugs on campus, but they're much less common than on other campuses. **They're easy to avoid**, because there's no pressure to try. In fact, if you want drugs you really have to look for them, because they aren't around very often."

## The College Prowler Take
### ON DRUG SCENE

As it turns out, the squeaky clean image that Furman students project is more than just an image. Drugs are a difficult thing to find on Furman's campus. Many students say they know of one or two people who use drugs, but a large majority have never even seen an illegal substance on Furman's property. Although there are drugs around, their users are hardly numerous enough to constitute an actual "drug scene."

Use among Furman students is also much quieter than at most colleges, because it is not a socially accepted norm. Although there may be more drug use than some students think, it has hardly any impact on Furman's social culture.

**A+**

The College Prowler™ Grade on
### Drug Scene: A+

A high grade on Drug Scene indicates that drugs are not a noticeable part of campus life; drug use is not visible, and no pressure to use them seems to exist.

# Overall Experience

Q "While I went through an early adjustment crisis and considered changing schools, I knew that Furman was a place where I would get a great education and make excellent friends. I was right, and I couldn't be happier that I stuck it out. I have incredible friends, incredible professors, and a major that I couldn't be more excited about. **The trick is to throw yourself into the new experience** and get involved quickly."

Q "After growing up with the Georgia Bulldog football scene, **game days often make me wish I'd gone to a bigger school**. That's only 10 days a year, though, and there's never another time when I'd rather be anywhere else!"

## The Lowdown
ON OVERALL EXPERIENCE

"It's a great education, but you don't get a good picture of what the real world is like. A lot of times, I wish I was somewhere else, but I've made good friends. You could do better, but you could definitely do worse."

Q "I was shocked at first by the 'Bible Belt' mentality that everyone seemed to have, but **you learn to find your own niche**. There are people who are not so conservative, and then you learn how to appreciate the ones who are. Learning how to overcome those differences had been a great life lesson."

Q "I love Furman! Everyone is really friendly. Academically, it is really competitive, but the education I have received has been great. **My favorite experience has been studying abroad in Chile**. I got to miss winter term in freezing, rainy Greenville, and spend two months in the sun down south! I only wish I was somewhere other than Furman when I have to write a 15-page paper or study all night for an exam."

## The College Prowler Take
ON OVERALL EXPERIENCE

Furman students are generally crazy about their school. Although it's not for everyone, the ones who decide to attend usually find it a great match. The academic programs at Furman are a huge draw. Students appreciate the quality of education they are getting and the personal attention they get from their professors. And although the workload can be stressful at times, Furman's idyllic campus makes it difficult to sustain any level of stress for too long.

It's true that those within the Furman bubble may seem out of touch with the real world at times. Other times, it may seem as if you are surrounded by homecoming queens, class presidents, and valedictorians. But despite a few drawbacks, no one seems to want to leave. Just ask anyone on campus. Furman students love to talk about why they love their school.

# Guilford College

5800 West Friendly Avenue, Greensboro, NC 27410
www.guilford.edu          (800) 992-7759

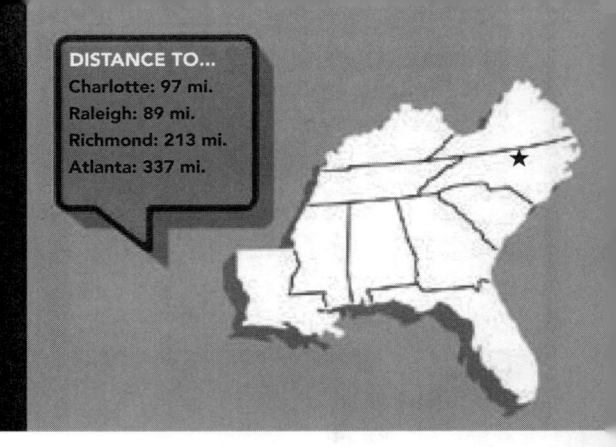

**DISTANCE TO...**
Charlotte: 97 mi.
Raleigh: 89 mi.
Richmond: 213 mi.
Atlanta: 337 mi.

*"Overall, Guilford College is a very positive place to spend four years of your life."*

**Total Enrollment:**
1,734

**Top 10% of High School Class:**
15%

**Average GPA:**
3.0

**Acceptance Rate:**
69%

**Tuition:**
$20,290

**SAT Range (25th-75th Percentile):**
| Verbal | Math | Total |
|---|---|---|
| 520 – 650 | 500 – 620 | 1020 – 1270 |

**ACT Range (25th-75th Percentile):**
Total
21-26

**Most Popular Majors:**
14% Business
11% Psychology
7%  English Language
7%  Education
6%  Computer and Information Sciences

**Students also applied to:***
University of North Carolina—Chapel Hill
University of North Carolina—Greensboro
Appalachian State University

*For more school info check out www.collegeprowler.com

## Table of Contents

| | |
|---|---|
| Academics | 519 |
| Local Atmosphere | 521 |
| Safety & Security | 522 |
| Facilities | 524 |
| Campus Dining | 525 |
| Campus Housing | 526 |
| Diversity | 528 |
| Guys & Girls | 529 |
| Athletics | 531 |
| Greek Life | 533 |
| Drug Scene | 534 |
| Overall Experience | 535 |

## College Prowler Report Card

| | |
|---|---|
| Academics | B |
| Local Atmosphere | B- |
| Safety & Security | B+ |
| Facilities | B |
| Campus Dining | C- |
| Campus Housing | B |
| Diversity | C |
| Guys | B |
| Girls | B+ |
| Athletics | C |
| Greek Life | N/A |
| Drug Scene | B- |

# Academics

## The Lowdown
### ON ACADEMICS

**Degrees Awarded**:
B.A. (Bachelor of Arts), B.S. (Bachelor of Science), B.F.A. (Bachelor of Fine Arts)

**Full-time Faculty**:
84

**Faculty with Terminal Degree**:
90%

**Student-to-Faculty Ratio**:
15:1

**Average Course Load**:
12-16 credit hours (3 or 4 classes)

**Sample Academic Clubs:**
Tri-Beta (Biology honor society), Health Sciences Club, Phi Alpha Theta (History honor society), Forensic Science Club

**Special Degree Options**:
Cooperative pre-professional program, 52 concentrations, integrative studies major

**AP Test Score Requirements**:
Possible credit/placement for scores of 3-5

**IB Test Score Requirements**:
Possible credit/placement for scores of 4-7 on higher level tests

## Did You Know?

The Academic Skills Center (ASC) is located in the library on the top floor. They will edit papers for you in any stage and can help find tutors for any academic subject. Call (336) 316-2253 to make an appointment.

Everyone at Guilford calls everyone else by their first name, including deans, staff, professors, and the president. It's some kind of eerie social phenomenon.

If you double-major, you will have an advisor in both departments. You can choose your advisor when you declare a major. Before you declare, your advisor will be your FYE course professor.

**Best Places to Study:**
Hege Library, main campus on the lawn, Founders (upstairs during the day), Bauman (if you need a computer)

## Students Speak Out
### ON ACADEMICS

> "My experiences with teachers have been wonderful. Most are smart, passionate, and interested in the students as individuals."

Q "Some teachers are good, and others aren't. Some teachers placed school policies above the importance of actual learning. Some teachers viewed themselves as always superior to students, whereas other teachers tried to view students on their level. There is a **fairly mixed blend** really."

Q "Some of them are **boring and don't care**, but that's only a few."

Q "Some teachers are too interested in **teaching their own philosophy**."

Q "Teachers are **accessible and easygoing**. They're extremely informative and actively involved in most students' lives."

Q "If you **keep an open mind** you will get something out of every class. One of the best things about Guilford is the teaching staff."

**COLLEGE PROWLER**

Need help deciding on a major? Check out www.collegeprowler.com for all the info on Guilford courses and professors.

## The College Prowler Take
### ON ACADEMICS

Most Guilford students see their classes and professors as the highlight of their college experience. Classes are kept small to promote discussion. You'll never have any 200-student "Intro" classes at Guilford—you'll hardly have any classes over 30, for that matter. Many classes are primarily discussion based, more so in some majors than others. Some classes require that you participate or risk a lower grade. Often, desks are arranged in a circle so everyone can speak equally and look at each other. In this respect, you are not only commenting for the sake of answering the professor's question, but also responding to the rest of the class. Everyone is on a first name basis, which, at the very least, gives the illusion of a friendly relationship with your teachers. Since most departments are small enough for you to repeat a professor, you might end up finding a favorite.

As with any college, you get more out of your education by actually doing as much of the work as possible. Expect to be assigned reading for basically all classes. Skipping class too often is not really an option for most Guilford classes. Generally, if you need help, professors are accessible. However, with some, you must take the initiative to speak with them if you are falling behind. Most will listen or make some attempt to assist you. Advisors are not always that helpful, so make sure you have a good grip on the core requirements and the requirements for your major. Guilford professors want you to improve and (get this!) even want you to succeed.

**B**

The College Prowler™ Grade on
### Academics: B

A high Academics grade generally indicates that professors are knowledgeable, accessible, and genuinely interested in their students' welfare. Other determining factors include class size, how well professors communicate, and whether or not classes are engaging.

# Local Atmosphere

**City Websites**
http://www.greensboro.com
http://www.greensboronc.org

## The Lowdown
ON LOCAL ATMOSPHERE

**Region:**
Southeast

**City, State:**
Greensboro, North Carolina

**Setting:**
On-campus woods, foothills of the Appalachians, semi-urban, suburban

**Distance from Chapel Hill:**
1 hour, 22 minutes

**Distance from Raleigh:**
1 hour, 48 minutes

**Distance from Durham:**
1 hour, 21 minutes

**Points of Interest:**
Revolutionary War Battleground, International Civil Rights Center and Museum, Weatherspoon Art museum, Greensboro Arboretum, Historic downtown, Tate Street, Jefferson Pilot Building, New Garden Friends Meeting

**Major Sports Teams:**
Greensboro Bats (baseball), Generals (ice hockey), Carolina Dynamo (soccer), Chrysler Classic of Greensboro (golf)

## Students Speak Out
ON LOCAL ATMOSPHERE

"Greensboro is a college town. If you look for fun in Greensboro, you'll find it. It's a great place."

Q "Greensboro is a city of about 200,000 people that **just keeps growing and sprawling**. It is very commercial with lots of chain restaurants and big-box stores. There are some really nice parks and public gardens though."

Q "I like Greensboro. There is more of a sense of community than what I was used to—downtown is fun. It can get **kinda wild at times**, too."

Q "There are many other schools in the vicinity, and the town is just the right size. The people here are **likeable and relaxed**."

Q "There's a saying here: 'Many colleges in town, but not a college town.' Let's just say that **most social interaction revolves around campus**."

## The College Prowler Take
### ON LOCAL ATMOSPHERE

Greensboro life is what you make it. There is a great arts and culture scene, but you have to actually get off campus and venture into other parts of the city to find it. However, many students are quite satisfied with the numerous activities on campus, and stay absorbed in the "Guilford Bubble." Some call Greensboro a college town, but others insist the opposite. The other colleges in the area also have events that are open to Guilford students and the public, such as speakers, theater performances, and art galleries. Other colleges and universities in Greensboro include: Bennett College (all-women), University of North Carolina at Greensboro (UNCG), Greensboro College, NC Agricultural and Technical State University College (A&T), and Guilford Technical Community College (GTCC). Guilford has a college-town atmosphere that is not completely driven by college folk, but also a young music community. Most of those who criticize Greensboro as horribly boring haven't really ventured much outside the Guilford campus area of town. There's a lot to do in Greensboro, if you look.

## Safety & Security

### The Lowdown
### ON SAFETY & SECURITY

**Number of Guilford Police:**
9 public safety officers, additional staff

**Phone:**
(336) 316-2908, office
(336) 316-2911 for on campus emergency
(336) 316-2909 for Public Safety Control
Dial 0 on campus for Campus Operator and Information

**Health Center Office Hours:**
Monday-Friday 9 a.m.-noon and 2 p.m.- 5 p.m. (Last appointment at 4 p.m.)

**Safety Services:**
Four blue-light phones – phone emergency polls around campus, on-campus escort services by request, Whistle Alert program, 24-hour public safety patrol, 24-hour control room dispatch/2911 emergency line center, key card limited access to dorms and some buildings, connection to city police and emergency services

**B-**

The College Prowler™ Grade on
## Local Atmosphere: B-

A high Local Atmosphere grade indicates that the area surrounding campus is safe and scenic. Other factors include nearby attractions, proximity to other schools, and the town's attitude toward students.

### Did You Know?

You can be charged if you lock yourself out of your room multiple times. It is free for the first time then $10 every time after that. Expect at least a 20-minute wait to get in. You may be better off trying to find your roommate.

### Students Speak Out
ON SAFETY & SECURITY

"I haven't had to deal directly with security, but I generally feel comfortable leaving my door unlocked if I'm leaving for a while."

Q "I've felt very safe being out on campus at any time of day or night. I've met most of [the security officers], and found them to be a **well-intentioned and helpful, if a bit disorganized**, group. I have known people who've had far worse experiences though, where their safety was a much less sure thing."

Q "[Security is] mostly really nice one-on-one, unless they get in **serious 'bust some peoples' mode**. Less lenient with party scene this year— Let us live!"

Q "Guilford is towards the western edge of Greensboro. People on campus are free-spirited, and **I have never felt threatened** at Guilford."

Q "Inefficient, lazy, unaccommodating, **unfriendly, anal-retentive**; all these words sum up Guilford Security."

### The College Prowler Take
ON SAFETY & SECURITY

Although most students feel very safe on campus, it is not necessarily because of security measures, but rather due to the side of town on which Guilford is located. Security is fairly visible, especially on the weekends. The campus is open (not fenced/walled), but few outside the Guilford community (or friends) wander randomly onto or through campus. The sidewalks throughout main campus are well-lit at night. In general, both males and females alike feel safe. Many say they have never felt threatened while walking alone, day or night. Main campus has areas that are fairly open, so it is easy to see anyone coming. Despite the lack of lighting, many even feel safe walking around in the woods—though, strictly speaking, this not recommended! More students have issues with security's response time for various calls, and some even feel intimidated by security's (or shall we say "big brother's") watchful eye. A common complaint is that security arrives rather quickly to break up parties, but takes longer when other, perhaps more serious, incidents occur.

**B+**

The College Prowler™ Grade on
### Safety & Security: B+

A high grade in Safety & Security means that students generally feel safe, campus police are visible, blue-light phones and escort services are readily available, and safety precautions are not overly necessary.

# Facilities

## The Lowdown
ON FACILITIES

**Student Center:**
Yes, Founders Hall

**Athletic Center:**
Alumni Gym, Ragan-Brown Field House

**Libraries:**
Hege Library

**Movie Theatre on Campus?**
No, but there are many televisions in the Underground and dorm lounges. The Leak Room in Duke Hall is used to show movies for clubs or classes.

**Bowling on Campus?**
No

**Bar on Campus?**
No, but several are right across the street.

**Coffeehouse on Campus?**
Yes, The Underground is in Founders.

**Favorite Things to Do:**
Walk in the woods, sit around campus, swing on the Hobbs porch, play Frisbee in the fields, listen to WQFS, jam on the lawn, sunbathe on the lawn or down by the lake

### Computers

**High-Speed Network?** Yes

**Wireless Network?**
Hege Library, soon in Founders Hall, some alternative houses

**Number of Labs:**
Two main labs in Bauman; others open off and on and for classes.

**Numbers of Computers:** N/A

**24-Hour Labs:** Two main labs in Bauman

**Charge to Print?**
There are only additional charges when you go over the 300 page limit per semester per student. One color page is equal to seven black and white pages.

### Popular Places to Chill
The woods and meadows, the Underground, Founders Lobby, the lake, porches of dorms and other buildings, the apartments.

The Underground is not as popular this year due to the recent removal of the booths and smoking area, as well as study tables for students. Hopefully the Underground will be better redecorated and designed with time, since many students are critical of the changes, and want to still use the space to study. Founders Lobby is also less populated now that the front entrance is under construction, but Founders still remains the center of campus for all, despite the construction.

## Students Speak Out
ON FACILITIES

"It's pretty beautiful. Some buildings are nice on the outside, but a little old on the inside."

"The student center [Founders] is being renovated right now, and although that is nice, that **money could also be used instead for good salaries of quality teachers**."

- "They're not extravagant, but **I feel like I've got what I need**. The only exception is laundry; the machines are usually in disrepair, and cost way too much."

- "Out **athletic facilities are pretty good**, and there have been recent changes, which have greatly improved them."

- "There **isn't much in the way of common space**—the lounges are mostly for watching TV—but in general the facilities are decent."

## The College Prowler Take
### ON FACILITIES

Some of the campus facilities are currently undergoing major renovations, and have been for the past several years. The reconstitution is moving slowly from one building to another, due to needed classroom and office space. The college tries to keep the dorms and housing up-to-date and clean, but they are quickly running out of on-campus housing for traditional students. This year, there are major renovations happening to the main student center, Founders Hall, and the long-term plan will hopefully make it more helpful and accessible to students, although it is unclear how. Recent renovations to the Underground seem to have had a detrimental effect, as it is less popular now than it used to be, but, in general, Guilford students enjoy their surroundings and consider the renovations on the facilities to be positive ones.

**B**

The College Prowler™ Grade on
## Facilities: B

A high Facilities grade indicates that the campus is aesthetically pleasing and well-maintained; facilities are state-of-the-art, and libraries are exceptional. Other determining factors include the quality of both athletic and student centers and an abundance of things to do on campus.

# Campus Dining

## The Lowdown
### ON CAMPUS DINING

**Freshman Meal Plan Requirement?**
Yes

**24-Hour On-Campus Eating?**
There are none, except vending machines. However, Harris Teeter across the street is open 24 hours.

**Meal Plan Average Cost**:
$3,080 per year, all plans are the same price.

**Student Favorites:**
The Co-Op

**Did You Know?**
Your weekly meal allotment turns over at the end of the week; it does not carry over.

## Students Speak Out
### ON CAMPUS DINING

"The cafeteria on campus is awful. It's only open during short and inconvenient windows of time."

Q "There are always **vegetarian and vegan options**, but they're not necessarily good ones."

Q "I believe a fair evaluation, pushing aside what bias I have, is that the dining hall provides a **decent range of menu items**, including vegetarian items for students. The quality of the food has seemed poor in the past, but I admit it has gradually gotten better as new equipment was brought in to replace the old antiquated cooking units."

## The College Prowler Take
### ON CAMPUS DINING

Many students suggest that you try to get off the meal plan by all means possible. However, others say that it is tolerable, for cafeteria food. The dining hall staff at least appears to be trying to improve things. Food and service has been getting progressively better, despite outsourcing to Sodexho and a reduction in open hours. It can be horrible, but any mass-produced food is difficult to make perfect. This year, workers have shown new strictness about not allowing food (besides fruit and bagels) out of the caf, so remember to give yourself enough time to gobble down a sandwich or a slice of pizza in between classes.

**C-**

The College Prowler™ Grade on
## Campus Dining: C-

Our grade on Campus Dining addresses the quality of both school-owned dining halls and independent on-campus restaurants as well as the price, availability, and variety of food.

# Campus Housing

## The Lowdown
### ON CAMPUS HOUSING

**Undergrads on Campus:**
73%

**Number of Dormitories:**
6 + alternative houses (6)

**Number of University-Owned Apartments:**
24

**Room Types:**
Singles, doubles, a few triples, suites, apartments (with single rooms only), room for those with special needs

**Laundry Service?**
Yes, Laundry Logic: (336) 316-3634. Otherwise, coin washers and dryers are available in every main dorm.

**You Get:**
Twin bed, desk, desk chair, dresser (sizes vary), closet or wardrobe, window blinds, network computer port, telephone port (free campus and local telephone calls), cable TV port

**Bed Type:**
Mattresses are twin extra-long. Some are bunkable, others are not.

## Also Available

Apartments are furnished in the common area with a couch, chair, lamp, kitchen table, and kitchen chairs. Most dorms have A/C and heating, but it is often not adjustable. There are sinks in English and Milner in every room.

## Cleaning Service?

All the major dorms are cleaned weekly or bi-weekly by Guilford staff. This includes bathrooms, hallways, and lounges, but not personal rooms. The apartments and the alternative houses are not cleaned by staff, except sometimes over breaks, and must be kept up by the residents. Toilet paper and other supplies are not included in residences not cleaned by staff. Only the bathrooms are cleaned in Bryan.

## Students Speak Out
### ON CAMPUS HOUSING

"The dorms are all different for different lifestyles. Some students like them, others don't."

Q "If you're a girl, **you definitely want to be in Mary Hobbs**; if for nothing else, you might get a room with two windows. The atmosphere there is also perhaps the best. I wouldn't recommend Bryan to freshman because of the suite-style arrangement—eight people to a common room with two people per bedroom. Think about it this way: if you live in a suite you have to be able to get along with seven different new people instead of just one."

Q "Guilford's decision two years back to **isolate Binford as an all-freshmen dorm** was a poor decision, as it did just that: 'isolate' the freshmen. And this led to a number of disgusting events in the dorm. Most years however, it is decent, and my first year spent there was a wonderful time where I got to meet many like-minded individuals."

Q "**Bryan is designed like a prison**, and quarters are tight. I wouldn't recommend it, although it has been traditionally the party dorm, so if you like late-night drunken carousing Wednesday through Sunday and don't need to go to bed before 3 a.m., then you might like it."

Q "If you can, **live in the apartments or get a single**. If that's not an option, Mary Hobbs has a nicer atmosphere; not so similar to public housing. Binford is very social, Bryan is the party dorm, and Milner just sucks."

## The College Prowler Take
### ON CAMPUS HOUSING

On-campus living is not a bad option and since it is basically required of traditional-age underclassmen, you make the best of it. Most of the dorms are on central campus, so you can roll out of bed and stumble to the major academic buildings in about two minutes. Two of the biggest dorms, which typically house lots of freshmen, are Milner and Binford. Both are co-ed, mostly separated by wings. The feeling inside has been likened to that of a mental institution—lots of long hallways and ominously closed doors. However, many antisocial folks love the small, cave-like rooms with little light. As do most of the sports types, since they seem to spend little time there. The furniture is suited for lofting, which might give you an extra couple inches of floor space. The lounge is spacious if your room makes you claustrophobic, which it will, but it is not a good place to study, as there is constant Ping-Pong and foosball action happening, as well as the big screen TV blaring in the background.

### The College Prowler™ Grade on
## Campus Housing: B

A high Campus Housing grade indicates that dorms are clean, well-maintained, and spacious. Other determining factors include variety of dorms, proximity to classes, and social atmosphere.

# Diversity

## The Lowdown
ON DIVERSITY

**African American:** 16%

**Native American:** 1%

**Asian American:** 1%

**Hispanic:** 2%

**White:** 80%

**Out-of-State:** 65%

### Minority Clubs
Blacks Unifying Society (BUS), Native American Club, International Relations Club

### Most Popular Religions
The most popular religions are Quaker, various Christian, atheist, and agnostic. Religious diversity is comfortable on campus. GCRO (the Guilford Council of Religious Organizations) promotes tolerance and understanding between the groups with discussions and meetings. Although the groups do not necessarily interact officially, members certainly do, and everyone attempts to be open-minded concerning issues of religion.

### Political Activity
Guilford likes to be considered politically active and interested in current events. Guilford is relentlessly liberal, and Democrats may find that they are even sometimes less extreme than other students.

### Gay Tolerance
The Guilford community is very open to GLBTTQA students (Gay, Lesbian, Bisexual, Transgender, Transsexual, Questioning, and Allies). They are a presence on campus, but not an overwhelming one.

### Economic Status
Most Guilford students come from middle-class backgrounds, although there are people from both economic extremes. Those who are rich do not tend to flaunt it. Many people come from hippie and liberal parents and sometimes at least want to act as if they could survive being "less well-off" than they may actually be.

## Students Speak Out
ON DIVERSITY

"The campus does have diversity and it promotes diversity on a regular basis. It is an issue that is always being addressed."

"There are lots of different genres of students who are all equally vocal. Also, the campus tries to be respectful of the diversity that exists at Guilford. I attended several workshops/training sessions/classes that were designed to critically look at racism, classism, various religions, etc. **I left Guilford much more aware** of how to look at diversity in a critical manner."

"There are a **significant number of minorities on campus**, and their presence is felt. However, nearly all of the minorities are African American. The Asian population does seem to be growing, though."

"As far as I can tell, **Guilford is mostly white**, but there is some diversity, and the atmosphere is accepting to all groups."

> "It's **not very diverse at all**, and the diversity that is there seems forced. It's rare to see black and white students sitting together in the cafeteria."

### The College Prowler Take
ON DIVERSITY

Guilford seems to have great diversity of mind and perspective, although most people are on the liberal side of the spectrum. For several years, one man was known as "the Republican," simply because he was outspoken about his mainstream conservative opinions, and was conspicuous because of this point of view. The activist groups are very devoted to what causes they see as currently critical. There are a good amount of people from all over the country, although primarily North Carolinians are attracted to the college. As in most groups gathered from around the country, people enjoy exploring their regional differences in speech, tradition, and lifestyle. As for racial diversity, groups do not always mix as well as they could, but it is in no way a threatening environment for minorities. In general, people get along well, and are unusually friendly to one another.

### The College Prowler™ Grade on
# Diversity: C

A high grade in Diversity indicates that ethnic minorities and international students have a notable presence on campus and that students of different economic backgrounds, religious beliefs, and sexual preferences are well-represented.

# Guys & Girls

### The Lowdown
ON GUYS & GIRLS

**Women Undergrads**: 51%

**Men Undergrads**: 49%

## Birth Control Available?

It is available by prescription or by local Planned Parenthood. Condoms are free from Student Health.

## Social Scene

One of the first things many freshmen say about Guilford is, "Everyone is so friendly." This is fitting, considering that the school's affiliation is the Society of Friends (Quakers). If this sounds rather idealistic to you, bear in mind that while most of the community acts very open-minded publicly, there are certainly complaints about other people later, in private. There may be some social wars between different peer groups, but they don't tend to be as vicious as they might be in other places, and are certainly not as bad as in high school. Guilford is a small community, however, and often social groups overlap, so rumors spread faster than lightning.

## Social Scene (Continued...)

People do tend to occasionally be cliquish in some respects, but there is more ruling out of certain social groups then sticking to one particular circle. For example, the sports people are often very alienated from the rest of campus, and live in a separate world. They do not normally associate with anyone else, unless necessary. This is truer for some sports, especially varsity football, than others. There seems to be some overlapping of certain social groups, as well. For example, the nerds and geeks (who proudly call themselves so) mix with the freaks and hippies, etc. Druggies and non-druggies overlap as well, although maybe not always to their knowledge. Everyone at Guilford seems to get along well, minus any animosity towards or from the athletic population. Overall, students are outgoing, interested in meeting new people, and welcoming.

## Hookups or Relationships?

Guys and girls mix, not just as dates or potential dates, but very much as friends. Not everyone here is looking to hook up all the time, although that is certainly possible. Those of various sexual natures mix often, as well. There are many people who have long lists of hookups. Be aware that with a small campus, you will likely see that person again, whether you like it or not. However, the campus is not so small that you'll run into them everyday, unless you have class together or something similar, even if you live in the same building. Sexuality isn't really a big issue. You can get through your four years at Guilford without ever really dating, and no one will criticize you too much.

Also, due to the size of the campus, friends' groups tend to re-circulate people in dating patterns, creating what some like to call "incestuous dating." Friends will date/hook up with each other, or their best friend's ex, or their friend's ex-roommate. This is not always the case, but it is often easy to play "connect the dots" or Kevin-Bacon-like degrees of association games with couples on campus.

## Dress Code

With Guilford students, pretty much anything goes. There isn't much of a standard and there is very little that is seen as offensive to either professors or other students. There is wide range of preference in dress, but, in general, people are relaxed and not very formal. Those who do dress up a bit have more sensible or artsy fashion. Professors are also not consistently formal, but some dress more business-like than others. It is not common to see anyone but administration men wearing a tie. Unless you work for the Admissions office, there are basically no dress code restrictions. Students have a preference for subculture-based apparel over pop culture. Many students have a personal and individual style. Influences include hippie, artsy, punk, and Goth. There are students representing most subcultures and stereotypes you can think of. The indie rocker/emo fashion has been on the rise over the past couple years, parallel to popular culture. Normal preppy comes out in the sports gear people and more recent underclassmen, but still seems unnatural for Guilford. Students do love their school, and Guilco logo items are seen among all groups. Guilford people love thrift stores, too! Students also occasionally share their wardrobes among friends.

## Students Speak Out
### ON GUYS & GIRLS

{ "Most people are open-minded and nice to talk to. There are definitely some hotties around!"

Q "What are the guys like? **Strange**. What are the girls like? Even stranger."

Q "For the most part, I'd say the **large majority of students on campus was nice**. Most students didn't go through their four years at Guilford without at least one relationship."

Q "There are more hot girls than guys, and there's a big **free-love bisexual community**. But it's not a show that you can turn into your own little pan-optic prison—creepy guys and average Joe sports players rarely get to see it."

## The College Prowler Take
### ON GUYS & GIRLS

Dating and the social scene on Guilford's campus have to do a great deal with the individualist nature of the students and the small, community centered campus. There are lots of different personalities, and someone for every type. People like to get to know each other, dating or not. Dating seems to go in circles, but many people get into long-term relationships or else numerous shorter hookups. Some playing around among friends' groups without as much guilt also takes place partly due to some sexually liberal students. There is a large lesbian population, more so than the gay population. Many bisexual or questioning women decide Guilford is a good time to try out having a girlfriend, since it is completely acceptable in the community. There is plenty of intermingling between the year levels as well. Overall, Guilford students are presumably about as sexuality promiscuous as most college-age people, although there are people from either extreme. It all depends on personal preference.

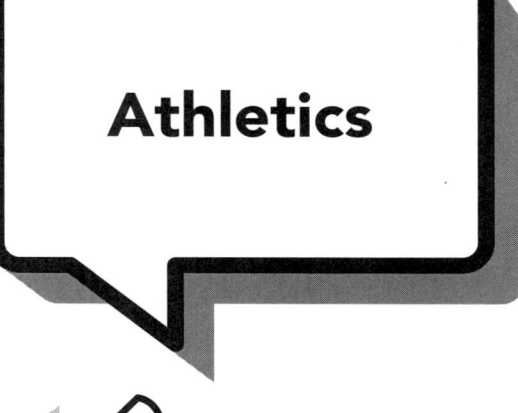

# Athletics

## The Lowdown
### ON ATHLETICS

**Men's Varsity Teams:**
Football
Baseball
Basketball
Tennis
Soccer
Cross Country
Lacrosse
Golf

**Women's Varsity Teams:**
Volleyball
Basketball
Tennis
Softball
Swimming
Cross Country
Soccer
Lacrosse

**Club Sports/ Intramurals:**
Ultimate Frisbee, Women's Rugby, Men's Rugby, Cheerleading, Bowling, Ping-Pong

**Most Popular Sports:**
Ultimate Frisbee, Rugby, Basketball, Bowling

**Overlooked Teams:**
Women's basketball; the women's basketball games are actually pretty exciting and showcase some talented athletes.

**Guilford College Sports Hotline:**
(336) 316-2500 (ext. 4107), 24 hours a day

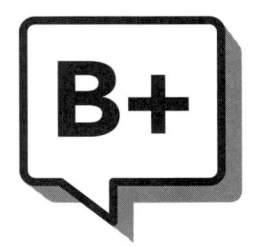

## B

## B+

**The College Prowler™ Grade on Guys: B**

A high grade for Guys indicates that the male population on campus is attractive, smart, friendly, and engaging, and that the school has a decent ratio of guys to girls.

**The College Prowler™ Grade on Girls: B+**

A high grade for Girls not only implies that the women on campus are attractive, smart, friendly, and engaging, but also that there is a fair ratio of girls to guys.

**Athletic Division:**
NCAA Division III

**Conference:**
ODAC (Old Dominion Athletic Conference) Division III

**School Mascot:**
The Quakers (unofficially, The Fighting Quakers)

**Fields:**
Baseball – 2 fields, Football, Soccer (also used for Rugby and Frisbee)

**Getting Tickets:**
It is extremely easy to get into any sporting event that you want. The only time tickets have been hard to get is when the women's basketball team was doing really well.

## Students Speak Out
### ON ATHLETICS

"Guilford students are divided between athletes and non-athletes more so than between races. So, sports have a presence on campus, but it is not as big as state schools."

Q "I don't know much about the athletics here. I really don't pay attention. I'm **not into competition**. Pssst, neither are Quakers!"

Q "Intramural sports (rugby, etc) are cool. Everything else is not. Jocks who come for scholarships are always in opposition to the rest of campus. My advice: **if you play sports, learn to be a hippie**, too, or be prepared to face some feelings of opposition from both sides."

Q "**What sports**? I didn't know varsity sports existed at Guilco."

Q "Varsity is its own thing—[there's a] big division between varsity sports and the rest of campus. **Club teams are amazing**, though, and have great people—i.e., ultimate Frisbee."

## The College Prowler Take
### ON ATHLETICS

Varsity sports are a sore point with the college and those who attend. Although varsity sports participants represent a significant part of the college population, few come to Guilford just to play sports. Several seniors commented on their surveys: "I have never been to a sporting event." Although Admissions has been recruiting an increasing number of varsity sports players, there still is a lingering rift on campus. The separation and friction is not as bad as it used to be, in part helped by the efforts of Student Senate and Student Activities to promote game attendance with special events and promotions. The popular club sports have increased the percentage of students that support organized competitive recreational activities. Many different types of students love and enjoy their club sports, in part because of the decreased social strain.

**The College Prowler™ Grade on**
## Athletics: C

A high grade in Athletics indicates that students have school spirit, that sports programs are respected, that games are well-attended, and that intramurals are a prominent part of student life.

# Greek Life

## The Lowdown
ON GREEK LIFE

**Number of Fraternities:**
0

**Number of Sororities:**
0

**Undergrad Men in Fraternities:**
0

**Undergrad Women in Sororities:**
0

### Did You Know?

There are several non-frat-based organizations that have public parties and events.

The whole campus joins together every spring for Serendipity—the wildest party of the year, which lasts the entire weekend.

## Students Speak Out
ON GREEK LIFE

"I am so happy there is no Greek life on campus. That is part of the reason I chose Guilford. There are plenty of other groups who put on functions throughout the year."

"I re**ally liked the absence of Greek life**. There were many groups of students, but since the school was so small, you sort of knew everyone and had friends in every clique. There are 'hippie' students, 'Goth' students, 'preppy' students, 'stoner' students, 'jocks,' 'nerds,' 'theater' students, etc., but most students fell into more than one of these categories and were friends with people in all groups."

"I like Guilford a lot; **I wish there were frats and sororities** on campus, but it's okay."

"The **Bryan parties make up for the absence of Greek life** in my opinion. There are plenty of clubs on campus for students to be involved in and get to know each other in similar ways, if they so desire. The student union puts on quite a few events each year, as does the yachting club."

"The absence of Greek societies on campus was one of the main draws for me. I feel as though this way of living opens up campus activity to everyone, and lessens the feeling of one person being better than another because of arbitrary membership. **Here, parties are open to everyone**, thrown by dorms or apartments, and no one can say that you can't participate because you weren't willing to wear a wig and an oversized bra. I think if Guilford were to integrate fraternities it would encourage even more cliquishness, and students would have less opportunity to interact with others."

## The College Prowler Take
### ON GREEK LIFE

Most Guilford students don't miss the Greek life. In fact, many students came to Guilford because it did not have frats or sororities. If you are really desperate to go to a frat party, you can always take a quick ride down to one of the ones at UNCG or A&T. Guilford has similar interest-based clubs like Greek societies. In the past two years, the alternative houses all had themes based around a service project or group-based community effort. Guilford also has the Bonners Scholars program, where students do volunteer work for their scholarships to Guilford.

**N/A**

The College Prowler™ Grade on
### Greek Life: N/A

A high grade in Greek Life indicates that sororities and fraternities are not only present, but also active on campus. Other determining factors include the variety of houses available and the respect the Greek community receives from the rest of the campus.

## Drug Scene

## The Lowdown
### ON DRUG SCENE

**Most Prevalent Drugs on Campus**: Nicotine, Alcohol, Marijuana, Adderall, Mushrooms, Caffeine

**Liquor-Related Referrals**: 118

**Liquor-Related Arrests**: 3

**Drug-Related Referrals**: 57

**Drug-Related Arrests**: 5

**Drug Counseling Programs**: Student Health offers drug-related counseling and a self-help library.

## Students Speak Out
### ON DRUG SCENE

"It is easy to be a part of the drug scene if you want to, and it's easy to ignore if that is your preference."

- "We have a **rep for being a pothead school**, but there are plenty of people who don't enjoy smoking it."

- "To give you an idea, you aren't going to walk down a dorm hall and see any drugs. The times when you see them are if you move within certain circles or start them yourself. It's **not an open thing on campus**."

- "**Mostly safe drugs** are done around here. Pot is up there in usage … more people have hospital visits for alcohol than pot."

## The College Prowler Take
### ON DRUG SCENE

Contrary to popular belief, Guilford is not a weed haven, but it's not exactly a convent either. If you want to do drugs, you can do drugs. If you want to ignore their existence, you can do this as well. You may not be able to ignore all the howling, staggering drunks on the weekend, but generally, everyone is quiet, reasonable, and respects each other's personal space. Many students are not even aware that drug circles exist on campus. Others commented they might know more potheads than the DEA, but they do not feel pressured or threatened by the presence of drugs. As long as you are careful, have knowledgeable friends, and stay safe, drugs will not be a dangerous issue.

**B-**

The College Prowler™ Grade on
## Drug Scene: B-

A high grade on Drug Scene indicates that drugs are not a noticeable part of campus life; drug use is not visible, and no pressure to use them seems to exist.

# Overall Experience

## Students Speak Out
### ON OVERALL EXPERIENCE

"Guilford has some problems; some of them need serious attention. But, it's still a great school with great faculty. I couldn't imagine spending my four years anywhere else."

- "I sometimes wish that the school's administration would get its act together, since they seem very confused about the school's identity. However, there are really awesome teachers and classes here, and **it's not hard to get in**. We're lucky."

- "I used to love it, but now, **I just want to be left alone by administration** sometimes."

- "I love Guilford, and passed up a full ride to the College of Wooster to stay here at Guilford. There is no other school like Guilford on the planet, in all respects: education, people, faculty, and sense of community. **I love it all and refuse to go anywhere else**."

- "So far, **Guilford rocks!** There's a lot of stuff to do and there are so many awesome people to meet. Everyone's nice and will help you out if they can. I don't know of a place where I'd rather be."

## The College Prowler Take
### ON OVERALL EXPERIENCE

Guilford is a wonderful place to be if you are looking for a small liberal arts college experience. Guilford does not attract the people who go to a standard, huge state school with frats and "semi-pro" athletic teams. Guilco is a personal, life-altering experience, for at least some aspect of your world perspective. In many different respects, students adore their school, the atmosphere, and people. Guilford allows (and expects) you to be independent academically, but you must work to maximize your education. Although it is harder to slip through the cracks at Guilford than it might be elsewhere, it is certainly possible to fail out. The majority of the student body feels sufficiently and appropriately challenged academically, although some say it really depends on your department (major). Others don't bother to do the work, or take the easiest classes possible and extra years to graduate—then complain about it, no less! Those that get the most out of their time on campus tend to be the happiest. Get involved in the Guilford community, have fun, and try to do most of your work. You won't be disappointed!

# Hampton University

Tyler Street, Hampton, VA 23668
www.hamptonu.edu    (800) 624-3328

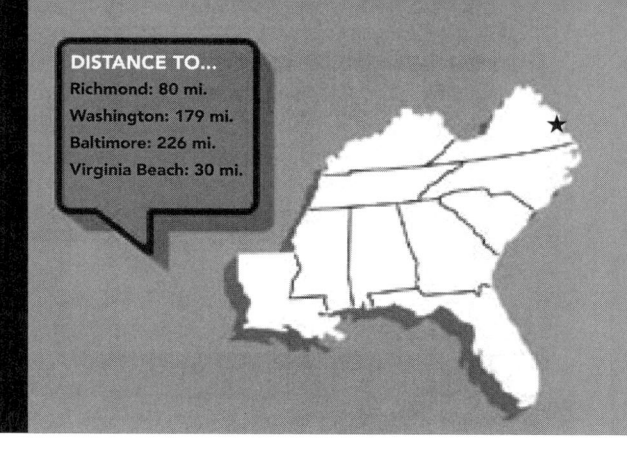

**DISTANCE TO...**
Richmond: 80 mi.
Washington: 179 mi.
Baltimore: 226 mi.
Virginia Beach: 30 mi.

"Hampton University is ranked one of the top HBCUs in the United States and is steadily gaining more recognition as years pass."

**Total Enrollment:**
4,644

**Top 10% of High School Class:**
20%

**Average GPA:**
3.0

**Acceptance Rate:**
60%

**Tuition:**
$13,506

**SAT Range (25th-75th Percentile):**
| Verbal | Math | Total |
|---|---|---|
| 470 – 560 | 460 – 550 | 930 – 1110 |

**ACT Range (25th-75th Percentile):**
| Verbal | Math | Total |
|---|---|---|
| 17-21 | 17-22 | 17-21 |

**Most Popular Majors:**
12% Biology
11% Psychology
10% Sociology
9% Business
6% Nursing

**Students also applied to:***
Howard University
Morehouse College
Spelnman College

*For more school info check out www.collegeprowler.com

## Table of Contents

| | |
|---|---|
| Academics | 538 |
| Local Atmosphere | 540 |
| Safety & Security | 541 |
| Facilities | 543 |
| Campus Dining | 545 |
| Campus Housing | 547 |
| Diversity | 548 |
| Guys & Girls | 550 |
| Athletics | 551 |
| Greek Life | 553 |
| Drug Scene | 554 |
| Overall Experience | 556 |

## College Prowler Report Card

| | |
|---|---|
| Academics | B- |
| Local Atmosphere | C+ |
| Safety & Security | B+ |
| Facilities | B |
| Campus Dining | C |
| Campus Housing | D+ |
| Diversity | D- |
| Guys | B- |
| Girls | A |
| Athletics | B- |
| Greek Life | C+ |
| Drug Scene | B- |

# Academics

## The Lowdown
### ON ACADEMICS

**Degrees Awarded:**
Bachelor, Master, Doctorate

**Undergraduate Schools:**
Journalism, Business, Liberal Arts and Education, Nursing, Architecture, Education, and Science and Technology

**Full-time Faculty:**
400

**Faculty with Terminal Degree:**
79.0%

**Student-to-Faculty Ratio:**
16:1

**Average Course Load:**
15 hours

**Special Degree Options:**
5-year MBA

**AP Test Score Requirements:**
Possible credit for scores of 4 and 5

**IB Test Score Requirements:**
Possible credit for scores of 6 and 7

## Did You Know?

Booker T. Washington went to Hampton University when it was Hampton Institute, and there's a statue of him on campus pointing to an unknown place or thing.

Blackboard is being implemented more at Hampton as a means of communication between students and teachers.

There's a myth that if a student walks across Ogden circle (a circle of grass across from Robert C. Ogden auditorium thought to be an ancient Indian burial ground), the student won't graduate on time, or may not graduate at all from Hampton University.

*Black Enterprise Magazine* lists HU as number three in leading colleges and universities for African American students.

*Black Issues in Higher Education* ranks HU in the top 10 for graduating African Americans with degrees in biology, business management, communications, English, journalism, and psychology.

The John Templeton Foundation named HU to its Honor Roll for Character Building Colleges four years in a row (1996-2000).

Originally the University opened as Hampton Normal, and Agricultural Institute.

Hampton University now has a Virginia Beach campus.

Hampton University has its very own history museum.

**Best Places to Study:**
Library, residence halls, student center

## Students Speak Out
### ON ACADEMICS

"There are too many foreign teachers at Hampton, and they are the ones teaching the hard stuff like math and science. It's hard to understand what they are saying with their accents."

Q "Most of the teachers I've had at Hampton have been helpful and understanding. I've had the occasional teacher who tries to act like they can't accept a valid excuse for a late assignment. I gave my opinion on that teacher at evaluation time, but **overall, I like my professors**."

Q "Most professors here are really cool. I had this one professor for a news class my sophomore year, and he was so cool. Even though the class was in the morning, and I hate the morning, I liked going to his class. I thought I wanted to do something production-related, but **he opened my eyes to news writing**, just from that class. I wonder what happened to him."

Q "I think it depends on your major for what kind of teachers you get. I'm an English major, so of course, I know I have to write, but I always seem to get the teachers that **expect perfection on each and every paper**."

Q "For real, one of the reasons I've stayed at Hampton is because most of my professors really do help me. **I like the fact that I'm not a number**. I'm a first and last name, and most of time when you see the professors on campus, they still remember your name, even after you've moved out of that class."

## The College Prowler Take
### ON ACADEMICS

The academics and reputation of this university are the main reasons students are attracted to HU. The small class sizes and the fine teachers, for the most part, are both big pluses. Hampton University is composed of six schools, 38 bachelor degree programs, 14 master degree programs, and doctoral or professional degree programs in nursing (Ph.D.), physics (Ph.D.), physical therapy (DPT), or pharmacy (Pharm.D.). However, some students feel like they aren't getting their money's worth out of their education. There are institutes in America that cost less where you can receive the same education as that of HU. You may ask yourself, "What am I paying for?" Well, you're mostly paying for the Hampton University name on a piece of paper. But, despite the gripes some students have about cost, the academics at Hampton University are great, mainly because of the wonderful teachers here—and for the cost of tuition, who wouldn't be motivated to learn something? The most recognized department is the School of Journalism and Communications, which is globally funded and has the newest building on campus (erected in 2002). Overall, the education you receive at Hampton University is top-notch, and well worth the cost financially.

**B-**

The College Prowler™ Grade on
### Academics: B-

A high Academics grade generally indicates that professors are knowledgeable, accessible, and genuinely interested in their students' welfare. Other determining factors include class size, how well professors communicate, and whether or not classes are engaging.

# Local Atmosphere

## The Lowdown
ON LOCAL ATMOSPHERE

**Region:**
North Southeast

**City, State:**
Hampton, Virginia

**Setting:**
Small city

**Distance from Washington, DC:**
3 hours

**Distance from Richmond:**
1 hour, 30 minutes

**Points of Interest:**
The Norva, Ikea, Nauticus, Jillian's by the waterside, Roger Brown's, Alice May's, Langley Airforce base, Hampton Coliseum, the American Theater, Charles H. Taylor Arts Center, Peninsula Fine Arts Museum, Chrysler Museum of Art, Harrison Opera House, Virginia Symphony, Virginia Stage Company in Wells Theater, Busch Gardens, Water Country USA, Virginia Zoo, Colonial Williamsburg, Salt Ponds Marina, Buckroe Beach, Grandview Nature Preserve, Fort Monroe, Fort Wool, Jamestown Settlement, Yorktown Victory Center, Hampton History Museum, Virginia Air and Space Museum, Virginia Living Museum, Langley Speedway

## Major Sports Teams
Hampton Roads Piranhas (Women's Professional Soccer), Hampton Roads Admirals (American League Hockey), Norfolk Tides (AAA Baseball), NASCAR at Langley Speedway, Norfolk Night Hawks (Arena Football)

## Did You Know?
Hampton was established in 1610, and is the oldest American English speaking city.

Hampton is the home to NASA Langley Research Center.

Hampton hosts the Hampton Cup Regatta, Hampton Bay Days, and the Hampton Jazz Festival.

## Students Speak Out
ON LOCAL ATMOSPHERE

"If you don't have a car, you don't see anything at all around here. This atmosphere is wack."

Q "I'm from California, so clearly **I'm not used to this drab town**. [There are], like, two clubs with the same locals there every other night."

Q "Hampton is pretty, but that's about it. **I'm always so bored** here, and it makes me kind of homesick when I think about the parties and stuff I used to do back home."

Q "I'm not really into the party scene or the nightlife like most people are. I don't have to be moving all the time, so **I'm quite content with the slowness** of Hampton."

Q "Hampton bores me to death. Like, I think I've seen everything in Hampton and in Norfolk for the most part. I only go to Norfolk when my big sister picks me up because I don't have a car. **I like going to Virginia Beach** a lot to get away from here."

## The College Prowler Take
### ON LOCAL ATMOSPHERE

Hampton is part of a larger area known as Hampton Roads, which consists of several cities that run together: Hampton, Newport News, Norfolk, Portsmouth, Virginia Beach, Suffolk, and Chesapeake. The area is primarily suburban sprawl that originated in Norfolk, which is home to the largest naval base in the world. The sprawl is split into two sides: "*This* side of the water," which consists of Hampton and Newport News, and "the other side of the water," which is mainly Norfolk, Portsmouth, and Virginia Beach. "This side" has a lot of cheaper stores, which do attract the many college students; across the long tunnels, on "the other side of the water," there are many up-scale malls, where many of the students would prefer to go for shopping, dining, and hanging out with friends—if only they weren't so costly and far away! Hampton itself, as many students were very quick to point out, is quite small and quickly becomes repetitive.

**C+**

The College Prowler™ Grade on
## Local Atmosphere: C+

A high Local Atmosphere grade indicates that the area surrounding campus is safe and scenic. Other factors include nearby attractions, proximity to other schools, and the town's attitude toward students.

# Safety & Security

## The Lowdown
### ON SAFETY & SECURITY

**Number of HU Police:**
20

**Phone:**
(757) 727-5000

**Health Center Office Hours:**
Monday-Friday 7 a.m.-5 p.m. Closed Saturday and Sunday.

**Safety Services:**
There are emergency posts scattered on campus. (Push the button and it signals the police immediately. A dispatcher also speaks to you from the post.) Self-defense classes also available.

### Did You Know?

Newport News is nicknamed "Bad News" because of the high crime rate in that area.

Hampton was selected as the most family-friend city in America by *Sesame Street Parents Magazine*.

Hampton is ranked number 25 by *Ladies Home Journal Magazine* for America's Best Cities for Women.

## Students Speak Out
### ON SAFETY & SECURITY

"I feel completely safe when I'm on campus. It's well-lit, and as a female I don't worry about anyone trying to grab me as I'm walking back to my dorm in the late-night hours from the library."

Q "I don't have any qualms with HU security, unlike other things on this campus. But, for real, I hang out with my girl a lot by the waterside, and **I don't fear anything but the water rats.** I either walk back to my dorm along the water, or through the campus, and either way I feel real safe."

Q "I can honestly say **Hampton's campus is one of the most well-lit campuses** that I've seen. I'm a night person, so I go to the 24-hour study a lot, so I'm going back to my room at two or three in the morning. Never have I ever worried about being raped and mangled by a stranger, although it would be nice to have, like, a shuttle or something pick me up."

Q "**I don't feel threatened** by anyone or anything on campus. The way the police are always around, it seems like they could almost spot someone who isn't a student anyway. I don't even hear of anything crime-related for the most part on campus."

Q "HU has pretty good police officers, so, like, I don't think there's a real high crime rate on campus. I heard **those emergency lights on campus don't work**, but what would be the point of them, anyway? If someone was chasing me, would I say 'hold on Mr. Ax-Murderer while I press this emergency button and talk to police'?"

## The College Prowler Take
### ON SAFETY & SECURITY

There is not a college campus anywhere that is crime or incident free, and HU is no exception. However, the incidents have been minimal over the years and overall the campus of HU is relatively safe, and the administration has been working to make the campus even safer. There are now 24-hour security guards at the main gate, and gates before every entrance and exit, to limit unauthorized vehicle access on campus. No one, other than students and those with proper verification, is allowed anywhere else on campus without going through security, and the main gate is the only entrance through which outsiders may enter the campus. The downfalls to this system are that there doesn't seem to be anything stopping people on foot from entering campus, and that students wish that there was easier access closer to their dorms or classrooms. Hampton has a comparatively low crime rate compared to the surrounding Hampton Roads cities, and has a crime rate lower than the national average for cities of its size.

**B+**

**The College Prowler™ Grade on**
## Safety & Security: B+

A high grade in Safety & Security means that students generally feel safe, campus police are visible, blue-light phones and escort services are readily available, and safety precautions are not overly necessary.

# Facilities

## Computers
**High-Speed Network?** Yes
**Wireless Network?** Yes
**Number of Labs:** 9
**Numbers of Computers:** 1,500
**24-Hour Lab?** No
**Charge to Print?** Yes, three cents per page

## The Lowdown
ON FACILITIES

**Student Center:**
The Student Center

**Athletic Center:**
Holland Gym & Convocation Center

**Libraries:**
1

**Movie Theatre on Campus?**
Yes

**Bowling on Campus?**
Yes

**Bar on Campus?**
No

**Coffeehouse on Campus?**
Yes, Lotta Java is located in the student center.

**Favorite Things to Do:**
Most students hang out in the Student Center between classes where there is Chick-fil-a, Zeros, and Planet Smoothie. Students can use the bowling alley for 50 cents, work out in the fitness center, play games in the game room, or watch television in the TV room, all located in the student center. The student center is always packed, and students are almost always able to find an acquaintance to share a meal or just a conversation.

**Popular Places to Chill:**
The Student Center, MLK Rotunda, outside the cafeteria, or in front of the Science and Technology (S&T) building.

## Did You Know?

Hampton University offers non-remedial tutoring, placement service, day care, health service, health insurance.

Career, military, personal, veteran student, academic, older student, and religious counseling services are offered.

The library has three satellite facilities.

Special or historical sites include: Hampton University Museum; Emancipation Oak, one of the Great Trees of the World National Landmarks; Mansion House, built in 1828; Virginia Cleveland, built in 1874; Wigwam Building, built in 1878; Academic Building, built in 1881; Memorial Chapel, built in 1886.

# Students Speak Out
## ON FACILITIES

{ "The facilities are okay. The computer labs are pretty much up-to-par. The gym is always clean, and the pool area is decent."

Q "**The facilities on campus are decent**. The pool could be bigger and lit up more sufficiently. Holland is always so dark and dim, even when it's sunny outside, and it's so hot, no matter what time of the year it is. I had a class over there last semester, and thought I was going to be cremated each time I went to class. You can simmer and come to a boil in those rooms. The computer labs are okay, and they would be better if I didn't have to pay to print. That is the biggest pain. I do like the student center, as far as the atmosphere and the things to do. The food is good, too."

Q "As far as the computer labs on this campus, I think there should be at least one 24-hour lab. I don't like having classes in MLK, because the **rooms are always crowded**, and you have to try and grab a chair from another room just to have a seat in the class. Then you have to sit all close and intimate in those tiny rooms. The student center is okay. At least it's always clean."

Q "I enjoy almost everything about this campus. There seems to be an adequate number of computers and labs. **The gym in Holland is a little small, but it's okay**. Convocation is a nice facility, and I think we should have more events in there. The student center is always crowded, and it's usually something like the hot spot on campus. I know I'm in there quite a bit."

Q "The facilities on campus are not that great to me. **Holland gym is actually one of the smallest gyms I've seen on a college campus**. At least I can say there are plenty of computers on campus, even though I really don't utilize them that much. The student center gets boring to me after a while. It's the same people hanging out in there for what seems like the entire day. It seems like they don't even go to class. I do love Planet Smoothie though. I faithfully buy my Captain Kid smoothie everyday."

Q "There's **plenty to do in the student center**, if you have time between classes, or if you stay off campus and don't want to make the commute to go all the way home and come back. The student center is the main attraction where everything is, and mostly everyone chills."

---

**COLLEGE PROWLER**™

Want to know more about the facilities at Hampton? For a detailed listing of all facilities on campus, check out the College Prowler book on Hampton available at www.collegeprowler.com.

## The College Prowler Take
ON FACILITIES

All of the administrative buildings are very attractive and somewhat luxurious. They are supplied with sufficient air conditioning for comfort, and there are always renovations in progress to make appearances even better. The Scripps Howard Building is two years old, and it's supplied with news-broadcasting televisions and very sufficient amenities catering to the faculty and students. This building brings a very positive impression to the campus, and has generated great funds toward the University. The student center is a great focus on campus as well. It's only a few years old and supplies students with a place to hang out, study, get a bite to eat, exercise, play games, and houses offices for student organizations to meet. Overall, the campus is one of the most attractive in the nation. However, the dormitories on campus are not as pleasing to the eye on the inside as the out. There are also some complaints that classroom sizes are a little small, and there are some buildings that still need air conditioning.

**B**

The College Prowler™ Grade on
## Facilities: B

A high Facilities grade indicates that the campus is aesthetically pleasing and well-maintained; facilities are state-of-the-art, and libraries are exceptional. Other determining factors include the quality of both athletic and student centers and an abundance of things to do on campus.

# Campus Dining

## The Lowdown
ON CAMPUS DINING

**Freshman Meal Plan Requirement?**
Yes

**24-Hour On-Campus Eating?**
No

**Student Favorites:**
Zeros and Planet Smoothie

**Meal Plan Average Cost:**
$3,084 per year

### Did You Know?

Off-campus students sometimes sneak in through the exit door to get a bite to eat between classes, or for Sunday brunch.

## Students Speak Out
### ON CAMPUS DINING

"How many ways can you say bad? Food is food, but I've been to schools that have some great food. This definitely is not one of them. The selection is small, and it seems like it's the same stuff all the time cafeteria."

Q "I rarely eat in the cafeteria because **the food is so bland and bad**. Plus, it seems like you need to be near a bathroom not long after eating in there. It's sad that you can almost predict what is going to be on the menu each and every day."

Q "I like the food in the student center, but the cafeteria definitely is a no-no. **I've gone broke buying food, so I don't go in there**. I just want to know how many different ways can you prepare a chicken every day?"

Q "I guess its okay. I hear people say it's bad, but it's okay to me. Of course **it's not a home cooked meal, but food is food**. On a scale of 1 to 10, I would give the cafeteria a five. The food in the student center is a little greasy for my taste. There should be more of a selection for on-campus students."

Q "**The food in the student center is bangin'**, but the cafeteria food is absolutely positively, by far, the most terrible food that has ever touched my tongue. It can't even compare to other colleges and universities I have visited. Other schools have a plethora of eateries and they can use their meal card. Not here, and that is the worst."

## The College Prowler Take
### ON CAMPUS DINING

"Gourmet Services" is what the HU cooking staff is called, but there is nothing gourmet about the food they serve at all. If you attend an event on campus that they are catering, you might be surprised to find that it is properly seasoned and actually tasty—because the fare they serve up in the cafeteria is surprisingly horrible. Many students want to cancel their meal plan—three meals a day, every day, each semester, when many students don't even want one! A few think the meal plan is great, primarily athletes, who wish they could eat more than three times a day, due to their strenuous activities and long days. But, by and large, the food is not appreciated on campus. Incredibly, the cafeteria is actually greatly improved from what it once was: there were many renovations done to the cafeteria after some violations were exposed on campus. Overall, food in the cafeteria could still stand to be healthier and a little tastier, and students should not be limited to the same thing every day.

**C**

The College Prowler™ Grade on
### Campus Dining: C

Our grade on Campus Dining addresses the quality of both school-owned dining halls and independent on-campus restaurants as well as the price, availability, and variety of food.

# Campus Housing

**Did You Know?**
Freshmen are on curfew until after homecoming and are not allowed visitation until the spring semester.

## The Lowdown
ON CAMPUS HOUSING

**Undergrads on Campus:**
68%

**Number of Dormitories:**
15

**Number of University-Owned Apartments:**
1

**Room Types:**
All residence halls have standard rooms assigned to two people of the same gender. All dorms (except two) have community bathrooms shared by eight to 15 people.

**Available for Rent:**
Nothing

**Cleaning Service?**
Yes, staff cleans the halls and bathrooms of the residence halls.

**You Get:**
Bed, dresser, desk, closet, pillow, cable and Internet access

**Bed Type:**
Twin beds

**Also Available:**
Some halls have microwaves on each floor for shared use.

## Students Speak Out
ON CAMPUS HOUSING

"The dorms have improved quite a bit lately. I used to hate them, because I just never felt clean in the showers, and the rooms were so small. Now I'm in McGrew, and it's nice. They put new furniture in there."

Q "On-campus housing is awful. **The bathrooms are the worst part**. When you have a community bathroom, you have to deal with the nasty ways of other people, and sometimes the resident assistants don't report the toilets being stopped up and other disgusting things. White is one of the nicer dorms, only because it's still pretty new, and people haven't had the chance to destroy it, yet. I would avoid Queen Street."

Q "These dorms are hideous. I think it's terrible that with all the money we pay to be here, we are not even allowed our own refrigerator and microwave in our rooms. **I've seen all types of critters and things with tails** in my tenure here. I would recommend Holmes for the boys and McGrew for the girls. I would stay away from Queen Street and James Hall."

Q "Our dorms are okay. I've seen better. They should put air in all the dorms, so at least living on campus can be comfortable in these hot summer months. **I don't like sharing a bathroom** with 10 or more girls. Some are very nasty, and leave their nasty little items in view for others. I heard horror stories about Queen Street, so I'd stay away from there."

> "I don't like our on-campus housing situation at all. People throw their food in the trash in the bathrooms, which causes them to stink, and also leave their trash exposed, which is why a lot of these dorms have mice and roaches. **Hampton shows the beauty that is on the outside**, but they don't mention the mice and other critters you may share your room with."

## The College Prowler Take
### ON CAMPUS HOUSING

It is a roof over your head and a place to lay your head, but the residence halls are not the most luxurious style of living. On-campus housing is great for some, and a horrible experience for others. Most people stay on campus because it is convenient to get to class, to take a quick nap between classes, or because their parents force them to. Staying on campus is a good thing, because it forces students to be immersed in their studies and not worrying about parties. Most students are thankful for their experience in the dorms, and feel that they wouldn't have adjusted well to HU without it. The most fun and happiness in a dorm is acquired during the freshman year.

# Diversity

## The Lowdown
### ON DIVERSITY

Native American: 0%
Asian American: 0%
African American: 95%
Hispanic: 1%
White: 3%
International: 0%
Unknown: 2%
Out-of-State: 65%

### Minority Clubs
The minority clubs are small because the small number of minorities Hampton has are not widely recognized.

### Most Popular Religions
There is a Student Christian Association widely recognized on campus, and they have noonday prayer in various dorms throughout the week. There is a chapel on campus that holds church on Sunday with a non-denominational practice.

### Gay Tolerance
There are no open gay support groups on campus, however, gays are accepted. The gays on campus are generally quiet and are not outwardly flamboyant with their lifestyle.

## D+

**The College Prowler™ Grade on**
## Campus Housing: D+

A high Campus Housing grade indicates that dorms are clean, well-maintained, and spacious. Other determining factors include variety of dorms, proximity to classes, and social atmosphere.

## Political Activity

Most students at Hampton are socially and politically liberal. There have not been a large number of protests on campus. Most students are quiet with their political views about things happening on campus, unless it is something major that will affect a large group.

### Did You Know?

Hampton University is home to one of the Ten Great Trees of the World: the Emancipation Oak. The tree marks the spot where, in 1863, the first southern reading of the Emancipation Proclamation took place. It was also the spot of the first classroom for African Americans at HU.

## Students Speak Out
### ON DIVERSITY

> "Hampton is an HBCU [Historically Black College and University], so there really is not a lot of diversity."

- "The small number of minorities here at Hampton stick together, and **you don't really see them much**."

- "I don't really see a large amount of diversity here. The few foreigners or whites **don't really hang out with the African Americans**. I can probably count the number of minorities."

- "**Hampton is far from being diverse**. The only diversity is really with the African Americans from different places in the world. That really offers no diversity, because most people I meet are either from New York, New Jersey, or Philadelphia."

- "I would like to see a little more diversity on campus, because right now, there isn't much at all. I see **a few international students**, but they are all on sports teams and hang out together."

## The College Prowler Take
### ON DIVERSITY

Any student looking for a diverse college would be disappointed with HU. Being a Historically Black College and University (HBCU), HU has little to no diversity. The campus consists of an average of 90 to 95 percent African Americans. The other 5 to 10 percent is either white or another race. Religiously, most students identify themselves as Christians. With 65 percent of the population from out-of-state, there are many students from the northeast, south, and west within the United States, which mixes up the general environment. The regional diversification can be heard in the way people speak, how they cook, and the unique identity they bring to campus. The City of Hampton is primarily a Caucasian and African American mix. There is great diversity within the city of Hampton and the surrounding cities, particularly due to the large military population, but definitely not within the University.

**The College Prowler™ Grade on**
## Diversity: D-

A high grade in Diversity indicates that ethnic minorities and international students have a notable presence on campus and that students of different economic backgrounds, religious beliefs, and sexual preferences are well-represented.

# Guys & Girls

## The Lowdown
ON GUYS & GIRLS

**Women Undergrads:** 62%

**Men Undergrads:** 38%

**Birth Control Available?**
No

**Social Scene**
Most students on campus are very social and friendly, even if they are not acquainted with you. It is not hard to find a niche, but it sometimes changes as the years pass, because people transfer, are dismissed, or graduate before you.

**Dress Code**
The University has a strict dress code, which they outline in every syllabus given to the students. This prohibits halters, net shirts, hoods in the classroom, baseball caps in the buildings, and "do-rags" for the males. This school is very fashion savvy, and can almost be compared to a modeling runway. Girls put on their best clothes with stiletto heels, and pile on the makeup to walk to the same classes each and every day. There are some females you will never see without makeup. Most guys are pretty casual, but have to have a fresh white T-shirt and fresh sneakers with every ensemble.

## Hookups or Relationships?
Freshmen tend to hook up almost immediately after they arrive. It could have a lot to with the fact that they arrive a week before the upperclassmen for orientation and all they have is each other. After that first week, some of the girls hook up with upperclass guys or with the local guys in the military. Some people prefer the "untitled" relationship, because it lessens the pressure and responsibilities a serious relationship can entail.

## Students Speak Out
ON GUYS & GIRLS

"The girls outnumber the guys here by a lot. The girls here go way too far to get all dressed up, and they put on all this makeup just to see the same guys each and every day."

"I love the scene with the girls. **There seems to be like 10 girls for every guy** here, and they're not ugly girls either. Hampton University is known for being exclusive for having beautiful women. From the short skirts, long legs, and other beautiful assets, it's a man's paradise."

"There are too many girls here, and **the guys are not of choice-cut quality**. All the dudes look alike with those stupid white T-shirts and jeans. It's like a uniform. You can be bombarded with all the different perfumes and colognes merged together that these people wear, and it can often be nauseating."

"**This might be the fashion capital if I've ever seen it**. I don't understand how some of these girls can get up in enough time to put on a face, stockings, and heels and truck it to class in a timely fashion. I thought school was supposed to be the place to learn, not bag a man."

"It would be a lot better if there was a more even amount of guys and girls on campus. **I don't see too many unattractive people**, though, and I think it's mainly because people take so much pride in their appearances."

## The College Prowler Take
### ON GUYS & GIRLS

HU girls are the talk of the town ... literally! All the locals get excited when they meet a female from HU, or an "HU chic." HU girls have the reputation of being "high-class, bourgeois" females. Some are even considered "ditsy" and materialistic. A lot, however, do happen to be very smart, love to party hard, and most go to church on Sundays. The high-spirited HU guys are always trying to snag an HU girl, however they are not always successful. Regardless, with a ratio of 5:1 (which sometimes seems as if it is 10:1), girls to boys, guys do not sweat the fact they cannot get a girl, because they will eventually, whether the girl is a student at HU or not. HU guys are typical guys who want to make money, have a nice-looking girl—or as they say a "bangin' female"—and are mainly business majors. Girls tend to think the guys need to start paying half as much attention to their appearance as they do; the guys tend to wear the baggy jeans and T-shirt, instead of being clean-cut looking.

**B-**

**A**

### The College Prowler™ Grade on
## Guys: B-

A high grade for Guys indicates that the male population on campus is attractive, smart, friendly, and engaging, and that the school has a decent ratio of guys to girls.

### The College Prowler™ Grade on
## Girls: A

A high grade for Girls not only implies that the women on campus are attractive, smart, friendly, and engaging, but also that there is a fair ratio of girls to guys.

# Athletics

## The Lowdown
### ON ATHLETICS

**Men's Varsity Teams:**
Tennis
Basketball
Football
Swimming
Track (indoor/outdoor)
Sailing
Cross Country
Golf

**Women's Varsity Teams:**
Basketball
Softball
Track (indoor/outdoor)
Ebony Fire
Volleyball
Cheerleading
Bowling
Tennis
Sailing
Cross Country
Golf

**Club Sports:**
Volleyball, Basketball, Softball

**Intramurals (IMs):**
Basketball, Softball, Tennis, Football, Bowling, Sailing

**Most Popular Sports:**
Football is the most popular sports event. Next would be men's basketball.

**Overlooked Teams:**
The girls' volleyball and softball teams often complain they don't get much support from students.

**Athletic Division:**
Division II

**Conference:**
MEAC

**School Mascot:**
Pirates

**Fields:**
Armstrong Stadium

**Getting Tickets:**
The cost of games is covered in tuition. Prices vary for the events for outside students.

# The College Prowler Take
ON ATHLETICS

Royal blue and white are HU's colors, but don't expect to come and see the people on campus covered in them. In general, students tend not to show off their school spirit and paraphernalia. There is some support for the football team, but overall the Pirates tend not to come out to support their teams. The most support comes during homecoming, but, even then, it tends to be more of a fashion show for meeting and greeting than about the game. It's usually in the athletes themselves that people will find the most school spirit. The Hampton Pirates have a decent athletics department, offering five varsity sports for men, and seven for women. Currently, the Pirates are a Division II team; however, those students that follow the sports hope to see them turn Division I in the future. And with the beautiful Armstrong Stadium and high-caliber facilities, HU should have no trouble luring Division I-caliber talent. As for non-varsity athletics, there is an intramurals program available to students, along with club sports, but few people seem to know anything about them. This is an area at HU that could use improvement.

# Students Speak Out
ON ATHLETICS

"Hampton has a great sense of team spirit and pride. You can see the Hampton pride stickers almost anywhere, and it truly shows. The athletes are actually not as big-headed as I've seen at other schools."

Q "**The football team always seems to do pretty well**. I enjoy going to a lot of football games, because the girls get all dressed up, and you can tell they're not there to watch the game. The setup of the stadium is okay. It's really easy to get distracted from the game."

Q "The teams are consistently strong, and they usually display a lot of teamwork. **They don't get as much recognition as they should**. The IM sports give people that usually don't have as much time to play organized team sports a chance to be full-time students, and also keep up their love of sports."

Q "**Hampton has some strong athletic teams**. That's one thing I can say, I'm proud when I represent the University. I love sports, and even if I don't go to every game, I like to know the stats, and what's going on with the teams."

**B-**

The College Prowler™ Grade on
## Athletics: B-

A high grade in Athletics indicates that students have school spirit, that sports programs are respected, that games are well-attended, and that intramurals are a prominent part of student life.

# Greek Life

## Students Speak Out
### ON GREEK LIFE

"I think Greek institutions are key to social interactions. They're important because they teach you how to bond with others, and you have long-standing traditions and legacies."

Q "Having a Greek organization on a black campus that is predominantly Christian is demeaning to how we want to represent ourselves. **We don't need Greek traditions to bring us together**; we have Christian values that support our black culture."

Q "**They promote a sense of unity**. Black Greek organizations start out as a hallmark in the community. Greek organizations are the descendents of movers and shakers in the black community. They continue to be a strong force in the community at large. They also serve as a symbol of academic excellence togetherness and culture. The Greeks on campus are scarce and dwindling."

Q "The Greeks don't do a whole lot on campus but flaunt their paraphernalia. When we had our R.A. association activities, **they showed us no support at all**. It's basically like they stick together, and don't venture out past their own group on campus."

Q "**Our Greek life is a mess**. A lot of them seem to continue to get banned from campus, or they seem to be letting in just anybody nowadays. The only time I really see the Greeks is during their designated week, when they are in the cafeteria and around campus wearing their letters. I don't see what they do, or what other organizations they support."

## The Lowdown
### ON GREEK LIFE

**Number of Fraternities:**
5

**Number of Sororities:**
5

**Undegrad Men in Fraternities:**
5%

**Undergrad Women in Sororities:**
4%

### Did You Know?

The Greek organizations on Hampton's campus seem to be dying off as the years pass.

## The College Prowler Take
### ON GREEK LIFE

The Greek life on the campus of HU is currently a dying culture. With sororities and fraternities being caught hazing and suspended from campus every year, the Greeks seem to be disappearing left and right. The only times students notice the Greeks wearing their paraphernalia or see them in uniform are for a big events like the Greek Step Show or homecoming. The Greeks remain virtually invisible on campus, giving little to the community and the school. They are rarely seen participating in community service or organizing student events. The Greeks at HU don't even seem to be a social center as they are on most campuses; they have no houses, and they throw no parties. One has to question what role, if any, the Greeks play in life at HU.

## Drug Scene

### The Lowdown
### ON DRUG SCENE

**Most Prevalent Drugs on Campus:**
Marijuana

**Liquor-Related Referrals:**
0

**Liquor-Related Arrests:**
5

**Drug-Related Referrals:**
0

**Drug-Related Arrests:**
2

**Drug Counseling Programs:**
Student Health Services
(757) 727-5315

### The College Prowler™ Grade on
### Greek Life: C+

A high grade in Greek Life indicates that sororities and fraternities are not only present, but also active on campus. Other determining factors include the variety of houses available and the respect the Greek community receives from the rest of the campus.

## Students Speak Out
### ON DRUG SCENE

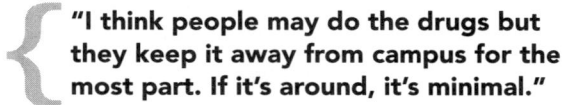

> "I think people may do the drugs but they keep it away from campus for the most part. If it's around, it's minimal."

Q "There are a lot of people that smoke marijuana on campus. Although HU tries to mask the fact that students smoke, they recognize the fact that many students do. As far as any other drugs, **I don't think a lot of people participate** in anything else other than that."

Q "**There's a lot of weed smoking** by students that attend the University, but as far as students doing it on campus, that's not too prevalent. What students do in their private quarters is their business and the University can't control that, but I think students respect the University by not doing it on campus."

Q "**They may as well legalize marijuana**, because it's everywhere. Some people take the chance of smoking on campus, and some people just do it in the confines of their or someone else's living quarters."

Q "Truthfully I don't see it too much around campus. I think the policy of being expelled if you are found with it is an excellent deterrent. **No one wants to call their parents and tell them they're on their way home**, because they've been expelled for doing some type of drug."

## The College Prowler Take
### ON DRUG SCENE

HU has no tolerance for any form of drugs on campus. If caught, you are "out by five." This refers to a student's dismissal by 5 p.m. if caught violating a major rule. If a student is found with any form of an illegal substance, it is confiscated immediately and the student is automatically expelled from the campus. The main drug on campus is alcohol. In conjunction with alcohol is marijuana. According to most students, marijuana has a highly visible existence on campus. Many students who do smoke tend to hide it in fear of the severe drug penalty; however, it's not hidden enough to go unrecognized. The strictness of the drug policy on campus, and the fact that there is little recognition of drugs being on the campus, is a plus for the University and its students. There is no apparent usage of "hard drugs" such as coke or ecstasy on campus.

**B-**

**The College Prowler™ Grade on**
**Drug Scene: B-**

A high grade on Drug Scene indicates that drugs are not a noticeable part of campus life; drug use is not visible, and no pressure to use them seems to exist.

# Overall Experience

## Students Speak Out
### ON OVERALL EXPERIENCE

"In going to HU, I experienced a culture shock. Coming from an area of many races and cultures, I was not used to seeing one race. It is a good educational experience, the school has its ups and downs, but I liked it."

Q "**Hampton University felt like being in high school again** on one hand, and on the other hand, it was an experience that will take me into the real world. I never experienced more irritation or drama before I got to HU. However, I've learned a lot about life at this university, and there are details of my life that I would not have been able to have had anywhere else."

Q "Where do I begin?—The first year was great and the second year was when all the confusion surfaced and **I experienced the 'HU run around.'** The third year, the true colors shine through, and halfway through that you start wanting to put together the pieces. The fourth year, after all the pieces are together, you try to graduate. It prepared me for the real world and made me realize that the real world wasn't going to be prepared for me."

Q "Though it has taken me five years to get out of this piece, **I don't hate HU, completely**. I've learned a lot of lessons, like studying will pay off, and how you react in college is how the real world will view you. I learned if you want to be somebody, you have to want to get to where you want to be, which will not be easy."

## The College Prowler Take
### ON OVERALL EXPERIENCE

Hampton University requires an acquired patience and has issues you would probably not endure at another university. The financial aid mix-ups, runaround, and the registrar's inability to provide answers can make any Hamptonian want to pack their bags and transfer elsewhere. The crazy weather, poor transportation and parking, and the great hunt for something to do at night, while frustrating, can also lead to some interesting memories and experiences, and can even make for a good story or two. On the other hand, the educational experience students receive is one of the best, with inspirational teachers and awesome classes. The friends you make and relationships you build at Hampton make any matriculating student or alumni proud to have had a Hampton University experience. Many meet their lifetime mates while attending Hampton, or meet a Hampton alumni later in life at a job or other event. Hampton students and alumni are everywhere, and can tell you about the good times and bad times they had at the University.

The HU experience is definitely one-of-a-kind, the only kind in the world, no less. At Hampton, you come with the feeling that this is going to be the best experience of your life, when in actuality it becomes a lesson in choice and decision-making. It is one you will not regret. The campus scenery entices you, the academics applaud you, the students enthrall you, and everything else falls into place. College, it's what you make it, and at Hampton you have the opportunity to make it everything you can possibly hope for ... and more!

# Loyola University New Orleans

6363 St. Charles Avenue, New Orleans, LA 70118-6195
www.loyno.edu          (800) 456-9652

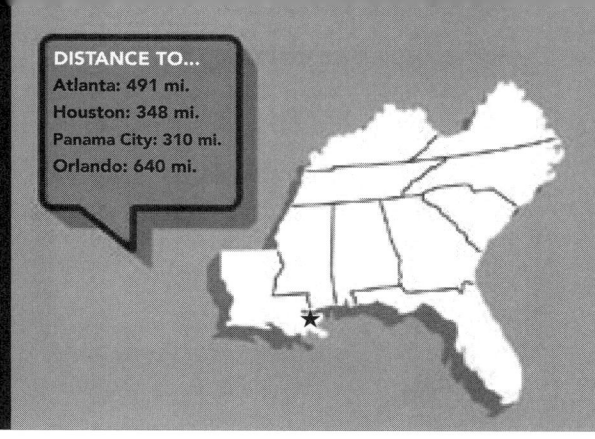

**DISTANCE TO...**
Atlanta: 491 mi.
Houston: 348 mi.
Panama City: 310 mi.
Orlando: 640 mi.

*"Loyola selects professors who possess a high level of excellence in their particular field, and readily make applications to daily living."*

**Total Enrollment:**
3,303

**Top 10% of High School Class:**
29%

**Average GPA:**
3.7

**Acceptance Rate:**
69%

**Tuition:**
$21,078

**SAT Range (25th-75th Percentile)**
| Verbal | Math | Total |
|---|---|---|
| 570 – 670 | 560 – 640 | 1130 – 1310 |

**ACT Range (25th-75th Percentile)**
| Verbal | Math | Total |
|---|---|---|
| 26-30 | 23-27 | 25-28 |

**Most Popular Majors:**
14% Communication Studies and Rhetoric
9% Psychology
5% Biology/Biological Sciences
5% Marketing/Marketing Management
5% Political Science and Government

**Students also applied to:***
Louisiana State University–Baton Rouge
Spring Hill College
Tulane University
University of New Orleans
Xavier University (LA)

*For more school info check out www.collegeprowler.com

## Table of Contents

| | |
|---|---|
| Academics | 558 |
| Local Atmosphere | 560 |
| Safety & Security | 561 |
| Facilities | 563 |
| Campus Dining | 564 |
| Campus Housing | 566 |
| Diversity | 567 |
| Guys & Girls | 569 |
| Athletics | 571 |
| Greek Life | 572 |
| Drug Scene | 574 |
| Overall Experience | 575 |

## College Prowler Report Card

| | |
|---|---|
| Academics | B+ |
| Local Atmosphere | A- |
| Safety & Security | C |
| Facilities | C |
| Campus Dining | B- |
| Campus Housing | C |
| Diversity | C+ |
| Guys | B |
| Girls | B+ |
| Athletics | D+ |
| Greek Life | C |
| Drug Scene | B- |

# Academics

### The Lowdown
ON ACADEMICS

**Degrees Awarded:**
Bachelor, Post-Bachelor Certificate, Master, Post-Master Certificate, First Professional

**Undergraduate Schools:**
College of Arts and Science, College of Business Administration, City College, College of Music College

**Pre-Professional Programs:**
Pre-Law, Pre-Dentistry, Pre-Medicine, Pre-Veterinary Science

**Full-time Faculty:**
293

**Part-time Faculty:**
176

**Faculty with Terminal Degree:**
259

**Student-to-Faculty Ratio:**
22:1

**Average Course Load:**
Most students take 15 or 18 credits.

**Special Degree Options:**
Loyola offers education for the working student through City College; also, there's the four-year Music Education degree program.

**Sample Academic Clubs:**
Advertising, Loyola Society of Criminology, MBA Association, Public Relations PRSSA

**Int'l Programs & Services:**
Center of International Education, Loyola Intensive English Program (IEP), Undergraduate Study Abroad Programs, Law Foreign Summer Programs

### Did You Know?

Loyola offers some kind of financial aid to 85 percent of the students.

Loyola University New Orleans is one of 28 Jesuit colleges and universities in the United States.

**Best Places to Study:**
Monroe Library, the Palm Court, the lounge in front of the Orleans Room in the Danna Center

## Students Speak Out
### ON ACADEMICS

"As a freshman, I was disappointed with the teachers, as I felt my high school teachers were more interesting. Now I am taking more business classes where I find professors up-to-par with my high school teachers."

Q "My classes are very interesting. **All my teachers are knowledgeable** and know their craft, yet they are skilled in delivering the information in a way that I can understand the concepts taught. Right now I am taking chemistry, which is a common curriculum class. My chemistry teacher makes everything pertinent to everyday life. Since I'm an English major, he doesn't force me to learn so much about a subject that I will not have to necessarily know for my future professional life."

Q "I pretty much like all my teachers. They all have a **genuine interest in what they are teaching**, and bring their experience from outside the classroom. The main reason I like Loyola is that they require philosophy and religious classes. It's something new and different from other universities. I think those classes help me see the world with a different point of view."

Q "Most teachers that I have had are pretty cool. They **allow the students to express their point of views**. However, some professors only like their opinions, and would rather that you adopt theirs then your own. Most teachers are pretty liberal, pretty cool."

Q "**Classes are really good here**. I like the psych department and the philosophy department. Dr. Matthews is really cool, and she's got lots of connections since she's been at Loyola awhile. Everybody knows her. Plus, she prepares her students for grad school. If you take her clinical psych class, you find that it's awesome. She actually tells you, 'Okay, this is what you can do with grad school. This is how you can apply.' You know, stuff that you need to know."

## The College Prowler Take
### ON ACADEMICS

The Jesuit education compels every person to reach a high level of human excellence. This results in an academic standard that challenges students to sharpen their critical thinking as they develop academic knowledge, and creates sensitivity to social justice in a way that many have not experienced before. The Jesuit tradition requires development of the whole person, body and soul, intellect and feelings, and requires that students learn how to "be critical, examine attitudes, challenge assumptions, and analyze motives." That high regard for academic excellence and social awareness, evidenced in the way professors teach here, makes Loyola attractive to prospective students. Depending on their major, students at Loyola choose how many extracurricular activities they want to involve themselves in. The Loyola student is also required to take common curricular classes like philosophy and religion, which are not required at other universities, as part of the Jesuit pursuit to build the whole person and promote critical thinking.

Competent professors, many of whom are notable professionals in their own right, generously offer counsel and guidance to ensure the student's academic success, as well as that the journey is a pleasant one. In general, Loyola students lean toward artistic endeavors, more so than purely technological pursuits.

**The College Prowler™ Grade on**
### Academics: B+

A high Academics grade generally indicates that professors are knowledgeable, accessible, and genuinely interested in their students' welfare. Other determining factors include class size, how well professors communicate, and whether or not classes are engaging.

# Local Atmosphere

## The Lowdown
ON LOCAL ATMOSPHERE

**Region:**
South

**City, State:**
New Orleans, Louisiana

**Setting:**
Mid-sized urban

**Distance from Baton Rouge:**
1 hour, 15 minutes

**Distance from Lafayette:**
2 hours, 10 minutes

**Points of Interest:**
Camellia Grill, D-Day Museum, Snug Harbor and the French Quarter, Audubon Park and Audubon Zoo, Magazine Street

**Sports Teams:**
Saints (football), Hornets (basketball)

**City Websites:**
http://www.neworleans.org
http://www.CityofNO.com

## Students Speak Out
ON LOCAL ATMOSPHERE

**"New Orleans is a very diverse and cultured city. Most students leave Loyola as a more open-minded, accepting individual."**

"New Orleans' atmosphere is really good. **People like to drink a lot, and they're pretty laid-back.** With Tulane University present there are a lot of Tulane kids, and some of them are very annoying. The stuff to stay away from would be the Quarter. There are a lot of extremely uncool people there. Definitely visit Frenchman Street, but skip Bourbon, unless you're going straight down to get to Frenchman."

"New Orleans is 'the' party town, and it can either teach you to manage your time, or destroy you. Plenty of people have to leave Loyola because they've wasted their time and money on booze and drugs, and it caught up with them eventually. **We're right next door to Tulane University**, and we've got an amiable relationship with their student body."

"I like that I can party downtown and do whatever I want, but then come back to uptown, where the area is quieter and a little cleaner. **I have Audubon Park to enjoy nature**, and everything else I would want in a city. Whether you like the suburbs or the city, there's something here for you."

"The atmosphere here is very fun and all-embracing. That's what I like about New Orleans and Loyola; both are pretty welcoming to everybody. I'm from a small town, so it's really exciting to meet **so many people of various cultural backgrounds** and discover different ways of thinking. Having Tulane and other schools nearby is also great."

## The College Prowler Take
### ON LOCAL ATMOSPHERE

There's no city quite like New Orleans. Students that attend Loyola receive the advantage of living in a major city, without dealing with the major disadvantages. Due to its size, just about anything in New Orleans is a walk or streetcar stop away and can be enjoyed in the four years you're here. While it may not feel like your typical college town, decked out with university memorabilia, you will find that New Orleans offers great escapades. If you have a free afternoon, Magazine Street is lined with original boutiques, rare bookstores, and quaint cafés. The Audubon Park is practically across the street from school, and if you really want to make a big day of sightseeing, you just hop the streetcar and head for downtown and the French Quarter, where you'll find plenty of sites, including sidewalk artists and street musicians.

New Orleans is a city, and, like in any city, safety must be the number one thought when setting out on any excursion. Yet, a unique aspect of New Orleans is that there is no one particular area that is deemed safe or otherwise. In the downtown and French Quarter areas there are Hospitality Police to ensure your safety and that you have proper directions. The streets easily get very crowded and dirty ... but that's New Orleans.

# Safety & Security

## The Lowdown
### ON SAFETY & SECURITY

**Number of Loyola Police Officers:**
13 officers

**Phone:**
(540) 865-3434

**Health Center Office Hours:**
Monday–Friday 8 a.m.–5 p.m.

**Health Assistants After Hours:**
Monday–Friday 11 p.m.–8 a.m., and weekends in the residence halls
(504) 865-3326

**Safety Services:**
Rape Defense class (RAD); Take Back the Night, shuttle, BOLO e-mails, Catwalk-escort service, blue-lights

**A-**

The College Prowler™ Grade on
## Local Atmosphere: A-

A high Local Atmosphere grade indicates that the area surrounding campus is safe and scenic. Other factors include nearby attractions, proximity to other schools, and the town's attitude toward students.

### Did You Know?

PAWS (Peers Advocating Wellness), a student organization, heightens student awareness on health and wellness issues. Any Loyola student can join by contacting http://www.mgtherio@loyno.edu.

### The College Prowler Take
**ON SAFETY & SECURITY**

Students say it loud and clear—on campus, Loyola is a safe place. You will notice a number of campus police roaming the grounds and checking the facilities. Lighting all over campus maintains good visibility for students who may still be practicing music in the communications building late at night, or heading for a midnight read at the library—where only the front doors are open at night and the 24-hour computer lab is monitored by campus police. Loyola's Public Safety and University Police try to make their presence known throughout campus, not only to deter possible crimes, but also to make students feel safe. Rather than offering a false sense of security to students, they work to make students aware of possible dangers around them by offering a variety of safety awareness programs.

### Students Speak Out
**ON SAFETY & SECURITY**

"I feel pretty safe walking across campus at night. Even though New Orleans is a very dangerous city, I can walk on campus and not get mugged."

Q "I think that the **security guards need to go to the gym** and work out, so they can catch the bad guys on campus. But overall, I don't really feel unsafe on campus, because there are always other people around."

Q "There is a particular offender who plagues the campus that has not been caught: the masturbator reported in the Monroe Library. Other than that I feel safe. **The campus is well-lit.**"

Q "A **student is robbed twice a month just off campus**. The campus police are a presence only on the Loyola campus, and I don't feel safe if I am not directly on the campus grounds."

Q "The security here at Loyola is very good. I walk by myself at night all the time and I don't feel unsafe at all. The **campus is closed off from the rest of the town**, and the campus police do a really good job of keeping it safe within the campus. Within the campus you are safe. However, it's not a good idea to walk at night on any of the streets surrounding the campus."

### The College Prowler™ Grade on
### Safety & Security: C

A high grade in Safety & Security means that students generally feel safe, campus police are visible, blue-light phones and escort services are readily available, and safety precautions are not overly necessary.

# Facilities

## The Lowdown ON FACILITIES

**Student Center:**
The Danna Center

**Libraries:**
2, plus Loyola and Tulane have a dual library membership program for students and faculties.

**Athletic Center:**
Recreational Sports Complex (Rec Plex)

**Movie Theater on Campus?**
Yes, there is screening in Bobet, Room 332

**Bar on Campus?**
No

**Coffeehouse on Campus?**
Yes. The Java Hut Coffee Bar at the Underground, the Danna Center, Starbucks in the Monroe Library.

**Popular Places to Chill:**
The Underground, the Palm Court and Peace Quad, balcony of Marquette Hall

## Computers
**High-Speed Network?** Yes
**Wireless Network?** Yes
**Number of Labs:** 8
**24-Hour Labs:** Monroe Library
**Charge to Print:** None

## Favorite Things to Do

There are endless student band gigs to hear, both on campus and at the local bars. Loyola students put on impressive operas and dramas throughout the year, as well as musical ensembles, and, by spring, there are the student recitals to attend. Thanks to the Film Buff Program, students also may watch movies almost every night free of charge (visit the school website for a movie list). Open Mic at the Underground is also a great way to spend an evening and share some laughs.

## Students Speak Out ON FACILITIES

"The computer labs are fine, but the student center is bland, and the athletic center is very outdated and under-supplied."

Q "I like the facilities here at Loyola, although **I wish that they were more like Tulane**. They've got really, really nice equipment and, generally speaking, a more up-to-date look."

Q "The facilities I use are nice. Some of the music facilities are state-of-the-art, and the **dorms are respectable**. I lived on the Honors floor, and it is definitely better than what I have seen at other schools—very well-kept."

Q "The facilities are very adequate. Especially the **library media rooms are really high-tech**. The only building with classrooms that I have a problem with is Monroe, but even there you can get Internet hookup. For the most part, it's nice and up-to-date."

Q "The **Rec Plex needs a lot of attention**. The Monroe Library, however, is one of the best buildings on our campus."

## Campus Dining

## The College Prowler Take
### ON FACILITIES

Most students feel as though Rec Plex, the athletic center, could use a little work; it needs to be renovated, and it needs some more equipment. The Monroe Business Building is, by far, the campus eye-sore, and contrasts from the Tudor-Gothic architecture of the other buildings that dominate the Loyola campus. Students often compare their facilities with those of rival school Tulane, but realize Tulane's facilities reflect what students pay in tuition. Despite needing a little bit of maintenance, students find their campus very comfortable and appealing. Lovely walks and an abundance of park benches and grassy spots invite students to sit and read, or engage in lively discussions. The school also overlooks the spacious Audubon Park, which is right across the street.

## The Lowdown
### ON CAMPUS DINING

**Freshman Meal Plan Requirement?**
Yes

**24-Hour On-Campus Eating?**
No

**Student Favorites:**
The Underground, Pizza Hut, Smoothie King

**Meal Plan Average Cost:**
$1,374 per semester

### Did you know?

The OR provides comment sheets that students can fill out. Whether positive or negative, the cards will be posted on the bulletin board in the dining hall along with the head concierge's gracious response.

Every dining area offers at least one vegetarian meal. In the Orleans Room, Loyola Dining Services has started the "Greenery," which offers a new vegetarian meal daily.

## C

**The College Prowler™ Grade on**
### Facilities: C

A high Facilities grade indicates that the campus is aesthetically pleasing and well-maintained; facilities are state-of-the-art, and libraries are exceptional. Other determining factors include the quality of both athletic and student centers and an abundance of things to do on campus.

## Students Speak Out
### ON CAMPUS DINING

"Food is average on campus. The OR's food is okay at lunch and horrible at dinner. One bright spot is Sandella's, where you can get great-tasting wraps."

"The food is all right on campus; it could be better. **It's not that healthy**, although they have made strides in the past few months to increase that level of healthiness. I visit the Underground fairly regularly, and I find that they serve nutritious food to a certain extent. I eat a lotta muffelattas!"

"After a while, you'll get sick of the OR, as the food is just okay. Loyola renovated the Underground, and the new food they serve now is wonderful; their wraps are delicious. The salad bowls are great, too. The food seems to be healthy and fresh. **It's a really remarkable improvement**, and all the students are very happy."

"**I really like what they did to the Underground**. They actually serve, not just decent food, but good food now, which is why there is always a line at the cash register. The OR has also improved in the last few years. They offer a vegan bar, and that's cool that they cater to people who don't eat meat. I do, however, think the C-Store is a rip-off."

"**Dining services has taken several key steps to improve** the quality of food options on campus. There's a Starbucks in the library that opened this summer. To have a coffee bar is great; to have a Starbucks is superb. We really needed that. I just wish it was open at night when students are trying to stay awake to study. Maybe they'll change that soon."

## The College Prowler Take
### ON CAMPUS DINING

There is a main dining hall where students eat lunch a la carte, and complain that it's slightly overpriced. Dinner there is an all-you-can-eat buffet that includes a vegetarian bar, many hot dishes, and always hamburgers and fries. There seems to be a variety of food services available throughout campus, but students end up going to the same place again and again, until they get bored of the food. The school tries to accommodate people with various eating habits, including the vegans and vegetarians.

The staff tries to meet the expectations and the desires of the student body, and even offers a comment sheet for students to list their requests or complaints. While the students appreciate the effort, they still seem to feel that the food selection is to repetitive.

**B-**

The College Prowler™ Grade on
### Campus Dining: B-

Our grade on Campus Dining addresses the quality of both school-owned dining halls and independent on-campus restaurants as well as the price, availability, and variety of food.

# Campus Housing

## Room Types

Residential housing on campus includes standard, suite-style, and apartment-style units. In standard units, students share a common bathroom facility and living area. In suite-style units, students share a bathroom and living area with no more than five people. In apartment-style units, students share a semi-private bathroom with no more than one person, and share a living area and kitchen with no more than six people.

## The Lowdown
### ON CAMPUS HOUSING

### Did You Know?
All campus residents get free cable and Ethernet connection.

**Undergrads on Campus:**
39% (1,381)

**Percentage of Women:**
68%

**Percentage of Men:**
32%

**Cleaning Service?**
Only for bathrooms of Biever Hall and Cabra Hall

**Available for Rent:**
Refrigerator

**You Get:**
Bed, closet, chest of drawers, desk and chair

**Bed Type:**
Twin extra-long, some lofts

## Students Speak Out
### ON CAMPUS HOUSING

"The dorms are kind of scary. New Res is nice; it's the apartment suite, the one that has a kitchen and everything. Buddig was really disgusting, though."

"I don't think the dorms are too bad. I lived in Biever last year, which was nice. I have visited New Res, and that's very nice. The **dorms are very spacious, and there are big windows**. I, personally, don't like Buddig. The dorms are very small, there aren't many windows, and the visitation rules suck. You couldn't check-in people. This year I am in Cabra, because after planning to live off campus, my friend bailed on me. Cabra is okay; there's a workspace in the dorms, and balconies. The whole campus that Cabra is on is pretty. I actually like the idea of being off the main campus, and at Cabra we have 24-hour visitation! Cabra isn't as horrible as everyone says it is."

"Avoid Cabra. Biever is better than Buddig. **New Res [Carrollton Hall] is the best** but reserved for upperclassman with good grades and no disciplinary record."

Q "Cabra sucks! Concrete jungle. It's a big block of concrete that has rooms in it, and it's cold and dirty. The **rooms are closets, but you have to cram two people in them**. It sucks. Luckily, when I lived there, everybody in my suite had one per room. That was livable, but to stick two people in one of those tiny rooms, you wanted to kill them."

Q "**Loyola's dorms, overall, rate higher than most schools**. They're large and climate-controlled, but scoring one of the upperclassmen apartments can be really tough. Freshmen are assigned to a double-occupancy room—boys have a common bathroom for each wing, while four girls in a suite have a private bathroom."

## The College Prowler Take
ON CAMPUS HOUSING

Though kept under control, the sheer number of students, plus having to share showers, makes many of the Loyola dorms less than enticing. The dorms are clean but old, and have a musty smell that is just a New Orleans trademark. Overall, the dorms are acceptable, and, of course, New Res is the Mecca for every student, which motivates them to maintain their high GPAs and not get a write-up. New Res is reserved for upperclassmen in good standing, and, as the name implies, is the new residence hall on campus—which means it has all the nicest accommodations. Of the underclassman housing, Biever is the most popular. One of the major benefits of the dorms is that they offer Ethernet and cable access to their students, along with several other perks.

**The College Prowler™ Grade on**
## Campus Housing: C

A high Campus Housing grade indicates that dorms are clean, well-maintained, and spacious. Other determining factors include variety of dorms, proximity to classes, and social atmosphere.

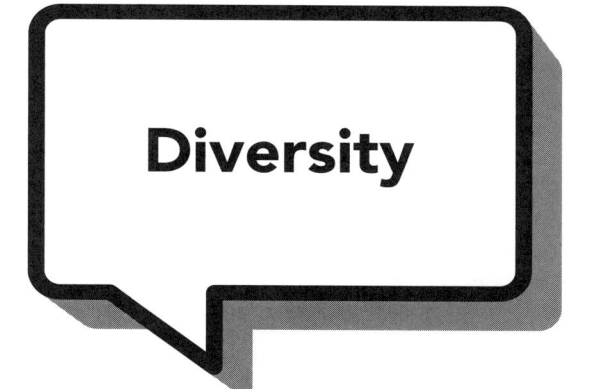

# Diversity

## The Lowdown
ON DIVERSITY

**Native American:** 1%

**Asian American:** 4%

**African American:** 10%

**Hispanic:** 10%

**White:** 72%

**International:** 3%

**Out-of-State:** 55%

## Minority Clubs
There are several student organizations, including the Black Student Union, Bridging the Gap, Etcetera, International Student Association (ISA), La Gente, Loyola Asian Student Organization (LASO), Muslim Students Association.

## Most Popular Religions
Most students on campus are Catholic.

## Political Activity

Most students are politically and socially liberal. There have been protests on campus in the past. However, students generally keep their political persuasions to themselves.

## Gay Tolerance

Loyola welcomes gay students and has Etcetera, a student-led organization open to gay, lesbian, bisexual, transgender, and straight people alike in an effort to promote tolerance.

## Economic Status

There is some diversity of socioeconomic status. However, most come from middle-upper-class families.

### Did You Know?

Loyola offers study-abroad programs during the academic semesters and summer. Students are able to study literature and other subjects relevant to the country they visit. Countries include Belgium, Ireland, Mexico, France, England, and Spain.

Want to hear more about the student groups on campus? Pick up a guidebook on Loyola at www.collegeprowler.com.

## Students Speak Out
### ON DIVERSITY

"As far as race goes, it's not diverse at all. It's mostly rich, white kids. People here are friendly. It's not that they don't want to be diverse, it's just the way it is at Loyola."

Q "Diverse personalities are prevalent on campus. People know they can be themselves, and don't have to conform to some notion of 'normality.' **Everything goes on Loyola's campus, which is really very cool**. However, ethnic diversity is next to nonexistent, but there's not much segregation of what little diversity there is here. It's pretty integrated."

Q "The Loyola campus is really diverse, and that's one thing I like about Loyola. However, people may stick together in their own ethnic group or region, and that sucks. I think it is definitely great to have friends from different countries, and from all over the country, in one classroom. It **brings many different perspectives to the subject studied**. It's cool to find out what life is like in Texas, or to visit my friend in another countr,y or in New York over fall break. It's a really good way to learn about the world."

Q "Loyola is very white. It might be a little diverse, but my roommate was the one who brought its non-diversity to my attention. I hadn't noticed. She is a sociology major, a hardcore one, so she's very aware of social differences. After her comment, I looked around and found that it's true. Most of my friends are white. Just look around on campus. **You don't see very many different shades of people**. It's a shame."

Q "The campus is the most diverse campus I've ever seen in my life. **The cultural groups are the most popular groups**. Everyone, regardless of color, has signed up for LASO [Loyola Asian Student Organization], and BSU [Black Student Union]. There's also a International Student Association, and they have all kind of cultural events."

## The College Prowler Take
### ON DIVERSITY

Don't let the categorization of Loyola as a Jesuit school fool you: Loyola openly accepts people from every walk of life, and slowly but surely is diversifying its population. While the campus is predominantly white, there are a fairly decent number of racial minorities visible on campus. And there are student group organizations and many international students that stay involved with special group issues.

Unfortunately, a lot of times, minorities remain in a clique together. Some students recognize this as natural part of identifying with your own culture, but others express concern for lack of team spirit. The school strives to teach its students acceptance and to embrace diversity, which is reflected in the personalities of the students. The people here are friendly, and it's not unusual to get a "hello" from someone you just pass on the way to the same class every day.

# Guys & Girls

## The Lowdown
### ON GUYS & GIRLS

**Women Undergrads:** 62%

**Men Undergrads:** 38%

**C+**

The College Prowler™ Grade on
## Diversity: C+

A high grade in Diversity indicates that ethnic minorities and international students have a notable presence on campus and that students of different economic backgrounds, religious beliefs, and sexual preferences are well-represented.

### Social Scene
It seems fairly easy to create a social circle, especially if you talk to students within your major, or join a student organization. Breaking that trend can be more difficult. Once you have made friends, by whatever means, you can expect to have to turn offers down on any given night. There is always so much to do: shop at the Riverwalk, jog in Audubon Park, listen to jazz, funk, or blues down at the Neutral Ground, watch a Broadway show, or cheer for the Saints down at the Superdome. The selection in New Orleans is endless.

### Hookups or Relationships?
While there are relationships that run strong, random hookups and non-committed forms of relationships are more common. Even more abundant are students that seem happiest single and free to concentrate on studies—and other points of interest.

## Dress Code

Most students dress casual since the weather in New Orleans is a steaming 70-plus degrees most of the time. Shorts or a skirt, T-shirts, and always flip-flops are the standard, but you won't feel out of place if you wear business casual. Since many students are "rich kids," they tend to wear the good brands. However, it's not unusual to find a group that loves the thrift store and eclectic trends. Some girls wear halter tops and miniskirts, or super tight jeans with stilettos. You'll find guys that look like they walked right out of the A&F ads. (Sorry, girls. They're probably gay.) There are those with piercings and pink hair, but not an excessive number. Naturally, everybody walks out looking amazing (and sometimes skanky) when it's time to party.

## Students Speak Out
### ON GUYS & GIRLS

"Everyone is really friendly here. Sometimes it can be hard to find an available guy or girl, but in general, people are friendly. They'll open doors for you, and say 'hi' in the hall."

"Dating life at Loyola is pretty good. You have your typical jocks that didn't fit in at your Big Ten school, so they decided to come to a little liberal arts college and run amuck with the fraternities that don't mean anything. The **girls are pretty cool** unless they are in sororities, but that's a little critical, and they are super hot."

"I think that when you come to Loyola, the first kind of people you notice is the sorority and fraternity type. Both guys and girls seem like they come from rich families, and seem like they don't know how to take care of themselves. I know a lot of people who didn't even know how to do their own laundry. It's kind of ridiculous. I mean, I know a lot of sweet, people but there are **definitely people here that have a lot to learn**. The short skirts and the tube tops with stilettos are kind of 'ugh'—especially when they have a beer belly!"

"**There are many, many hot girls on campus**. You just have to walk around campus and you'll see them. Or, you can go to Audubon Park and watch the joggers jog down St. Charles Avenue. That's a good activity. It's kinda fun just to hang out on St. Charles Avenue. You can meet a lot of interesting girls."

## The College Prowler Takes
### ON GUYS & GIRLS

Any student at Loyola will frankly state that there are a few attractive students on campus. Due to the warm climate, they needn't wear tons of clothes, and you'll notice that most have a fit physique. Staying cool seems to be more important than trying to dress to impress, but since Loyola tends to have an upper-class vibe, there are always those who do dress in a business casual style. The unbalanced male-to-female ratio, coupled with the disinterest in steady relationships, makes for less of a focus on looks and more of a focus on—academics. People are also looking for those that know how to get out and have some fun. Students know that if they really want to find the hotties, it's time go visit the neighbors at Tulane.

**B**

**B+**

**The College Prowler™ Grade on**
## Guys: B

A high grade for Guys indicates that the male population on campus is attractive, smart, friendly, and engaging, and that the school has a decent ratio of guys to girls.

**The College Prowler™ Grade on**
## Girls: B+

A high grade for Girls not only implies that the women on campus are attractive, smart, friendly, and engaging, but also that there is a fair ratio of girls to guys.

# Athletics

## The Lowdown
ON ATHLETICS

**Men's Varsity Teams:**
Baseball
Basketball
Cross Country
Track and Field

**Women's Varsity Teams:**
Basketball
Cross Country
Soccer
Track and Field
Volleyball

**Athletic Division:**
NAIA Division I

**Conference:**
Gulf Coast Athletic Conference (GCAC)

**School Mascot:**
The Wolf

**Getting Tickets:**
Plan to buy tickets at the door since any sports event at Loyola is only sporadically attended.

**Fields:**
Basketball and Volleyball Arena: The Loyola Den (800), Baseball Stadium: Segnette Field (1,000), Turchin Stadium (5,000), Track and Soccer Stadium: Tad Gormley Stadium (20,000), Soccer Field: NOSA Soccer Field (1,000)

**Club Sports:**
Cheerleaders, Loyola Dance Team, Loyola Golf Association, Men's Lacrosse, Men's Rugby Team, Men's Soccer Team, Sports Officials Club, Ultimate Frisbee Club

**Intramurals:**
Basketball, Racquetball, Soccer, Softball, Swimming, Tennis, Volleyball, Water Polo

**Most Popular Sports:**
Students will know the latest on women's and men's basketball or volleyball games, if they read the campus e-mail that provides all the information. There is an indoor court for both.

**Overlooked Teams:**
Some students wish Loyola formed an official soccer team and had its own field, rather than practicing inside at the arena shared by the basketball team.

## Students Speak Out
ON ATHLETICS

"We are not really big on sports. I've never been to any kind of Loyola game, but I have seen the games advertised. People try to get their friends to go to the games, but not many do."

"I don't play any sports, but from what I understand, **Loyola is not known for its sports teams**. Sometimes when I go to the gym, I see students at volleyball practice, but that's about it. I do work out. The facilities like the treadmills and machines are well-kept."

"It seems like for the number of students Loyola has, **we have the adequate number of machines**. Of course, before spring break and the holidays, it's always a little more crowded."

💬 "We have a **newly formed men's basketball team** now, so it's on the rise since we're offering scholarships. Volleyball is what everyone likes here. Although there is a volleyball club, there is currently no real team."

💬 "Our school is not competitive because we are not in a big district. If I had to choose, **I think soccer and basketball are most competitive**. Cross country teams have more star-quality members. There are a lot of people who do intramural sports, but it's all really laid-back. Go play, and then go grab some beers for the team."

# Greek Life

## The College Prowler Take
### ON ATHLETICS

Loyola's athletic teams have been struggling to rebuild since they were reinstituted back in 1991. The school has about 20 years worth of missing athletics to make up for. Slowly but surely, the Wolves athletic teams are trying to make a comeback. Overall, the athletics department at Loyola is currently not up-to-par, which may contribute to the lack of team spirit on Loyola's campus. (LSU makes us look like we are in hibernation!) Perhaps the sporadic attendance at school sporting events is also due to the atmosphere found off campus, which offers so many fun alternatives to athletics; the preoccupation with scholastic achievement by much of the student body; or the cost of tickets for the major sports. The administration has been working hard to attract new athletes to the school. The athletic scholarships now offered to three men and three women for basketball make sports-oriented students hopeful of a change for the better.

## The Lowdown
### ON GREEK LIFE

**Number of Fraternities:**
5

**Number of Sororities:**
6

**Undergrad Men in Fraternities:**
7%

**Undergrad Women in Sororities:**
18%

### The College Prowler™ Grade on
## Athletics: D+

A high grade in Athletics indicates that students have school spirit, that sports programs are respected, that games are well-attended, and that intramurals are a prominent part of student life.

### COLLEGE PROWLER™

For a detailed listing of all the fraternities and sororities, check out the College Prowler book on Loyola available at *www.collegeprowler.com*.

## Students Speak Out
### ON GREEK LIFE

"**We aren't the stereotypes that most sororities are.** I just joined to get involved in extracurricular stuff and to meet people. We're not as hardcore and cliquish about it as other schools. We're awesome."

Q "Greek life absolutely does not dominate the social scene. If anything, it's the lamest scene on campus. The best parties, the best groups of kids, the most lively personalities are not in the fraternities. It's a waste of time on Loyola's campus. I probably wouldn't say that about big schools, but **on campus, there is absolutely no need to join** a frat or sorority."

Q "I think Greek life is a lot better than many of the sororities in other schools; it's not like LSU's, which is quite ridiculous. My sister is part of Kappa Zeta, there and they just seem really sleazy in the things they would do. But here at Loyola, it seems that they do a lot for the community. They're nice people, and I don't have any bad feelings toward them. When you first go to college you think, 'Ugh, sorority girls, fraternity boys—they're all idiots.' But **here they're actually really smart people**."

Q "I think Loyola is 20 percent Greek. It doesn't dominate the social scene. I know a lot of people who are in sororities, but the good thing is that you can always go to parties, and even have friends in a sorority or fraternity, without being a part of the group activities. **The parties are not exclusively for the Greeks**. For instance, everyone is invited to Red Tide. They always charge, but it's like five to seven bucks, not that expensive. If you choose not to be in a sorority or a fraternity, that doesn't mean you won't have a life."

Q "Sometimes, I feel like fraternities and sororities rule this school. But there are enough individuals to make up for the sheep. I've met so many interesting people here. The Greek thing is **just something you get used to after a while**."

Q "I joined a sorority because I wanted to meet people, but it's nice because everything is still laid-back. Our sorority is certainly important to us, but Greek life here is not like one group of girls goes Gamma Phi. It's very diverse. **The Greek community here is close** because it's so small. We make up about 18 percent of the student body. We're not the huge majority."

## The College Prowler Take
### ON GREEK LIFE

According to most students, Greek life at Loyola is far different from Greek life on larger campuses: Loyola Greeks, while still fairly visible on campus, tend to be a bit more laid-back and less the epicenter of social life. A student receives an entirely different view of Greeks once they come to Loyola. Despite the visibility, most students say the Greeks aren't the center of social life, nor are their parties the only ones to attend.

Greek life puts a strong emphasis on community service, and the Greeks often tend to be the leaders the community service opportunities Loyola has to offer. There may be cliques, but the overall attitude is very friendly and non-imposing.

**The College Prowler™ Grade on**
## Greek Life: C

A high grade in Greek Life indicates that sororities and fraternities are not only present, but also active on campus. Other determining factors include the variety of houses available and the respect the Greek community receives from the rest of the campus.

# Drug Scene

## The Lowdown
### ON DRUG SCENE

**Most Prevalent Drugs on Campus:**
Marijuana

**Liquor-Related Referrals:**
18

**Liquor-Related Arrests:**
0

**Drug-Related Referrals:**
34

**Drug-Related Arrests:**
1

### Drug Counseling Programs
**Counseling and Career Services Center**

Phone: (504) 865-3835

Services: Individual and group alcohol and drug abuse screenings, psychological evaluations, outpatient alcohol and drug counseling, and referrals to outside treatment agencies, alcohol and drug education classes to students at possible risk, library of substance abuse material, AA, Al-Anon

## Students Speak Out
### ON DRUG SCENE

"Many people do have alcohol problems, but they are usually out-of-town freshmen who are trying to get used to New Orleans, 'Party Capital of the World.'"

Q "Related to the drug scene on campus, it's definitely available, but I find that there are two paths you can go by, and in the long run, **you should stay away from the harder drugs**. Don't associate your friends with those things. Also, don't use it as a ghost writer for the work that you do in school."

Q "I honestly don't know enough to comment—**the problem must not be a problem**, because I know very many people on campus, and have never heard anything about it."

Q "I guess I cannot really compare what goes on at Loyola to any other campus, but **there are people here who do drugs' and you know they do**. There are many students who do recreational stuff, but there aren't coke-heads walking the halls. Pretty much if they do drugs, students make sure it does not interfere with their school or academic life."

Q "**Drug use is pretty prevalent in the dorms**, but it is off campus, too. You definitely find people in parks smoking weed. On campus you know where to go if you needed anything, and I mean just about anything, pharmaceuticals to hard drugs. That's just the dorms. When you live off campus, it's a little bit harder. You have to know people. It's not blatantly obvious, you have to ask around."

## The College Prowler Take
### ON DRUG SCENE

Alcohol is one of the most abused drugs on campus, but its use is almost a way of life in New Orleans, and there is not a strict policy against the use of alcohol. Loyola is not a dry campus; according to policy, they follow whatever state and federal laws allow. This means anyone 21 and over is allowed to purchase, publicly consume, or possess alcoholic beverages, and on top of that, if you are 18, you can consume alcoholic beverages in private residences; the University has deemed dormitories to be private residences, so if students are 18 they can drink in the dorms.

While the alcohol policy is fairly lenient, the drug policy is fairly harsh. Due to the proximity to an elementary school, those found with drugs can be prosecuted for a federal crime, and the University has unannounced canine drug searches of dorms. Drug abuse, and drug use in general, is not always visible on campus. But, there are those students who have no qualms about using drugs, and say they are very accessible. If there is one drug that is used most, it is weed. However, more than that, there is a wide and prevalent use of alcohol.

**B-**

**The College Prowler™ Grade on**
### Drug Scene: B-

A high grade on Drug Scene indicates that drugs are not a noticeable part of campus life; drug use is not visible, and no pressure to use them seems to exist.

# Overall Experience

## Students Speak Out
### ON OVERALL EXPERIENCE

"There are things at Loyola that I wish would change, but they're always open to the students' opinions. They really try hard to please us, and that's good because I can try to make the change happen."

Q "**I really like Loyola**. It's a good experience being far away from home and being out on my own. I have met so many different kinds of people here that I wouldn't have met if I had gone to school in Georgia. I would have met a lot of Georgia people, a lot of Georgia things. I am happy here."

Q "**My professors are sincerely interested in my progress** and success as a student and as an individual. This town of New Orleans is awesome. I keep finding out new stuff about the 'Big Easy,' and I look forward to this fall semester. This is more than an academic experience ... it's an amazing adventure."

Q "I feel like a lot of questionable activities occur within the Office of Student Affairs. Students are often used to serve the interest of administrators. However, **I wouldn't want to be in a different city** or surrounded by different students and faculty. I love Loyola, New Orleans, and the idea of a Jesuit education."

Q "The day I registered for classes I was so stressed out I completely canceled my registration! As I made my way to the dorm to pack, my residential life 'mom' stopped me on the balcony.' I heard you're leaving. What's going on?' She was genuinely concerned. We talked, and I turned around and registered! I am glad I did. The school is small, about 3,500 undergraduates, **so I easily made friends**. Even people that I just pass as I go from one class to the next give a friendly 'hello!'"

## The College Prowler Take
### ON OVERALL EXPERIENCE

Loyola's friendly and knowledgeable professors, great student body, and amazing city setting make it very attractive. It offers a generous amount of scholarships and financial aid, which makes its expensive private-school tuition more feasible. The spirit of Loyola reflects a strong sense of personal identity, independence, and free thinking, and the school offers an environment that is conducive to such an experience. It is a liberal arts college in every sense of the word. From academics to extracurricular activities, Loyola connotes a certain elevation of utilitarianism that makes it stand out from other schools. Much of what Loyola has to offer is a reflection of its surrounding area; New Orleans is a unique blend of culture and activity that no other place in the world can compare to. Despite its downfalls, those that attend Loyola claim that it is the best choice they have ever made, and, if given the opportunity, they would do the same again.

Students who come to Loyola are confident that what they find here will be useful in their professional and private lives on many different levels. Loyola offers students the opportunities they need to grow into well-rounded individuals, ready to take on the world. Students sometimes become so absorbed in the daily grind of writing papers and attending mandatory meetings for their major, that they don't see how great they have it. But, in the end, they realize that this academic experience, coupled with the incredible multicultural New Orleans setting, has helped create and reinforce a palpable evolution in the way they view life, and that the process of that experience is both memorable and life changing, as well.

# Rhodes College

2000 N. Parkway, Memphis, TN 38112
www.rhodes.edu          (800) 844-5969

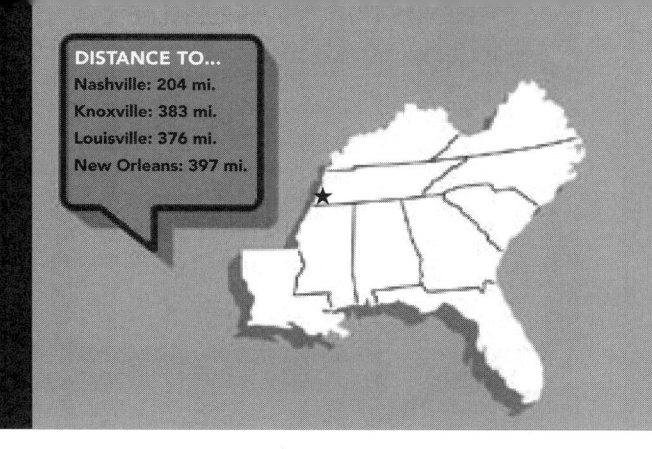

**DISTANCE TO...**
Nashville: 204 mi.
Knoxville: 383 mi.
Louisville: 376 mi.
New Orleans: 397 mi.

*"Rhodes is one of the South's most distinguished institutions of higher education."*

## Table of Contents

| | |
|---|---|
| Academics | 578 |
| Local Atmosphere | 580 |
| Safety & Security | 581 |
| Facilities | 583 |
| Campus Dining | 585 |
| Campus Housing | 586 |
| Diversity | 588 |
| Guys & Girls | 589 |
| Athletics | 591 |
| Greek Life | 592 |
| Drug Scene | 594 |
| Overall Experience | 595 |

**Total Enrollment:**
1,520

**Top 10% of High School Class:**
59%

**Average GPA:**
3.7

**Acceptance Rate:**
72%

**Tuition:**
$24,274

**SAT Range (25th-75th Percentile)**
| Verbal | Math | Total |
|---|---|---|
| 600 – 690 | 590 – 670 | 1190 – 1360 |

**ACT Range (25th-75th Percentile)**
| Verbal | Math | Total |
|---|---|---|
| 26-32 | 25-29 | 26-30 |

**Most Popular Majors:**
38% Social Sciences
12% Business
11% English
10% Biology
7% Foreign Language

**Students also applied to:***
Davidson College
Emory University
Sewanee–University of the South
Vanderbilt University
Washington University in St. Louis

*For more school info check out www.collegeprowler.com

## College Prowler Report Card

| | |
|---|---|
| Academics | B |
| Local Atmosphere | B+ |
| Safety & Security | B- |
| Facilities | B |
| Campus Dining | D+ |
| Campus Housing | B+ |
| Diversity | D |
| Guys | B- |
| Girls | B |
| Athletics | C |
| Greek Life | A- |
| Drug Scene | B+ |

# Academics

## Special Programs
Dual-Degree Programs in collaboration with Rhodes' affiliate colleges: Vanderbilt University - Master of Education, Master of Science in Nursing; Washington University (St. Louis) - Bachelor of Science in Engineering; University of Memphis/University of Tennessee - Master of Science in Biomedical Engineering

## Sample Academic Clubs
The American Chemical Society, the American Marketing Association, the Legal Society, Model NATO, the Philosophy Club, and the Society of Physics Students.

## The Lowdown
ON ACADEMICS

**Degrees Awarded:**
Bachelor, Master (in Accounting only)

**Full-time Faculty:**
135

**Faculty with Terminal Degree:**
94%

**Student-to-Faculty Ratio:**
11:1

**Average Course Load:**
14-16 hours

**AP Test Score Requirements:**
Possible credit for scores of 4 or 5

**IB Test Score Requirements:**
Possible credit for scores of 5, 6, or 7

### Did You Know?
Fifty-five percent of Rhodes' 2007 graduating class were members of their high school's National Honor Society chapters, 11 percent were either valedictorian or salutatorian, and seven percent were either a National Merit or Achievement Finalist or Semi-Finalist.

It's mandatory for Rhodes students to take Bible-based courses in order to fulfill graduation core requirements. Two different tracks are offered in order to do this. There is the "Search" track, which examines the development of Christianity in relation to other influential, ancient religions and philosophies, and the "Life" track, which focuses mainly on reading and interpreting biblical scripture.

**Best Places to Study:**
Top floors of the library, Rollow Row of Oaks, the Conservatory, the social rooms

## Students Speak Out
### ON ACADEMICS

> "Rhodes makes it purposely hard to maintain scholarships; they depend upon the money that is lost to fund the scholarships for incoming freshmen. It's frustrating, and the administration does not seem sympathetic."

Q "Most of the professors at Rhodes truly care about your learning progress. They know you by name and love to meet for lunch or coffee outside of class time. I would say that the **professors at Rhodes are mentors, rather than simply teachers**."

Q "The teachers are some of the greatest. Not only are they wonderful in class, but they do their best to **make you feel like you're not just a student, but an important member of the community**. They are our professors, our mentors, our friends, and at times, our employers (baby-sitting and house-sitting). I love the fact that I've had class at my professors' houses, gone to Grizzlies games with them, eaten lunch with them on several occasions, and can just go to their offices when I need to chat."

Q "Professors at Rhodes are fantastic. They're here to teach, first and foremost, and have a **genuine concern for their students' success**. They are extremely well-qualified, many could teach anywhere, including Ivy League schools, or work outside academia if they choose. Classes are largely discussion-oriented and on the whole very interesting. Professors encourage you to think, not just imbibe what they say and regurgitate it."

Q "Many of the teachers at Rhodes invite students to participate in classroom discussion. However, there is a large number of **teachers who ignore students both in and outside of class.** They give a cold feeling of non-commitment to their job and feel justified in teaching at Rhodes because they have been published."

## The College Prowler Take
### ON ACADEMICS

What really makes Rhodes' academics so phenomenal are the professors. They vary a lot in regards to personality and teaching style, but they all possess an undeniable passion for what they do. Most, if not all, grade hard as well. If you make a good grade, you've earned it. They put a lot of effort into their work, and they expect to get just as much back from you. They're experts in their fields, are highly gifted, most are published, but the best part of all—they are all extremely approachable. Professors won't hesitate to call students on their slacking and will always push you to push yourself, but they will also joke around with you, and enjoy meeting up with their students for some coffee and good conversation.

Rhodes is well-known for its tough academics, which is the selling point for many students who chose to attend the college. The international studies, political science, and biology departments lure many students, and are held in high esteem on campus, as many of their majors have received national acclaim. The humanities are likewise popular and award winning. No matter your major, it's a given that you're going to have to work hard to succeed here. There aren't any "breeze courses," so if you come to Rhodes, be prepared to use your brain if you want to maintain a high GPA.

**The College Prowler™ Grade on**
## Academics: B

A high Academics grade generally indicates that professors are knowledgeable, accessible, and genuinely interested in their students' welfare. Other determining factors include class size, how well professors communicate, and whether or not classes are engaging.

# Local Atmosphere

## Students Speak Out
### ON LOCAL ATMOSPHERE

"Memphis has a rich cultural heritage. It's the birthplace of rock and roll and home to the best BBQ in the world. Visitors should visit St. Jude's Research Hospital and Sun Studios."

Q "**Watch out for gas stations at night**, you are sure to get mugged. I am now a senior, and have had the unpleasant experience twice. Other than that, Memphis is a nice, small community. All Rhodes students must take at least one trip to Graceland during their four years here—it is a rite of passage of sorts."

Q "It's easy to judge Memphis too harshly, but if you spend the time to get to know it, it's pretty cool. Subculture is hard to find, but it does exist. So does **good local music of all types**, if you know where to look. Go to the Caravan, the New Daisy, and the Riot, if you like rock. Go to Beale as often as possible. Even if you can't drink, you can just sit around and listen to music."

Q "Memphis is a very hard city to live in if you are unfamiliar with it. There are a lot of fun things to do, but they are hard to locate for those who do not come from the area. Living in the dorms at Rhodes is great because you almost automatically live with someone from the area who can show you around. The **class divisions and racial divisions are prevalent** and sad, but most students at Rhodes, fortunately, don't typically come into contact with these things."

Q "The Memphis atmosphere is one of a kind. It may not be as big of a commercial center like some of the bigger metro areas in the United States, but the **skyline and the city lights in the evening are enough to give it the edge**. There are plenty of places tucked away all over the city for you to discover and make your own, and that's a lot of the fun of living in Memphis."

## The Lowdown
### ON LOCAL ATMOSPHERE

**Region:**
Mid-South

**City, State:**
Memphis, Tennessee

**Setting:**
Large city

**Distance from Nashville:**
3 hours

**Distance from Little Rock:**
2 hours, 30 minutes

**Points of Interest:**
Beale Street, Sun Studios, National Civil Rights Museum, Mud Island, Pink Palace and IMAX, Memphis Zoo, Graceland, Gibson Guitar Factory, Memphis Botanical Garden, Rock 'n' Soul Museum, St. Jude, Peabody Place, the Orpheum, the Pyramid, AutoZone Park, and the Arts District.

**City Websites:**
http://www.memphismojo.com

**Major Sports Teams:**
Grizzles (basketball), Redbirds (baseball), Riverkings (hockey)

## The College Prowler Take
### ON LOCAL ATMOSPHERE

Memphis isn't the paradigmatic college town, but that's part of its charm. From the blues and bars on Beale, to the quirky antique and vintage shops in the Cooper-Young District, Memphis has just about anything for anyone. There's an endless array of hole-in-the-wall places to discover in the city, which is one of Rhodes students' favorite weekend hobbies. The music scene is terrific, and you're almost guaranteed an impromptu concert somewhere if you walk around and explore long enough. Midtown has a large variety of good restaurants and shopping areas, you can always find a party downtown. If you're in the mood for a ritzy night out, Germantown's only a half hour away. The city has a lot to offer if you're willing to go and look for it, but it's not without its downfalls. Crime is high, and it's advised to use the buddy system whenever you go out. And, as a rule, don't drive down any roads named after dead presidents or states after nightfall, unless you have a very stout and burly man with you (or are one yourself), or unless you are fond of getting robbed.

## Safety & Security

### The Lowdown
### ON SAFETY & SECURITY

**Number of Rhodes Police:**
15

**Phone:**
(901) 843-3880 (non-emergencies)
911 (emergencies)

**Health Center Office Hours:**
Registered nurses are available Monday through Friday 8:30 a.m.–4:30 p.m.; physicians are available 1:30 p.m.–4:00 p.m.

**Safety Services:**
24-hour safety watch, escort service, after-hour access service, emergency phones, special programs throughout the year, including Rape Awareness workshops and seminars on personal protection

### Did You Know?

Although Memphis doesn't boast the lowest crime rate in the nation, Rhodes is considered, by far, the safest college campus in the city.

## B+

**The College Prowler™ Grade on**
### Local Atmosphere: B+

A high Local Atmosphere grade indicates that the area surrounding campus is safe and scenic. Other factors include nearby attractions, proximity to other schools, and the town's attitude toward students.

## Students Speak Out
### ON SAFETY & SECURITY

{ *"The security is horrible. Last year, my dorm had over $10,000 worth of stuff stolen in one week because of vandals breaking into campus."*

Q *"When I'm parking my car at someplace other than Rhodes, it **feels odd to have to roll my windows up and lock my doors**. I'm totally not used to doing that here, and I love the fact that I can get away with it with no worries."*

Q *"I feel absolutely safe on campus. But, the area surrounding campus is not the safest. I personally **know of people who have been robbed off campus**. As great as life can be at Rhodes, all a student has to do is look through the fence to see that life is not great for everyone."*

Q *"Safety on campus is good, and I've never felt unsafe. **Since we're on an honor code, lots of kids leave their doors unlocked**, leave their backpacks at the entrance of the Rat, and walk around at night with little apprehension. There's a guard at the gates to check cars coming on campus, and you can call campus safety at any time for just about anything, including locking yourself out of the dorm."*

Q *"I feel fairly safe on campus, and have never been wary of walking around, regardless of the hour. However, the **security guards are not always in the booth or awake at late hours**. They also don't really check carefully who is coming on campus. Although I haven't heard of any incidents, it does seem to be a potential problem, and it has made me feel uneasy."*

## The College Prowler Take
### ON SAFETY & SECURITY

There's a running joke at Rhodes that says the campus couldn't be any more secure unless campus safety had hounds to release. Given that, the extremely low crime rate, and the fact that you can't walk anywhere on campus without seeing at least one campus safety officer every five minutes, the vast majority of students seldom if ever feel unsafe within the gates. There are some questionable neighborhoods surrounding the college, and the biggest concern of the student body is definitely infiltration. The main entrance has a guard 24 hours a day, but sometimes security can get lax, and unless there's a big event going on, almost everyone is just waved through. Recent efforts have been made, however, to improve this problem. It's sometimes easy for students to forget just how much crime is outside of the gates, and how much is stopped everyday from getting in.

**B-**

**The College Prowler™ Grade on**
### Safety & Security: B-

A high grade in Safety & Security means that students generally feel safe, campus police are visible, blue-light phones and escort services are readily available, and safety precautions are not overly necessary.

# Facilities

## The Lowdown
ON FACILITIES

**Student Center:**
The Brian Campus Life Center (BCLC)

**Athletic Center:**
Mallory and Hyde Gymnasiums (in the BCLC)

**Libraries:**
One main library (the Burrow), but in the spring of 2005, a new $40 million dollar, high-tech library will be opening.

**Movie Theatre on Campus?**
No. However, the college often reserves an entire theater at the Peabody and offers discounted tickets for $1 or $2 when students show interest in an upcoming film.

**Bowling on Campus?**
No

**Bar on Campus?**
No, but the Lynx Lair sells beer.

**Coffeehouse on Campus?**
Java City

**Popular Places to Chill:**
Java City, the pool, the amphitheater, Lynx Lair

## Favorite Things to Do
There are lots of things to keep you occupied between classes and papers, but most students really just like to relax and hang out. The beauty of the campus is phenomenal, and on any given day you'll find students sitting beneath the oaks, stretching out on the grass, or playing Frisbee on the field behind Buckman. Lounging in Java City, playing a quick game of basketball, sunbathing by the pool, or swinging outside of Briggs is also very popular.

### Computers
**High-Speed Network?** Yes
**Wireless Network?** Yes
**Number of Labs:** 2 in Buckman and 1 in the Burrow Library
**Number of Computers:** 105
**24-Hour Labs:** None
**Charge to Print?** No

## Students Speak Out
ON FACILITIES

"The facilities on campus are top-notch and very versatile. No matter what your interests are, there is probably some place to accommodate them."

Q "The gym is rather big, and has a good variety of equipment. The rowing machines are great. The pool is also really awesome. In the winter they put a big bubble over it and it's heated, I think. All the facilities are convenient. **The buildings in general are gorgeous** with all the Gothic architecture."

Q "Aesthetically, Rhodes is a great school. The BCLC is a little out of place on the Rhodes campus due to its sheer size, but the facilities it offers are amazing. It has four basketball courts, three racquetball courts, a **great gym for cardiovascular workouts and a fully equipped weight room**. The only problem is that it closes early, and cannot be accessed at all times."

Q "**The music practice rooms suck!** Let me repeat—suck! There aren't enough, the pianos are terrible, and the rooms are so un-soundproof that you listen to every other person in the building practice at the same time. I love the Rhodes architecture, but I'm sad that Rhodes is losing its little college appeal. My favorite parts of campus are the old parts around Palmer, Clough, Burrow, and the Rat. The new buildings are massive, and take over the campus. The huge empty green spaces with little bushes for trees don't give the campus the same feel."

Q "Be warned: the walk between Hassell and the BCLC is miserable in the winter because it's a wind tunnel—no trees!—and sweltering in the summer—big open space in 100-degree heat with no shade. **The new library is gorgeous and something we need**, but they're putting in too many 'walking paths' and such things. I wish they'd stick to the original designs for the college."

Q "The gym and the BCLC are really nice. The training staff is excellent, and provides services even to non-athletes. The practice rooms in the music building are functional, but not soundproof by any stretch of the imagination. It's kind of cool that way, though—you can always find your friends just by listening for them. The recital hall is pretty nice, with a good live sound. I don't know a whole lot about science, but the astronomy lab seems pretty well-equipped, especially when they open up the gigantic telescope. The campus is beautiful, with the newer buildings being the most beautiful, of course, but **each building has its own charms**."

# The College Prowler Take
## ON FACILITIES

The BCLC is the main center for student activity on campus. A few of the facility's highlights include the Lair, weight rooms and workout facilities, basketball, racquetball, and squash courts, the ballroom, and the pool. The second floor of the BCLC is a great place to study or catch up on some leisurely reading, and it's also where the aerobics and activity rooms are located. The building itself is only a few years old, and the sheer size of it is quite impressive. The workout rooms are well-equipped and immaculately maintained for the most part, as are most of the other facilities on campus. It's hard to find a dirty bathroom (unless you swing by one in Glassell) or a piece of equipment that's broken for more than a day or two. The college offers state-of-the-art, convenient facilities wrapped up in stunning exteriors, while continuing to expand and upgrade each year.

**B**

The College Prowler™ Grade on
## Facilities: B

A high Facilities grade indicates that the campus is aesthetically pleasing and well-maintained; facilities are state-of-the-art, and libraries are exceptional. Other determining factors include the quality of both athletic and student centers and an abundance of things to do on campus.

# Campus Dining

## The Lowdown
### ON CAMPUS DINING

**Freshman Meal Plan Requirement?**
Yes

**Meal Plan Average Cost:**
$2,346

**24-Hour On-Campus Eating?**
No

**Student Favorites:**
The Lair is a favorite for students who are on the go, or are just plain tired of eating at the Rat. It has a collegiate atmosphere, complete with pool tables, comfy sofas and lounge chairs, a foosball table, TVs, and a buy-by-the-ounce candy station.

### Did You Know?
Like fried chicken? How about catfish? Fried Chicken Fridays and Catfish Wednesdays at the Rat are something Rhodes students look forward to each week. And the free espresso shot day at Java City isn't half bad either.

## Students Speak Out
### ON CAMPUS DINING

"The food sucks. The Rat is horrible and repetitive. The Lair is greasy and unhealthy. You will gain weight."

"The campus food is pretty good, considering. **Hours are restrictive, but food is generally good**, except on weekends. Rat food on the weekends should be avoided at all costs. Other than that, I like the dining options. The Rat could stand to be bit more efficient with serving and keeping lines down. Also, I'd like to see more healthy options here. But it tastes good, so at least that's something."

"**The food here is horrible**. You are forced to pay for the meal plan if you live on campus, and because of possible class schedules, one is apt to miss two meals a day due to the times they are served at."

"I am very impressed with the **diversity of food available in the Rat**, as well as the genuine helpfulness and concern about what the students want to eat. The message board is truly paid attention to."

"**If you're health-conscious or vegetarian, you're out of luck**. The Lair is a danger zone unless you're used to ingesting ridiculous amounts of grease. The Rat can be okay, but it's not consistent."

## The College Prowler Take
### ON CAMPUS DINING

If you were to go around and ask students what they dislike the most about Rhodes, the main complaint you'd get would have something to do with the dining options. If you live on campus, you have to be on a meal plan, and, unless you live in EV, the cheapest plan you can purchase is 15 meals per week. The only two places to eat using your plan are the Rat and the Lair, and both have very specific time restrictions. Because of the inflexible hours and sparse options, it's nearly impossible to make the most of your meal plan, and you usually end up wasting a lot of money each week. The Rat offers a large variety of decent food, but most of it is a bit on the unhealthy side. Also, you're only allotted $4.85 per meal for the meal plan at the Lair, so trying to buy a full meal with their ridiculously high prices is pretty much out of the question. A number of students even claim that the dining options are what drove them to move off campus.

## Campus Housing

### The Lowdown
### ON CAMPUS HOUSING

**Undergrads on Campus:**
75%

**Dormitories:**
15

**University-Owned Apartments:**
1

### Room Types

Singles, doubles, triples, quads, and townhouses (six students per townhouse) are available. Bathrooms are either common (one bathroom per hall), suite-style (where a private bathroom is shared between four or five people), or townhouse-style (where six people share two bathrooms). Each residence hall has at least one social room, complete with a TV, VCR, and microwave.

### Did You Know?

Room descriptions and floor plans for most residence halls can be found on the Residence Life website at http://www.stuaffairs.rhodes.edu/housing/index.htm.

**D+**

### The College Prowler™ Grade on
### Campus Dining: D+

Our grade on Campus Dining addresses the quality of both school-owned dining halls and independent on-campus restaurants as well as the price, availability, and variety of food.

**Cleaning Service?**
All public areas and common bathrooms are cleaned every other day, and suite-style bathrooms are cleaned once a week.

**You Get:**
Bed, desk (usually with attached bookshelf), chair, dresser, wardrobe or closet, blinds, cable TV jack, Ethernet connection, free on-campus and local phone calls, caller ID, call waiting, and voicemail service

**Bed Type:**
Twin extra-long (39"x80"), some bunk-beds

**Also Available:**
There are three special themed housing options available to students: Substance-Free Housing, Quiet Study Housing, and Restricted Visitation Housing.

## Students Speak Out
ON CAMPUS HOUSING

{ "Williford should be avoided. Trezevant is amazing—there are sinks in your room, and plenty of room to make you feel like you're not living in a closet."

Q "Most of the **residence halls are comfy and cozy.** The rooms can take a little getting used to, but over all, the size is adequate. I like Trezevant because it is in the middle of everything, but kind of off the traditional beaten path, and so can be a little quieter. I would avoid Voorhies unless you like a somewhat claustrophobic and darker atmosphere. Also, I would stay away from Stewart. Sure it's one of the newer ones, but who wants to walk across the street all the time?"

Q "Despite the ritualistic moaning about living in a relatively small dorm room that can be heard from many students, I would say that **Rhodes provides top-of-the-line housing** that is excellent in comparison to what other schools have."

Q "The residence halls are pretty awful—**they are old, smelly, and moldy. But, who cares?** Everyone's stuck in them. I lived in Robinson and I loved it. The social room is newer and it's close to Java City, the Lair, and the sorority houses. The bathrooms get so gross by the end of the year, though. I've heard that the Williford girls bond with each other, because they live in quad-style rooms. The social room is awful and they have common bathrooms. Glassell is the place to be if you're a freshman guy—you can arrange the rooms so there's lots of privacy, and it's right by the frat houses."

## The College Prowler Take
ON CAMPUS HOUSING

Most Rhodes students are moderately happy with their on-campus housing arrangements. The college has been recognized numerous times for its spacious residence halls and rooms, and the student body, though they complain sometimes, know that they have it better than the bulk of other college students. All Rhodes students must live on campus for at least two full academic years, so having big rooms and clean amenities is a plus. Living on campus also helps new students form bonds, get involved in the social scene, and become adjusted to college life.

**B+**

**The College Prowler™ Grade on**
## Campus Housing: B+

A high Campus Housing grade indicates that dorms are clean, well-maintained, and spacious. Other determining factors include variety of dorms, proximity to classes, and social atmosphere.

# Diversity

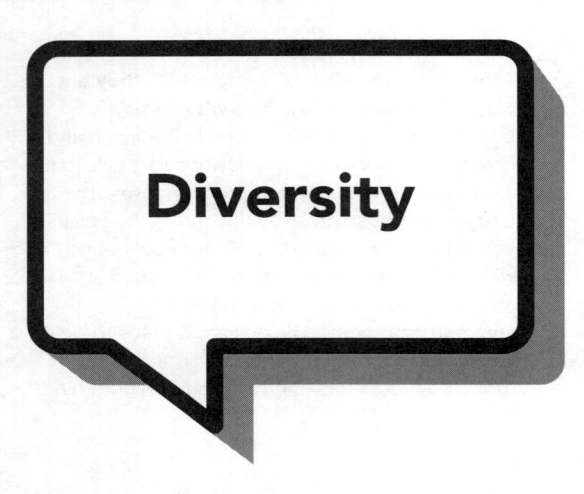

## The Lowdown
ON DIVERSITY

**Native American** 1%

**Asian American:** 3%

**African American:** 4%

**Hispanic:** 1%

**White:** 87%

**International:** 1%

**Unknown:** 3%

**Out-of-State:** 71%

## Political Activity
Most students are politically conservative or moderate, though there is a liberal presence on campus (which includes a number of the professors). While Rhodes doesn't host many (if any) protests, the student body is generally outspoken about their political views. If you're looking for a first-rate political debate or just a friendly discussion, anyone on campus will be more than happy to provide you with one.

## Minority Clubs
Rhode's minority clubs are few, but they do have a definite place on campus. Organizations such as the Rhodes Indian Cultural Exchange (RICE) and Black Student Association (BSA) throw parties and sponsor a number of different events each year that the entire campus is invited to participate in.

## Most Popular Religions
Rhodes is predominantly Christian, and a lot of religious activity takes place on campus through organizations such as Rhodes Christian Fellowship (RCF), Pizza Bible Study, and the Catholic Student Association (CSA).

## Economic Status:
Rhodes students come from a variety of economic backgrounds, but the majority seems to be of a primarily wealthy breed. Not everyone is a "rich kid," but the on-campus abundance of BMWs, Escalades, and yes, even Hummers gives a fair indication of most of the student body's economic status.

## Students Speak Out
ON DIVERSITY

"Most people here are white, middle-class, from private schools or really good public or magnet schools. Most people here grew up in the suburbs. Everyone is basically the same."

"I think that there is a lot of diversity here, but sometimes **it's economic or cultural diversity instead of racial** diversity. It's pretty hard to define diversity, but I think that there are a lot of different people and different outlooks at Rhodes."

"Um … **diversity doesn't really exist**. It is getting better, but there is not much ethnic or religious diversity, aside from Protestant vs. Catholic. I would say there is more socioeconomic diversity than anything, but even that seems small."

> "There is plenty of campus diversity. Integration, however, seems to be the problem. Diversity doesn't matter if **the minorities and the majority don't mix.** If we would stop having a 'black table' at lunch, or stop the idea of fitting professors and students into a race category to meet a quota, maybe diversity would be better."

> "Diversity is fine, as long as you like it being **90 percent WASPs [White Anglo-Saxon Protestants].** I really think that the campus is this way not because anyone has done anything wrong, like oppose diversity. It's the diversity that hasn't come to Rhodes, not the fact that Rhodes hasn't opened the doors to diversity."

## The College Prowler Take
ON DIVERSITY

The only real shortcoming within the student body would be its lack of cultural diversity. On average, each class you take will have only one or two minority students in it, at best. Many students claim that there is more diversity in areas outside of race, religion, and economic background. This is true. The range of different opinions, interests, and beliefs within the student body is evidenced by the plethora of student organizations, as well as by the countless discussions and debates that take place all over the campus each day.

The College Prowler™ Grade on
## Diversity: D

A high grade in Diversity indicates that ethnic minorities and international students have a notable presence on campus and that students of different economic backgrounds, religious beliefs, and sexual preferences are well-represented.

# Guys & Girls

## The Lowdown
ON GUYS & GIRLS

**Women Undergrads:** 58%

**Men Undergrads:** 42%

### Birth Control Available?
No. Female students can make appointments for pelvic exams and birth control prescriptions, but Health Services does not issue the contraceptives. Students must go to a community pharmacy and have the prescription filled, and they are responsible for the payment of their prescription.

### Social Scene
Initiating social interaction on campus is one of the easiest and best-loved pastimes of Rhodes students. The student body is extremely outgoing and friendly. Though most students are academically minded and focused on their studies, there is no lack of social butterflies. Mingling with students outside of your major, Greek affiliation, social background, or academic interests is a very common occurrence on campus, and is openly sought after for the most part. Striking up a conversation with someone you see in the mailroom or pass on the way to class isn't unusual or awkward.

## Hookups or Relationships?

A good amount of students on campus are in relationships, though not always with other Rhodes students. The dating scene is mostly found off campus, as the majority of Rhodes students are either in serious relationships or just hooking up at parties.

## Dress Code

Practically anything goes here: jeans and a T-shirt, wearing your PJs to class, ponchos and Salvation Army skirts, Louis Vuitton handbags and designer ensembles—you name it. Rhodes students sport a variety of styles, and your look usually doesn't determine the people you hang out with. If you dress eclectically, snazzy, or just bum it and go for the unkempt look, it's all the same here.

## Students Speak Out
### ON GUYS & GIRLS

"I think Rhodes is, in general, very attractive. The vast majority are good looking, intelligent, and motivated. Most are very nice too, especially if you get to know them."

Q "There will be people you don't mesh with. I think the guys are great, but as a female senior, **I don't find them dateable** anymore."

Q "There are more girls on campus then guys. There is no dating scene. The guys are preppy frat boys who wear polo shirts and loafers, and have not had a hair cut in a year. If you are into preppy frat guys who are **chain smokers and have beer bottles permanently attached to their hands**, then you will love the guys here, if not, sorry, there is nothing else. There is a little more diversity with the girls. Some are brainy, some are nice, and some are southern snobs."

Q "Rhodes girls are average. The hottest girl at Rhodes would only be considered mildly attractive at any big state school. On top of that, they believe that the world is made for them, and they should be treated like queens. **All the good girls transfer after freshman year**. If you are looking to get a smart, attractive, and courteous woman, Rhodes is not the place for you."

Q "I'm really not quite sure where Rhodes finds all these attractive people. There are **tons of well-dressed, smart, cute guys and girls**. Kids are really friendly here, especially to new people. Being a freshman girl was crazy! I've never gotten so much attention from guys in my life."

Q "The guys ... there aren't that many. Half of them are fun and nice, and the other **half are just weird and here only for the academics**. There are some cute ones, but I wouldn't say, in general, Rhodes has hot guys. There are a lot more girls, and I think the girls for the most part are very pretty. I can't really say if they are hot, but they are a lot of fun."

## The College Prowler Take
### ON GUYS & GIRLS

In general, the student body at Rhodes is well over moderately attractive. But, then again, "to each his (or her) own." As for the guys, you'll see many excellent physiques, a fair amount of tousled hair, and the occasional dimple. You'll also see some artsy, intellectual types, a few who want nothing better than to be transported back to the sixties, and a number who are clean-cut and sport capped teeth. The girls are similarly assorted according to their own style, personalities, and genetic blessings. Nearly everyone is outspoken and intelligent, and generally people are sincere and maintain a commendable level of integrity. All this loveliness, however, is occasionally laced with arrogance.

**B-**  **B**

**The College Prowler™ Grade on**
### Guys: B-

A high grade for Guys indicates that the male population on campus is attractive, smart, friendly, and engaging, and that the school has a decent ratio of guys to girls.

**The College Prowler™ Grade on**
### Girls: B

A high grade for Girls not only implies that the women on campus are attractive, smart, friendly, and engaging, but also that there is a fair ratio of girls to guys.

# Athletics

## The Lowdown
### ON ATHLETICS

**Men's Varsity Teams:**
Football
Basketball
Baseball
Soccer
Swimming
Golf
Tennis
Indoor Track
Outdoor Track
Cross Country

**Women's Varsity Teams:**
Softball
Golf
Field Hockey
Volleyball
Basketball
Tennis
Soccer
Indoor Track
Outdoor Track
Swimming
Cross Country

## Club Sports
Cheerleading, Rhodes Outdoor Organization (ROO), Ultimate Frisbee, Equestrian, Rugby, Crew, Fencing, Lacrosse

## Intramurals (IMs)
Flag Football, Volleyball, Basketball, Ultimate Frisbee, Soccer, Squash, Racquetball, Tennis

## Getting Tickets
Tickets aren't necessary when attending a Rhodes sporting event. Even though some of the teams are actually quite good, spectators are usually mysteriously sparse.

## Most Popular Sports
On the varsity level, soccer, tennis, and basketball seem to be the most popular, but to Rhodes students, varsity sports aren't nearly as appealing as most club and intramurals are. Ultimate Frisbee, crew, and lacrosse are very well established on campus, and ROO and fencing attract a number of students as well.

## Overlooked Teams
Sadly, many of the varsity teams aren't given enough credit. The men's golf team won first place in the 2004 SCAC Championship, and both the men and women's soccer teams have had excellent records over the past couple years.

**Athletic Division:**
NCAA Division III

**Conference:**
SCAC

**School Mascot:**
The Lynx

**Fields:**
Fargason Field (Football), Soccer Field, Baseball Field, Softball Field, Field Hockey Field, Intramural Fields (Back Forty), Soloman Practice Field

## Students Speak Out
### ON ATHLETICS

"The sports program is as close to nonexistent as it can be while still existing. Sports are not important to me at all—no one goes to games, and we don't win any."

"I don't care about the sports. I work for the athletic department and several of my friends are on teams and they're really into it, but sports are definitely **not a campus-wide interest**."

💬 **"Intramural sports are fairly big**, but varsity sports are kind of a joke. No one goes to the games, as far as I can tell."

💬 "Even if you don't play sports, you can still get into the spirit because there are always friends who play, **tailgate parties, and fun games** to go to! I love spending Saturdays in the fall tailgating and watching football in the sunshine."

💬 "Varsity sports are for those who love the game and want to be competitive. I love sports, but think at the varsity level, **they take too much away from other college things** like studying and having fun. IM sports are great fun, and a good outlet for competitive people, but also friendly for those who don't have much or any experience at a sport."

## The College Prowler Take
### ON ATHLETICS

Rhodes status as a Division III school plays a large role in the general apathy of the student body towards sports and sporting events. It seems that varsity sports are only important to those athletes who are involved in them, while the rest of the student body couldn't care less. However, the number of students who participate in intramural and club sports is quite shocking considering the school's academics-only reputation. If you're looking for a big sports-oriented college where students paint themselves in the school colors each weekend and cheer on the football team, Rhodes isn't the place you're going to find it. The bleachers at Rhodes are never packed and chanting the fight song is only done at freshman orientation.

The College Prowler™ Grade on
## Athletics: C

A high grade in Athletics indicates that students have school spirit, that sports programs are respected, that games are well-attended, and that intramurals are a prominent part of student life.

# Greek Life

## The Lowdown
### ON GREEK LIFE

**Number of Fraternities:**
7

**Number of Sororities:**
6

**Undergrad Men in Fraternities:**
51%

**Undergrad Women in Sororities:**
58%

### Did You Know?

Each year, Rhodes students gather to watch and participate in the Kappa Delta All-Sing, a musical competition that has become a Rhodes tradition.

It's not always "All Greek" to Rhodes students. Many of the events hosted by the Greek organizations on campus are open to all students, including parties, service activities, and pageants.

## Students Speak Out
### ON GREEK LIFE

{ "Greek life is great, but really, it's just another activity to be a part of. Students can find multiple activities to which they can devote their time and meet interesting people."

Q "I'm Greek, so I'm partial. At Rhodes, Greek life is good. **It's a strong, but not overbearing, force** with good intentions. I hope we [Greeks] are as open as I think we are—to other Greeks and non-Greeks alike. Yes, we dominate the social scene, but I think more in the sense of providing much of what happens socially for students on campus and concerning leadership; most of your strong campus leaders are Greek. There is, in fact, a correlation between Greeks and student involvement on campus. The same people are always involved and many, if not most, are Greek."

Q "Although sororities and frats aren't exclusive, it's probably a good idea to rush and **pledge, unless you're totally into staying in and studying** on the weekends. It's not impossible to meet people and have fun without being Greek, but the Greeks definitely have more fun. Although the stats say that only half the campus is Greek, it feels like more people are Greek. I think it's because the non-Greeks are studying, off campus, or more introverted. It's also harder for a girl to be independent than for a guy to be independent."

Q "I found that in a sorority as well as some other organizations, I can safely say that just about every Greek person has several friends who are either not Greek or in another sorority or fraternity. The **Greek organizations do host some events for the entire campus**, which include bus parties to fun places off campus, like bars and clubs. I think Greek life is important to the social scene of the college for Greeks and non-Greeks alike."

Q "Greek life is a joke. I belong to a fraternity and I wish I had never joined. I have friends in all different aspects of the campus including other fraternities. **Fraternities try to take themselves too seriously**, and try to play it off like Rhodes is a big Greek school, when really, the best option is to rush and remain independent."

Q "Greek life is lame at Rhodes. Not that anyone should expect it to be great, but it is far from any Greek system at a large state school—where it is actually beneficial to find a place in a group of people with similar interests and statistics as you. Here, Greek parties are open to all and the campus is small enough [that] you will have a chance to literally meet everyone within your freshman year. **Rushing isn't even necessary**, and I don't recommend it."

## The College Prowler Take
### ON GREEK LIFE

Greek life at Rhodes is unlike anything you would normally find when investigating fraternity and sorority involvement on other college campuses. While over 50 percent of the college is part of the Greek system, there is no division within the student body in terms of who is and who isn't in a frat or sorority. Everyone hangs out with each other, no matter their affiliation or non-affiliation. This is probably due mostly to the fact that Greeks aren't allowed to live in their houses, so there's no sense of them being separated from the rest of the campus. Fraternity and sorority members definitely show pride in their chosen organizations, but there's no rivalry between members of different Greek affiliations, and independents don't get the cold shoulder either.

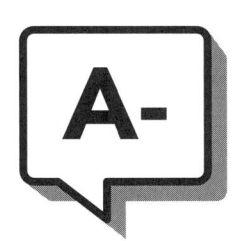

**A-**

**The College Prowler™ Grade on**
## Greek Life: A-

A high grade in Greek Life indicates that sororities and fraternities are not only present, but also active on campus. Other determining factors include the variety of houses available and the respect the Greek community receives from the rest of the campus.

# Drug Scene

**The Office of Student Affairs/Student Life**

Phone: (901) 843-3815

Services: educational programming for groups/organizations, alcohol and drug-related literature, referrals to counseling services

## Students Speak Out
### ON DRUG SCENE

## The Lowdown
### ON DRUG SCENE

"I hear that cocaine is a problem, but I have never actually seen it. Drugs are definitely used here, but it is not really out in the open, and it's easy to avoid if that is not your scene."

**Most Prevalent Drugs on Campus:**
Alcohol, Tobacco, Caffeine, Marijuana

**Liquor-Related Arrests:**
45

**Drug-Related Arrests:**
5

Q "Other than cigarettes and alcohol, I have seen **very little drug use on campus**. Maybe I'm just sheltered."

Q "**Pot is probably the most prevalent drug** on campus, but there are stories of fraternity members getting a hold of crack and the like. It's not overwhelmingly common, though."

Q "I don't mean to give the impression that Rhodes students are stoners, but there are **more drugs here than you would think**. When I came I just assumed that no one did drugs, but that's definitely not the case. I respect that people have made their own choices, though there's no pressure to do drugs or to not do drugs, and I think people don't let it get out of hand."

Q "Though I'm sure it's not—all colleges have drugs to an extent—the **drug scene here seems almost nonexistent**. I've never come into contact with or heard of any hard drug use here on campus."

## Drug Counseling Programs

### The Counseling and Student Development Center

Phone: (901) 843-3894

Services: alcohol dependency assessment and support services, short-term personal counseling and group counseling, alcohol and drug-related literature, referrals to community mental health providers, crisis intervention, personal development programs

### Charter Lakeside

Phone: (901) 377-4733

Services: counseling and referral services, alcohol and drug-related literature, in-patient and out-patient treatment of addictive diseases

## The College Prowler Take
### ON DRUG SCENE

As on any college campus, if you're looking for drugs, you're going to be able to find them. However, at Rhodes you're probably going to have to look pretty hard, or be in the right circle of people to do so. Everyone seems to have heard of someone who does drugs, but few actually admit to it. Likewise, the availability and abuse of really hard drugs by some students is rumored, but no one ever says they've actually seen anyone do them or have obtained any themselves. Eyewitness accounts of drug use are close to nonexistent. Rhodes is not completely drug-free, but drugs are definitely not a dominant force on campus. There's no pressure for anyone at Rhodes to partake in drugs if they don't want to, and the majority of the student body doesn't want to.

### B+

**The College Prowler™ Grade on Drug Scene: B+**

A high grade on Drug Scene indicates that drugs are not a noticeable part of campus life; drug use is not visible, and no pressure to use them seems to exist.

## Overall Experience

### Students Speak Out
### ON OVERALL EXPERIENCE

"You will not receive a better education—inside or outside of the classroom—anywhere. Rhodes may be equaled by some, but it is excelled by none."

Q "Honestly, it's hard to tell if I have made the right choice so far. I'm thinking about transferring. I love my friends and living in Memphis, but **the classes seem pretty average for all the money that I am spending**. I'm also confused about my major—it seems like there isn't a wide variety of majors to choose from. The people are great, but sometimes they can be fickle. Rhodes is like a big family, everyone knows everyone's business, but we all love each other."

Q "I wish I had transferred after one semester. Rhodes is bad in all aspects of the word. I feel like very few teachers truly care about the students, the administration is like a big brother government who tries to make examples out of people they see as 'disposable,' and the **students here are shallow and care little of their fellow man**—they just want to look good, and sometimes do so by making other people look bad."

Q "I love it here. Though there isn't a lot of diversity, and there are definitely some things I would like to change. There is also **a great group of people and professors.** The people here are down-to-earth, and I feel like I am getting a good education in a fun and comfortable environment."

Q "I absolutely adore Rhodes, and wouldn't want to be at any other college campus anywhere. It was my first choice, and **I am pleased with it on a daily basis**. The classes, the society, and the friends around which I live provide the atmosphere that I believe the college experience is all about."

## The College Prowler Take
### ON OVERALL EXPERIENCE

When assessing their college experience, most students feel that Rhodes is the right place for them, and that they'd rather not be anywhere else. The incredible academics, boundless opportunities, and one-of-a-kind atmosphere that the college offers are hard to be disappointed with. At Rhodes, students are constantly challenged to reach their potential, explore their interests, and take advantage of their talent. In the beginning, it's sometimes difficult for students to take all of this in. Students who are unhappy at Rhodes and decide to transfer, often don't find their niche right away. They get frustrated with the hefty workload or unnerved by other students' unbridled ambition and decide to leave.

At some point during their time at Rhodes, every student is going to dislike something about the college—the massive amount of work, the social scene, the food, even the weather. But overall, most students are very satisfied with their decision to attend Rhodes. The college's sincere dedication to knowledge and integrity can't be found anywhere else. Rhodes provides a truly unique college experience for anyone who chooses to become a part of its community.

# Rollins College

1000 Holt Avenue Winter Park, FL 32789-4499
www.rollins.edu          (407) 606-2161

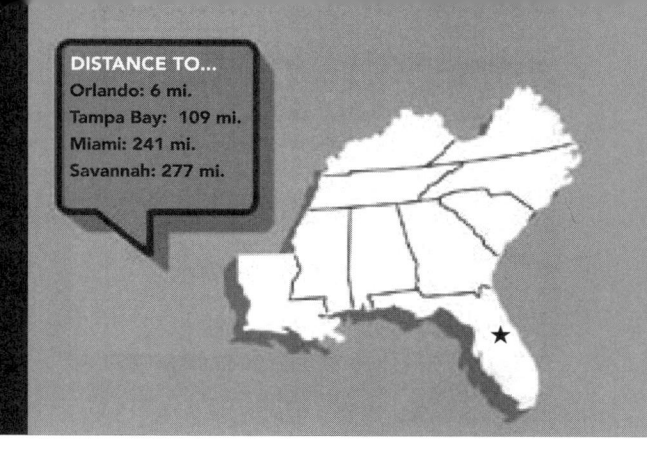

**DISTANCE TO...**
Orlando: 6 mi.
Tampa Bay: 109 mi.
Miami: 241 mi.
Savannah: 277 mi.

*"Mentioning Rollins tends to conjure up the image of a serene country club with students lounging in the sun."*

**Total Enrollment:**
1,733

**Top 10% of High School Class:**
38%

**Average GPA:**
3.4

**Acceptance Rate:**
66%

**Tuition:**
$27,700

**SAT Range (25th-75th Percentile):**

| Verbal | Math | Total |
|---|---|---|
| 540 – 630 | 540 – 630 | 1080 – 1260 |

**Most Popular Majors:**
12% Psychology
11% International Business/Trade/Commerce
9% English Language and Literature
9% Economics
6% Political Science and Government

**Students also applied to:***
Guilford College (NC)
Davidson College (VA)
University of Florida
Florida State University

*For more school info check out www.collegeprowler.com

### Table of Contents

| | |
|---|---|
| Academics | 598 |
| Local Atmosphere | 599 |
| Safety & Security | 601 |
| Facilities | 602 |
| Campus Dining | 603 |
| Campus Housing | 605 |
| Diversity | 606 |
| Guys & Girls | 608 |
| Athletics | 609 |
| Greek Life | 611 |
| Drug Scene | 612 |
| Overall Experience | 613 |

### College Prowler Report Card

| | |
|---|---|
| Academics | B+ |
| Local Atmosphere | A- |
| Safety & Security | C+ |
| Facilities | A- |
| Campus Dining | B- |
| Campus Housing | B |
| Diversity | D- |
| Guys | B |
| Girls | A |
| Athletics | B |
| Greek Life | A |
| Drug Scene | C |

# Academics

## Did You Know?

A national academic syndicate ranked Rollins first in the state of Florida in the Great Schools at Great Prices category.

Each semester, during finals, Rollins holds Al's Free Pancake Flip at night; students enjoy a delicious breakfast that holds them over while studying into the wee hours of the morning.

**Best Places to Study:**
Library, Dave's Down Under

## The Lowdown
### ON ACADEMICS

**Degrees Awarded:**
Bachelor, Master

**Undergraduate Schools:**
Arts and Sciences, Hamilton Holt School

**Full-time Faculty:**
186

**Faculty with Terminal Degree:**
92%

**Student-to-Faculty Ratio:**
11:1

**Special Degree Options:**
Dual-Degree Programs: Master of Business Administration; Pre-Engineering; Environmental Management/Forestry

**Special Programs:**
Honors Degree Program, Pre-Engineering, Rollins Conference, Self-Designed Major; Preprofessional: Pre-Dental, Pre-Law, Pre-Medical

**AP Test Score Requirements:**
Possible credit for scores of 4 or 5

**IB Test Score Requirements:**
Possible credit for scores of 5, 6, or 7

## Students Speak Out
### ON ACADEMICS

"Professors are very encouraging at Rollins. One thing you get at a school of this size is teacher interaction. When I go to class, my teacher knows my name; that's not something you get at larger schools."

Q "The professors at Rollins are academically stimulating, interesting, and challenging, for the most part. **They are generally enthusiastic and impassioned about their area of expertise**, happy to help a student when needed, and genuinely concerned about bestowing their knowledge upon students."

Q "Most Rollins students find their classes at least somewhat interesting. Beware though: in larger classes, **students are rarely participatory**, while smaller, upper-level courses provide more intellectual and open discussions."

Q "Almost always, you have teachers that you either like or dislike. **I have yet to find a teacher at Rollins I dislike**. The teachers are always so excited to be teaching their specific subject that they make you excited too. There's never a dull moment."

💬 "**Most are excited about the classes they teach,** available outside of class for help, and are friendly and respectful towards students. Some classes are interesting and others are just boring and miserable."

### The College Prowler Take
ON ACADEMICS

This small liberal arts school owes its reputation for academic excellence to the quality of its faculty. The school's small size facilitates close interaction between students and faculty. At Rollins, no student is just a number. Teachers here generally know not only your name, but your major, plans after college, and academic strengths. They are always available to help, or simply to talk. Of course, there are always exceptions. Some teachers are boring, a few exhibit lack of respect towards students, and occasionally you hear of teachers who really don't teach at all. However, the majority of professors at Rollins are here because they have a genuine desire to impart knowledge.

Most students will agree that Rollins professors are exceptional, perhaps the greatest strength of the college. Complaints are common, however, concerning the limited majors offered, especially in the business area and in performing arts. A considerable number of students create their own major for this reason. Rollins students often find the workload here relatively heavy, but certainly doable. Teachers tend to be flexible as well, or at least willing to take student's concerns into account. Overall, the college at least meets, and generally exceeds, the expectations of entering students for academic quality.

**B+**

### The College Prowler™ Grade on
## Academics: B+

A high Academics grade generally indicates that professors are knowledgeable, accessible, and genuinely interested in their students' welfare. Other determining factors include class size, how well professors communicate, and whether or not classes are engaging.

# Local Atmosphere

### The Lowdown
ON LOCAL ATMOSPHERE

**Region:**
South

**City, State:**
Winter Park, Florida

**Setting:**
Suburban

**Distance from Orlando:**
10-15 minutes

**Distance from Miami:**
4 hours

**Points of Interest:**
Leu Gardens, Disney World, Universal Studios, Charles Hosmer Morse Museum of American Art, Sea World, Gatorland, Dixie Stampede, Tchoup Chop (Emeril Lagasse's restaurant), Pointe Orlando

**Major Sports Teams:**
Orlando Magic (basketball), Orlando Predators (football), Orlando Seals (hockey)

**City Websites:**
http://www.ci.winter-park.fl.us
http://www.cityoforlando.net

## Students Speak Out
### ON LOCAL ATMOSPHERE

"Rollins is next to Orlando, the home of Mickey Mouse and other tourist traps. Downtown Orlando's scene has its highlights, but the 2 a.m. alcohol curfew is quite a buzz kill."

Q "Winter Park is a nice quiet place to be. **The nightlife in Orlando is pretty hot**, but you always have to be aware of your safety, like everywhere else in the United States. Travel in groups. Besides, where's the fun in being by yourself?"

Q "**UCF is right down the road**, well, a few miles down the road, and if someone tells you they go to Full Sail [School of Film, Art, Design, Music, and Media Production], turn and run as fast as you can!"

Q "I'm from the Orlando area originally, so nothing is new to me, but I love this town. There is always something to do. There are other universities present, such as UCF and Stetson. Of course, since you're in Orlando, you should visit the theme parks, and **take advantage of the beaches**."

Q "Winter Park is an affluent suburb. Directly next to Rollins is a posh area that often makes students of lower incomes feel inadequate. But, if one explores Orlando itself, there are scenes for everyone. UCF is close, too. **Try to avoid the 'Pike' fraternity at UCF**, they are some scary boys."

## The College Prowler Take
### ON LOCAL ATMOSPHERE

Winter Park itself is a small, relatively quiet town abutting the bustling city of Orlando. This provides the best of both worlds, as Rollins students can relax in the small town atmosphere surrounding the college, and also visit the multitude of attractions Orlando has to offer with just a 15 minute drive on I-75. Within walking distance of campus are a variety of upscale clothing stores and elegant restaurants. Also in Orlando, you can visit Disney World and relive your childhood. Rollins is located relatively close UCF (University of Central Florida), and many students party there frequently for a break from the usual Rollins scene. UF (University of Florida) isn't too far from campus either.

Though the quaint town of Winter Park is beautiful and ritzy, you really need a car to experience more of the area. Downtown Orlando offers the best (and just about only) nightlife. There, popular clubs line the streets, and bars are literally everywhere. Oh yeah, beaches are less than a two-hour drive. All in all, Rollins is well-situated, and most students find the immediate area charming with, dare we say, a paradise-like quality.

**A-**

The College Prowler™ Grade on

### Local Atmosphere: A-

A high Local Atmosphere grade indicates that the area surrounding campus is safe and scenic. Other factors include nearby attractions, proximity to other schools, and the town's attitude toward students.

# Safety & Security

> "Rollins is really a pretty safe campus, but **the security is not top-notch**, by any means. You usually have to wait about 10 or 15 minutes to get an escort, even if you go to the office in person."

> "I've never really needed assistance from campus safety, but I haven't really heard good things about them. Basically, better security at Rollins is needed, but **I feel safe for the most part**. It's a very well-lit campus."

> "**The security on campus is adequate for its size** and I generally feel safe, although it is common to learn of sexual assaults that are covered up by the administration."

> "Rollins is located in one of the wealthiest parts of Central Florida. **I feel safe walking to my car at 2 a.m.**, though the dangers of the world lurk behind any corner, regardless if it is in the vicinity of multi-million dollar homes."

## The Lowdown
### ON SAFETY & SECURITY

**Number of Rollins College Police:**
22

**Phone:**
(407) 646-2999

**Safety Services:**
Late-night transport/escort service, 24 hour emergency telephones (blues-phones), lighted pathways/sidewalks, controlled dormitory access (key, security card, etc.), 24-hour foot and vehicle patrols.

**Health Center Office Hours:**
Monday - Friday 8 a.m. to 12 p.m., weekends 1 p.m. to 3 p.m.

## The College Prowler Take
### ON SAFETY & SECURITY

Most students feel safe on campus, due largely to the extremely small size of the college and infrequent crime instances. Campus safety seems to always be a presence (whether students want them to be or not). Call-boxes are located all around campus, though it seems officers don't always respond as quickly as they should. Winter Park itself is a very safe area with low instances of crime. Though theft does occur, it's usually a result of students feeling so safe they fail to lock their dorm room doors, and come back to a missing laptop or jewelry.

## Students Speaks Out
### ON SAFETY & SECURITY

{ "Security is okay. The campus safety officers are always willing to help you. Unfortunately, they can't keep all the 'bad guys' out." }

**The College Prowler™ Grade on**
### Safety & Security: C+

A high grade in Safety & Security means that students generally feel safe, campus police are visible, blue-light phones and escort services are readily available, and safety precautions are not overly necessary.

# Facilities

## The Lowdown
ON FACILITIES

**Student Center:**
The Cornell Campus Center

**Athletic Center:**
Cahill-Sandspur Field, Alfond Sports Center, Alfond Swimming Pool, Alfond Boathouse, Alfond Stadium at Harper-Sheperd Field, Bert W. Martin Tennis Complex

**Libraries:**
1

**Movie Theatre on Campus?**
No

**Bowling on Campus?**
No

**Bar on Campus?**
No, however a number are within walking distance.

**Coffeehouse on Campus?**
Yes, there is Dianne's Cafe.

**Popular Places to Chill:**
The Cornell Campus Center, Dave's Down Under, Alfond Pool, Alfond Sports Center

## Favorite Things to Do
Most students visit the gym or the pool at least once a day. Both of these destinations attract students looking to socialize, as much as they do those who want to work out or get a tan. Around noon, the Cornell Campus Center teems with students getting lunch and meeting up with friends. Soccer games attract large crowds, as do plays, and it seems weeknights, there are always students in the Olin Library concentrating on their work.

### Computers
**High-Speed Network?** Yes
**Wireless Network?** Yes
**Number of Labs:** 8
**Numbers of Computers:** 200
**24-Hour Labs:** Olin Library
**Charge to Print?** 1,000 pages (per student) are allotted per year.

## Students Speak Out
ON FACILITIES

"The athletic center is a great place, and it offers free group exercise classes that are really fun."

Q "The student center always has something going on where you can meet a ton of people. The clubs are always holding some program or another. It depends what you're interested in, but **you'll always find something**."

Q "**The facilities are nice, for the most part**. The campus center, library, and the gym are the nicest. The dorms and some of the buildings, such as Orlando hall, need to be redone."

Q "The gym is small, but nice. **Girls, like myself, tend to fight over a certain machine**, of which there are only two. Time limits are instilled and followed, though, to much success. Our student center, Dave's Down Under, is well-equipped with a large projection television and a late-night food grill. The campus is unparalleled in aesthetic quality."

Q "The facilities are fabulous! They're one of the best parts of the school. The student center is brand-new and overlooks a lake. **The sports center is brand-new and gorgeous**. The grounds are beautiful. You can always find a nice spot on campus to sit around."

Q "The facilities are amazing on campus, and provide **a great place to escape dormitories** and be social."

## The College Prowler Take
### ON FACILITIES

It isn't uncommon to hear people visiting Rollins for the first time remark something like, "This looks more like a country club than a college!" Indeed, Rollins' campus is a picture of paradise, combining traditional Florida flair with a northeastern feel that's origin is difficult to pinpoint. The Cornell Campus Center offers breathtaking views, which almost make the common cafeteria food served there feel like more upscale dining (not quite!). Many pay at least one visit to the pool or to the lake everyday; Rollins is a sun-worshiping campus.

Many students are initially drawn to Rollins for its beautiful campus, and it is hard to surpass the sheer aesthetic splendor of this little tropical paradise. Rollins takes great care to build and maintain its facilities, and it's rare to find a college so clean and new. Few people can complain about the facilities on campus for this reason.

# A-

The College Prowler™ Grade on
## Facilities: A-

A high Facilities grade indicates that the campus is aesthetically pleasing and well-maintained; facilities are state-of-the-art, and libraries are exceptional. Other determining factors include the quality of both athletic and student centers and an abundance of things to do on campus.

# Campus Dining

## The Lowdown
### ON CAMPUS DINING

**Freshman Meal Plan Requirement?**
Yes

**24-Hour On-Campus Eating?**
No

**Student Favorites:**
The Market Place, Domino's, the Grille, Dianne's Cafe

**Other Options:**
Many restaurants on Park Avenue, including Sunrise Deli and Tropical Smoothies, will deliver to the dorms at no cost, so students can receive the food they're craving without leaving their rooms.

### Did You Know?

Students can place money on a Flex account that can be used for buying food on campus, as well as for vending machines, items in the bookstore, copiers, and laundry.

Don't be surprised when you hear the Marketplace referred to by nearly everyone as Beans, though no one seems to know how the name originated.

## Students Speak Out
ON CAMPUS DINING

> "The food at Beans is some of the best college cafeteria food anywhere. The vegetarian place is great, and the pizza slices are huge!"

Q "Well ... the food here isn't exactly bistro quality. It's definitely edible. The cafeteria is always a good place to meet people when you're new on campus. I'd say though, that **the best place to eat is the Grille**. Who doesn't like burgers and curly fries!?"

Q "The food can be iffy. In the cafeteria, I usually found myself eating just a salad or sandwich. The Grille has some good options; however they get tiresome after a while because **it's all greasy**."

Q "The food is quite atrocious. This is common in college, since Sodexho controls much of the business market. I have an allergy to sugar, and often find myself complaining about the lack of simple foods—most meat is served marinated in the 'sauce of the week.' The school attempts to accommodate you, though, and **the staff is fabulous**."

Q "The Grille at night is your best bet, and Dianne's Cafe has pretty good stuff during the weekdays. Remember: **You can order Domino's pizza with your meal plan card**. It will serve you well."

Q "**The food is expensive**, but better than most schools."

## The College Prowler Take
ON CAMPUS DINING

Campus dining is generally not criticized heavily, and many students find the food at Rollins far superior to that of other colleges. The meal plan at Rollins will allow you to purchase food at all on-campus restaurants, as well as Domino's. Most students head to the Cornell Campus Center when they get hungry. Inside, there's cafeteria style food, a grocery store, and fast food. "Beans," the cafeteria, is great for breakfast and offers variety that changes daily. Since Beans closes relatively early, the Grille, open till 2 a.m., is the late-night snack spot. This restaurant provides students with the gratifying, and also extremely greasy, food they often crave after a night of studying or partying.

Food on campus can be extremely overpriced, and it is easy for students to pay little attention to the cost of meals, only to find themselves without meal plan money left by the end of the semester. The campus grocery store, the C-Store, is notorious for raising prices astronomically, such as charging $8 for a small can of peanuts! Unfortunately, the inflated prices cause more cash conscious students to forego the meal plan, and turn to the variety of off-campus food sources.

**B-**

The College Prowler™ Grade on
## Campus Dining: B-

Our grade on Campus Dining addresses the quality of both school-owned dining halls and independent on-campus restaurants as well as the price, availability, and variety of food.

# Campus Housing

## The Lowdown
### ON CAMPUS HOUSING

**Room Types:**
Resident rooms are all standard. Students share a central bathroom facility. Most first year students are assigned to these rooms. Apartments are located on campus. These units are either two bedroom (housing four students) or one bedroom (housing two) and have in-room kitchens.

**Best Dorms:**
Ward Hall, Elizabeth Hall

**Worst Dorms:**
McKean, Rex Beach

**You Get:**
Bed, desk and chair, closet or wardrobe, dresser, Ethernet or broadband Internet connections, free campus phone calls and mailbox, free cable

**Available for Rent:**
Steel Safes

**Cleaning Service?**
Public areas, including community bathrooms, are cleaned daily.

**Also Available:**
Special-interest housing

## Students Speak Out
### ON CAMPUS HOUSING

"I'd say the best dorm, if you want quiet, is Holt. It's always clean, and the people are so friendly. If you want constant parties, check out Ward."

"For the money, **the dorms could be better**, and they could turn on the heat when it gets cold in Ward; but they are decent enough—it could be worse—and the cleaning people work really hard."

"Yikes! The dorms are not the brighter side of Rollins. Ward is probably one of the nicer ones. I lived in McKean my freshman year. It wasn't that great. So, now I'm living in the Sutton apartments, which are definitely an upgrade from the dorms, but **they're for mainly upperclassman**."

"I thought I hated the dorms freshmen year, and lived off campus for a year after. I ended up returning though because of its central location, and its easy one-time payment at the beginning of the year. I currently live in Holt, which is **the preferable dorm for those who want to meet diverse people**, not the stereotypical preppy, wealthy Rollins student, and also get some quiet time, since parties are nearly nonexistent."

"Dorms at Rollins could be a lot better. They look really nice from the outside, but once you're inside they lose their appeal. **A lot of them are old and dirty-looking**. But it's really what you make out of it. I feel comfortable in my dorm, and I enjoy living there."

"Many dorms have been renovated, so Elizabeth and Ward are very nice. I would **stay away from McKean**, though."

## The College Prowler Take
### ON CAMPUS HOSPITING

Rollins now requires all students with fewer than 50 credits to live on campus, which essentially forces most freshman and sophomores to live in the dorms. For a college with immaculate facilities, the dorms are a source of disappointment for some students. Many freshman dorms have tiny rooms and always seem dirty, despite the genuine efforts of the cleaning staff. The dorms that have been recently renovated receive rave reviews, though. Due to dorm dissatisfaction, students often fight for a spot in the Sutton Place apartments. Here residents are chosen through a lottery, which takes year and GPA into consideration, and those provided with a room seem happy with having their own kitchen and more private living space.

Despite the fact that many criticize the dorms, freshman dorm life is an essential part of integrating into the Rollins community. Rollins students seem to look back with fond memories on their dorm years, because of the people they met, the friendships forged, and the parties thrown, regardless of the condition of their actual dorm building.

## B

### The College Prowler™ Grade on
### Campus Housing: B

A high Campus Housing grade indicates that dorms are clean, well-maintained, and spacious. Other determining factors include variety of dorms, proximity to classes, and social atmosphere.

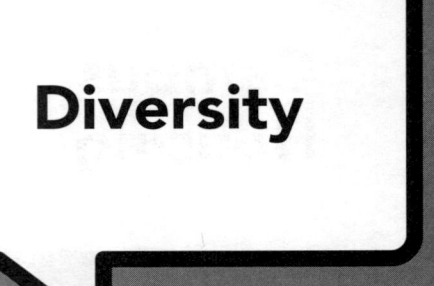

# Diversity

## The Lowdown
### ON DIVERSITY

**Native American:** 1%

**Asian American:** 3%

**African American:** 4%

**Hispanic:** 7%

**White:** 81%

**International:** 4%

**Out-of-State:** 57%

### Political Activity
The student body at Rollins is relatively divided on the political spectrum. Outspoken liberals and extreme conservatives can both be found in masses.

### Most Popular Religions
The most prominent religions are Catholicism and Christianity. The church on campus offers services for both of these denominations.

## Economic Status

Rollins seems to consist predominantly of students from wealthy economic backgrounds. Much of the student criticism concerning Rollins centers on the believed excess of "snobby rich kids." This is a generalization, however, and far from all of the students here would classify themselves as rich.

## Minority Clubs

The minority clubs at Rollins are quite active on campus, though often their membership is small.

## Students Speak Out
### ON DIVERSITY

{ "I think we could definitely use a much more diverse group of people on our campus."

- "The first half of the student body is all **extremely rich kids who come here to party**. The second half is a more diverse population who made it on scholarship. Race-wise, it's not that diverse, and, gender-wise, there's a lot more females here on campus. How many times have I been asked, 'So how do you like going to an all-girl's school?' Too many to count!"

- "Rollins is not diverse at all. There are currently only about **five black professors**, and the amount of non-white or non-affluent students is slight."

- "At times, **everyone here starts to look the same**."

- "Diverse is a funny word at Rollins. **Do you mean diverse as in BMW, Mercedes, or gargantuan SUV?** Or, in student body makeup? Or, in 'will anyone go and watch a movie that isn't a sequel' diverse?"

- "I usually see at least one or more person of color **every other day**."

## The College Prowler Take
### ON DIVERSITY

The demographics speak for themselves: our campus is not an extremely diverse one. As one student accurately put it, "Sometimes, everyone starts to look the same." Rollins has the reputation of consisting mainly of stereotypical, rich, preppy, white kids, and it's easy to understand how this came about—a significant number of students fit this profile. But, it's important to recognize that an almost equal number of students are nothing like the Rollins stereotype. Politically, the campus seems pretty much split, and during election times, things can get heated. An abnormally large portion of students come from the Northeast, while international students are underrepresented. It takes some effort and patience for students drastically different from the mold to find those similar to themselves at Rollins, but the many clubs and special interest housing help greatly in the process.

The College Prowler™ Grade on
## Diversity: D-

A high grade in Diversity indicates that ethnic minorities and international students have a notable presence on campus and that students of different economic backgrounds, religious beliefs, and sexual preferences are well-represented.

# Guys & Girls

## Dress Code

Fashion sense is of great importance at Rollins. The majority of students dress preppy, and nearly all those with "style" buy top-name designer brands. The stereotypical dress code for a Rollins girl on any given day would be a Lily Pulitzer skirt paired with a Lacoste polo shirt, Down East sandals, and a Louie Vuitton purse to match. Guys dress slightly more casual, frequently in jeans, khakis, or shorts and a polo shirt as well. Outfits for going out are often chosen well in advance with stunning results. There are also plenty who could care less about fashion, and go to class in their pajamas, preferring sleep to immaculate dress.

## The Lowdown
### ON GUYS & GIRLS

**Women Undergrads:** 61%

**Men Undergrads:** 39%

**Birth Control Available?**
Yes

**Social Scene**
Rollins has an active social scene, and meeting students never seems to be a problem. With only about 1,700 students attending Rollins, it's easy to feel like you know, or at least recognize, just about everyone. Clubs are not a huge part of Rollins life, and it more often occurs that people meet in the dorms, at parties, or sometimes simply sitting outside the cafeteria. People are extremely outgoing and always willing to initiate interaction.

**Hookups or Relationships?**
Freshman year, weekend parties revolve, for the most part, around random hookups. At Rollins, commitment free hookups are common and quite accepted. By sophomore year, however, people start to date more often. Relationships range from extremely short-lived and drama-filled, to couples planning their wedding by senior year. Those who preferred the non-committal hookups of freshman year will have no problem continuing this till the end, as well.

## Students Speak Out
### ON GUYS & GIRLS

"The guys are pretty good-looking. But, I have to say that the selection isn't so huge."

Q "Everyone knows the stereotype of the Rollins girls and guys. **The guys are all frat boys or soccer players** who own at least 10 pink shirts, and the girls are all blonde with Louies. However, I have met a great deal of people who do not fit in this category, including myself. I'm not really going to comment on the guys ... they're nice, but I enjoy dating my boyfriend, who does not go here."

Q "The 'stereotypical' Rollins guy is as follows: cocky, good-looking, rich, Republican, non-monogamous, lacking in intelligence, and often drunk. **The girls are pretty much the same**. Throw in some cocaine and you have the stereotypical Rollins relationship."

Q "When I first came to Rollins, we were voted in the top five for hottest girls on campus in *Playboy*, *Maxim*, and I'm sure some other similar magazines. I think it depends on taste, but **we have a decent-looking crowd**."

> "Although the guys and girls would most likely be considered hot, **a lot of them are very snobby**. It's sad to say that if I were to leave Rollins, it would most likely be because of the people. I do not, however, feel targeted specifically. I think that these people are just rude in general."

### The College Prowler Take
**ON GUYS & GIRLS**

The student body at Rollins is an unusually attractive one. Girls are typically thin, dressed in designer clothing, and immaculately done-up. Guys are preppy, rich, and many are very good-looking. Girls are also known to be snobby, and guys generally cocky. But these are all stereotypes, and far from everyone conforms to these generalizations. One student said, "If you look, you can find any social atmosphere you desire at Rollins." This is true, but it does take some effort.

Entering Rollins, you quickly realize that this campus has extremely materialistic tendencies, and an abnormal number of students with excessive wealth. Dress is important here, and contributes greatly to social status. Designer brands are a must, and most dress as preppy as possible. Popped collars on guys and Lily Pulitzer for girls are major fashion trends at Rollins. Though many scorn the materialism at Rollins, it does make for an attractive student body that parents approve highly of.

**The College Prowler™ Grade on**
## Guys: B
A high grade for Guys indicates that the male population on campus is attractive, smart, friendly, and engaging, and that the school has a decent ratio of guys to girls.

**The College Prowler™ Grade on**
## Girls: A
A high grade for Girls not only implies that the women on campus are attractive, smart, friendly, and engaging, but also that there is a fair ratio of girls to guys.

# Athletics

### The Lowdown
**ON ATHLETICS**

**Men's Varsity Teams:**
Soccer
Basketball
Baseball
Crew
Cross Country
Golf
Rowing
Sailing
Tennis
Water Skiing

**Women's Varsity Teams:**
Soccer
Basketball
Softball
Volleyball
Crew
Cross Country
Golf
Rowing
Sailing
Tennis
Water Skiing

### Intramurals (IMs)
Basketball, Volleyball, Soccer, Softball, Flag Football, Tennis, Golf, and Bowling

### Getting Tickets
Tickets are easily obtained and never sold out. For most events you can get in free, but for the few that charge it is a minimal price.

### Most Popular Sports
Soccer and baseball are two of the most popular varsity sports. The men's soccer team has a huge following, and regularly packs the stands on big game nights. Of the intramural sports, flag football gets a lot of people involved.

**Athletic Division:**
NCAA Division II

**Conference:**
Sunshine State Conference

**School Mascot:**
Tars

**Fields:**
Cahall-Sandspur Field, Alfond Stadium at Harper-Sheperd Field

## Students Speak Out
### ON ATHLETICS

> "The soccer games are a blast, especially since the guys' soccer team is fabulous!"

Q "A sport's popularity depends on the crowd. The spirit on campus is miniscule in anything. However, our sports teams win many competitions, and are of good quality. **IM sports are fairly popular** on campus, but there is always room for more people."

Q "Sports are definitely supported, but not very big on campus. **We don't even have a football team**, but our soccer boys and girls are pretty good."

Q "**Sports are pretty big**—soccer especially. There's also volleyball, crew, basketball, and a ton I know I'm missing."

Q "They do a pretty good job promoting varsity sports. **I've seen some IM action**, but it doesn't seem like those are really promoted or well-known."

Q "Varsity sports are big. Soccer, baseball, golf, and basketball are the big four that always do well. IM is so-so. Since Rollins is so small, **most of the good athletes are already on teams**, and don't do much IM stuff."

## The College Prowler Take
### ON ATHLETICS

Rollins has some amazing athletes, and many of our varsity teams consistently rank well in their divisions. There is a pretty big population of varsity athletes on campus, although the student body doesn't always support them like at larger universities (University of Florida, Florida State). There is no football team, so maybe that is one reason for lack of spirit. IM sports exist, but are not promoted as much as they should be.

Simply put, if you are the kind of sports fanatic who craves big conference basketball and wild tailgate parties before weekend football games, then Rollins probably isn't the school for you. However, our soccer teams have won numerous division championships and our basketball team is on the rise.

**B**

The College Prowler™ Grade on
### Athletics: B

A high grade in Athletics indicates that students have school spirit, that sports programs are respected, that games are well-attended, and that intramurals are a prominent part of student life.

**COLLEGE PROWLER™**

Want to join a team? Check out the complete College Prowler guide on Rollins at *www.collegeprowler.com*.

# Greek Life

## The Lowdown
ON GREEK LIFE

**Number of Fraternities:**
5

**Number of Sororities:**
6

**Undergrad Men in Fraternities:**
38%

**Undergrad Women in Sororities:**
40%

**Other Greek Organizations:**
Greek Council, Greek Peer Advisors, Interfraternity Council, Order of Omega, Panhellenic Council

## Students Speak Out
ON GREEK LIFE

"Greek life is the social scene for the most part. Personally, I stay as far away from it as possible."

"Frat parties are **where everyone goes to get wasted**."

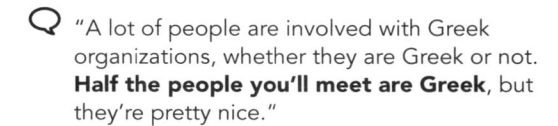

"For me, Greek life doesn't dominate the social scene. I'm not into the whole fraternity and sorority scene. **For those who want to avoid it, you can**. For those who embrace it, you definitely can."

"**You don't have to be a part of Greek life** to be popular and have fun on campus."

"Greek life is very big, and I'd say, yes, it does dominate. From what I've heard, **most of the parties are hosted by frats** and are usually held in their houses."

"A lot of people are involved with Greek organizations, whether they are Greek or not. **Half the people you'll meet are Greek**, but they're pretty nice."

## The College Prowler Take
ON GREEK LIFE

If you like the whole Greek idea, chances are it could work to your benefit. It is worth mentioning that there are some people that do the whole Greek thing that you wouldn't necessarily expect. Greek life, whether students want to admit it or not, is a dominating force at Rollins. Frat parties here are infamous, and they are not limited to just the weekends. Throw in the frats and sororities at nearby UCF, and you have yourself a real Greek fest!

The College Prowler™ Grade on
### Greek Life: A

A high grade in Greek Life indicates that sororities and fraternities are not only present, but also active on campus. Other determining factors include the variety of houses available and the respect the Greek community receives from the rest of the campus.

# Drug Scene

> "There are always stories about drugs on campus, but I've never witnessed anything. **It's not a huge problem**, but it's something to expect from certain college students."

> "Like everywhere else in the world, there are drugs at Rollins. However, unlike everywhere else in the world, coke seems to be in style every year at Rollins. A girl wants to lose weight to fit in? Her friends convince her to start paying large sums of money to snort white lines up her nose and destroy her life. **Marijuana is everywhere**; if you want it, you can get it at any time of day."

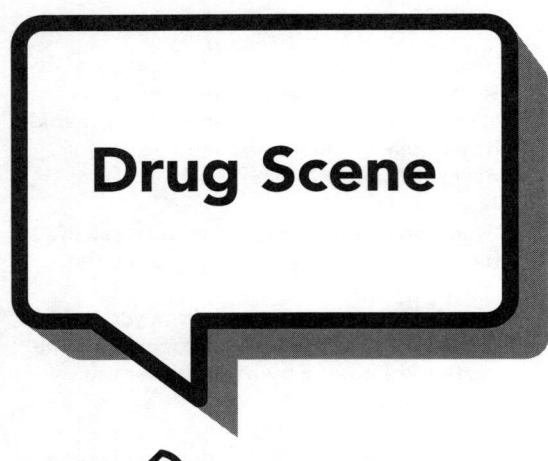

## The Lowdown
ON DRUG SCENE

**Most Prevalent Drugs on Campus:**
Alcohol, Marijuana, Cocaine, Adderall

## Students Speaks Out
ON DRUG SCENE

> "The drug scene definitely exists here. People smoke all over—I think that it's disgusting."

> "Tell me one college where drugs don't appear? Personally—and I'm a junior—**I've never run into a problem** with them."

> "Drugs are prevalent at Rollins. **It's often said it's 'snowing in Florida,'** referring to Rollins' cocaine problem. Painkillers such as Valium are popular, as is Adderall. I'd estimate that at least 50 percent of the students here do some sort of drug, including pot."

## The College Prowler Take
ON DRUG SCENE

**Drugs are certainly a presence on campus, and they are easily obtained. Alcohol is, of course, the most prevalent drug and as one student put it, "Alcohol is the only source of entertainment on the weekends." Rollins wasn't ranked the number two party school by *Playboy* magazine for nothing. Marijuana runs a close second in popularity. Pot users range from the typical frat guy, to even the best of students that secretly light up in their rooms. Though a lot of people smoke and drink, most students don't feel pressured to join in.**

**Cocaine is also widely used on campus and, as one student said, it's common to hear the phrase, "It snows at Rollins," referring to the coke problem. With so much money floating around, some students choose to invest in drugs, and coke seems to be most popular.**

The College Prowler™ Grade on
### Drug Scene: C

A high grade on Drug Scene indicates that drugs are not a noticeable part of campus life; drug use is not visible, and no pressure to use them seems to exist.

# Overall Experience

## Students Speak Out
### ON OVERALL EXPERIENCE

> "I love going to school at Rollins. The atmosphere, classes, food, and people make me feel like I go to school in paradise."

> "Even though it has its faults, like everything does, **I love the campus, the people, and my experience here at Rollins**. I don't think I would be enjoying myself this much if I went to another school."

> "Besides the profound capitalist nature of Rollins, it is pretty decent. If there was another school that is in the South with a small campus, small classes, wonderful professors, and my major, but has normal people, I would be there in a flash. But I don't know of any, so **I suppose I'm stuck here**."

> "I used to hate Rollins. I realized later that this was due to a bad roommate, not a bad school. If you are not the stereotype—I'm not—you do have to work a bit harder to meet people. Live in dorms, and **you will find at least a handful of people you like**. I met most of my friends this way, with the exception of two I met in upper-level classes, where students usually share interests. I'm glad now I didn't transfer."

> "This is my third school and, for one, I'm not a big fan of the student body. This is not to say that I do not love the academics at Rollins. **I have yet to have a bad professor**, and the bio and chemistry departments are top-notch. The small class sizes are also a plus. I can't say I miss elbowing people out of the way to check my latest bio test grade, which is listed by social security number."

> "My overall experience at Rollins has been good. My biggest gripe is with the student body. You may encounter students who think they're better because they have the Gucci. **I advise just finding your niche**, and not minding any of the snobby, image-based students on campus."

## The College Prowler Take
### ON OVERALL EXPERIENCE

Although many students gripe about the arrogant, capitalist, Louis Vuitton-sportin' student body, just about everyone admits that the academics are top-tier and the campus, at times, can feel like a spa or resort. Although this has been said many times throughout, it can't be stressed enough—not everyone here fits the stereotype! All it takes is a little soul searching and you will be sure to find your crowd at Rollins.

You will find however, that many students who enroll at Rollins will withdraw within their first semester, because they just couldn't take the stress and strain of living up to one of two things: the arduous task of keeping up with the rigorous academics, and/or keeping up with a certain social crowd. However, the students who decide to stick it out, even after (initially) feeling extremely depressed, isolated, or stressed out, normally find that they have made the right decision. Life at this little paradise we call Rollins College really is what you make of it.

# Tulane University

6823 St. Charles Avenue, New Orleans, LA 70118
www.tulane.edu        (504) 865-5731

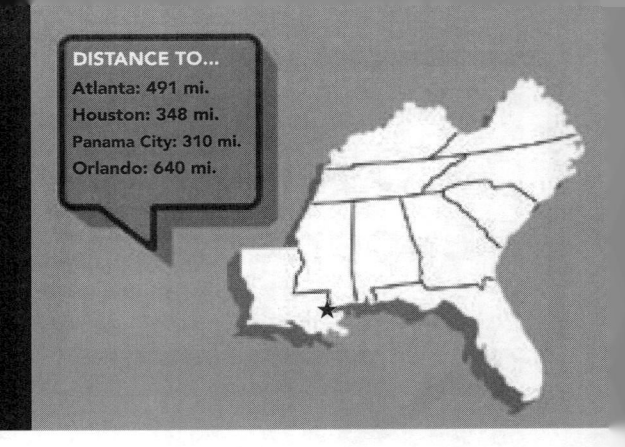

**DISTANCE TO...**
Atlanta: 491 mi.
Houston: 348 mi.
Panama City: 310 mi.
Orlando: 640 mi.

---

*"A popular Tulane motto is, 'You're either a smart kid here on scholarship, or you're a rich kid looking for the ultimate party school.'"*

**Total Enrollment:**
5,989

**Top 10% of High School Class:**
65%

**Average GPA:**
3.5

**Acceptance Rate:**
55%

**Tuition:**
$31,210

**SAT Range (25th-75th Percentile)**
| Verbal | Math | Total |
|---|---|---|
| 610 – 730 | 630 – 690 | 1240 – 1420 |

**ACT Range (25th-75th Percentile)**
| Verbal | Math | Total |
|---|---|---|
| 24-30 | 22-32 | 28-32 |

**Most Popular Majors:**
- 21% Business Management and Marketing
- 17% Social Sciences
- 9% Engineering
- 8% Psychology
- 7% Biological and Biomedical Sciences

**Students also applied to:***
- Boston University
- Duke University
- Emory University
- Vanderbilt University
- Washington University in St. Louis

*For more school info check out www.collegeprowler.com

## Table of Contents

| | |
|---|---|
| Academics | 615 |
| Local Atmosphere | 617 |
| Safety & Security | 618 |
| Facilities | 619 |
| Campus Dining | 621 |
| Campus Housing | 622 |
| Diversity | 624 |
| Guys & Girls | 625 |
| Athletics | 627 |
| Greek Life | 628 |
| Drug Scene | 630 |
| Overall Experience | 631 |

## College Prowler Report Card

| | |
|---|---|
| Academics | B |
| Local Atmosphere | A- |
| Safety & Security | C+ |
| Facilities | B+ |
| Campus Dining | C+ |
| Campus Housing | C |
| Diversity | D+ |
| Guys | B- |
| Girls | B+ |
| Athletics | B- |
| Greek Life | B |
| Drug Scene | C+ |

# Academics

## The Lowdown
ON ACADEMICS

**Degrees Awarded:**
Associate, Bachelor, Master, Doctorate

**Undergraduate Schools:**
Tulane College, Newcomb College, A.B. Freemen School of Business, School of Architecture, School of Engineering, School of Social Work, University College

**Full-time Faculty:**
747

**Faculty with Terminal Degree:**
98%

**Student-to-Faculty Ratio:**
9:1

**Average Course Load:**
13.6 credits

**AP Test Score Requirements:**
Possible credit for scores of 4 or 5

**IB Test Score Requirements:**
Possible credit for scores of 5 or greater

## Special Degree Options

BSE/MSE 5-Year Degree in Engineering

This program is run by the engineering department and the honors program; it results in a B.S. in engineering or computer science and a M.S. in the same field after five years.

Engineering-Master of Business Administration

This is a program to earn a B.S. in engineering and an MBA after five years.

Bachelor of Science/Arts and Master's Degree in Public Health (BS/MSPH).

This is a program to earn dual degrees in the field of environmental health. During the third year, students enrolled in this program begin to take graduate level courses in the environmental health sciences department downtown at the SPHTM.

## Sample Academic Clubs

American Institute of Architecture Students, American Marketing Association, American Society of Civil Engineers, Association of Pre-Dental Students, Biomedical Engineering Society, Philosophy Club, Pre-Law Society, Pre-Medical Society, Society of Women Engineers

## Did You Know?

In 1886, Josephine Louise Newcomb founded Newcomb College, the first degree-granting women's college in the nation to be established as a division of a university.

**Best Places to Study:**
Howard-Tilton Library, the PJ's patio on Willow Street, or outside on a sunny day on one of the many quads

## Students Speak Out
### ON ACADEMICS

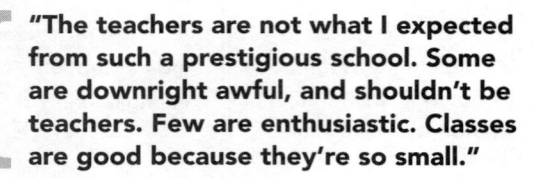

"The teachers are not what I expected from such a prestigious school. Some are downright awful, and shouldn't be teachers. Few are enthusiastic. Classes are good because they're so small."

Q "I usually end up enjoying the classes that are taken by choice, but the ones that I take due to a requirement I don't enjoy as much because they don't spark my interest. **The teachers are pretty decent** for the most part."

Q "Take this piece of advice: **research your classes and teachers before you commit** to a schedule. There's usually more than one section of a class for each course, and different teachers will be better than others. Talk to upperclassmen and find out who they liked and didn't like before you get into a class. If you start to get the feeling that you don't like a teacher, drop the class and take it with someone else, or do it another semester. Oh yeah ... and be careful with math courses. It's the worst department at Tulane."

Q "I have now attended classes at three universities, and the Tulane professors have the highest probability of **knowing what they're talking about.**"

Q "It's evident that most of my teachers have a lot of **experience working outside of Tulane** in their respected fields. Their international, 'real world' examples make the classes interesting."

## The College Prowler Take
### ON ACADEMICS

As with any school, you're going to hate some professors and love others. Some of Tulane's faculty members are very influential, both in the general academic world and in their particular fields. The accessibility of these professors, however, often depends on class size. At Tulane, you'll find a mixture of small-group classes and huge lectures. The core classes required for most majors and many of the science requirements (chemistry, for example) have classes upwards of 150 students. If you take a foreign language or a class in the 300 or 400 level, however, the class will not exceed 25 students, in order to allow for more teacher-student interaction. Many professors of smaller classes let class run outside on one of the many quads on a pretty day.

Contacting professors is usually very easy at Tulane. They are very accessible through the Blackboard (Internet) system, e-mail, or office hours. Most are very helpful and friendly when you have a problem or a question with the material. Because of the prestigious name, they do not let just anyone teach at Tulane. Most professors are very intelligent and knowledgeable about their subject. The main problem that many students express is a feeling that some faculty members don't understand the best way to teach their material, and that this makes classes harder than they have to be. Getting in touch with your professors and TAs is, by far, the best way to overcome such problems.

**B**

The College Prowler™ Grade on
### Academics: B

A high Academics grade generally indicates that professors are knowledgeable, accessible, and genuinely interested in their students' welfare. Other determining factors include class size, how well professors communicate, and whether or not classes are engaging.

# Local Atmosphere

## The Lowdown
### ON LOCAL ATMOSPHERE

**Region:**
South

**City, State:**
New Orleans, Louisiana

**Setting:**
Urban

**Distance from Baton Rouge (LSU):**
1 hour, 30 minutes

**Points of Interest:**
Bourbon Street, Magazine Street, D-Day Museum

**Major Sports Teams:**
Saints (Football), Voodoo (Arena Football), Hornets (Basketball)

## Students Speak Out
### ON LOCAL ATMOSPHERE

"The atmosphere is awesome. New Orleans is the perfect college town. There's always something going on, things to do, and places to see."

"**There are tons of cultural places to visit**, and even more fun things to do. There are other universities, and a city that draws people that are laid-back and looking for a good time."

"The atmosphere in this town is one which seems to pressure citizens into extreme drinking habits. There are other universities present, like Loyola. **Stuff to avoid: being by yourself at night.** Stuff to visit: the cemeteries, Magazine Street."

"The best way to describe New Orleans is as a developing country. The richest people live two blocks from the poorest. There are multiple universities in the area; however, they don't compare to Tulane. Stay away from Audubon Park at night, and make sure to **visit the D-Day museum**."

## The College Prowler Take
### ON LOCAL ATMOSPHERE

There are very few cities in the US that can match New Orleans' abundant culture, quaint architecture, amazing food, and party scene. Whether or not you plan to attend Tulane, New Orleans is a great city to visit. In terms of sports, New Orleans has football, baseball, and basketball teams to root for. For a more artsy feel, there are plenty of quiet jazz cafes and small bookstores all over the city. Local and famous bands come through to perform throughout the year—many musicians and artists make their home in the streets of New Orleans. No matter where you're from, by the end of your first year at Tulane, you'll agree that New Orleans is one of the liveliest cities in the world.

**A-**

The College Prowler™ Grade on
## Local Atmosphere: A-

A high Local Atmosphere grade indicates that the area surrounding campus is safe and scenic. Other factors include nearby attractions, proximity to other schools, and the town's attitude toward students.

# Safety & Security

## Did You Know?
Tulane Emergency Medical Service (Tulane EMS) is an ambulance service run by students who are basic- and intermediate-level emergency medical technicians.

## The Lowdown
ON SAFETY & SECURITY

**Number of Tulane Police:**
36 full-time, commissioned officers; about 40 part-time, student employees

**Phone:**
865-5381 (non-emergency); 865-5200 or campus extension 5200 (emergency)

**Health Center Office Hours:**
Monday-Friday: 8:30 a.m.-4:30 p.m.,
Tuesdays: 8:30 a.m.-6 p.m.
Saturday: 9 a.m. - noon
Sunday: Closed
Summer Hours: 9 a.m.-3 p.m.

**Safety Services:**
There are 33 blue-phones on campus. Many residence halls maintain a 24-hour exterior door-locking system; entrance into buildings is by key or card. Visitors use security phones to call the person they are visiting, and are allowed into the halls only when escorted by a resident. Other halls, including freshman halls, have desk assistants on duty from 8 p.m. to 7 a.m.; residents of those halls must show identification and sign in guests. Officers and student marshals on foot patrol offer a personal escort service anywhere on campus, anytime (request escorts through

## Students Speak Out
ON SAFETY & SECURITY

*"I always feel safe on campus. It is when I'm off campus late at night that I feel threatened."*

Q *"Security is excellent on campus, but nonexistent off campus. Even just a few blocks off campus, **there have been several muggings** and sexual assaults this year—almost all were young women walking alone at night."*

Q *"The TUPD isn't the sharpest force, but **they do their job well**. I don't feel unsafe on campus at all."*

Q *"If you're ever in River Ridge or old Metairie, **watch your back**. I cannot tell you the amount of times I have come close to something bad happening."*

Q *"I have never felt insecure on campus. **At night, there are multiple lights on** and many security guards around campus."*

## The College Prowler Take
### ON SAFETY & SECURITY

Students all concur that they feel safe while walking on Tulane's grounds, but feel threatened or scared when in the city at night. Theft of bikes, purses, cell phones, and Tulane student IDs happen on a daily basis, and this is even a form of entertainment in *The Hullabaloo*'s (Tulane's student newspaper) Crime Watch section. The best advice for anyone in New Orleans, especially students, is to stay in groups—this goes double at night. The worst safety threats happen to people walking by themselves, especially in areas outside of the Tulane campus. A little bit of common sense goes a long way toward making the city a safer place and getting the most out of New Orleans' many cultural districts.

**C+**

### The College Prowler™ Grade on
## Safety & Security: C+

A high grade in Safety & Security means that students generally feel safe, campus police are visible, blue-light phones and escort services are readily available, and safety precautions are not overly necessary.

# Facilities

## The Lowdown
### ON FACILITIES

**Student Center:**
The UC is under construction, but there is the Pavilion (a.k.a. "the Bubble") and Bruff commons.

**Athletic Center:**
Reily Recreation Center

**Libraries:**
9

**Bar on Campus?**
Students 21 and up can buy beer at the Big Easy Café.

**Coffeehouse on Campus?**
There are two PJ's coffeehouses on Willow Street, in Willow Hall, and in Percival Stern Hall on the academic quad.

**Favorite Things to Do:**
IM sports or getting some friends together to throw a Frisbee or a football; a lot of people go out to parties, local clubs and bars; sunbathing is done pretty much all year round, as is working out at Reily.

**Popular Places to Chill:**
There isn't really a core meeting place for students. People go to the Pavilion or mostly hang out in PJ's on Willow.

### Computers

**High-Speed Network?** Yes

**Wireless Network?** Yes (it works everywhere except for some of the older dorms).

**24-Hour Labs:** Willow Cyber Café

**Main Labs:**
Richardson Lab, Room 201: Technology Services' main computing lab; has on-site lab assistants to help with computer issues, and offers color and black and white printing.
Willow Cyber Café – 22 computers are located in the Willow multipurpose room, right next to PJ's Coffee.

**Charge to Print?** $0.10 black and white pages, $1.00 color pages; each student has a $25 printing allowance and printing is billed through a debit of the student ID card.

## The College Prowler Take
### ON FACILITIES

Back in the good old days, Tulane had a Subway, Pizza Hut, and Chick-fil-A. That's all gone now because of UC construction. Simply put, the Pavilion—the other main alternative—doesn't cut it, and many students do not like it because of its lack of restaurant choices and the cramped layout of the bookstore. Once the UC construction is complete, there will be a much better place for students to gather on campus; with a March 2006 opening date, however, current and upcoming students are going to have to cope for awhile. Some residence halls (especially those for freshmen) and other buildings are in obvious need of renovations, but, overall, the University seems to be continually improving its facilities. Most buildings on campus, especially on the academic quad, are beautiful and go well with the green spaces and the large trees surrounding them.

## Students Speak Out
### ON FACILITIES

"**The facilities here are superb. However, with the renovation of the University Center, it has posed a bit of an inconvenience.**"

Q "**Some of the facilities are amazing**, like the Reily Center and the business school. Others are horrible. The freshman dorms and the dance/theater department definitely get the shaft on financing."

Q "Compared to the other schools in the area, **the facilities are really nice**."

Q "The facilities for athletes, technology, etc. are excellent and **the new student center is under construction**."

Q "I'm at Reily every day. It's the best gym I've ever had a membership to. **There are a lot of good classes,** like abs and such, that are free."

**B+**

The College Prowler™ Grade on
## Facilities: B+

A high Facilities grade indicates that the campus is aesthetically pleasing and well-maintained; facilities are state-of-the-art, and libraries are exceptional. Other determining factors include the quality of both athletic and student centers and an abundance of things to do on campus.

# Campus Dining

## Students Speak Out
ON CAMPUS DINING

"Bruff really is not that great. It gets old real fast; but then again, that is the case with any college. The Pavilion is great. I am obsessed with Einstein's Bagels."

Q "There isn't much variety on campus and **the campus stores offer very little selection**. It's also expensive to eat at places other than Bruff. They make is seem like you're getting a good deal, but you aren't."

Q "Food on campus is pretty good, though it can become repetitive. **Late-night dining is good at the Big Easy Café**, though the name is quite cheesy. Dining halls are decent and fairly clean."

Q "The food is substantial, but if you want to eat healthy, your options are very limited. **Better get used to sandwiches!**"

Q "The food on campus is decent. **Bruff has its good days and bad days**. The best on-campus establishment is the Drawing Board that's in the architecture building."

## The Lowdown
ON CAMPUS DINING

**Freshman Meal Plan Requirement?**
Yes

**Meal Plan Average Cost:**
$1,685

**24-Hour On-Campus Eating?**
Nothing is open 24/7, but there's always something available. If the Big Easy isn't open, then Bruff or something in the Bubble is.

**Student Favorites:**
Le Gourmet, Einstein Brothers' Bagels

### Did You Know?

Students have the option of putting Greenbuck$ or debit money onto their Tulane cards to eat in the Pavilion. (It's best to go with the debit option, because you can only spend Greenbuck$ on food and you can't use them for laundry, coffee at PJ's, or at the bookstore, as you can with debit.) There are also Kosher meal plans available.

## COLLEGE PROWLER

Want to know more about campus dining? For a detailed listing of all dining facilities on campus, check out the College Prowler book on Tulane available at *www.collegeprowler.com*.

## The College Prowler Take
### ON CAMPUS DINING

No one you talk to on campus is going to tell you that Bruff is the best and has really great food. Most will say simply that it is food, and you eat it not because it's good, but because you must eat. For what it's worth, Bruff Commons is all-you-can-eat dining, and the other eateries on campus are set up so that meal dollars (or "Greenbuck$") buy essentially the same things as real cash. However, for the most versatility, it's best to choose the "debit" option over the Greenbuck system—you can use the cash you put on your student ID to buy much more than food this way, so it's a lot more convenient (and still safer than carrying cash).

**The College Prowler™ Grade on**
## Campus Dining: C+

Our grade on Campus Dining addresses the quality of both school-owned dining halls and independent on-campus restaurants as well as the price, availability, and variety of food.

# Campus Housing

## The Lowdown
### ON CAMPUS HOUSING

**Undergrads on Campus:**
55%

**Dormitories:**
12

**University-Owned Apartments:**
1

**Room Types:**
Single; Double; Super Single; 2, 4, and 8 person suite; 3, 4, and 5 bedroom apartments

**You Get:**
Carpeted rooms, cable TV/Internet/telephone hookup, kitchen facilities, common areas, and air conditioning

**Bed Type:**
Some have extra-long twin, other have twin beds, and Leadership Village has lofts.

**Available for Rent:**
Micro-Fridges

**Cleaning Service?**
JaniKing, the cleaning service on campus, cleans the community bathrooms daily and the suite bathrooms every other day.

### Did You Know?

The dorms New Doris and Zemurray were recently destroyed, and are now being constructed into new co-ed freshman dorms for future classes. After that construction, there will be seven dorms for freshman on campus (and the five still for upperclassmen).

### Students Speak Out
ON CAMPUS HOUSING

"JL, Warren, and Phelps are very nice dorms. However, Sharp and Monroe are the center of freshman life. It's a give-take situation."

Q "The dorms are gross but so much fun, a totally perfect college experience. I would **avoid the all-girl dorms** [JL and Warren] and the honors dorm [Butler]."

Q "Sharp and Monroe are the two major freshman dorms [co-ed], and **Sharp is slightly nicer**. For girls, the all-girls dorm JL is very nice."

Q "**The dorms are crap**. I can't believe that I have to pay to live in them. The bathrooms are disgusting, and the rooms are not soundproof at all. To prove my point, there was puke outside my room in Butler for two weeks before it was cleaned up, and when they did clean it, it was one in the morning."

Q "I think the dorms are fairly typical. The dorms to avoid are Monroe and Sharp. JL and Warren are nice for women, and **New Doris is the only freshman dorm with suite-style rooms**."

### The College Prowler Take
ON CAMPUS HOUSING

Students have few good words to say about Monroe and Sharp. They are old, ugly, and pretty gross, but there's a big social factor about living in these two dorms. JL and Warren are nice all-girls dorms; they're quiet and most of the rooms have sinks in them, but they're usually less social than the co-ed dorms, and you have to go out of your way to meet boys. For upperclassmen, Irby and Phelps are the two dorms that people hate the most. These look like motels because the doors to the rooms face outside, and they are older buildings. You are guaranteed housing only for freshman year, so don't be surprised if you get waitlisted for housing your sophomore and junior year (last year, there were more than 500 people on the housing waitlist!). Tulane students largely think the dorms are gross, but livable.

### The College Prowler™ Grade on
### Campus Housing: C

A high Campus Housing grade indicates that dorms are clean, well-maintained, and spacious. Other determining factors include variety of dorms, proximity to classes, and social atmosphere.

# Diversity

## The Lowdown
ON DIVERSITY

**Native American:** 0.47%

**Asian American:** 5.45%

**African American:** 9.85%

**Hispanic:** 3.88%

**White:** 79.55%

**International:** 2.65%

**Out-of-State:** 64.62%

### Economic Status
You cannot go to school here without a scholarship and not be rich. With tuition and room and board costing around $40,000 a year, Tulane is extremely expensive. However, a lot of students here are on scholarship, so there is a certain population of middle- and lower-class students.

### Gay Tolerance
MOSAIC is a gay-straight alliance club, and the dominant group on campus for promoting tolerance based on sexual orientation. New Orleans and Tulane are both fairly liberal climates, so sexuality isn't a broad problem on campus.

### Political Activity
On average, Tulane is an apathetic campus when it comes to politics. However, there is a large following of both the College Republicans and Democrats, and the USG (Undergraduate Student Government) is taken seriously. If you're into politics, there are a lot of groups you can get involved with. There is the newspaper, *The Tulane Hullabaloo*, which is pretty liberal—especially the magazine. There is also *The Arcade*, that comes out every other week. *The Hullabaloo* always devotes space to cover the weekly USG meeting, and has had articles about local and national politics. Tulane is mostly liberal, but if you are a conservative, you'll definitely find a big niche of your own.

## Students Speak Out
ON DIVERSITY

> "Tulane's campus is somewhat diverse. I think its better than most state schools."

> "I find it has **spurts of diversity**, but a lot of the same kind of people."

> "Tulane is not very diverse at all, unless you are talking in terms of diverse parts of the country. Most of **my classes aren't ethnically diverse**, and in general, the campus isn't either."

> "A lot of the literature may say it's diverse, but it's generally made up of **a lot of well-off white kids from New York or New Jersey**. It's nothing that takes away from the campus, and there are multicultural organizations, but if you're looking for a melting pot of a campus, then Tulane isn't exactly that."

> "Although Tulane tries to portray itself as a diverse university, the majority of the students are upper-class white guys and girls. There are a lot of students that **come from countries all over the world, too.**"

## The College Prowler Take
### ON DIVERSITY

Does Tulane have a lot of diversity? The way you answer this question all depends on your past experiences. Naturally, if you went to an elitist private academy with less than a handful of minorities enrolled, you'll get here and see a couple of African Americans and Indian students, and will be amazed at the amount of diversity. However, if you went to an inner-city high school or a public high school where the white population was slowly becoming a minority, you'll come to Tulane and think this is the largest white population at a school you've seen in a long time. After all, the white population is 80 percent of the total makeup. Racially and ethnically, this school is lacking in diversity. The diversity of Tulane comes from the amount of kids hailing from all over the country. It is a type of diversity that is only found in this part of the country, and, in a sense, the city itself makes up for Tulane's lack of diversity.

**The College Prowler™ Grade on**
### Diversity: D+

A high grade in Diversity indicates that ethnic minorities and international students have a notable presence on campus and that students of different economic backgrounds, religious beliefs, and sexual preferences are well-represented.

# Guys & Girls

## The Lowdown
### ON GUYS & GIRLS

**Women Undergrads:** 53%

**Men Undergrads:** 47%

### Birth Control Available?
ECP, Depo-Provera injections, and birth control pills are available by prescription in the women's clinic. Condoms are also available in the men's heath clinic.

### Social Scene
People love to drink here, so a lot of the social scene revolves around one of the many bars near campus. Students attend frat parties in the fall in order to meet new people. However, there are a lot of groups that are into music and go to concerts, and there are some people that are into art or politics and do things with their group of friends. Basically, your social scene revolves around what group of people you hang out with most,

### Hookups or Relationships?
Both. A lot of hookups happen all year 'round, but a lot of people have boyfriends/girlfriends that go to different schools, and there are a lot of relationships on campus, as well. (A word of advice: 33 percent of people on campus have an STD—this is above the national average, and a good thing to keep in mind.)

### Dress Code

A lot of girls dress up practically every day, and it's an unstated rule that the official Tulane shoe is the flip-flop. The bookstore sells Tulane flip-flops, and guys and girls alike own a pair or two (they are very comfortable). A lot of girls carry around big tote bags as backpacks, and are constantly seen talking on cell phones or smoking cigarettes.

The average, straight, college guy has a pretty bland collection of clothes, and they all dress the same. There are a lot of gay and metrosexual guys at Tulane, so you'll often see a guy walking down McAlister with shoes on that you wish you owned. It's also cool to wear your collar flipped up, and Abercrombie is really popular with the preppy kids.

Then there are kids that come to class every day in jeans and a hoodie with their hair everywhere.; there are some who blatantly don't care about their appearance, but a lot do. So, if you're looking for a girl or guy, you'll probably need to go the extra mile when getting ready, because there's a lot of competition.

### The College Prowler Take
**ON GUYS & GIRLS**

Tulane is not an ugly campus by any means, but there is a minority of really, radiantly hot babes. Most guys look average and have an average wardrobe—the most attractive men on campus are gay. The girls tend to dress up more than at your average college campus, and put a lot of effort into their appearance. There are a lot of cool and interesting people to meet, and a lot like to have a good time along with studying and being typical, intellectual college students. There are more hookups than actual committed relationships, but you'll find a lot of people with significant others that live elsewhere. There's not an abundance of nerdy kids or really preppy kids—you see a lot of everything. No matter what your type is, you'll find something that you like at Tulane.

### Students Speak Out
**ON GUYS & GIRLS**

Q "Beware, most of the guys at Tulane seem hot … until you get to know them. Then it's a different story."

Q "Not the most attractive student body. Some girls are more ritzy than others. I would say the majority are pretty laid-back with image … that may not be right. Put it this way, I'm not concerned about looking good every day, and **there's no pressure to, so it's nice**."

Q "Guys tend to be smart and pushy, and it seems that all **the hot, cute guys are quickly snatched up**. The girls are overall very cute."

Q "Like anywhere else, there are nice people as well as jerks. The guys are not hot, but there's a small population of hotties. **Most of the girls look anorexic**."

Q "Every now and then you'll find an interesting, smart, good-looking guy. But, in general, the combination is scarce. **Most of the girls are spoiled rich kids** with way too many clothes and too much free time."

**B-**

**B+**

The College Prowler™ Grade on
### Guys: B-

A high grade for Guys indicates that the male population on campus is attractive, smart, friendly, and engaging, and that the school has a decent ratio of guys to girls.

The College Prowler™ Grade on
### Girls: B+

A high grade for Girls not only implies that the women on campus are attractive, smart, friendly, and engaging, but also that there is a fair ratio of girls to guys.

# Athletics

## The Lowdown
### ON ATHLETICS

**Men's Teams:**
Baseball
Basketball
Cross Country
Football
Golf
Tennis
Track

**Women's Teams:**
Basketball
Volleyball
Soccer
Cross Country
Track
Golf
Tennis
Swimming & Diving
Track

**Athletic Division:**
NCAA Division I

**Conference:**
C-USA

**School Mascot:**
Riptide the Pelican, Green Wave

**Getting Tickets:**
Tickets are free to students, and easy to get.

**Fields:**
Tad Gormley Stadium and the Superdome – Football
Brown, Newcomb, UC Quads – Intramural sports/club sport practices
Fogelman Arena – Basketball
Turchin Stadium, Zephyr Field – Baseball
Goldring Tennis Stadium – Tennis
George G. "Sunny" Westfeldt, Jr. Facility – Soccer, club sports

### Club Sports
Ballroom Dancing, Baseball, Capoeira, Cricket, Dodge Ball, Fencing, Field Hockey, Gymnastics, Ice Hockey, Judo, Karate, Men's and Women's Lacrosse, Martial Arts, Rock Climbing, Rowing, Rugby, Volleyball, Water Polo, Wrestling

### Intramurals (IMs)
Flag Football, Indoor and Outdoor Soccer, Volleyball, Dodge Ball, Racquetball, 3-on-3 Basketball, Basketball, Softball, Ping-Pong

### Most Popular Sports
Football is probably the most popular sport on campus, followed by men's basketball.

### Overlooked Teams
Most athletic teams at Tulane are overlooked. In fact, the administration almost cut out athletics entirely for the 2003-2004 school year.

## Students Speak Out
### ON ATHLETICS

"Varsity sports have little momentum, but some students show up to the games. People participate in IM sports, but it's not huge."

Q "Varsity and IM sports are as big as you make them. **A lot of people get really into it**, but if you're not, it doesn't matter."

Q "Sports get less support from students than other colleges. **There are a lot of intramural sports**."

Q "**Varsity sports are not so good** and IM sports are probably worse."

Q "Club sports are the best way to go. **They're more organized then IMs**, but less intense than varsity. I've met some of my closest friends through playing club sports."

## The College Prowler Take
### ON ATHLETICS

Tulane's athletic department almost got shut down a few years ago, so that gives you an idea of how widely supported and successful the teams are. The baseball and women's basketball teams are some of the best in their divisions, but never have won a championship. Some of the University's baseball and football games are played in the Superdome, the stadium for the city's football team (the Saints), and there is usually a good showing for games that are held there. A lot of students are involved in club sports because there are so many more sports offered in club than varsity, and they are much more laid-back. Intramurals are fun to participate in, but these tend to be much less organized, and they do not last very long.

**B-**

**The College Prowler™ Grade on**
## Athletics: B-

A high grade in Athletics indicates that students have school spirit, that sports programs are respected, that games are well-attended, and that intramurals are a prominent part of student life.

# Greek Life

## The Lowdown
### ON GREEK LIFE

**Number of Fraternities:**
15

**Number of Sororities:**
11

**Undergrad Men in Fraternities:**
19%

**Undergrad Women in Sororities:**
33%

**Multicultural Colonies:**
Alpha Kappa Alpha, Alpha Phi Alpha, Delta Sigma Theta, Delta Xi Nu

### Did You Know?

There is a no-hazing policy at Tulane.

## Students Speak Out
### ON GREEK LIFE

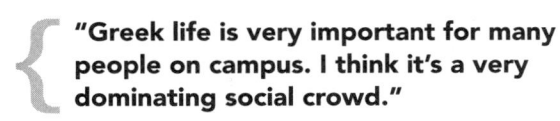

*"Greek life is very important for many people on campus. I think it's a very dominating social crowd."*

Q "It dominates my social scene because I let it, and **all of my good friends are in the same sorority and frat**, but one could just as easily be a part of the same social scene without being in a sorority or frat. Two of my good friends didn't pledge, and they're out with us every night."

Q "For me, Greek life does dominate the social scene, however **there are plenty of other things to do**. There are lots of students that are not involved in Greek [life], but I feel like you gain access and knowledge of more parties."

Q "It doesn't dominate at all. If you're in it, you can get into it, and have fun with it. If you're not, it really doesn't matter. **It can be a personal preference**, which is cool."

Q "I am involved in Greek life, and I love it. You can put as much time into it as you want, and it's not too intense. **It doesn't dominate**, and if you don't want to go Greek, then it won't hinder your social life."

**COLLEGE PROWLER™**

Planning to go Greek? Pick up the College Prowler guide on Tulane at *www.collegeprowler.com* and find out which house is best for you.

## The College Prowler Take
### ON GREEK LIFE

If you go Greek, it will likely be a dominant part of your college life, but if you decide that it isn't your thing, the Greek scene won't affect you at all. There is the option of going to frat and sorority parties during the fall semester, and the opportunity to rush and pledge in the spring semester. Other than being bombarded with people wearing Greek T-shirts, flip-flops, pins, etc., there is not much Greek on the Tulane campus. People who are in fraternities and sororities are very loyal to their organization, and make it a priority right up there with schoolwork. At Tulane, you won't feel pressured to join one of these organizations, and your social life isn't going to suffer if you choose to avoid pledging. Being in a sport or a club can provide almost the same network as any sorority or fraternity, and can be just as fun.

**B**

**The College Prowler™ Grade on**
### Greek Life: B

A high grade in Greek Life indicates that sororities and fraternities are not only present, but also active on campus. Other determining factors include the variety of houses available and the respect the Greek community receives from the rest of the campus.

# Drug Scene

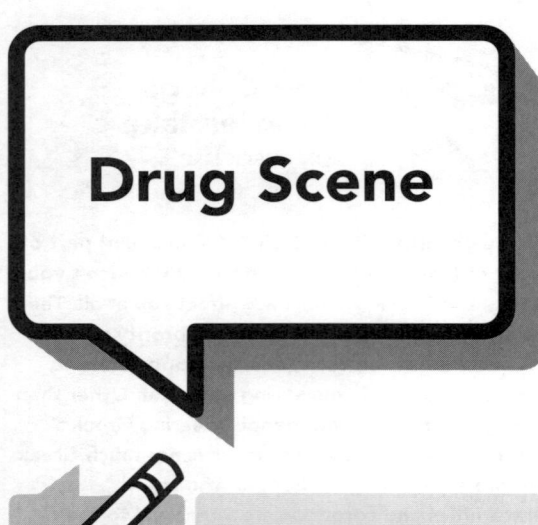

## The Lowdown
ON DRUG SCENE

**Most Prevalent Drugs on Campus:**
Alcohol, Marijuana, and Cocaine

**Liquor-Related Referrals:** 46

**Liquor-Related Arrests:** 0

**Drug-Related Referrals:** 34

**Drug-Related Arrests:** 15

**Drug Counseling Programs:**
Peer Health Advocates of Tulane (PHAT) – PHATs are Tulane student volunteers who provide information about abstinence, safe sex and contraception, nutrition, alcohol and drugs, and other health issues.

## Students Speak Out
ON DRUG SCENE

"If you want something, it's accessible. If you don't want to do them, it's not a big deal."

Q "**There is a lot of alcohol**. Marijuana is present, but less prevalent than alcohol. A select few do cocaine, but it is very easy to avoid it."

Q "It is definitely there, but not plainly out in the open. When you go to any expensive private school, **you get kids spending money on drugs**."

Q "**Drugs are prevalent**, but in no way an intricate part of social life. As long as you know how to drink, you're good."

Q "I hear a lot of talk about a lot of people doing coke, but I haven't seen it. **There's a pretty big dealing scene**, mostly pot, and there are a lot of stoners here."

## The College Prowler Take
ON DRUG SCENE

There are not that many drugs that are heavily used on campus. However, alcohol is considered a drug, and a lot of students abuse it. Tulane EMS is constantly picking up people for alcohol poisoning, and there are plenty of drunks walking around on Thursday, Friday, and Saturday nights. If you don't like harder drugs, they are easily avoided, but trying to avoid the prevalence of alcohol is nearly impossible. An important thing to remember, especially at Tulane, is that you can't assume who's involved in the drug scene. With any rich school, students have more money to buy drugs, and intelligent, affluent students are just as likely as anyone else to be buying or selling drugs.

**The College Prowler™ Grade on**
## Drug Scene: C+

A high grade on Drug Scene indicates that drugs are not a noticeable part of campus life; drug use is not visible, and no pressure to use them seems to exist.

# Overall Experience

> "At first, I hated this school. I thought that the people were shallow and drunk, the professors were below par, and I didn't like the New Orleans lifestyle at all. I couldn't find anyone who listened to music, or liked going to the same things as I did. My first semester was really rough. However, once we got back from Christmas break, everything changed for the better. **I got more involved in things that I liked, and I changed my major**."

## Students Speak Out
### ON OVERALL EXPERIENCE

> "As far as New Orleans is concerned, I would be nowhere else. The name counts in school, so go to the best place you can. I wish I were at Harvard, but I couldn't take the weather or afford to live there."

> "My experience has been very good. Difficult at times, amazing at others—a wide range of new experiences and emotions, which I think is a wonderful thing. **Overall, I'm very happy to be here**. I think it's an ideal place to be for college for four years, and then move on. Coming here has enabled me to explore my interests in an inspiring, encouraging environment with little or no discouraging people or attitudes."

> "I have truly enjoyed my first year at Tulane; opportunities were thrown my way, and **I have met some very interesting people**. With my major in international relations and international development, I could not ask for more from a university."

> "I've really enjoyed my experiences thus far. No school is going to be perfect. I've definitely met some very interesting people, and the setting of New Orleans as a college town makes it an amazing experience. **There's so much to do if you look for it**. I'm happy where I am."

## The College Prowler Take
### ON OVERALL EXPERIENCE

It takes a very intelligent and well-balanced person to attend Tulane. The nightlife and 24/7 party scene can tempt students to blow off classes and just have a good time. It is quite hard to find the right balance between partying and schoolwork. Contrary to popular belief, this isn't high school glorified; college is actually going to be a lot of work. Even the so-called "blow off classes" that you take for humanities credit will make you read one long-winded book after the other, and write 10 to 15 page research papers by the end of the semester.

You'll never sit at home on a weekend for lack of something to do, and holidays—especially Halloween and (obviously) Mardi Gras—are some of the best parts about living in New Orleans. The live jazz music and the food is also fantastic—if Bruff's food tasted anything like it does out in the city, the average student's weight would rival that of Anna Nicole Smith (pre-TrimSpa!).

Not only will you get a well-balanced education at Tulane, but you will also meet some of your best friends, become involved in things you never could have imagined at home, be a leader of a group when you never had that chance in high school, and be introduced to a new, unique environment and culture that cannot be found in any other place in the country. There is no other school like Tulane, and there is no other city like New Orleans.

# University of Miami

PO Box 248025, Coral Gables, FL 33124
www.miami.edu          (305) 284-4323

**DISTANCE TO...**
Orlando: 242 mi.
Tampa Bay: 256 mi.
Key Largo: 58 mi.
Savannah: 495 mi.

"The academics at UM have been steadily improving since the '70s, back when it was known to beach-loving hippies as 'Suntan U.'"

**Total Enrollment:**
9,184

**Top 10% of High School Class:**
44%

**Average GPA:**
4.0

**Acceptance Rate:**
60%

**Tuition:**
$27,840

**SAT Range (25th-75th Percentile)**
| Verbal | Math | Total |
|---|---|---|
| 550 – 660 | 580 – 680 | 1120 – 1340 |

**ACT Range (25th-75th Percentile)**
| Verbal | Math | Total |
|---|---|---|
| 25-30 | 24-30 | 25-30 |

**Most Popular Majors:**
23% Business, Management, Marketing
12% Visual and Performing Arts
10% Biological and Biomedical Sciences
10% Communication and Journalism
8% Social Sciences

**Students also applied to:***
Boston University
Duke University
Florida State University
New York University
University of Florida

*For more school info check out www.collegeprowler.com

## Table of Contents

| | |
|---|---|
| Academics | 633 |
| Local Atmosphere | 635 |
| Safety & Security | 636 |
| Facilities | 638 |
| Campus Dining | 640 |
| Campus Housing | 641 |
| Diversity | 643 |
| Guys & Girls | 645 |
| Athletics | 646 |
| Greek Life | 648 |
| Drug Scene | 650 |
| Overall Experience | 651 |

## College Prowler Report Card

| | |
|---|---|
| Academics | B |
| Local Atmosphere | A |
| Safety & Security | B |
| Facilities | B+ |
| Campus Dining | C+ |
| Campus Housing | B- |
| Diversity | A- |
| Guys | B+ |
| Girls | A- |
| Athletics | A |
| Greek Life | B+ |
| Drug Scene | B- |

# Academics

## The Lowdown
ON ACADEMICS

**Degrees Awarded:**
Bachelor, Master, Doctorate

**Undergraduate Schools:**
Architecture, Arts and Sciences, Business, Communication, Education, Engineering, Music, Nursing

**Full-time Faculty:**
2,152

**Faculty with Terminal Degree:**
96%

**Student-to-Faculty Ratio:**
13:1

**AP Test Score Requirements:**
Possible credit for scores of 3, 4, or 5

**IB Test Score Requirements:**
Possible credit for scores of 4, 5, 6, or 7

**Special Degree Options**
Dual-Degree Honors Programs: Biomedical Engineering, Marine Geology, Physical Therapy, Medicine, Latin American Studies

**Honors Program in Medicine**
Six-Year Accelerated Bachelor of Science and Doctorate of Medicine

**Sample Academic Clubs**
Florida Engineering Society, Filmmakers' Association, German Club, Honors Student Association, National Broadcasting Society, School of Architecture Student Council

### Did You Know?

Feel trapped in your dorm room? Many students, armed with wireless Internet on their laptops, head outside to study by the lake or under a tree.

At the end of every semester, students receive surveys asking them to rank each of their professors in various categories. The results are tallied and posted on the school network to help students select their courses.

Teaching assistants are rare in most courses at UM. Even freshmen lecture classes are almost always taught by full-time faculty members.

**Best Places to Study:**
Library, dorm study lounges, University Center, outside

## Students Speak Out
### ON ACADEMICS

> "The teachers vary by department. For the most part, however, the material covered in classes is intriguing. That is, when you can comprehend what is being taught."

Q "Most of the teachers are extremely well-prepared about the classes they are teaching. Only one teacher I've had really has not been geared for UM because of his teaching methods. **The classes have been very interesting** throughout the years, and I feel that I have learned a lot."

Q "The teachers at UM are, for the most part, pretty cool. There are, of course, some that are better than the others. I find that **all the teachers are accessible**, and that is a positive. They are also more than willing to help with any questions."

Q "The teachers here are very friendly, but you can make them into whatever you want. **If you want a friend, that's an option**, and so is being the person in the back of the room, learning in your own quiet way. Either way, they will stimulate your mind. Most classes are very interesting, and some professors are very entertaining in their teaching methods."

Q "The teachers are willing to spend a lot of time with you personally, maybe because this is a private school. **Classes are interesting once you get past the intro level** if you're doing something you like, but they're pretty good about AP credits here, so it's easy to AP-out of intro level courses."

## The College Prowler Take
### ON ACADEMICS

Back in the 1970s, the University of Miami was known as "Suntan U." Fun-loving hippies flocked from around the country to party on their parents' money for four years. Since that era ended, UM has done a great job in climbing its way into the top tier of American colleges. Although Miami is still a great party town, most of UM's students are here with academics in mind, as well as nightlife and beaches. As a school becomes more prestigious, it builds a strong faculty, and that's exactly what UM has done. Students seem to like their professors, even if they complain regularly about homework and exams. Although complaints about the amount of work and grading are common, it's rare to hear anyone claim that a professor does not know the subject he's teaching.

It's not hard to see that UM is never going to be one of the strongest colleges in the country academically. Harvard, Princeton, and Yale don't need to worry about losing professors to UM, unless they really hate the New England cold. But, Miami is building a great university by combining academics with other aspects of college life. It's safe to say, then, that while academics are not hurting UM, they're not the best thing about it. The professors are mostly good, and there are a few great ones, but overall it feels like a place that's going to teach you what books say you need to know, not necessarily what you actually want to know.

**The College Prowler™ Grade on**
## Academics: B

A high Academics grade generally indicates that professors are knowledgeable, accessible, and genuinely interested in their students' welfare. Other determining factors include class size, how well professors communicate, and whether or not classes are engaging.

# Local Atmosphere

## The Lowdown
ON LOCAL ATMOSPHERE

**Region:**
Southeast

**City, State:**
Coral Gables, Florida

**Setting:**
Coastal

**Distance from Orlando:**
3 hours, 30 minutes

**Distance from Key West:**
3 hours, 30 minutes

**Points of Interest:**
South Beach, Coconut Grove, Sunset Place, Florida Keys, Everglades, Lowe Art Museum, American Airlines Arena, Bayside, Pro Player Stadium, Vizcaya Mansion, Miami Jai Alai, Little Havana, Venetian Pool, Metro Zoo

**Major Sports Teams:**
Dolphins (football), Marlins (baseball), Heat (basketball), Panthers (hockey)

**City Websites:**
*http://ci.miami.fl.us*
*http://miami.citysearch.com*
*http://www.digitalcity.com/southflorida*

## Students Speak Out
ON LOCAL ATMOSPHERE

"There are a few neighborhoods to avoid, but it's like any town, anywhere in America. I feel perfectly safe here."

Q "**Miami is a very fast-paced city**. There is always something to do. I would recommend going to Coconut Grove many times, South Beach once, and always avoid Grand Avenue. Coconut Grove is always a fun place to shop, eat, and catch a movie. South Beach is fun to people-watch, and spend $100 on your individual meal!"

Q "**There are areas where it is dangerous**, and you should not stray from main streets in certain areas, however, for the most part, the city is definitely a safe place."

Q "The town is **perfect for a college campus**. It has its great spots, good spots, and the ones you need to avoid as well. Other universities are present, and are a noticeable factor in the community. The city atmosphere provides a good cultural, as well as career-oriented, atmosphere."

Q "The atmosphere here in Miami is great. **It's very lively, and there are a lot of things to do** all the time—for example clubbing on South Beach, dining out, going to the beach, going to football games, and shopping (Sunset Place and the Grove). FIU is the other big school in the greater Miami area."

## The College Prowler Take
### ON LOCAL ATMOSPHERE

It's hard not to be impressed by the aura of Miami. Whether it's the authentic Cuban culture in Little Havana, or the neon frenzy of South Beach, Miami has plenty to do and see. Sports fans will be impressed by the mixture of professional and collegiate athletics, while entertainment-savvy students will love the music and art scenes. There is definitely not a shortage of things to do, and few cities can match Miami's 24-hour atmosphere. There are things to watch out for, including some bad neighborhoods and insane traffic, but the positives far outweigh the negatives when it comes to Miami's atmosphere. One of the negatives of having such a great city around the campus is that a true "college town" has never been born. Colleges in rural areas usually tend to have small cities spring up around them to accommodate the thousands of students. But, with so much to do around town, Coral Gables seems to be carrying on daily without thinking too much about the big college next door.

The College Prowler™ Grade on
### Local Atmosphere: A

A high Local Atmosphere grade indicates that the area surrounding campus is safe and scenic. Other factors include nearby attractions, proximity to other schools, and the town's attitude toward students.

# Safety & Security

## The Lowdown
### ON SAFETY & SECURITY

**Security Phone:**
(305) 284-6666

**Health Center Office Hours:**
Monday, Tuesday, Wednesday, and Friday 8:30 a.m.-5 p.m., Thursday 9 a.m.-5 p.m.

**Safety Services:**
RAD, Adopt-A-Cop, escort, security request, emergency phones, silent witness

### Did You Know?

After 10 p.m., no one is allowed into the residential colleges unless they are a resident or are signed in by a resident.

There are over 70 emergency phones located throughout campus. The phones are easy to spot because of their blue lights, and they dial directly to the Department of Public Safety.

## Students Speak Out
### ON SAFETY & SECURITY

"Security is maintained at a fairly high level. Check-in booths at all entrances ensure safety. You must swipe your ID at three spots before you enter your dorm after 10 p.m., so there is a real sense of safety, especially at night."

Q "**The campus is very secure**. There are several places on campus that have emergency phones, in case an emergency ever arises. Also, police are always walking or driving around campus. After 10 p.m., each student entering a residential college must present their ID to make sure they live in that college. People that do not have proper identification must be signed in prior to entering a residential college. I have always felt very safe at the University."

Q "I believe that **security on campus does vary based on gender**. If you are a guy, it does not really matter, however some girls feel that walking alone at night is not the most safe thing to do. I believe that the campus is pretty safe; I have not felt insecure yet."

Q "I feel very safe and secure on this campus, regardless of the incident reports we get about crimes. They're very rare, and **I haven't heard of a problem in months**. It is a big city, so there is some need for concern, but I feel very safe here."

Q "I would say that the security on the UM campus is **above average** and that our campus is in a safe neighborhood. I'm not worried by e-mails regarding crimes that happened on campus. Actually, I'm proud to have our school post warnings like that to let us be aware of what's going on."

## The College Prowler Take
### ON SAFETY & SECURITY

The majority of students on campus feel safe walking around at night, and there are tons of cops and security guards, as well as emergency phones in case there is ever a problem. Even though Miami can certainly be a dangerous city at times, UM is located in Coral Gables, which is a fairly nice neighborhood. Still, this doesn't hide the fact that several incidences occurred on campus recently, and people were talking about it. The crimes that were committed, which included burglary and sexual assault, were recognized because of UM's policy of e-mailing the entire student body whenever a serious crime occurs on campus.

Although UM officials are very concerned with crime on campus and heavily investigate any threats, it's important for students to know that crime is, at times, an issue. The most important thing is that an overwhelming majority of students feel safe on campus, and that there is very little risk of extremely serious crimes (rape, manslaughter, murder, etc.).

**B**

The College Prowler™ Grade on
### Safety & Security: B

A high grade in Safety & Security means that students generally feel safe, campus police are visible, blue-light phones and escort services are readily available, and safety precautions are not overly necessary.

# Facilities

**Computers**
**High-Speed Network?** Yes
**Wireless Network?** Yes
**Number of Labs:** over 60 total labs
**Numbers of Computers:** 218
**24-Hour Labs:** None (except during exams)
**Charge to Print?** No

## The Lowdown
ON FACILITIES

**Student Center:**
The Whitten University Center (UC)

**Athletic Center:**
Wellness Center, Hecht Athletic Center, IM Fields

**Libraries:**
12

**Movie Theater on Campus?**
Yes, Bill Cosford Cinema, Memorial Building

**Bowling on Campus?**
No

**Bar on Campus?**
Yes, the Rathskellar; it also hosts live bands and comedians.

**Coffeehouse on Campus?**
Yes. The Coffee Company (Starbucks), Hurricane Food Court (closes early though).

**Popular Places to Chill:**
The UC, The Rat, The Rock, UC Patio, Storm Surge Cafe

### Favorite Things to Do
Some students gather in the Storm Surge Café at the UC to shoot pool or play Ping-Pong. Others enjoy working out at the Wellness Center or playing sports on the massive IM fields. Of course, there are also numerous Division I-A sporting events on and off campus, all of which are free to UM students with their ID cards.

**COLLEGE PROWLER**

Wanna know more? For a detailed description of all buildings on campus, check out the College Prowler book on the University of Miami available at www.collegeprowler.com.

## Students Speak Out
### ON FACILITIES

"The facilities, which span all interests, are all top-notch. The Wellness Center is top-of-the-line, sporting amenities for any activity, the bookstore, University Center, and dining halls are all clean and technologically sound."

Q "**The buildings are uglier than sin**, but the landscape makes up for them. Inside, most of the major buildings are very nicely decorated and kept up, and you forget what the outside looks like. The new buildings are nicely-designed."

Q "The facilities are very nice. The Wellness Center offers students the opportunity to lift weights, run or swim, and play basketball, volleyball, or racquetball. **The library has a wide variety of sources for students to access**. The Whitten University Center is a nice place for students to just sit around and relax. The Storm Surge Café is a place where students can hang out, play billiards, and eat. The UC also has a lap pool for students to work on their tan."

Q "The facilities on campus are **ridiculously nice**, being either brand new or newly renovated. For instance, our Wellness Center is under five years old and is unbelievable. Computers aren't performance-oriented, so they're as technically advanced as necessary, and a little more beyond that."

Q "The fitness facilities are outstanding, some of the best I have ever seen. While I usually prefer to do my workouts outside, **the gym is equipped with everything someone would need**—indoor track, indoor pool, sauna, classrooms for any class-type workouts like yoga, racquetball courts, volleyball courts, the fully-equipped weight and cardio section, and a juice bar. The student center is adequate, with many places to eat or talk to friends."

## The College Prowler Take
### ON FACILITIES

Although most of the classroom buildings around UM are hideously ugly, the insides are generally decent and the new buildings are very nice. The highlight of UM's facilities is, by far, the Wellness Center—a huge gym located next to the dorms where most freshmen live. The building stays open until midnight on weeknights, allowing for late-night games of basketball, squash, or racquetball, which can provide a great study break. The UC is a nice enough place, although it lacks some cool features that are present at other schools, like a bowling alley. There is a movie theater on one corner of campus, which shows relatively new movies free to students, as well as art-house fare. Students seem to appreciate the campus facilities, especially the Wellness Center, but any new renovations to the UC or campus buildings would certainly be welcome. The good news is that UM is always making changes and improvements, and if something is getting rundown or old, it's likely to be updated soon.

**B+**

The College Prowler™ Grade on
### Facilities: B+

A high Facilities grade indicates that the campus is aesthetically pleasing and well-maintained; facilities are state-of-the-art, and libraries are exceptional. Other determining factors include the quality of both athletic and student centers and an abundance of things to do on campus.

# Campus Dining

## The Lowdown
ON CAMPUS DINING

**Freshman Meal Plan Requirement?**
Yes

**24-Hour On-Campus Eating?**
No

**Student Favorites:**
Subway, Sbarro's, The Rathskellar, Taco Bell, Jamba Juice

**Meal Plan Average Cost:**
$3,318 per year

### Did You Know?

The dining halls stay open late once per semester for a "midnight breakfast" to help students who are up late studying for final exams.

The dining halls are stocked with current issues of the student newspaper, as well as free copies of the local papers and *USA Today* for students to read while eating.

## Students Speak Out
ON CAMPUS DINING

**"The dining hall food is annoying and repetitive, plain and simple. However, the University does have a 'center' that has many fast food places, offering a change from the everyday monotony of dining hall food."**

Q "The food on campus varies **depending on where you eat**. The dining dollars used at places like Taco Bell, Panda Express, Subway, and fast food places are always a good choice for the lazy college student, but the real dining hall gets really old quick. It serves the same dishes many times in the week, and it feels like the food they get is not always the best quality. I have friends who have boycotted the cafeteria for long periods of time."

Q "**Residential dining is respectable**, but it gets old very quickly. If your parents were good cooks, you probably won't like it, but if they weren't, you'll be impressed."

Q "I like the dining halls because there are a lot of choices and you can either eat healthily or not, whatever you like. Besides the dining halls, dining on campus gets really boring because there is only one other food court, and the menu there doesn't vary much. **We do have an on-campus Friday's-type place**, the Rat."

Q "The dining halls are, contrary to popular belief, actually not that bad. The food quality itself is usually decent, though **the menu gets repetitive**. If the dining halls are not what someone wants, there is also the on-campus Subway, Burger King, Taco Bell, Starbucks, Jamba Juice, Sbarro's, Panda Express, and more."

## The College Prowler Take
### ON CAMPUS DINING

The school has two dining halls, both with pretty standard college-buffet food. The variety sounds good—pizza, pastas, made-to-order sandwiches, hamburgers, hot dogs, fries, salad, and ice cream are only a few of the daily staples—but none of it is very high quality. Most students don't mind the food at first, but get really sick of it sometime around Halloween of their freshman year. This is about how long it takes to realize that all the different foods have the same greasy taste. Freshmen usually start with the comfortable 14-meal plan, which allows for 14 meals at the dining hall per week. If you don't use all of your dining dollars by the end of the semester, you can always head over to the campus convenience store and spend the remainder on junk food and prehistoric donuts.

### The College Prowler™ Grade on
### Campus Dining: C+

Our grade on Campus Dining addresses the quality of both school-owned dining halls and independent on-campus restaurants as well as the price, availability, and variety of food.

## Campus Housing

### The Lowdown
### ON CAMPUS HOUSING

**Undergrads on Campus:**
41%

**Dormitories:**
5 (not including apartments)

**University-Owned Apartments:**
35

**Cleaning Service?**
In public areas; floor bathrooms, study lounges, hallways, and common areas are cleaned daily by staff. Shared bathrooms between suites are not cleaned by staff.

**You Get:**
Bed, desk and chair, dresser, bookshelf, closet space, trash can, window coverings, cable TV connection, Ethernet connection, free campus and local phone calls (phone not included).

**Bed Type:**
Twin extra-long (39"x80")

**Also Available:**
Quiet floors, cart and vacuum loans

## Room Types

Residences have either standard rooms or suites.

**Standard**—Each floor contains a large, multiple-person bathroom that is shared by about 40 students (most freshman are placed in these halls).

**Suite**—Two rooms with two students in each share a connecting bathroom.

**On-campus apartments**—It can have two or three bedrooms, and hold up to six students who share kitchen and bathroom facilities.

## Did You Know?

The campus cable network was upgraded recently to include HBO and 60 other stations that are free to students.

There is at least one resident assistant living on each floor, whose job it is to help new students feel comfortable and encourage friendly relations among floormates.

Under a newly-passed law in Florida, there is no smoking allowed in campus buildings, including the residential colleges. Picnic tables and benches are set up for smokers outside of each of the dorms.

The front desk of each residential college has laundry carts and vacuums that students can check out for a short period. Some dorms even have movies that students can borrow from the desk.

## Students Speak Out
### ON CAMPUS HOUSING

"It is impossible to avoid community bathroom 'freshmen dorms,' but once the first year is over, Eaton and Mahoney/Pearson sport double suite-type rooms, each with their own bathroom."

"**I like the dorm life**. It's the easiest time in the world to meet random people. I lived in Hecht for freshman year and loved it, because there are a large variety of people. I heard Mahoney is the where all the pretty people live, with all the athletes, and Eaton is the place to live if you want somewhere in between."

"I do not mind the dorms at all. In fact, **I strongly recommend living on campus**. It has been a lot of fun living with several people of different backgrounds, and I have enjoyed getting to know all of them. Some people complain about communal bathrooms, but they are cleaned twice a day. Other people complain about roommates, but I have not had a bad experience with my roommate."

"The dorms are a great environment. There are **freshman dorms, Stanford and Hecht**, that were a really fun time. They are co-ed by floor, and the rooms are doubles. There really is not a set of dorms to stay away from; they are pretty much all the same set up."

"I currently reside in Eaton Residential College, which is for sophomores and upperclassmen. It is a suite setup, and connects through the restroom. I like living on campus, and **all of the benefits that come with it**, which include waking up and going to class without worrying about parking, and meeting more people through the residence halls."

"Most freshmen live in the Towers, and **they're not as bad as you would imagine**. They have bathrooms down the hall, but they're generally really clean for shared bathrooms. Then, there are the suite-style rooms, which involve cleaning your own bathroom. That sucks, but the rooms are better-shaped and brighter. There are also on-campus apartments."

## The College Prowler Take
### ON CAMPUS HOUSING

If you decide to attend UM, there will be a form you fill out ranking the residential colleges by preference. This seems to be basically useless, as almost all freshmen are placed in Hecht or Stanford, also called the Towers. A few students may end up elsewhere because of overcrowding, but almost everyone lives in the Towers for their first year. Although the other dorms are bigger and don't have whole-floor bathrooms, most students agree that spending a year in the Towers is a good experience because it forces you to meet people. When you're living with 40 other people who are looking to make friends, and you all have to share a bathroom, you get to know people quickly, which is great for freshmen. Expect to live in the Towers for a year, and make sure to leave your door open for the first few days so people know you're open to making friends.

**B-**

**The College Prowler™ Grade on**
## Campus Housing: B-

A high Campus Housing grade indicates that dorms are clean, well-maintained, and spacious. Other determining factors include variety of dorms, proximity to classes, and social atmosphere.

## Diversity

### The Lowdown
### ON DIVERSITY

**Native American:** 0%

**Asian American:** 6%

**African American:** 10%

**Hispanic:** 24%

**White:** 54%

**International:** 6%

**Out-of-State:** 40%

### Minority Clubs
Minority students will feel right at home in the diverse atmosphere of Miami. Clubs like OASIS, Asian American Students Association, and African Students Union will help students meet others from their ethnic background.

### Most Popular Religions
Religion isn't a major issue at UM, although there are plenty of clubs for more spiritual students on campus, regardless of their religions.

### Political Activity
The student body seems more interested in going to the beach than protesting controversial political decisions. Although the city of Miami is known for its mixed political feelings, UM students don't seem to care much.

### Gay Tolerance
Miami is famous for its wide-spread homosexual culture, especially in the South Beach area. Citizens are very accepting of the gay community, and UM mirrors that tolerance with organizations like SpectrUM.

### Economic Status
Given the high cost of attending UM and the fancy clothing seen around campus, many students seem to come from wealthy homes. This doesn't mean that there aren't plenty of students with modest backgrounds, but those really struggling with finances may want to consider a public university.

## Students Speak Out
ON DIVERSITY

"I read somewhere that we have one of the most diverse campuses in the United States, and that's evident from just walking around campus for a short amount of time."

"We have a very diverse campus. **Over 100 nations are represented**. I actually chose this school because this was the only time in my life where I would have the chance to get to know so many people from different places."

"UM consistently ranks among the top five schools in the United States for the amount of diversity within its student body. It is one of the greatest things about the University, knowing that I will be able to meet, talk to, and **learn with people from all around the country**, as well as the world. Each person makes the school more unique."

"Our campus sucks when it comes to diversity. **There are not many other ethnic groups** other than white and Hispanic."

"**Every style of person is represented here**. I believe there is someone from every state at least in the school, if not in my class level."

## The College Prowler Take
ON DIVERSITY

Like most big cities, Miami has areas that are very cultural, and visiting these areas might feel like stepping into another world. Instead of Chinatown, Miami has Little Havana, the world's largest collection of Cubans outside of Cuba. The huge Hispanic population in Miami is not limited to one area. You'll overhear conversations spoken in Spanish almost everywhere in the city, and sometimes the accents are hard to understand, and you end up with totally preposterous things in your McDonald's bag after an unsuccessful trip to the drive-thru. Miami has so many different ethnicities represented that students coming from non-diverse backgrounds may feel uncomfortable at first. As the numbers prove, only half of the students in most classes will be white. This is a great experience for students of any ethnicity. It basically forces you to understand different cultures and people from various backgrounds.

**A-**

The College Prowler™ Grade on
## Diversity: A-

A high grade in Diversity indicates that ethnic minorities and international students have a notable presence on campus and that students of different economic backgrounds, religious beliefs, and sexual preferences are well-represented.

# Guys & Girls

## The Lowdown
ON GUYS & GIRLS

Women Undergrads: 58%

Men Undergrads: 42%

### Birth Control Available?
Condoms are always available for free in a basket at the Student Health Center, and there are conferences and campaigns to promote awareness of teen pregnancy and birth control methods.

### Social Scene
The school is very social and most guys and girls don't have trouble meeting people if they want to. Since almost all freshman live in the Towers their first year, they will often meet other students on their floor when they share bathroom facilities. Usually guys and girls live on alternate floors, so the opposite sex is never too far away. Since most students come to UM looking to make friends, it's never hard to find someone to hang out with, even if it takes a couple weeks to build a friendship.

### Hookups or Relationships?
As is expected, most freshmen come to school without being in relationships. Random hookups are common in the beginning, but after a few months or a year, relationships take over. Miami is a great town for dating, with plenty of romantic spots and restaurants.

### Dress Code
The clothing seen on campus is almost as diverse as the students that go here. For every guy that falls out of bed five minutes before class and throws on sandals and jeans, there's a girl wearing the latest fashions to her math lectures. For daily life, pretty much anything goes. Most of the guys stick with shorts and T-shirts during the day, and the girls wear jeans and tank tops. Bring some preppy clothes for going out at night, when the standard dress is slacks and formal shirts for guys, and skirts and nice tops for girls. The heaviest thing you'll need as far as the weather goes is a hooded sweatshirt and jeans. Make sure to bring a comfortable pair of sandals, a UM staple for both guys and girls.

## Students Speak Out
ON GUYS & GIRLS

"The girls are amazing. They're all beautiful, but the question is if it's on the inside or just outer beauty. The friends I've made are not supermodels, but they're quality girls."

Q "**The guys are short**, like me, for the most part, unlike a northern school, where the shortest guy is six feet tall."

Q "**The girls are awesome**. Watch out for personality. Some girls in Miami lack it! But, beauty is definitely not a problem."

Q "People here are interesting. **A lot of eastern attitude comes out**, in my opinion. As a midwesterner, I am used to a little more hospitality. However, I do believe that this is no different from any other campus."

Q "The girls are incredible. **There is no hotter place on earth than here**, with beautiful women from all over the world that sometimes have the attitude to go with it. I must say, that is on the negative side. I have many friends and I simply believe that it is about finding your comfort zone."

> "The thing about U. of Miami is that the same sort of people are looking for **a group that suits their needs** or the type of friends that they are used to from back home. I think it is important to find your niche, and you will be happy. I found mine in a fraternity and have been loving it since."

# Athletics

## The College Prowler Take
### ON GUYS & GIRLS

The opinion of most UM students seems to be that the student body's bodies are great to look at, but that this is not a school to meet your future spouse. Temporary flings or random hooking up is common among freshmen who are basking in their post-high school freedom. But once everyone gets settled and makes the friends they'll have for the next four years, relationships kick in. The school can be as promiscuous as you want it to be. If you're looking for a quick hook-up, it's not hard to head to a bar or club and find it. Most students don't make this a habit, as it obviously complicates things a great deal. Your best bet is to make a bunch of friends that are of the opposite sex in the beginning of your freshman year, and then you'll have plenty of connections to guys or girls for the rest of college. Overall, the guys and girls look great, and, to be fair, some are great all around.

## The Lowdown
### ON ATHLETICS

**Men's Varsity Teams:**
Baseball
Basketball
Cross Country
Football
Swimming & Diving
Tennis
Track and Field

**Women's Varsity Teams:**
Basketball
Cross Country
Golf
Rowing
Soccer
Swimming and Diving
Tennis
Track and Field
Volleyball

### B+

**The College Prowler™ Grade on Guys: B+**

A high grade for Guys indicates that the male population on campus is attractive, smart, friendly, and engaging, and that the school has a decent ratio of guys to girls.

### A-

**The College Prowler™ Grade on Girls: A-**

A high grade for Girls not only implies that the women on campus are attractive, smart, friendly, and engaging, but also that there is a fair ratio of girls to guys.

## Club Sports
Aikido, Badminton, Baseball, Bowling, Fencing, Field Hockey, Golf, Karate, Lacrosse, Racquetball, Roller Hockey, Rowing, Rugby, Sailing, SCUBA, Soccer, Swimming, Table Tennis, Tae Kwon Do, Tennis, Ultimate Frisbee, Volleyball, Water Polo

## Intramurals
Arena Football, Basketball, Dodgeball, Fantasy Football, Flag Football, Floor Hockey, Golf, Indoor Soccer, Inner tube Water Polo, Kickball, Soccer, Softball, Team Billiards, Team Racquetball, Tennis Singles, Ultimate Frisbee, Volleyball, Wallyball, Whiffle Ball

**Athletic Division:**
NCAA Division I

**Conference:**
Atlantic Coast Conference

**School Mascot:**
Hurricanes

**Fields:**
IM Fields, Orange Bowl (Football)
Convocation Center (Basketball)
Mark Light Stadium (Baseball)

## Most Popular Sports
There's no questioning what the most popular sport is on campus. Football dominates every weekend during the season, with students donating their Saturday afternoons to supporting the team. It also helps to have a program that's continually ranked among the top in the country. The baseball team is also one of the country's best but doesn't get nearly the amount of attention the football team does. Other sports are very competitive in their divisions, but don't get the student support they likely deserve.

## Overlooked Teams
The women's basketball team is among the top in its division and even in the country, but few pay attention to it. The baseball team gets great recognition nationally, but you're more likely to see Sportscenter anchors talking about it than you are to hear it in a conversation among students.

## Getting Tickets
Attending UM is a sports-lover's dream. Students get free access to any UM sporting event with their ID card. Tickets to football bowl games are also available for students to purchase, and the school puts together packages to get students to attend away games during football season. The basketball arena and baseball stadium on campus are fun places to see a game for free.

# Students Speak Out
## ON ATHLETICS

"Football is huge, since we have one of the best teams in the nation, and basketball is getting there. IM sports are also huge, with large programs occurring each spring and fall."

Q "Athletics are an essential part of on-campus life. **Sportsfest is great fun**, and you really connect with your teammates. It's definitely worth doing IM sports, if you are into it."

Q "**Varsity football and basketball are very popular** on campus. Everyone goes to the football games, and over half of the students attend the basketball games. IM sports are also very popular. Many people participate in IM football, soccer, or racquetball."

Q "Miami is **one of the nation's leading sports programs**. There is nothing like Hurricane football and the history that comes with it. I am a huge sports fan, and one of the main draws was coming to watch the sports here. Although the basketball team is not necessarily all I wished it to be, they have a new facility on campus, which makes it convenient to go to games, unlike the Orange Bowl which is located in a shady area of town."

Q "**Intramurals are as big as you want them to be**. They are well formed, and have a place just to organize and get together. I am the IM chair for my fraternity and am a huge supporter of IMs on campus. They are really competitive and well-officiated."

Q "The IMs on campus offer indoor and outdoor flag football, basketball, dodgeball, kickball, water polo, indoor and outdoor soccer, softball, tennis, and many others. **It is definitely a great program**."

## The College Prowler Take
### ON ATHLETICS

Although UM students might be lazy when it comes to academics, politics, or national events, one thing they take seriously is football. It helps, of course, that UM has one of the most dominant college football programs in the country, and that the team shows no sign of dropping out of the nation's top tier. A true sign of a college student's devotion is how early they're willing to wake up. For noon games on Saturdays, students line up outside the Orange Bowl gates as early as 8 a.m. to ensure good seats. By the mid morning, the lines wind out into the parking lot, and the massive student section of the Orange Bowl is generally buzzing. Intramurals also play a big part in campus life. There's a yearly competition between the residential colleges called Sportsfest, where teams from the dorms compete in dozens of games over a weekend. There are also intramurals during the fall and the spring, where the activity is dominated by fraternities, but can also include various other organizations. The most important thing will always be the football team, proven by the funeral-like silence the day after any rare loss.

**The College Prowler™ Grade on**
## Athletics: A

A high grade in Athletics indicates that students have school spirit, that sports programs are respected, that games are well-attended, and that intramurals are a prominent part of student life.

# Greek Life

## The Lowdown
### ON GREEK LIFE

**Number of Fraternities**:
10

**Number of Sororities**:
6

**Undergrad Men in Fraternities**:
12%

**Undergrad Women in Sororities**:
12%

### Did You Know?

Fraternities and sororities participate in two major competitions per year. In the fall, there's Homecoming, when they battle for victory by attending volunteer events, building floats, and staging skits called Organized Cheer. In the spring is Greek Week, when similar events are held, along with more sports-oriented games and contests.

The 12 percent of students who are Greek hold 85 percent of the campus leadership positions.

UM has a very strict anti-hazing policy and monitors all Greek organizations.

## Students Speak Out
### ON GREEK LIFE

"**Greek life is very interesting. It gives you the chance to meet so many new people and find out things about yourself that you never would have otherwise. There is no raw dominance by the Greeks on campus.**"

Q "Greek life is a lot of fun, and I would recommend that everyone check out the fraternities and sororities represented on campus. **Fraternities do throw parties often**, but unfortunately people usually go to non-Greek sponsored parties."

Q "I waited a semester before joining, since **there is both fall and spring rush for fraternities**, and found the right fraternity for me. I believe that it was the best move to figure out what each fraternity stands for. It is also a very good way to meet people, as well as the opposite sex. There are different fraternities or sororities, and each has something to offer according to what you are looking for."

Q "**Greek life does not dominate the social scene**, which is good in that it forces the fraternities and sororities to have higher standards. In general, though, most of the Greek organizations are involved in their own activities and do not interact with the rest of the student body."

Q "Greek life is only a fraction of the campus, but **everything done socially either has their name on it officially or unofficially**. The social level of the campus does rest on the Greek's shoulders, being that if it's doing poorly, the Greeks are to blame."

## The College Prowler Take
### ON GREEK LIFE

Greek life is not a disruptive force on campus, but it is sizeable enough to make a difference. Although UM does not have the massive Greek system of some universities, there are plenty of fraternities and sororities for students to choose from. If you want to stay away from Greek life, you won't have to try hard at UM. The fraternity houses are lined up on a road on the edge of campus, and the sorority and fraternity suites are in a building in a quiet part of UM. If not for the letter shirts seen around school, non-Greek students could easily forget that there are even fraternities and sororities at UM. But, behind the scenes, the Greek system here is very important. The social aspect of Greek life is present at UM, but is not overwhelming. If you want a Greek system that is quiet but still important, you will like UM's.

**B+**

The College Prowler™ Grade on
### Greek Life: B+

A high grade in Greek Life indicates that sororities and fraternities are not only present, but also active on campus. Other determining factors include the variety of houses available and the respect the Greek community receives from the rest of the campus.

# Drug Scene

## Students Speak Out
### ON DRUG SCENE

"I can honestly say that I have never run into anyone attempting to buy, sell, or use drugs. I'm sure that they're out there, but I suppose they hide themselves very well."

"**Miami is full of drugs**. I haven't had the chance to be in that scene, but they are definitely around."

"I have not seen too many people doing drugs. The handful of times I have witnessed someone doing drugs was at an off-campus event, and **they were smoking marijuana**."

"In Miami, there are many drug problems with such drugs as ecstasy. However, **I have not seen very much**, as I have never been around or really been introduced to a drug beyond marijuana. I have been told there are pretty heavy drugs around, I just don't know what and where. It is definitely avoidable though."

"**There is a drug problem on campus**. Many of the students are wealthy, and think they have nothing better to spend daddy's money on than marijuana or crack, or alcohol for that matter."

## The Lowdown
### ON DRUG SCENE

**Most Prevalent Drugs on Campus:**
Alcohol, Marijuana, Ecstasy, Cocaine

**Liquor-Related Discipline Cases**:
234

**Liquor-Related Arrests**:
0

**Drug-Related Discipline Cases**:
20

**Drug-Related Arrests**:
4

### Drug Counseling Programs
**PIER 21**
Phone: (305) 284-6120
Services: alcohol and drug education, prevention, and intervention

**Student Counseling Center**
Phone: (305) 284-5511
Services: general psychological counseling service, referrals to specialized counseling

**BACCHUS** (Boosting Alcohol Consciousness Concerning the Health of University Students)
Services: alcohol education, focused primarily on college students

## The College Prowler Take
### ON DRUG SCENE

College mirrors reality in that, if you want drugs, you can always find them. Miami, like any big city, has its fair share of bad neighborhoods and drug addicts. But, it's easy to stay away from them, especially around the campus in upscale Coral Gables. The only drug that's really being abused on UM's campus is alcohol, and that's true of almost all colleges. There are groups of students that are into marijuana, cocaine, ecstasy, or various other drugs, but dealing is not really a problem on campus, and most RAs are pretty strict about looking out for drug use in the dorms. Given UM's fairly difficult classes, most hardcore drug users aren't going to be around for long. Most students don't seem to be too concerned with drugs while on campus. While UM isn't going to make any top ten lists of schools with drug problems, there is certainly a dependency on alcohol at social events and in the lives of most students. Turning down alcohol at UM can be more difficult, as it plays an extremely important part in most students' social lives.

**B-**

The College Prowler™ Grade on
### Drug Scene: B-

A high grade on Drug Scene indicates that drugs are not a noticeable part of campus life; drug use is not visible, and no pressure to use them seems to exist.

## Overall Experience

### Students Speak Out
#### ON OVERALL EXPERIENCE

"I love it here. There is no place on earth I'd rather be getting my education. The only thing I gripe about is physics, but hey, we all have issues! Overall I'd give the school 4.5 stars out of 5."

Q "I really like this school a lot. There are times when I wish I was back with my friends at home, and sometimes **I think that the girls are looking for the perfect hard body**, which really sucks. But, I have plenty of friend; and the school is great."

Q "When you find the right situation, **everything works out great**. I strongly suggest people come and enjoy everything this city has to offer and the amazing experience that is Miami."

Q "I made the best choice of my life choosing Miami, and I have no regrets. My overall experience has been so positive, **words can't describe it**. The friends I've made, the learning I've done, and the culture I've become accustomed to have made me much closer to the person I strive to be."

> "Overall, UM is okay. **I am not really happy with how much I pay to go to this place**. Sometimes I wish I was somewhere else, when I consider the money that I pay, but otherwise it's a great school."

## The College Prowler Take
ON OVERALL EXPERIENCE

Despite daily griping about tuition costs, parking, thunderstorms, and hard classes, most students really seem to enjoy UM. Excellent attributes like the nightlife, weather, and culture seem to cancel out some of the bad things about being in Miami. For some students, these bad things include the unapproachable "hot" girls and guys on campus, while others find life in the dorms to be a challenge. The complaints about college are basically what you'd expect to hear anywhere. It appears that the grass is always greener on the other side—even if your "side" consists of bright beaches, blonde bombshells, and coconut-pineapple Italian ices. In other words, for many teenagers and 20-somethings, the downside to living in Miami and attending UM isn't much of a downside at all. Miami is one of the coolest cities in the world for a college student, and that goes deeper than just the superficial bar and club scene.

Students who are unhappy here generally figure it out within a semester and transfer, usually to somewhere closer to home. But these are probably the type of people who would have been unhappy anywhere. College is tough, especially the first couple weeks, if you come without knowing anyone. Making a whole new group of friends for the first time since kindergarten is one of the hardest and most stressful things you may ever have to do. But the end result of this process is friendships that you'll likely maintain for the rest of your life. Whether it's with your roommates, classmates, fraternity brothers, or sorority sisters, college is a time when you should make friends and have fun. Despite the initial challenges of coming to college, there are few cities in the world that are as fun as Miami.

# University of Richmond

**DISTANCE TO...**
Ocean City: 234 mi.
Washington: 109 mi.
Baltimore: 155 mi.
Virginia Beach: 116 mi.

28 Westhampton Way, Univ. of Richmond, VA 23173
www.richmond.edu          (800) 700-1662

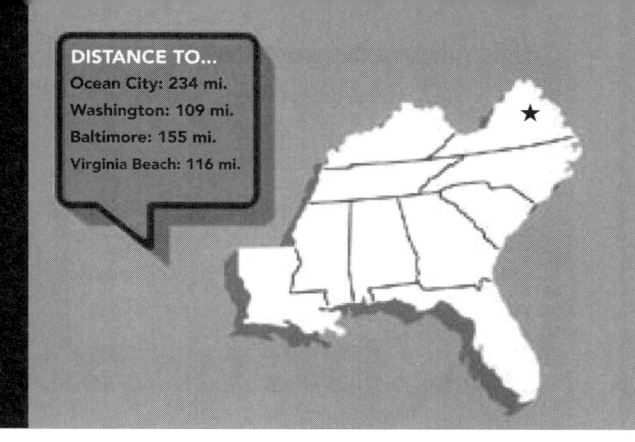

*"UR graduates are very employable and can look forward to great starting salaries, thanks to the quality of education they receive."*

**Total Enrollment:**
2,873

**Top 10% of High School Class:**
60%

**Average GPA:**
3.5

**Acceptance Rate:**
42%

**Tuition:**
$26,520

**SAT Range (25th-75th Percentile):**

| Verbal | Math | Total |
|---|---|---|
| 610 – 690 | 630 – 700 | 1240 – 1390 |

**ACT Range (25th-75th Percentile):**

| Verbal | Math | Total |
|---|---|---|
| N/A | N/A | 27-30 |

**Most Popular Majors:**
33%  Business
20%  Social Sciences
9%   English
7%   Biology
7%   Foreign Languages

**Students also applied to:***
Boston College
College of William and Mary
University of Virginia
Vanderbilt University
Wake Forest University

*For more school info check out www.collegeprowler.com

## Table of Contents

| | |
|---|---|
| Academics | 654 |
| Local Atmosphere | 655 |
| Safety & Security | 657 |
| Facilities | 658 |
| Campus Dining | 660 |
| Campus Housing | 661 |
| Diversity | 662 |
| Guys & Girls | 664 |
| Athletics | 665 |
| Greek Life | 667 |
| Drug Scene | 668 |
| Overall Experience | 667 |

## College Prowler Report Card

| | |
|---|---|
| Academics | B |
| Local Atmosphere | B- |
| Safety & Security | A- |
| Facilities | B |
| Campus Dining | C- |
| Campus Housing | B- |
| Diversity | D+ |
| Guys | A- |
| Girls | A |
| Athletics | B |
| Greek Life | A |
| Drug Scene | B+ |

# Academics

## The Lowdown
ON ACADEMICS

**Degrees Awarded:**
Associate, Bachelor, Master

**Undergraduate Schools:**
Robins Business School, School of Arts & Sciences, Jepson Leadership School

**Full-time Faculty:**
327

**Student-to-Faculty Ratio:**
10:1

**Average Course Load:**
5 courses, 15 credits

**AP Test Score Requirements:**
Possible credit for scores of 4 or 5, depending on subject

**Sample Academic Clubs:**
Omicron Delta Epsilon, Omicron Delta Kappa, Golden Key, Accounting Society, American Chemical Society, American Marketing Association, Areopagus

## Did You Know?

UR has an endowment of almost $1 billion. That is one of the highest in the nation, and allows the school to attract the best teachers and subsidize the tuition so it isn't too outrageous.

The Jepson Leadership School is the first undergraduate school in the nation devoted entirely to educating and training students in leadership studies.

**Best Places to Study:**
Boatwright Library, Whitehurst Study Lounge, Music Library

## Students Speak Out
ON ACADEMICS

*"The history department is very strong. I have had some fantastic teachers, and they make history, which can be a boring topic, seem interesting and useful."*

*"I've found just about all of my teachers to be understanding, interesting, and knowledgeable. The classes that aren't requirements are fun and interesting as well. **General education requirements can be boring**, and CORE is terrible."*

*"**The teachers with tenure don't really seem to care**. I like it when I have a young teacher, because he tries to make the class interesting, and still seems excited about the subject. Fortunately, there seem to be a lot of energetic young professors here, even if you do have to deal with the occasional old, boring one."*

*"Because of the small student-to-teacher ratio, **classrooms tend to have an intimate feel**. You certainly have the opportunity to know your professors on a personal level, and vice versa. As a student, you absolutely get the feeling that the professors want you to learn."*

## The College Prowler Take
### ON ACADEMICS

UR is a liberal arts school, so students are required to fulfill general requirements in all aspects of academics—from visual and performing arts, to science and history. This gives every student a solid background in every field. There's such a wide selection of classes available that students can usually find a course that interests them. Another benefit of this program is that it allows undecided students to explore several disciplines and try to find one that suits them. Freshmen are also required to take CORE, a course designed to introduce them to what college courses are like. When the general education requirements are out of the way, students can focus on their chosen field. Each field requires certain classes, but also offers a wide variety of electives that are more specialized and interesting. The business and leadership schools are two of UR's strengths. Graduating from the leadership school will open doors to hundreds of top-notch companies. The business school is one of the top schools in the country, and alumni of the school often look to UR grads first when recruiting. Professors are very approachable because class sizes are small and intimate. This allows students to develop personal relationships with their professors, and it is not uncommon for a professor to invite his entire class to dinner at his house.

**B**

The College Prowler™ Grade on
### Academics: B

A high Academics grade generally indicates that professors are knowledgeable, accessible, and genuinely interested in their students' welfare. Other determining factors include class size, how well professors communicate, and whether or not classes are engaging.

## Local Atmosphere

### The Lowdown
### ON LOCAL ATMOSPHERE

**Region:**
Southeast United States

**City, State:**
Richmond, Virginia

**Setting:**
Suburban

**Distance from Philadelphia:**
4 hours, 30 minutes

**Distance from Washington, DC:**
2 hours, 30 minutes

**Points of Interest:**
Maymont Park, Edgar Allan Poe Museum, Annabelle Lee Riverboat, Richmond National Battlefield Park Civil War Visitor Center, Tredegar Iron Works, Brown's Island Park, Pony Pastures, the Diamond, Capital Building, Patrick Henry Courthouse, Shockoe Slip, Carytown

**City Websites:**
*http://www.ci.richmond.va.us*
*http://www.richmond.com*

**Major Sports Teams:**
Richmond Braves (minor league baseball), no major sports teams

## Students Speak Out
ON LOCAL ATMOSPHERE

"Richmond is a great city with a lot to do. I recommend visiting the river as often as possible. The only other college around is VCU, but UR students hardly ever hang out with them."

Q "Campus is in the suburbs of the city and feels that way. There is not a presence of other universities until you move downtown by VCU. There are definitely areas of the city to stay away from, but there is no reason to be in those places anyway, and **there's a pretty good bar scene downtown** to visit. Virginia Beach also is not too far away."

Q "Richmond is a little too southern for me. I am from Boston, and I would be permanently pissed off if I lived down here all the time. **Things move way too slowly**. People who wait on you in restaurants take forever, and fast food is just food, not very fast. Don't even get me started on the driving situation—there are nothing but Sunday drivers here."

Q "**There are some real shady areas** of the city that are scary, but UR is far enough outside the city that it really isn't a big deal. The bar area of the city, Shockoe Slip, is great, and so is the River District."

Q "For all intents and purposes, the University of Richmond could be located on the moon. Hardly any of the students venture outside of the 'UR Bubble,' which is the **invisible barrier that seems to keep everyone on campus** all the time."

## The College Prowler Take
ON LOCAL ATMOSPHERE

Richmond is a lovely historic city that provides a wonderful setting for UR. Visiting one of its many parks, museums, or battlefields is a great way to spend an afternoon. For those who are into less recreational activities, there is shopping and several movie theaters. Public transportation is disappointing, and it is important to either have a car or have access to one in order to enjoy Richmond to the fullest. Also, depending on what region of the country you are from, Richmond's slow pace may be too much to bear at times. Overall, Richmond is a lovely city with a lot to see and explore. One can easily be here for four years and not run out of things to do.

**B-**

The College Prowler™ Grade on

## Local Atmosphere: B-

A high Local Atmosphere grade indicates that the area surrounding campus is safe and scenic. Other factors include nearby attractions, proximity to other schools, and the town's attitude toward students.

# Safety & Security

## The Lowdown
### ON SAFETY & SECURITY

**Number of Police:**
15 sworn officers and 7 security officers
Phone: (804) 289-8715, or dial 911 (on-campus emergency)

**Health Center Office Hours:**
Monday-Friday (except Thurs.) 8:30 a.m.-12:00 p.m. & 1 p.m.-5 p.m. Thursday 8:30 a.m.-11:30 a.m. & 1 p.m.-5 p.m. Closed on weekends.

**Safety Services:**
Safety shuttle, 911 emergency phone number on campus, blue-light emergency phones

### Did You Know?
The University is one of only six private institutions in the country (and three colleges) that has a full-service law enforcement agency accredited by the Commission on Accreditation for Law Enforcement Agencies.

## Students Speak Out
### ON SAFETY & SECURITY

"I've had beer stolen from my refrigerator, but that is the extent of the criminal activity at UR. It is as safe as a school gets."

Q "In yet another example of UR's gender bias, **the Safety Shuttles are only available to female students.** The female students usually take the shuttles to avoid having to walk across campus in bad weather, not because they don't feel safe. I think UR needs to extend this service to male students as well."

Q "**It's very safe**. I am from Philadelphia, and it was a change for me to come here, and not have to worry about locking my door or chaining up my bike. You never need to worry about your personal safety here, and the only incidents that you have to deal with are petty vandalism and some theft."

Q "I have never locked my door in three and a half years at this school. This campus is safe. **Theft is occasionally a problem**, but not unreasonably so."

Q "The police patrol campus 24 hours a day on foot and by vehicle. **They don't hassle the students unreasonably**, but if you do get caught doing something illegal, you go to jail."

### College Prowler
How safe will you be at UR? To find out how students feel about campus security, visit www.collegeprowler.com and pick up *University of Richmond—Off the Record*.

## The College Prowler Take
### ON SAFETY & SECURITY

Most students agree that aside from some minor vandalism and theft, UR is incredibly safe. One of the biggest deterrents to crime is that the campus police maintain a very visible and active presence 24 hours day. The most common incident reports are for theft of University property. Laptops and other equipment are often reported missing from classrooms and labs. Students often refer to the "UR Bubble." It really does seem as though the campus is isolated from the outside world, and it is easy to forget that 15 minutes away is the city of Richmond, which led the nation in homicide percentage per population a few years ago. But, at UR you are safe.

**A-**

**The College Prowler™ Grade on**
### Safety & Security: A-

A high grade in Safety & Security means that students generally feel safe, campus police are visible, blue-light phones and escort services are readily available, and safety precautions are not overly necessary.

# Facilities

## The Lowdown
### ON FACILITIES

**Student Center:**
Tyler Haines Commons

**Athletic Center:**
The Robins Center

**Libraries:**
4; Boatwright (main library), science, music, and law libraries

**Movie Theater on Campus?**
No, although movies are shown occasionally on a large screen in the Pier. Students can also rent DVDs for free from the Media Resource Center in the library.

**Bowling on Campus?**
No

**Bar on Campus?**
Yes, the Cellar, but it only serves beer.

**Coffeehouse on Campus?**
Yes. Boatwright Library on the first floor. It's named "The 8:15 at Boatwright."

**Popular Places to Chill:**
The Cellar, Whitehurst, The 8:15 at Boatwright, IM Fields (in nice weather)

## Favorite Things to Do

The Cellar is the number one on-campus hang-out for students over 21. It has a great selection of beers and food and hosts live bands or open mic nights. Happy hour is from 7 to 9 each night. The coffee shop is conveniently located on the first floor of the library and is a great place to go on a study break.

### Computers

**High-Speed Network?** Yes
**Wireless Network?** Yes
**Number of Labs:** 5
**Numbers of Computers:** 400
**24-Hour Labs:** Boatwright Basement
**Charge to Print?**
250 free printing credits per semester; printing costs 10 cents a page after that.

## Students Speak Out
### ON FACILITIES

"The Robins Center is a really nice basketball stadium with recreational ball courts and racquetball. The weight room is disappointing and should be expanded with new equipment."

Q "**I would love a movie theater on campus**. The Pier shows films, but it's not comfortable at all, and they show movies that are out of the theaters already. The closest movie theater is all the way down Broad Street, and that's not very convenient."

Q "The student center is lacking a lot, and I don't think that it is all that great. It has a bookstore, which usually has long lines, and a game room with only a few pool tables and Ping-Pong tables, and the headquarters of some of the student organizations—on the third floor and hard to find—but that is it. **They could do more** to make it a nice place to hang out."

Q "The facilities, especially the student center and the gym, are undergoing some much-needed renovations. The blueprints of the campus recreational center looked phenomenal. **I think they're putting in an indoor track** and updating the entire facility."

Q "The athletic facilities are nice, but the weight lifting gym is a little small. **The computers are fabulous**, and the students center is average, but in a nice spot because it looks over the majestic lake that is on campus."

## The College Prowler Take
### ON FACILITIES

UR has more than adequate facilities that are convenient and readily available to students. There is plenty to do: exercise, swim, play basketball, tennis, shoot pool, watch movies—the list goes on and on. Even though several basketball courts are available, along with racquetball, one drawback to the facilities at University of Richmond is the weight room. The weight room is small and just does not measure up to some of the nicer recreational facilities at other colleges across the country. With the exception of a few possible additions, the facilities at UR are extensive enough that you will never run out of things to do.

**B**

The College Prowler™ Grade on
### Facilities: B

A high Facilities grade indicates that the campus is aesthetically pleasing and well-maintained; facilities are state-of-the-art, and libraries are exceptional. Other determining factors include the quality of both athletic and student centers and an abundance of things to do on campus.

# Campus Dining

## The Lowdown
ON CAMPUS DINING

**Freshman Meal Plan Requirement?**
Yes

**24-Hour On-Campus Eating?**
No

**Student Favorites:**
The Cellar, Papa John's, Chinese Kitchen Express

**Meal Plan Average Cost:**
Very flexible, it ranges from $250 per semester (for Spider Blue) to $1,625 per semester (for Spider Max).

## Students Speak Out
ON CAMPUS DINING

Q "I've heard people complain about D-Hall, but I like it. The selection is wide enough that I haven't got tired of it yet, and since it is buffet-style, **you can eat until you explode** if you want to. I love the Cellar, and the Pier isn't bad either—it's good overall."

Q "Food services wants to make the students happy, and it shows. The problem with the food on campus is that **there are only two main places to eat**. There is the main dining hall, which is located on one side of the lake—a hike for those on the other side—and Tyler's Grill, a fast food place in the student center in the middle of campus. Tyler's Grill, a.k.a. the Pier, is almost always packed."

Q "Not enough variety at D-Hall, but I do like the salad bar and the wrap bar. **The vegetarian selection is miserable**, but it is nice that the school tries. The Pier offers salads, but they are usually gross, and the Cellar doesn't have much to offer except greasy food."

"The Pier has incredibly long lines all the time. They really need to come out with a new system for taking orders and giving out the food. You can be in line for a half hour, and the food is definitely not worth it."

## The College Prowler Take
ON CAMPUS DINING

**There really isn't much selection at all as far as on-campus dining is concerned. Underclassmen usually eat all their meals at the main dining hall (D-Hall). The food isn't half bad there, especially at breakfast. There are also theme nights where exotic food is served. The University hires outside companies to cater these events. Aside from these meals, the food is edible, but not amazing. After about a year, students get sick of the food at D-Hall and look to the other options, the Pier and the Cellar.**

The College Prowler™ Grade on
## Campus Dining: C-

Our grade on Campus Dining addresses the quality of both school-owned dining halls and independent on-campus restaurants as well as the price, availability, and variety of food.

# Campus Housing

## Room Types

There are singles, doubles, triples and suites.

Singles—usually reserved for upperclassmen; some have private bathrooms.

Doubles—the majority of rooms; bathrooms are shared by everyone on floor.

Triples—not many; bathrooms are shared by floor.

Suites—only in Gray Court; semi-private bathroom between two rooms.

## The Lowdown
ON CAMPUS HOUSING

**Undergrads on Campus:**
92%

**Number of Dormitories:**
15

**University-Owned Apartments:**
168 individual apartments

**Bed Type:**
Twin or extra-long twin (only available to students 6'4" and taller).

**Cleaning Service?**
No, public areas only; Community bathrooms are cleaned daily, except on weekends. Semi-private bathrooms are not, neither are UFA bathrooms.

**You Get:**
Bed, desk and chair, bookshelf, dresser, closet or wardrobe, cable TV jack, Ethernet or broadband Internet connections, free campus and local phone calls

**Also Available:**
Smoke- and substance-free housing

## Students Speak Out
ON CAMPUS HOUSING

"My biggest problem with the dorms is that they are noisy, and the walls are paper thin. Good luck getting any sleep if you live in Gray Court or Marsh."

Q "Dorms are pretty standard, and **the quality doesn't vary too much** between them. Gray Court features two-room suites sharing a bathroom, while other dorms feature mostly double rooms, with the occasional single or triple, with community bathrooms."

Q "In general, the dorms are nice because they provide a lot of variety for students to arrange their room in the most comfortable way possible. **Dorms such as Marsh and Jeter are spectacular**, and generally all the dorms are now receiving air conditioning and the other amenities, so I would choose them all."

Q "Living in the apartments [UFAs] is great. It might be a long walk to classes, but it is worth it to have your own kitchen and bathroom. **Try to live near the IM fields, if you can** because they seem to be the center of the action."

Q "The dorms can get hot in the summer—really hot. Several of them have air conditioning, but Robins, Dennis, and Freeman Halls do not. The air conditioning is also turned off at the end of September so a warm October can make dorm life miserable. **You can never have too many fans**."

## The College Prowler Take
### ON CAMPUS HOUSING

Dorms are basically the same at all colleges, and the dorms at UR aren't any worse or better than average. Perhaps the biggest disadvantage to on-campus housing is that the dorms are segregated by gender. Only one dorm, Keller Hall, currently houses both male and female students, and this is part of a trial experiment to determine whether to expand the program to all dorms. Although separate housing makes it possible to walk around in your underwear, many students feel that it would be better if students of the opposite sex were right down the hallway, instead of in a whole different building.

**B-**

The College Prowler™ Grade on
### Campus Housing: B-

A high Campus Housing grade indicates that dorms are clean, well-maintained, and spacious. Other determining factors include variety of dorms, proximity to classes, and social atmosphere.

# Diversity

## The Lowdown
### ON DIVERSITY

Native American: 0%

Asian American: 3%

African American: 5%

Hispanic: 2%

White: 86%

International: 4%

Out-of-State: 84%

### Minority Clubs
The Multicultural Student Union (MSU) has the greatest visibility on campus, but there are several traditionally black sororities that have UR chapters, and there has been a great deal of discussion recently about forming a black fraternity.

### Most Popular Religions
Catholicism and Christianity, although there is a sizeable Jewish population as well. Weekly non-denominational services are held in the UR chapel, and are well-attended.

## Gay Tolerance

Although there aren't any obvious examples of intolerance toward gay students, there isn't an outpouring of acceptance either. There are several groups such as GLAD and SafeZone, but the gay community is not extremely visible on campus, with the exception of Coming Out Week, when the campus is full of tolerance-promoting activities.

## Economic Status

UR is notorious for being the "University of Rich Kids." Although this is not completely true, for the most part students come from wealthy or at least above average economic backgrounds. Some of the cars students drive are ridiculously expensive.

## Political Activity

The campus is divided politically, with both conservatives and liberals strongly represented. People who enjoy politics will find a place to debate ideas, and a chance for activism, but, for the most part, students could care less about politics. This is another symptom of the UR Bubble, and the campus political groups are often frustrated by the apathetic nature of most students.

## Students Speak Out
ON DIVERSITY

"I've never been to a place where that the lack of diversity is as bad as it is here."

"I would like to see more diversity at UR, and although I'm sure the school makes an attempt to recruit a more diverse student body, it doesn't seem to be working too well."

"I have a very diverse group of friends and feel that even though there might not appear to be a great deal of diversity at UR, if you give it a chance, you will find that there is. **Join MSU and attend the international club events** if you want to meet people from different cultures—you won't regret it."

"When the school imported actors to pretend to be UR students and show a more diverse face, I wasn't surprised. **There aren't any minorities here**."

"I know a lot of international students from all over the world. They all have interesting insights into American culture, and it is fascinating to hear about their home countries."

## The College Prowler Take
ON DIVERSITY

There is little to no diversity at UR. Most of the minorities on campus are involved with sports or are international students, and they tend to socialize only with one another. This is unfortunate, because it is doesn't allow students to meet new people with different beliefs, backgrounds, and cultures. The school is a bit too conformist, and you really have to go out of your way if you want to meet a diverse group of people. A few years ago, there was a scandal at UR because the University hired actors to come and pose for photos to be placed in the school's guidebook. Many of these actors were minorities, and it gave the appearance that UR is a more diverse school than it actually is. As sad as it is, at UR, you really have to make an effort to get to know people from different races. You definitely should make that effort, however, because you can learn a lot about the world, and about yourself, through fostering these relationships.

The College Prowler™ Grade on
## Diversity: D+

A high grade in Diversity indicates that ethnic minorities and international students have a notable presence on campus and that students of different economic backgrounds, religious beliefs, and sexual preferences are well-represented.

# Guys & Girls

## Dress Code
Real preppy. Whatever the latest new, hip brand is, UR kids have it—Hollister or Abercrombie. It's bad enough that people wear collared shirts to class, but it has also become a tradition to dress up for pre-football game tailgates. No one complains when the weather is nice and girls wear sundresses, but the dress code is far too preppy for the most part. It would be nice to just roll out of bed and go to class in sweats, but at UR you have to dress to impress.

## The Lowdown
### ON GUYS & GIRLS

Women Undergrads: 51%

Men Undergrads: 49%

**Birth Control Available?**
Yes

**Social Scene**
Two years ago UR finally integrated housing so that men and women at least live near one another, although still not in the same building. Before that, it was incredibly hard for the men, who lived on one side of the lake, to interact with the women, who lived on the other side. Students are fairly outgoing and don't just socialize within the groups or organizations to which they belong. Obviously, there are shy people here as well, but even they can join one of the University's many organizations and get to meet people.

**Hookups or Relationships?**
Relationships dominate the upperclassmen scene, while the underclassmen prefer hooking up. It seems like all the students get it out of their system by the end of their sophomore year and settle down in relationships. Most people are in relationships with other UR students. If you are an upperclassman who isn't in one, you should either get in one or look to the underclassmen for hookups.

## Students Speak Out
### ON GUYS & GIRLS

"**The girls are hot, but also spoiled and stuck-up. Most of the guys are cool, except for the real rich ones who think they are better than everyone.**"

Q "The people I have met at Richmond are fantastic. **I've met a lot of genuine people** that come from the same kind of background as I do, so everyone relates pretty easily. The girls are the same as the guys, they are very nice as well and very attractive, except they study a lot harder than the guys do in general."

Q "I wish the school were bigger, so that it wasn't as easy to get a reputation as it is. **Girls are branded sluts for no reason at all**, and that can really hurt them. If you hook up with someone and aren't in a relationship with them, you are called a slut."

Q "Most of the girls here are daddy's girls who have been spoiled their entire lives and expect guys to spoil them, too. **They are extremely high maintenance.**"

Q "You'll learn quickly **not to judge a book by its cover**. The girl you label a stuck-up snob because she has BMW keys dangling from her Prada purse might turn out to be one of the most down-to-earth people you've ever met."

## The College Prowler Take
### ON GUYS & GIRLS

One of the best and worst parts about UR is that it is full of beautiful people. Don't worry—there are also a lot of average ones. There does seem to be an exceptionally large number of hot girls and guys though. There are more girls than guys, but the difference is negligible and doesn't exactly make for easy pickings. Even though there are lots of attractive people, there is still a good deal of competition for the most attractive ones. If you are average looking, don't worry, chances are you will do just fine for yourself. The bad part is that students are very concerned with appearance—maybe too much so. It is also very easy to get a bad reputation because the school is small enough that word will get around if a person hooks up a lot with many different people. However, if you want a relationship, the average girls are usually much cooler than the drop dead gorgeous ones. The same goes for the guys as well.

**The College Prowler™ Grade on**
## Guys: A-

A high grade for Guys indicates that the male population on campus is attractive, smart, friendly, and engaging, and that the school has a decent ratio of guys to girls.

**The College Prowler™ Grade on**
## Girls: A

A high grade for Girls not only implies that the women on campus are attractive, smart, friendly, and engaging, but also that there is a fair ratio of girls to guys.

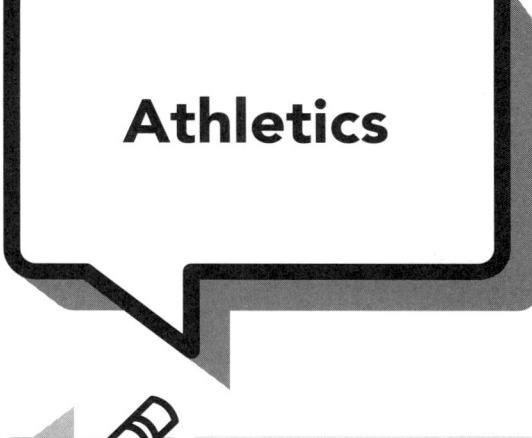

# Athletics

## The Lowdown
### ON ATHLETICS

**Men's Varsity Teams:**
Basketball
Cross Country
Football
Golf
Soccer
Tennis
Track and Field

**Women's Varsity Teams:**
Basketball
Cross Country
Diving
Field Hockey
Golf
Soccer
Tennis
Track and Field

### Club Sports
Baseball, Basketball, Crew, Equestrian, Field Hockey, Ice Hockey, Lacrosse, Martial Arts, Rugby, Soccer, Synchronized Swimming, Ultimate Frisbee, UR Spinners/Dance, Volleyball, Water Polo

### Intramurals
Basketball, Handball, Touch Football, Hockey, Horseshoes, Racquetball, Soccer, Softball, Squash, Swimming, Table Tennis, Tennis, Volleyball, Water Polo, Wrestling

### Getting Tickets
UR students get in free when they show their SpiderCard. Other fans need to buy tickets from the box office.

**Athletic Division:**
NCAA Division I

**Conference:**
Atlantic-10

**School Mascot:**
The Spider

**Fields:**
Intramural (IM) Field, First Market Stadium (Soccer), Crenshaw Field (Lacrosse/Field Hockey), Pitt Field (Baseball), UR Stadium (off-campus site of football games)

### Most Popular Sports
The men's basketball program is rising rapidly in national recognition. The baseball team is nationally-ranked, and produced five players who were drafted by Major League Baseball within the last few years.

### Overlooked Teams
The women's soccer team doesn't get as much attention as it deserves. It is a great program that is consistently nationally-ranked. The synchronized swimming team and cross country teams are also nationally-ranked but receive little attention.

## Students Speak Out
### ON ATHLETICS

"Other than Spider basketball and tailgating before football games—and not going to them—varsity sports go basically unnoticed on campus. IM sports are very popular, especially among students in the Greek system."

"UR is the opposite of most schools. In some ways, **intramural sports are bigger than varsity ones**. The I-AA Spiders football team rarely draws a crowd to its games, although pre-game tailgating is crowded. Students will drive to the stadium and tailgate for two hours, only to leave when the game begins."

"Varsity sports are not that huge on campus. The football team is a joke, no one goes to the games, and I would say **the basketball team is the most legitimate 'big/popular' sport** that everyone goes to see."

"I'm in a sorority, and I participate in most IM sports. Varsity sporting events like basketball games are fun to go to sometimes because they are huge social events. **I wish that cheerleading was bigger than it is here**. The team is real small and doesn't do anything exciting."

"The club teams here are very intense. I play club rugby, and our team is nationally-ranked. It's great. **We get to travel and compete** against the nation's best teams. I think we practice almost as much as, if not more than, a varsity team."

## The College Prowler Take
### ON ATHLETICS

The biggest drawback to Spider athletics is the football program. It's boring and sad to watch the team lose year after year. Basketball and baseball are the strong points of UR athletics, and games are always highly-attended. For students not gifted enough to play a varsity sport, club sports are a fun way to meet people, exercise and compete against other schools. It's fairly easy to make a team, and once you are on one, you get to travel to other schools to compete in tournaments. Intramural sports are even bigger than club sports, and in some cases, bigger than varsity sports.

**B**

**The College Prowler™ Grade on**
## Athletics: B

A high grade in Athletics indicates that students have school spirit, that sports programs are respected, that games are well-attended, and that intramurals are a prominent part of student life.

# Greek Life

## The Lowdown
ON GREEK LIFE

Number of Fraternities: 10

Number of Sororities: 8

Undergrad Men in Fraternities: 32%

Undergrad Women in Sororities: 49%

Multicultural Colonies: The Global House

## Students Speak Out
ON GREEK LIFE

"Sororities are a waste of money because they rarely have social events or do anything as a sisterhood. Fraternities throw all the parties, so it isn't necessary to be in a sorority."

Q "If you want nothing to do with Greeks, there is still plenty to do. **It's much easier to be an independent guy than an independent girl**, I think, because of the nature of the sexes. I was very much independent, lived with several Greek girls, and still had a blast."

Q "Greek life is very entertaining for people who are interested in it. The Row is where all the fraternities, except for the off-campus fraternities, have weekly parties. **It basically dominates the social scene**, because there are not a lot of other school groups who can attract as many people as the fraternities do."

Q "Every party I go to is thrown by one fraternity or another. **The campus social scene would suck if they weren't around**. This is sad because it looks like the University is trying to get rid of them, and views them as more of a liability than a good thing."

Q "It by no means dominates the social scene, but it does play a major part. **The Greeks are not 100 percent exclusive**. Many Greeks have independent friends, so there is a definite mixture when it comes to social events."

## The College Prowler Take
ON GREEK LIFE

Greek life dominates the campus social scene. Some students have even transferred because they didn't get into a frat or sorority. Since UR is so small, it is easy to get a reputation, and a bad one can lead to being blacklisted from certain frats or sororities. It is a little too much like high school. If you are involved with the Greek system, and it seems like most students are, then you have it made. You become close to the other 50 or so people in your fraternity or sorority, and you never have to worry about finding something to do on the weekends. When the Row is open, it is the place to be. Lately however, due to more restrictive list procedures, it has lost some of its luster.

### The College Prowler™ Grade on
### Greek Life: A

A high grade in Greek Life indicates that sororities and fraternities are not only present, but also active on campus. Other determining factors include the variety of houses available and the respect the Greek community receives from the rest of the campus.

# Drug Scene

## The Lowdown
ON DRUG SCENE

**Most Prevalent Drugs on Campus:**
Marijuana, Ritalin/Adderall, Ecstasy, Cocaine

**Liquor-Related Referrals:** 556

**Liquor-Related Arrests:** 17

**Drug-Related Referrals:** 1

**Drug-Related Arrests:** 7

**Drug Counseling Programs:**
Counseling and Psychological Services (CAPS) provides various services for free.

## Students Speak Out
ON DRUG SCENE

Q "**Cocaine is big in some circles**, but isn't really a threat to the average student. I think it is mostly a case of rich kids with too much money on their hands trying coke because they are curious."

Q "Lots of kids smoke weed occasionally but few use it regularly. **The campus is dry** and without weed most of the year, except for right after breaks when people will bring it back with them to try and make some money. Once they sell out, campus is dry again."

Q "**The drug scene is pretty low**, or at least it's discrete. Marijuana is probably the drug of choice, though it is rumored that the women take a liking to coke."

Q "The only real big drug is Ritalin or Adderall. Everyone uses these to study or if they need energy. Weed isn't big, but I know a few people who smoke regularly."

## The College Prowler Take
ON DRUG SCENE

UR actually doesn't have that big of a drug scene. This is probably because of the strictness of the University. Of course, it is possible to get marijuana if you want it, and weed is definitely the most widely used drug (besides alcohol). The prices are higher than at most schools because the students here are wealthy and can afford to pay for it. It is also a question of supply and demand, and the fact that the dealer is taking a huge risk by selling drugs. A lot of people use Ritalin or Adderall as a study aid. Few students at UR think that using these pills without a prescription counts as drug abuse. Non-users won't feel pressured to use drugs because the scene is so underground that no one wants to admit new members.

**The College Prowler™ Grade on**
**Drug Scene: B+**

A high grade on Drug Scene indicates that drugs are not a noticeable part of campus life; drug use is not visible, and no pressure to use them seems to exist.

# Overall Experience

> "The friendliness took me by surprise my first semester—everyone says hello and is willing to help you out. Overall, **I feel proud having graduated from such an esteemed institution**, and I feel honored to have worked with, and been challenged by high-caliber professors. I feel blessed to have been around and established friendships with the people there."

## Students Speak Out
ON OVERALL EXPERIENCE

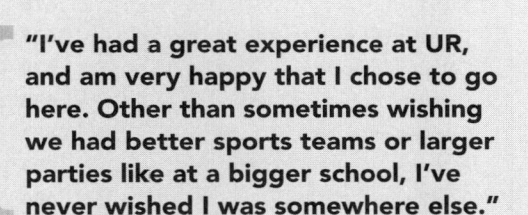

## The College Prowler Take
ON OVERALL EXPERIENCE

"I've had a great experience at UR, and am very happy that I chose to go here. Other than sometimes wishing we had better sports teams or larger parties like at a bigger school, I've never wished I was somewhere else."

> "I love Richmond, except **I wish it was a little bigger**. There are always things you like or dislike about a school, but overall, I am getting a good education. I have met good people, and I am having a good time. I just wish our sports teams were a little better."

> "My freshman year I absolutely hated school. But, I had the presence of mind to know that it had little to do with the actual school and more to do with myself. I would have been miserable anywhere. After four years at the University of Richmond, **I would not have done it any differently**."

> "The school is small enough that you will at least recognize most of the people you pass throughout the day. **It's not so small that you can't escape, or everyone knows your business**. And, it's not too big that you would ever feel lost or overwhelmed."

Students really seem to enjoy UR, and its retention rate of 91 percent reflects that. Those who just don't feel like they fit in transfer out after freshman year, so by the time senior year comes around, everyone in your class likes the school and knows one another, for the most part. There is also an influx of students who transfer into the school at the beginning of sophomore year. The best part about UR is the intimate atmosphere that it has, being a somewhat small, private university. It is a comfortable atmosphere that allows students to study in peace and relax when they need to. You get to know a lot of people and develop close friendships with many of them. The campus is gorgeous, and so are the people.

Students at UR rarely have much to complain about, and few could see themselves at any other school. They realize how lucky they are to be here and try to make the most of their opportunity by taking advantage of the great education, strong alumni network, and career preparation activities that the school provides. There are students who don't particularly like the school when they first arrive, but by the end of their time here they don't regret their original choice to attend the University of Richmond.

# Vanderbilt University

2201 West End Avenue, Nashville, Tennessee 37235
www.vanderbilt.edu     (800) 288-0432

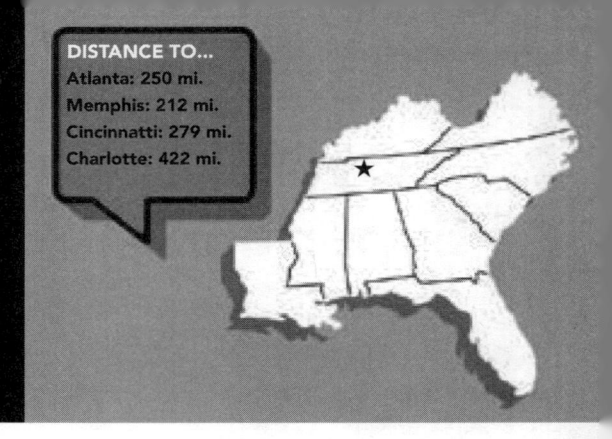

**DISTANCE TO...**
Atlanta: 250 mi.
Memphis: 212 mi.
Cincinnatti: 279 mi.
Charlotte: 422 mi.

"Everyone is very conscious of preserving the spirit of Vanderbilt, which in large part comes from its southern heritage."

### Table of Contents

| | |
|---|---|
| Academics | 671 |
| Local Atmosphere | 673 |
| Safety & Security | 674 |
| Facilities | 676 |
| Campus Dining | 677 |
| Campus Housing | 678 |
| Diversity | 680 |
| Guys & Girls | 681 |
| Athletics | 683 |
| Greek Life | 684 |
| Drug Scene | 685 |
| Overall Experience | 687 |

**Total Enrollment:**
6,231
**Top 10% of High School Class:**
77%
**Acceptance Rate:**
40%
**Tuition:**
$29,990
**SAT Range (25th-75th Percentile):**
Verbal       Math         Total
610 – 710    640 – 720    1250 – 1430
**ACT Range (25th-75th Percentile):**
Verbal       Math         Total
28-33        26-32        28-32
**Most Popular Majors:**
36%  Social Sciences
13%  Engineering
8%   Psychology
6%   Biology
6%   Foreign Languages
**Students also applied to:***
Duke University
Emory University
University of North Carolina–Chapel Hill
University of Virginia
Washington University in St. Louis

*For more school info check out www.collegeprowler.com

### College Prowler Report Card

| | |
|---|---|
| Academics | A- |
| Local Atmosphere | B+ |
| Safety & Security | B+ |
| Facilities | A |
| Campus Dining | C- |
| Campus Housing | B+ |
| Diversity | D |
| Guys | B |
| Girls | A+ |
| Athletics | B |
| Greek Life | A+ |
| Drug Scene | B+ |

# Academics

## Did You Know?

Vanderbilt takes pride in its honest grades; you won't find runaway grade inflation here. Unlike the 92 percent of Harvard grads that graduated with honors, if you graduate from Vandy with honors, it will be a significant distinction.

**Best Places to Study:**
Biomedical Library, Baseball Glove Lounge, Sarratt Student Center, Branscomb Study Lounge, the Pub

## The Lowdown
### ON ACADEMICS

**Degrees Awarded:**
Bachelor, Master, Doctorate

**Undergraduate Schools:**
College of Arts and Science, Blair School of Music, School of Engineering, Peabody College of Education, School of Nursing

**Full-time Faculty:**
2,066

**Faculty with Terminal Degree:**
97%

**Student-to-Faculty Ratio:**
9:1

**Average Course Load:**
15 to 17 hours (5 courses)

**Special Degree Options:**
5-year Undergraduate/MBA program

**Sample Academic Clubs:**
Phi Beta Kappa, Pre-Law Society, Investment Club, Society of Female Engineers

Need help choosing a major? Check out the College prowler book on Vanderbilt available at collegeprowler.com

## Students Speak Out
### ON ACADEMICS

"Professors are good, professional, and smart. Several of the departments have had major problems, especially the political science department."

"In the four years of classes I had, every professor was highly accessible and eager to help me. They never passed me off to a teaching assistant and were always willing to work around my schedule. **Many even give you their home number** and only ask that you refrain from calling late."

## The College Prowler Take
### ON ACADEMICS

Q "I think that one of Vanderbilt's greatest strengths is the amount of student-faculty interaction. I have found my professors to be both approachable and genuinely interested in helping the students. **Almost all of my classes have centered on class discussion**, and participation, and this provides a good opportunity to get to know other students, as well as the professors."

Q "The professors are very smart. **They expect a lot out of you**, and you have to put in the work. They aren't going to give you anything for free. Probably in your freshman year, you will get in that one class where you swear your teacher hates you and you can't seem to do well, but here at Vanderbilt, teachers work with you. If they see you're working hard, they will give you the benefit of the doubt. I encourage you to get to know your professors, and drop them e-mails every now and then so that they know your name. You need to make yourself stand out."

Q "Some teachers are really tough; **some are more down-to-earth**. It all depends on whom you get for which class. Classes are usually pretty small, but intro classes can get big. You'll find that even if you have a TA or grad student instructing your lab or discussion group, the actual professor still isn't too hard to find."

It goes without saying that an institution like Vanderbilt will boast a tremendous faculty, since teachers are truly at the heart of any high-level university. What makes Vanderbilt so special is the interaction between faculty and students, a category where Vandy is an anomaly—in the absolute best sense of the word.

As a research university, the offerings are unlimited, and between all the departments and post-graduate schools, there is ample opportunity for a student to fully explore any discipline he or she so chooses. Combine this with a reasonably small student body and a fabulous student-to-teacher ratio, and you have a learning environment in which undergrads are treated like upper division students from the moment they step onto Vandy's campus their freshman year.

**A-**

The College Prowler™ Grade on
### Academics: A-

A high Academics grade generally indicates that professors are knowledgeable, accessible, and genuinely interested in their students' welfare. Other determining factors include class size, how well professors communicate, and whether or not classes are engaging.

# Local Atmosphere

## Students Speak Out
### ON LOCAL ATMOSPHERE

"It's a pleasant atmosphere. There are many opportunities to find work around campus or downtown. There are some state universities around, but they all keep to themselves."

Q "I don't really like Nashville. I'm from a small city, and I wanted to move to a big, fast city. Nashville got much of its big city notoriety from Opryland, and the country music scene. **It can be described as a big small town**. Yes, there are lots of clubs, but I'm sure you won't be spending your weekends there. After a while, the club scene gets boring."

Q "**Nashville is the sort of city that needs to be given a chance**. Many people from larger cities, notably New Yorkers—Yankees in the southern vernacular—are predisposed to disliking Nashville, and as a result miss out on what it has to offer. Truth be told, it is a smaller city, but that doesn't mean it is devoid of cultural events or good nightlife; it is just on a smaller scale than a San Francisco or New York."

Q "There's really not anything to do here. If you are looking for lots of stuff to do, this is not the place. Your friends are really important, and **you'll gain friendships that will last for a lifetime**. The other colleges here are Tennessee State, Belmont, David Lipscomb, Fisk, and Meharry Medical College. We don't really mingle with the other schools, though."

Q "Nashville is a great emerging and developing town with many options. It's a southern town in Tennessee, but **the people are very cosmopolitan, with a hick here and there**. Many times, you forget you are in Tennessee. There are great restaurants, bars, clubs, theater, and of course, amazing music—and only a part of it is country."

## The Lowdown
### ON LOCAL ATMOSPHERE

**Region:**
Southeast

**City, State:**
Nashville, TN

**Setting:**
Urban

**Distance from Memphis:**
2 hours, 30 minutes

**Distance from Knoxville:**
3 hours

**Distance from Atlanta:**
3 hours, 30 minutes

**Points of Interest:**
Grand Ole Opry, Ryman Auditorium, Frist Art Center

**Major Sports Teams:**
Nashville Predators, Tennessee Titans, Nashville Sounds (Minor League Baseball)

**City Websites:**
*http://www.nashville.gov*
*http://www.nashville.net*

## The College Prowler Take
### ON LOCAL ATMOSPHERE

Nashville is an insider's town. If you know the ins and outs of the city, then there's something to do every day and night. This is a lot of fun, because knowing about the cool restaurant or the special nights at various clubs makes you feel like you're privy to privileged information. The problem is, of course, finding everything to begin with. Making fun of Nashville and the local population is very fashionable for Vanderbilt students, but it should be noted that these same critics can never be found in their rooms on a weekend night, because they are out taking advantage of what the city has to offer.

# Safety & Security

## The Lowdown
### ON SAFETY & SECURITY

# B+

**The College Prowler™ Grade on**
## Local Atmosphere: B+

A high Local Atmosphere grade indicates that the area surrounding campus is safe and scenic. Other factors include nearby attractions, proximity to other schools, and the town's attitude toward students.

**Number of Vandy Police:**
102

**Phone:**
(615) 322-2745

**Health Center Office Hours:**
8 a.m.- 4:30 p.m.

**Safety Services:**
Escort service, shuttle service, Safe Trips

### COLLEGE PROWLER™

Want to know more about local hot spots near Vanderbilt? For a detailed listing of all bars and clubs, check out the College Prowler book on Vanderbilt available at www.collegeprowler.com.

### Did You Know?

Vanderbilt police are actually a division of the Nashville Metro Police, and are therefore real policemen, unlike the security guards at many other universities.

## Students Speak Out
### ON SAFETY & SECURITY

> "I feel like crime in the Vanderbilt community has risen. Sometimes I doubt whether VUPD can be effective addressing something other than parking violations."

Q "Safety has gotten better in the last few years. Vanderbilt University Police Department has been trying to make it a safer place, especially for women. **They offer police escorts at any hour**, if you want to stay at the library late studying. There is also a service called Safe Trips that runs at night."

Q "**There is still a lot of work to do**, but the administration has been treating sexual assault cases more seriously. The Women's Center just received a federal grant to raise awareness about sexual assault on campus, as well as to provide fun programming and counseling services."

Q "Security is a big issue, and I know that VUPD is working closely with other campus organizations to increase our safety, but it's hard. There are services available for students, but they often get overlooked for the quick, sometimes risky, walk alone. **A lot of students generally feel safe**, even when walking alone at night. The most common occurrence I think is theft and larceny, followed by indecent exposures."

Q "There are very few incidents that affect students on the campus. The police notify the entire community whenever an incident does occur. This past year, I believe there were **two robberies, and four or five indecent exposures**. Relatively, it isn't that bad. The areas of Nashville that students inhabit or frequent are also very safe."

## The College Prowler Take
### ON SAFETY & SECURITY

Vanderbilt is very safe in that there isn't a great deal of crime in spite of its urban location. However, many students feel that the community is very vulnerable to more serious incidents than the oft-joked-about string of indecent exposures. Truth be told, the main campus is very poorly lit, and the emergency blue-phones are too few and far between. This, mixed with the general naiveté of the student body, is troublesome. However, Vanderbilt administration and the campus police force are very well equipped to handle any problems (and the statistics back this up). One just wishes that they'd spend more time patrolling the walkways and entrances to campus.

**B+**

The College Prowler™ Grade on
### Safety & Security: B+

A high grade in Safety & Security means that students generally feel safe, campus police are visible, blue-light phones and escort services are readily available, and safety precautions are not overly necessary.

# Facilities

## Computers

**High-Speed Network?** Yes
**Wireless Network?** Yes
**Number of Labs:** 6
**Numbers of Computers:** 204 (in labs)
**24-Hour Labs:** No
**Charge to Print?** The first 10 pages are free; after that, it's 10 cents a page. The only place on campus where printing is free is the Wyatt Center.

## The Lowdown ON FACILITIES

**Student Center:**
Sarratt Student Center

**Athletic Center:**
Student Recreation Center

**Libraries:**
8

**Movie Theater on Campus?**
Yes

**Bowling on Campus?**
No

**Bar on Campus?**
Yes

**Coffeehouse on Campus?**
Yes

**Favorite Things to Do:**
Student Rec Center, Sarratt Movie Theater

**Popular Places to Chill:**
The Wall, Alumni Lawn, the 'C' Room, Rand Hall, Sarratt Student Center

## Students Speak Out ON FACILITIES

"I love all the facilities except the laundry rooms. They're always crowded, the machines are broken, and it costs two bucks a load. But, I guess that's the price you pay for four channels of HBO."

Q "**The recreation center is really nice**. It's large, and there is a lot to do. The labs in the engineering building and on Peabody are the best, though. Vanderbilt is a very scenic school, so just about everywhere you go is really nice."

Q "They are currently completely remodeling many of the athletic facilities for varsity athletes, and the recreational center for student usage is very nice with a great workout room. **We get new equipment every year**, and we have five squash courts, outdoor and indoor tracks, four basketball courts, a climbing wall, and a pool."

Q "**The facilities on campus are beautiful**. Because of the school's enormous endowment, they are able to continually build new buildings and renovate old ones, so it is very rare that you will find yourself in an architecturally unappealing or dated building or facility."

## Campus Dining

Q "Everything is top-notch. **Vandy's got tons of money**, and the people in charge put lots of it into having a nice rec center, computer facilities, and libraries. They recently renovated Sarratt Student Center."

### The College Prowler Take
ON FACILITIES

Vanderbilt takes great pride in both aesthetics and functionality. With the endowment and tuition prices as high as they are, the school is continually improving its facilities, and does an excellent job in discerning both what is necessary, and what is the most effective solution. With regards to facilities, students are continually amazed by the school's ability to allow the history of the University, and the classic feel that comes along with it, to coexist with the need for the modern and high-tech. There is something very special about stepping out of the garden environment of the campus into a perfectly maintained, seemingly antebellum, building and being able to access a high-speed, wireless network on your laptop.

### The Lowdown
ON CAMPUS DINING

**Freshman Meal Plan Requirement?**
Yes

**24-Hour On-Campus Eating?**
No

**Student Favorites:**
The Pub, Stonehenge, the 'C' Room

**Meal Plan Average Cost:**
$690 per semester

### Students Speak Out
ON CAMPUS DINING

"**Food ranges from gross to barely edible. Freshman food is horrible.** I ate salad the entire first year because it was the only decent thing. I almost never ate at Rand after that."

Q "Cafeteria food is good, except **you get tired of eating it every day**. The Divinity School Refectory has really good food, and no one knows about it."

### The College Prowler™ Grade on
### Facilities: A

A high Facilities grade indicates that the campus is aesthetically pleasing and well-maintained; facilities are state-of-the-art, and libraries are exceptional. Other determining factors include the quality of both athletic and student centers and an abundance of things to do on campus.

# Campus Housing

Q: "Food is great, if you aren't eating dinner on the Rand dinner plan. **The student center has several great eateries**: Stonehenge serves incredible sandwiches and soup bowls, but only during lunch; the Pub is open 24 hours with good pub food, like grilled sandwiches, salads, hamburgers, soup bowls, chicken strips, nachos, and free popcorn."

Q: "It's good if you realize it's going to be cafeteria food and **lower your expectations accordingly**. The only complaint I ever had was that the meals were repetitious. Regardless, students are always going to complain about the meal plan."

Q: "**Food has been top-rated**, and when Dining prepares a special event, it's usually excellent. The day-to-day service tends to be mass-produced and repetitive, like anywhere else. Residential colleges will change dining and no doubt spruce it up."

## The College Prowler Take
### ON CAMPUS DINING

Other than dinner at Rand, students are very positive about the quality of the food. Fortunately, you only need to eat there freshman year, and, like most traumatic experiences, it only brings people closer together for having gone through it. Vanderbilt has recently overhauled its meal plan system, which will give students a great deal more flexibility in their food options. However, despite the high quality and selection of what is available, the prices are ridiculously inflated and there isn't a grocery store within walking distance—the cost of living is very high within the "Vanderbubble."

## The College Prowler™ Grade on
## Campus Dining: C-

Our grade on Campus Dining addresses the quality of both school-owned dining halls and independent on-campus restaurants as well as the price, availability, and variety of food.

## The Lowdown
### ON CAMPUS HOUSING

**Undergrads on Campus:**
84%

**Number of Dormitories:**
32

**Number of University-Owned Apartments:**
0

**Room Types:**
Singles, doubles, triples, four-person townhouses, six-person apartment-style, 10 person houses

**Available for Rent:**
Refrigerators, microwaves, fans, bookshelves

**Cleaning Service?**
Yes

**You Get:**
Desk, chair, bookshelf, full-length mirror, dresser, closet, waste bin, bed, mattress, cable TV (includes cable and five HBOs)

**Bed Type:**
Twin extra-long, bunkable

**Also Available:**
Phone

## Students Speak Out
ON CAMPUS HOUSING

"Vandy/Barnard is the nicest dorm on campus. There is a laundry facility, Munchi Mart, and a kitchen. If you're lucky, you might get a corner room, which is a single that's the size of a double."

Q "They've changed things for freshman housing, so **you don't get to pick which building you live in**, just whether you'd like a single or a double. Vandy/Barnard, which is nice, but small, is singles and doubles; Branscomb is all doubles, and Kissam is all singles. You don't want to end up in Kissam, so don't check the box for a single room."

Q "What summarizes Kissam the best is an article that was run by Vanderbilt's humor magazine *The Slant*, which juxtaposed two photos, one of a Kissam building and the other of some of the worst projects in New Orleans. I can honestly say I wasn't able to distinguish between the two images. Did I mention that **it doesn't have laundry**, either?"

Q "As with most of the buildings on campus, dorms are well-maintained and relatively nice. Each dorm develops its own personality each year, so I can't say which to avoid or to request. When talking to other people, remember that **no matter what dorm you get, you will be happy**; I guarantee it."

Q "Kissam Quad is far from the fraternity row and the gym, but it's close to classes. I lived in Kissam and loved it. I like having my own room, but the hall is small, so you feel close to others on your hall. Vandy/Barnard is the nicest dorm, but **the singles are tiny**. Brandscomb is where the doubles are; people love to live there because it's the party dorm."

## The College Prowler Take
ON CAMPUS HOUSING

Most Vanderbilt students live on campus for their entire college career, and it is pretty easy to see why. Undergrads are, for the most part, very well taken care of. The University has changed the way freshmen are assigned, so as to promote more mixing of different types of students, since dorms tend to develop reputations. Odds are, you'll still end up in the sort of place you're looking for. With the exception of a moldy room in Kissam or being banished to Peabody as a sophomore, you probably won't feel the need to live off campus, though some people do get fed up and leave. The key thing to remember as an incoming freshman is that the dorm you live in doesn't dictate the sort of friends you'll make. Even though roommates and hallmates tend to become close, don't overreact if you end up somewhere far from where you think you want to be—after about the first month of school, it won't even be an issue.

**B+**

**The College Prowler™ Grade on**
## Campus Housing: B+

A high Campus Housing grade indicates that dorms are clean, well-maintained, and spacious. Other determining factors include variety of dorms, proximity to classes, and social atmosphere.

# Diversity

## The Lowdown
ON DIVERSITY

**Native American:** 0%

**Asian American:** 7%

**African American:** 7%

**Hispanic:** 4%

**White:** 74%

**International:** 2%

**Unknown:** 6%

**Out-of-State:** 81%

## Minority Clubs
Black Student Union, Muslim Student Association, Asian American Students Association, Masala South Asian Cultural Exchange, Vanderbilt Association of Hispanic Students, African Student Association

## Most Popular Religions
Most of the students on campus are Christans, with the most popular demonitations being Protestant and Catholic.

### Political Activity
There are occasional rallies at Vanderbilt for a wide variety of causes. It seems that about half of the school is passionately and actively involved in politics, while the other half remains apathetic. Not much of a middle ground exists.

### Gay Tolerance
There is a growing gay community at Vanderbilt, and they have a very noticeable and positive presence on campus.

### Economic Status
Vanderbilt comes with a hefty price tag, and that reflects in the student body. Most are middle to upper-class.

## Students Speak Out
ON DIVERSITY

"It isn't diverse at all. Unfortunately, different groups stick to themselves. There are lots of multicultural festivals, but not many students from other races go to these functions."

"**We have people from all over the world**. No matter what you're into, you'll find a close-knit group with the same interests. Plus, it's cool just to talk to people with all sorts of ideas and cultures."

"The diversity on campus is good but the self-segregation is what hurts the campus. All the races on campus stay to themselves and **never mingle with anyone else**. It kind of defeats the purpose of forming a diverse student body."

"Diversity has been a problem. Vanderbilt is continuously improving its diversity, though getting over the stereotype with recruitment is a problem that is slowly being solved. Ethnically, **minorities comprise a very small percentage of the campus**."

"At Vanderbilt, even as a minority, **I never feel like I don't belong**."

## The College Prowler Take
### ON DIVERSITY

Diversity and integration are extremely touchy subjects. It is one thing to have diversity on paper, but quite another to actually achieve true diversity. Obviously, you cannot have real diversity if different kinds of people are not well represented, but once that has been achieved, it is up to the students to follow through. Vanderbilt has become more diverse over the last few years, and the admissions board has made a real point of trying to continue to bring different kinds of people into the Vanderbubble. They have made really good progress—what remains to be seen, however, is whether or not the students (of all groups) at Vandy are interested in making a concerted effort. Right now, the answer is no.

**The College Prowler™ Grade on**
## Diversity: D

A high grade in Diversity indicates that ethnic minorities and international students have a notable presence on campus and that students of different economic backgrounds, religious beliefs, and sexual preferences are well-represented.

Want to know more about diversity on campus? Pick up a College Prowler guidebook on Vanderbilt available at *www.collegeprowler.com*.

# Guys & Girls

## The Lowdown
### ON GUYS & GIRLS

**Women Undergrads:** 52%

**Men Undergrads:** 48%

### Birth Control Available?
Yes. Birth control is available at the Student Health Center. (615) 322-2427.

### Social Scene
Very active. Regardless of whether it is Friday night or Tuesday night, there will generally be something big happening on campus. In the rare event that the campus is dead, it is a near certainty that you will be able to find some large groups of Vandy students downtown.

### Hookups or Relationships?
It's hookups for freshman and sophomores and relationships for juniors and seniors. Alcohol seems to play a large role in this process. For the younger students who are spending a huge amount of their time living it up and drinking on multiple nights of the week, the hookup scene is huge. Juniors and seniors tend to be a little more relationship oriented, but there is still a lot of random "interaction."

## Dress Code

Preppy—J. Crew and Polo shirts for guys and J. Crew and Kate Spade bags for girls. Vandy students waffle between two main fashion styles, the first being the traditional prep style and the other being a trendy designer style. Regardless of your fashion IQ coming in, you will be able to spot a fake Gucci bag in no time.

## Students Speak Out
### ON GUYS & GIRLS

"Like any school, we have a wide range of guys and girls. We have a lot of good-looking people; most of them work out."

"Both guys and girls have **a huge amount of pressure to be attractive and stylish**. It's amazing how easy it is to maintain a good upkeep when you have the money to spend on it."

"**The guys are not as hot as the girls**, and if they're hot, they lose all their points when they open their mouths."

"Average guy: Momma's boy who did well in high school, but wasn't exceptionally popular. Average girl: Daddy's girl who was the prom/homecoming queen, head cheerleader/debutante, and the most popular girl at her high school. **Beauty and brains mix** when you find valedictorians that are striking."

"Guys are kind of full of themselves for the most part. It's kind of hard to find some people who are down-to-earth, but once you do they will become the best friends ever. **Girls are okay once they get older.** I think they come in on way too high a horse, either morally or egotistically. After they settle down, they're much better."

## The College Prowler Take
### ON GUYS & GIRLS

No one has ever disputed that Vanderbilt girls are beautiful and talented—the only problem is that they all tend to go for the same look, which, after a while, diminishes their individuality. It seems like there is a definite burden on Vandy girls to live up to this high standard. Guys are, by comparison, not quite at the level of the girls, but are, in their own right, pretty impressive. There is a greater variety of the types of guys, but, still, both men and women at Vanderbilt are not incredibly diverse, being preppy for the most part.

### The College Prowler™ Grade on
## Guys: B

A high grade for Guys indicates that the male population on campus is attractive, smart, friendly, and engaging, and that the school has a decent ratio of guys to girls.

### The College Prowler™ Grade on
## Girls: A+

A high grade for Girls not only implies that the women on campus are attractive, smart, friendly, and engaging, but also that there is a fair ratio of girls to guys.

# Athletics

## Most Popular Sports
Football and basketball get the most fan support.

## Overlooked Teams
While they don't draw many fans, Vanderbilt consistently excels at the "country club" sports. Both of our tennis and golf teams have placed nationally and consistently rank among the top in the SEC. The Vanderbilt baseball team has a brand-new stadium, and has competed strongly in SEC play.

## The Lowdown
ON ATHLETICS

**Men's Teams:**
Baseball
Basketball
Cross Country
Football
Golf
Soccer
Tennis

**Women's Teams:**
Lacrosse
Basketball
Cross Country
Golf
Soccer
Tennis
Track

**Athletic Division:**
Division I

**Conference:**
Southeastern Conference

**School Mascot:**
Commodores

**Fields:**
Three student intramural fields, baseball field, soccer and lacrosse stadium, football field, football practice field

## Club Sports
Aikido, Angling, Aussie Football Badminton, Balloon Bowling, Crew, Cycling, Disc, Golf, Equestrian, Fencing, Field Hockey, Ice Hockey, Judo, Karate, Kung Fu, Lacrosse, Paintball, Racquetball, Roller Hockey, Rugby, Sailing, Soccer, Squash, Swimming, Table Tennis, Tae Kwon Do, Thai Boxing, Track, Triathlon, Ultimate Frisbee, Volleyball, Water Polo, Water Skiing, Wrestling

## Intramurals (IMs)
Basketball, Flag Football, Frisbee, Softball

## Getting Tickets
Tickets to games are for students. Usually your student ID card will get you into any Vanderbilt sporting event for free.

## Students Speak Out
ON ATHLETICS

*"School spirit for our sports teams is booming, and women's teams are awesome."*

Q "Students love to go to varsity games. Vanderbilt is in the most competitive conference in the nation, so we often lose. Nonetheless, it's a great social event that students love attending. As for IMs, they are extremely popular and offer tons of sports. If the rec center doesn't offer your sport, and there is a demand, **they'll create a league for you.**"

> "There are so many kids at Vandy who were great athletes in high school, but aren't quite good enough to compete in the SEC. Similarly, there are a lot of sports that don't exist at the varsity level that do exist at the club level, so if there's something you want to play, **you'll be able to play it at a pretty high level**."

> "Varsity sports aren't big on campus, mainly because **everyone would rather root for their home SEC team** because everyone seems to be from Kentucky, Alabama, or Georgia. IM sports are very good and very available to everyone. I really think that the IM sports have a substantial impact on the morale of the campus."

## The College Prowler Take
### ON ATHLETICS

**Vanderbilt seems to get made fun of a lot for the support it gives its teams. A lot of this has to do with the size of the student body. Even if every single Vanderbilt student and grad student showed up, we couldn't fill our own basketball arena. Compare this to the public schools of the SEC, which are three times bigger and have tons of alumni that live, and have always lived, within 20 minutes of their school. There are some of us, however, that take pride in our football team, despite the two-win, ten-loss campaign last year. Nearly 100 percent of our football players graduated, and none of our programs have ever been on probation. Vandy remains the lovable and respectable underdog.**

## B

The College Prowler™ Grade on
### Athletics: B

A high grade in Athletics indicates that students have school spirit, that sports programs are respected, that games are well-attended, and that intramurals are a prominent part of student life.

# Greek Life

## The Lowdown
### ON GREEK LIFE

**Number of Fraternities:**
12

**Number of Sororities:**
17

**Undergrad Men in Fraternities:**
31%

**Undergrad Women in Sororities:**
53%

## Students Speak Out
### ON GREEK LIFE

> "Greek life runs the show, but the relations between the Greeks and the independents are really good, and most things are open to everyone."

> "Greek life dominates Vanderbilt social life. If you don't join a frat or know someone in a frat, **you'll be hard-pressed to find a party** ever. This is just a part of being a Vanderbilt and is unavoidable."

Q "One major stereotype of Vanderbilt is that **the Greek scene dominates the social life**. Many students are not Greek. However, the Greek scene does provide a great option for everyone in weekend activities. That, along with the fact that the houses are non-residential, keeps the Greeks from becoming the elitists they tend to be at other colleges."

Q "About half the females at Vandy rush a sorority, and about a third of the males join a fraternity. While many people believe it dominates the social scene, **one can be independent and still have a social life**. One thing the Greeks bring is free parties on campus where you can dance, be crazy, and hang with all your friends."

Q "**I wish there was more to do on the weekends**—frat parties get so old. I also have a couple best friends that aren't Greek and are only excluded from the sense of belonging."

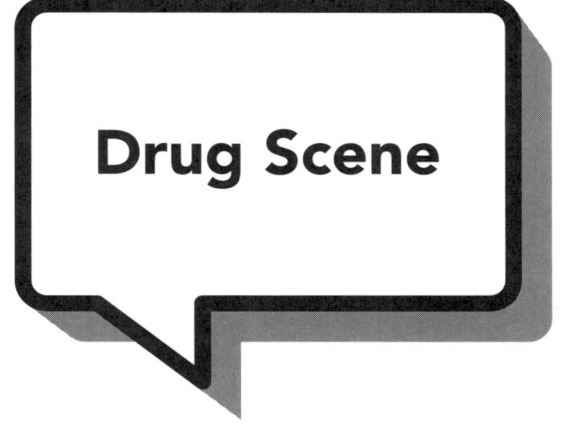

## Drug Scene

### The Lowdown
ON DRUG SCENE

### The College Prowler Take
ON GREEK LIFE

It is undeniable that the Greeks play a major role at Vanderbilt. A lot of people are frustrated with this, and like to come down on the Greeks—they call them sheep or people who buy friends. It is easy to be negative about the Greek system because it is so prevalent, but because all the parties are open to everyone, and there is an honest sense of inclusion, the Greeks actually provide a really good service to the community by planning and organizing parties and events. The pressure to join a fraternity or sorority is definitely there.

**Most Prevalent Drugs on Campus:**
Marijuana, Adderall, Cocaine

**Liquor-Related Referrals:**
Not available

**Liquor-Related Arrests:**
7

**Drug-Related Referrals:**
Not available

**Drug-Related Arrests:**
17

**Drug Counseling Programs:**
Available through Student Health and Student Psychological Services, (615) 322-2571

### The College Prowler™ Grade on
# Greek Life: A+

A high grade in Greek Life indicates that sororities and fraternities are not only present, but also active on campus. Other determining factors include the variety of houses available and the respect the Greek community receives from the rest of the campus.

## Students Speak Out
### ON DRUG SCENE

> "All in all, there isn't a drug scene, unless you count tobacco, caffeine, or alcohol. However, it does exist, and if you want to find it you can. Largely, students stick to those."

Q "Drugs aren't as big as I thought they'd be, but then again I don't hang out with the major druggies on campus. **I heard they're really bad**, but I wouldn't know for sure."

Q "Drugs really aren't that big at Vanderbilt because **the drug of choice for the Vandy student is alcohol**. There is a problem with binge drinking and alcohol abuse, but drug use is hardly a speck on the radar."

Q "You will not hear stories about 'pot parties' or drug-related date rape cases. That's not to say it doesn't happen, but **it's not prevalent on campus**. I think the main thing that students do is marijuana, but I don't think it's very dominant, and you probably will never find yourself in a peer pressure situation. I think the dominant 'drug' on campus is beer."

Q "There are a lot of drugs on campus, but that's the same everywhere. I have been around a lot of drugs, and it's very easy to make the decision about whether or not to partake. I, personally, never felt pressured. **It's easy to find drugs, and easy to stay away from them** at the same time."

## The College Prowler Take
### ON DRUG SCENE

Unless you're a pothead who also happens to be a genius, it'd be downright impossible to succeed at a school like Vanderbilt while supporting a drug habit. But, then again, if you were a genius, you wouldn't be doing drugs in the first place. There is a small drug scene on campus, so if you really need to find drugs, you can without too much difficulty. The poison of choice on Vanderbilt's campus, however, is alcohol. Like at any university, there are problems with binge drinking, but if you're smart enough to get into Vanderbilt then you're smart enough to make your own decisions.

**B+**

### The College Prowler™ Grade on
### Drug Scene: B+

A high grade on Drug Scene indicates that drugs are not a noticeable part of campus life; drug use is not visible, and no pressure to use them seems to exist.

# Overall Experience

Q "I think a lot of people come into Vanderbilt with a bit of a chip on their shoulder. Either because they feel an Ivy League school snubbed them, or [because] they got into an Ivy League school and couldn't afford it, but Vanderbilt gave them a scholarship. What's amazing is, given that, **everyone ends up falling in love with Vandy** and cannot imagine themselves anywhere else."

## The Lowdown
ON OVERALL EXPERIENCE

"I'm having a lot of fun, and I'm being challenged by some of the best minds in the world; I can't think of any way I could improve my college life."

Q "I have never regretted being at Vandy for a minute. **I have found a lot of very good friends** here, and I have had a lot of fun partying here. Nashville is a fun city with a lot going on, too. I would definitely recommend this school."

Q "Vanderbilt is the place for me, and I'm glad I came here. My experience here so far is worth a lifetime and I have two years left. **I'm just really happy I didn't go to Duke** ... I would be miserable."

Q "Even though a few friends are like family to me now, I think I would've enjoyed my college years more if I had transferred that first year or taken a more active interest in my college search. **I needed somewhere more liberal, less preppy, and less Greek.** However, I excelled in my classes and graduated with honors, and even spent time abroad, so maybe it all worked out in the end."

## The College Prowler Take
ON OVERALL EXPERIENCE

Initial impressions of the school are not always favorable. Even if you enjoy your visit and love the beautiful campus when you arrive here, you may still spend some of your first semester wondering what you are doing in a place so different from where you grew up. However, once you get past the initial culture shock and make a few steps outside of your comfort zone, you'll realize that Vandy is a great place to be.

Every now and again, southern culture will do something new to throw you for a loop, but even when that happens you should enjoy the exposure to something new. At every turn, there is something to enjoy at this college and in this town. From the academic opportunities to the social scene, Vanderbilt offers everything that you could ask for.

# Wake Forest University

Box 7305, Reynolda Station,
Winston-Salem, NC 27109
www.wfu.edu        (336) 758-5255

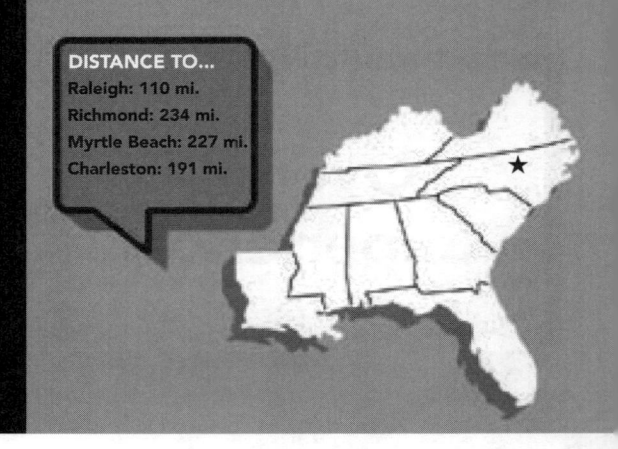

**DISTANCE TO...**
Raleigh: 110 mi.
Richmond: 234 mi.
Myrtle Beach: 227 mi.
Charleston: 191 mi.

*"Wake Forest has surpassed its reputation as a solid school for southern kids and has become an elite institution with national appeal."*

### Table of Contents

| | |
|---|---|
| Academics | 689 |
| Local Atmosphere | 691 |
| Safety & Security | 692 |
| Facilities | 694 |
| Campus Dining | 695 |
| Campus Housing | 697 |
| Diversity | 698 |
| Guys & Girls | 700 |
| Athletics | 701 |
| Greek Life | 703 |
| Drug Scene | 705 |
| Overall Experience | 706 |

**Total Enrollment:**
3,930

**Top 10% of High School Class:**
65%

**Acceptance Rate:**
45%

**Tuition:**
$28,310

**SAT Range (25th-75th Percentile):**

| Verbal | Math | Total |
|---|---|---|
| 610 – 690 | 630 – 700 | 1240 – 1390 |

**ACT Range (25th-75th Percentile):**

| Verbal | Math | Total |
|---|---|---|
| N/A | N/A | N/A |

**Most Popular Majors:**
12% Business
12% Communication
10% Political Science and Government
9% Psychology
8% Biological Sciences

**Students also applied to:***
Duke University
Emory University
University of North Carolina–Chapel Hill
University of Richmond
Vanderbilt University

*For more school info check out www.collegeprowler.com

### College Prowler Report Card

| | |
|---|---|
| Academics | B+ |
| Local Atmosphere | C+ |
| Safety & Security | A+ |
| Facilities | A |
| Campus Dining | C+ |
| Campus Housing | B |
| Diversity | D- |
| Guys | B+ |
| Girls | A- |
| Athletics | A |
| Greek Life | A+ |
| Drug Scene | A |

# Academics

## The Lowdown
**ON ACADEMICS**

**Degrees Awarded:**
Bachelor, Master, Doctorate, First Professional

**Undergraduate Schools:**
Wake Forest College, Wayne Calloway School of Business and Accountancy

**Full-time Faculty:**
440

**Faculty with Terminal Degree:**
91%

**Student-to-Faculty Ratio:**
10:1

**Average Course Load:**
14 hours

**AP Test Score Requirements:**
Possible credit for scores of 4 or 5

**IB Test Score Requirements:**
Possible credit for scores of 6 or 7

## Sample Academic Clubs
Accounting Society, Alpha Epsilon Delta (health professions), American Society for Personnel Administration, Anthony Aston Players, Anthropology Club, Beta Beta Beta (biology), Circolo Italiano, Communications Association, Delta Alpha Phi (German), El Club Hispanico, Eta Sigma Phi (classics), Euzelian Academic Society, French Club, Golden Key National Honor Society (community service), Kappa Kappa Psi (band), American Marketing Association, Mortar Board (seniors), Omicron Delta Epsilon (economics), Omicron Delta Kappa (leadership), Phi Beta Kappa, Phi Mu Epsilon (mathematics), Philomathesian Literary Society, Pi Sigma Alpha (politics), Politics Club, Pre-Law Society, Russian Club, Sigma Tau Delta (English), Sociology Club, Student North Carolina Association of Educators, and Upsilon Pi Epsilon (computer science)

## Special Degree Options
Dual-Degree Programs: Biomedical Engineering (with Virginia Tech), Medical Technology, and Microbiology (with the Wake Forest School of Medicine), Engineering (with North Carolina State University and other approved schools of engineering), Forestry and Environmental Studies (with Duke University), Latin American Studies (with Georgetown University)

Accelerated Master's Programs: Five-year BS/MS in accountancy

Intercollege Programs: Interdisciplinary Honors Seminars, American Ethnic Studies, Classical Studies, International Studies, Humanities, Women's Studies

## Did You Know?
Wake Forest has study abroad programs in more then 20 different countries, and nearly 50 percent of all students study abroad at some point during their four years.

Wake Forest's accounting students pass the CPA exam at a higher rate than those at any other school.

**Best Places to Study:**
Z. Smith Reynolds Library, Benson Center, Carswell Hall

## Students Speak Out
### ON ACADEMICS

"**The teachers are great! They really are there to teach, and not to do research. Wake gives you an amazing education when you graduate because of all of the liberal arts divisional requirements.**"

Q "Grading at Wake Forest is really tough. Many **professors will make up their own grading scale** that's harder than normal, or will only give out a certain number of As. It's very challenging here, more so than you would think."

Q "**It depends upon the course**, but I think that you can take any course at Wake, and at least one section will be taught by a truly great teacher. My mom has been a teacher for almost 30 years, so I'm harsh when judging teachers. While I have found a few I don't get along with, I have also encountered some of the best I've ever had. As a whole, they're an excellent group."

Q "The professors are incredible. **They come from all over the world**. In my freshman year seminar, during the Arab-Israeli conflict, my teacher was actually a visiting professor from Palestine. He wrote the three books that we read for the class, and the class was outstanding. My religion professor specialized in Buddhism and Hinduism. He had been to the base camp of Mt. Everest and was fluent in Japanese. He was incredible and an inspiration to me."

Q "The professors at Wake Forest are impressive, both intellectually and in terms of their diversity. While the vast majority of professors are experts in their field, every now and then you'll have a professor who has difficulty getting the material across. Even though Wake has an extensive liberal arts requirement, **the professors usually keep your attention**, even in classes that you have no interest in."

## The College Prowler Take
### ON ACADEMICS

Possibly the most attractive feature of the vast majority of Wake Forest's faculty is their accessibility. In a technology-obsessed environment, professors are never more than an e-mail away. The majority of teachers upload the syllabus, coursework, and assignments onto either a personal Website or the Blackboard intranet. You'll find that professors, in addition to posting a series of set office hours, are more than willing to accommodate advance requests to meet with you at a more suitable time. Wake Forest professors are generally regarded as brilliant, but modest. In a university primarily concerned with undergraduate education, there are very few haughty, intellectual snobs who feel that teaching a bunch of freshman is a shameful waste of their talent. Instead, almost all professors actively teach intro classes at some point or another, and do so with enthusiasm, rather than throwing a series of TAs upon you.

Wake has certainly earned its reputation as "Work Forest," as the workload is incredibly demanding, and the average GPA hovers dangerously below a 3.0. However, that very reputation makes success here that much more valuable and rewarding, and most students agree that while they're often steamrolled by a landslide of work, it only makes them stronger and better equipped to face a new series of challenges.

**B+**

The College Prowler™ Grade on
### Academics: B+

A high Academics grade generally indicates that professors are knowledgeable, accessible, and genuinely interested in their students' welfare. Other determining factors include class size, how well professors communicate, and whether or not classes are engaging.

# Local Atmosphere

## The Lowdown
ON LOCAL ATMOSPHERE

**Region:**
Southeast

**City, State:**
Winston-Salem, NC

**Setting:**
Suburban/small city

**Distance from Charlotte:**
1 hours, 30 minutes

**Distance from Washington DC:**
5 hours

**Distance from Atlanta:**
5 hours

**Points of Interest:**
Old Salem, Museum of American Art, North Carolina Zoological Park, Ernie Shore Field, Lawrence Joel Veterans Coliseum, Groves Stadium, Tanglewood Park, Ziggy's, The Garage

**Major Sports Teams:**
Warthogs (minor league baseball), Parrots (minor league hockey)

**City Websites:**
http://www.winstonsalem.com
http://www.visitwinstonsalem.com

## Students Speak Out
ON LOCAL ATMOSPHERE

"Winston-Salem is kind of dead. I was expecting a city atmosphere, and it's definitely not. There are smaller schools in Winston, but we don't really mingle too much. I would stay away from any clubs downtown. They're sketchy."

Q "UNC-Chapel Hill and Duke are about an hour or so away in Raleigh-Durham. **There's a huge social scene over there**. North Carolina State isn't far away either. In Winston-Salem, there are a few small schools, but Wake dominates. Winston-Salem is not a bad city by any means, but if you want the really big entertainment options, you'll have to go to Raleigh or Charlotte, which are just under two hours east and south of here."

Q "A lot of people say Winston-Salem is boring. It isn't really a college town or anything. We have things like movies, and putt-putt. However, a lot of people stay on campus most of the time because **there are a lot of things to do on campus**. We have a movie theater, nature trails, and shops you can walk to in less than five minutes."

Q "There are tons of restaurants, a few clubs, bars, movie theaters, bowling alleys, and a mall. **It isn't exactly the most interesting college town**, but most things occur on campus anyway, so that isn't much of a loss. There are other universities like Winston Salem State, but I haven't visited any."

Q "If you are from a small town, then you'll be happy. But if you're from a city and are used to the party life, you may be disappointed. Basically, **there's always something to do**. You just have to go find it."

## The College Prowler Take
### ON LOCAL ATMOSPHERE

Winston-Salem is, as many students would attest, decidedly mediocre. A city of roughly 180,000, W-S doesn't quite have the resources to be considered an exciting place by any means, but it isn't exactly a cultural wasteland either. While the downtown area is generally dead, the outlying areas feature enough bars to keep students generally content, and an impressive array of restaurants. While Winston's athletic scene is generally dominated by the Demon Deacons, the area does feature a pair of minor league teams, baseball's Warthogs and ice hockey's Parrots. Essentially, some fun can be found in Winston, but it may require some looking. Remember, if you're desperate for a college town, UNC isn't too far east, and most Wake students will likely end up there more than once over the course of four years.

## C+

The College Prowler™ Grade on
### Local Atmosphere: C+

A high Local Atmosphere grade indicates that the area surrounding campus is safe and scenic. Other factors include nearby attractions, proximity to other schools, and the town's attitude toward students.

# Safety & Security

## The Lowdown
### ON SAFETY & SECURITY

**Phone:**
911 (emergencies), 311 (non-emergencies)

**Health Center Office Hours:**
Monday through Friday 8:30 a.m.-12 p.m. and 1:30 p.m.-4 p.m.

**Safety Services:**
Rape Defense classes, Campus Watch, R.I.D.E. shuttle/escort van, emergency phones, victim assistance, C.A.R.E. Women's Safety

### Did You Know?
The Wake Forest community has endured only 14 violent crimes over the past few years.

## Students Speak Out
### ON SAFETY & SECURITY

{ "Campus police are never too far away, and there are blue-lights around campus. Safety is definitely not something that really worries anybody at all, though maybe we take it for granted."

Q "We close-off campus at 10 p.m., so **you have to have a Wake Forest parking pass to get in** or have someone call down for you. Also, all the doors to the suites and dorms are locked at all times, and the only way to get in is to have a Wake Forest key card. Honestly, I feel relatively safe, and the police on campus are really helpful. If you decide to come, I suggest that you take RAD—it's a self-defense course for women, and it's really fun! You get to know the police officers through RAD, and it makes me feel much more confident."

Q "If you live on campus, you have almost nothing to worry about. You can walk around campus any time of the day or night and not worry. If you're walking around really late at night, though, it's still a good idea to have someone with you. **Campus police are always accessible**, and very friendly. I have never felt uncomfortable in my dorm. Lock your door when you're sleeping or not there, and you'll be fine."

Q "I can honestly say that at Wake, **I feel safer than I do at home**, which is a nice area of New Jersey. Through all the mandatory orientation meetings and required health classes, they give you statistics and information on crimes that occur on campus—stuff you would find everywhere like violence, theft, or rape, etc. Besides some fights and people drinking too much, I haven't heard of anything really bad happening."

Q "The first thing you need to know about Wake Forest is that it is called the 'bubble.' Basically, **WFU is surrounded on all sides**. There are three entrances, and after 10 p.m., police block all of the gates to the entrances. This means that anyone, besides WFU students, who enters campus after 10 p.m. must be approved."

## The College Prowler Take
### ON SAFETY & SECURITY

Considering Winston-Salem's less-than-admirable crime record, Wake Forest's campus is just about as good as it gets in terms of overall safety. The campus is essentially closed to outside traffic after 8 p.m., requiring a visitor's pass or prior permission for non-students to enter at night. Granted, every few months there will be an incident in which someone has been mugged in a remote parking lot in the dead of night. However, these incidents have been exclusively non-violent, and usually involve more of a lack of common sense on the part of the victim than anything else. Barring these few minor issues, Wake's campus is overwhelmingly safe, and with a touch of common sense, you'll coast through your four years incident-free.

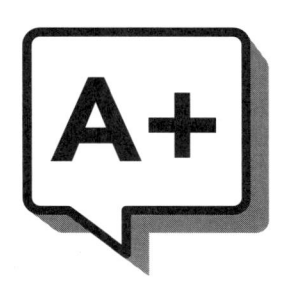

**A+**

The College Prowler™ Grade on
## Safety & Security: A+

A high grade in Safety & Security means that students generally feel safe, campus police are visible, blue-light phones and escort services are readily available, and safety precautions are not overly necessary.

# Facilities

## Favorite Things to Do

Athletics and music are generally the most popular Wake Forest sponsored events. While ACC basketball is certainly the king here, and students will camp out days in advance for tickets against Duke and UNC, football games are very popular on Saturdays. Soccer and baseball games tend to draw a decent following as well. Wake attracts a few major acts each year to play on campus, and hosts tons of lesser known artists and student bands weekly.

## The Lowdown
### ON FACILITIES

**Student Center:**
Benson University Center (the UC)

**Athletic Center:**
Miller Athletic Center and Reynolds Gym

**Libraries:**
Z. Smith Reynolds Library and various departmental libraries

**Numbers of Computers:**
One for every student, plus labs

**Movie Theater on Campus?**
Yes, Pugh Auditorium and Benson University Center have theaters.

**Bowling on Campus?**
No

**Bar on Campus?**
Yes, there is Shorty's Bar and Grill.

**Coffeehouse on Campus?**
Not currently, but one will be constructed during this upcoming year.

**Popular Places to Chill:**
Benson University Center, Reynolda Cafeteria (the Pit)

## Students Speak Out
### ON FACILITIES

"Facilities are all great. Wake has a ton of money, and makes the campus and buildings look immaculate."

Q "I love the facilities on campus. The Miller Center is one of the nicest buildings on campus. **The fitness center has tons of machines**, such as weight machines, free weights, treadmills, elliptical machines, bikes, etc. The only problem is that it always tends to be crowded with masses of students trying to work out. The other buildings are all quality too. I have no complaints."

Q "The facilities are very nice and **are constantly being renovated**. The campus is gorgeous in general."

Q "The facilities are really nice. We just got a huge new exercise building that offers classes and has a ton of exercise equipment. **We have a free movie theater on campus**, Starbucks, Office Depot, Wachovia, small grocery stores, and a really nice bookstore."

Q "Facilities are amazing in all aspects. **No school that I've ever been to compares** to Wake's facilities, and I visited some of the top schools in the nation, such as Stanford, Duke, and USC."

## The College Prowler Take
### ON FACILITIES

The academic buildings at Wake Forest are, for the most part, excellent. New buildings, such as Greene Hall, are something of a fusion of modern architecture and traditional southern Georgian brick. In addition, built into each seat in nearly all classrooms are personal Ethernet connections and power outlets. You will be using your laptop quite a bit. The lab facilities are as you'd expect, functional and fairly sterile. Students here certainly aren't surprised that Wake's campus is consistently rated one of the top in the nation.

## Campus Dining

### The Lowdown
### ON CAMPUS DINING

**A**

**Freshman Meal Plan Requirement?**
Yes

**24-Hour On-Campus Eating?**
No

**Student Favorites:**
Chick-fil-A, Tortilla Fresca, Pan-Geo's

**Meal Plan Average Cost:**
$1,300 per semester

### The College Prowler™ Grade on
### Facilities: A

A high Facilities grade indicates that the campus is aesthetically pleasing and well-maintained; facilities are state-of-the-art, and libraries are exceptional. Other determining factors include the quality of both athletic and student centers and an abundance of things to do on campus.

**Did You Know?**
No one at Wake ever buys silverware. Walk into the Benson Center, grab 50 plastic forks, and walk out like you own the place.

## Students Speak Out
**ON CAMPUS DINING**

"The food is great at the beginning, because everything's new and awesome, but after a while it does get a little boring. Subway is huge and there's always a long line."

"On campus, the food is **very satisfactory**. Among the big names, we have a Subway, a Chick-fil-A, Freshens, and Pizza Hut; they offer all the things they do normally. There is also the Sundry Shop, a mini grocery store on campus that sells almost anything and everything you can't get in the cafeterias. There is also Shorty's, an on-campus coffeehouse that covers all your caffeine needs, as well as desserts and some slightly more formal dinners."

"**The food on campus is lousy**; the only unfriendly workers on campus are those who serve the food. The food options lack diversity, and the hours are poor. While the Mag Room is available for a quality 'help yourself' style lunch, and 'the Pit' has the most dinner options, students quickly get tired of the food on campus, and since the prices are mostly outrageous, many choose to take advantage of the cuisine off campus."

"Wake lacks a 24-hour food option, as well as an all-you-can-eat buffet style. **While it has its disadvantages, it does allow you to enter the food areas as often as you'd like**, as you are not constrained to only a certain amount of visits, as other campus's meal plans dictate."

"The food is decent, although not overly healthy. **There is a pretty good variety of options** of styles of foods and different places to eat, but the availability of healthier food could definitely be improved. The Benson cafeteria has an especially nice atmosphere."

"Food on campus is okay, for a while. A company called Aramark basically has **a monopoly on the food services**, so they have little incentive to provide high quality or low prices. I cook most of my meals now."

## The College Prowler Take
**ON CAMPUS DINING**

What does it say about Wake's food service when the main dining hall is openly referred to as "the Pit"? Well, despite its name, the main food court at Wake Forest isn't too bad. Stocked with a Subway, Italian, Mexican, southern, and "World's Faire" stations, along with a typical burger joint, a bakery, Freshen's frozen yogurt, and a salad bar, you can find anything from chicken Parmesan to portobello fajitas or homestyle turkey with gravy and mashed potatoes. While the food's quality has actually exceeded many students' expectations over the years, watch out for the bill. Ouch! You can run your total up over 10 dollars before you even know what hit you.

**C+**

The College Prowler™ Grade on
### Campus Dining: C+

Our grade on Campus Dining addresses the quality of both school-owned dining halls and independent on-campus restaurants as well as the price, availability, and variety of food.

# Campus Housing

## Room Types

Residence rooms are configured into halls, suites, and apartment-style suites.

Halls—students, living in double occupancy rooms, share a large, central bathroom facility (typically thirty students will live together on a hall).

Suites—students share a private or semi-private bathroom with no more than eight students; these rooms may be either doubles or singles.

Apartment-Style Suites—four single rooms share a common living area, kitchen and bathroom.

## The Lowdown
### ON CAMPUS HOUSING

**Undergrads on Campus:**
80%

**Number of Dormitories:**
18

**Number of University-Owned Apartments:**
3

**You Get:**
Bed, desk and chair, dresser, closet, window coverings, cable TV jack, Ethernet connections, free campus and local phone calls, mini-fridge and microwave combo

**Bed Type:**
Twin extra-long (39"x80"); bunk-beds

**Also Available:**
Substance-free and special-interest housing

**Cleaning Service?**
In public areas. Community and semi-private bathrooms are cleaned by staff approximately once a week, as are the common hallways in suites.

## Did You Know?

All residents get free cable and all dorm rooms have both air conditioning and heat.

## Students Speak Out
### ON CAMPUS HOUSING

"Don't live in substance-free housing, even if you use no substances. Trust me on this one."

Q "The dorms are pretty nice. Luter is a nice dorm, but not a lot of fun people live there. The freshman dorms are fun because you hang out with people in your class and bond. Upperclassmen prefer to live on the quad. Davis, Taylor, Poteat, and Kitchin are the dorms to be in after freshman year, but stay away from Effird or Huffman—they're weird. But, **anywhere you're placed as a freshman is fine**. You'll have lots of other freshmen with you and you'll love it."

Q "The dorms are all pretty nice. I stayed in Bostwick, and I loved it. **I had a corner room in the basement so it was really big**. Collins and Babcock have sinks in their rooms, and Johnson is substance-free. I don't think you have a choice in housing assignments freshman year, but you can try. They are all co-ed by floor or by hall."

> "The dorms on campus are, for the most part, great. Most of the freshman dorms are very similar, except for location—beware of Palmer and Piccolo; for they are far removed from the rest of the campus. **Some dorms have sinks and bathrooms in or between rooms**, which is very convenient."

> "All the dorms are nice. About 85 percent of students live on campus. Freshmen are put together on South Campus. Collins is the louder freshman dorm because it has the most people. Johnson is substance-free. You can only choose to live in Johnson. Otherwise, it's just random placement. **As a freshman, you can't pick your roommate**. You fill out a questionnaire and Wake pairs you up with someone who has similar answers."

## The College Prowler Take
### ON CAMPUS HOUSING

Fortunately, most of Wake's freshman halls aren't bad. You should expect nothing smaller than a roughly 14' by 9' room at worst. Every room at Wake includes a microwave and mini-fridge, an added perk you soon won't be able to live without. Collins, Bostwick, and Johnson are decent, and are set up in a communal hall style, in which bathrooms are shared by roughly 30 students. Each of the freshman dorms has at least one kitchen on each floor, numerous well-equipped study lounges, laundry rooms, and vending machines. In general, there is no point worrying about room selection as a freshman, because barring Johnson, you can't choose where your room will be; your rooming fate is left to the luck of the draw.

## B

### The College Prowler™ Grade on
### Campus Housing: B

A high Campus Housing grade indicates that dorms are clean, well-maintained, and spacious. Other determining factors include variety of dorms, proximity to classes, and social atmosphere.

# Diversity

## The Lowdown
### ON DIVERSITY

**Native American:** 0%

**Asian American:** 4%

**African American:** 9%

**Hispanic:** 1%

**White:** 83%

**International:** 3%

**Out-of-State:** 75%

### Minority Clubs

WFU's minority clubs are a very active social force on campus. Minority student organizations include the Black Student Alliance, the Asian Student Interest Association, the Gospel Choir, El Club Hispanico, and the Black Christian Fellowship. The Office of Multicultural Affairs advises four chartered, historically African American Greek organizations: Alpha Phi Alpha, Omega Psi Phi, Alpha Kappa Alpha, and Delta Sigma Theta.

## Most Popular Religions
The most commonly represented religious group on campus is Baptist, followed by Methodist. There are also pockets of Catholics as well as Jews.

## Political Activity
The majority of students are politically conservative. Though the campus does have active Campus Democrat and Campus Republican student groups, students are generally not overly outspoken about their political views. Many consider the student body to be generally apathetic.

## Gay Tolerance
The campus is generally accepting of its gay students, and has on-campus student groups such as the GSSA (Gay-Straight Student Alliance). However, the percentage of homosexuals on campus is fairly low, so the GSSA doesn't play a major role in campus affairs.

## Economic Status
Many of the students at Wake are downright filthy rich, and you'll see plenty of BMWs around campus. There are plenty of middle-class people as well, however, so don't worry if your parents' income doesn't exceed that of a small country.

## Students Speak Out
### ON DIVERSITY

"Wake takes students from all over the country. There are only two states not represented, and I think there are 12 other countries represented."

Q "The school isn't diverse at all, which I don't like. However, many people are very open-minded, which is great. **Every year, the school gets more and more diverse**, so the administration is definitely trying to change the lack of diversity issue."

Q "The campus is not at all diverse. **Mainly white, upper-class Republicans go here**. There is a small minority population, but personally, I was hoping for much more diversity than I found at Wake."

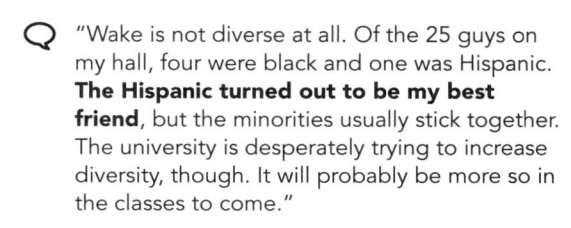

Q "Wake is not diverse at all. Of the 25 guys on my hall, four were black and one was Hispanic. **The Hispanic turned out to be my best friend**, but the minorities usually stick together. The university is desperately trying to increase diversity, though. It will probably be more so in the classes to come."

Q "**Diversity is somewhat of a problem**. It's basically white upper-class, and that's the norm. There are obviously minorities, but a lot less than there should be, in my book."

## The College Prowler Take
### ON DIVERSITY

Upon arriving at Wake, you're sure to notice a general trend in the student body here. Roughly 80 percent of the students at Wake Forest are white, and diversity is something that could certainly be improved upon. Fortunately, race relations are generally quite good, which can't be said about every school. Wake Forest does feature many cultural student groups for those so inclined, which are attended fairly well and are very active on campus. Wake Forest is certainly aiming to improve the sub-par diversity on campus; the students are generally open-minded, and recognize the administration's attempts to improve the situation.

The College Prowler™ Grade on
## Diversity: D-

A high grade in Diversity indicates that ethnic minorities and international students have a notable presence on campus and that students of different economic backgrounds, religious beliefs, and sexual preferences are well-represented.

# Guys & Girls

## The Lowdown
ON GUYS & GIRLS

**Women Undergrads:** 51%

**Men Undergrads:** 49%

### Birth Control Available?
Yes. Student Health offers several forms of birth control including pills and shots. They also have an unlimited supply of free condoms.

### Social Scene
Social interaction on campus lives and dies with the Greek system. Like it or not, the vast majority of students will hit the frats before even considering the bars or clubs. Fortunately for everyone, the parties are generally open, so there will be plenty of independents in addition to the Greeks.

### Hookups or Relationships?
There's a rumor that some Wake students were caught actually dating a few years back, but for all we know it hasn't happened since. At Wake Forest, hookups are king. You will find that upperclassmen do eventually develop a few relationships however.

### Dress Code
Wake Forest students could single-handedly keep Abercrombie & Fitch in business. Don't be surprised if many of your classmates dress up to go to class, and expect more than a few people to show up to football games in shirts and ties or sundresses.

## Students Speak Out
ON GUYS & GIRLS

"Guys are typically the rich Abercrombie mold, and girls the same. There is, I'm sorry to say, very little variety. This is pretty different for me, given that I'm from a public, more diverse, background."

Q "Generally, guys and girls on campus are very wealthy and trendy. A lot of people dress up to go to class, instead of wearing pajamas. A lot of the guys are hot. Some of the fraternities act 'too cool' sometimes, and it's annoying. **The dating scene is not so fabulous**—people hook up a lot, but don't date so much. I think that there are a lot of really pretty, skinny girls at Wake, more than ordinary. But that's the kind of people Wake attracts: good-looking, white, upper-class conservatives."

Q "One of the main reasons I came to Wake is because of how hot the girls were when I visited. **I've met tons of cool guys and girls**, but there are also tons of guys and girls that suck. That's because it's an expensive private school in the South, and there are a lot of snobs. Half the girls are daddy's little princesses. And some of the guys are like, 'Look at my nice, expensive car.' They can be cool, but most of my friends are from the north."

Q "Wake Forest has some of the prettiest people I have ever seen—both guys and girls. **It's really hard to find an ugly person**. People at Wake work out a lot, too. All my friends from other colleges always comment on how odd it is when they visit—they notice."

Q "All I can say about the guys is **there are a lot of scrawny nerds**, but there also some pretty cool guys. The same goes for the girls. It is obvious some have never stepped foot out of their sheltered world, while some are extremely snobby. Wake is one of those places where you can walk around and know almost everybody."

## The College Prowler Take
### ON GUYS & GIRLS

As many students would attest, the campus could easily be featured in a J. Crew catalog. Many boast that everyone is gorgeous and in shape, but some admit this can be intimidating and creates competition. If fitness is an indication of the overall "attractiveness" of a school, Wake is in seriously good shape. The gym is packed with both guys and girls at any time of day, and physical appearance seems to be at a premium. Almost everyone is trendy and preppy, although there are certainly varying levels. Not all students live and die with the new Abercrombie catalog. If you're looking for an attractive student body across the board, this is the place to be. Wake is generally regarded as having one the best-looking collective student bodies in the Southeast. However, if you're looking for considerable variety beyond the typical upper-class white look and the occasional middle-class frat look, you may be disappointed, as the alternative scene is dismal at best.

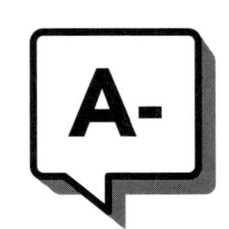

**B+**

**A-**

**The College Prowler™ Grade on**
## Guys: B+

A high grade for Guys indicates that the male population on campus is attractive, smart, friendly, and engaging, and that the school has a decent ratio of guys to girls.

**The College Prowler™ Grade on**
## Girls: A-

A high grade for Girls not only implies that the women on campus are attractive, smart, friendly, and engaging, but also that there is a fair ratio of girls to guys.

# Athletics

## The Lowdown
### ON ATHLETICS

**Men's Varsity Teams:**
Baseball
Basketball
Cheerleading
Cross Country
Football
Golf
Soccer
Tennis
Track and Field

**Women's Varsity Teams:**
Basketball
Cheerleading
Cross Country
Field Hockey
Golf
Soccer
Tennis
Track and Field
Volleyball

### Club Sports
Ballroom Dancing, Karate, Swimming, Lacrosse, Tennis, Crew, Cycling, ORAC (Rock Climbing), Ultimate Frisbee, Equestrian, Rugby, Fencing, Unified Rythms (competitive dance), Field Hockey, Running Club, Volleyball

### Intramurals (IMs)
Basketball, Bowling, Indoor Soccer, In-line Hockey, Softball, Floor Hockey, Team Tennis, Flag Football, Water Polo, Soccer, Volleyball

**Athletic Division:**
NCAA Division I

**Conference:**
ACC (Atlantic Coast Conference)

**School Mascot:**
Demon Deacon

**Fields:**
Lawrence Joel Veteran's Memorial Coliseum, Groves Stadium, Hooks Stadium, Spry Stadium, Ketner Stadium, Reynolds Gym, Water Tower Field, Poteat Field

## Most Popular Sports
Certainly basketball, which is by far the most sought-after ticket in town, followed by football, which manages to draw crowds of 30,000 against NC State and Florida State.

## Overlooked Teams
The baseball team, which is one of the nation's best. They don't enjoy much of a home field advantage due to the fact that many of their games occur while students are still in class.

## Getting Tickets
For the majority of sports, such as soccer, tennis, and even football, tickets aren't even required for students; you can simply show up immediately before the game and walk right in. However, basketball tickets are a different story entirely. For games against Duke or UNC, students camp out for two days in order to get quality seats. There is a fan club, the Screamin' Deacons, that allows all members entry to the games, but it costs $15 to join, and you must attend every game and sit in a specified area while wearing the club shirt.

# Students Speak Out
## ON ATHLETICS

"The main sports on campus are football and men's basketball. Those are huge, and people go crazy over them. Other than that, sad to say, most people don't pay much attention."

Q "Varsity sports are huge at Wake, especially because **we're the second smallest Division I college** besides Rice. Intramural sports are also very popular, and I believe about 80 percent of the students on campus are involved in an intramural sport."

Q "Thanks to Tim Duncan, **basketball is very popular**. Our football team is not exactly dominating, but we went to a bowl game two years ago, and there always seems to be some support in the stands. Women's field hockey is consistently the best in the country. IM sports offer almost any sport you can think of, and I would say that a large percentage of students participate in them."

Q "Sports are huge. Football and basketball games are widely attended. We're in the top 25 in basketball. I also go to some baseball games. Everything's easy to get to and close to campus. **IM sports are fun** and a good way to get to know people. I've heard that over half the school participates in some kind of IM sport."

Q "IM sports are pretty popular. There are so many people who participate, and it's a lot of fun. They're also a great way to meet people. **They get pretty competitive** sometimes. There are also club sports, which are a level between varsity and IM. They practice and are funded by the University. They even compete against other schools. However, the commitment level is not as high as varsity sports."

## The College Prowler Take
### ON ATHLETICS

If you're not familiar with the game of basketball, odds are you will be once winter rolls around in Winston-Salem. Wake students live and die with the success of Demon Deacon basketball, and there isn't a better show in town than when Wake plays UNC or Duke. Expect campus to empty out on nights of a home basketball game, as students and fans pack the Lawrence Joel Arena, a large off-campus stadium a mile down the road, which seats roughly 16,000. Football plays second fiddle to the basketball team at Wake, but it still draws quality crowds numbering between 20 and 30 thousand at Groves Stadium, across the street from "the Joel." The atmosphere isn't quite as rowdy as what you'd expect at Tennessee or Michigan, but considering Wake's size, the attendance is solid. For those who would rather play than watch, the intramural leagues at Wake Forest are very popular and can be very competitive. Whether you're a Greek or independent athlete, you should become very active in intramurals, which are easily some of the most popular activities on campus and an excellent way to meet people.

**A**

**The College Prowler™ Grade on**
## Athletics: A

A high grade in Athletics indicates that students have school spirit, that sports programs are respected, that games are well-attended, and that intramurals are a prominent part of student life.

# Greek Life

## The Lowdown
### ON GREEK LIFE

**Number of Fraternities:**
11

**Number of Sororities:**
8

**Undergrad Men in Fraternities:**
39%

**Undergrad Women in Sororities:**
50%

### Did You Know?

Once a year, the fraternities and sororities participate in a competition called Greek Week.

## Students Speak Out
**ON GREEK LIFE**

Q "Greek life dominates the party scene; all the good on-campus parties are at the fraternity lounges. It doesn't rule the social world, though. It's an extremely diverse social scene, and Greeks are only one of many groups."

Q "The Greek life definitely dominates the social scene. The only parties are Greek parties. I am in a sorority, and most of my friends are as well, though I do have independent friends. It's weird, because at most other schools, it's not really like this, and being Greek is more of an elitist thing. I'm not really what you'd call a 'typical' sorority girl. and no one ever thought I'd join, but **it's more low-key at Wake**. Still, it's a big deal and most girls rush in the spring."

Q "At Wake Forest, Greek life seems like everything. Unless you're going off campus on a weekend, the only thing to do is go to frat parties. **There're no rivalries** or anything between the sororities. They all have their stereotypes, though—one is all rich girls, one is all party girls, etc. You should definitely check it out, but if it's not your thing, that's not a problem."

Q "I know plenty of girls who are independent, and are still into the social scene. It's a little tougher with guys, because **the only thing to do on weekends is go to frat parties**, and if you're not in the frat, they won't give you beer. They give it to the girls for obvious reasons. Six of my closest friends pledged the same fraternity, but I didn't. I still had a good time being an independent, but I'm seriously considering joining in the fall."

Q "Greek life is pretty big on campus. You definitely don't have to be involved in it, though. I am, but **I have lots of independent friends**, and it really makes no difference. They have a deferred rush process, which means you don't rush until second semester freshman year. All Greek parties are open on campus. So whether you're Greek or independent, you can still hang out with everyone!"

Q "The Greek life dominates the social scene almost to an extreme. Barring an occasional varsity or club sport party, **frat parties are the only option**, which many students quickly tire of. Fraternities and sororities do, however, hold many other functions besides parties, which may capture your attention. Whether you become Greek or not, most students have friends that will, which allows for easy access to parties and alcohol."

## The College Prowler Take
**ON GREEK LIFE**

The student body at Wake Forest is nearly 50 percent Greek, and, as expected, the party scene revolves around fraternities like the earth around the sun. Everyone is either in one of the 11 fraternities and eight sororities, or knows several people who are. Some parties are consistently dry, while others serve enough alcohol to get the entire population of a small country drunk, and of course, there are plenty in between. Wake has a deferred rush process, allowing freshmen to become better acquainted with the school before rushing into a poor decision. Greek life is certainly a major deal here, and students generally have a positive attitude toward the Greek community. Whether you're Greek or independent, you'll fit in just fine.

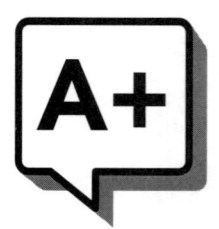

The College Prowler™ Grade on
### Greek Life: A+

A high grade in Greek Life indicates that sororities and fraternities are not only present, but also active on campus. Other determining factors include the variety of houses available and the respect the Greek community receives from the rest of the campus.

# Drug Scene

## The Lowdown
ON DRUG SCENE

**Most Prevalent Drugs on Campus:**
Alcohol, Marijuana

**Liquor-Related Referrals:**
0

**Liquor-Related Arrests:**
14

**Drug-Related Referrals:**
0

**Drug-Related Arrests:**
2

## Students Speak Out
ON DRUG SCENE

"Drugs are not huge at all at Wake. Pot is the only thing that has a presence. If you want it, you can find it. If you don't, no one cares."

"There are no drugs. **Some people live in substance-free housing**. People at Wake are here to learn, not to get high. There are people who go to law school or medical school. We don't fool around."

"Drugs are here, but **they're not prominent**. Just watch out at the big parties, and don't drink anything that you didn't watch come out of a can."

"A couple people I know smoke weed, but it's not big. **There's a pot-smoking frat**, but they got kicked off campus a few years ago and run underground. If you're into pot, there are ways to get away with it. I wouldn't recommend smoking in your room. Anything beyond that, I know nothing about. Most people just drink."

"I'm sure there are drugs on campus. I just don't see them. It all depends on who you surround yourself with. I don't think that they have a heavy presence at Wake. **The biggest problem is definitely alcohol**."

## Drug Counseling Programs

### Student Health Services
Phone: (336) 758-5218
Services: alcohol dependency assessments, evaluation of alcohol on physical well-being

### The University Counseling Center
Phone: (336) 758-5273
Services: one-on-one counseling, alcohol and drug dependency assessment services, short-term and long-term counseling

### The College Prowler Take
**ON DRUG SCENE**

There aren't enough drugs on campus to even consider it part of a "scene," and you could argue that most students aren't even aware of a drug presence on campus. You'll occasionally hear a few rumors of parties involving a bit of cocaine, but no one ever seems to have been to one, so prevalence of that type of activity is doubtful. There is still, mind you, a decent amount of students that will smoke pot, but their impact on the campus is negligible. "Harder" drugs are practically unheard of at Wake. Odds are, you won't ever see them used, nor will you know anyone who uses them. Non-users feel very little pressure to indulge in drugs.

**The College Prowler™ Grade on**
### Drug Scene: A

A high grade on the Drug Scene indicates that drugs are not a noticeable part of campus life; drug use is not visible, and no pressure to use them seems to exist.

## Overall Experience

### Students Speak Out
**ON OVERALL EXPERIENCE**

"Overall, Wake is nice. There are things I hate, like the lack of diversity, and there are some scary, close-minded southern people. Would I be happier somewhere else? Possibly. I wouldn't transfer, though."

Q "There are things that I wish I knew before I made the decision to come here. I wish I'd known that there was so little diversity, and I wish I'd known how ridiculously hard the academics are in some departments. I also wish I'd known that **there isn't a lot to do in Winston-Salem**. I find that everyone is very similar here, and if you want a lot of diversity, it's not the place to be. But, you just have to make the effort. I've grown to like it a lot."

Q "Honestly, there are times I wish I was somewhere else, but **I don't regret it at all**. Sometimes it's called 'Work Forest' because of all the work, but it's manageable. Work hard, party hard."

Q "I love Wake Forest. The business school is providing me with a top-notch education, with which I am almost guaranteed a job, **the campus is overwhelmingly beautiful**, and the athletics, both club and varsity, have made Wake my perfect college choice. Even though its price tag is expensive, Wake is consistently rated as one of the 'best buys' of private school education, and I have absolutely no regrets taking out school loans. Thus far, I'm convinced that attending Wake Forest has been one of the best choices I've ever made."

Q "You have to work hard if you come to Wake. I didn't expect it to be this much work. But, everyone else works hard, too. It felt good to know that I had earned my grades, and **I'm getting the education I'm paying for**. The people are wonderful, and it's easy to get involved in anything and everything you want."

## The College Prowler Take
ON OVERALL EXPERIENCE

Students unquestionably agree that a Wake Forest education is rewarding, and most attribute their decision to attend this university to Wake Forest's reputation as an academically demanding institution that has an excellent track record of graduate school and job placement. Known as "Work Forest," the school's challenging curriculum provides a valuable well-rounded education that not only prepares students for a career, but teaches them to think in a novel and resourceful manner. Students never cease to be impressed by their idyllic campus and top-notch facilities, as well as by the excellent fusion of athletics and academics that seems to be injected into the soul of the school. However, students do have a fair share of gripes. Wake's academic reputation is certainly warranted, and students claim that the excessive, and often obscene, amount of work required is nearly insufferable at times, which can often cripple the overall social vitality of the school. Winston-Salem's general lack of entertaining options does nothing to alleviate this concern. Finally, the poor diversity on campus is assuredly the most common complaint, and, while efforts are being made to improve the ethnic diversity at Wake Forest, as things stand, diversity is certainly sub-par.

The majority of students will openly profess their love for Wake Forest, and many say that choosing Wake was the best decision they've ever made. For an intense and ultimately rewarding education, this is a great choice. But, if you're looking for a party school, you'd be better off giving someplace else a shot.

# Washington and Lee University

116 North Main Street, Lexington, VA 24450
www.wlu.edu          (540) 458-8710

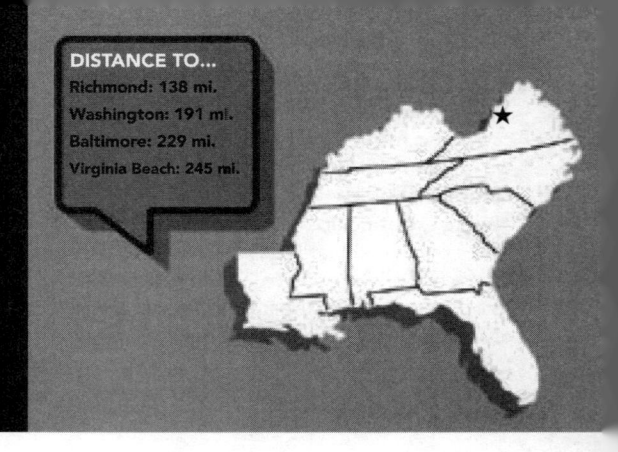

**DISTANCE TO...**
Richmond: 138 mi.
Washington: 191 mi.
Baltimore: 229 mi.
Virginia Beach: 245 mi.

*"Professors are eager to help, the surroundings are beautiful, and students trust their peers."*

### Table of Contents

| | |
|---|---|
| Academics | 709 |
| Local Atmosphere | 711 |
| Safety & Security | 712 |
| Facilities | 714 |
| Campus Dining | 715 |
| Campus Housing | 717 |
| Diversity | 718 |
| Guys & Girls | 720 |
| Athletics | 722 |
| Greek Life | 724 |
| Drug Scene | 725 |
| Overall Experience | 727 |

**Total Enrollment:**
1,738

**Top 10% of High School Class:**
78%

**Acceptance Rate:**
31%

**Tuition:**
$25,760

**SAT Range (25th-75th Percentile):**
Verbal      Math         Total
650 – 720   650 – 720    1300 – 1440

**ACT Range (25th-75th Percentile):**
Verbal   Math   Total
N/A      N/A    28-31

**Most Popular Majors:**
13% Economics
12% History
11% Business
8% Political Science
6% Journalism

**Students also applied to:***
College of William and Mary
Dartmouth College
Davidson College
University of Virginia
Vanderbilt University

*For more school info check out www.collegeprowler.com

### College Prowler Report Card

| | |
|---|---|
| Academics | A |
| Local Atmosphere | C- |
| Safety & Security | A |
| Facilities | B+ |
| Campus Dining | C+ |
| Campus Housing | B |
| Diversity | D- |
| Guys | B |
| Girls | A- |
| Athletics | C+ |
| Greek Life | A+ |
| Drug Scene | B- |

# Academics

## The Lowdown
### ON ACADEMICS

**Degrees Awarded:**
Bachelor of Arts, Bachelor of Science

**Number of Majors Offered:**
40

**Number of Courses Offered:**
900+

**Undergraduate Schools:**
The College; Williams School of Commerce, Economics, and Politics

**Full-time Faculty:**
206

**Faculty with Terminal Degree:**
193

**Student-to-Faculty Ratio:**
10.1:1

**Average Class Size:**
15

**Faculty's Average Annual Course Load:**
7

### Special Degree Options
Interdisciplinary majors include East Asian Studies, Medieval and Renaissance Studies, Neuroscience, Public Policy, Russian Area Studies, Teacher Licensing (collaboration with Mary Baldwin College)

### Special Non-Major Programs
Environmental Studies, Global Stewardship, Women's Studies, Washington Term

### AP Test Score Requirements
There is possible credit for scores of 4 or 5 (3 for mathematics). Check with specific academic departments for requirements.

### IB Test Score Requirements
There is possible credit or advanced placement for scores of 5 or above on Higher-Level exams. Decisions made by the department on an individual basis.

### Did You Know?
W&L is the ninth-oldest college in the country; it traces its founding to 1749 (it started as Augusta Academy). Come back in 2049 for the opening of the mysterious time capsule.

Washington and Lee's honor system is legendary. Professors say the honor system gives them confidence in students, who can schedule their own exams and sometimes take them home overnight. Students say it lets them leave valuables around campus without fear.

**Best Places to Study:**
For productivity, try the Science Library, Leyburn Library, and the Commons cubicle farm (upstairs offices for student organizations). For fun studying/procrastination, try the Journalism School computer lab, the Commerce School computer labs, and the Commons.

## Students Speak Out
### ON ACADEMICS

"Every teacher I've had—and I'm a senior—has been extremely accessible. All have set office hours, but they also have no problem if you drop in on them unannounced to ask a question or just chat."

"**Professors are extremely approachable**; they love to interact with students. I hadn't even been here a week before I had been invited to a professor's house for dinner. Since W&L expects professors to spend a lot of time teaching, and not quite as much time doing research, the school attracts professors who prize prof-student interaction."

"Classes tend to be **small and discussion-based**. Freshmen can anticipate a lot of choice in their class selections, and professors and advisors are eager to help them navigate individual classes and general education requirements. As you get into your major, you tend to know more and more of your fellow classmates. Professors frequently consult upperclassman majors when they plan courses or consider changing teaching strategies."

"All professors administer and consult **end-of-course evaluations**, and some even do mid-term evaluations to find ways of better teaching their students."

"**Freshmen can expect to be challenged**. And, they need to get over the fact that they were 4.0 students in high school because the reality is that they may never see that number again, no matter how hard they try."

## The College Prowler Take
### ON ACADEMICS

Make no mistake: academic work at Washington and Lee is intense. Professors expect a lot of effort, and take great pride in not inflating grades. If you get an A+ here, cherish it, because it might be the only one you'll see. On the positive side, students build personal relationships with the faculty and can rely on them for help whenever they hit a rough spot. Professors keep ample office hours and have students over for some down-home cooking. Certain old-school history profs have also been known to share a few drinks with their pupils at the Palms, but that's another story. Classes at Washington and Lee are taught exclusively by professors—no teaching assistants allowed.

At Washington and Lee, that students are required to take a broad selection of classes—general education credits, or "gen eds"—outside of their majors. This kind of work typically makes up one-third of the course load. Some of W&L's coolest programs are interdisciplinary—the courses cut across the usual majors and create hybrid offerings that attract all kinds of students. The Shepherd Poverty Program combines economics, politics, and philosophy in academic study, and volunteer work helps students get their hands dirty with real-world problems. Students can dip into economics, literature, and science in the Environmental Studies Program, or peruse philosophy, music, and art in the Medieval and Renaissance Studies major.

**The College Prowler™ Grade on**
### Academics: A

A high Academics grade generally indicates that professors are knowledgeable, accessible, and genuinely interested in their students' welfare. Other determining factors include class size, how well professors communicate, and whether or not classes are engaging.

# Local Atmosphere

**City Websites**
http://www.lexva.com/
http://www.ci.lexington.va.us/
http://www.lexingtonvirginia.com/

## Students Speak Out
ON LOCAL ATMOSPHERE

## The Lowdown
ON LOCAL ATMOSPHERE

"Lexington has a lot to do, and there are beautiful little towns nearby like Staunton, Charlottesville. that are fun to walk around, if you want to get off campus for a day."

**Region:**
Shenandoah Valley

**City, State:**
Lexington, Virginia

**Setting:**
Rural

**Population:**
6,910 (Census Bureau, 2004)

**Distance from Washington, DC:**
3 hours

**Distance from Richmond, VA:**
2 hours

**Distance from Roanoke, VA:**
50 minutes

**Points of Interest:**
Lee Chapel and Museum, Natural Bridge and Caverns, George C. Marshall Museum at the Virginia Military Institute, carriage tours of Lexington, the Stonewall Jackson House, the Virginia Horse Center, Rockbridge Vineyard, the Theatre at Lime Kiln

Q "**The town can be a little stifling at times**, just in terms of size, but the atmosphere is good. The college has a good relationship with the surrounding city and the Virginia Military Institute. In a town this size, you are bound to run into friends and professors everywhere you go, from the grocery store to local shops. Sometimes it seems as if the town is an extension of the school."

Q "I like the small town atmosphere, particularly being nestled among the trees and along the little creek. **If you are a big city person, then it might take some getting used to**."

Q "The orchestra concerts together with plays, choir concerts, and movies in the school theater provide **more refined opportunities** for entertainment."

Q "The Lexington area is **one of the most beautiful places I've ever been**. The population is rural, but the town is charming, old, and full of intrigue. Everything in town is basically within walking distance, although a car is necessary to get to places like Wal-Mart. The outdoors is definitely a plus in the area—there is a river hot spot about a half an hour from town where you can go tubing, swimming, and sunbathing. And there are plenty of places to hike—we're in the Shenandoah Valley, after all."

> "There are lots of things to do outdoors like **hiking, kayaking, biking, running, and camping**. We have House Mountain nearby, the New River is a couple of hours away in a car—great white water rafting and kayaking—and Natural Bridge is a 20-minute drive."

# Safety & Security

## The College Prowler Take
### ON LOCAL ATMOSPHERE

W&L is nestled in historic Lexington, deep in the heart of Virginia's Shenandoah Valley. This is definitely a small town, rich in heritage and boasting panoramic views of the valley and mountains—some of Virginia's most stunning natural surroundings. History is palpable here—you can catch a horse-drawn carriage tour and see the former homes of "Stonewall" Jackson and Robert E. Lee. The University's main lawn, with massive white columns fronting the line of academic buildings, served as the backdrop for a scene in *Gods and Generals*. But, many students complain that, beyond the bubble of W&L, Lexington and the surrounding area offer little to keep them amused and engaged. Unfortunately, there isn't much interaction with the one other college in town, the Virginia Military Institute (VMI) which is right next door but worlds away.

## The Lowdown
### ON SAFETY & SECURITY

**Number of security guards:**
13

**Phone:**
(540) 458-8999

**Student Health Center/Infirmary contact:**
It is located in the basement of the Gilliam and Davis dorms. (540) 458-8401

### Health Center Hours
Open 24 hours a day, seven days a week when undergraduate classes are in session. Registered nurse is on duty and a physician is on call during these times, except for one-hour breaks for lunch and dinner.

### Safety Services
Self-defense PE class (for ladies only), Traveler Safe-Ride program, CAIR (Confidential and Impartial Resources—for mediation in sexual misconduct cases), nightly patrols of dorms and academic buildings, emergency phones in parking lots.

## C-

**The College Prowler™ Grade on**
## Local Atmosphere: C-

A high Local Atmosphere grade indicates that the area surrounding campus is safe and scenic. Other factors include nearby attractions, proximity to other schools, and the town's attitude toward students.

### Did You Know?

The Infirmary has 10 beds for students who need some supervision but aren't sick enough for the hospital.

According to official statistics, on-campus resident halls were really safe last year—no burglaries, robberies, or aggravated assaults reported. Three burglaries were reported on campus, the most recent for which the school releases statistics.

### Students Speak Out
ON SAFETY & SECURITY

"I only lock my dorm room when I'm going to be away an extended period of time. Otherwise, I keep my door open, even if I go to class. The honor code really does result in a safer campus and a great deal of trust between students."

Q "Whether campus security guards are strict or lenient depends on the relationship you develop with them. **If you're polite, make conversation**, and get to know them, they'll usually give you a hand. But, if you're rude, enjoy blatantly breaking the rules and acting like a moron, they'll come down and be as strict as they need to be."

Q "I have had better luck calling my sober friends or finding a random sober person at a party than getting Traveler to pay attention to me. **The drivers are usually pretty polite, but they're not necessarily punctual**."

Q "**I feel like Lexington's a bubble**, and because of our honor code, nothing bad can happen—I'm sure I'm being naïve, but I have no reason to think otherwise."

Q "**Security is amazing**. The campus is safe, so our security team is here to make sure that we feel safe. We have blue-light phones as well as available escort service. Members of campus security are friendly and dedicated to their jobs. Campus security will have your car towed, but they will also drive you to the impound lot to reclaim it. The Lexington police handle off-campus incidents. For the most part, they are consistent and fair and don't seem to have an axe to grind when it comes to W&L students."

### The College Prowler Take
ON SAFETY & SECURITY

Lexington is a sleepy little town at heart, an insulated cocoon with a very low rate of reported violent crime. Partly because of the one-strike honor system, students feel free to trust each other with their property. That trust seems to be justified nearly all of the time. Most freshmen don't lock the doors to their dorm rooms, and some upperclassmen keep the habit even after they move into town. In the days of yore, students could leave their laptops, purses, or wallets in full view in the library for days on end, and find them undisturbed when they came back. Or so the story goes. Today, it's probably not smart to take those chances. Security guards are not exactly omnipresent on campus, but they respond quickly to calls, and their relations with students tend to be friendly. They also come in handy, often helping distressed students with a variety of problems, like pumping up a run-down car battery, or opening up a locked door.

**The College Prowler™ Grade on**
### Safety & Security: A

A high grade in Safety & Security means that students generally feel safe, campus police are visible, blue-light phones and escort services are readily available, and safety precautions are not overly necessary.

# Facilities

## The Lowdown
### ON FACILITIES

**Student Center**
John W. Elrod University Commons ("the Commons") comes complete with a baby grand piano, movie theater, pool tables, Internet kiosks, darkroom, table tennis, café, and dining hall.

**Athletic Facilities**
Warner Center (includes Fitness Center), Doremus Gymnasium, Duchossois Tennis Center

**Libraries**
3—James G. Leyburn Library, Science Library, Law Library

**Movie Theater on Campus?**
Yes—the Commons theater is the biggest, baddest entertainment system on campus, perfect for movies and football games.

**Bowling on Campus?**
No—but it is available just outside town.

**Bar on Campus?**
No—but beer is on tap (for students with valid ID) in the Commons Café.

**Coffeehouse on Campus?**
No, but the Café has coffee and downtown Lexington has several coffee shops.

**Computers**
**High-Speed Network?** Yes
**Wireless Network?** Yes
**Number of Labs:** 14
**Numbers of Computers:** 335, plus kiosks
**24-Hour Labs:**
Huntley Hall (C-School), Reid Hall (J-School), Gaines Hall, Newcomb Hall, Robinson Hall, Leyburn Library (first floor and reference area), Commons, Science Building (Science Library, Howe Hall, Parmly Hall)

**Charge to Print?**
10 cents per black and white page, 35 cents for color

### Did You Know?

Washington and Lee's libraries contain over one million hard-cover volumes and electronic documents, plus over 6,000 serial subscriptions. Get busy reading!

The 11,000 square-foot Fitness Center holds 38 cardiovascular training stations and 13,000 pounds of free and fixed weights.

## Students Speak Out
### ON FACILITIES

"Although some facilities are considerably older than others, they are well-kept. There aren't any ceiling tiles falling on our heads or anything."

"If you're talking computers and general technology, **the C-School and J-School have the best facilities**, and the J-School beats out the C-School."

💬 **"The library is the ugliest building I've ever encountered.** Most people think it's an architectural atrocity. I've seen alumni come in there and look and say, yeah, the carpet's still the same."

💬 "Many of the classrooms are in historical sites, so **they are kept in immaculate condition**—though historical furniture is not the most comfortable to sit in for long periods of time."

💬 "**We have only one dining hall and one co-op**, so dining options are rather limited. Social options are also very limited, though it's getting a lot better. The social life revolves around the fraternity system, which is unfortunate. But with the new Commons, new movies are shown almost every day of the week, and bands are brought in to play on weekends."

## Campus Dining

### The College Prowler Take
ON FACILITIES

Only three years ago, the facilities at W&L were seriously lacking. The weight room, for example, looked like something off the set of "Rocky" (before he made it big): torn carpet, smeared windows, and rusty equipment. Now, thanks to a spending binge that would make a Washington politician proud, W&L's campus sports a sparkling new exercise facility, a $30 million Student Commons, and a journalism school wired for the 21st century. The school works hard at making up for what Lexington lacks in the area of social entertainment. The administration has been investing a lot of money in building up the school, and creating an environment that appeals to students.

### The Lowdown
ON CAMPUS DINING

**Freshman Meal Plan Requirement?**
Yes

**24-Hour On-Campus Eating?**
No

**Student Favorites:**
Commons Café for quick bites, the Marketplace for leisurely breakfasts

**Meal Plan Cost:**
$3,600 for full meal plan (first-year requirement); upperclassmen meal plans range from $3,600 to $500 per year.

### B+

**The College Prowler™ Grade on**
## Facilities: B+

A high Facilities grade indicates that the campus is aesthetically pleasing and well-maintained; facilities are state-of-the-art, and libraries are exceptional. Other determining factors include the quality of both athletic and student centers and an abundance of things to do on campus.

**Did You Know?**
Students with special dietary needs just need to talk to the chefs, and they will set up meal plans that meet the requirements.

## Students Speak Out
ON CAMPUS DINING

**"The quality of the food in the Commons is excellent. At the fraternity houses, the quality drops a little, but is still pretty good. On campus, there is plenty of variety for the health-conscious."**

"**Nothing on campus is open 24 hours**, and something of this nature could be a big help to students studying all night."

"The food is pretty good. **The D-Hall has been upgraded to the Marketplace**, and there are more options for students. There is always a variety of pizza. There is also a deli bar, a different type of soup every day, a salad bar, hot dogs, burgers, and grilled chicken. The main course varies from day to day."

"**I think the food is food**; people just complain because they feel the need to complain about something."

"The food at W&L basically depends on what year you are. The new Marketplace, **mainly where freshmen eat**, offers a wide variety of choices at each meal. Some upperclassmen choose to eat in the Marketplace during the rest of their time at W&L."

"Our Café, the short-order restaurant that is open most of the day, is **great for meals and snacks**. Many upperclassmen eat at fraternities or sororities. Each house has a different cook, and there is enough variety in the food choice to make it worthwhile. The meal plans are for those who may just want a few meals a week, as well as for those who can't even boil their own water."

## The College Prowler Take
ON CAMPUS DINING

Students on campus have a few options when it comes time to grab some munchies or a sit-down meal. Freshmen have to purchase the full meal plan, 21 meals per week. Very few students actually eat all this food—for example, many feel that sleep is often more valuable than breakfast—so some of this money goes down the drain. But, upperclassmen can choose from a variety of meal plans, some of them much less expensive than the freshman plan. One option that a lot of students choose involves eating at their respective fraternity or sorority. The Greek houses each have their own cook and offer a variety of different foods to eat.

The College Prowler™ Grade on
### Campus Dining: C+

Our grade on Campus Dining addresses the quality of both school-owned dining halls and independent on-campus restaurants as well as the price, availability, and variety of food.

# Campus Housing

### Did You Know?
About 60 percent of the freshman rooms in Gilliam, Davis, Baker, and Graham-Lees residence halls are doubles; the rest are single rooms. W&L students are so sociable!

There are substance-free halls available, in which residents agree to strict rules about alcohol, drugs, and smoking.

## The Lowdown
ON CAMPUS HOUSING

**Undergrads on Campus:**
61%

**Dormitories:**
5, plus 3 separate Woods Creek Apartment buildings

**University-Owned Apartments:**
40

**Room Types:**
Singles and doubles; Gaines and Woods Creek facilities are apartment-style, with up to five people in a suite.

**Available for Rent:**
Bed linens, micro-fridge (contains a microwave, refrigerator, and freezer); Incoming students are contacted with rental forms.

**Cleaning Service?**
Only public areas are cleaned.

**You Get:**
A closet, chest of drawers, study desk, desk chair, mirror, and single bed; Students provide their own bed linens and other furnishings as desired.

**Bed Type:**
Most are extra-long and can be bunked.

## Students Speak Out
ON CAMPUS HOUSING

"You get the unforgettable dorm experience your freshman year. You can roll out of bed at 8:47 and be in class at 9 with a minute to spare."

Q "Walking at a normal clip from the dorms, it doesn't take more than five minutes to make it to the main portion of campus, maybe a bit more for the far side where the Science Center is located. **You could probably cut this down to three minutes**, if you made a dash for it."

Q "**Freshman housing is a little scary** and rather plain, but once you get beyond the first year, housing improves significantly. Upper-class housing is in suite units, so it is like living in an apartment with two to four other people."

Q "Your chances of being housed on campus all four years are good if you want it, but **most students live off campus as upperclassmen**."

> "**My freshman room was a nightmare**. It was far too small for a roommate and me to live in. We tried to work it out until Thanksgiving, but then we gave up. The room was just too small—we couldn't even fit our two beds in the room without them blocking the door. On the other hand, when we contacted our dean of freshman about the problem, she resolved all of the issues very quickly. We were each given our own rooms and life became a lot more pleasant. Freshmen are not alone—the administration is there to help them."

# Diversity

## The College Prowler Take
### ON CAMPUS HOUSING

W&L students have to live on campus for their first two years at the University (the fraternity and sorority houses, as well as the dorms, qualify as on-campus, and are open to sophomores). Students confront a whole range experiences in on-campus housing—sometimes it's good, sometimes it's pretty bad. The rooms themselves are generally unexceptional, so whether students enjoy their accommodations depends a lot on roommates, dorm counselors, and neighbors down the hall. Students can make lasting friendships during their time in the freshman halls. When there are problems, students say that the administration usually gets right on it and resolves issues ranging from roommate problems to space issues.

## The Lowdown
### ON DIVERSITY

**Native American:** 0%

**Asian American:** 2%

**African American:** 4%

**Hispanic:** 1%

**White:** 88%

**International:** 5%

**Out-of-State:** 85%

### Minority Clubs

Minority students are very active in several organizations that know how to have good, clean fun. The Minority Students Association helps to promote minority recruitment and sponsors an annual cabaret, complete with great food in a swanky setting—bring a date and dance to soul and R & B music till the wee hours. Club Asia, after getting off the ground just recently, put on a very cool cultural fair (hint: lots of martial arts weapons). The Student Association for International Learning (SAIL) helps international students get accustomed to Lexington. It also sponsors a Model United Nations and international relief projects, as well as internationally themed parties.

### The College Prowler™ Grade on
### Campus Housing: B

A high Campus Housing grade indicates that dorms are clean, well-maintained, and spacious. Other determining factors include variety of dorms, proximity to classes, and social atmosphere.

## Most Popular Religions

Catholic, Episcopal, Presbyterian, and Methodist, in declining order are the most popular. The General's Christian Fellowship and Reformed University Fellowship are the two largest Christian groups, and they often attract about a hundred people for services. Students declaring a religious preference hit 70 percent in 1998 but that percentage has now declined to 55 percent. Just over half of all undergrads list a Christian religious preference.

## Political Activity

W&L students are no longer as reliably conservative as they once were—there is now some competition on the political front. During the 2004 election year, Young Democrats helped to get out the vote for the local party, and College Republicans countered with their own speakers and volunteer drives. But the political scene is typically fairly low-key: students from both sides can cooperate and mingle with each other. You hardly ever see a protest or demonstration of any kind.

## Gay Tolerance

There is not a large gay presence on campus, but many students here seem fairly accepting of others who have come out. A chapter of the Gay-Straight Alliance was established in the fall of 2002 and since then has brought a lot of attention to the issue.

## Economic Status

Although W&L doesn't keep detailed or scientific records of how much its students' families earn, the students here are pretty clearly not hurting for cash. Mighty SUVs and late-model sedans abound in the parking lots, and only about 35 percent of undergrads ask for financial assistance. From all appearances, this is a well-off campus.

## Students Speak Out
### ON DIVERSITY

"Diversity isn't really a hot topic on campus since there isn't much. However, it's becoming increasingly discussed due to the administration's 'branding' effort to increase diversity."

Q "Unfortunately, **this is not a very diverse campus on a broad scope**, but it's certainly improving. The main demographic stereotype here is southern, rich, and white. However, just this Parents' Weekend, my mom commented on how noticeable the increase in African American and Asian students was. This is great, because W&L has a 'good old boy' stigma attached to it. Diversity is good, because it makes campus more interesting."

Q "**Students naturally tend to segregate themselves**, mainly because of the Greek system. 'I'm an SAE' or 'I'm a Chi-O' is almost always attached to somebody's identity, whether it's good or bad. Don't get me wrong, the Greek system is great, and I really enjoy it, but it certainly has its stereotypes."

Q "Lack of diversity is a major deficiency at W&L, but **it is changing for the better**. Minority groups are not abundant enough. I wish we had way more diversity in socioeconomic backgrounds, intellectual and cultural viewpoints, and national origins. Right now, W&L is too homogeneous, and you have to actively seek intellectual stimulation. However, the University is taking steps to increase diversity, and I think the trend is toward more intelligent students, as well as more interesting and unique ones."

Q "**There is tolerance of different races and ethnicities**, but don't expect much more than just tolerance. Most people don't go out of their way to embrace. Don't get me wrong, there is very little open discrimination on campus, but you don't often see minority students at Greek parties unless they are members of a Greek organization."

## The College Prowler Take
### ON DIVERSITY

Washington and Lee has acquired a partially-deserved reputation for being a place where everyone talks the same (in a southern drawl), dresses the same (sandals, pastel polo shirts with popped collars), votes the same (Republican), and looks the same (white). However, much of that may be changing. The percentage of minority students has been on the rise and is currently about 10 percent. A dean of multicultural affairs was hired last year to spread the word that W&L welcomes minorities. There have been serious discussions about forming an African American Studies program, which would involve faculty and students from a range of departments, including history, politics, music, and English. There are also rumblings about students forming chapters of historically African American sororities in the near future, but this seems to be farther off. While students find diversity in interests, the numbers really don't lie; W&L just isn't too diverse, but it is working on it.

**The College Prowler™ Grade on**
## Diversity: D-

A high grade in Diversity indicates that ethnic minorities and international students have a notable presence on campus and that students of different economic backgrounds, religious beliefs, and sexual preferences are well-represented.

# Guys & Girls

## The Lowdown
### ON GUYS & GIRLS

**Women Undergrads**: 49%

**Men Undergrads**: 51%

### Birth Control Available?
Yes, it is at the Student Health Center.

### Social Scene
The social scene is huge here—students shouldn't expect to lock themselves in their room and study all the time. Even studying and writing papers sometimes become social activities, as students congregate in the C-School or J-School to commiserate. Introverted kids have a tougher time finding a niche in the midst of pretty frantic social activity, especially during the first term or two, but most eventually seem to adjust. Similarly, non-Greeks and students who never go out to frat parties can feel like the life of the University is passing them by. Advice: students should at least try the Greek scene a little bit, and sample the growing options for alternative entertainment if the frat scene doesn't measure up. The Commons has become the central meeting place on campus—students filter through by the hundreds every hour.

## Hookups or Relationships?

The dating scene is extremely sparse until junior and senior years, when some students move into steady relationships. Hookups predominate on campus throughout the four years.

## Dress Code

Preppy dress is standard issue here. When the weather permits, ladies often wear skirts and spring dresses to class, accessorized with calf boots or heels. On balmy days, the stereotypical W&L man sports a slightly ruffled haircut, a polo shirt (preferably pastel), khakis, and sandals. (In nastier weather, the campus runs amok in grey North Face jackets.) However, mad props to the iconoclasts who wear cowboy boots and suede jackets to class. You know who you are.

### Students Speak Out
**ON GUYS & GIRLS**

"There aren't any set visiting hours for members of the opposite sex in the dorms. Individual halls or suites can set policies if they want, but everyone tends just to operate under the general rules of common courtesy."

"The division after freshman year between frats and sororities leads to mutated relationships and it is very difficult to date someone in the conventional sense. **People are very focused on status and popularity**, rather than platonic intimacy or actually getting to know each other. Maybe this is a vestige of times when W&L was not co-ed and women were brought in from other schools."

"The male-female ratio doesn't really play into the social scene, since the ratio is about even. But **it is like you're back in high school**, because W&L is so small almost everyone has hooked up or dated one another—lots of overlapping, which can be obnoxious and leads to high school type dramatics."

"**There are way more attractive girls than attractive guys**. I've seen gorgeous girls compete for guys they wouldn't look twice at if we were at a state school."

"Student Health Services both **provides and encourages contraception** very actively. You can get free condoms at the Student Health Center, or through 25-cent vending machines, if you'd like anonymity."

### The College Prowler Take
**ON GUYS & GIRLS**

Maybe it's the result of an unspoken admissions office policy, but W&L is blessed with more than its fair share of attractive ladies. And perhaps it's a "southun thang," but most of these ladies take great pride in fixing themselves up for every special (and not-so special) occasion. Pearls, heels, and spring dresses at a football game. The guys can be impressive when they want to be: a blazer, khakis, and a tie—preferably a bow tie—are standard fare at the aforementioned football games and fraternity-sorority mixers. Students give mixed signals about whether W&L is a promiscuous campus. But, a huge online survey sponsored by the school in March 2004—the National College Health Assessment—showed that, on average, students here are actually less sexually active than their peers nationwide.

**B**  **A-**

The College Prowler™ Grade on
## Guys: B

A high grade for Guys indicates that the male population on campus is attractive, smart, friendly, and engaging, and that the school has a decent ratio of guys to girls.

The College Prowler™ Grade on
## Girls: A-

A high grade for Girls not only implies that the women on campus are attractive, smart, friendly, and engaging, but also that there is a fair ratio of girls to guys.

# Athletics

## The Lowdown
ON ATHLETICS

**Men's Varsity Teams:**
Baseball
Basketball
Cross County
Football
Golf
Lacrosse
Soccer
Swimming
Tennis
Track
Wrestling

**Women's Varsity Teams:**
Basketball
Cross Country
Field Hockey
Lacrosse
Riding
Soccer
Swimming
Tennis
Track
Volleyball

### Club Sports
Cycling, Soccer, Ping-Pong, Rugby (M), Ultimate Frisbee, Volleyball, Boxing, Martial Arts, Squash

### Intramurals (IMs)*
Badminton (M), Basketball (MW), Bowling (MW), Golf (MW), Softball (M), Swimming (MW), Ping-Pong (M), Racquetball (M), Squash (M), Tennis (M), Ultimate Frisbee (M), Volleyball (MW), Wrestling (M), Flag Football (M)

*M—Men only, W—Women Only, MW—Men and women's teams offered, No designation— mixed teams

**Athletic Division:**
Division III

**Conference:**
Old Dominion Athletic Conference (ODAC)

**School Mascot:**
The Generals (a.k.a. Washington and Lee) Unfortunately, an actual mascot hardly ever makes an appearance.

**Fields:**
Alumni Field (illuminated, turf), Cap'n Dick Smith Baseball Field, Liberty Hall Fields (soccer), Soccer/Lacrosse Stadium, tennis courts (14), Wilson Field (football)

**Most Popular Sports:**
Men's lacrosse, club rugby

**Overlooked Teams:**
Men's basketball—too many rebuilding woes have cut into the support from student fans, although professors still come to games somewhat regularly.

**Getting Tickets:**
No tickets required!

## Students Speak Out
ON ATHLETICS

{ "The attitude toward sports could be much stronger than it is. The heavy workload that students have is probably the main reason for this."

"School spirit with regards to sports is unfortunately low. At a school based around tradition, **it's sad that more people don't go to games** and support their classmates."

## The College Prowler Take
### ON ATHLETICS

Q "Athletes work hard and deserve a good fan base, but the general attitude of most athletes is that **not enough fans show up**. It is hard to make it out to all of the games. This is either a result of the lack of emphasis our school places on athletics or just the sheer volume of work that most students have, which doesn't allow them to attend games, especially on the weekdays."

Q "**There are a lot of athletes on campus**, but you will definitely fit in if you don't play a sport. Basically, sports at our school are not taken all too seriously. The athletes take them seriously when they are in season, but every athlete is also a student, and because we know that we're not going to be professional athletes, we realize that it is also important to do well in school. This creates the general attitude about sports that they aren't all that important, which might explain the lack of a strong fan base at the major sporting events."

Q "There are a variety of different club sports at W&L that give students who don't want a varsity level commitment a chance to stay active. **Certain club sports are more popular than others**. The rugby team currently holds sixpercent of the male population at W&L and travels to DC, Richmond, Norfolk, Lynchburg, and even Savannah to compete. Other clubs like ultimate Frisbee, lacrosse, and squash also travel for competition. Some clubs are taken more serious than others, depending on how competitive they are."

Washington and Lee puts the "student" in "student-athlete." The University doesn't award athletic scholarships, and athletes are expected to carry their academic weight. This sometimes makes it tough for W&L to field successful teams, particularly in football and basketball. Attendance is pretty light at most sporting events, but people turn out en masse for Homecoming and Parent's Weekend football games. No tickets are required for athletic events—just find a seat and start cheering. Unfortunately, W&L tradition mandates that spectators leave football games after the first half. Alas, school spirit only runs so deep. W&L sponsors a variety of intramural (IM) sports, from basketball to flag football to softball. Combined with club sports, this gives nearly every student an opportunity to play a sport on some level.

C+

Want to get some time in on the field or the court? Pick up *Washington and Lee—Off the Record* from www.collegeprowler.com to find out more about sports on campus.

The College Prowler™ Grade on
### Athletics: C+

A high grade in Athletics indicates that students have school spirit, that sports programs are respected, that games are well-attended, and that intramurals are a prominent part of student life.

# Greek Life

## Students Speak Out
### ON GREEK LIFE

"Fraternity membership hit a 20-year low last year, due partly to a fraternity suspension. Sorority membership, as a percent of female students, climbed to an all-time high."

Q "**Fraternities and sororities—to a lesser degree—are the social scene**. Official party nights are Wednesdays, Fridays, and Saturdays—you are guaranteed to have a big fraternity party on each of those nights. Alternatives are few and far between: the University tries to lure students to low-key events like acoustic evenings or outdoor activities, but to no avail."

Q "**You will have more fun** if you are involved in Greek life. Sororities aren't as crucial, but I don't know what independent guys do for fun."

Q "We get our social scene from the frats and sororities because **there are no clubs or bars** or other colleges of any significance; without the fraternities, this school would be very boring."

Q "You shouldn't necessarily join a frat or [sorority] in order to fit in. **As long as you're confident with yourself**, you can do fine without joining a Greek organization."

Q "In my opinion, fraternities are way too important here. **Often, guys' friends are determined mainly along frat lines**, or at least those in fraternities spend the most time with with guys in their frat. Sororities and fraternities, through the rush process, create unnecessary and hurtful barriers. This process can get very competitive and can cause rifts among upperclassmen and freshmen alike. Hopefully, the Greek system's importance is starting to decline here."

## The Lowdown
### ON GREEK LIFE

**Number of Fraternities**:
14

**Number of Sororities**:
5

**Undergraduate Men in Fraternities**:
75%

**Undergraduate Women in Sororities**:
76%

**Multicultural Colonies**:
There are no multicultural/minority fraternities or sororities on campus, but W&L does have non-Greek minority organizations (see Diversity section).

### Did You Know?

Every year, the frats and sororities sponsor Lip Sync, perhaps W&L's most debauched, and definitely its most legendary, "charity" event. Each house's most, uh, talented performers put on incredible acts of choreographed lip-syncing and dancing that would put Ashlee Simpson to shame. The proceeds go to a local food drive.

## The College Prowler Take
### ON GREEK LIFE

Fraternities are absolutely huge at W&L, and have been for generations. About three out of every four guys joins a fraternity. Sororities, since coming to campus in the last decade, now attract about the same percentage of W&L women. What explains this? Students say that the small-town environment, where everything seems to shut down early, pushes them into "frats" or "srats" in order to get their share of nightlife and socializing. Plus, students try to continue the friendships they make in their first term at W&L; groups of friends often decide to join the same fraternity together. Despite the best efforts of the school administration to provide alternative entertainment, the Greek system still drives the social scene. The frats hold parties nearly every weekend, and lay it all out for a few special occasions (Homecoming, Christmas Weekend, Parents' Weekend). The fraternity parties are open to all students who want to come; the only closed parties are fraternity-sorority mixers.

**A+**

The College Prowler™ Grade on
## Greek Life: A+

A high grade in Greek Life indicates that sororities and fraternities are not only present, but also active on campus. Other determining factors include the variety of houses available and the respect the Greek community receives from the rest of the campus.

# Drug Scene

## The Lowdown
### ON DRUG SCENE

**Most Prevalent Drugs on Campus:**
Alcohol, Nicotine

**On-Campus Liquor-Related Violations:**
34

**Off-Campus Liquor-Related Arrests:**
51

**On-Campus Drug-Related Violations:**
8

**Off-Campus Drug-Related Arrests:**
0

## Drug Counseling Programs

### Student Health Center
Phone: (540) 458-8401
Services: Free counseling for depression, drug and alcohol dependency, referrals to specialists

### University Counseling Program
Phone: (540) 458-8590 or (540) 458-8401 (after hours or emergency)
Services: Confidential appointments with a licensed psychologist or psychiatrist

## Students Speak Out
ON DRUG SCENE

{ "I am the only member of my pledge class who does not drink. While I have never felt pressured to drink, W&L's social scene largely revolves around alcohol. I think that many students are indirectly pressured to drink."

Q "Drug use is very prevalent, especially the use of marijuana. **It's kept pretty undercover**, and there's certainly no pressure to use drugs, but a lot of students do, and it's easy to get drugs if you want them. Students rarely get caught, though."

Q "**Up until this year, I didn't drink**. Even if you go out, I don't think there's a negative attitude towards people who don't drink. I've seen frat brothers ask people who don't drink if they'd like water or soda."

Q "**Alcohol is easier to find than water at a frat party**. Marijuana is pretty easy, too, assuming you know who to ask."

Q "**Drug abuse seems prevalent around campus**, in the sense that if you want drugs, you can probably find them. But, it isn't obvious or being passed around the basement of a frat party."

## The College Prowler Take
ON DRUG SCENE

Some of the information about the presence of drugs around campus is anecdotal and gossipy—not cold, hard facts. Marijuana use does occur, although most of this may happen off campus, where houses aren't patrolled by security guards (as the freshman dorms and fraternities are).

According to the National College Health Assessment survey (March 2004), Washington and Lee students proved less likely than their peers (from 73 compared universities) to entirely avoid alcohol, cigarettes, and marijuana. But, over 90 percent of students at W&L say they've never used harder drugs like cocaine or ecstasy. Investigators with the regional drug task force say they suspect marijuana use on W&L's campus, but can't prove it. Alcohol is the drug of choice at W&L, and it is extremely prevalent both on and off campus.

**B-**

**The College Prowler™ Grade on**
## Drug Scene: B-

A high grade on Drug Scene indicates that drugs are not a noticeable part of campus life; drug use is not visible, and no pressure to use them seems to exist.

# Overall Experience

Q "W&L has **an unfortunate reputation as a hard partying and hard drinking school**. And to an extent, this is true. Anyone who ignores the University because of this does himself or herself a great disservice. Academics are exceedingly important at W&L, and the courses are typically very tough. Partying is important, but it never eclipses the more important reasons for being here for most students."

Q "Incoming students should be aware they'll be in a small southern town, and **they're not going to get urban culture** or a club scene."

## Students Speak Out
ON OVERALL EXPERIENCE

"W&L is not for everybody. I've ended up really liking it because I've found people who share my interests. But, then there are some people that the school's just not suited for."

Q "I knew that I wanted to come to W&L from the second I drove up, and **it's met every single expectation that I had**. The honor system is everything I expected, and the profs were more challenging, and yet more genuine, than I expected."

Q "Make sure you look into the school extensively—spend the night if you can. Know that **it's almost exclusively Greek**—you have to be a really independent person to thrive here, if you're not going to get involved in the Greek system."

Q "**W&L is not high school**, and anyone entering as a freshman should expect to struggle somewhat integrating themselves into campus during their first year. Also, the academic expectations are much higher than those of a public high school. Almost every W&L student has the experience of receiving a bad mark on their first paper. This difficulty in adjusting, though, does pass and eventually people find ways of fitting in here."

## The College Prowler Take
ON OVERALL EXPERIENCE

Year after year, Washington and Lee has been remarkably successful at producing happy students. Freshmen usually come in starry-eyed, and leave four years later content, happy, grateful, and nostalgic for all the good times gone by. The demanding expectations don't seem to put a serious damper on the general feeling of good cheer. One objective gauge of this is W&L's remarkably active and supportive alumni network, which supports the University, stays in touch to get jobs for students, and most recently chipped in cash to the tune of $240 million for massive modernization projects.

Students give high marks to the educational quality here, as well as to the natural setting and the sense of community and respect engendered by the honor system. But, as their comments have shown, some students are put off by the small-town environment and the dominance of Greek life on campus, as well as by recent friction between students and the administration over alcohol policies and changes to their beloved spring term. Most biting is some of the criticism leveled at the Greek system for allegedly crimping the social options for students who don't really want to party all the time.

Still, the overall impression is a positive one. Many students here believe their school is like no other—an example of what college life should be—and they plan to keep it that way.

# Southern USA Weather Map

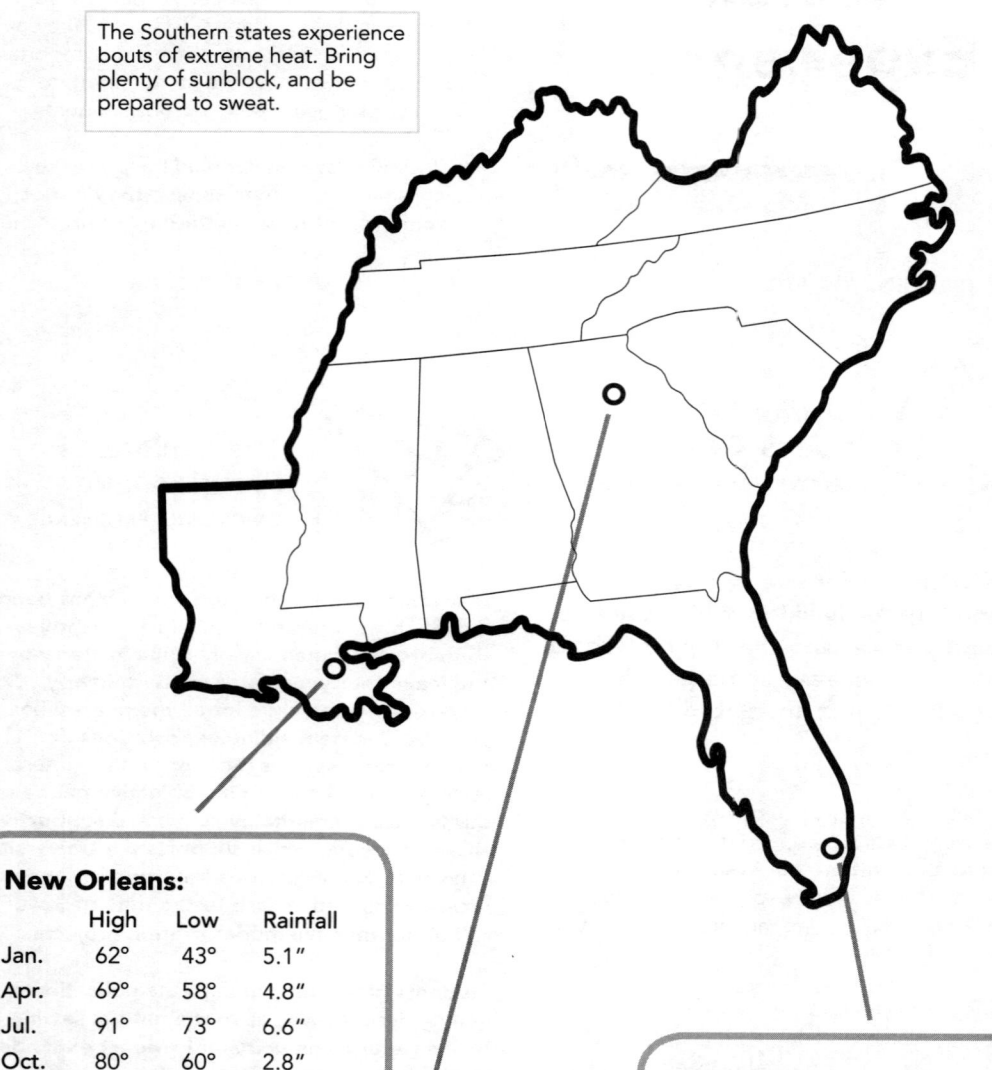

The Southern states experience bouts of extreme heat. Bring plenty of sunblock, and be prepared to sweat.

### New Orleans:

|      | High | Low | Rainfall |
|------|------|-----|----------|
| Jan. | 62°  | 43° | 5.1"     |
| Apr. | 69°  | 58° | 4.8"     |
| Jul. | 91°  | 73° | 6.6"     |
| Oct. | 80°  | 60° | 2.8"     |

### Miami:

|      | High | Low | Rainfall |
|------|------|-----|----------|
| Jan. | 76°  | 60° | 2.0"     |
| Apr. | 83°  | 68° | 3.0"     |
| Jul. | 89°  | 76° | 6.0"     |
| Oct. | 95°  | 72° | 7.0"     |

### Atlanta:

|      | High | Low | Rainfall |
|------|------|-----|----------|
| Jan. | 52°  | 33° | 4.7"     |
| Apr. | 73°  | 51° | 4.1"     |
| Jul. | 89°  | 70° | 5.3"     |
| Oct. | 73°  | 53° | 3.0"     |

# REPORT CARD SUMMARY
# Academics

**Academic Atmosphere**
As many as 1 in 4 college students drop out after or during freshman year. One of the reasons for this trend is that many incoming freshman just aren't prepared for the enormous academic transition from high school to college; it's a huge change.

| | | | | |
|---|---|---|---|---|
| **A** | DUKE UNIVERSITY | | | |
| **A** | WASHINGTON AND LEE UNIVERSITY | | **B** | UNIVERSITY OF FLORIDA |
| **A-** | COLLEGE OF WILLIAM & MARY | | **B** | UNIVERSITY OF MIAMI |
| **A-** | DAVIDSON COLLEGE | | **B** | UNIVERSITY OF RICHMOND |
| **A-** | EMORY UNIVERSITY | | **B** | VIRGINIA TECH |
| **A-** | UNIVERSITY OF VIRGINIA | | **B-** | AUBURN UNIVERSITY |
| **A-** | VANDERBILT UNIVERSITY | | **B-** | COLLEGE OF CHARLESTON |
| **B+** | ELON UNIVERSITY | | **B-** | FLORIDA STATE UNIVERSITY |
| **B+** | GEORGIA TECH | | **B-** | FURMAN UNIVERSITY |
| **B+** | LOYOLA UNIVERSITY NEW ORLEANS | | **B-** | HAMPTON UNIVERSITY |
| **B+** | ROLLINS COLLEGE | | **B-** | UNIVERSITY OF ALABAMA |
| **B+** | UNIVERSITY OF NORTH CAROLINA | | **B-** | UNIVERSITY OF CENTRAL FLORIDA |
| **B+** | WAKE FOREST UNIVERSITY | | **B-** | UNIVERSITY OF GEORGIA |
| **B** | CLEMSON UNIVERSITY | | **B-** | UNIVERSITY OF KENTUCKY |
| **B** | GUILFORD COLLEGE | | **B-** | UNIVERSITY OF MISSISSIPPI |
| **B** | JAMES MADISON UNIVERSITY | | **B-** | UNIVERSITY OF SOUTH CAROLINA |
| **B** | RHODES COLLEGE | | **B-** | UNIVERSITY OF SOUTH FLORIDA |
| **B** | TULANE UNIVERSITY | | **B-** | UNIVERSITY OF TENNESSEE |

# REPORT CARD SUMMARY
# Local Atmosphere

**Around Town**
When you're not studying, you'll probably want to be doing something other than sitting around. Every school offers different surroundings, and while visiting is important, hanging around for a few hours won't give you all the information you'll need about what other students do for fun off campus.

| Grade | School |
|---|---|
| A | UNIVERSITY OF CENTRAL FLORIDA |
| A | UNIVERSITY OF MIAMI |
| A- | EMORY UNIVERSITY |
| A- | GEORGIA TECH |
| A- | LOYOLA UNIVERSITY NEW ORLEANS |
| A- | ROLLINS COLLEGE |
| A- | TULANE UNIVERSITY |
| A- | UNIVERSITY OF GEORGIA |
| A- | UNIVERSITY OF MISSISSIPPI |
| A- | UNIVERSITY OF SOUTH FLORIDA |
| B+ | FURMAN UNIVERSITY |
| B+ | RHODES COLLEGE |
| B+ | UNIVERSITY OF FLORIDA |
| B+ | UNIVERSITY OF KENTUCKY |
| B+ | UNIVERSITY OF NORTH CAROLINA |
| B+ | UNIVERSITY OF SOUTH CAROLINA |
| B+ | VANDERBILT UNIVERSITY |
| B | CLEMSON UNIVERSITY |
| B | COLLEGE OF CHARLESTON |
| B | FLORIDA STATE UNIVERSITY |
| B | UNIVERSITY OF ALABAMA |
| B | UNIVERSITY OF TENNESSEE |
| B | UNIVERSITY OF VIRGINIA |
| B- | GUILFORD COLLEGE |
| B- | JAMES MADISON UNIVERSITY |
| B- | UNIVERSITY OF RICHMOND |
| B- | VIRGINIA TECH |
| C+ | AUBURN UNIVERSITY |
| C+ | COLLEGE OF WILLIAM & MARY |
| C+ | DAVIDSON COLLEGE |
| C+ | HAMPTON UNIVERSITY |
| C+ | WAKE FOREST UNIVERSITY |
| C | DUKE UNIVERSITY |
| C- | WASHINGTON AND LEE UNIVERSITY |
| D | ELON UNIVERSITY |

# REPORT CARD SUMMARY
# Safety & Security

**Staying Safe and Secure**
The presence of crime on campus is something you should strongly consider when choosing a college. Your chosen school may look like Pleasantville when the tour guide shows you around campus, but there may be more to the picture than what you're shown. Your safety and security should not be taken for granted.

- **A+** DAVIDSON COLLEGE
- **A+** WAKE FOREST UNIVERSITY
- **A** EMORY UNIVERSITY
- **A** JAMES MADISON UNIVERSITY
- **A** UNIVERSITY OF FLORIDA
- **A** WASHINGTON AND LEE UNIVERSITY
- **A-** AUBURN UNIVERSITY
- **A-** COLLEGE OF WILLIAM & MARY
- **A-** ELON UNIVERSITY
- **A-** FURMAN UNIVERSITY
- **A-** UNIVERSITY OF ALABAMA
- **A-** UNIVERSITY OF CENTRAL FLORIDA
- **A-** UNIVERSITY OF MISSISSIPPI
- **A-** UNIVERSITY OF NORTH CAROLINA
- **A-** UNIVERSITY OF RICHMOND
- **A-** VIRGINIA TECH
- **B+** CLEMSON UNIVERSITY
- **B+** GEORGIA TECH
- **B+** GUILFORD COLLEGE
- **B+** HAMPTON UNIVERSITY
- **B+** UNIVERSITY OF GEORGIA
- **B+** UNIVERSITY OF SOUTH CAROLINA
- **B+** UNIVERSITY OF VIRGINIA
- **B+** VANDERBILT UNIVERSITY
- **B** COLLEGE OF CHARLESTON
- **B** FLORIDA STATE UNIVERSITY
- **B** UNIVERSITY OF MIAMI
- **B** UNIVERSITY OF TENNESSEE
- **B-** RHODES COLLEGE
- **B-** UNIVERSITY OF KENTUCKY
- **B-** UNIVERSITY OF SOUTH FLORIDA
- **C+** ROLLINS COLLEGE
- **C+** TULANE UNIVERSITY
- **C** DUKE UNIVERSITY
- **C** LOYOLA UNIVERSITY NEW ORELANS

# REPORT CARD SUMMARY
# Facilities

**A Beautiful Campus**
Okay, you've paid the school thousands of dollars. Now you expect them to give you a little something in return—nice buildings, up-to-date computer labs, a decent gym or two. In the College Prowler guidebooks, students speak out on the quality of the facilities each school has to offer.

- **A** EMORY UNIVERSITY
- **A** FLORIDA STATE UNIVERSITY
- **A** JAMES MADISON UNIVERSITY
- **A** UNIVERSITY OF CENTRAL FLORIDA
- **A** UNIVERSITY OF FLORIDA
- **A** UNIVERSITY OF NORTH CAROLINA
- **A** VANDERBILT UNIVERSITY
- **A** WAKE FOREST UNIVERSITY
- **A-** CLEMSON UNIVERSITY
- **A-** DAVIDSON COLLEGE
- **A-** DUKE UNIVERSITY
- **A-** ROLLINS COLLEGE
- **A-** UNIVERSITY OF ALABAMA
- **A-** UNIVERSITY OF GEORGIA
- **A-** UNIVERSITY OF SOUTH CAROLINA
- **B+** AUBURN UNIVERSITY
- **B+** ELON UNIVERSITY
- **B+** FURMAN UNIVERSITY
- **B+** TULANE UNIVERSITY
- **B+** UNIVERSITY OF MIAMI
- **B+** UNIVERSITY OF SOUTH FLORIDA
- **B+** UNIVERSITY OF TENNESSEE
- **B+** VIRGINIA TECH
- **B+** WASHINGTON AND LEE UNIVERSITY
- **B** COLLEGE OF CHARLESTON
- **B** COLLEGE OF WILLIAM & MARY
- **B** GEORGIA TECH
- **B** GUILFORD COLLEGE
- **B** HAMPTON UNIVERSITY
- **B** RHODES COLLEGE
- **B** UNIVERSITY OF KENTUCKY
- **B** UNIVERSITY OF MISSISSIPPI
- **B** UNIVERSITY OF RICHMOND
- **B** UNIVERSITY OF VIRGINIA
- **C** LOYOLA UNIVERSITY NEW ORLEANS

# REPORT CARD SUMMARY
# Campus Dining

**Grade "F" Meat**
The food a school offers probably doesn't seem particularly important, does it? When considering a school, students often fail to consider that they'll be living (and eating) at the mercy of the institution for at least the next four years.

- **A-** UNIVERSITY OF SOUTH CAROLINA
- **B+** AUBURN UNIVERSITY
- **B+** DUKE UNIVERSITY
- **B+** JAMES MADISON UNIVERSITY
- **B+** VIRGINIA TECH
- **B** ELON UNIVERSITY
- **B** FURMAN UNIVERSITY
- **B** UNIVERSITY OF ALABAMA
- **B** UNIVERSITY OF CENTRAL FLORIDA
- **B** UNIVERSITY OF GEORGIA
- **B** UNIVERSITY OF TENNESSEE
- **B-** COLLEGE OF WILLIAM & MARY
- **B-** LOYOLA UNIVERSITY NEW ORLEANS
- **B-** ROLLINS COLLEGE
- **B-** UNIVERSITY OF FLORIDA
- **B-** UNIVERSITY OF KENTUCKY
- **B-** UNIVERSITY OF SOUTH FLORIDA
- **C+** CLEMSON UNIVERSITY
- **C+** COLLEGE OF CHARLESTON
- **C+** FLORIDA STATE UNIVERSITY
- **C+** TULANE UNIVERSITY
- **C+** UNIVERSITY OF MIAMI
- **C+** UNIVERSITY OF NORTH CAROLINA
- **C+** WAKE FOREST UNIVERSITY
- **C+** WASHINGTON AND LEE UNIVERSITY
- **C** DAVIDSON COLLEGE
- **C** HAMPTON UNIVERSITY
- **C-** GEORGIA TECH
- **C-** GUILFORD COLLEGE
- **C-** UNIVERSITY OF MISSISSIPPI
- **C-** UNIVERSITY OF RICHMOND
- **C-** UNIVERSITY OF VIRGINIA
- **C-** VANDERBILT UNIVERSITY
- **D+** EMORY UNIVERSITY
- **D+** RHODES COLLEGE

www.collegeprowler.com

# REPORT CARD SUMMARY
# Campus Housing

> **Dorm Atmosphere**
> Living in a dorm is going to be a huge part of your college life. Your living situation will influence almost everything about your four years in college. The people you live with and the comforts you're afforded will affect your personal and academic life.

| Grade | School |
|---|---|
| A- | DAVIDSON COLLEGE |
| A- | ELON UNIVERSITY |
| A- | FURMAN UNIVERSITY |
| B+ | JAMES MADISON UNIVERSITY |
| B+ | RHODES COLLEGE |
| B+ | UNIVERSITY OF NORTH CAROLINA |
| B+ | VANDERBILT UNIVERSITY |
| B | COLLEGE OF CHARLESTON |
| B | DUKE UNIVERSITY |
| B | GUILFORD COLLEGE |
| B | ROLLINS COLLEGE |
| B | WAKE FOREST UNIVERSITY |
| B | WASHINGTON AND LEE UNIVERSITY |
| B- | EMORY UNIVERSITY |
| B- | FLORIDA STATE UNIVERSITY |
| B- | UNIVERSITY OF ALABAMA |
| B- | UNIVERSITY OF CENTRAL FLORIDA |
| B- | UNIVERSITY OF FLORIDA |
| B- | UNIVERSITY OF GEORGIA |
| B- | UNIVERSITY OF MIAMI |
| B- | UNIVERSITY OF RICHMOND |
| B- | UNIVERSITY OF TENNESSEE |
| B- | UNIVERSITY OF VIRGINIA |
| C+ | CLEMSON UNIVERSITY |
| C+ | COLLEGE OF WILLIAM & MARY |
| C+ | UNIVERSITY OF KENTUCKY |
| C+ | UNIVERSITY OF MISSISSIPPI |
| C+ | UNIVERSITY OF SOUTH CAROLINA |
| C+ | VIRGINIA TECH |
| C | AUBURN UNIVERSITY |
| C | LOYOLA UNIVERSITY NEW ORLEANS |
| C | TULANE UNIVERSITY |
| C- | UNIVERSITY OF SOUTH FLORIDA |
| D+ | HAMPTON UNIVERSITY |
| D | GEORGIA TECH |

# REPORT CARD SUMMARY
# Diversity

**The Melting Pot**
College isn't just supposed to be high school with more buildings. It's supposed to be an experience that broadens your horizons, and it's hard to do that if you only meet people exactly like you.

| Grade | School |
|---|---|
| A- | UNIVERSITY OF MIAMI |
| B+ | DUKE UNIVERSITY |
| B- | FLORIDA STATE UNIVERSITY |
| B- | GEORGIA TECH |
| B- | UNIVERSITY OF CENTRAL FLORIDA |
| B-. | UNIVERSITY OF SOUTH FLORIDA |
| C+ | EMORY UNIVERSITY |
| C+ | LOYOLA UNIVERSITY NEW ORLEANS |
| C+ | UNIVERSITY OF FLORIDA |
| C+ | UNIVERSITY OF NORTH CAROLINA |
| C | GUILFORD COLLEGE |
| C | UNIVERSITY OF VIRGINIA |
| C- | UNIVERSITY OF SOUTH CAROLINA |
| D+ | COLLEGE OF WILLIAM & MARY |
| D+ | TULANE UNIVERSITY |
| D+ | UNIVERSITY OF ALABAMA |
| D+ | UNIVERSITY OF RICHMOND |
| D+ | VIRGINIA TECH |
| D | CLEMSON UNIVERSITY |
| D | COLLEGE OF CHARLESTON |
| D | FURMAN UNIVERSITY |
| D | RHODES COLLEGE |
| D | UNIVERSITY OF MISSISSIPPI |
| D | UNIVERSITY OF TENNESSEE |
| D | VANDERBILT UNIVERSITY |
| D- | AUBURN UNIVERSITY |
| D- | DAVIDSON COLLEGE |
| D- | ELON UNIVERSITY |
| D- | HAMPTON UNIVERSITY |
| D- | JAMES MADISON UNIVERSITY |
| D- | ROLLINS COLLEGE |
| D- | UNIVERSITY OF GEORGIA |
| D- | UNIVERSITY OF KENTUCKY |
| D- | WAKE FOREST UNIVERSITY |
| D- | WASHINGTON AND LEE UNIVERSITY |

# REPORT CARD SUMMARY
# Guys

**Guys Gone Wild**
College guys are very different from the high school guys you're used to; they're a different breed. College should offer you an entirely new and engaging social scene, and with that comes members of the opposite (or same) sex who are not only attractive, but also fun and personable. College Prowler guidebooks offer you a variety of student opinions about the guys on each campus.

| Grade | School |
|---|---|
| A | CLEMSON UNIVERSITY |
| A | UNIVERSITY OF FLORIDA |
| A | UNIVERSITY OF GEORGIA |
| A- | FLORIDA STATE UNIVERSITY |
| A- | UNIVERSITY OF KENTUCKY |
| A- | UNIVERSITY OF RICHMOND |
| A- | UNIVERSITY OF SOUTH CAROLINA |
| A- | UNIVERSITY OF SOUTH FLORIDA |
| A- | UNIVERSITY OF TENNESSEE |
| B+ | AUBURN UNIVERSITY |
| B+ | DAVIDSON UNIVERSITY |
| B+ | DUKE UNIVERSITY |
| B+ | ELON UNIVERSITY |
| B+ | FURMAN UNIVERSITY |
| B+ | UNIVERSITY OF ALABAMA |
| B+ | UNIVERSITY OF CENTRAL FLORIDA |
| B+ | UNIVERSITY OF MIAMI |
| B+ | UNIVERSITY OF NORTH CAROLINA |
| B+ | UNIVERSITY OF VIRGINIA |
| B+ | VIRGINIA TECH |
| B+ | WAKE FOREST UNIVERSITY |
| B | GEORGIA TECH |
| B | GUILFORD COLLEGE |
| B | JAMES MADISON UNIVERSITY |
| B | LOYOLA UNIVERSITY NEW ORLEANS |
| B | ROLLINS COLLEGE |
| B | VANDERBILT UNIVERSITY |
| B | WASHINGTON AND LEE UNIVERSITY |
| B- | COLLEGE OF CHARLESTON |
| B- | COLLEGE OF WILLIAM & MARY |
| B- | EMORY UNIVERSITY |
| B- | HAMPTON UNIVERSITY |
| B- | RHODES COLLEGE |
| B- | TULANE UNIVERSITY |
| B- | UNIVERSITY OF MISSISSIPPI |

# REPORT CARD SUMMARY
# Girls

**Pretty Woman**
Guys, you're going to have a hard time enjoying your next four years if there just aren't any worthwhile girls on campus. College should offer you an entirely new and engaging social scene, and with that comes members of the opposite sex who are not just attractive, but fun and personable as well. College Prowler guidebooks offer you a variety of student opinions about the girls on each campus.

| Grade | School |
|---|---|
| A+ | UNIVERSITY OF CENTRAL FLORIDA |
| A+ | UNIVERSITY OF GEORGIA |
| A+ | VANDERBILT UNIVERSITY |
| A | CLEMSON UNIVERSITY |
| A | COLLEGE OF CHARLESTON |
| A | FLORIDA STATE UNIVERSITY |
| A | HAMPTON UNIVERSITY |
| A | ROLLINS COLLEGE |
| A | UNIVERSITY OF ALABAMA |
| A | UNIVERSITY OF FLORIDA |
| A | UNIVERSITY OF KENTUCKY |
| A | UNIVERSITY OF MISSISSIPPI |
| A | UNIVERSITY OF RICHMOND |
| A | UNIVERSITY OF SOUTH CAROLINA |
| A | UNIVERSITY OF SOUTH FLORIDA |
| A | UNIVERSITY OF TENNESSEE |
| A- | ELON UNIVERSITY |
| A- | FURMAN UNIVERSITY |
| A- | JAMES MADISON UNIVERSITY |
| A- | UNIVERSITY OF MIAMI |
| A- | UNIVERSITY OF NORTH CAROLINA |
| A- | UNIVERSITY OF VIRGINIA |
| A- | WAKE FOREST UNIVERSITY |
| A- | WASHINGTON AND LEE UNIVERSITY |
| B+ | GUILFORD COLLEGE |
| B+ | LOYOLA UNIVERSITY NEW ORLEANS |
| B+ | TULANE UNIVERSITY |
| B | AUBURN UNIVERSITY |
| B | COLLEGE OF WILLIAM & MARY |
| B | DAVIDSON COLLEGE |
| B | DUKE UNIVERSITY |
| B | RHODES COLLEGE |
| B | VIRGINIA TECH |
| C | EMORY UNIVERSITY |
| C | GEORGIA TECH |

# REPORT CARD SUMMARY
# Athletics

> **Be a Good Sport**
> Even if you're not a hardcore athlete, a school's athletics can still be important to you. School spirit can be an exhilarating feeling, and intramural sports offer you a social outlet and a break from the academic routine.

- **A+** CLEMSON UNIVERSITY
- **A+** UNIVERSITY OF ALABAMA
- **A+** UNIVERSITY OF FLORIDA
- **A+** UNIVERSITY OF NORTH CAROLINA
- **A+** UNIVERSITY OF TENNESSEE
- **A** AUBURN UNIVERSITY
- **A** FLORIDA STATE UNIVERSITY
- **A** GEORGIA TECH
- **A** UNIVERSITY OF GEORGIA
- **A** UNIVERSITY OF KENTUCKY
- **A** UNIVERSITY OF MIAMI
- **A** UNIVERSITY OF MISSISSIPPI
- **A** UNIVERSITY OF SOUTH CAROLINA
- **A** UNIVERSITY OF VIRGINIA
- **A** VIRGINIA TECH
- **A** WAKE FOREST UNIVERSITY
- **A-** DUKE UNIVERSITY
- **B** DAVIDSON COLLEGE

- **B** FURMAN UNIVERSITY
- **B** ROLLINS COLLEGE
- **B** UNIVERSITY OF RICHMOND
- **B** UNIVERSITY OF SOUTH FLORIDA
- **B** VANDERBILT UNIVERSITY
- **B-** COLLEGE OF CHARLESTON
- **B-** ELON UNIVERSITY
- **B-** HAMPTON UNIVERSITY
- **B-** JAMES MADISON UNIVERSITY
- **B-** TULANE UNIVERSITY
- **B-** UNIVERSITY OF CENTRAL FLORIDA
- **C+** WASHINGTON AND LEE UNIVERSITY
- **C** COLLEGE OF WILLIAM & MARY
- **C** GUILFORD COLLEGE
- **C** RHODES COLLEGE
- **C-** EMORY UNIVERSITY
- **D+** LOYOLA UNIVERSITY NEW ORLEANS

# REPORT CARD SUMMARY
# Greek Life

**Going Greek**
Whether or not you plan on joining a fraternity or sorority, it is possible that Greek life could still be a huge part of your college experience; Greek events are major social functions. You may discover that joining a Greek organization is a much more enriching and worthwhile experience than you'd ever expected (or much

| Grade | School |
|---|---|
| A+ | VANDERBILT UNIVERSITY |
| A+ | WAKE FOREST UNIVERSITY |
| A+ | WASHINGTON AND LEE UNIVERSITY |
| A | COLLEGE OF WILLIAM & MARY |
| A | DUKE UNIVERSITY |
| A | ELON UNIVERSITY |
| A | ROLLINS COLLEGE |
| A | UNIVERSITY OF ALABAMA |
| A | UNIVERSITY OF FLORIDA |
| A | UNIVERSITY OF GEORGIA |
| A | UNIVERSITY OF MISSISSIPPI |
| A | UNIVERSITY OF NORTH CAROLINA |
| A | UNIVERSITY OF RICHMOND |
| A | UNIVERSITY OF VIRGINIA |
| A- | FLORIDA STATE UNIVERSITY |
| A- | FURMAN UNIVERSITY |
| A- | RHODES COLLEGE |
| A- | UNIVERSITY OF SOUTH CAROLINA |
| A- | UNIVERSITY OF TENNESSEE |
| B+ | AUBURN UNIVERSITY |
| B+ | CLEMSON UNIVERSITY |
| B+ | EMORY UNIVERSITY |
| B+ | GEORGIA TECH |
| B+ | JAMES MADISON UNIVERSITY |
| B+ | UNIVERSITY OF KENTUCKY |
| B+ | UNIVERSITY OF MIAMI |
| B+ | UNIVERSITY OF SOUTH FLORIDA |
| B+ | VIRGINIA TECH |
| B | TULANE UNIVERSITY |
| B | UNIVERSITY OF CENTRAL FLORIDA |
| B- | DAVIDSON COLLEGE |
| C+ | COLLEGE OF CHARLESTON |
| C+ | HAMPTON UNIVERSITY |
| C | LOYOLA UNIVERSITY NEW ORLEANS |
| N/A | GUILFORD COLLEGE |

# REPORT CARD SUMMARY
# Drug Scene

**Drugs, Drugs Everywhere**
Drugs have been an issue ever since people discovered that they could grind up, inject, smoke, melt, or swallow various kinds of stuff to change the way they feel. College Prowler guidebooks address the prominence of the drug scene on campus, and the student attitudes, to let you know how visible the threat of drug use actually is at each school. Here, a high grade means that drugs are not a noticable part of campus life.

| Grade | School |
|---|---|
| A+ | FURMAN UNIVERSITY |
| A | COLLEGE OF WILLIAM & MARY |
| A | WAKE FOREST UNIVERSITY |
| A- | AUBURN UNIVERSITY |
| A- | DAVIDSON COLLEGE |
| A- | ELON UNIVERSITY |
| A- | GEORGIA TECH |
| B+ | CLEMSON UNIVERSITY |
| B+ | RHODES COLLEGE |
| B+ | UNIVERSITY OF NORTH CAROLINA |
| B+ | UNIVERSITY OF RICHMOND |
| B+ | UNIVERSITY OF SOUTH CAROLINA |
| B+ | VANDERBILT UNIVERSITY |
| B | COLLEGE OF CHARLESTON |
| B | DUKE UNIVERSITY |
| B | UNIVERSITY OF FLORIDA |
| B | UNIVERSITY OF VIRGINIA |
| B- | GUILFORD COLLEGE |
| B- | HAMPTON UNIVERSITY |
| B- | JAMES MADISON UNIVERSITY |
| B- | LOYOLA UNIVERSITY NEW ORLEANS |
| B- | UNIVERSITY OF ALABAMA |
| B- | UNIVERSITY OF GEORGIA |
| B- | UNIVERSITY OF KENTUCKY |
| B- | UNIVERSITY OF MIAMI |
| B- | UNIVERSTY OF MISSISSIPPI |
| B- | UNIVERSITY OF SOUTH FLORIDA |
| B- | UNIVERSITY OF TENNESSEE |
| B- | VIRGINIA TECH |
| B- | WASHINGTON AND LEE UNIVERSITY |
| C+ | EMORY UNIVERSITY |
| C+ | FLORIDA STATE UNIVERSITY |
| C+ | TULANE UNIVERSITY |
| C | ROLLINS COLLEGE |
| C | UNIVERSITY OF CENTRAL FLORIDA |

# Financial Aid

> This section of the book has advice and important information for funding your college education.

### FAFSA Deadline:

The application period opens January 1 for the following year, so if a class begins in September 2006, you could apply for aid as early as January 1, 2006. The application period closes in June, at the end of the academic year.

## Federal Aid

The FAFSA (Free Application for Federal Student Aid) is the application you must complete to get federal aid. You can apply online, or get an application at *http://www.fafsa.ed.gov/*.

Federal aid comes in two forms: grants and loans. Grants are awards with nothing to pay back, while federal loans need to be repaid down the road at a low (or zero) interest rate.

### Federal Grants

Pell Grants are awarded to low-income students, while Federal Supplemental Educational Opportunity Grants (FSEOG) are for low-income students with exceptional financial need.

### Federal Loans

- Unsubsidized Stafford Loan—Available to any student regardless of financial need, but the student pays the interest.
- Subsidized Stafford Loan—A loan that is interest-free until six months after you graduate from college (the government pays the interest until that time). These are available to students who meet financial requirements and attend school more than half-time.
- Plus Loans—Available for the parents of students attending college.
- Perkins Loans—Administered by the college, these are for students with exceptional financial need.

# Students with Special Needs

Colleges and universities are required by federal law to meet certain physical and educational needs unique to those with disabilities. The degree to which schools accommodate both learning and physically challenged students varies. Schools often have a staff member especially knowledgeable of such issues who will best answer questions about access, education, and housing.

### Auburn University

Contact:
Dr. Kelly Haynes
Director, The Program for Students with Disabilities
(334) 844-2096
haynemd@auburn.edu

Is a smaller course load available? - **Yes**
Is more time given to finish your degree? - **Yes**
Is credit given toward the degree for remedial courses? - **No**
Services offered to students with learning disabilities: **reading machines, tape recorders, note-taking services, readers, extended time for tests, tutors, other**
Services offered to students with physical disabilities: **note-taking services, special transportation, tape recorders, tutors, adaptive equipment, reader services, Braille services, interpreters for hearing-impaired, talking books**
Is the campus accessible to students with physical disabilities? - **100%**
Is housing available for disabled students? - **Yes**

### Clemson University

Contact:
Jane B. Greenawalt
Program Director, Student Disability Services
(864) 656-6848
janeg@clemson.edu

Is a smaller course load available? - **Yes**
Is more time given to finish your degree? - **Yes**
Is credit given toward the degree for remedial courses? - **No**
Services offered to students with learning disabilities: **other testing accommodations, tape recorders, diagnostic testing service, note-taking services, oral tests, readers, extended time for tests, other**
Services offered to students with physical disabilities: **note-taking services, special transportation, tape recorders, special housing, tutors, adaptive equipment, reader services, Braille services, interpreters for hearing-impaired, talking books**
Is the campus accessible to students with physical disabilities? - **Partially**
Is housing available for disabled students? - **Yes**

### College of Charleston

Contact:
Bobbie Lindstrom
Director, Center for Disability Services
(843) 953-1431
lindstromb@cofc.edu

Is a smaller course load available? - **Yes**
Is more time given to finish your degree? - **Yes**
Is credit given toward the degree for remedial courses? - **No**
Services offered to students with learning disabilities: **reading machines, tape recorders, diagnostic testing service, learning center, extended time for tests, tutors**
Services offered to students with physical disabilities: **note-taking services, tape recorders, tutors, adaptive equipment, reader services, Braille services, interpreters for hearing-impaired, talking books**
Is the campus accessible to students with physical disabilities? - **Mostly**
Is housing available for disabled students? - **N/A**

### College of William & Mary

Contact:
Lisa Bickley
Assistant Dean of Students
(757) 221-2510
ljbick@wm.edu

Is a smaller course load available? - **No**
Is more time given to finish your degree? - **No**
Is credit given toward the degree for remedial courses? - **No**
Services offered to students with learning disabilities: **tape recorders, diagnostic testing service, note-taking services, readers, extended time for tests**
Services offered to students with physical disabilities: **note-taking services, tape recorders, adaptive equipment, reader services, Braille services, interpreters for hearing-impaired**
Is the campus accessible to students with physical disabilities? - **Mostly**
Is housing available for disabled students? - **Yes**

## Davidson College

Contact:
Kathy Bray-Merrell
Assoc. Dean of Student Life
(704) 894-2225
kamerrell@davidson.edu

Is a smaller course load available? - **Yes**
Is more time given to finish your degree? - **Yes**
Is credit given toward the degree for remedial courses? - **N/A**
Services offered to students with learning disabilities: **other testing accommodations, tape recorders, diagnostic testing service, note-taking services, oral tests, readers, extended time for tests, tutors**
Services offered to students with physical disabilities: **note-taking services, tape recorders, tutors, adaptive equipment, reader services, talking books**
Is the campus accessible to students with physical disabilities? - **90%**
Is housing available for disabled students? - **Yes**

## Duke University

Contact:
N/A

Is a smaller course load available? - **N/A**
Is more time given to finish your degree? - **N/A**
Is credit given toward the degree for remedial courses? - **N/A**
Services offered to students with learning disabilities: **N/A**
Services offered to students with physical disabilities: **N/A**
Is the campus accessible to students with physical disabilities? - **N/A**
Is housing available for disabled students? - **N/A**

## Elon University

Contact:
Priscilla Lipe
Disabilities Service Coordinator
(336) 278-6500
plipe@elon.edu

Is a smaller course load available? - **Yes**
Is more time given to finish your degree? - **Yes**
Is credit given toward the degree for remedial courses? - **Yes**
Services offered to students with learning disabilities: **remedial math, remedial English, remedial reading, note-taking services, extended time for tests, other**
Services offered to students with physical disabilities: **note-taking services, tape recorders, special housing, tutors, reader services, interpreters for hearing-impaired, talking books**
Is the campus accessible to students with physical disabilities? - **Mostly**
Is housing available for disabled students? - **N/A**

## Emory University

Contact:
N/A

Is a smaller course load available? - **Yes**
Is more time given to finish your degree? - **Yes**
Is credit given toward the degree for remedial courses? - **No**
Services offered to students with learning disabilities: **other testing accommodations, other special classes, note-taking services, oral tests, readers, extended time for tests, tutors**
Services offered to students with physical disabilities: **note-taking services, tape recorders, adaptive equipment, tutors**
Is the campus accessible to students with physical disabilities? - **N/A**
Is housing available for disabled students? - **Yes**

## Florida State University

Contact:
Lauren Miller
Director of Student Disability Resource Center
(850) 644-9566
SDRC@admin.fsu.edu

Is a smaller course load available? - **Yes**
Is more time given to finish your degree? - **Yes**
Is credit given toward the degree for remedial courses? - **No**
Services offered to students with learning disabilities: **remedial math, remedial English, reading machines, remedial reading, tape recorders, diagnostic testing service, untimed tests, note-taking services, oral tests, readers, tutors, other**
Services offered to students with physical disabilities: **note-taking services, special transportation, tape recorders, tutors, reader services, interpreters for hearing-impaired, talking books, other**
Is the campus accessible to students with physical disabilities? - **99%**
Is housing available for disabled students? - **Yes**

## Furman University

Contact:
Ms. Susan Clark
Director, Disability Services
(864) 294-2322
susan.clark@furman.edu

Is a smaller course load available? - **Yes**
Is more time given to finish your degree? - **Yes**
Is credit given toward the degree for remedial courses? - **No**
Services offered to students with learning disabilities: **tape recorders, note-taking services, oral tests, readers, extended time for tests, tutors, other**
Services offered to students with physical disabilities: **note-taking services, tape recorders, tutors, note-taking services, tape recorders, special housing, tutors, adaptive equipment, reader services, Braille services, interpreters for hearing-impaired, talking books**
Is the campus accessible to students with physical disabilities? - **98%**
Is housing available for disabled students? - **Yes**

**Georgia Tech**

Contact:
Tameeka Hunter
Disability Services Specialist
(404) 894-2564
tameeka.hunter@upss.gatech.edu

Is a smaller course load available? - **Yes**
Is more time given to finish your degree? - **Yes**
Is credit given toward the degree for remedial courses? - **No**
Services offered to students with learning disabilities: **other testing accommodations, tape recorders, videotaped classes, diagnostic testing service, note-taking services, learning center, readers, extended time for tests, tutors, other**
Services offered to students with physical disabilities: **note-taking services, special transportation, tape recorders, special housing, tutors, adaptive equipment, reader services, Braille services, interpreters for hearing-impaired, other**
Is the campus accessible to students with physical disabilities? - **Partially**
Is housing available for disabled students? - **Yes**

**Guilford College**

Contact:
Sue Keith
Director of Academic Skills Center
(336) 316-2200
skeith@guilford.edu

Is a smaller course load available? - **Yes**
Is more time given to finish your degree? - **Yes**
Is credit given toward the degree for remedial courses? - **No**
Services offered to students with learning disabilities: **other testing accommodations, reading machines, tape recorders, other special classes, untimed tests, note-taking services, oral tests, learning center, readers, extended time for tests, tutors**

Services offered to students with physical disabilities: **note-taking services, tape recorders, special housing, tutors, adaptive equipment, reader services, talking books**
Is the campus accessible to students with physical disabilities? - **Mostly**
Is housing available for disabled students? - **N/A**

**Hampton University**

Contact:
Mrs. Janice Halima Rashada
Director of Testing and 504 Compliance officer
(757) 727-5493
janice.rashada@hamptonu.edu

Is a smaller course load available? - **Yes**
Is more time given to finish your degree? - **No**
Is credit given toward the degree for remedial courses? - **No**
Services offered to students with learning disabilities: **remedial math, other testing accommodations, remedial English, remedial reading, tape recorders, untimed tests, note-taking services, oral tests, readers, extended time for tests, tutors, other**
Services offered to students with physical disabilities: **note-taking services, tape recorders, tutors, adaptive equipment, reader services, interpreters for hearing-impaired, talking books, other**
Is the campus accessible to students with physical disabilities? - **98%**
Is housing available for disabled students? - **N/A**

**James Madison University**

Contact:
N/A

Is a smaller course load available? - **Yes**
Is more time given to finish your degree? - **Yes**
Is credit given toward the degree for remedial courses? - **No**
Services offered to students with learning disabilities: **other testing accommodations, reading machines, tape recorders, diagnostic testing service, note-taking services, oral tests, learning center, readers, extended time for tests, other**
Services offered to students with physical disabilities: **note-taking services, special transportation, tape recorders, special housing, adaptive equipment, reader services, Braille services, interpreters for hearing-impaired, talking books, other**
Is the campus accessible to students with physical disabilities? - **85%**
Is housing available for disabled students? - **N/A**

## Loyola University New Orleans

Contact:
Sarah Mead Smith or Kacey McNalley
Director or Special Needs Counselor
(504) 865-2990
ssmith@loyno.edu

Is a smaller course load available? - **Yes**
Is more time given to finish your degree? - **Yes**
Is credit given toward the degree for remedial courses? - **No**
Services offered to students with learning disabilities: **remedial math, other testing accommodations, reading machines, tape recorders, diagnostic testing service, untimed tests, note-taking services, special bookstore section, oral tests, learning center, readers, extended time for tests, tutors**
Services offered to students with physical disabilities: **note-taking services, special transportation, tape recorders, special housing, tutors, adaptive equipment, reader services, Braille services, interpreters for hearing-impaired, talking books, other**
Is the campus accessible to students with physical disabilities? - **Mostly**
Is housing available for disabled students? - **Yes**

## Rhodes College

Contact:
Melissa Butler
Coordinator, Disability and Career Services
(901) 843-3994
mbutler@rhodes.edu
Is a smaller course load available? - **Yes**
Is more time given to finish your degree? - **Yes**
Is credit given toward the degree for remedial courses? - **N/A**
Services offered to students with learning disabilities: **other testing accommodations, reading machines, tape recorders, note-taking services, extended time for tests, tutors**
Services offered to students with physical disabilities: **note-taking services, tape recorders, special housing, tutors, adaptive equipment, reader services, Braille services, interpreters for hearing-impaired, talking books**
Is the campus accessible to students with physical disabilities? - **90%**
Is housing available for disabled students? - **N/A**

## Rollins College

Contact:
Dr. Karen Hater
Director, Thomas P. Johnson Student Resource Center
(407) 646-2354
klhater@rollins.edu

Is a smaller course load available? - **Yes**
Is more time given to finish your degree? - **Yes**
Is credit given toward the degree for remedial courses? - **No**
Services offered to students with learning disabilities: **other testing accommodations, reading machines, tape recorders, untimed tests, note-taking services, learning center, readers, extended time for tests, tutors**
Services offered to students with physical disabilities: **note-taking services, tape recorders, special housing, tutors, interpreters for hearing-impaired**
Is the campus accessible to students with physical disabilities? - **75%**
Is housing available for disabled students? - **Yes**

## Tulane University

Contact:
Katie Heidingsfelder
Accommodations Coordinator
(504) 862-8433
KHeiding@tulane.edu

Is a smaller course load available? - **No**
Is more time given to finish your degree? - **No**
Is credit given toward the degree for remedial courses? - **No**
Services offered to students with learning disabilities: **other testing accommodations, tape recorders, diagnostic testing service, untimed tests, note-taking services, oral tests, readers, extended time for tests, tutors**
Services offered to students with physical disabilities: **note-taking services, tape recorders, special housing, tutors, reader services, interpreters for hearing-impaired, talking books**
Is the campus accessible to students with physical disabilities? - **Partially**
Is housing available for disabled students? - **Yes**

## University of Alabama

Contact:
Judy Thorpe
Director; Office of Disability Services
(205) 348-4285
jthorpe@aalan.ua.edu

Is a smaller course load available? - **Yes**
Is more time given to finish your degree? - **Yes**
Is credit given toward the degree for remedial courses? - **No**
Services offered to students with learning disabilities: **remedial math, reading machines, note-taking services, oral tests, learning center, extended time for tests, tutors**
Services offered to students with physical disabilities: **note-taking services, tape recorders, tutors, reader services**

Is the campus accessible to students with physical disabilities? - **90%**
Is housing available for disabled students? - **Yes**

## University of Central Florida

Contact:
Dr. Philip Kalfin
Director of Student Disability Services
(407) 823-2371

Is a smaller course load available? - **N/A**
Is more time given to finish your degree? - **N/A**
Is credit given toward the degree for remedial courses? - **No**
Services offered to students with learning disabilities: **other testing accommodations, reading machines, tape recorders, videotaped classes, diagnostic testing service, note-taking services, readers, extended time for tests, tutors, other**
Services offered to students with physical disabilities: **note-taking services, special housing, tutors, reader services, Braille services, interpreters for hearing-impaired**
Is the campus accessible to students with physical disabilities? - **95%**
Is housing available for disabled students? - **Yes**

## University of Florida

Contact:
John Denny
Director, Disability Resources
(352) 392-1261
jdenny@ufl.edu

Is a smaller course load available? - **Yes**
Is more time given to finish your degree? - **Yes**
Is credit given toward the degree for remedial courses? - **No**
Services offered to students with learning disabilities: **other testing accommodations, reading machines, tape recorders, diagnostic testing service, note-taking services, readers, extended time for tests**
Services offered to students with physical disabilities: **note-taking services, special transportation, tape recorders, tutors, adaptive equipment, reader services, Braille services, interpreters for hearing-impaired, talking books, other**
Is the campus accessible to students with physical disabilities? - **95%**
Is housing available for disabled students? - **Yes**

## University of Georgia

Contact:
Patricia Marshall
LD Specialist
(706) 542-7034

Is a smaller course load available? - **Yes**
Is more time given to finish your degree? - **Yes**
Is credit given toward the degree for remedial courses? - **No**
Services offered to students with learning disabilities: **remedial math, other testing accommodations, remedial English, reading machines, remedial reading, tape recorders, diagnostic testing service, note-taking services, oral tests, learning center, readers, extended time for tests, tutors**
Services offered to students with physical disabilities: **note-taking services, tape recorders, note-taking services, special transportation, tape recorders, special housing, tutors, adaptive equipment, reader services, Braille services, interpreters for hearing-impaired, talking books**
Is the campus accessible to students with physical disabilities? - **Mostly**
Is housing available for disabled students? - **Yes**

## University of Kentucky

Contact:
Leisa Pickering
Cognitive Disabilities Specialist
(859) 257-2754
lmpick@uky.edu

Is a smaller course load available? - **No**
Is more time given to finish your degree? - **N/A**
Is credit given toward the degree for remedial courses? - **No**
Services offered to students with learning disabilities: **other testing accommodations, reading machines, tape recorders, diagnostic testing service, extended time for tests**
Services offered to students with physical disabilities: **special transportation, tape recorders, special housing, adaptive equipment, reader services, interpreters for hearing-impaired, talking books**
Is the campus accessible to students with physical disabilities? - **95%**
Is housing available for disabled students? - **Yes**

## University of Miami

Contact:
Judith Antinarella
Director Disability Services
(305) 284-2374
jantinarella@miami.edu

Is a smaller course load available? - **N/A**
Is more time given to finish your degree? - **N/A**
Is credit given toward the degree for remedial courses? - **N/A**
Services offered to students with learning disabilities: **other testing accommodations, tape recorders, learning center, readers, extended time for tests, tutors**

Services offered to students with physical disabilities: **note-taking services, tutors, adaptive equipment, interpreters for hearing-impaired**
Is the campus accessible to students with physical disabilities? - **95%**
Is housing available for disabled students? - **No**

## University of Mississippi

Contact:
N/A

Is a smaller course load available? - **N/A**
Is more time given to finish your degree? - **N/A**
Is credit given toward the degree for remedial courses? - **N/A**
Services offered to students with learning disabilities: **N/A**
Services offered to students with physical disabilities: **N/A**
Is the campus accessible to students with physical disabilities? - **N/A**
Is housing available for disabled students? - **N/A**

## University of North Carolina

Contact:
Jane Benson
Director, Learning Disability Services
(919) 962-7227
lds@unc.edu

Is a smaller course load available? - **No**
Is more time given to finish your degree? - **Yes**
Is credit given toward the degree for remedial courses? - **No**
Services offered to students with learning disabilities: **other testing accommodations, reading machines, tape recorders, note-taking services, learning center, readers, extended time for tests, other**
Services offered to students with physical disabilities: **note-taking services, special transportation, reader services, Braille services, interpreters for hearing-impaired**
Is the campus accessible to students with physical disabilities? - **94%**
Is housing available for disabled students? - **Yes**

## University of Richmond

Contact:
Mary M. Churchill, Ph.D.
Staff Psychologist
(804) 289-8119
mchurchi@richmond.edu

Is a smaller course load available? - **Yes**
Is more time given to finish your degree? - **N/A**
Is credit given toward the degree for remedial courses? - **N/A**

Services offered to students with learning disabilities: **other testing accommodations, tape recorders, learning center, extended time for tests, tutors, other**
Services offered to students with physical disabilities: **other**
Is the campus accessible to students with physical disabilities? - **Mostly**
Is housing available for disabled students? - **Yes**

## University of South Carolina

Contact:
Deborah C. Haynes
Director, Student Disability
(803) 777-6142
debbieh@gwm.sc.edu

Is a smaller course load available? - **Yes**
Is more time given to finish your degree? - **Yes**
Is credit given toward the degree for remedial courses? - **No**
Services offered to students with learning disabilities: **reading machines, tape recorders, untimed tests, note-taking services, readers, extended time for tests**
Services offered to students with physical disabilities: **note-taking services, special transportation, tape recorders, special housing, adaptive equipment, reader services, interpreters for hearing-impaired, other**
Is the campus accessible to students with physical disabilities? - **95%**
Is housing available for disabled students? - **Yes**

## University of South Florida

Contact:
Mary Sarver
Director, Student Disability Services
(813) 974-8135
Msarver@admin.usf.edu

Is a smaller course load available? - **Yes**
Is more time given to finish your degree? - **Yes**
Is credit given toward the degree for remedial courses? - **No**
Services offered to students with learning disabilities: **other testing accommodations, reading machines, tape recorders, note-taking services, oral tests, readers, extended time for tests, other**
Services offered to students with physical disabilities: **special transportation, tape recorders, special housing, tutors, adaptive equipment, reader services, Braille services**
Is the campus accessible to students with physical disabilities? - **Fully**
Is housing available for disabled students? - **Yes**

## University of Tennessee

Contact:
Learning Disabilities Coordinator
(865) 974-6087
ods@utk.edu

Is a smaller course load available? - **No**
Is more time given to finish your degree? - **No**
Is credit given toward the degree for remedial courses? - **N/A**
Services offered to students with learning disabilities: **other testing accommodations, reading machines, tape recorders, diagnostic testing service, note-taking services, oral tests, readers, extended time for tests**
Services offered to students with physical disabilities: **note-taking services, special transportation, tape recorders, special housing, adaptive equipment, reader services, interpreters for hearing-impaired, talking books, other**
Is the campus accessible to students with physical disabilities? - **95%**
Is housing available for disabled students? - **No**

## University of Virginia

Contact:
N/A

Is a smaller course load available? - **N/A**
Is more time given to finish your degree? - **N/A**
Is credit given toward the degree for remedial courses? - **N/A**
Services offered to students with learning disabilities: **other testing accommodations, tape recorders, diagnostic testing service, untimed tests, note-taking services, oral tests, learning center, readers, extended time for tests, tutors**
Services offered to students with physical disabilities: **note-taking services, tape recorders, tutors, reader services, talking books**
Is the campus accessible to students with physical disabilities? - **Fully**
Is housing available for disabled students? - **N/A**

## Vanderbilt University

Contact:
N/A

Is a smaller course load available? - **Yes**
Is more time given to finish your degree? - **Yes**
Is credit given toward the degree for remedial courses? - **Yes**
Services offered to students with learning disabilities: **other testing accommodations, diagnostic testing service, note-taking services, oral tests, learning center, readers, extended time for tests, tutors**
Services offered to students with physical disabilities: **note-taking services, tape recorders, special housing, tutors, adaptive equipment, reader services, Braille services, interpreters for hearing-impaired, talking books**
Is the campus accessible to students with physical disabilities? - **98%**
Is housing available for disabled students? - **Yes**

## Virginia Tech

Contact:
N/A

Is a smaller course load available? - **N/A**
Is more time given to finish your degree? - **N/A**
Is credit given toward the degree for remedial courses? - **N/A**
Services offered to students with learning disabilities: **N/A**
Services offered to students with physical disabilities: **N/A**
Is the campus accessible to students with physical disabilities? - **N/A**
Is housing available for disabled students? - **Yes**

## Wake Forest University

Contact:
Van Westervelt, Ph.D
Director, Learning Assistance Center
(336) 758-5929

Is a smaller course load available? - **Yes**
Is more time given to finish your degree? - **Yes**
Is credit given toward the degree for remedial courses? - **No**
Services offered to students with learning disabilities: **learning center, extended time for tests, tutors, other**
Services offered to students with physical disabilities: **note-taking services, special housing, reader services, talking books**
Is the campus accessible to students with physical disabilities? - **Mostly**
Is housing available for disabled students? - **Yes**

**Washington and Lee University**

Contact:
http://www.wlu.edu

Is a smaller course load available? - **Yes**
Is more time given to finish your degree? - **Yes**
Is credit given toward the degree for remedial courses? - **No**
Services offered to students with learning disabilities: **other testing accommodations, reading machines, tape recorders, untimed tests, extended time for tests, tutors**
Services offered to students with physical disabilities: **special housing, tutors, interpreters for hearing-impaired**
Is the campus accessible to students with physical disabilities? - **Mostly**
Is housing available for disabled students? - **N/A**

# Southern Admissions Counseling

Source: Independent Educational Consultants Association

**College Prowler Counseling**
Our network of former college admissions officers use evaluation tools and methods employed by universities nationwide to provide you with an insider analysis of your admission case. Learn more at www.collegeprowler.com.

There are also several local counselors registered in the south, which you'll find listed below. Don't forget to tell them College Prowler sent you!

## Alabama

**Rosalind P. Marie, Ed.S.**
Certified Educational Planner
Marie Associates
2759A Jeff Road
Harvest, AL 35749
256-852-4688
consultrm@aol.com
www.educationalavenues.com

**Paulette R. Pearson, M.A., Ed.S.**
Paulette Pearson Consulting Inc.
537 Oakline Drive
Hoover, AL 35226
205-978-4090
ppearson@bellsouth.net

## Florida

**Robin G. Abedon, M.A.T.**
Certified Educational Planner
12904 Mizner Way
Wellington, FL 33414
561-790-5462
rabedon@takingtheNextStep.com
www.takingtheNextStep.com

**Betty Jean Arsenault, Ed.D.**
Educational Consulting Services
165 Sabal Palm Drive, Suite 111
Longwood, FL 32779
DrBetty@bellsouth.net

**Sandy Bercu, M.A.**
Sandy Bercu College Consulting
14043 Shady Shores Drive
Tampa, FL 33613
813-963-6342
sbercu@aol.com

**Mary B. Consoli, B.S.Ed.**
Certified Educational Planner
Mary B. Consoli Associates
111 2nd Avenue NE
St. Petersburg, FL *
727-896-5022
mbconsoli@aol.com
www.mbconsoli.com
*Send all mail to TN office.

**Louise Kreiner**
Certified Educational Planners
New England Educational Advisory Service, LLC
7301-A Palmetto Park Rd., Suite 206-B
Boca Raton, FL *
727-896-5022
www.teenproblem.com
*Send all mail to MA office.

**Shirley H. Grate, Ed.D.**
Certified Educational Planner
SG, Inc. (GRES)
PO Box 17623
West Palm Beach, FL 33406-7623
561-906-9715
sgrate@aol.com

**Janet I. Greenwood, Ph.D.**
Certified Educational Planner
Greenwood Associates, Inc.
310 S. Brevard Avenue
Tampa, FL 33606
813-254-5303
www.GreenwdAssoc.com

**B.J. Hopper, M.Ed.**
Certified Educational Planner
264 Magnolia Bay Drive
Eastpoint, FL (Tallahassee)
850-670-8007
BHopper719@aol.com

**Midge Lipkin, Ph.D.**
Certified Educational Planner
Schoolsearch
161 Orchid Cay Drive
Palm Beach Gardens, FL 33418 *
561-630-3666
mlipkin@schoolsearch.com
*Send all mail to MA office.

**Martha Moses, M.A.**
Certified Educational Planner
Martha Moses & Associates
8100 SW 81st Drive, Suite 277
Miami, FL 33143
305-273-0014
mmoses@gate.net

**Judi Robinovitz, M.A.**
Certified Educational Planner
Judi Robinovitz Associates
3010 N. Military Trail, Suite 220
Boca Raton, FL 33431
561-241-1610
JudiRobino@aol.com
www.ScoreAtTheTop.com

**Joan Tager, M.S.**
Certified Educational Planner
121 St. Edward Place
Palm Beach Gardens, FL 33418
561-627-4243
capstager1@aol.com

## Florida

**Mark L. Fisher, Ed.D.**
Certified Educational Planner
Fisher Educational Consultants, Inc.
10 Glenlake Parkways-S. Tower #130-182
Atlanta, GA 30328
678-222-3444
mfisher@mindspring.com

**Jean P. Hague, M.A.**
Certified Educational Planner
400 Colony Square
1201 Peachtree Street N.E., Suite 200
Atlanta, GA 30361
404-872-9128
jeanhague@aol.com

**B.J. Hopper, M.Ed.**
Certified Educational Planner
3400 Peachtree Road, Suite 1539
Atlanta, GA 30326
404-814-1394
BHopper719@aol.com

**George G. Kirkpartick, M.A.**
Certified Educational Planner
The George G. Kirkpartrick Co.
3210 Peachtree Road NE, Suite 12
Atlanta, GA 30305-2400
404-233-3989
kirkeducon@aol.com
www.theggkco.com

**Sandra G. Lawrence, M.Ed.**
Independent College Consultant
2952 Foxhall Circle
Augusta, GA 30907
MrsL31747@aol.com

**Teed M. Poe, M.S.**
Educational Consultant
501 Manor Ridge Drive
Atlanta, GA 30305
404-351-9557
teedmp@comcast.net

**Vic Spigener, III**
Educational Consultant
8045 Sandorn Drive
Roswell, GA 30075
770-650-6864
spigenerv@bellsouth.net

**Leigh Ann Spaetz, LPC**
Educational Consultant
Greenwood Associates, Inc.
730 Mallory Manor Court
Alpharetta, GA 30022
678-336-3265
laspraetz@comcast.net
www.greenwdassoc.com

## Kentucky

**Paul Levitch**
Levitch Associates, LLC
7508 New LaGrange Road, Suite 9
Louisville, KY 40222
502-412-7244
paul@levitch.net
www.levitch.net

**Jane Schoenfeld Shropshire**
Certified Educational Planner
3079 1/2 Royster Road
Lexington, KY 40516
859-396-9508
jshrop@att.net

## Louisiana

**Nancy W. Cadwallader, M.F.A.**
Certified Educational Planner
Collegiate Advisory Placement Service, LLC
PO Box 66371
Baton Rouge, LA 70896
225-928-1818
cadwallader@att.net

**Kathie Livaudais Carnahan**
Carnahan & Associates
4904 Magazine Street
New Orleans, LA 70115
504-894-1008
collegepro@bellsouth.net

**Farron G. Peatross, M.A.**
Certified Educational Planner
Educational Placement Services, Inc.
3839 Betty Virginia Circle
Shreveport, LA *
318-869-0088
peatross@bellsouth.net
www.educplacement.com
*Send all mail to TN Office.

**Christie Theriot Woodfrin, M.Ed., LPC**
Certified Educational Planner
Woodfin & Associates, LLC
6221 South Claiborne Avenue, #439
New Orleans, LA *
866-942-0345
cwoodfin@bestschoolforyou.com
www.bestschoolforyou.com
*Send all mail to Texas office.

## North Carolina

**R. Gordon Bingham**
Certified Educational Planner
Bingham Associates
173 Tullyries Lane
Lewisville, NC 27023 (Winston-Salem)
336-946-2819
gbingham2@triad.rr.com

**Mary Jane Freeman, M.A.Ed.**
Certified Educational Planner
The Davidson Center for Learning and Academic Planning
PO Box 550
452 South Main Street
Davidson, NC 28036-0550
704-892-4533
MaryjaneF@aol.com
www.davidsoncenter.com

**Milton Daniel Little, Ph.D.**
Certified Educational Planner
Burke-Little & Associates, Inc.
411 Morris Street
Durham, NC 27701
919-688-5785
burklittle@aol.com
www.burke-little.com

**Linda McMullen, M.S.**
Certified Educational Planner
Licensed Professional Counselor
3435 Lakeview Trail
PO Box 6278
Kinston, NC 28501
252-523-2769
mcmullen@eastlink.net

**Ann Crandall Sloan, M.A.**
Certified Educational Planner
Triangle Educational Planners
3820 Meton Drive, Suite 215
Raleigh, NC 27609
919-786-9003
acsloan@bellsouth.net
www.triangleeducationalplanners.com

## South Carolina

**William S. Dingledine, Jr., M.S.**
Certified Educational Planner
Educational Directions, Inc.
PO Box 5249
Greenville, SC 29606
864-467-1838
WSDingle@educdir.com
www.educdir.com

**Ann Carol Price, M.Ed.**
Certified Educational Planner
Licensed Professional Counselor
3104 Devine Street
Columbia, SC 29205
803-252-5777
anncarolprice@yahoo.com
www.thepricegroup.com

## Tennessee

**Mary B. Consoli, B.S.Ed.**
Certified Educational Planner
Mary B. Consoli Associates
624 Reliability Circle
Knoxville, TN 37932
865-675-1997
mbconsoli@aol.com
www.mbconsoli.com

**Farron G. Peatross, M.A.**
Certified Educational Planner
Educational Placement Services, Inc.
5130 Greenway Cove
Memphis, TN 38117
901-685-3156
peatross@bellsouth.net
www.educplacement.com

**Bunny Porter-Shirley**
Certified Educational Planner
Educational Planning Services
801 Lynnbrook Road
Nashville, TN 37215
615-269-3322
eduplanners@comcast.net
www.eduplanners.com

**Anne Thompson, M.A.**
Certified Educational Planner
Christian Psychological Center
3978 Central Avenue
Memphis, TN 38111
901-458-6291
athompson@cpcmemphis.net
www.cpcmemphis.net

## Virginia

**Samuel Barnett, Ph.D.**
Certified Educational Planner
School Futures
227 Nutley Street, NW
Vienna, VA 22180
703-938-1787
sbarnett@schoolfutures.com
www.schoolfutures.com

**Shirley A. Bloomquist, M.Ed.**
A Second Opinion
11136 Rich Meadow Drive
Great Falls, VA 22066
703-406-8034
sbloomqu@aol.com

**Milton Daniel Little, Ph.D.**
Certified Educational Planner
Burke-Little & Associates, Inc.
1513 Confederate Avenue
Richmond, VA
804-278-9055
burklittle@aol.com
www.burke-little.com

**Emily Snyder, M.A.**
Know Your Options
9154 Bloom Court
Burke, VA 20015
emily@knowyouroptions.com
www.knowyouroptions.com

# Words to Know

**Academic Probation** – A student can receive this if they fail to keep up with their school's academic minimums. Those who are unable to improve their grades after receiving this warning can possibly face dismissal.

**Beer Pong / Beirut** – A drinking game with numerous cups of beer arranged in a particular pattern on each side of a table. The goal is to get a Ping-Pong ball into one of the opponent's cups by throwing the ball or hitting it with a paddle. If the ball lands in a cup, the opponent is required to drink the beer.

**Bid** – An invitation from a fraternity or sorority to pledge their specific house.

**Blue-Light Phone** – Brightly colored phone posts with a blue light bulb on top. These phones exist for security purposes and are located at various outside locations around most campuses. If a student has an emergency or is feeling endangered, they can pick up one of these phones (free of charge) to connect with campus police or an escort service.

**Campus Police** – Policemen who are specifically assigned to a given institution. Campus police are not regular city officers; they are employed by the university in a full-time capacity.

**Club Sports** – A level of sports that falls somewhere between varsity and intramural. If a student is unable to commit to a varsity team but has a lot of passion for athletics, a club sport could be a better, less intense option. If a club sport still requires too much commitment, intramurals often involve no traveling and a lot less time.

**Cocaine** – An illegal drug. Also known as "coke" or "blow," cocaine often resembles a white crystalline or powdery substance. It is highly addictive and dangerous.

**Common Application** – An application that students can use to apply to multiple schools.

**Course Registration** – The time when a student selects what courses they would like for the upcoming quarter or semester. Prior to registration, it is best to have an idea of several back-up courses in case a particular class becomes full. If a course is full, a student can place themselves on the waitlist, although this still does not guarantee entry.

**Division Athletics** – Athletics range from Division I to Division III. Division I-A is the most competitive, while Division III is considered to be the least competitive.

**Dorm** – Short for dormitory, a dorm is an on-campus housing facility. Dorms can provide a range of options from suite-style rooms to more communal options that include shared bathrooms. Most first-year students live in dorms. Some upperclassmen who wish to stay on campus also choose this option.

**Early Action** – A way to apply to a school and get an early acceptance response without a binding commitment. This is a system that is becoming less and less available.

**Early Decision** – An option that students should use only if they are positive that a place is their dream school. If a student applies to a school using the early decision option and is admitted, they are required and bound to attend that university. Admission rates are usually higher with early decision students because the school knows that a student is making them their first choice.

**Ecstasy** – An illegal drug. Also known as "E" or "X," ecstasy looks like a pill and most resembles an aspirin. Considered a party drug, ecstasy is very dangerous and can be deadly.

**Ethernet** – An extremely fast Internet connection that is usually available in most university-owned residence halls. To use an Ethernet connection properly, a student will need a network card and cable for their computer.

**Fake ID** – A counterfeit identification card that contains false information. Most commonly, students get fake IDs and change their birth dates so that they appear to be older than twenty-one (of legal drinking age). Even though it is illegal, many college students have fake IDs in hopes of purchasing alcohol or getting into bars.

**Frosh** – Slang for "freshmen."

**Hazing** – Initiation rituals that must be completed for membership into some fraternities or sororities. Numerous universities have outlawed hazing due to its degrading or dangerous requirements.

**Intramural Sports (IMs)** – A popular, and usually free, student activity where students create teams and compete against other groups for fun. These sports vary in competitiveness and can include a range of activities—everything from billiards to water polo. IM sports are a great way to meet people with similar interests.

**Keg** – Officially called a half barrel, a keg contains roughly two hundred twelve-ounce servings of beer and is often found at college parties.

**LSD** – An illegal drug. Also known as "acid," this hallucinogenic drug most commonly resembles a tab of paper.

**Marijuana** – An illegal drug. Also known as "weed" or "pot." Besides alcohol, marijuana is one of the most commonly-found drugs on campuses across the country.

**Major** – The focal point of a student's college studies; a specific topic that is studied for a degree. Examples of majors include physics, English, history, computer science, economics, business, and music. Many students decide on a specific major before arriving on campus, while others are simply "undecided" and figure it out later. Those who are extremely interested in two areas can also choose to double-major.

**Meal Block** – The equivalent of one meal. Students on a "meal plan" usually receive a fixed number of meals per week. Each meal, or "block," can be redeemed at the school's dining facilities in place of cash. More often than not, if a student fails to use their weekly allotment of meal blocks, they will be forfeited.

**Minor** – An additional focal point in a student's education. Often serving as a compliment or addition to a student's main area of focus, a minor has fewer requirements and prerequisites to fulfill than a major. Minors are not required for graduation from most schools; however, some students who want to further explore many different interests choose to have both a major and a minor.

**Mushrooms** – An illegal drug. Also known as "shrooms," they look like regular mushrooms but are extremely hallucinogenic.

**Off-Campus Housing** – Housing from a particular landlord or rental group that is not affiliated with the university. Depending on the college, off-campus housing can range from extremely popular to non-existent. Those students who choose to live off campus are typically given more freedom, but they also have to deal with things such as possible subletting scenarios, furniture, and bills. In addition to these factors, rental prices and distance often affect a student's decision to move off campus.

**Office Hours** – Time that teachers set aside for students who have questions about the coursework. Office hours are a good place for students to go over any problems and to show interest in the subject material.

**Pledging** – The time after a student has gone through rush, received a bid, and has chosen a particular fraternity or sorority they would like to join. Pledging usually lasts anywhere from one to two semesters. Once the pledging period is complete and a particular student has done everything that is required to become a member, they are considered a brother or sister. If a fraternity or a sorority would decide to "haze" a group of students, these initiation rituals would take place during the pledging period.

**Private Institution** – A school that does not use taxpayers dollars to help subsidize education costs. Private schools typically cost more than public schools and are usually smaller.

**Prof** – Slang for "professor."

**Public Institution** – A school that uses taxpayers dollars to help subsidize education costs. Public schools are often a good value for in-state residents and tend to be larger than most private colleges.

**Quarter System** (sometimes referred to as the Trimester System) – A type of academic calendar system. In this setup, students take classes for three academic periods. The first quarter usually starts in late September or early October and concludes right before Christmas. The second quarter usually starts around early to mid–January and finishes up around March or April. The third quarter usually starts in late March or early April and finishes up in late May or mid-June. The fourth quarter is summer. The major difference between the quarter system and semester system is that students take more courses but with less coverage.

**RA** (Resident Assistant) – A student leader who is assigned to a particular floor in a dormitory in order to help to the other students who live there. An RA's duties include ensuring student safety and providing guidance or assistance wherever possible.

**Recitation** – An extension of a specific course; a "review" session of sorts. Because some classes are so large, recitations offer a setting with fewer students where students can ask questions and get help from professors or TAs in a more personalized environment. As a result, it is common for most large lecture classes to be supplemented with recitations.

**Rolling Admissions** – A form of admissions. Most commonly found at public institutions, schools with this type of policy continue to accept students throughout the year until their class sizes are met. For example, some schools begin accepting students as early as December and will continue to do so until April or May.

**Room and Board** – This is typically the combined cost of a university-owned room and a meal plan.

**Room Draw/Housing Lottery** – A common way to pick on-campus room assignments for the following year. If a student decides to remain in university-owned housing, they are assigned a unique number that, along with seniority, is used to choose their new rooms for the next year.

**Rush** – The period in which students can meet the brothers and sisters of a particular chapter and find out if a given fraternity or sorority is right for them. Rushing a fraternity or a sorority is not a requirement at any school. The goal of rush is to give students who are serious about pledging a feel for what to expect.

**Semester System** – The most common type of academic calendar system at college campuses. This setup typically includes two semesters in a given school year. The "fall" semester starts around the end of August or early September and finishes right before winter vacation. The "spring" semester usually starts in mid-January and ends around late April or May.

**Student Center/Rec Center/Student Union** – A common area on campus that often contains study areas, recreation facilities, and eateries. This building is often a good place to meet up with fellow students and is most commonly used as a hangout. Depending on the school, the student center can have a huge role or a nonexistent role in campus life.

**Student ID** – A university-issued photo ID that serves as a student's key to many different functions within an institution. Some schools require students to show these cards in order to get into dorms, libraries, cafeterias, and other facilities. In addition to storing meal plan information, in some cases, a student ID can actually work as a debit card that allows students to purchase things at bookstores or local shops.

**Suite** – A type of dorm room. Unlike other places that have communal bathrooms that are shared by the entire floor, a suite has a private bathroom. Suite-style dorm rooms can house anywhere from two to ten students.

**TA** (Teacher's Assistant) – An undergraduate or grad student who helps in some manner with a specific course. In some cases, a TA will teach a class, assist a professor, grade assignments, or conduct office hours.

**Undergraduate** – A student who is in the process of studying for their bachelor's (college) degree.

# About the Authors

### Lindsey Nolan—Auburn University

I had a really good time writing this guidebook for you, and I sincerely hope that it has helped you out in your search for your perfect college! This is my first publication ever, but hopefully it won't be my last. I'm currently a sophomore at Auburn University studying English. I've lived in Auburn, Alabama for several years now and have grown to love the school as well as the town. Although I've lived in many places all over the country, I can honestly say that Auburn has been one of my favorites. I hope that this guidebook is helpful to you and gives you a better perspective on what Auburn University is about. If you have any questions or comments, you can e-mail me at lindseynolan@collegeprowler.com.

I must give thanks to my parents, Hollie, Kathleen, Emily, Katie, Lee Ann, and everyone at College Prowler!

### Andrew D. Coleman—Clemson University

I had a good time writing this book. I was eager to help other students make a more informed decision in selecting a college because I know how challenging the process can be. Right now, I am a junior at Clemson University majoring in history. I have spent the fall semester of my junior year studying and doing an internship in Washington, DC. It has been an insightful and very educational experience—I would recommend a program like this to anyone. I hope this book has been useful and will help you make an informed decision when it comes time to choose a school. I give special thanks to my parents for their support and to all the folks at College Prowler, who have helped me along the way.

E-mail the author at andrewcoleman@collegeprowler.com

## Melanie Murray—College of Charleston

Before anything else is said, I want to express how thankful I am to have been given this opportunity. This project has given me insight into a field that I know for sure I want to be doing for the rest of my life and has helped me develop a beginner's work ethic for writing that I know will only grow as time goes on. I'm a junior at the College of Charleston pursing a major in English and a double-minor in creative writing, with an emphasis in non-fiction and communications. This is more than a first step for me, more than just an excuse to storm around the house like a weathered professional screaming, "I'm up against a deadline!" It has shown me what hard work really can accomplish. I hope you enjoyed reading this book and that it has given you a more honest and insightful glimpse into C of C.

Even though I was a crabby hermit locked in a room with a computer for months, I have many people to thank, people who have helped in more ways than one: Mom and Dad of course, Lauren, Nick, Becca, Sarah, Britt, Kathy, Jimmy, Mamie, Bo, Lauren, Leah, Liz, and everyone at College Prowler!

E-mail the author at melaniemurray@collegeprowler.com

## Camille Thompson—College of William & Mary

Writing this book was an exercise in patience, as I wrote it while holding down two other jobs. It was a good experience, though, and it reminded me of how much I love W&M and can't wait to return to classes as a junior. I am pursuing a degree in English, with a minor in women's studies. I aspire to become a print journalist. To that end, I'm currently participating in an internship at the *Free Lance-Star* newspaper in Fredericksburg, Virginia, writing stories for the Life section.

When I return to W&M this fall, I will proudly serve as Assistant News Editor of *The Flat Hat*. I earned this position after writing stories for the News section nearly every week last year.

I hope this book was helpful in your quest for the right college and that you enjoy wherever you end up as much as I enjoy W&M. Feel free to contact me at camillethompson@collegeprowler.com with any questions.

Thanks to:

Mom and Dad for putting up with me, David for all his love, help, and encouragement, the rest of my family for loving me, David, Matt, Jon, Erin, Dillon, and Wendy for filling out my survey, the entire *Flat Hat* staff, especially Meghan and Stephen for putting up with me at 4 a.m., Mr. Olson, Mrs. Stovall, Glenn Barclay, Mrs. Woodcock, Mr. Stebar, Dr. Walker, Mr. L, Dr. Scholnick, Professor O'Dell, and every other teacher I've ever had, for your guidance and wisdom.

## Colin Eagan—Davidson College

Colin Eagan is a senior at Davidson College, where he divides his time between majoring in English and pondering life's intricacies. Colin is an editor at the college newspaper, and recently launched a new humor feature called *The Yowl*. He spent his second semester of his junior year studying antiquities in Cyprus, Egypt, and Rome. If everything goes according to plan, Colin will graduate in the spring of 2004, and hopefully move somewhere other than back home to Baltimore, Maryland (although secretly his mom would just love that).

He dedicates this book to Lauren—who makes Davidson what it is.

Colin can be reached at colineagan@collegeprowler.com.

## Margaret Campbell—Duke University

Most of this you must already know. If you're researching colleges, you've probably already come across rankings, descriptions of campuses, and admissions and financial aid statistics. This book may give you a lot more of the same, but that is not exactly its aim. You will find more information about Duke than I ever knew existed before writing this book. There are some vital questions about everyday life answered here, and more importantly, a lot of student opinions have been revealed. So it's best to take what you can find. If you're looking to spend the next four years of your life here, then you have every right to know how "real" Duke students feel about their school. This book will give you that information, and then some.

Good luck in your college hunting, and when the admissions letters come in, you should celebrate—and then feel free to thank College Prowler for making your decision that much easier.

E-mail the author at margaretcampbell@collegeprowler.com.

## Amy Mahon—Elon University

This was a very interesting and fun opportunity for me! I am currently a freshman here at Elon, double-majoring in elementary education and theater arts, so learning more and more about my school was very interesting. It was also great that I got to meet a lot of the administrators that I will be working with in the coming years!

Aside from studies, I am also involved in the Service Learning Community here on campus for my freshman year only, and will take part in Elon Volunteers! next year (yes, with the exclamation mark). I love the opportunities for service on this campus and the encouragement from people to get involved. I am also in the Isabella Cannon Leadership Program, where we do workshops to not only learn how to be effective leaders, but how to be good listeners, followers, and workers. After all, part of being a good leader is listening to new ideas. Elon University is big on accepting new ideas and trying them out. You cannot be a leader of tomorrow if you cannot face the challenges of today with an open mind!

I strongly encourage any high school juniors or seniors to come and visit the campus, sit in on a class, talk with students and admissions counselors, and get a good feel for the school. Elon is not for everyone. Some people prefer to be on a much larger or smaller campus. Some do not want to be in a mainly conservative environment. Elon is amazing, so I challenge you to step outside the box and see for yourself whether or not you can call it home. Best of luck!

You can reach Amy at amymahon@collegeprowler.com.

## Jordan Pope-Roush—Emory University

I've had a fun time writing this guidebook and hope that it was informative and educational. Anyone who knows me knows that I have had an interesting four years at Emory, but I have always kept a positive outlook and tried to keep things fun. I am currently a senior Creative Writing major and hope to one day become President of Namibia. I am from Dayton, Ohio, and I have two last names.

Thanks to everyone who helped, to my parents for having sex that one time and thereby creating me, to my brother and sister, my dead dog Max, Pike, Avery the pit bull, Snoop Dogg, Boomer Esiason, Jesse Jackson, Thomas Jefferson, Cameron Diaz, Outkast, Barry Larkin, Jesus, all the robots, the U.S. government for always being there for me, everyone who ever looked at me, the squirrels, and Ohio for being the eighth-most populated state.

jordanpoperoush@collegeprowler.com

## Richard Bist—Florida State University

Writing this guidebook has been both fun and challenging. As a creative writing major at Florida State University, I've been challenged in most of my classes, and that in turn has helped to prepare me for writing projects such as this one. I'm looking forward to beginning my senior year this fall, and I know that when I graduate next spring, I will be ready to move on to my next challenge: graduate school. I have been lucky enough to have had this opportunity to grow as a writer, and I hope that this is only the beginning of a fruitful writing career, both in fiction and non-fiction.

Of course, I wouldn't have made it this far if it weren't for the support, encouragement, and guidance of numerous individuals. I wish to express love and gratitude to my wife, Alecia; my parents, Paul & Joni; my in-laws, Carter & Janet; and the rest of my family. I would also like to thank Mark Winegardner, Dr. Claudia Johnson, Dr. Cadence Kidwell, Elizabeth Stuckey-French, and Dr. Russ Franklin for their guidance, both in and out of the classroom. I don't want to forget the folks at College Prowler for bestowing me with this opportunity.

And last but not least, I'd like to extend a tip of the hat to the friends and well-wishers who help to keep me sane, and especially Erica, Michelle, Terri, Roosevelt, Lynette, Kristina, and Ed the Head (you know who you are!).

E-mail Richard at richardbist@collegeprowler.com.

## Debra A. Granberry—Furman University

I've appreciated the opportunity this book has given me to try my hand as a writer. I hope reading it has been an enlightening, and at times, perhaps entertaining experience. I'm now a senior at Furman trying to finish up degrees in both communication studies and English. I lived in Dallas, Texas my entire life, until the calling of higher education caused me to pack up my car and move a thousand miles away to Greenville. Who knows what's next?

And because I have now reached the point in my literary career where I am allowed to thank people, I would like to profusely thank several people. First, my remarkable family for always letting me go and always letting me come back. And especially my brother, a recent graduate of Furman, without whom I probably could not have finished this book. Thanks to all my friends at home, school, and elsewhere. Nicole, my roommate who put up with me while I spent all summer writing, and everyone else at Furman who helped me out with this book.

Debra can be contacted by e-mail at debragranberry@collegeprowler.com.

## Jonathan Trousdale—Georgia Tech

Jonathan Trousdale is a recent graduate of Georgia Tech and currently resides in Riverdale, Georgia, near the Atlanta Airport. He spent five years at Tech studying toward a degree in public policy and economics. During much of his time at Georgia Tech, Jonathan was employed under the School of Public Policy, and gained experience assisting professors with their research in the areas of economics and public policy. He recently worked for the Office of Governor Sonny Perdue in Atlanta, assisting the governor's personal advisors, and also was heavily involved in several campus organizations. In the near future, Jonathan plans to begin work with Campus Crusade for Christ, Int'l as a campus ministry intern at the University of Sarajevo, in Bosnia.

E-mail the author at
jonathantrousdale@collegeprowler.com.

## Elizabeth Laird—Guilford College

I sincerely enjoyed writing this book. I still find myself rather involved with the college, so the Prowler has been fun to research. It was entertaining to catch up with students during the surveys. So many Guilford folks were excited by the opportunity to talk about the college outside of the Guilford Bubble, and without having to worry about the administration.

While at Guilford, I was involved in several different activities, all of which I loved dearly, despite the somewhat obsessive amount of time I devoted to them. I was editor of *The Piper* twice, as well as art editor; news director and goth/industrial music director for WQFS; religious organizations rep and ICC member for Student Senate; and a clerk and co-founder of the Pagan Mysticism Group. I deeply enjoyed my time with my various organizations throughout my years at Guilford. I also worked for Student Activities for several years, which helped me to recognize all that Guilford has to offer.

I graduated with a degree in English and philosophy with a concentration in photography. Junior year, I had a simply amazing semester abroad in London. I am currently still living in Greensboro, in part to continue to be around Guilford folk during my year off before graduate school. I plan to pursue a career in writing and attend grad school for magazine journalism. I am a fourth-generation Florida native, and some of my favorite things in the world are the Cure and cats.

Thank you to my parents and Guilford friends for your support and love. Thanks to Rebecca Saunders for giving me such a fun and wonderful job with Student Activities. My love to all the people who made my time at Guilford an important and lovely part of my life.

Feel free to contact me at
elizabethlaird@collegeprowler.com.

## Candace Renee'—Hampton University

Candace Renee' Means was born March 31, 1983, in the Motor City, Detroit, Michigan, where she lived until she moved to her "home by the sea." While attending Cass Technical High School, Candace knew she wanted to go into the field of communications. Her freshman year of high school, after sneaking into a college day for only juniors and seniors and seeing a breathtaking presentation by Hampton University, it was then she knew she wanted to obtain a Hampton University degree.

In 2001, upon graduating from Cass Tech, Candace entered Hampton University as a broadcast journalism major. During that year, she met people from all across the world in search of the same dream as her—a Hampton degree. In her sophomore year, she would become a resident assistant; a member of the sophomore executive council, student government's women's caucus, and Hampton University's dean's list; as well as become an on-air announcer at the Hampton University radio station WHOV. This is the year her love for Hampton grew to the level of adoration it is at today. During this time, she continued to mold her writing skills and began to focus on her dream of being a journalist.

Today, Candace is a 21-year old senior at Hampton, with plans of attending graduate school. She is still an on-air announcer for WHOV. She is still undecided on the specific field she wants to pursue, but knows it will be some form of journalism.

You can reach the author at candancerenee@collegeprowler.com.

## Sylvia Florence—James Madison University

What a great opportunity to use my creativity and writing skills, while helping out wandering high school seniors and their parents, all searching for their school of choice. I am now a junior at James Madison University, relentlessly pursuing a career in print journalism, working as the assistant style/focus editor at *The Breeze* (our school paper), and fire fighting in the summers in Oregon. Just as I couldn't have told you my freshman year that I'd be in Virginia a couple years later, I can't tell you where in the world I will be after graduation. However, I feel confident that wherever I end up, my life has been enriched by living in Harrisonburg and attending JMU. Whether or not you decide to join the Madison ranks is your choice to make; I hope this guidebook has helped you out, answered some of your questions, and perhaps even entertained you.

With the knowledge that I haven't won an Oscar or a Pulitzer yet, I still have a list of people I would love to recognize. Thank you God, first of all, for this opportunity; thank you Mom and Dad for bugging me about this book and for always believing in and supporting me with your love, encouragement, and humor; Kyle, my favorite lil' big bro; Susan, the Machine, for being my intellectual twin and my soul sister; all of my awesome friends at IUP and SOU for making my freshman and sophomore years unbeatable; Kelly, Natalie, Kate, Corey, Nini, and all my L-Town homies for being the amazing friends that you are; my roommates, Kim, Brook, and Chris for putting up with me and my silly questions; my roomies for next year, Carly, Kelsey, Kemper, Diana, and Katie for all their love and prayers; all my JMU friends who are too numerous too name, but too precious to leave out; and all the people at College Prowler, especially for their patience and flexibility. Thank you!

Reach Slyvia by e-mail at slyviaflorence@collegeprowler.com.

## Jessica Manzo—Loyola University New Orleans

An Oklahoma native, I am a junior at Loyola University. I love to travel and experience very different places, so after a nearly four-year stint in Chicago where I worked as editor for a non-profit organization, I found my way down to the Big Easy, where I pursued a degree in English writing and a minor in music. The experience in the Deep South continues to be wonderful—though somehow I still consider Oklahoma home base.

I find that one of the joys in writing on a specific topic is the simple pleasure of discovery. I truly gained insight into Loyola and its student body that I otherwise may not have recognized. I learned that Loyola students are bottom-line and unpretentious. Students at Loyola readily share their opinions, as well as their skepticisms. They are sincere and at the core there is a spirit of service in them. The time and patience they gave in answering my seemingly endless questions meant the bulk and completion of this guidebook.

When I am not reading and analyzing literature or other academics at an uptown café, I can be found at home singing arias or playing sonatas, swimming at the Rec Plex, teaching applied piano lessons at a local girls' school, or if it's a beautiful day with no threats of sudden showers, writing a screenplay in Audubon Park.

I wish a very sincere thanks to my Loyola friends who cheered me on in this writing adventure. Even more appreciation is in order to my friends at College Prowler, especially Omid, my faithful and always friendly advisor, whose direction and understanding in the process made everything that much better.

Any questions, please contact me at jessicamanzo@collegeprowler.com.

## Sara Rutherford—Rhodes College

I'm currently working towards a double-major in English with a writing focus and anthropology/sociology. And, if I have enough time and brainpower in the next three years, I'd like to minor in psychology, too. I hope to utilize all of the information and skills I acquire to become a professor of English later on in life. Either that, or I want to be an independently wealthy recluse in Ireland and spend my days writing and herding sheep. Seriously. Hopefully, I'll be able to publish more in the future, and I look forward to growing as both a writer and a person in the coming years.

Rhodes was a huge change for me. I come from a very small town in rural Georgia and the size of Memphis was a little intimidating at first. I adapted quickly enough, though, and I've really grown to love the city. Rhodes academics are much more challenging than my high school ever thought of being, and I'm very happy about that, as well. I can't wait for the really tough classes to start. All in all, my college experience so far has been great, and I only plan for it to get better.

All right, I think that's quite enough of the vaingloriousness. Now it's time to thank everyone who so greatly deserves it. For all their help and support, I'd like to thank Daney Kepple and Dean Bob Johnson first and foremost; Carol Casey, Brian Hummer, and all the other Rhodes staff who were so quick to give me information; Michelle, Andrea, Rachel, Lisa, Chen-Chen, Tulisha, Diane, and Erin for helping spread the word and giving me the inside info; my mom and dad because they're the greatest; and Jacquelyn Johanna for curbing my procrastination and helping me finish up. Thank you guys so much!

If anyone has any questions or comments, I'd love to hear from you. You can reach me at sararutherford@collegeprowler.com. Best wishes to all in the college hunt!

## Brittany Lee—Rollins College

Working on this book was a great experience. It was so nice to finally be able to write something other than term papers! I'm a sophomore at Rollins College, trying to dual-major in English and psychology with an honors degree. I grew up in Connecticut and came down to Florida, mostly to escape the snow. Now that I'm here, though, I've come to love far more about my college than the region's weather. I hope this book helps you in making the often difficult decision of where to go to college. I would additionally like to thank all those at College Prowler for giving me the opportunity to create this guidebook and for answering all the questions I had along the way.

If you have any questions, please contact me at brittanylee@collegeprowler.com.

## Kate Dearing—Tulane University

Born and raised in Houston, Texas, Kate Dearing joined the Tulane Community in the fall of 2003 after graduating with honors from Langham Creek High School. She is currently a double-major in communications and Spanish at Newcomb College, the secretary of the women's ultimate Frisbee team, and one of the news editors for the *Tulane Hullabaloo*.

I'd like to thank all my lab rats (a.k.a. Tulanians) who made this possible. Thank you to my mom and dad, all my siblings, my favorite cousin Jillian who left science for Spanish (good choice), all my friends from past and present—especially Sunny and Elaine who were the ones to get me through my first year, and all the people here at Tulane who have made my first year at college something I'll never forget. My section of this book is dedicated to my best friend Stan, who has always believed in me more than I've ever believed in myself.

Dear reader,

I leave you now with some advice that I've learned while being here. Get involved. I know of so many kids who came here and left after first semester because they didn't feel like they were a part of the community. Go out there and play a sport you have never played (like ultimate Frisbee, perhaps), or join a religious or culture group to understand something you were never exposed to back at home. Make friends and enemies. This is a part of your life that you will always look back on and wish you were still there. Take advantage of what it has to offer. Good luck with all that senior year of high school includes, and hopefully I'll see you in the fall.

P.S. If you have any questions, comments, or perhaps donations, e-mail me at katedearling@collegeprowler.com. I love mail, so send some my way.

## Merrick Wiedrich—University of Alabama

I hope as you read this book you were able to get a better understanding of the University of Alabama. After being on this campus for two years, I thought I knew all there was to know. But, even I learned so much from writing this book. I was able to see how the students as a whole feel about their school, and how this school has and is changing their lives. Now that you have read the thoughts of UA students, I hope that you, too, will come and see why so many of us have so much to say about Alabama.

I am now a junior here at the University of Alabama, studying to be a journalist. When I am not studying, I spend all of my time gaining experience for my future and living life as a UA college student to the fullest. I am currently writing for *The Crimson White*, the University's newspaper, and I am a member of Phi Mu sorority. I have learned so much from the classes I have taken, but also from the people that I have met while being here. In the future, I plan to take my brilliant education and the experiences I have had here, and continue to write and inform others about the world.

While working on this book, I have learned that college is what you make out of it. Everyone's experience is different but in the end we are all here for the same reason—Roll Tide!

Before I go, I have to thank the people that have put up with me for so long. My accomplishments and life would not be the same without the help and support from these amazing people. Thank you Mom, Dad, Roger, Guy, Aaron, Christina, Libbie, Brooke, Dejha, Megan, Adam (my biggest fan), Brian Brantley, UA's administration, Phi Mu, and College Prowler, thank you for this opportunity!

Merrick can be contacted at merrickwiedrich@collegeprowler.com.

## Lily Barrish—University of Central Florida

I am starting my fifth year at UCF, and will be graduating with a degree in English/creative writing. I hope to continue writing forever, and eventually hope to land a job as an editor. I grew up in New York state with my parents and younger sister and plan on leaving Orlando after I graduate. The world is too big to stay in one place for too long.

There is no way that I could have completed this book with out my very wonderful friends—Susan Baxter and Cassandra Lafser. They put in a tremendous amount of time with me and through many laughing attacks and bouts of almost crying with frustration, we ended up with a finished project. I am very proud of the work that all three of us have done, and can't wait to be a published author.

Susan graduated in the summer of 2004 with a degree in hospitality management. She grew up in New York state before moving to Jacksonville, Florida at the age of 13. Susan plans to travel around the world before settling down with a career. She hopes to be her own boss and run things her way.

Cassandra also graduated with a double-degree in advertising and public relations. Cassandra grew up in Jacksonville, Florida with her parents and younger sister. She plans to move closer to the beach, and take on the world.

We have lived the UCF life and loved every moment of it! Good luck!

Reach the author by e-mail at lilybarrish@collegeprowler.com.

## Regine Rossi—University of Florida

I finished my bachelor's degree in English, and graduated with my Master of Education degree in English education (both from the University of Florida, of course!). I'm now teaching at the south Florida high school I attended, which is a neat, challenging, fun experience, but I loved UF and academic life so much, that it made me want to become a professor —no, really. I'm hoping to go back to graduate school to get my Ph.D. in a few years, and maybe someday I'll get to go back to the fabulous town that has its Gator teeth firmly sunken into my soul.

I want to take a second to thank some important people: all the folks at College Prowler, naturally, for giving me the opportunity to tell everyone what a great place UF is; Carolyn Stana, John Bengston, and the whole English Proteach crew for making it that way for me; and above all else, my family and especially my terrific Ma—without whom, of course, I never even would have had a chance to try it all out. Last but not least, dear reader, I would like to thank you—yes, you!—for taking a look at this book and (I assume) considering the University of Florida.

Good luck in your search for the perfect school, and if you pick UF, maybe I'll see you around Gainesville!

Any questions, contact
reginerossi@collegeprowler.com

## Nicole Gross—University of Georgia

Working on this book was a great way for me to collect everything I want to remember from my experience and condense it down, kind of like my own little scrapbook. It has allowed me to gain writing experience and has shaped my career goals in the process. I am hoping to continue writing, in all its forms, throughout my career. I am currently a rising senior at the University of Georgia and a consumer journalism major, with an emphasis in fashion merchandising and advertising. The thing I love about writing for advertising is the search for human truths and little insights that you can convey to other people. I hope this guide has offered some kind of insight into real life at UGA, so you can get an idea of what to expect, rather than vague, meaningless descriptions from a brochure.

I guess the best way to describe my college experience so far is to call it an adventure of sorts. I have made huge mistakes, gotten arrogant, and consequently been humbled. I have learned how to meet people, give presentations to groups of 300, and make decisions like an adult. I think college is a really important time for self-discovery, and I hope wherever you choose to go, you become more of the person you want to be as an adult.

I would like to thank all my homies who gave me tips for writing this book and were continually excited for its publication. You all are the biggest reason for my many great times. Also, I would like to thank everyone at College Prowler, especially Christina and Kai who have helped me out many times. Finally, I would like to dedicate my section of this book to my mom, who will always be my biggest inspiration.

Nicole Gross

nicolegross@collegeprowler.com

## Mandy Langston—University of Kentucky

Mandy Langston didn't always enjoy every moment of her time at Kentucky, but by the end of it all was sad to leave. She worked at the *Kentucky Kernel* newspaper as a staff writer and columnist and was voted Favorite Kernel Writer in 2004. She spent much of her time reading and writing poetry at Common Grounds coffeehouse in Lexington during college.

I wish to thank my favorite "Maestro," who the University of Kentucky should be thanking as well, Buck Ryan. If you are lucky enough to have him in class, tell him I said thank you and bring a guitar—he's cool like that.

Also, I wish to thank my choir director, Dr. Lori Hetzel, for giving me a chance to make music with the most talented women on campus. You put a song in my heart and a smile on my face. Thank you to the staff of the *Kentucky Kernel* for reminding me that work can be as fun as you let it be. Thanks to the staff of Jimmy John's for all the late-night subs, and the Ale-8-One bottling company for all the caffeine.

Thanks Mom for all the support and rosary prayers on test days in college, and to Figgins for the late-night tailgate counseling sessions and ice cream. Amanda, Erin, Rachel, and Valarie: you girls know what loyalty means.

Thanks to the singles ministry at Victory Baptist Church for showing me Christ's love. You guys are my heart. Thank you Jesus for loving me enough to come down here to this messed up world to fight to win me.
Romans 12:2.

She can be reached at mandylangston@collegeprowler.com

## Shawn Wines—University of Miami

At whatever college you end up attending, you will find things you like and things you hate. The College Prowler guidebooks are a terrific example of this. There are no colleges with straight As, and none with straight Fs. If there were perfect colleges out there, everyone would flock there, and if there were totally miserable schools, they'd be empty.

The trick to enjoying college is finding a place that excels in the areas that you find important. For me, nightlife is not as important as academics. Chances are, if you narrow down what you're looking for, there will be a few schools that are right for you. Making the final decision on where to go involves a ton of factors, but you should know that there isn't just one college in the world that will make you happy. Unless you make a terrible mistake, wherever you end up going is probably going to suit your needs. You will seek out the kind of people you want to be friends with, even if you don't mean to. Your senior year of high school is a great time to have fun, but it also involves the biggest decision you've ever had to make. The best advice I can give is to do research, visit campuses, talk to students, and follow your heart. If you end up hating it, just transfer.

I'll close this out by saying thanks to the many people who've helped me complete this thing. Thanks to Julian, Sasha, Guy, Jacob, Matt, and Carey. Special thanks to Rich for driving around with me and finding out the hours of all the local restaurants who refuse to answer questions over the phone. Thanks to Rosh and Anthony for your advice and comments on all those clubs I've never been to. Thanks to Mike for your knowledge about all the bars and for being a cool enough roommate to let me sit at my computer and write this thing for four weeks, even though I know my chair blocks your view of the TV. And of course, thanks to my parents and all of my family for their never-ending love, support, advice, and friendship. Please send money.

shawnwines@collegeprowler.com

## Ricki N. Renick—University of Mississippi

When I first got to Ole Miss, my first roommate was nuts, I had no friends to speak of, and all I could think about was going home, and how much I missed my friends. I thought I had made the biggest mistake of my entire life. The first year went by, and I found that I had a ton of friends and had begun to love Mississippi. But, since I was going into engineering, I thought that I should go somewhere that was more reputable, and I left Ole Miss and went to NC State. I got there and immediately loved the city, but the classes all had over 200 students in them. My teachers didn't know me, and when I had a question, I was too intimidated by them and their snippety ways to ask anything. I realized that engineering was not what I was meant to do. I was meant to be a writer; it was what I truly loved.

Back I went to Mississippi. None of my friends knew I was coming back, and I had decided not to go back to my Greek organization. I thought that I should find new friends outside of the Greek community. I went back and was meeting new people left and right once again. My classes were amazing, the journalism school embraced me, and I was getting involved in many facets of the student media. I was having a great time. One warm fall night, during the first semester I was back, I went out to a concert in the Grove with some friends, when all of a sudden I was tackled to the ground by an enormous hug from one of my former sorority sisters whom I hadn't seen in about a year. She was elated to see me, and begged me to come to lunch with her the next day at the sorority house. I agreed, but I was a little skeptical because I didn't want to be sucked back in. I went the next day to the house and sat down to have lunch, and a bunch of new members who had been initiated when I was gone came and sat down. They said, "Someone told us you were Ricki, and we just wanted to meet you because we have heard so many stories about you." At that moment, I knew that as long as I was at Ole Miss I would never leave it behind again.

E-mail the author at rickirenick@collegeprowler.com.

## Adrianna Hopkins—University of North Carolina

It has been really fun to look over my past two years at UNC and review what I had been through and the opportunities I have yet to face. I'm a junior at UNC-Chapel Hill with a major in electronic communications (broadcast journalism) and a minor in Spanish. I'm considering another major in political science, sociology, or African American studies. I've done a lot of traveling to different universities for leadership programs, internship opportunities, and summer classes. I must say that UNC-CH is by far the most interesting, diverse, and friendly university I have visited. Of course I had to adjust to the school, just like everyone else. I've always had a room to myself, so living with a roommate was something new to me. High school academics were a breeze, but in college, I actually have to study days in advance for a test. It's weird to see TAs teaching you when they're literally only a couple of years older than you. But, UNC has such a nice and friendly atmosphere that the transition from home to college wasn't too terrible. I love UNC. And I'm so glad that I made the choice to attend this school. I hope this book gives you an inside look into and a heads-up about UNC. If you have any questions or comments please contact me by e-mail at adriannahopkins@collegeprowler.com.

I'd like thank my mom, "Moshie," and my father for supporting me in all my endeavors and for their unconditional love; my brother, "my heart," for making me laugh; my extended family for supporting me; my close friends at UNC-CH and my friends from Kansas for always having my back! Much thanks to everyone at College Prowler for giving me this opportunity. Last, but definitely not least, thanks to God.

## Peter K. Hansen—University of Richmond

I had fun working on this book and look forward to publishing more in the future. I want to thank the folks at College Prowler for this opportunity and say that I feel bad because I enjoyed writing this so much that it hardly seemed like work. I graduated from UR with a major in journalism and minors in philosophy and sociology. I'm originally from Pennsylvania (go Eagles), but I currently reside in Honolulu, Hawaii, and couldn't be happier. If you have any questions or comments on my work—or want to give me a job—please  e-mail me peterhansen@collegeprowler.com.

But, enough about me; I also want to thank several people for their help and support, especially Laz, Elo, Swilson, Jon E. Madden, Gerald Holden, VinBeth, *The Paper Moon*, Shadow, the BVC, the inspirational music of Jefferson Starship as well as everyone in my family—Mom & Dad, Krista, Grandmom, Steve, Ann and Chuck and everyone else I didn't mention. Mahola!

## Jessica Foster—University of South Carolina

I'm really excited to have had the opportunity to inform people about USC. As a second-year print journalism major I take advantage of every chance to get experience writing and improve my skills, and helping to author this book has allowed me to do all of this while having fun at the same time! Born in Missouri, but raised in the Southeast, USC was a natural choice for me, considering that I live within a half-hour drive from campus. Little did I know then how many amazing people I would meet here, how many fun experiences I would have, and how much I would learn. Going to USC has been a great adventure for me thus far, and I hope that this book will help others make the college choice that is right for them, whether that college is USC or not.

I would like to give a quick thanks to some important people who have provided me with so much love and support. Thank you Mom, Dad, Lori, Michelle, Donna, Steve, Fred, Cotter's, Aunt Carmen, Luke, the many teachers who have inspired me along the way to work hard to achieve my goals, and the people at College Prowler for making this all possible.

Email Jessica at jessicafoster@collegeprowler.com.

## Whitney Meers—University of South Florida

I hope that all of the weekend nights I have sacrificed to work on this guidebook will help you in your mission to find the college that is right for you. If you decide to attend USF (and I hope that you do), you can find me riding around campus on my skateboard, working in the newsroom at *The Oracle*, or taking the night off to party with my friends in Ybor City.

I plan to graduate from USF with B.A. degrees in anthropology and mass communications. After graduation, I hope to take some time to travel the world before I come back to Tampa to pursue a Ph.D. in anthropology.

I encourage readers to remember that life isn't all about test scores and grade point averages. Have fun in college, but be responsible and don't get carried away. I'd like to give many thanks to my family, which extends far beyond those who I am related to by blood. A special thank you goes to Mom, Dad, John, Julie, and Janalise, because without you guys I would be nothing. Thanks to all of my homies who helped me keep my sanity by religiously meeting me at the Park and Ride Ledges at 9 p.m. on weeknights to skate the box, especially Keith. Many thanks go to Todd for the summertime coastal outings and for being my best friend of eight years. Thanks to Robin Jones, Dr. Joe Callon, and Dr. Jonathan Gayles for being such outstanding role models; I hope to make you proud someday. Finally, thanks to all of my friends around the world who have helped shape me into the person I am today. Much love to all of you.

Send any questions or comments to whitneymeers@collegeprowler.com.

## Jacob W. Williams—University of Tennessee

As a lifetime resident of East Tennessee, and a fifth-year senior at the University of Tennessee, I have spent a lifetime absorbing the culture here. I have been fortunate enough to experience other cities and colleges in small enough doses to make me realize how great I have had it in Knoxville all along. While I have given many a high school senior advice about pursuing further education, College Prowler has allowed me to reach a broader audience to share my experience and knowledge.

I currently plan to graduate with a B.A. in economics as well as a business minor in December. I feel that UT has started to prepare me for my ultimate career aspiration of becoming an entrepreneur. I believe that the lessons I have learned outside of the classroom are equally as valuable as textbooks and professors. Among my greatest memories are the beautiful, autumn game days I spent cheering on the Volunteers, the practical jokes I am still laughing about that I played on my fraternity brothers, and the night I spent throwing homecoming float pomps at the wonderful girl who would soon after become the love of my life.

I hope that the knowledge I have shared with you will prove advantageous as you embark on your college career. It was with purpose that I included carefully-selected excerpts of student insight. Mere statistical information and college brochures alone do not truly reflect the environment you are about to enter, and you have made a wise choice by choosing College Prowler. My goal throughout my section of this book was to answer the questions that take others a semester, or in some cases years as a student, to learn.

E-mail the author at jacobwilliams@collegeprowler.com.

## Miriam Nicklin—University of Virginia

Having just graduated from the University of Virginia this past May with a B.A. in English, it has been a pleasure for me to reflect on my college experience as a whole and share that with you in this book. I know much of it, in fact most of it, is incredibly subjective, but perhaps that is the best way for you to truly get a taste of any place. So, in this book I give you my (as well as many other students') very personal experiences at UVA—by all means take them in and learn from them. And now as I close these words and the final chapters of my college career, I am sad and excited. I take with me my writing and my thriving memories of Virginia and wish that you, potential students of UVA, will come to love this place as much as I have.

I thank everyone and everything that went into making this book possible. If you have any questions, comments, or words of flattery please contact me at miriam@collegeprowler.com.

## Matt Woolsey—Vanderbilt University

This is my first crack at informational writing on any kind of notable scale. Hopefully, I painted an image of the school that was helpful (either in getting you to choose Vandy or in discovering this is not the college for you). A university is not simply the bricks and mortar of the buildings, but rather the life the students breathe into them. I wish that before attending, I had been able to learn from a Vandy student for a few hours—my motivation to assemble this guide.

Enough about the school! I'm originally from the San Francisco Bay Area and am really happy with my second home in Nashville. I am a double-major in literature and philosophy, with honors in Arts and Sciences and the department of English (both fingers crossed). For the last two years I've been on the Vanderbilt water polo team, though, after being replaced by a freshman, I'm now part of the Vanderbilt Triathlon Club. Starting in the fall, I'll be acting as the chief editor of the Lifestyles section of Vanderbilt's student newspaper, *The Vanderbilt Hustler* (named in honor of our robber baron founder).

To prevent this from becoming a resume, I'd like to thank some members of the band (so to speak): Julie Jacobs, Katie Irish, Eugene Montoya, Josh Gess, Josh Cooper, Keeley Valentino, Jennifer Montesi, Justin Elliott, Darian Duckworth, and Jeremy Sowers.

Send any questions to Matt at mattwoosley@collegeprowler.com.

## Elisabeth Grant—Virginia Tech

I have to admit that I've been very lucky to be able to have opportunities like writing for College Prowler. When I became an English major at Tech, I did so just because I enjoyed writing and reading novels. I really found a direction when I decided to have a concentration in professional writing. I took classes that caught my attention and then was able to participate in internships and organizations that allowed me to actually try out what I was studying.

I've written for *Forester's Incorporated*, designed and contributed work to *Happenings* (an engineering science and mechanics department publication), and participated as a staff member for two separate literary magazines at Tech (*Silhouette* and *The Brush Mountain Review*). While I've gained a strong academic foundation at Tech, I really feel that a lot of my education has come from doing work for these internships and organizations. I've challenged myself while at Tech and decided to get two degrees: a B.A. in English and a B.S. in psychology. As graduation approaches, I'm hoping to get out in the workplace and concentrate on a career in professional writing.

I hope you've enjoyed this guidebook; I had a lot of fun working on it. Let me know what you thought about the book or ask me questions about Tech. You can e-mail me at elisabethgrant@collegeprower.com.

I definitely have a few people I'd like to thank for helping me get where I am today. I'd like to thank my mom, dad, and my brother Jonathan for their constant support and encouragement. Thanks to Dr. Marie Paretti, who taught me how to find my audience and then provided me with opportunities to do so. Thanks to the English Students' Society for all the fun times. I'd also like to thank Justin, Steph, Shannon, Deanna, the lifeguards at McComas and War, and everyone else who's made my time at Tech so much fun. But, most of all, thank you College Prowler for such a great opportunity!

## Aaron Mass—Wake Forest University

I'm currently a junior at Wake Forest, majoring in both biology and economics, with a minor in chemistry. There's no defined goal as of yet, but I am certainly taking suggestions. Moving to Winston-Salem from New York certainly required a considerable period of adjustment, however, it was more than worthwhile and has definitely broadened my perspective. Your years at college are like no others, in terms of the excessive freedom you gain along with only limited responsibility, and that experience is priceless. I hope that this book has provided some element of insight into how Wake Forest students regard their school and everything that comes with it, and that you'll consider Wake when applying to schools. If you have any questions or comments please contact me by e-mail at aaronmass@collegeprowler.com.

Finally, and most importantly, I'd like to recognize everyone who helped me in any way, shape, or form. Thanks Alex, Archie, Brad, Brett, Brian, Bryan, Bubba, Chris, Coach, Donk, Gilligan, Emily, Ethan, Frenchie, Harman, Haser, Katie, Kathleen, Kenny, Kristin, Lindsay, Mojo, Morgan, Paco, Plaza, Riley, Sack, Sean, Squeaks, Tess, TJ, Tyler, Mom and Dad. I'd also like to thank my mentors, Anthony, Chris, Dan, and George for their invaluable advice, Powerbars for providing my exclusive source of sustenance and, of course, everyone at College Prowler!

# Jeremiah McWilliams—Washington and Lee University

You've read this far and haven't given up? I congratulate you.

Students here care deeply about what the school will look like next year, and 10 years down the road—whether it will stay true to the sense of honor, trust, and community that sets it apart. The majority of this book belongs to this student generation because without them the project would not have been possible. I hope their enthusiasm and honesty brought W&L to life for you, the reader.

Special thanks to Mom and Dad—Tim and Linda McWilliams—for pushing me to finish this project, and also to Mom for her sharp editing eye. Once an English teacher, always an English teacher. Thanks also to Jonny, Joy, and Johannah for being a lot of fun, and to Omid Gohari for being an all-around swell guy, who is flexible and understanding.

So, what now? Is there life after writing a college guidebook? Let's hope so. I'm hoping to convert my politics and journalism degrees into a job as a reporter after graduation this year. I hear CBS might need an anchor, some new blood at the news desk. In the meantime, I hope to keep writing for the *Trident* (W&L's feistiest campus paper) and playing plenty of Halo 2.

I wish you all the best in your search to find the right college, whether that search leads you to Washington and Lee or not. Just remember, there is a place for you, and you will eventually find it. Do your homework and get lots of good advice, and things will work out. Don't hesitate to contact me to chat about W&L.

If you have any questions or comments for Jeremiah, send them to jeremiahmcwilliams@collegeprowler.com.

[ LIBRARY
M.S PERF. & VIS.
ARTS ]

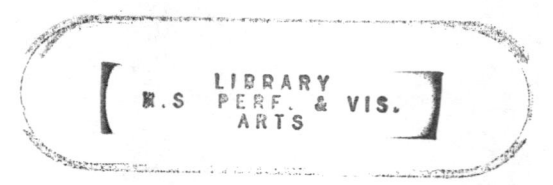

**DATE DUE**

|  |  |  |  |
|--|--|--|--|
|  |  |  |  |
|  |  |  |  |
|  |  |  |  |
|  |  |  |  |
|  |  |  |  |
|  |  |  |  |
|  |  |  |  |
|  |  |  |  |
|  |  |  |  |
|  |  |  |  |
|  |  |  |  |
|  |  |  |  |
|  |  |  |  |
|  |  |  |  |
|  |  |  |  |
|  |  |  |  |

POLLETT